D
6-90

JACKSON COLA

D0758422

HD	Louis, J.C.
9348	The cola wars
.U540634	

Learning Resources Center
Santa Fe Community College
Santa Fe, New Mexico
(505) 471 8200

DEMCO

The Cola Wars

The Cola Wars

J. C. LOUIS AND HARVEY Z. YAZIJIAN

Everest House, Publishers, NEW YORK

Library of Congress Cataloging in Publication Data
Louis, J. C.
    The cola wars.
    Includes index.
        1.   Coca-Cola Company.   2.   PepsiCo, Inc.
I.   Yazijian, Harvey Z., joint author.   II.   Title.
HD9348.U540634   1980   338.7'66362'0973   79-51190
ISBN: 0-89696-052-8

Copyright © 1980 by J. C. Louis and Harvey Z. Yazijian
All Rights Reserved
Published simultaneously in Canada by
Beaverbooks, Pickering, Ontario
Manufactured in the United States of America
Designed by Joyce Cameron Weston
First Edition   RRD1080

Contents

ACKNOWLEDGMENTS

We wish to express our deepest gratitude to Professor Peter Dale Scott of the University of California, whose work was an inspiration and perhaps the cornerstone on which we built.

We also want to express our heartfelt appreciation to David Solomon for his devoted editorial service to portions of this book, and to Steven Weeks, whose unerring counsel was an indispensable assistance at many, many junctures.

Mr. Robert Windt of Cunningham and Walsh and Mr. Jesse Meyers, publisher of *Beverage Industry Magazine,* were never too busy to give of themselves, and the same was true of Mr. Tom Greer of the U.S. International Trade Commission, to whom we owe a very special vote of thanks. Mr. Bill Backer of Backer and Spielvogel generously shared his many memories as the guiding light of Coke's advertising.

Dr. Roy Stout of Coca-Cola, Mr. John Koten of the *Wall Street Journal,* author Richard Walton of New York City, Mr. Bob Hall, editor of *Southern Exposure,* and Professor George Evica of the University of Hartford were extremely helpful sources, as well. Dr. Roy Morse of Rutgers University and Norris Lyle, a San Francisco attorney, made immeasurable contributions to our story, as did the North American Congress on Latin America, David Tobis of the Mayor's Office of New York City, Bob Norris and William Wipfler of the Interfaith Center on Corporate Responsibility, Boston journalist Henry Schipper, Gordon Addams of the Council on Economic Priorities, Michael Locker of Corporate Data Exchange, Dr. Sidney Wolf of the Health Research Group, Dr. Louise Light and Margaret Glavins of the United States Department of Agriculture, and Marilyn Hamilton Light of the Hypoglycemia Foundation.

Mr. Philip Marquar of Owens-Illinois, Mr. Robert Nagel of California and Hawaii, Mr. Bud Coons of Central Investment, Mr. John Weingarten of Goldman-Sachs, and Professor Richard Buel of Wesleyan University were all extremely helpful in their guidance.

A very special thanks to Jean De Sapio and Bill Granberg of *Leisure Beverage Insider,* Frank Mastropolo of the Clio Awards, Vicki Bales of *Beverage Industry,* author Jim Hougan of Washington, D.C., attorney Leo Kayser, and Delia Fernandez-Rey of ABC News.

Lastly, we would like to acknowledge the support of Carl Oglesby, David Williams, Professor James Kostman, Bob Katz, Jeff Goldberg, Jeff Cohen, Jeff Gottlieb, and others connected with the Assassination Information Bureau of Cambridge, Massachusetts and Washington, D.C.

And we are here as on a darkling plain
Swept with confused alarms of struggle and flight,
Where ignorant armies clash by night.

—MATTHEW ARNOLD, "DOVER BEACH"

PART ONE

CHAPTER ONE

Before the Deluge

THE COCA-COLA COMPANY was barely a decade old when it had attained a stature normally reserved for beloved figures and cherished institutions of our national heritage. More than any of our other industrial companies, more than our most powerful churches, more, perhaps, than even our most splendid natural wonders, Coca-Cola has long enjoyed an unsurpassed identification with the heart and soul of America. William Allen White, the prestigious newspaper editor from Kansas, dubbed the drink "the sublimated essence of all that America stands for," and Robert Woodruff, Coca-Cola's guiding light and principal stockholder since 1923, once pronounced his product "the essence of American capitalism." American POWs during World War II wrote home that merely thinking of a Coca-Cola gave them the will to go on.

"Probably more than any other product in history," said *Dun's Review*, in October of 1966, "it has been copied and castigated, eulogized, and boycotted . . . Coca-Cola—one product, one size, one Georgia-green bottle—has . . . been celebrated in song and verse . . . the subject of countless editorials, cartoons . . . and the prop in hundreds of thousands of photographs. It has been clutched, fondled, and sipped by kings and queens, presidents and prime ministers, maharajahs and monks, astronauts and aborigines. The product . . . has symbolized everything from free enterprise and the American way of life, to Imperialism and the American way of death." The leaders of the company seldom resist embracing such kudos. In a memo in 1959, a company vice-president, responding to the widespread hostility toward Coca-Cola in the Communist bloc countries, remarked, "Apparently, some of our friends overseas have difficulty distinguishing between the United States and Coca-Cola. Perhaps we should not complain too much about this."

Why this persistence in equating Coca-Cola with America? The company can certainly be expected to magnify the connection, but did it invent it? Public relations aside, what was it about the histories of Coke and America that has made the two universally synonymous to generation after generation for nearly a century?

In May 1886, the very month Coca-Cola was invented in Atlanta, Georgia, thousands of workmen in the otherwise Puritanical South broke a sacred Sabbath to shorten the axles on thousands of railroad cars and move one rail a few inches closer to its counterpart along some thirteen thousand miles of track. By day's end, a major portion of the railway system matched the standard gauge of the North so that the cotton, iron, steel, tobacco, coal, and other riches of the subjugated South could flow freely to the dominant Yankee states. This moment marked another birth pang of the New South—that curious amalgam of Northern industry and the remains of antebellum culture that was born again after the Civil War in the relentless development of the region by Yankee financiers and their Southern hosts. During its first forty years, Coca-Cola charted a meteoric rise from a storefront operation, spawned in the redemptive soil of the Reconstruction, to a major multinational corporation which fully embodied and symbolized this New South. The Northern impact notwithstanding, the New South would bear many signs of the Old until after World War I. Full-scale Yankee participation in Coca-Cola would not come about until the 1920s. In the meantime, the company rode into history on the crest of a gradual but unrelenting wave of transition and by co-opting the vestiges of the Southern social character.

The key factor in Coca-Cola's remarkable rise in this early period was the profound degree of resiliency of the South's traditional social allegiances. Under the pressures of Reconstruction, many former landowners fell into tenant farming, then sharecropping and, finally, bankruptcy, but in heart and soul they held to the Southern aristocratic ideal with a fierce nostalgia. Industrialism would spread with the help of Southern spokesmen, whose platform—the Compromise of 1877—rested on the implicit promise that the South could retain at least the semblance of its former grandeur in its frontier values and agrarian independence.* Southerners took that promise seriously. Georgia, the home of Coca-Cola, was a leader in the rhetoric and promotion of the New South.†

Shorn of the leisure and secure ease of plantation days, the Southerner became zealously sentimental. Reduced to laboring beside freed slaves, he turned first to vagrancy laws and "black codes," then violence and wholesale lynchings in a grotesquely misdirected attempt to reassert former values. Deeply religious, the Southerner was beset by a newly felt sense of guilt after the war; never was Jehovah so stern during plantation days as he was in Reconstruction times. Southerners flocked to "that old-time religion" to cleanse themselves of sin. Forced to change, the Southerners responded grudgingly, clinging where they could to established social patterns between rich and poor, white and black, in order to preserve the contours of the folk culture at the very outset of industrialization. It was this set of cultural conditions that would sweep Coca-Cola across the South at an otherwise impossible pace.

Coca-Cola entered the market originally as one of thousands of exotic medicinal products belonging to the nationwide patent medicine industry. The proprietary medicine field sprang up in various regions around the country in the mid-nineteenth century. The name "quack doctor" was born of a widespread mistrust of the worldly healers, which led millions to turn to self-medication.‡

---

* C. Vann Woodward, *American Counter-point* (Boston: Little, Brown 1971). p. 43

† In the states to the west, a breach of that promise led to the brief Populist Revolt of the 1890s, uniting migrated Southern farmers—black and white—with city laborers against the New South proponents of Northern industry. The revolt ended, leaving old alignments more entrenched than ever.

‡ Mary Baker Eddy and her Christian Science movement created a spiritual alternative within this trend.

The industry received its greatest push, though, from the illness, disease, and in-juries arising from the war. The vanquished South spawned its own distinct market rooted in deep-seated psychosomatic disorders—melancholy, catatonia, hysteria, impotence, and simple irritability were all common, along with neural-gia, insomnia, biliousness and heart palpitations. Northerners also suffered from these afflictions, but were generally more affected by diseases arising from indus-trialization and domestic inactivity: bronchitis, tuberculosis, rheumatism, partial deafness, overwrought nerves, sore throat, etc.*

Many medicinals included vegetable and herbal ingredients and each region was endlessly resourceful in its search for relief. The North tended to stick with the old standby, alcohol. Because of the widespread alcoholism, the South for-swore drink after the Civil War and turned more toward cocaine and opium. Unlike opium, cocaine did not become popular until the 1880s, showing up then in such New South nostrums as Dr. Tucker's Specific, Dr. Mitchell's Coca-Bola, AZ-MA-SYDE, Ryna's Hay-Fever-n-Catarrh Remedy, and Nyal's Compound Extract of Damiana. While still a young neurologist, Sigmund Freud noted in his *Uber Coca* that American physicians had grown enthusiastic over coca's effectiveness in dealing with chronic alcoholism as well as morphine addiction. Ever watchful for a new opportunity to penetrate an already crowded field, the Southern patent medicine makers read the handwriting on the wall.

The creation of Coca-Cola in May 1886 followed six months of painstaking experimentation by John Styth Pemberton, a fifty-three-year-old former Confed-erate officer and proprietary druggist bent on removing the alcohol from his "French Wine Coca—Ideal Brain Tonic." This unsuccessful elixir seems to have been patterned after the enormously successful French import, Vin Mar-tiani, a red Bordeaux amply laced with whole-leaf extract of coca. Late in 1885, Pemberton foresaw that the growing disenchantment with alcohol would inhibit sales of his own potables as well as the dozens of other coca wines that soon ap-peared on the market. He found three backers who came up with $160,000, and the Pemberton Chemical Company was formed.

By the following spring, Pemberton was manufacturing his panacea in the company's new headquarters in a red-brick house on Marietta Street in Atlanta. He had already made some vital changes toward developing a new formula. Eliminating the wine, he added an extract from the African kola nut, a stimulant brought over with the slaves, reputed to work miracles on a hangover. He blended the extract of coca with the kola extract to form a syrup base for a new and wondrous "Brain Tonic," but the bitter taste of his two featured ingredients needed to be masked. For months on end, the gray-bearded druggist mixed and stirred dozens of concoctions in a thirty-gallon brass kettle hung over a backyard fire. In May, he finally hit upon a combination of oils and flavors of the extracts that suited his taste. The result was the syrup base for Coca-Cola.

Flavor chemists in England had been dabbling in cola drinks for a decade, just as Pemberton and others had been working with coca. But Pemberton's de-

* Gerald Carson, *One For a Man, Two For a Horse* (New York: Doubleday, 1961). Chs. 1–4

cision to blend the two was boldly original, for it brought together two of the most massive stimulants known to pre-industrial cultures. Coca leaves, which became quite accessible in the United States during the 1870s, had long been a favorite condiment of Bolivian Indians who chewed them constantly while working. Later, cocaine, a derivative of coca leaves, was likewise used by work gangs throughout the South. Kola produced much the same effects among West African native "kola chewers," who were reputed to double their work load without any fatigue at all.* As used, the stimulant was so powerful that certain sects feared the "Hell Seed" and completely abstained. Thus, a pastime of the Indian and the African became a product in the hands of an American—and Coca-Cola was born.

In early June, Pemberton and his backers successfully persuaded several Atlanta drugstore owners to feature his new "Intellectual Beverage and Temperance Drink" during the summer. Packaged in recycled pint-size beer bottles, Coca-Cola syrup went on sale at several soda counters for twenty-five cents. Noted Coca-Cola historian John Graff tells of an incident at Jacob's drugstore that summer that ". . . changed the course of civilization. According to Willis E. Venable, the soda-fountain man at Jacob's, a customer came in complaining of a headache and asked for a bottle of Coca-Cola syrup. As he was handed the bottle, the man asked Venable to open it and mix up a glass on the spot so he could get immediate relief. Venable was near the soda fountain and, rather than walk to the water tap clear at the other end of the counter, he suggested that soda water be used. The anxious customer was not particular. He took a long historic pull of the world's first Coca-Cola, and remarked that it really tasted fine— much better than mixed with tap water as the label suggested . . . Word got around town and a few other soda fountains followed."†

By the 1870s, consumption of soda water with fruit juice and flavored syrups had become quite popular at fountains and spas. Pemberton and his associates had never imagined that their medicine would be sold in the same fashion as these early flavored beverages. Nevertheless, they seized the opportunity, changing the instructions on the labels and modifying their marketing strategy. In the wake of the happy accident at Jacob's and the July 1886 passage of Atlanta's first dry laws, the deluge was conceived. Syrup sales jumped from 25 gallons to 1,049 gallons the following year. Pemberton's ads began to emphasize that Coca-Cola "makes a delicious, exhilarating, refreshing, and invigorating beverage," in addition to being a cure "for all nervous afflictions—Sick Headache, Neuralgia, Hysteria, Melancholy, Etc. . . ."

Coca-Cola was—first and foremost—a medicine. The panoply of symptoms it was meant to relieve, occurring in a rural, physically active populace, was easily attributable to the widespread despair following the Civil War. Fortunes—large

---

* George B. Beattie, "Soft-Drink Flavours: Their History and Characteristics," *Perfumery & Essential Oil Review*, December, 1956. p. 437-38
† John Graff, "The Coca-Cola Conspiracy," *High Times Magazine* August, 1977. p. 46

and small—had been lost, the economy wrecked, cities and towns burned and abandoned, ports fallen into decay, and much of the land devastated. Worse, there was the humiliation of defeat and the collapse of the old order. The masters of the great plantations were fast becoming the landless poor. By and large, they had sprung from origins identical to those of the yeomen and the poor whites, and in many critical ways they came to share a fate no different.* In a word, it was abject poverty or, in the case of the wealthier planters, the ever-present threat of it. For them, making a living never came easily again.

It was a life quite different from anything these Southerners had known. Their New World roots were in the frontier, their heritage from the back country. Except for the older colonial baronies of Virginia, the entire plantation system was nothing more than the backwoods grown prosperous under the settlement of two generations of pioneers. Contrary to the aristocratic legend of gentility, the planters were as aggressive, mean, and vulgar as their lower-class brethren, and a good deal more ambitious.† Living off the labor of slaves, the planters, along with the independent farmers and crackers (poor whites), were free to dabble in aristocratic pretension and idle pastimes rather than bearing the yoke that shaped Yankee industrial society.‡ Even the slaves' irregular work habits fit the plantation pattern. Later, under the Northern emphasis on routinized labor, the urbanizing, wage-oriented New South offered an important avenue for the spread of Coca-Cola by directing this age-old bent for leisure and idleness toward recreation and active consumption.

Meanwhile, Coke's earliest popularity as a medicine grew directly out of the cruel shock of postwar events. With the Yankee pillage of the plantations, the planters and yeomen fell into debt-ridden sharecropping in a desperate attempt to stave off starvation. Once as free and idle as the razorbacks that were the meat of their diet, the poor whites were suddenly consumed by low-paying work, often beside the freed blacks in the fields and the burgeoning factories, from dawn until dusk, from infancy through old age.

These universally desperate conditions spawned a mood of terminal gloom across every corner of Southern society. The nervous disorders which afflicted the Southerners in the war's wake were thus a product of their despair and hope-

---

* W.J. Cash, *The Mind of the South* (New York: Knopf, 1941). p. 14-21, 147-56
† Historian Eugene Genovese called them "parvenus," whose acquisitiveness was channeled into the accumulation of property—slaves and land—rather than money, as in the North. Property bred prestige, including military honors and political status, and so a quasi-aristocracy arose, opposed to money-oriented Yankee capitalism. Eugene Genovese, *Roll, Jordan, Roll: The World the Slaves Made* (New York: Pantheon, 1974). p. 140-41
‡ In his brilliant opus, *The Mind of the South*, W. J. Cash informs us— "[the planters] were much concerned with seeing the ponies run, with hearing the band, with making love, with dancing, with extravagant play . . .", while "[the cracker was] one of the most complete hedonists . . . ever recorded. To stand on his head in a bar, to toss down a pint of raw whiskey at a gulp, to fiddle and dance all night, to bite off the nose or gouge out the eye of a favorite enemy, to fight harder and love harder than the next man, to be known far and wide as a hell-of-a-fellow. . . . To lie on his back for days and weeks, storing power as the air he breathed stores power under the sun of August . . . in such sweet fashion would he make life not only tolerable, but infinitely sweet."

lessness and an unremitting hatred for their conquerors. With its array of hallu-cinogenic, curative, and euphoric tonics, the huge proprietary medicine indus-try, which sired the original Coca-Cola, catered to the Southerner's immediate psychic needs as well as his long-standing appetite for the "unreal." Plantation life had stripped him of any socio-economic focus, and as W. J. Cash stressed, "the southerner was inevitably driven back upon his imagination, his world-con-struction [is] bound to be mainly a product of fantasy, and his credulity is lim-ited only by his capacity for conjuring up the unbelievable."* Indulging this preference for "the extravagant, the flashing, and the brightly colored," Coca-Cola and the other elixirs provided a psychotropic distraction for the principal pastime of the imagination of the New South—the Cult of the Old South.†

A defiant stroke in the aftermath of defeat, this cult affected every area of Southern society, including Coca-Cola's inventor. In *Coca-Cola*, author Pat Watters comments, "Dr. Pemberton's whole life may be said to have been one of endless defeat."‡ A former Confederate officer, he was a well-schooled drug-gist, and his products were as lively as their names suggest—Extract of Styl-linger, Gingerene, Triplex Liver Pills, Globe of Flower Cough Syrup, Indian Queen Hair Dye, and the fateful French Wine of Coca. But Pemberton was a creature of the laboratory, not the marketplace. What progress he did make was due largely to the efforts of one of his backers, Frank M. Robinson, who created Coca-Cola's first ads and staged its original point-of-sale promotions. Robinson, in fact, had been at Pemberton's side that spring day in 1886 when Coca-Cola was created. Just as the druggist looked up from his kettle, satisfaction brimming in his pale-blue eyes and the taste of the Real Thing fresh in his mouth, Robin-son coined the name of the drink and later inked out the Spencerian-script logo that went on to become the world's best-known trademark.

In July 1887, Pemberton's health began to fail. With Coca-Cola still not bringing in the money he needed to meet his financial obligations, he sold two-thirds of his interest in the Pemberton Chemical Company to Willis Venable, mixologist extraordinaire of that first carbonated Coke. Venable and an associ-ate moved the equipment and the advertising paraphernalia from Pemberton's Marietta Street home to the basement of the pharmacy. The inventory that ac-companied the transfer, written in Pemberton's own wavering hand, depicts the sad end of his last real chance for success. Among the items listed are the big brass stirring kettle, 1 stencil plate, 500 street-car signs, 1 large poster, 1 wood-cut, 14 oilcloth fountain signs, 5 Coca-Cola cards, and a glimpse of the more exotic stuff of Pemberton's art: oil of nutmeg, fluid extract of nutmeg, fluid ex-tract of coca leaves, oil of spice, oil of lemon, oil of lime, vanilla, citric acid, or-ange elixir, oil of neroli, and caffeine. Total value: $283.24.§

Having sold the very last of his Coca-Cola stock for barely more than a song,

---

* ibid. p. 45
† C. Vann Woodward, *Origins of the New South* (Baton Rouge: Louisiana State University Press, 1951). p. 155
‡ Pat Watters, *Coca-Cola: An Illustrated Biography* (Garden City, Doubleday, 1978). p. 3
§ ibid. p. 20

the destitute Pemberton died on August 16, 1888, and was buried in his native Columbus, Georgia in a grave that went unmarked for the next seventy years.

Out of respect for their departed colleague, a convocation of Atlanta druggists closed their shops and met in the store of Asa Candler, a prosperous druggist, who had sought his first job with Pemberton after arriving in Atlanta in 1873. Along with the owner of Jacob's Pharmacy and a former Pemberton salesman, Candler had acquired all of the Coca-Cola stock from Venable and the dying Pemberton. "Our profession has lost a good and active member," eulogized Candler.

Pemberton's descendants would later undertake lengthy litigation, claiming that they had been deprived of ownership, but a clear chain of documents would describe the story of how Pemberton signed away the rights to Candler and others, whom Candler would later buy out through a series of shrewd inventory swaps. By 1891, he had acquired full ownership of the properties, titles, patents, assets, and formula of Coca-Cola for a paltry $2,300.

Asa Griggs Candler was born on December 30, 1851, in Villa Rica, Georgia, one of eight children of Samuel and Martha Candler. Samuel had an eclectic career as gold prospector, Indian fighter, sheriff, member of the Georgia State Legislature, and was later owner of a small slaveholding plantation. During the Civil War, young Candler experienced the hardships of poverty and became well acquainted with the South's legacy of frustration. In these years, Martha took over the children's formal education and imparted her deep religious convictions. Asa had always wanted to become a doctor, and he apprenticed himself to two physicians in Cartersville, Georgia. There he learned pharmaceutical skills and by the age of twenty-one had decided to pursue a career as a druggist. His parents' land was lost at this time and Candler became part of a whole generation of plantation progeny who were forced to turn toward the cities.

The Southerners gradually surrendered to the outer changes forced on them, but in their hearts they continued to despise the Yankee model. "Progress," wrote W.J. Cash, "stood quite accurately for a sort of new charge at Gettysburg." Asa Candler himself was a devoted member of the Atlanta Horse Guard, whose bugle-filled ceremonies were but a few of the hundreds of Confederate reunions that filled the region's greatest cities in the heyday of the New South. Coca-Cola's first ads appeared in newspapers alongside articles that commemorated the courage of Rebel soldiers, often quoting their reminiscences and dying words. With its sentimental, cavalier extravagance, the soldierly ideal was Candler's deepest personal tie to the Old South, and it helped inspire some of Coca-Cola's first major advertising campaigns. All this nostalgia doubtless obscured the irony that kola had been a favorite stimulant among the Africans, whose toil in slavery gave life to that dream of old, beloved Dixie.

Success in the post-Reconstruction era was rooted in something far more tangible than the chivalry and graceful manners of Southern folklore. The pastoral life of the planters extolled in legend was quickly vanishing. The man of leisure and extravagance was replaced by the hard-driving, ascetic man whose undeviating acquisitiveness was now directed at money instead of property and whose growing thrift fueled a single-minded devotion to business. Even as a boy, Asa showed signs of developing in this mold. Often, he would buy pins in Atlanta and sell them at a profit in the countryside. After killing a mink that strayed into the farmhouse, and selling the pelt for a dollar, he became a self-employed trapper and even encouraged his playmates to set lines while he operated as a middleman in the sales. One of the very few New South magnates to arise from a plantation background, Candler joined the other entrepreneurs in occasioning a renewal of the rural industriousness of the earliest Southern settlers, some of whom gave birth to coarse and cunning breeds like the "shark" and the "horse-trader."[*]

Candler exhibited a good deal of this horse-trading mentality in his management of Coca-Cola. For years, he stinted on his own personal luxury while plowing all the profits back into the business. Wages were kept to an absolute minimum. In 1894, an office boy received "$3.00 per week and lots of Coca-Cola" while, in 1899, members of the heralded sales force were paid $12.50 a week plus travel expenses.[†] If a clerk erred and sent a shipment to the wrong town, Candler would force him to pay the freight himself. In 1898, Candler enforced the original construction contract on a new company headquarters that cost twice what the builder had estimated. The builder was driven into bankruptcy, and wound up with marginal employment at Coca-Cola. Ten years later, Candler resold the structure for nearly five times what he had paid.[‡]

During the mid-1890s, Candler looked for men equal to the tremendous task of spreading his product throughout the South. According to Pat Watters, he found some of his most successful salesmen among the cotton buyers of the region, who worked the off-season and were eventually used to augment the company's staff in the busy summer months.

The cotton buyers were closely allied to the supply merchants and cotton brokers, who formed the key link in a chain leading back to the Yankee lords of credit. This credit chain financed the desperate Southerners' conversion from self-sufficient agriculture to single-staple cotton farming in a last-ditch effort to avoid starvation. The helpless farmers were only too glad to get credit at any price, and so willingly put up as collateral both their unplanted crop, and the title of ownership to their land as well. Because of the risks involved, the creditors could justify setting interest rates at 40 to 80 percent while exacting strict stipulations on the lien. Even the farmer whose crop made it to market often passed into a state of total vassalage and indebtedness to the creditor.[§] Asa Candler knew that many creditors still managed to go broke. "But," wrote W.J. Cash, "let a man have a firm eye for the till . . . let him remember that the price

* Cash, op. cit., p. 18; p. 149-53
† Watters, op. cit., p. 37
‡ Watters, ibid. p. 38
§ Woodward, *Origins*, p. 180–81

of sentimental weakness was disaster, to return a quiet 'no' to the client who was hopelessly involved, not to flinch from the ultimate necessity . . . to which he must often come of stripping a father of ten children of his last ear of corn— and his prospects of growing rich were bright."*

During the crucial early years, Asa Candler organized Coca-Cola's already thriving business. The 1890 total fell just short of nine thousand gallons, and two years later Candler chartered the Coca-Cola Company as a Georgia corporation. One thousand shares of capital stock were issued at $100 each. Candler acquired nearly all of them with the proceeds of the sale of his booming drug company. Frank Robinson and Samuel Candler Dobbs, who handled sales and advertising, held minority interests, along with certain favored retailers.

Candler concentrated first on perfecting the quality of his product. (A devoutly religious man and a complete teetotaler, Candler wholeheartedly approved of Coca-Cola's status as a temperance drink and a medicinal.) Cocaine remained an essential ingredient, but Candler made numerous changes to improve the taste and to increase the shelf life of the syrup, which some pharmacists reported to be unsuitably short. Frank Robinson's acute faculties of taste and smell were invaluable, and he and Candler sniffed, tasted, and mixed until they arrived at the unique formula for Coca-Cola. The two continued this ritual of tasting and smelling for every batch of syrup brewed until Robinson's retirement in 1914.

The development of a system that assured high quality was a constant preoccupation, and Candler moved his company several times in search of a facility that could handle the vast demand for the unwieldy syrup. One factory over a pawnshop consisted of two forty-gallon copper kettles atop a square brick furnace. A platform enclosed the furnace on three sides where workers rolled barrels of sugar on skids. After pouring the sugar into the prerequisite amount of water, the workers stirred the sugar and water solution with a wooden paddle to prevent it from scorching. They then ladled the thick substance out with an immense measuring pot and poured it into fifty-gallon barrels.

Secluded from the workers, Candler and Robinson now performed their alchemical magic. Combining the other ingredients in precise order and amounts determined by their exacting experiments, they transformed sugar water into almighty Coca-Cola. Once the molten batch had cooled, the workers returned to decant the syrup into containers ranging from pint and quart sizes for over-the-counter sales to one-gallon jugs, as well as five- and ten-gallon kegs. Candler had secondhand whiskey kegs painted bright red to disguise their disreputable origins.

* The credit line system was a Southern tradition even before the war, when it operated somewhat less severely. At least two major investment-banking fortunes were built on the windfall profits of pre-war cotton financing . One belonged to an Alabama family who allegedly helped underwrite the first public offering of Coca-Cola stock in the early 1920s, the other to the founders of Lehman Brothers, the prominent Wall Street concern, which also appears later in the Coke and Pepsi story. Cash, op. cit., p. 163–164

The crudeness of the operation and the recurrent syrup leaks into the stores below led Candler to move the company to a spacious mansion on Ivy Street in the fall of 1893. Formerly a church for the local Methodist parish, the building must have had a special appeal to Candler, himself a devout Methodist and Sunday School superintendent. It offered two floors of office and storage space as well as a basement where a new hundred-gallon copper kettle rested, its top even with the first floor to expedite the dumping of sugar. An important addition was a fifteen-hundred-gallon rectangular wooden tank, which allowed for greater uniformity of product. Sugar water was siphoned from the kettle into the wooden tank to make twelve-hundred-and-fifty-gallon batches, measured by depth with a graduated wooden stick. After the addition of vital ingredients, two workers would climb onto ladders or kegs at each end of the tank and push the syrup back and forth with wooden paddles for an hour.

After five years, even the Ivy Street headquarters proved insufficient to meet the insatiable demand for Coca-Cola. This time, Candler built a new facility from scratch, a spacious, triangular building on Edgewood Avenue, which he intended to be the company's home for all time. The basement factory was a marvel of early twentieth-century automation. A hydraulic elevator for lifting barrels of sugar and syrup replaced the old rope-hoisting method; the furnace disappeared, replaced by a steam boiler. The copper kettle was steam-jacketed and outfitted with a steam-powered stirring apparatus which ended the laborious manual stirring, and was enclosed by a huge wooden platform for the loading and dumping of sugar. Hot sugar water was now piped into square copper-lined cypress cooling tanks suspended from the ceiling and then into cylindrical tanks also equipped with steam-driven paddles.

The crucial mixing of the vital, secret ingredients was still done by hand in total seclusion, by Candler and his trusted colleague.

From the very beginning, Frank Robinson proved to be a boon for Coca-Cola. His keen nose and sharp taste notwithstanding, Robinson was, first, last, and always a promoter. He had come to Pemberton initially to sell him real estate, only to be sold by the good doctor on the profitable possibilities of his new Ideal Brain Tonic. When the ailing Pemberton started to sell off his interest, it was Robinson who rushed to the prosperous druggist urging him to buy the company. He then oversaw a sales force made up of Samuel Candler Dobbs, Daniel Candler, both nephews of Asa, George W. Little, and a handful of others. The force soon included the cotton buyers, which by the early nineties had carved out territories across the nation.

Robinson and Candler were by then holding several training meetings a year for the new men, instructing them to emphasize the importance of quality drinks and the profitability of Coca-Cola. Each salesman was provided with ample supplies of lithographic fountain signs which he carried in a hefty fiber trunk. Salesmen taught soda-fountain operators how to properly mix a Coca-Cola, checked the carbonation systems, and hung the displays in the store. Extensive lists of every drugstore along the route were also supplied, and salesmen were expected to report why orders were not placed.

Robinson and his salesmen used every incentive known and invented some of their own to boost orders. In addition to paying freight, offering year-end rebates on large orders, and providing discounts for prompt payment, they used a dazzling variety of premiums including decorative advertising clocks, porcelain urns, prescription scales, and cabinets. Coca-Cola guaranteed soda-fountain operators and druggists a sizeable profit on their first order by sending out coupons good for a free Coke to everyone on a mailing list prepared by the fountain operator. The company redeemed the coupons, taking an initial loss but winning itself customers for life. Since fountain patrons often bought other items once in the store, Coca-Cola became synonymous with higher profits in the minds of the merchants. Pat Watters notes the strategy of "pounding everlastingly into the public's mind through printed display the words 'Drink Coca-Cola, Delicious and Refreshing—5 cents!' "

The public was a pliable and enthusiastic target for this marketing effort. Syrup sales in the first ten months of the massive push of 1892 jumped to 35,-360 gallons from the 9,000 mark of 1890. The advertising budget of $11,401 adopted at the annual meeting amounted to almost a quarter of that year's total revenues of $49,676.50. Candler never deviated from this precedent of total commitment of Coca-Cola's resources to advertising. Sales climbed at a dizzying pace in the 1890s, reaching 281,055 gallons in 1899, and over 360,000 gallons in 1902. Company revenues rose with the tide, surpassing $400,000 in 1900 and with an ad budget exceeding $120,000 in 1902, Coca-Cola became the best-known product in America.

Coca-Cola leapt into national prominence on the heels of its fantastic growth in the New South, but the instant success it enjoyed there was not so easily duplicated elsewhere. Besides the physical obstacles and marketing difficulties of mass distribution, there was a unique commingling of regional factors in the culture of the New South, which provided the fertile soil in which Coke thrived. The preservation of certain Southern ideals in the Cult of the Old South cut across class lines, enabling Coke ads to appeal to a broad public sector in a single stroke. Another factor was much more significant. Though it arose from the same postwar emotionalism which fueled Southern nostalgia and sentiment, it appealed to something deeper and older in the Southern psyche—religion, specifically Methodism.

Whereas the visual appeal in many early Coke ads was based on the legend of the Old South, the slogans stressed themes of religious import, such as "temperance" or "purity." Not only was the spirit of Methodist revivalism harnessed in the service of higher sales, but a good deal of political influence was gained by the Coca-Cola Company through its immersion in the affairs of the Southern Methodist Church.

Asa Candler was steeped in Methodist fundamentalism from an early age. His mother took the children to Sunday School at the Primitive Baptist Church in Villa Rica until Samuel Candler joined the Methodist church. Despite his mother's stern brand of fundamentalism, which exposed Asa to a more repressive version of Calvinist doctrine than other plantation children, he could not escape the emotional quality of frontier religion. Asa and his brothers were later attracted to the frenetic fits, jerks, loud "hosannas" and other ecstatic expressions of revivalist faith. He converted to Methodism in 1869 at the feet of a maimed Confederate veteran who had baptized his father, and throughout his life enthusiastically partook in the revival meetings of the most spellbinding evangelists of the day. Charles Candler, Asa's son and the second president of Coca-Cola, later wrote, "He never missed a service, joined unrestrainedly in the singing, and was wont to approve with fervent 'Amens' the compelling appeals of the speaker. The rising excitement and the near hysteria of these revivals was like a potent wine to his nervous system. . . . His eyes would shine, his body become tense, and his whole being pulse with the exhilaration . . ."*

After entering the drug business in Atlanta, Candler became a Methodist Sunday School teacher and then superintendent. Meanwhile, his brother Warren was graduated from Emory College, an all-white institution in Oxford, Georgia controlled by the Church since 1824. He later became editor of the Methodist newspaper, the *Christian Advocate*, and then president of Emory in 1888. By 1898, Warren was a Methodist bishop. Though it is denied in his biography, Warren, according to nephew Charles, was a Coca-Cola stockholder at this time. He owned one share given him by his brother in 1892, which he sold back to Asa in 1906 after being severely criticized by Church elders for owning a security that was also part of the Church endowment.† At the time, a share of Coca-Cola was worth about $3000.

The following year Asa began a practice which he would continue for the rest of his life—the financing of major Methodist enterprises. After a modest contribution to Emory, Candler was urged by his brother, then board president, to become an Emory trustee. Within a year Asa had become chairman of the board's finance committee. Six years later he was the board president.

The Church appointed an educational commission to start a new university. Bishop Candler became its chairman and Asa Candler the treasurer. Asa donated $1 million to it—then the largest gift ever made by a Southerner to education—and prevailed on Atlanta's Chamber of Commerce to come up with an additional half million dollars. The commission declared that Emory would move to Atlanta on a seventy-five-acre site donated by Asa. Remaining as board president until his death in 1929, Candler would pump some $8 million into Emory to build the Candler School of Theology, a library, and a medical school, as well as to transplant from downtown Atlanta an entire Methodist hospital, which he and his brother had built. The law school housed a bust of the principal donor, brother J.S. Candler, Coca-Cola's legal counsel and, later, a Georgia Supreme Court justice. Charles Howard Candler, who succeeded his father as Emory board president, would give another $7 million by 1957.

* Charles Howard Candler, *Asa Griggs Candler* (Atlanta, Emory University, 1950). p. 353–54
† Charles Howard Candler, *Asa Griggs Candler; Coca-Cola and Emory College, 1888* (Atlanta, Emory University, 1953). p. 16–21

Such largesse paved the way for Asa Candler's son and the sons of three Coca-Cola directors to join the Emory board along with nine directors of the company's local bank, the Trust Company of Georgia. During this period, Coca-Cola financed more church and school construction than any other donor in the state. Emory became a training ground for professional and middle-class leaders in the South, producing more Methodist ministers than any other seminary, 60 percent of the doctors, and 80 percent of the dentists.

Many political benefits arose from this alliance of church and company, but none was contributed more to Coca-Cola's explosive growth in the 1890s than the surge of widespread conversions. The rural Southerners had always had a strong religious tradition, whose overtones toward the supernatural coexisted comfortably with their romantic, emotional, and hedonistic sensibilities. The Puritan anxiety over original sin was not so prominent in their pre–Civil War outlook. The evangelism, camp meetings, and gatherings that mingled rich with poor, and slave with master, capitalized successfully on this powerful sense of the supernatural, and were further complemented by the pantheistic Christianity of the slaves.

In contrast, the religious movements that followed the Civil War were fueled more by the pressing sensation of original sin, of imminent judgment, of apocalypse—of terror before the Deluge. The anxiety over sin and the longing for absolution were as common and compelling now as they had ever been in seventeenth- and eighteenth-century New England. Religion was powerful; it drew men together in great hordes to listen to ministers risen from their own midst preach the doctrine of a passionate, personal God, a God for the individualist, the whimsical tyrant of the Old Testament who could cast them into the pit of hell or draw them back into the fold.* Closely paralleling Old South nostalgia, the Revivals were the pause that refreshed the depleted souls of the Southerners.

Coca-Cola regularly placed ads in religious publications until 1913. Asa Candler was distraught when the *Wesleyan Christian Advocate,* the leading Methodist publication, refused Coca-Cola's advertising, presumably because of the company's special relationship with the Church. Candler was so convinced of the effectiveness of such advertising that when Coca-Cola shifted its account from the Massengale Agency, producer of the elegant lithographic ads of the 1890s, it retained the firm specifically to handle the religious market. These ads employed slogans that harnessed religious fervor: "Coca-Cola revives and sustains," "Full of vim, vigor, and go," ". . . refreshes the weary, brightens the intellect," "the drink that quenches the heart's desire," and various associations with "pure," "clean," "wholesome."

Coca-Cola benefitted most from the crucial emphasis the revivals placed on temperance. Dr. Pemberton was in search of a nonalcoholic tonic when he discovered Coca-Cola, and the earliest ads proclaimed the drink's virtues as "The Great National Temperance Drink." Deriving momentum from their war on li-

* Cash, op. cit., p. 56

quor, the Revivals effectively played on the same sense of humiliation that had driven Southerners to drink in the first place. This kind of religious manipulation found some marvelous practitioners in preachers like Billy Sunday—"I tell you, the curse of almighty God is in the saloon"—and the legendary Sam Jones—"Every barroom is a recruiting office for hell."

Candler craved the stimulation of these men, and contributed substantial sums to their ministries.* Allied with leading temperance organizations, such as the Anti-Saloon League founded by Methodist Bishop James Cannon, these men perfected their revivalist tactics in hundreds of local campaigns. Mobs of singing women and children could trigger converts by the thousands. Whole counties would often call for a dry vote in the wake of these revivalist barnstormings. By 1907, some 825 of the 994 counties of the ex-Confederate states had gone dry.

The native-born, rural Protestant element, which comprised over 80 percent of the populace, was the spine of Southern temperance.† The voices of Southern progressive crusaders cried out against the miserable lot of the farmer, the worker, and the child laborer. Liquor, they said, was a vice that rendered the Southerner powerless to resist the Yankee's corrupting morals or subjugation under the Yankee urban machine. Prohibition was thus mainly a countryman's movement which stirred up old Southern ideals even in the heart of the city dweller. Atlanta became the nation's first city to go dry late in 1885, and John Graff cites one historian who credits "certain Atlantans" with a sixth sense for anticipating the long drought which made the city the soft-drink capital of the world by 1920 and Candler a millionaire many times over.

It was a simple thing really. Coca-Cola provided a lift-giving alternative for hundreds of thousands of converts. It was the sinless drink for the saved sinner—the *soft* drink known by no mistake of history as the "Holy Water of the South." The ministers held sway over public opinion, and their power to exact proper conduct led toward a rigid conformity and a pronounced intolerance of dissent. The wretched drank alcohol not only on pain of ruin and damnation, but of moral opprobrium as well. But the new code could hardly erase entrenched social patterns, and in some ways even augmented the pleasure to be had in secrecy and the furtive sense of mischief. Graff observed: "Alcohol and cocaine became a favorite mix at wet and dry watering holes alike. While city slickers dumped sparkly powders into their shot glasses of Pemberton's elixir, discreet drinkers in drier towns were dumping bootleg hootch into every sparkling cup of temperance Coke. Its dark reddish brown color and spicy sweet taste were a perfect masquerade mixer for any barnyard buzz no matter how

* Candler (1950), op. cit., p. 354

† Despite much clamor to the contrary, historian C. Vann Woodward denies that the success of Prohibition rested on anti-black sentiment. Alcoholism had never been a serious problem among the slaves, and was not a basis for large-scale conversion among the freed blacks. Woodward, *Origins*, p. 390

crude it turned out to be."* The complexity of Southern ways worked to Coca-Cola's advantage, and drinking Coke became an inextricable part of the calculus of salvation, making the company's relationship with the Methodist Church all the more reasonable and self-serving.

Such commercial alliances were shunned immediately after the Civil War by Warren Candler and others who warned against the Yankee's money-mania. Yet as Southern Methodism came to have institutions of higher education, like Emory and Vanderbilt, as well as its own philanthropic endowments and publishing houses, Candler and the other clergy who had crucified the Northern "trusts" quite naturally came to imitate the Northern model.† The Methodist Church, along with those of other sects, came to reflect the prerogatives of business, in several important respects. Churches competed vigorously with one another, often with the help of indigenous businesses like the tobacco trusts or the railroads. Like many of the other militantly evangelical sects, Southern Methodism had a particularly well-endowed patron in Coca-Cola, and the alliance was one of the last bastions of a "solid" South.

Though Prohibition materially benefitted the Candlers far more than anyone else, its rampant popularity was by no means their own brainchild. On the contrary, the dry movement was the most common meeting ground for men of the cloth and commerce. While ministers like Warren Candler developed a passion for ever greater numbers of converts and ever larger organizations, industrialists like brother Asa typically exhibited a burning concern for grace, soul-winning, and personal salvation. Ignored at first, Prohibition came to receive the widest support from businessmen who struck their "bargain with Heaven" by ostentatiously supporting the ministers, financially and politically.‡ Mere wealth could not free them from their sincere feeling of sin, but they might well obtain *both* their personal salvation and earthly ambitions through a dedicated, if calculated, patronage of the religious establishment.

That patronage became possible only as commercial activity, once the exclusive province of the Yankee, moved toward the center of Southern social life. Though he was swept up in this process as no Southerner had ever been, Candler retained a typically Southern ambivalence toward capitalistic endeavor that only gradually surrendered to Northern attitudes. Despite his Puritan upbringing, Candler wrote his son Charles in the voice of the Old South prejudice against incessant work and materialism. "I have thought it wise not to involve your life in a mere money-getting machine," and he repeatedly warned him not to restrict his activities "to the narrow compass of a five-cent soda." Charles, who, like his father, traded a career in medicine for one with Coca-Cola, later commented in Asa's biography that "... there is reason to believe that he felt wealth was a dangerous thing." As Coca-Cola spread across the country and the South rejoined the Union, Candler's attitudes were tempered with a dash of the

* Graff, op. cit.
† Woodward, *Origins*, p. 173
‡ Cash, op. cit., p. 222–27

Yankee as he wrote that "Commerce is not the selfish and groveling thing which many esteem it."

Indeed, by the time Charles set down the story of Asa's life in 1950, the legend of the Southern aristocrat had long since given way to the log-cabin romance of lowly origins, and Asa has forever been remembered as a Horatio Alger type who arrived in Atlanta in 1873 with $1.75 in his pocket rather than as the direct descendant of a line of substantial slaveholding landowners and Southern politicians. Indeed, though his parents' land had been lost, he still had a former Georgia governor for a cousin, two brothers who went to the U.S. Congress, and another destined in 1906 to sit on the bench of the Georgia State Supreme Court. For these Yankeeized Southern aristocrats, money joined family ties and property as measures of social position, and surpassed them as a vehicle for piety.

This equation also embraced politics. By dimming the voice of the more liberal reformist sects in the North, the Revivals effectively hindered the social gospel reform movement in the South. Thus, in 1908, just four years before laws barring child labor under the age of twelve were passed in every major Southern state, the outspoken Asa Candler told a convention of beleaguered Southern activists "... the most beautiful sight we see is the child at labor; as early as he may get at labor, the more beautiful, the more useful does his life get to be." Candler perfectly expressed the self-serving relationship between conservative economic thinking and revivalist theology when he observed that "Jesus did not and does not propose to remove the inequities of life. On the contrary, these inequities are a part of the divine order ordained by Him for the promoting of the brotherhood of man."* Methodist philosophy as espoused by the Candlers had a pronounced influence on the New South's budding generation of tenant farmers, sharecroppers, mill workers, and urban wage earners who were the first Coca-Cola consumers.

The formula of intervention and industrialization in underdeveloped economies was duplicated outside of the United States even before the process turned the Southern economic landscape into one vast franchise operation of branch plants, branch banks, captive mines, and chain stores. Coca-Cola and Methodism played a crucial role. Soon after becoming a Methodist bishop, Warren Candler was charged with starting a mission in Cuba, currently claimed by the United States for its victory in the Spanish-American War.† The United States

___

* In his *Great Revivals and the Great Republics,* Warren Candler rendered one of the classic tributes to the "Chosen Race" in a passage which declared the Anglo-Saxons divinely appointed to lead the march of evangelical religions in the world. Echoed time and again by the church leaders, this nativist sentiment equating Americanism with Anglo-Saxon ancestry and militant protestantism, played on the Southerners' bitterness and dislocation during the Reconstruction and was one of the prime impulses behind the revival of the Ku Klux Klan in 1915, by one-time Methodist minister, Colonel William Joseph Simmons. George Brown Tindall, *Emergence of the New South* (Baton Rouge, Louisiana State University Press, 1967). p. 196

† Bob Hall, "Coca-Cola and Methodism," *Southern Exposure,* Fall, 1976. p. 98–101

had entered the final phase of Cuba's war for independence from Spain, proclaimed itself liberator, and labeled the territory an American protectorate. Bishop Candler journeyed to Cuba and, when he returned, proclaimed the island "our ripest, nearest, readiest mission field. America did not intervene too soon. . . . A wretched population stretches out its hand to us appealingly." Candler was referring to the Cubans' "Romanism," to their inability to read the Bible, their "dullness," and their lack of church-sanctioned marriages and funerals. "With twenty-five thousand dollars the first year," he wrote, "what a harvest could be gathered."

While his Methodist colleagues in the North started missionary movements in the Philippines and Puerto Rico, the bishop marched into Cuba "with Bible in one hand and bread in the other." "But," writes Bob Hall in *Southern Exposure* magazine, "Bishop Candler's other hand didn't have bread; rather, he introduced Cuba to brother Asa." Together, the two sought to make the peasants converts to Christ and consumers of Coke. In 1906 the first bottling plant opened in Havana, catering to American tourists and maintained by Cuban public works projects. A second plant went up in Santiago in 1913 to supply the large American naval base at Guantanamo.

Asa told his relatives and stockholders in 1898 that Coke would be popular "wherever there are people and soda fountains." Though sales were impressive, winning the Cuban market turned out to be more complicated than Asa predicted. Despite social conditions of civil rebellion, colonial poverty, and despair, all of which the Cubans shared with post-Civil War Southerners, their country lacked the revivalist fever so necessary to Coca-Cola's rapid early growth. An agent for the company complained to Atlanta that the advertising themes captured in words like "hygienic," "pure," and "cleanliness" had no meaning to the Cuban. Bishop Candler perceived the problem more clearly than his brother when he recognized that before becoming converts or consumers, Cubans would have to "think and feel like Americans." Coca-Cola and Methodism could not themselves industrialize the island, but the alliance could preside over the social climate of modernization as it did in the New South. At the bishop's insistence, a Methodist college was immediately founded in Havana, taking its name from its first and greatest benefactor, Asa Griggs Candler.

Candler College sought to imbue Cuban ministers with what Asa called "the type of Christianity that makes for a wholesome conservatism politically and socially." The Cuban effort was not initially successful for either the Church or the company, as the economic stranglehold of an American presence inhibited the kind of social development of a consumer class that would later occur in other third-world countries. The Cuban chapter was an early expression of the American imperial formula that made the pursuit of wealth a "holy science" and harnessed the soul's restless urge to conquer, to absolve, to endure. Pleading for funds for Methodist missions in 1915, Asa Candler revealed the quintessential calculus of salvation and intervention that fueled Coca-Cola's rampage across the New South and into the international arena: "The wealth of America must, by its very nature, curse our own land or bless all other nations. . . . Either good or bad—with it we must save the world or destroy ourselves."*

During the fateful intervention by the United States in the Cuban struggle for independence, a young American fighting man named Benjamin Franklin Thomas often saw the Cubans drinking something called Pina Fria from a bottle. Coca-Cola was unavailable in Cuba, and Thomas missed the beverage he loved. There on the front lines of a war that in its wake would bring Coca-Cola to the island nation, Thomas had a historic idea: bottle it.

By some accounts, Candler had paid an undisclosed amount of money for the same advice whispered in his ear by an acquaintance who approached him with "the secret" for vastly enhancing his business. But he avoided following the advice on any large scale because of the cumbersome bottles then in use. The pronounced pop that resounded when the cork on the bottle was pushed down made him fearful of damage suits resulting from bottles that occasionally exploded. So it was left to Thomas, returned from the war, and his new law partner, Joseph Brown Whitehead, to persuade Asa Candler.

Candler warned them that he had no confidence in that aspect of the business, but nevertheless gave them a six-hundred-word contract that ranks as one of the most important documents in corporate history. The two attorneys acquired the rights to set up bottling plants, as well as to purchase syrup, throughout the nation at no expense or liability to the Coca-Cola Company. The company agreed to sell the syrup to them exclusively (except for one or two small bottling operations already in existence), to grant them the sole rights to use the trademark, and to furnish labels and advertising materials.

Only one obstacle remained, which even their enthusiasm could not remove: they didn't have the capital to set up even one bottling plant, much less the cash necessary for opening plants across the nation. Whitehead sold one-half of his 50 percent share to John T. Lupton—a lawyer friend in Chattanooga, Tennessee—for $5,000. Late in 1899, the first Coca-Cola bottling plant began operations in that city. As the twentieth century began, Thomas and Whitehead surveyed the territory before them with awe. Still they lacked the means to administer the herculean task before them, and so settled, with Candler's approval, on a franchise system that has survived to this day as the foundation of Coca-Cola's omnipresence. The partners divided the country into two vast regions, Whitehead taking the Southern, Southwestern, mid-Western states, while Thomas took the Northeastern, mid-Atlantic, and far Western.

Thomas and Whitehead approached enterprising individuals who had sufficient capital to establish a bottling operation. Each franchise was granted an exclusive territory for all time. This gave Coca-Cola a local presence in hundreds of communities across the nation while establishing a close kinship between the bottlers and the parent company. Unlike the economy of branch banks and chain stores that dominated much of the New South, the bottlers were the fran-

* ibid., p. 98–101

chised principals of their own operations, responsible only for standards of quality and uniformity as well as the purchase of syrup. They had a real stake in earning the respect of the community and maintaining the pure and wholesome image that had grown up around the product. Most important, because the franchise was granted "in perpetuity," it customarily passed from father to son, generation after generation. It was common for one man to invest $5,000 or so to start up a franchise, and then to set up a son, brother, cousin, or nephew in another one out of the profits from the first. A whole lore has developed around such Coke lineages as the Luptons, the Rainwaters of Florida, and the Montgomerys of Atlanta. Thus, the franchise system effectively spread the dynastic style of the Candler era throughout the corporate family.

The plants in the South multiplied quickly, but franchises operating in the North struggled through harder times, changing ownership frequently before becoming stabilized. New York was a prize which Thomas finally awarded in 1904 to Arthur W. Pratt, a seasoned Alabama bottler who had proved his mettle by starting a franchise in Newark, New Jersey. Pratt pushed Coke tirelessly in Manhattan for a decade, and demand increased beyond his capacity to fill it. In 1918, he sold out for $160,000 and moved to a less demanding West Coast territory. The New York territory continued to prosper under Pratt's successor, who died several years later. When asked if he regretted the sale, Pratt denied it with a wink. "I'm worth $160,000 living, and Charlie Culpepper is worth $4.5 million dead."

Quality control and standardization came to preoccupy the bottlers. In 1913, a minor crisis was precipitated when some of the bottlers' product went sour. Charles Candler and a company chemist located the problem in improper methods of sterilization, and not in the syrup, as the bottlers had claimed. Continuing suits from consumers alleging that roaches and bugs were turning up in bottled Coke led the bottlers to form the Coca-Cola Bottlers' Association in 1915.

For years, Thomas and Whitehead had been in search of a bottle that would let Coke stand out as something unique. Thomas once reportedly told his nephew and eventual successor that ". . . we need a bottle which a person will recognize as a Coca-Cola bottle even when he feels it in the dark. The bottle should be so shaped that, even if broken, a person could tell at a glance what it was." Charles Rainwater, Whitehead's successor at the parent company, along with representatives from the Bottlers' Association, rejected nine other entries in favor of a new bottle design by the C.J. Root Company, of Terre Haute, Indiana. The designers from Root had copied the shape of what they thought was the coca bean. Actually, they had copied the cacao bean, from which cocoa is made, but the end result was splendid—a bottle with bulged sides and parallel longitudinal ridges, tapered at the ends. Manufacturing designer Raymond Loewy once dubbed the bottle "the most perfectly designed package in use." Patented by Root in 1915, it became a Coca-Cola trademark in 1960, and has remained a symbol of the company to this day.

The arrival of a distinctive, easily recognizable bottle was none too soon, for that year witnessed the peak in a dangerous trend that dated back to Candler's earliest days: the proliferation of Coca-Cola imitations. Dr. Pemberton himself was alleged by the Candlers to have made and sold an imitation based on the original formula. After his death numerous other brews with logos that looked and sounded like Coca-Cola's appeared on the scene. Similarly, Coke's ads and promotional schemes were also plagiarized. Neither Candler nor Robinson—said to have been able to tell a fraud from a quick whiff of the syrup—had any intention of letting pretenders reap the benefits of their hard work.

In 1916 alone, 153 impostors were struck down in the courts, including Fig Cola, Candy Cola, Cold Cola, Cay-Ola, Koca-Nola, as well as Coca and Cola. Precedent proved no deterrent to the pretenders as they kept up the barrage through the years—Caro-Cola, Coca-Kola, Kora-Nola, Kola-Nola, KoKola, Co Kola, Coke Ola, Kos Kola, Toca-Cola, Sola Cola, and King Kola. As many as seventy of the imitators on the scene in 1909 still contained cocaine, such as Kel Kola ("It Has the Kick"), and Kaw-Kola ("Has the Kick").* The analogous problem of soda fountains and diners selling substitutes when Coca-Cola was ordered by a customer has persisted down to the present, and the company has continued its long tradition of the staunchest trademark protection in business history. An entire department at the Atlanta headquarters is devoted solely to instituting these kinds of suits, which the company properly insists are legally required to keep the copyright from falling into the public domain.

There were imitators, and there was the Real Thing. From the moment he took possession of the company, Candler devoted himself to his product with religious fervor. Candler was concerned that the imitators' fraudulent claims for their products would undermine Coca-Cola's credibility as an effective medicine. Even when Coca-Cola proved ineffective in dealing with his own chronic headaches, Candler still took extraordinary care to protect his secret formula, for it was the foundation of his business success, and the equivalent of his "calling," his worldly mission. He and Robinson exercised every precaution by unpacking the essential oils and other vital ingredients in complete seclusion and then scratching the labels and any identifying characteristics from the bottles and containers. Invoices were withheld from the bookkeeper and kept under lock and key.

Candler personally prepared some key solutions, including the all-important extracts of coca and kola. These and other ingredients form the core of the formula, one of the best-kept secrets of American industry—"Merchandise 7X." Charles Howard Candler recollects: "I was initiated into the secrets of the product which have passed down by word of mouth only to the most trusted employees. . . . The total number of persons who have known the secret formula since Dr. Pemberton's day can be added up on the fingers of one hand. . . . One of the

---

* In addition to the courts, Candler fought the menace of imitators in ad campaigns, with such slogans as "Get the Genuine" (1906), "Get what you ask for and see that you get it" (1910), and "Ask for it by its full name—then you will get the genuine" (1913).

proudest moments of my life came when my father . . . initiated me into the mysteries, inducting me, as it were, into the 'Holy of Holies.' No written memorandum was permitted. No written formulae were shown. . . . Containers of ingredients, from which the labels had been removed, were identified only by sight, smell, and remembering where each was . . . on the shelf. . . . To be safe, father stood by me several times while I compounded these distinctive flavors . . . with particular reference to the order in which they should be measured out and mixed . . . and I thereupon experienced the thrill of making up with his guidance a batch of Merchandise 7X."[*]

Reflecting on this passage, Pat Watters queries, "Wars have raged, thrones have toppled, but how many sons of men have known such a moment with a father? . . . And what a feeling it must have been for Mr. Candler and Mr. Robinson to have that secret knowledge, the secret transcending even the other magic of the company."

Preserved today in written form in a security vault at the Trust Company of Georgia, the "secret" amounts to a kind of pristine, esoteric knowledge, an ancient revelation with which no one tampers. Any alteration or disclosure of the formula has been fought with all the strength of a Fundamentalist encountering Darwin. Coca-Cola is the timeless product that was created perfect, imparting a unique experience to the participant which can be preserved and duplicated, but never improved. To drink a Coke was to partake in the clean, wholesome, and refreshing qualities proclaimed in the company's gospel of "truth in advertising." Gathering momentum from its roots in the Revivals, Coca-Cola quickly became a religion of its own, complete with a creation myth, a system of consecrating values, and a pronounced ethic for its propagation.

As with all organized religions, Coca-Cola had both its disciples and its enemies. For the unbelievers as well as the orthodox, the major focus was on the feature that gave Coke its kick—cocaine. As its market expanded, Coca-Cola passed through its medicinal phase to embrace both the rural-based temperance movement and the beautiful ladies and elegant gentlemen afflicted with a touch of the postbellum blues. It experienced a growing urban market during the 1890s among the uprooted farmers and sharecroppers as well as the black freedmen, who moved off the land to become wage earners in the mill towns and new industrial cities. An urban language grew up around Coca-Cola, so that a soda jerk quickly reached for the syrup when asked for "coke," "dope," "cold dope," a "shot," or a "shot in the arm." Drugstores were suddenly "hop joints" and the bright red and white horse-drawn drays that doled out the syrup were known far and wide as "dope wagons."[†]

The Coca-Cola Company has never subscribed to the Madison Avenue adage that there is no such thing as bad publicity, perhaps owing to its early experience

---

[*] Candler (1950) op. cit., p. 119; 122–23
[†] Graff, op. cit.

with cocaine. When he took over the company, Asa Candler continued Pemberton's lengthy struggle to cover up the taste of the coca and kola extracts with oils that would preserve the syrup's shelf life. Shrouded in secrecy, the formula itself was based on concealment. The genius of Coca-Cola was the masking of its pungent essence behind the artful blending that catered to "good taste"—a feature which early imbibers mirrored in the clandestine consumption of their own cocaine added to the drink. Meanwhile, the company made no secret of the fact that small amounts of cocaine were in the product, but it never considered that presence something to shout about.

Despite a brief but powerful romance with cocaine shortly before the turn of the century, the public was treated to a particularly strong dose of anticocaine reportage, such as an 1891 newspaper article alleging thirteen deaths due to cocaine "poisoning."[*] Similar indictments of cocaine as "the third scourge of the human race"—after morphine and alcohol—resulted in a proclamation by Candler, in 1892, that he would give up Coca-Cola if cocaine could ever be shown to be addictive. Candler was especially sensitive about references to Coca-Cola as "dope," but the otherwise vast success his product enjoyed during the last decade of the nineteenth century overshadowed the anticocaine rumblings.

Whereas the use of opium had enjoyed a somewhat lengthy period of growth before the storm over it set in, the use of cocaine after a decade or more of marginal control by physicians was met by mounting opposition—from the physicians![†] Coca-Cola and the flood of over-the-counter patent medicines were stealing their patients en masse, and the pharmaceutical manufacturers of prescription drugs were equally incensed.

However much their long-term interests were opposed to the over-the-counter drug trade, these groups' short-term profits were tied to the promotion and provision of patent medicines in their medical journals and stores. What was needed was a clever, quiet means of doing away with most of the medicines without disrupting the trade as a whole. Beginning in 1899, the solution took form in what became a fifteen-year propaganda campaign in Northern medical periodicals that amounted to a clear-cut case of pitting the ever-growing urban culture against the entrenched, rural folk-medicine habits of the Southern and Northern countryside. The campaign highlighted the false link between cocaine-crazed blacks and the racial violence then exploding in the South.[‡] It spread quickly to congressional hearings, crime commission reports, and respected newspapers, which presumably spoke for the entire Northeast. In reality, the fear in the North was more of spreading addiction and the depletion of the work force than blacks gone amok. The medical profession and the Northern ruling elite thus used Southern blacks as scapegoats to dramatize the need—their need—for regulation at the federal level.

[*] Richard Ashley, *Cocaine* (New York: Warner Books, 1975). p. 75
[†] ibid., p. 69; 75–77
[‡] ibid., p. 80–89. c.f. David Musto. *American Disease: Origins of Narcotics Control* (New Haven: Yale University Press, 1973). p. 5–7

The cocaine-wise Southerners deeply feared the violent reprisals of the mis-treated black far more than any myths of the drug's addictiveness. After all, white foremen had been doling out cocaine to black work gangs for years in the hope of improving their productivity; in 1914, a Maryland journal reported co-caine usage among blacks to be *below* that of whites. Even the American Phar-maceutical Association, one of the prime beneficiaries of the campaign, admit-ted in a 1903 study that cocaine use cut across all sectors of society.* Nevertheless, the patent lies and illusions that the campaign was built on—that cocaine was especially suited to blacks, making them better marksmen and en-dowing them with insatiable lust and an uncontrollable paranoia as well as su-perhuman strength—eventually elevated the Southern whites' perennial fear of the blacks over their cherished states' rights and their own cocaine palate. In 1914, the South largely supported passage of the Harrison Narcotics Act, the first federal antidrug law.

Coca-Cola took much of the heat generated by this campaign from the very beginning. As early as 1902, doctors, pharmacists, and patients began reporting incidents of poisoning, near suicide, and death from drinking this leading medic-inal. Despite findings by a government chemist that the drink, even with co-caine, was not addictive, the state of Virginia considered a ban on Coca-Cola. In 1903, an article in the New York *Tribune* alerted the country to the dangers of cocaine usage among blacks, and called for legal action against the sale "of a soda-fountain drink manufactured in Atlanta, and known as Coca-Cola." The pressure of being associated with both violence and addiction was too much for Asa Candler. Later that year, without announcement, Coca-Cola switched to the use of spent coca leaves (the remains from the preparation of cocaine) and removed forever all trace of the controversial substance.†

Consumption of Coca-Cola did not abate in the least after the cocaine contro-versy. Candler slowly shied away from the special demographics of Coke's auspi-cious beginnings in Southern society. Coca-Cola's ads in the early 1900s shifted their appeal, stressing bodily appetites rather than bodily ills. The temperance claims aimed at revivalist converts were also dropped, but the ads retained the pious missionary quality aimed at propagating the faithful consumption of Coca-Cola as a pure, lift-giving refreshment. The Massengale agency, which had handled the vastly successful postbellum campaigns for a decade, was replaced by the St. Louis firm of W. C. D'Arcy in 1904. Contemporary sports figures like Ty Cobb appeared in ads praising the product. The elegant ladies were trans-planted to more informal surroundings, stressing the relaxed atmosphere of the beach, the tennis court, or the picnic. The pitch was to the work-play cycle of

---

* Harvey W. Wiley, *The History of a Crime Against the Food Law* (H. W. Wiley, 1929). p. 376–81

† By a stroke of political luck, exemptions in the drug laws passed from 1914 to 1922 permit-ted importation of coca leaves for medicinal purposes only, and ever since, Coca-Cola has been able to procure the spent leaves from the Stepan Chemical Co. in New Jersey, the only legal importer of coca leaves in the United States.

industrial society which replaced the older pattern of hedonistic amusement and idleness.

The first national magazine advertisement in 1904 was followed by vast regional campaigns over the next four years. By 1908, the company had hung Coca-Cola signs on 2.5 million square feet of walls and buildings in every major city, and billboards were designed by D'Arcy for the New York/Philadelphia railroad run. Ten thousand window displays were erected in 1908, a year when the company spent well over half a million dollars on advertising. In 1911, as the budget hit $1 million for the first time, D'Arcy ads started taking to the hard sell with such slogans as "It's clean and pure, that's sure" (1909), "Good to the last drop" (1908), "The best drink anyone can buy" (1913), and "The ballplayer's best beverage" (1914). In 1912, the Advertising Club of America cited Coca-Cola as having the best-advertised product in the United States.

Meanwhile, the company itself continued its promotional activities. In 1913 alone, the company distributed over 120 million novelties including eight-day clocks, paper napkins, matches, thermometers, door plates, pocketknives, decals, watch fobs, blotters, pencils, mirrors, doilies, change trays, window displays, fountain festoons, baseball cards, umbrellas, and the first in a long line of trays and calendars illustrated with bathing beauties. A robust trade in these memorabilia flourishes today under the auspices of the company and a private group of collectors called the Coca-Cola Clan.

Nevertheless, the shackles of government regulation began to take hold. Dr. Harvey Wiley, a government chemist who had led the assault on patent medicines, headed the famous "poison squad," and campaigned tirelessly for wholesome foods untainted by additives and artificial ingredients.

The Pure Food and Drug Act was passed in 1906, and three years later an agent from the Bureau of Chemistry seized a shipment of Coca-Cola syrup in a prologue to the celebrated case, "The U.S. vs. Forty Barrels and Twenty Kegs of Coca-Cola." In his book, *The History of a Crime Against the Food Law*, Wiley indicated that the Bureau of Chemistry, which he headed, was actually forbidden by then Secretary of Agriculture David Franklin Houston from prosecuting the Coca-Cola Company. The case moved forward only when a crusading newspaper owner from Atlanta confronted the secretary at Wiley's suggestion and wanted to know why Coca-Cola was exempted from the Pure Food Act when prosecutions were moving ahead against other manufacturers. Wiley and the Bureau soon found that the prevailing pressure was to try the case in Chattanooga, where, said Wiley, ". . . the whole environment . . . was favorable to the Coca-Cola industry." He thought that the case belonged in Washington, especially considering the effort and cost of sending all the government scientific personnel to Tennessee. "It was equivalent to trying the case in Atlanta."

The case dragged on as one Southern judge after another struck down Wiley's charges that caffeine was not an essential ingredient, as the company claimed, but an additive, which the new law prohibited. Coca-Cola lost in the Supreme Court in 1918, but sentencing was remanded to the Chattanooga court where Coca-Cola had earlier prevailed. After fining the Coca-Cola Company $90,000 to cover the court costs, the judge forbade the sale of Coca-Cola contrary to the provisions of the Food and Drug Act, but indicated that the "judgment shall not be binding . . . except as to this case and to the particular goods seized herein." In other words, those forty barrels and twenty kegs could not be sold, but the government would have to bring suit again and again under the federal statute for each violation in the future. Obviously, no attempt could be made to enforce the decree against Coca-Cola products every time they crossed a state line. Allegedly driven from his post by retaliatory investigations, Wiley subsequently pondered the outcome "if the Supreme Court could have passed an opinion on the immunity granted the Coca-Cola Company . . ."

The strain of these years took a heavy toll on Asa Candler. A contemporary of John D. Rockefeller, J. P. Morgan, and Andrew Carnegie, Candler had become rich—some say the richest man in the South—at a time of unbridled economic freedom. The horse-trading brand of individualism he embodied was the moral equivalent of freedom itself, so that "in a very real sense," wrote his son Charles, "the Coca-Cola Company was Asa G. Candler, and the line between his personal property purchases and those of the company was frequently undefined." He was simply not prepared to handle the new Federal Income Statute of 1915 which sharply defined that line by requiring the company to divest itself of its nonbusiness-related real estate holdings. These properties, erected or acquired with reinvested profits, included over a dozen skyscrapers—usually known as The Candler Building—in major cities, such as Atlanta, New York, Toronto, Los Angeles, Havana, Baltimore, and Kansas City. The forced liquidation netted over $5 million which was divided among the stockholders. Such strictures left Candler with the helpless feeling that he could no longer run Coca-Cola as he saw fit. Frank Robinson's retirement in 1914 had already precipitated an emotional letdown, and in 1916 Candler surrendered Coca-Cola to his sons and turned briefly to politics.

Candler's path to the mayoralty of Atlanta in 1916 had been cleared by his involvement in philanthropic enterprises. Emory University had placed Candler at the zenith of Atlanta's civic elite. The call from the business community to run for mayor came on the heels of a crop price-support system he devised for the region's depressed, prewar economy. Willing to put up millions, he proposed to keep cotton off the market by lending small farmers and large growers alike up to six cents per pound for storing their cotton in one of his warehouses. This was not the first time Candler had spoken for the little man. During the 1907 real estate panic in Atlanta, he bought up millions of dollars worth of residential property and resold it to people of moderate income under quite favorable terms. In both instances, he helped avert disaster in a vital sector of the economy. The beneficiaries were not really the lower middle class—Candler's campaign was markedly antilabor—but rather the small, independent businessman. (His plan to help the cotton growers resembled the more far-reaching proposal of the Populists a quarter century before, and probably stemmed from his own oppression by taxation and government regulation.)

In any event, he was out of Coca-Cola. The death of his wife, Lizzie, in February of 1919, sent him into a deep depression from which he never fully recovered. Though he remarried six years later, he spent most of the interim in Europe, lost in loneliness. The tireless activity of competitors and the repeated assaults on the sacred formula had led the Candler sons to a dramatic move. While Asa grieved over the death of their mother, the sons quietly sold the company in September 1919 for $25 million to Ernest Woodruff, an Atlanta entrepreneur, who put together a consortium of banks for the purchase. It was the largest business transaction the South had ever seen, the most crucial in Coca-Cola's thirty-three-year history, and Asa Candler had not even been told. Perhaps, speculates Pat Watters, this was because Woodruff was a next-door neighbor of the Candlers, and also because his sons knew the depth of his grief. After learning of the sale, he kept whatever bitterness he felt to himself, saying only that he disapproved of it, though the price was fair.

His kingdom come and gone, Candler lived out the 1920s in retirement. He was named "First Citizen of Atlanta" in 1923. At that time he was certainly among its greatest tycoons and most generous benefactors. He died on March 12, 1929, after a stay of several months in a quiet room at Wesleyan Memorial Hospital on the Emory University campus, the church-held institution he had built. Despite all that had happened, he could never imagine the totality of what Coca-Cola would later become. In light of the trials and hardships of his final years, it seems unlikely he cared as he once did. But perhaps Coke's destiny revealed itself to him out of the fullness of the past, as he prayed in his room or gazed peacefully between the Methodist pillars at the rolling Southern hills.

CHAPTER TWO

Wall Street Yankees in King Coke's Court

NO ASPECT of the company more epitomized the New South's emergence into mainstream America than the consortium that bought out the Candlers. Spearheading this syndicate was Ernest Woodruff, president of the Trust Company of Georgia, the son of George Woodruff, an ambitious New Englander who had sought his fortune as a Georgia mill operator before losing everything in the Civil War. Ernest went on to become an urban industrialist with interests in steel, coal, and railroads. As a banker he was even more in the Yankee mold, assembling syndicates and trusts whose acquisitions were turned over for a handsome profit.

Woodruff's purchase of Coca-Cola was a titanic feat requiring the participation of the Trust Company of Georgia, the Chase National Bank and the Guaranty Trust Company, the latter two among the wealthiest financial institutions in the United States, and forerunners of the New York banking giants Chase Manhattan and Morgan Guaranty Trust. This deal was another watershed in the "Yankeeizing" of the New South, a process singled out by one of its earliest apostles who said, ". . . the ambition of the South is to out-Yankee the Yankee."

The banks involved (later controlled by the Rockefellers and the Morgans) were suddenly in league with the financial elite of Atlanta. A litany of ties developed between these two groups which drew them closer as the century advanced. Overnight the Trust Company of Georgia became Coca-Cola's bank. Its original holdings of 24,900 shares—valued at about $110,000—increased through stock splits almost a hundredfold, yielding over 2 million shares (of common stock) worth a handsome $69.3 million. In addition, the bank manages a larger block of common shares than any other bank—over 10 percent of the company—and consequently, Trust Company of Georgia's board is amply populated with Coca-Cola's directors who see that its services are used advantageously by the company and its bottlers. The bank also provides the safe-deposit vault where the secret formula for the drink is kept. Both Chase Manhattan and Morgan Guaranty Trust hold Coca-Cola stock and also provide the company with key financial services. Coke's former chairman, J. Paul Austin, served on the boards of Morgan Guaranty Trust and the Trust Company of Georgia. As we shall see elsewhere, the increasingly integrated interests of this Yankee-Southern nexus have been well represented in Democratic administrations from Roosevelt to Carter.

Woodruff's great success lay in engineering the purchase of Coca-Cola, but it fell to his son Robert to run the company. A former Sunday School pupil of Asa

39

Candler, Robert Winship Woodruff was exposed to the "wholesome conservatism" his teacher thought a Christian education should impart. After graduating from a military academy, Woodruff attended college for a year, and then dropped out to work, much to his father's displeasure. Since he was paying college debts, his father gave him a job as purchasing agent at his coal company, where Robert's first acquisition was an entire truck fleet from White Motor Company. Walter White, the owner of the Cleveland firm, was enough impressed with young Woodruff to offer him a job and by 1923, at the age of thirty-three, Woodruff had become the nation's top truck salesman as well as a director of the Trust Company of Georgia. Woodruff was earning $85,000 a year at his job with White Motors when he heeded the call to come home.

Things were not going well for Coca-Cola. In 1920, Samuel Candler Dobbs, who stayed on briefly as president of the company, had made an untimely purchase of sugar at twenty-eight cents a pound, just before it plummeted to its pre–World War I price of seven cents. The stock dove from $40 to $18 a share and the company was suddenly faced with the staggering prospect of borrowing $22 million just to stay in business, undoubtedly helped in part by the quick profit taking of insiders who had bought stock at $5 per share. The bottlers, meanwhile, hurled charges of fraud and bad faith at the company. The company had approached the bottlers with the cursory suggestion that the time had come to raise the cost of the syrup, an item permanently fixed in their original franchise contract. The matter wound up in court, where a compromise was reached of a fixed price for syrup adjusted to the current price of sugar. A convention was needed to heal the wounds, and for the first time in thirty-five years, annual sales volume actually diminished. From the 1919 high, it dipped slightly in 1920, then more sharply during the next year, where it held at 15 million gallons until the arrival of Robert Woodruff.

When he took over as president, Woodruff blossomed under the invaluable assistance of the middle management which had weathered the storm of the last four years. The company had scored some victories: an imitator using the name "Koke" was struck down in court in a celebrated opinion by Justice Oliver Wendell Holmes, and new corporate headquarters were constructed. Declaring a unity of interest with the bottlers, Woodruff inaugurated a spirit of loyalty to the product rather than to the company. That loyalty was not misplaced. Profits were on the rebound, reaching $5 million on sales of $24 million in 1923.

Woodruff reorganized the sales department into a service department that stressed quality control and efficient maintenance of fountain accounts rather than simply filling orders. Perhaps a customer was stocking too much syrup, or his carbonator was not working properly, his refrigeration coils were clogged, or his advertising poorly displayed. Solving these problems and attaining maximum marketing efficiency became the core of the sales effort by which demand was increased. To back up this program, special training sessions for new servicemen were instituted at resort hotels.

Woodruff exhibited the same strong leadership as Asa Candler, but he seemed to possess an especially keen intuitive sense, and he never hesitated to ruffle a few feathers in order to implement it. When he decided to reorganize the sales department, Woodruff called all his salesmen together and announced that the department was to be disbanded and their services would no longer be needed. After letting the shock sink in, Woodruff added that a new service department was to be organized, and anyone interested could apply the following morning. With a style as imposing as his vision, Woodruff began where Candler left off, leading one executive to remark, "Asa Candler gave us feet, but Woodruff gave us wings." Like Candler, he insisted that Coca-Cola remain a one-product institution, which would not diversify into sugar plantations, bottle manufacturing, or any other related field. The parent company would manufacture syrup and oversee advertising and promotion, while the bottlers and jobbers serving fountains would handle the distribution. With no outlay of its own capital, Coca-Cola continued to expand, winning wide support which further facilitated the process. By 1926, there were 1,250 domestic bottlers and 2,200 jobbers who served over 900,000 retail outlets. The bottlers and jobbers were served, in turn, by 39 warehouses and 13 company-operated syrup factories scattered across America. Woodruff's most pragmatic considerations perfectly matched his strongest philosophic conviction, the idea that "[he] wanted everyone connected with Coca-Cola to make money."

Woodruff directed technological and packaging developments to enhance efficiency of bottler operations, point-of-sale promotions, and retailers' profits. The famous top-loading coolers, designed in 1929 by the company, were sold at cost to retailers for $12.50, against the $90 tag on competitive models. These became prototypes for the coin vending machines that came out in 1932, the same year in which the automatic dispenser appeared, ensuring uniformly mixed Coke at soda fountains everywhere. Quality control at bottling operations included intensive work to guarantee the use of pure water as well as avoidance of alkalinity and other foreign matter that might flatten or alter the taste. Most important, the six-pack, conceived in 1924, was fast becoming the company's major trump card in Woodruff's formula for success in the twenties: wholesale, cost-cutting marketing efficiency.

Although the country was saturated with retail fountain outlets, Woodruff saw that the best opportunities and future success lay with the bottlers. His view was confirmed in 1928, when bottlers' sales surpassed those at fountains for the first time. As the bottlers' progress accelerated, Woodruff strengthened his allegiance to them as the very embodiment of the competitive, free-enterprise system. It has often been said that the holder of a bottling franchise, with its conditions of perpetuity and exclusivity, has a license to print money. The awarding of franchises tended to duplicate the dynastic style of the Candlers. In Chattanooga, Tennessee, a banker estimated that three-quarters of all the town's fortunes were Coke related. Rare was the franchise that was not passed from father to son. The offspring of major bottlers were christened by their fathers after Coke bottlers from the South. Nor did death necessarily sunder a Coca-Cola family; the niece of an early bottler outlived two husbands—both bottlers—only to marry the head of the Chattanooga Glass Company, the local manufacturer of Coca-Cola bottles. So many nephews, nieces, and cousins have been connected with some phase of Coca-Cola by lineage, marriage and remarriage, that the wife of a bottler was once led to wonder, "Where would I be without this family? Coke is my entire life."

The bottlers were thus "one big happy family" that Woodruff exhorted to "march with a song in their hearts." One bottler declared in his credo, "I shall always try to do my best for the name I love and serve—Coca-Cola. I did not make Coca-Cola, Coca-Cola made me." Often known as "The Most Important Businessman in Town," the bottler was frequently a celebrity—such as golfer Bobby Jones or Woodruff's close friend, baseball great Ty Cobb, the "Georgia Peach." Woodruff preached that he should be active in community and civic work, so that he might become "not merely the representation of the product, but the personification of the institution."

Samuel Candler Dobbs believed that the real market for Coca-Cola was still in the countryside, among those who in his day had emerged as tenant farmers, sharecroppers, and cotton workers in the outlying mill towns. Dobbs's intuition was not entirely without merit. Farmers and cotton workers enjoyed relative prosperity both during and after World War I, a condition that permitted their indulgence in anything that appealed to their love of pleasure and show. From fancy foods to ten-cent cigars, from bright clothing to the new moving pictures, these folks could be expected by buy Coca-Cola with the same abandon as any other simple luxury.

However much Coca-Cola was drawing from rural tradition in its advertising or corporate mores, the demographics of its market had shifted. Far from being the favorite of teetotalers during Prohibition, Coca-Cola became the target of dry movement leaders such as the Women's Christian Temperance Union (WCTU). During the 1920s, these groups launched numerous attacks on the Coca-Cola "curse" and claimed the drink to be every bit as sinful as demon rum. They apparently felt Coke had lost its religious aura, and was catering to the degeneracy of modern, urban society. Without giving up its origins, Coke had indeed spread to the city along with most of the population of the industrial New South, leaving the WCTU and other Fundamentalist-inspired groups back in the rural Reconstruction, with only the heavenly powers to fight off the dangers of Darwin and the decadence of modern life. Coke's past ties were not to be forgotten. As late as 1933, when Prohibition was finally repealed, an *Atlantic Journal* editor saw problems for the "Great National Temperance Beverage." Woodruff was unperturbed by the attacks and imagined liabilities. He termed the latter "nonsense"; repeal could also help Coca-Cola, whose sales were magnificent in wet Canada during the height of Prohibition.

Like the changing South, the Coca-Cola Company had found its own place between country and city, between the old inclinations of Samuel Candler Dobbs and the Woodruffs' modern preferences. Just as they had endured among the bottler clans, elements of the old folk culture survived in the city—as they do to this day—and were of inestimable value in the company's transition, stability, and prosperity in the Great Depression. Referring to Coca-Cola's distinctly Southern nature, a 1931 *Fortune Magazine* article borrows from the language of one of advertising's greatest slogans to describe the ancient Southern penchant for idle amusement. Recalling a half dozen gentlemen sitting in an Atlanta candy store discussing cotton prices and drinking Coca-Cola, the article observes that "the Southerner exhibits an inexhaustible capacity for pausing and an inexhaustible capacity for being refreshed. To both these needs, Coca-Cola lovingly ministers."

During the Depression, the simple means of Coca-Cola's production protected the company's profits, which hit a record $3½ million in 1930 on sales of well over $41 million. The company had no labor problem, since there were, at most, only seventy-five unskilled laborers in the Atlanta plant, which produced one-fourth of that year's 30 million gallons of syrup. Most workers were involved with the manufacture of barrels to hold the syrup. There was no major investment in machinery, no heavy power consumption, and no assets to depreciate. The dumping of sugar into the 2,500-gallon tanks and the loading of finished syrup constituted the whole of the operation. Commenting on the languid production pace, the *Fortune* article pointed out that "Waiting for the sugar to go into solution is the major operation in the Coca-Cola plant."

From an examination of Coca-Cola's ads before and during the Depression, one can scarcely tell that a national catastrophe was at hand. Many of them were the creation of Archie Lee, an enterprising former newspaperman from Atlanta eager to leave his literary mark on the world. Working closely with Robert Woodruff from the early twenties, Lee designed one brilliant campaign after another, and over the years captured the spirit of America as no other figure in advertising has ever done.

Born and raised in North Carolina, Lee was an idealistic youth dedicated to the principles of unfettered freedom and liberty for the individual. Like many of the disillusioned Southern writers of the post–Civil War generation, he seemed resigned to the unfortunate reality that freedom was something lost with the Civil War. In a letter to his parents shortly after World War I, the serious-minded young journalist sounded the vigilant alarm of the patriot who sees a foreign menace masking the greater threat from within—the powerful, warlike government in Washington, engulfing freedom at home in order to defend it abroad. "The curse of money is upon the world," he declared passionately, but then promptly left journalism for advertising in the hope that the spirit of freedom might yet still flicker in riches and glory. "I want to do something really worthwhile. I would die happy if it should be just one recognized and lasting thing. . . . A man who can see life in its true colors and describe it in words can gain fortune and fame. . . . Fortune and fame—they make a lot of difference."

Archie Lee joined the D'Arcy Advertising Agency in 1920, and wrote home soon after wanting to invest $1,000 in the depressed Coca-Cola stock, which was selling well under the $40 price of the year before. At that time he was already working on the Coke account, and was very confident in both his abilities and his prospects for large financial rewards. A year later he wrote, "The way to make money, of course, is to get in with people who have broad visions and are making it in large quantities." Lee was strongly attracted by the scope of Woodruff's vision, as well as his humble, almost somnolent style of management. The *Fortune* piece placed it in the Southern tradition of idleness by observing: "Mr. [Robert] Woodruff forever appears to be about to go to sleep (which he seldom does). . . ." Woodruff was completely devoid of the "arrogance of ignorance" that nurtured what Lee saw as freedom's gravest enemies—Republican administrations, religious prejudice, Prohibition, divorce, and the impending railroad strikes. Conversely, Coca-Cola's leading ad man was staunchly Democratic, nonsectarian, urban, family oriented (Woodruff was the best man at his wedding), and antilabor. Two years after joining D'Arcy he wrote, "We are in competition with the best minds in America. . . . I am making a reputation in advertising."

Lee's campaigns refined those of earlier years and broke new ground. There was still an occasional reference to the old appeal of purity—"Nature's purest and most wholesome drink" (1926), "A drink of natural flavors" (1928), or "A perfect blend of pure products from nature" (1928). The sociability campaign of 1925—"Enjoy the Sociable," "The Sociability of Thirst," "Refreshment Time"—became outright companionship in the 1930s, with such slogans as "The pause that brings friends together," "The best friend thirst ever had," and "Friend for life"; Lee expressed his own social vision in these ads. Coke was not only part of nature, but part of the great national destiny as well—"Life, liberty and the pursuit of thirst" (1926), "The national family drink" (1927), "Every day is election day for Coca-Cola" (1936).

The rhetoric of the Candler days became slogans in Lee's ads, and the art work followed the predominant trend of the period, shifting away from the formal, static elegance of the Massengale lithographs. With the improvement of color-printing techniques, Coca-Cola's ads started turning up in the glossy mass-circulation magazines, employing such well-known artists as Fred Mizen, Norman Rockwell, Hayden Hayden, Haddon Sundblom, and N.C. Wyeth.

Beyond their simplistic memorability, many of Lee's ads were marked by a punchy, hard-selling rhythm which attempted to make Coca-Cola the measure of life's quality: "It had to be good to get where it is" (1925), "The drink everybody knows" (1939), and "Ice-cold Coca-Cola is everywhere else—it ought to be in your family refrigerator" (1934). In an era of uncertainty, Coke was an old reliable standby: "Thirst come—thirst served" (1932), "Bounce back to normal" (1933), "Feel fit for what's ahead" (1934).

America's feet were still on the ground and her head in the skies in early 1929, with "High Sign of Refreshment" and "Off to a Fresh Start," and the go-getting "Meet Me at the Soda Fountain." In February of that year, Coke unveiled the brainchild of Lee's career. Coming only months before the bottom dropped out,

"The Pause That Refreshes" would be put to almost unlimited use over the next thirty years by the Coca-Cola people, who still regard it as the greatest product slogan ever coined.

The number of permutations of "The Pause . . ." that the company and the bottlers employed during the thirties is impossible to say. Through 1933 alone, there was "4 P.M.—The Pause That Refreshes," "Pause and Refresh Yourself," "That Refreshing Pause," "Dear Santa, Please Pause Here," "Any time is the right time to pause and refresh," "Coca-Cola—the pause that brings friends together." It was an endless variation on the same sales message, and the company's extensive use of it was prompted, at least in part, by the numerous research and market psychology studies which Coca-Cola undertook in the 1920s. By the end of the decade, the company had developed a comprehensive advertising manifesto based on the rest-work cycle that practically amounted to a creed. Borrowing from the language of its advertising, an early 1940s company pamphlet claimed that Coca-Cola fit perfectly into this cycle, and the body's natural inclination to "pause and be refreshed."

In a 1953 address to an association of English industrialists, company vice-president Hammond Nicholson spoke of the ever-growing trend of "living-at-work" in which the whole gamut of the workers' freedoms and pleasures (the prime example in this case being that of drinking Coca-Cola) was increasingly to be found in the work place. Nicholson's audience was undoubtedly intrigued by this line of reasoning, especially since widespread labor revolts of the Depression were a painful reminder of the importance to the economy of a cheap, orderly, productive labor force. Though Coca-Cola itself had no labor problem, a 1932 ad sought to identify it with the concerns of its corporate peers: "Big Business Pauses for Refreshment."

And pause it might over Coca-Cola, for the company was in an enviable position. Except for a 30 percent drop in earnings between 1932 and 1933, every year of the decade set a new record. Profits were over $14 million in 1934, and had fully doubled by 1940, at just under $29 million. While banks failed, Coke's profits soared. Whole industries ground to a halt, but Coke's sales simply surged ahead. In the South, even King Cotton encountered a glutted world market, and precipitated financial disaster throughout the economy, worsening the already dire straits of bankers, businessmen, and laborers, along with the farmers and sharecroppers.

Whether from his beloved Ichuay plantation in southern Georgia or at Coca-Cola's Atlanta headquarters, Robert Woodruff could still look out on an America that justified his bedrock faith in laissez-faire capitalism and the old individualist heritage. This faith formed his fundamental opposition to socialism and later, to Franklin Delano Roosevelt.

Roosevelt, however, was a Democrat, and that was reason enough to welcome him in 1932. The South had long been solidly Democratic and so had Coca-Cola. Candler's clan sent two congressmen to Washington, and Asa's father, Samuel, had been a delegate to the 1860 Democratic National Convention. The calamitous changes the South underwent in the Reconstruction at the hands of the Republicans were second only to the Civil War itself. Desperate as Southerners were for federal aid during the Depression—aid which Roosevelt heaped in ever greater amounts on their unrelievable poverty—his leadership quickly came to threaten the power structure of the South with overzealous labor and agricultural reforms. Conservative Southern leaders who held decisive congressional votes which the President needed, enacted measure after measure of Roosevelt's New Deal programs, as long as he went along with their vision of race relations and traditional free enterprise. By 1936, however, Southern rulers were sounding the alarm; it was a matter of the New Deal versus the New South, and there was little question where the heart of old Dixie lay.

Perhaps owing to Coca-Cola's success in these years, Woodruff's opposition to Roosevelt was motivated more by principle than passion; national politics did not particularly interest him at this time. Beyond running Coca-Cola, he furthered the company's patronage of the Methodist establishment through a series of charitable donations, administered by the Trust Company of Georgia. The object of this patronage has been the same over the years. Woodruff's gifts to Methodist-owned Emory College have surpassed $150 million, primarily to the huge medical complex, to create new diagnostic clinics, a dental department, and other hospital divisions. Over half of Emory's $277 million endowment is in Coca-Cola stock. Emory reciprocated Coke's patronage with scientific support rather than religious blessings, producing numerous medical spokesmen who have defended the drink against repeated charges of its harmfulness.

Enduring as the relationship between these two corporate entities had been, the Fundamentalist soil that so enriched their earlier growth had shifted. Southerners now lived in cities. The primitive emotionalism of revivalist religion gave way to more formalized social behavior; Southerners tended to see themselves in a less personal and more social context. The Depression Era produced a good deal more rage and outer-directed anger than the deep-seated feelings of pain and inadequacy which provided Methodism with its converts and Coca-Cola with its first generation of consumers. Regardless of the ministers' proclamations that the Great Blight was punishment for the people's sins, the hysterical fever of the Revivals was no answer to the despair of the Depression. Coca-Cola, however, moved with the changing times, and a great many people found temporary escape in the solace of the Pause That Refreshed.

Ever since Asa Candler exhorted his sons to go forward and "map out new conquests" for Coca-Cola in their travels abroad, the company had shown a decided trend toward foreign markets. During the Candler era, soda fountains and bottling operations were instituted in Cuba, Canada, Germany, Hawaii, Bermuda, Mexico, France, England, Puerto Rico, and the Philippines. Charles Howard Candler secured a few small orders on a trip to England in 1900, and in 1919, a Frenchman undertook a belated "war effort" by selling the drink to American servicemen in Bordeaux. He also tried to peddle the syrup in Paris cafés, where an American proprietor shunned him saying, "That's what made the States go dry, and that's why I'm over here." Catering only to the American tourist market in the provinces, the overseas operations were also victimized by delays in shipping.

Woodruff's determination to fulfill Coke's global potential was very much in keeping with a general movement toward internationalism in Southern business and politics since World War I. Primarily a raw materials economy, the South was heavily engaged in world economics and, except for certain tariff-protected industries such as sugar and textiles, was steeped in the laissez-faire tradition. The South voted heavily in favor of such free-trade agreements as those proposed in 1934 by Cordell Hull, FDR's secretary of state and a Southerner himself. Despite the isolationism of the general populace, the South's ancestral ties to Great Britain promoted the region's emergence as a leading proponent of American internationalism, especially in areas affecting the Atlantic alliance.

In 1925 Woodruff traveled to Europe to study marketing possibilities, and in 1926 he established the Foreign Department to facilitate wholesale production abroad. Company technicians perfected a way to condense syrup into concentrate in order to facilitate shipping. Woodruff also hired an international team of scientists to develop a refining process for beet sugar to allow widespread syrup manufacture in plants that lacked easy access to large quantities of cane sugar.

In 1930, when there were sixty-four bottlers in twenty-eight countries, Coke expanded its quest for foreign markets by forming the Coca-Cola Export Corporation. With distribution in the Far East by a bottler in Hong Kong, Coke dominated the Pacific market until the outbreak of World War II. At that time, Coca-Cola could boast nearly a hundred bottling plants in seventy-eight countries. Unlike the domestic franchises, whose proven markets justified large capital investments, many of the early foreign operations were direct subsidiaries of the Export Corporation. Yet the men in the international field hustled with the drive and resourcefulness of fully franchised domestic bottlers. Ray Powers, for example—a personal friend of Woodruff's—began in Germany in the darkest hour of 1929 with a fleet of trucks, a powerful sales pitch, and high hopes that were crushed in the Depression. His successor, Max Keith, overcame many obstacles, including the Germans' preference for beer and their habit of drinking their beverages at room temperature. These difficulties did little to arouse investor interest in bottling franchises, and Keith was forced to sell through small wholesalers, whom he infected with his enthusiasm for the product. During his first year in 1933, sales nearly doubled to 111,000 cases, and a year later, a second plant was opened in Frankfurt. But the real boom came with the 1936 Olympics. Despite the Nazi health authority's disapproval of the caffeine content, the drink sold heavily, and by 1939 sales reached 4,500,000 cases.

Other European territories were administered through the Canadian operation. A separate territory was set up in Britain in 1934, run by the aforementioned Hammond Nicholson. The bottling plants were small and not fully automated, and the truck fleet in London was scattered over twenty disorganized routes. Sales were low in the summer and nearly nonexistent in winter. France, Belgium, and Norway were only somewhat better. Except for Germany, Australia was probably the most successful prewar operation.

But the groundwork was laid, and by the late thirties, with more than 94 percent of the world's population living outside the United States, it was not difficult for Woodruff and the managers of the Export Corporation to see where their real future lay. What they failed to realize was that the international preeminence they sought would arrive overnight with the coming of World War II.

CHAPTER THREE

Brave New Cola

PEPSI-COLA'S ROOTS, like those of Coca-Cola, were in the New South. Caleb B. Brabham, a gregarious man from the South's emerging middle class, was forced to leave medical school when his father's business failed and, in 1893, started a pharmacy in New Bern, North Carolina. His drugstore prospered mainly because of its popular soda fountain. An alternative to the out-of-favor saloon, such fountains provided many of life's amenities, from a pick-me-up to the latest gossip. Here, Brabham was able to revive his thwarted medical aspirations by tinkering with new concoctions and remedies.

One of his elixirs, patterned after the successful Coca-Cola, became particularly popular with the locals. With a taste derived from sugar, vanilla, oils, spices, and the African kola nut, "Brad's Drink" as it was known, was intended to relieve dyspepsia—upset stomach—and peptic ulcers. Brabham knew a good thing when he drank it, and in 1893 he changed its name to the more stylish "Pepsi-Cola." In 1902, he incorporated the Pepsi-Cola Company with the back room of his drugstore as its headquarters. Within a year, he sold 7,969 gallons of syrup and carefully invested $1,888.78 in advertising. In 1904, Brabham relocated in larger quarters, and employed a franchise system remarkably similar to that of the Coca-Cola Company to market Pepsi in bottles as well as soda-fountain syrup.

Though young Pepsi suffered the same ambivalence between medicinal virtues and leisure refreshment that beset early Coca-Cola, success came quickly for the infant company, as it was nurtured by the same temperance movement that fed its Southern sibling. By 1909, Brabham could boast a little barony of 250 bottlers in twenty-four states, and the company was well on its way to becoming a multi-million-dollar business.

World War I changed all of that, as it staggered the global economy and sent the cost of labor and materials soaring. In particular, the price of sugar jumped from 5½ cents a pound during the war—thanks to government price controls—to 22½ cents by 1920, catching Pepsi and its bottlers in the squeeze. In a desperate hedge against future price increases, Brabham, like Samuel Candler Dobbs at Coca-Cola, invested heavily in sugar at the latter price, only to watch it plummet within months to 3½ cents a pound. The damage had been done. The 1921 stockholders meeting noted that Brabham's decision had cost the Pepsi-Cola Company $150,000 at a time when the Pepsi apparatus was already crippled. Brabham had been unable to cope with the complexities of a rapidly changing postwar economy, and the company bottomed out in 1922. Bankrupt, Caleb Brabham humbly returned to his drugstore.

49

Pepsi was resurrected by Roy C. Megargel, a Wall Street financier who envisioned Pepsi as a nationally distributed product. He salvaged the trademark and assets from the ruins and started a new Pepsi-Cola Company in Richmond, Virginia. For several years he struggled to revive the company with investment capital. However, insufficient funds limited all-important advertising, which in turn kept volume low. In 1932, despite Megargel's efforts, the Pepsi-Cola Company went bankrupt again.

The company's remains came to the attention of Charles Guth, lord and master of Loft, Inc., a bustling candy concern in Long Island City, New York. A square-jawed, steely-eyed despot with an ego as grand as his ambitions, Guth had been rebuffed by the Coca-Cola Company when he demanded a discount on the 31,000 gallons of Coke syrup sold annually in his chain of 115 retail stores throughout the East. Guth stubbornly decided to market his own beverage, and bought the trademark and assets of Pepsi out of bankruptcy.

Guth used $10,500 of Loft's capital to buy Pepsi-Cola's proprietary rights for $10,500 and established a new Pepsi-Cola Company, with himself and Megargel, a silent partner, as sole stockholders. After altering the drink's taste, he began making the concentrate at Loft's Long Island City laboratory, housed in the building named for the gentleman who reportedly once owned it, Asa Candler.

Although the new Pepsi-Cola Company amounted to less than a drop in Coke's bucket, the stage was set for their first confrontation. Coke's management began complaining that customers at Loft stores were unknowingly served Pepsi-Cola when they had ordered Coca-Cola. To substantiate the charge, undercover agents sent by Atlanta on Coke-and-dagger missions to Loft stores later testified that they witnessed the practice. Guth dispatched his own spies, who claimed that Coke's soda spooks were agent provocateurs sent to harass and malign Pepsi-Cola. The struggle was taken into the courts, where, as we shall see, it would not be decided until 1942.

With Loft stores the sole outlet, the Pepsi-Cola Company was sinking steadily. Guth suddenly wanted out, and even offered to sell Pepsi to the Coca-Cola Company, whose refusal was certainly the blunder of its history. Furthermore, Megargel sued for funds owed him, but Guth bought him out for $35,000, $34,500 of which he simply took from Loft's treasury. Guth now owned 91 percent of a very shaky soft-drink company.

As Pepsi was about to fold for a third time, a used bottle dealer suggested to Guth that Pepsi be put in used beer bottles. Although beer bottles were twelve ounces, twice the size of Coke's six and a half ounces, their costs were minimal and Guth agreed. Sales still lagged when he charged ten cents, twice the Depression price, but when he lowered it to a nickel, giving twice the soda at his competitor's price, sales instantly skyrocketed. "Two large glasses in each bottle," boasted ad copy. Twice as much for the same money was a compelling deal for most folks during the great Depression. Within six months, Pepsi became a force to be reckoned with and Guth learned a fundamental tenet: sales were a direct result not only of promotion, but of packaging and price as well. He hadn't changed his product at all, but simply merchandised it more effectively.

Sales boomed and Guth became aware of another industry equation: volume was a direct result of expanding markets. Thereafter, he tightened relations with his remaining bottlers and aggressively sought new ones. Coke had amply demonstrated that it was the bottlers who would anoint the world with the beverage and in 1934, Pepsi had its first foreign bottling plant in Montreal. King Coke was still number one, but young Pepsi was now an earnest competitor.

Guth had ignored the candy business while tending to his up-and-coming star. The resultant financial chaos saddled Loft with a labor strike and stockholder revolt in 1935, amid which Guth judiciously resigned his post. Unfortunately for Loft's new president, James W. Carkner, Guth still controlled enough Loft stock to dictate company policy. Carkner began frantic efforts to keep the company solvent while extricating it from Guth's influence.

After an initial audit, Carkner discovered that Guth had wantonly used Loft money and resources to acquire and nurture the Pepsi-Cola Company for his own gain. Fearing that Guth's discovery of his suspicions would cost him his job, Carkner sneaked his legal counsel into the offices in the dead of night to examine the records. Two weeks later they reported that Guth's Pepsi-Cola had indeed drunk deeply from Loft's corporate veins. To save their failing company, Carkner and his fellow directors at Loft launched a bold last-minute gambit: they sued Guth for the ownership of Pepsi-Cola.

Loft vs. Guth, a landmark case, addressed the question of rightful ownership, which had traditionally been defined in a narrow literal way. The fact that Guth had actually owned the Pepsi-Cola Company without challenge would normally make him legally impervious. However, Loft attorneys argued that because Loft had actually assumed the risks for Guth's venture, the company should in turn reap the benefits.

Clever as the suit was, Loft could barely meet its payroll, let alone engage in a lengthy, hotly contested civil suit, and Carkner knew that Guth would move to fire him at the upcoming stockholders meeting, terminate the suit, and reinstall himself as president. Carkner anticipated the result of this struggle when he turned to Phoenix Securities Corporation, a Wall Street consulting and investment firm.

Like its namesake, the mythological bird, Phoenix Securities rescued corporations from the ashes of bankruptcy and nursed them back to life. It supplied needed cash to the ailing concern by buying up large quantities of stock, usually at a depressed price, with options to buy more. A Phoenix official was then placed on the board of directors to provide an incisive, tough-minded analysis of management and its policies. Phoenix would then reorganize the firm and implement the proper cures, hoping that the value of its stock would rise, making Phoenix's original stock purchase and its options very profitable. Phoenix played the game well and, by 1933, had acquired a handsome portfolio that included large chunks of some fair-sized businesses.

Phoenix's method is not recommended for the timid or uninitiated. Its leadership possessed inordinate business skills, gambler's nerves, and pit-boss toughness. Chairman of the board was Wallace Groves, a cunning man with a propensity for high risks and big ventures. In 1941, he was convicted of mail fraud and ended up in Federal prison for five months. Ironically, Groves hailed from Atlanta, and his family knew Ernest Woodruff. However, center stage belonged to his ambitious partner, Walter Staunton Mack, Jr.

Although Mack intended to sell Loft candies in the retail chain of the United Cigar/Whelan Drug Company, in which Phoenix Securities held an interest, he was gambling for the gleam in his eye—the Pepsi-Cola Company, the child wonder of the industry. From 1934 to 1937—when a dime bought two soft drinks—Pepsi netted over $9½ million. By 1938, there were 313 franchised bottlers and profits were $4 million, double that of 1936. Mack had been impressed with Loft's prospects of winning the Pepsi-Cola suit, provided the candy firm didn't go bankrupt or that Guth didn't regain power in the interim.

With characteristic zeal, Mack began preparing a strategy for the embattled candy company by purchasing 31,000 shares (or one-sixth of Loft), for needed leverage in the anticipated proxy fight. The polemics became quite heated, but when the dust settled and the proxies were counted, it was found that the stockholders had endorsed the Phoenix/Loft team. Carkner remained as president, and joined Loft's board of directors with Mack, Groves, and nine other handpicked candidates.

The first battle was won: Loft was securely controlled by Carkner and Mack. Yet Guth remained a formidable opponent. He already had an eye on foreign distribution for Pepsi, and in his hectic world the only real worry was the trial. Mack began to shore up Loft so it might survive the ensuing legal battle. Phoenix loaned Loft $400,000, and provided collateral for another $600,000 worth of notes in return for an equivalent amount of stock options.

The trial convened on November 10, 1937 in the Delaware Court of Chancery. For forty-six days, cadres of attorneys marshaled their arguments. When it was over, the court agreed with Loft that Guth could not have acquired the Pepsi-Cola Company had he not summarily expropriated Loft's resources. Down to the last bottle cap, the Pepsi-Cola Company belonged to Loft. In the wake of the news, Loft stock rose $5 per share and Phoenix immediately exercised its options, purchasing nearly 375,000 shares at the previously agreed-upon price of a little over $1.50 per share. Within several months, the stock reached $11. Guth appealed the decision and, in the interim, the Court appointed representatives from both sides to manage Pepsi. Mack was appointed president, a position he would enjoy for more than a decade. Guth was named general manager, all the time preparing for a possible loss of Pepsi by clandestinely establishing a new soft-drink company in Canada under the unctuous name of Noxie-Cola. But the scheme was uncovered and Guth was removed from his position.

On April 11, 1939, the Delaware Supreme Court upheld the lower court ruling. As settlement, Guth was given an estimated $300,000 and shown the door, with the stipulation that he stay out of the cola business for five years. Phoenix's strategy had worked brilliantly. Having bought nearly half of Loft when it was all but worthless, Phoenix now owned a thriving multi-million-dollar operation spread across the United States and Canada and gearing up in Cuba and England.

The Pepsi-Cola Company would have a long history of strong-willed and controversial leaders, and Walter Mack was one of the best. He was the right man at the right time. With his bowlers or wide-brimmed straw hats, a six-foot, one-inch frame often draped in trendy suits of his own design, sad blue eyes, and a resolute mouth, Mack cut a dashing if not heroic figure. He was a creative and freewheeling showman who gave the company a desperately needed sense of style and identity. To borrow from Alexander Pope, he was "a being darkly wise and rudely great."

Much of Mack's determination and flair trace back to his youth. His father was in the frenzied textile business and his mother was the daughter of a Texas Ranger. He learned how to be tough on the streets of New York City. Bright as well as streetwise, Mack attended Harvard where he studied economics and mathematics. After his Ivy League training, he enlisted in the Navy in 1917 and served on destroyers and transports on the Atlantic. When the war ended, he met success but not challenge in the textile and investment banking businesses, and moved on to the more venturesome Phoenix Securities.

With boundless energy, Mack began repairing the damage suffered during the strenuous fight with Guth. Pepsi-Cola's 1939 sales were up 39 percent from the previous year with net earnings at a robust $5.6 million. The candy business, which had seen more than its share of difficulties over the years, was finally divested from Pepsi. The future lay in soda.

Mack quickly grasped the unique properties of the soft-drink industry. He understood the interdependent relationship between the soft-drink manufacturer and its licensed bottlers. Consequently, he scoured the country for prospective bottlers, but in every locality found only lean and tottering local soft-drink operations laboring in the shadows of corpulent Coke franchises. One by one, Mack wooed the best of the small fry to bottle Pepsi-Cola. In addition, Mack set out to reassure his existing bottlers, whose confidence had been eroded by Guth's one-man show.

His efforts also included periodic meetings with stockholders, an unpopular move among corporate presidents at that time. He explains with typical assurance: "A lot of big corporations are scared to death of their stockholders, and their executives say to me, 'Walter, why the hell do you go out of your way to expose yourself to your stockholders, anyway?' Well, there isn't anything I've done for Pepsi-Cola that I'm ashamed to talk about. The stockholders may not always agree with what I do, but I'm not afraid to tell them why I've done it." His act was impressive and his enthusiasm contagious. In his dapper but earthy fashion, Mack endeared many to the company and himself, and the Pepsi-Cola Company grew faster than ever.

However, there was some unfinished business. Once Pepsi had dared to be more than a regional cola manufacturer, the showdown with King Coke was inevitable. For years, the gentlemen from Atlanta kept a wary eye on the startling performance of the upstart, and by the late thirties they had seen enough. They escalated their struggle with Pepsi from occasional jousts at Loft stores to international conflict. The Coca-Cola Company attacked in the same way it had struck the other cola infidels—by going for the trademark, the legal identity of a product. The issue was Pepsi's use of the word "cola," to which Coke claimed proprietary rights.

According to Mack, Coke's first trademark violation suit against Pepsi was filed in New York in 1938. "Coke put on a great show" by hauling into court impressive stacks of brown legal briefs detailing Coke's successes against all other cola heretics. Fortuitously, Pepsi appeared so helpless, claims Mack, that the widow of a former victim came to offer her condolences during the trial. Her husband had been president of Cleo Cola, a New Jersey company recently smitten in court by Coke. Mack asserts that in the midst of her sympathies, she inadvertently revealed that Coke had given her husband a $35,000 check. Sensing payoff, Mack obtained a copy and found it drawn from the special account of Coke's legal counsel. The next day in court, says Mack, Pepsi's attorney requested a discussion of Coke's victorious Cleo Cola case and inquired into the $35,000 check. Coke's counsel requested and received a two-day delay to respond.

That afternoon, as Mack tells it, Robert Woodruff called Mack. He just happened to be in Manhattan and invited Mack to the Waldorf Towers for breakfast the next morning. The only available account of what took place comes from Mack.

"Mr. Mack, I've been thinking about this lawsuit, and I think we ought to settle it. Is that agreeable to you?"

"It is, under one condition."

"What is that condition?"

Mack took a piece of Waldorf stationery and wrote, "I, Robert Woodruff, president and chief executive officer of the Coca-Cola Company, hereby agree that the corporation will recognize the Pepsi-Cola trademark and never attack it in the United States."

Mack handed it and the pen to Woodruff.

"Sign it," he said.

Woodruff did, a second agreement was drafted whereby Pepsi agreed to recognize Coke, and their lawyers later made it official.

The case was settled and the secret of Coke's $35,000 check was safe. Yet the truce was momentary. Coke claimed the agreement applied only to the United States and, assuming that Pepsi couldn't defend itself overseas, dispatched attorneys to file trademark violation suits in a dozen countries.

Coke drew the first blood when a Canadian court declared that the name Pepsi-Cola was indeed an infringement on the Coca-Cola trademark. Pepsi-Cola parried in 1939 with an appeal to the Canadian Supreme Court, which reversed the lower court's decision, ruling that cola is a generic word descriptive of any beverage derived from the cola nut. In 1942, staggered by the prospects of its first legal defeat, Coke petitioned the exalted Privy Council in London, the highest court in the British Commonwealth.

"It was a hell of a dirty trick," said Mack, "because it was during the war and they had lawyers over there. The Privy Council had set a date and they felt we couldn't get anyone over there."

Mack countered decisively by garnering the services of a brilliant trial attorney and the Republican Party's 1940 presidential candidate—the Honorable Wendell Willkie. Mack himself had been active in Republican circles and shared Willkie's yearning for an American presence in international affairs and, for a $25,000 retainer plus contingency fees, Willkie agreed to defend Pepsi against its rival's portentous copyright suit. Arrangements were made for Willkie to speak in England for the war effort, and thus he was flown over in an Air Force bomber to strike out against fascism and monopoly.

The Privy Council finally decided in favor of Pepsi, and requested both companies to coexist in peace. Coke's attack failed. To the disappointment of trademark attorneys throughout the world, an armistice was reached between the two soft-drink leaders and scores of suits and countersuits were dropped. The Coca-Cola Company could only salvage the word "Coke" which it began inscribing on its bottles by the end of 1941. In the beginning of 1942, the company ran ads that said, "Coca-Cola, known too as Coke . . ., the friendly abbreviation for the trademark 'Coca-Cola.' "*

Some whispered darkly, says Coke biographer E.J. Kahn, that the Privy Council upheld the Canadian court's decision out of fear of straining the unity of the Commonwealth at a time when Britain was faring poorly in World War II. Regardless, Coke had committed a strategic blunder by not attacking Pepsi when it was a helpless orphan. Young Pepsi had staked out a real piece of the soft-drink market, demonstrating that King Coke was anything but invincible.

---

* The Pepsi-Cola Company wasn't the only victor. A Delaware court arrived at a similar decision in a suit involving the Nehi Corporation, makers of Royal Crown Cola. Overjoyed, Nehi took out full-page magazine and newspaper ads touting the ruling: "Court Decides In Favor of Royal Crown Cola."

CHAPTER FOUR

Coke Was My Co-Pilot

IN 1940, Coca-Cola was under a successful challenge by an earnest competitor. At the same time, America's isolationism was being challenged by political forces at home and abroad. Market domination was going the way of manifest destiny. No longer a matter of blind forces, both would have to be protected and maintained by careful planning in a complex, chaotic world.

Coke continued to be part of Southern tradition where it began, in Atlanta, the cultural center of the region and the South's second largest industrial center. The 1939 opening of *Gone With the Wind* in Atlanta's Civic Center was the occasion for the most ebullient outpouring of Southern nostalgia in this century. "We may be certain," writes Pat Watters, "that the people of Coca-Cola were among the happiest and most charming of the celebrants." Although a swastika was displayed on Peachtree Street during an international Baptist convention in 1939, Atlantans were probably as unmindful as any of the debacle ahead. The acute recession had passed and the recovery brought prosperity in its wake. President Roosevelt laid the New Deal to rest, desiring now simply to preserve its reforms. Across the Atlantic, the conflagration raged; at home, barely an inkling.

When America went to war, Coke went to war. Pearl Harbor was still ablaze when Robert Woodruff declared the Coca-Cola Company would make Coke available to American servicemen for a nickel a bottle anywhere in the world.

It was meant to be a grand gesture, patriotic and inspiring beside the shock and grim resignation over the war. Coke was to march with the infantry, sail the seas, and soar the wild, blue yonder, the Georgia-green bottle in battle fatigues. Woodruff's pronouncement bubbled with a fearless idealism rarely heard since the doughboys rolled into battle in the last war. It extended two of the most prominent themes of its ad campaigns—universal availability and the nickel price—to the war campaign. Beside this surging patriotism, the decision was a master stroke of public relations with far-reaching implications for the company. Though the company would undoubtedly have footed the bill for this massive project, it was spared much expense when a War Department circular, signed by General George C. Marshall, informed theater commanders that they could order entire bottling plants directly to the front lines with the food and munitions.* Elevating Coca-Cola to the status of a wartime priority item, this order relieved the company of the dreaded sugar rationing that had so hindered its sales during World War I. Coca-Cola otherwise destined for Main Street in peacetime was rerouted to the troops overseas.

* Watters, op. cit., p. 164

This order reflected the Chief of Staff's conviction that nothing would perk G.I. morale like ice-cold Coke. The company would hardly disagree. "When a soldier has a Coke," said one company vice-president, "it satisfies his need to identify with the American tradition and way of life. It reminds him of what he's fighting for." Stories and letters flowing back from the battlefront indeed revealed the nostalgia and heroic sensibilities aroused by the mere thought of a Coke, much less the real thing itself. Beside the family and the flag, Coca-Cola was a slice of America, that little piece of home for which G.I.s fought.

The indelible mark the drink had left in their hearts was the flowering of Coke's relationship with the American Way. Millions of dollars of advertising spread across half a century had inextricably woven Coke into that experience to a point where the two were virtually inseparable. To the fighting man, Coke seemed to say more of freedom and high ideals than any Roosevelt or Churchill speech. In the heat and urgency of the times, the soldiers could not have realized that when the shooting was over, the world would be not only safe for democracy, but ready for an American presence spearheaded by the champion of wartime morale—the Coca-Cola Company.

Coke's campaign was prodigious. Sixty-four bottling plants were established behind Allied lines, and bottling machines that would have lain idle at home due to wartime sugar rationing were reportedly purchased from the bottlers by the company, dismantled, and flown to the front. Beginning in North Africa and moving up into Italy, the bottling plants followed the battlefronts, picking up and relocating as the fighting advanced through Europe and the rest of the world. Plants were established in France, Germany, India, the Philippines, England, and Australia. Ice-making machines and portable dispensers were devised for the various terrains, including a specially adapted jungle dispenser for General Douglas MacArthur's Pacific campaigns (MacArthur attended the opening of the first postwar plant in Manila and signed a commemorative tag attached to the first bottle). Thinner, lighter dispensers were designed for submarines and some fighter planes. When a plant was needed in China, another in India was dismantled and flown over the Himalayas piece by piece. After D-Day, the plants followed the Army columns as they blasted on to Berlin. When the government requested qualified personnel to help run the plants, the Coca-Cola Company dispatched 148 men to the Army as "technical observers." Known affectionately as the "Coca-Cola Colonels," they were assigned officer status and quickly became an integral part of the war effort (three were killed). During the Battle of the Bulge in 1944, one arrived to oversee the installation of a $250,000 plant and found to his dismay that a crane line had broken, leaving a thirty-five-ton, sixty-spout bottle filler on the bottom of the harbor. With a case of Coke, the "Colonel" bribed an officer to procure a tank retriever and recruit a reconnaissance team to haul it up and restore it to its original condition. When the first portable dispensers arrived in Australia, another Coke Colonel had to reorder dozens of new parts when he discovered that the British and American screw threads didn't fit together. "Things like that . . .," he mused, and "you lose the war."

Coke's greatest wartime champion was General Dwight Eisenhower, Supreme Allied Commander. He demanded abundant supplies of Coke wherever his armies went. For example, in a cable known as the "Eisenhower Cable," he requested eight Coke plants immediately after his armies landed on the beaches of North Africa. He even gave a case of Coke to Marshall Zhukov at the Potsdam Conference in 1945. Fortunately for the Coca-Cola Company, Ike would carry his sweet tooth right into the White House.

Indeed, Coca-Cola serviced the Axis as well as the Allies. Max Keith, whose successful German operation for Coca-Cola Export was just gathering momentum after the 1936 Olympic Games, continued undeterred by the outbreak of conflict. When the Nazis placed restrictions on imports, Keith was able to bring in the syrup concentrate through "contacts" in Air Minister Hermann Goering's office, which he established through the European representative of an American bank.* Shortly after the war began, Keith's lawyer in Berlin succeeded in having the Office of Enemy Propaganda appoint him an official administrator of soft-drink production in occupied territories. He was thus able to move easily in Luxembourg, Belgium, France, Holland, Norway, Switzerland, and Italy.

To keep up the beverage flow during the syrup shortage, Keith himself concocted a formula from available ingredients, which he named Fanta, short for fantastic. The product name survives to this day. When air raids threatened the bottlers in the city, Keith arranged for "siding plants," farmhouses, and dairy barns to be set up in the countryside. Spurred by small bottling machines, plenty of electricity, and good country water, sales of Fanta maintained an even level no matter how severe the bombings. Keith filled his empty Coke bottles with fresh drinking water and delivered them to the beleaguered cities. In return, the German authorities permitted him to keep his trucks, and even supplied them with gasoline.

Keith's dealings with the Nazis were by no means secure. At the outbreak of the war, Coca-Cola was targeted as a Jewish-American company when a German competitor bandied about some Coca-Cola crown corks with a kosher sign on them. Keith was under constant pressure to join the Nazi party, but managed to resist. Sugar was as vital to the Reich's armies as it was to American troops, and Keith continuously aided bottlers in Nazi territories who were suspected of hoarding sugar. Under threat of severe penalties if discovered, he helped them conceal bags of sugar behind hundreds of Coca-Cola cases stacked to the ceilings of the plants. Wishing to avoid any undue attention, Keith and his bottlers kept a low profile by maintaining an even sales volume and a reasonable profit margin. Toward the end of the war, Keith avoided expropriation of company holdings and deportation to a concentration camp only after two German officers separately met with sudden deaths, each less than twenty-four hours before they were to interrogate Keith. In 1945, Max Keith was liberated by the U.S. Marines and a team of Coca-Cola Colonels.

The Coca-Cola Company claimed that "next to wives and sweethearts and

---

* Watters, Coca-Cola, op. cit., p. 164

letters from home, among the things our fighting men overseas mention most [in their letters] is Coca-Cola." There was certainly truth to this claim. Coke was a taste of back home, of everything good and God-fearin', of Mom, of Main Street, of—Coca-Cola. "I can truthfully say," declared a soldier, "that I haven't seen smiles spread over a bunch of boys' faces like they did when they saw the Coca-Cola in that God-forsaken place. I don't know what I'm saving the Coke for, but I guess it keeps my morale up just to have it and look at it."

Stories about Coke during the war abound. Legend has it that chaplains were required to dole out the drink in times of scarcity. Coke biographer E. J. Kahn recounts some of the remarks in his book *The Big Drink**: "A young lady who lived in the Bronx passed along an excerpt from a love letter that her one and only, an Army corporal had written in Europe: 'Well, I guess you want to know now what it is I want so much, outside of you. Well, darling, it is a bottle of Coca-Cola.' A private first class in Burma wrote his Aunt: 'To my mind, I am in this damn mess as much to help keep the custom of drinking Cokes as I am to help preserve the millions of other benefits our country blesses its citizens with. . . . May we all toast victory soon with a Coke—if flavored with a little rum, I'm sure no one will object.' The Japanese tortured our Marines in the Southwest Pacific by dwelling interminably on the forsaken pleasures of drinking Coke ('Can't you just hear the ice tinkling in the glass?'). It was fiendish."

Bottles of Coke were valued at four dollars in the Solomon Islands, ten dollars in Casablanca, and as high as forty at a remote Alaskan base. A Navy lieutenant in the Pacific thought Coke was the "nectar of the gods"; a sailor in the Mediterranean asked his girl friend to scent her next letter with a drop of Coke. The first bottle of Coke to land at Anzio was carefully shared by nineteen G.I.s, and Colonel Robert Scott, author of *God Is My Co-Pilot*, was touched when fellow pilots awarded him a bottle of Coke for shooting down his fifth Japanese Zero. The story has it that he gave it to a surgeon who operated on him, who in turn gave it to a native boy recuperating from cholera.

At home, Coke's promotions strongly identified the drink with the war effort. Advertisements captured the mood and zeal of Americans at war. Three weeks after Pearl Harbor, an ad showed a hand thrusting a Coke bottle from an Air Force fighter wing; the copy read: "A time of crisis comes to America. The rising tempo of emergency is felt in factory and camp. It reaches into home and school. . . . Americans must be fit . . . avoid the tensions that lower efficiency." Of the things that made one "fit," one of them was the "pause that refreshes. On sea and land, it follows the flag." Even before sugar rationing went into effect, the company published a propaganda pamphlet that reiterated the theme of Coca-Cola's central role in the working place. Entitled "Importance of the Rest-Pause in Maximum War Effort," the booklet reprinted a batch of letters from civilian war workers suggesting that they could hardly survive without a Coke: "True, all nature moves in a rhythm of rest and action, and momentary

---

* E. J. Kahn, *The Big Drink* (New York: Random House, 1960).

pauses are biologically essential." Another pamphlet proclaimed, "And we, identifying ourselves with this rhythm, are to that degree essential." The pitch to wartime workers was ceaseless: "Our fighting men are delighted to meet up with Coca-Cola in many places overseas. Coca-Cola has been a globe-trotter since way back when. Even with war, Coca-Cola today is being bottled on the spot in over thirty-five Allied and neutral nations." (Sometimes the company went beyond the call of duty such as when it produced and distributed a film for the War Department entitled *The Free American Way*, which urged citizens to invest heavily in war bonds.)

Just after the outbreak of the war, as reported in *Beverage Industry*, the federal government asked the Coca-Cola Company for management assistance, and Ed Forio, a former syrup salesman and assistant to the executive vice-president, was sent to Washington to serve as the industry's consultant to the Beverage and Tobacco section of the War Production Board. One trade veteran credits Forio with smoothing the adjustment to wartime production: ". . . he kept the industry going during those critical years."* Forio served his country for a token dollar a year, and in light of his prior allegiances and subsequent politics, it seems possible that he remained on the company payroll during this period. In 1943, while hard at work in Washington, Forio was elected vice-president of the Coca-Cola Company.

Walter Mack recalls Forio's activities differently. "Forio," says Mack, "used his leverage in Washington directly to help Coke and hinder Pepsi." For example, one of Forio's first directives was to limit industrial sugar users to 80 percent of their 1941 consumption. While this was acceptable for Coca-Cola bottlers who had been doing a robust business, it sounded the death knell for many struggling Pepsi bottlers. "Eighty percent of nothing is nothing," said Mack, "and they thought they had me out of business." In response, Pepsi, in 1943, paid $3 million for a sugar plantation in Cuba, the country from which most of America's sugar was imported. However, the Cuban government's own wartime rationing prevented the plantation from providing Pepsi with any sugar until 1947. Furthermore, the ships in which Pepsi's sugar was imported from Cuba and the Philippines were being diverted to the war effort. As a war priority item, Coca-Cola syrup could travel with, and often ahead of, food, provisions, and ammunition on these boats. Consequently, the only source for additional sugar open to Mack was Mexico, where he made a deal to buy the entire surplus Mexican crop for five years. Ever resourceful, Mack circumvented Pepsi's sugar quota by building a plant in the Mexican town of Monterrey, a short distance from the border, and began shipping a sugar solution into the United States. When a shortage of barrels developed, Mack bought a forest and made his own.

Mack remembers that when Forio tried to put an end to his scheme, Mack went straight to the head of the Office of Price Administration with an offer to sell the government all the Mexican sugar it wanted at cost. As Mack relates it, if

---

* Interview, Michael Locker, Corporate Data Exchange, New York

the government refused the offer, he would use the sugar for Pepsi, and if additional attempts were made to enjoin him, he would take out full-page ads in major newspapers across the country showing how, in times of need, the government would not import the sugar or permit Pepsi to do so. At the same time, Mack approached a prominent government official of the War Production Board, Charles Wilson, former head of General Electric, and complained about Forio's favoritism in the area of sugar rationing. When Mack threatened to publicize the issue, Forio resigned and returned to Atlanta. Mack asserts that the Coca-Cola Company was in no rush to see sugar rationing end after the war, and that efforts to normalize sugar supplies, as we shall see, had to be taken by Pepsi.

Coke's wartime status was the culmination of fifty years and millions of dollars of high-powered advertising. Although it lacked any nutritional value, Coke was a highly esteemed commodity because it was one of the very institutions America was defending. Coke was the deity of consumer products, and thus, the nonessential had become the indispensable.

Woodruff's decision to supply the war effort greatly enhanced the vision of a world afloat on Coca-Cola. To the dismay of other competitors, World War II was a spectacular marketing bonanza for Coke. G.I.s quaffed ten billion bottles of Coke during the war as 95 percent of all soft drinks served on American bases were products of the Coca-Cola Company. An American Legion poll on soft drink preferences found that two-thirds of five thousand veterans queried chose Coca-Cola, and a similar poll conducted by the company itself found the percentage even higher among those who served overseas. Sixty-four new Coke plants stood amid the rubble of Europe, Asia, and Africa, waiting to quench the thirsts of rebuilding nations. Fifty-nine were installed at U.S. government expense. One Coke vice-president commented on Coke's strengthened product loyalty: "What we did during the war . . . sure did make those guys love us."

Any other company would have been accused of war profiteering, but the Coca-Cola Company was unique. Because of America's incorrigible faith in the goodness and universality of Coca-Cola the company was granted a greater latitude in its political and economic dealings than was enjoyed by nearly any other company. "Coca-Cola became the global high sign," according to one company brochure. "It accomplished in World War II what would have [otherwise] taken twenty-five years and millions of dollars." Yet this achievement was built on a great deal more than the public's love of Coca-Cola. For example, the House of Representatives, acting on a Treasury Department proposal, passed a bill that called for a war tax on all soft drinks sold. This bill, opposed by the soft-drink industry, was killed by the Senate Finance Committee. As E.J. Kahn observed, the committee's chairman, Walter F. George, considered Robert Woodruff his best friend.

Moreover, in 1940, Coca-Cola plucked from the leadership of the Democratic Party one of the standard-bearers of the New Deal, James Aloysius Farley. Farley was the consummate old-school politician who, it was said, never forgot a face. Weaned on the backslapping politics of New York's Rockland County, he rose quickly through the ranks of the state democratic machine to become chairman of the Democratic National Committee in 1932. He remained a convention delegate for twenty-four years.

Farley enjoyed an intimate relationship with Franklin Roosevelt as his advisor and political drummer. During the 1932 campaign, Farley canvassed the country recruiting delegates, and F.D.R. credited him as one of the two men most responsible for his victory in his first presidential election. A biographer once remarked, "I believe that if Roosevelt had decided upon the Koran as a subject of discourse, Farley would have enthusiastically sold the product." F.D.R. expressed his appreciation by appointing him U.S. Postmaster General. From this office, he lobbied for the New Deal by aligning many disparate forces, including some conservative Southern Democratic lawmakers. Once the New Deal was underway, Farley acted as a peacemaker between the administration and opponents of the programs, which included, among others, the powerful Morgan family, which would one day hold a significant interest in the Coca-Cola Company.* It was perhaps in this role as mediator that Farley made his deepest impression on Robert Woodruff, himself an early critic of the Roosevelt Administration.

In 1940, Farley and Roosevelt parted ways in one of the most famous disputes in the Democratic Party's history. Roosevelt's quest for an unprecedented third term was strenuously opposed by Farley in principle, and perhaps because it stymied his own presidential aspirations. Himself nominated at the Democratic Convention, Farley had many supporters, including a powerful Massachusetts contingent led by Joseph P. Kennedy, Jr. Kennedy was the only delegate not to switch his vote from Farley to make Roosevelt's first ballot nomination unanimous. Despite the defeat, the tremendously popular Farley reached the height of his political career with the nomination. A month later, after rejecting at least one other corporate offer, he accepted the chairmanship of the Coca-Cola Export Corporation. He resigned his cabinet post and the chairmanship of the Democratic National Committee, but remained as head of the New York State Democratic Chapter.

In an interview before his death in 1976, Farley reflected on why he joined Coca-Cola: "It would be understood that if I went there, I wasn't going with a company where the political influence I was supposed to have would interfere with my association with the company . . . because they didn't need any influence."* On the contrary, the influence he was "supposed to have" would enhance their association. As Woodruff pointed out, "I don't care where Jim goes—Spain, England, Italy, wherever—he's entertained by the government. He keeps up all those political connections."†

Indeed, Farley proved to be as well connected in the private sector as he had

* Watters, Coca-Cola, op. cit., p. 189
† Kahn, op. cit., p. 139

been in the public. During his first months on the job, he continued efforts begun in the summer of 1940 to purchase the New York Yankees from the estate of Colonel Jacob Ruppert.* The purchasing group involved major oil magnates including a big Roosevelt backer in 1936 and the lawyers for this transaction were F.D.R.'s former law partners.

The timing of the proposed $3 million purchase led to a great deal of speculation that Farley was merely paving the way for a major investment in the baseball franchise by Coca-Cola or its major stockholders. These rumors were further fueled by the company's ownership of the Southern Association's Atlanta baseball club; Woodruff's friendship with Ty Cobb, himself a Coca-Cola bottler; and by the apparent participation in the purchase by Farley's friend, W.L. "Chip" Robert, a Coca-Cola stockholder and secretary of the Democratic National Committee.† Despite denials by Coke president A.A. Acklin, the speculation continued until the deal fell through.

Farley's first task at Coke was to increase foreign revenues beyond the current 8 to 10 percent level of total sales. Because of its remoteness from the war, Woodruff chose to send his new ambassador to the relatively stable Latin America which was not only an attractive market for Coca-Cola, but an area of deep strategic concern for America's most influential policy makers, including the prestigious Council on Foreign Relations.‡

The Council's mammoth War-Peace Studies were conducted from 1939 to 1946 in formal consultation with the State Department's Advisory Committee on Post-War Foreign Policy. The Council itself had a major hand in creating this body, ten of whose fourteen members belonged to the Council. Roosevelt acknowledged that members of the Advisory Committee were my "postwar advisors," an admission confirmed by Council and government documents which reveal unquestionably that the Council totally dominated the State Department's planning of war aims and postwar priorities. With virtually unlimited access to sensitive state secrets that were unavailable to other private organizations, it has been claimed that the Council's influence may have amounted to a de facto control of the state in the wartime era.§

Not only were the priorities adopted by the Council perfectly suited to the goals of the Coca-Cola Company, but Coke's fabulous wartime prosperity actually helped create the kind of world the Council deemed favorable to American interests. Just three months before Farley's January 1941 departure on an eighteen-nation Latin America tour for the Coca-Cola Company, the Council circulated a memorandum on the foreign policy essentials "to achieve military and economic supremacy for the United States within the nonGerman world." Hitler's sweep across Europe in mid-1940 had shocked the Council and govern-

---

* *The New York Times*, November 16,1940, p. 11
  † ibid., August 11, 1940. p. 3
  ‡ Laurence Shoup, "Shaping the Post-War World: The Council on Foreign Relations and United States War Aims During World War II," *Insurgent Sociologist*, Vol. V, #III; Spring, 1975
  § ibid.

ment planners. They determined that the United States would urgently need to consolidate the entire Western Hemisphere, including Latin America, the British Empire, and the Far East into a cohesive trading block if the existing American economic structure were to survive. Once safe from Nazi economic competition and political penetration, this "Grand Area" could coexist with Hitler, and later become an organized center for unifying the German-controlled regions into a one-world economy.

Helping to secure the "Grand Area" seems to have been at least one aspect of Farley's Latin American mission. In fact, coverage of his tour reveals quite clearly that the former cabinet officer was not only attending to the business of Coca-Cola, but to the affairs of state as well. The new chairman of Coca-Cola Export had a great deal to say in support of Latin American loans and Secretary of State Cordell Hull's reciprocal trade agreements, but remained largely silent on the Coca-Cola matters which he had ostensibly been sent to explore.* His silence tended to create the impression that the vital interests of Coca-Cola were less of a priority than those of the country. In fact, they seem to have been skillfully intertwined, and nowhere was this more apparent than in Brazil, the first leg of Farley's Latin tour.

Long considered the hub of Latin America, Brazil was the leading candidate among policy analysts to become that peculiar creature of twentieth-century foreign policy, the client state. The country enjoyed a "special relationship" with the United States in return for help in achieving certain goals within the region. Brazil was part of a unique bilateral 1939 trade agreement which was based on a long-range policy of importing consumer goods, including Coca-Cola, and exporting capital goods and raw materials to the United States. Large-scale loans and commercial credits to promote gradual internal development and a stable currency were made available with the aim of creating a mature consumer society, rather than merely a source of cheap labor and raw materials.†

Coca-Cola was a direct beneficiary of the 1939 trade agreements. In an October 31 decree, Brazilian law covering chemical compounds in soft drinks was changed to allow the use of phosphoric acids, without which Coca-Cola could not be produced. Later that year, the government gave further incentive to Coca-Cola by reducing the tax on all 6½-ounce soft-drink bottles by 44 per-

---

* The New York Times, February 23, 1941. p. 18; March 11, 1941. p. 25; February 27, 1941. p. 22; March 30, 1941. p. 42

† Other Latin American countries more directly competitive with America, such as Argentina and Uruguay, were wrenched from the threat of possible Nazi economic control with generous gold dumping, spending, and loans that in the short term made these economies "bloom with the flush that is not the substance of prosperity." This eleventh-hour strategy, promulgated by the Council, drew harsh reaction from one Harvard analyst, who warned against harnessing our "Latin American sister republics to the economic chariot of the Arsenal of Democracy." Brazil, meanwhile, enjoyed its special relationship, signified by the fact that its trade agreement was the first ever linked to a loan policy, and its loans were the first to be made directly from the U.S. Treasury, rather than traditional sources—the banks. J. Anton De Haas, "Buying Latin American Loyalty," in Cecil Fraser (ed.) Industry Goes to War (New York: McGraw-Hill, 1941). p. 11, 116–117

cent.* Until this time, the ubiquitous Coke bottle was unheard of in Brazil. The local soft-drink industry protested vehemently that the minimum size of their bottles was nearly twice that of Coke, and could not easily be switched. Moreover, their products contained only natural caffeine derived from guarana, made from the seeds of a local shrub, and because of pasteurization, did not require the use of phosphoric acid, artificial coloring, and other additives. Nevertheless, the Brazilian government brushed aside their protests with an appeal to their patriotism and the intimation that failure to give commercial advantages to Coca-Cola would upset the conduct of foreign policy during a period of extreme world conflagration.

The stage was set for Farley's auspicious round of meetings with President Getulio Vargas, which had been arranged through Farley's personal acquaintance, then Foreign Minister Oswaldo Aranha.† Vargas had accomplished an illustrious and meteoric rise, overthrowing the coffee oligarchy in the mid 1930s. He subsequently forswore his sympathies for the fascists in favor of an alliance with the United States, on whom Brazil was already economically dependent. Under Vargas, Brazil supplied the only Latin American contingent to the Allied War effort, and by 1939, was already engaging the Nazis and Italians over the control of the country. It was Vargas who negotiated the 1939 bilateral agreements with the United States, and issued the favorable soft-drink decrees.

When he met with Vargas in 1941, Farley carried a personal letter from President Roosevelt which he delivered only after the negotiations.‡ According to Farley, Vargas was "greatly impressed" that he did not use the influence of the presidential letter until afterwards. Judging from the outcome of events that year, Farley was not so much conducting company business as he was furthering national foreign policy. Later in 1941, American military bases were established in the northeastern sector of Brazil, and in 1942 the first Coca-Cola appeared in Rio de Janeiro.

The congruity of goals shared by Coca-Cola and the Council was on a truly global scale. The haunting memory of the Depression compelled planners to think in terms of an international economy tied to massive export markets, the loss of which would cause another drastic dip in national income and a return of large-scale unemployment. Major General George V. Strong, who worked on the War-Peace studies, pointed out as early as May 1942, that America must emerge from the war with a settlement that "will enable us to impose our own terms, amounting perhaps to a pax-Americana."§ The overnight conversion of Coca-Cola's sixty-four overseas bottling plants to peacetime production in new foreign markets at the close of the war was not only a fortuitous development for the company, but an instantly decisive step toward achieving long-range na-

---

* Robert Ledogar, *Hungry for Profits* (New York: IDOC/North America, 1975). p. 111–17
† Watters, *Coca-Cola*, op. cit., p. 169
‡ ibid. p. 169
§ Shoup, op. cit.

tional priorities articulated by the Council almost two years before America officially entered the war.

The marked coherence between Farley's prewar movements and policy initiatives in Latin America and the Council's own recommendations for that region raise the equally intriguing possibility that Coca-Cola was a witting and willing participant in the Council's overall strategy extending back to 1939. The Coca-Cola Company was not only the maker of the consumer product most perfectly tailored to lead American exports, but it also had interlocking ties to the Council through the banking house of J.P. Morgan & Co., the principal financial affiliation of the Council, according to high government officials in the State Department and the Federal Trade Commission.* Two long-time directors of J.P. Morgan, George Whitney and Thomas W. Lamont, sat on the board of New York's Guaranty Trust Co. at least as far back as 1928. Guaranty Trust had participated in Ernest Woodruff's 1919 purchase of Coca-Cola, and remained one of the very largest of the company's shareholders throughout this period. Robert Woodruff represented Coke's interests while serving on the bank's board during the mid-twenties, and by 1928 he was succeeded by Coke director E.W. Stetson, who remained a director with Lamont and Whitney until after the outbreak of the war in Europe.†

Thus, the government's overtly sudden and favorable decision to promote Coca-Cola to a wartime priority item may have actually been formulated not after the Japanese attack on Pearl Harbor, but several months before, during the summer of 1941. At that time, Council leaders were giving up the viability of the "Grand Area" concept and, because of Japanese and German belligerence, were increasingly accepting the inevitability of war. They even recommended the drafting of a public statement of war aims, known later as the Atlantic Charter, which would literally conceal the Council's self-admitted imperialistic bias in defining American war aims behind more universally appealing propaganda. Following the widespread shock of Pearl Harbor, this universal chord resonated with the American people, and was as much in evidence in Woodruff's declaration of the fighting man's five-cent Coke as it was in Roosevelt's declaration of war. Swift and decisive, their public proclamations were guided by the extreme urgency for getting on with the war while their long-range considerations were influenced by the private vision of a tiny elite that aspired to shape the peace that followed. While unaware of this group and the ulterior forces at work, the American people rallied to their country's defense.

Jim Farley and Coca-Cola were made for each other. At home and abroad, his political contacts were unsurpassed, and for thirty years he traveled the globe meeting with kings, queens, emperors, sheikhs, princes, prime ministers—leaders of every imaginable persuasion. He was one of America's most prominent lay

* ibid.

† In 1959, J.P. Morgan & Co. acquired the Guaranty Trust, changing its name to Morgan Guaranty Trust Co. In 1978, Morgan Guaranty was the third largest Coca-Cola stockholder, controlling 2.84 percent of the corporation.

Catholics and was intimately involved with the Vatican, receiving papal audiences often every year. With an annual average of 120 banquets, 100 luncheons, and frequent trips overseas, he was Coke's supersalesman and spokesman for world affairs, providing the company with indispensable entrees into the loftiest realms of political power.

Coca-Cola's roots in the American character came to full bloom during the greatest test of the company's, and the country's, mettle. Coke fulfilled its economic imperative and historic mission foreshadowed in its position as one of the world's earliest multinational consumer corporations. Its access to political might provided it with heady successes of which Pepsi's leaders could scarcely dream. Yet Mack and his cohorts were bent on a course composed of far more than mere dreams.

CHAPTER FIVE

More Pounce to the Ounce

WALTER MACK had foreseen the titanic struggle looming between Coke and Pepsi for the hearts and nickels of the world, and perceived its deepest implications when he said, "The fight between Coca-Cola and us is a fundamental American struggle." He looked forward to it.

Mack understood that Coke had been identified for so long with the country's major social institutions that it had become one itself. Half a century and millions of advertising dollars had earned it a finely wrought identity and pervasive familiarity. One Pepsi executive remembers: "Coke dominated the field as hardly anybody can do today and still stay out of the clutches of the Federal Trade Commission on charges of monopoly." Pepsi, on the other hand, was a relative newcomer. Guth's once-successful nickel strategy stranded sales within the poorer lower classes without developing any other markets. Pepsi's image needed to be revitalized and to this end Mack awarded the Pepsi account to the Newell-Emmett advertising agency. Then, he dove head-on into promotional campaigns fully intent on catching the Coca-Cola Company.

Mack's genius lay in his ability to grab the public's attention, as seen in his first and most spectacular success. In 1939, an advertising executive approached Mack with a jingle worked up by a couple of daffy free-lance writers. A few days later, he was listening to an adaptation of "John Peel," a traditional English hunting song, with Pepsi-Cola lyrics. Sensing a novelty, Mack promptly bought the jingle for $2500 and despite protests from Newell-Emmett, ordered it to be aired on independent stations in New York and New Jersey. At a time when all radio commercials (there was no television then) were spoken in a bland, rhetorical style, Pepsi played the first fifteen-second jingle, replete with a catchy and fully orchestrated tune.

Public reaction was swift and decisive; the jingle was phenomenally successful and soon became the advertisement to which all others of the day would be compared. In retrospect, it is arguably one of the most successful ad campaigns ever and was called the "most famous oral trademark of all time." It exploited Pepsi's favorite theme—value—and the public took to its merry lyrics like carbonation to water in those dreary, financially strained war years. "What made the jingle great," said a Newell-Emmett executive, "and what saved it from dying long ago, was Mack's decision to play the song alone. He has an unusual instinct for sensing something new that will be successful."

Mack was hardly shy with successful formulas. All told, the jingle, for which its authors were compensated another $2,500, was played an estimated six million times. In 1941 alone, the ad was broadcast in one form or another over 469 radio stations in all variations and tempos and for all occasions from concerts and theater to the World Series. By popular demand, copies were sent to the owners of fifty thousand juke boxes. A survey conducted in 1942 revealed that the jingle was the best-known tune in America. In one fell swoop, Mack revolutionized radio advertising and gave Pepsi a good dose of pizazz. The stodgy gentlemen at Coke must have been mortified, and Mack was just beginning. (One later brainstorm wasn't so popular. In 1948, Mack installed a set of gargantuan electronic chimes atop Pepsi's Long Island City plant which blasted the first seven notes of the jingle every half hour. Within days, protests from ten square miles of Manhattan silenced Mack's clarions. "All I wanted to do was help people out by letting them know the time in a very pleasant and amusing way," he said puckishly.)

If Pepsi were to broaden its appeal, the "Twice as Much for a Nickel" campaign had to be augmented by a message espousing the drink's qualitative virtues. Consequently, America was introduced to "More Bounce to the Ounce," a saucy slogan highlighting Pepsi's quality while implicitly repeating the idea of greater quantity. Defying sugar rationing and its projected effect on sales, Mack sharply increased Pepsi's 1942 ad budget to emphasize the theme of quality. Ads extolled Pepsi's purity with photos of the bottling process and purification techniques. This campaign was executed for maximum reach through 205 Sunday newspapers.

Mack also understood the importance of proper packaging when marketing consumer products. The container is the interface between the consumer and the product, and must transmit the right image as well as the right feel. Nowhere in merchandising history was there a better example of this than Coke's pixieish 6½-ounce bottle. Though Mack persistently chided Coke's smallish container ("Look at this ridiculously tiny thing! Look at that false bottom! Fourteen ounces of glass and only six ounces of juice!"), he knew it was far superior to Pepsi's big bland bottles. For many years, Pepsi bottlers pasted their labels on any bottles they could get, and in fact, were the country's largest consumers of secondhand beer bottles.

The design of the label was something of an issue. An official of the Food & Drug Administration allegedly once asked Mack to print Pepsi's ingredients on the label. He promptly agreed, but only if Coke agreed to do likewise. According to Mack, the flustered official left, hardly willing to insist that the King replace its baked-on labels with paper labels just to identify its ingredients.

With typical verve, Mack commissioned the designer responsible for the interior of Tiffany's to create a personable and distinct Pepsi-Cola flask. The Pepsi logo was baked onto the new bottles, which were crowned with a dashing red, white, and blue bottle cap, purportedly of Mack's own design. This flashy package was then standardized throughout the bottling network.

To complete Pepsi's new face-lift, Mack moved his offices from Long Island City to a more fashionable 57th Street address in Manhattan, and began an aggressive public relations campaign, much of which was focused on the immense metropolitan New York market.

Mack exploited every opportunity to place Pepsi before the public. "We had very little money to spend on advertising, so we had to use ingenuity." Indeed, Mack's ad budget for 1939 was $600,000, meager when compared to Coke's estimated $15 million. Therefore, Mack couldn't afford conventional advertising like Coke's tepidly sexy women in bathing suits or the bottle propped in a snowbank. Instead, the company explored new promotional outlets like art shows, square dances, scholarships, and community activities of all kinds. It began the Walter Mack Jobs Awards for American Youth, winners of which were employed by the company, and Pepsi financed college scholarships which were open to blacks as well.

During the war, special recreational centers were visited by servicemen some 29 million times for a shave, shower, a nickel hamburger, and free Pepsi. Annual painting contests entitled "Portraits of America" featured some of the finest artists of the day and were assembled into a Pepsi-Cola promotional calendar. In 1938, Mack once again broke new advertising ground when Pepsi penned an exclusive contract with the sole holder of the patent of the skywriting smoke-producing device. Year after year, planes embellished the heavens over the country's major cities with "Pepsi-Cola," and in 1947 there were 6,390 sorties in forty-eight states as well as Cuba, Canada, and Mexico. Each scrawled signature cost Pepsi $55.

Sometimes Mack's imagination became overheated: he encouraged writers of pulp fiction to keep a bottle of Pepsi on their characters' night table beside the gin and .38 revolver. Once, he tried to buy the rights to the Popeye cartoon strip so he could replace the feisty sailor's spinach with Pepsi-Cola. After the rights to Popeye were found to be too expensive, Newell-Emmett scoured the countryside to come up with the Pepsi-Cola Cops, whom Mack promptly dubbed Pepsi and Pete. Whenever the pair were on the brink of disaster, they outwitted the villains with fortification miraculously supplied by Pepsi-Cola.

Pepsi's national magazine campaigns, which began in 1939, were often full of catchy humor, owing as much to Mack's tastes as his insistence that the ads be strictly tailored to fit the magazine's readership. Mack sought out the nation's premier cartoonists to produce ads worthy of the smart and stylish readers of *The New Yorker*, *Time*, *Collier's*, and others. Peter Arno came up with racy drawings for *The New Yorker*, including one showing a formal dinner where an ebullient man with a long, pointed nose peered pleasantly into the cleavage of a lady holding a glass of Pepsi, and said, "Mmmmmm—it looks good. What is it?" An artist named Soglow did a strip in which a sailor was heatedly necking with a young lady on a park bench. The word Pepsi-Cola flashes across the horizon, and the sailor is off and running with a tremendous burst of speed, his lips still pressed to the girl who still lies horizontally in his arms. Robert Day turned out topical ads, including a most prophetic one in *Time* depicting an elderly, smiling couple sitting in their apartment beside a radio pouring out a Pepsi commercial. A picture of Stalin hangs on the wall, confirming that the imposing towers looming in the distance are indeed those of the Kremlin.

Mack immersed himself in a host of such civic and social organizations as the Red Cross, U.S.O., the Elks, and the New York World's Fair Committee, and encouraged his bottlers to do the same. Later, he even sent each one an oratory kit complete with ten speeches on community issues. Mack was convinced that the enthusiastic support of community services would enhance the public's respect for Pepsi-Cola. By 1947, Mack invested a million of Pepsi's ballooning $4,500,000 ad budget in community services, declaring, "I'd rather have my community services than Frank Sinatra."

Mack first introduced the Pepsi-Cola Company to national politics and sparked its general proclivity toward Republicanism. He began as a Republican Party canvasser during the early twenties, advanced to district captain, and in 1930 was elected president of the Republican Club of the 15th Assembly District. Two years later, with his Wall Street career well underway, he was nominated for the New York State Senate seat for the 17th Senatorial District and endorsed by none other than Calvin Coolidge, the businessman's president, who said of Mack, "I'm glad to see a businessman who knows the value of a dollar going into politics." Hiring his own personal press agent, Mack put on an impressive campaign, but the bandwagon effect of F.D.R.'s election catapulted Mack's opponent into office along with many other Democrats.

Nevertheless, Mack might have won had he played ball with Dutch Schultz, the legendary New York mobster who wanted to buy the election for Mack. As Mack told E.J. Kahn of *The New Yorker*, two unsavory characters came to his campaign headquarters and advised him that if he wanted to win, he would do well to meet with their boss, Dutch Schultz. Mack agreed and was taken to a billiard parlor at 116th St. and Park Ave. in New York City. Surrounded by six armed men, Schultz offered to bet Mack $5,000 that he would win the election. "If you're not elected, you win the bet, and I'll owe you $5,000. You won't win the bet." Not willing to forge such a questionable alliance, Mack refused, only to discover on election night that the votes he lost in Schultz's territory cost him the victory. "If I'd won," Mack said, "I'd probably be senator from New York today instead of president of Pepsi-Cola."

In 1939, Mack became treasurer of the Republican Committee of New York, but was later narrowly defeated in his bid for the presidency of the National Republican Club. Conservative Hoover supporters viewed him as a radical because of his avid support of Wendell Willkie at the Republican convention of 1940. As a delegate from New York, Mack requested that his delegation be polled during the third ballot, a move that swung fourteen votes from Thomas Dewey to Willkie, who prevailed on the sixth ballot.

Political support became business ties the following year when Mack retained the unsuccessful GOP presidential hopeful to defend Pepsi-Cola against Coke's copyright suit in the United Kingdom. Willkie's liberal sympathies were as appropriate for Pepsi as his political priorities. He believed in the underdog—indeed, in the moral superiority of those who struggled—and if such thinking geared his instincts against the stodgy, self-righteous, insulated America with which Coke was so intimate, so much the better for Walter Mack and Pepsi-Cola. The outcome of the suit would have implications in territories around the world which Pepsi wanted to cultivate. Mack was drawn by the depth of Willkie's internationalist outlook, which included economic and social considerations, and the successful outcome of the suit enabled Pepsi to cultivate territories throughout the world. "Had he made the presidency with his ideas of 'one world,'" said Mack, "we would have had an entirely different world." If nothing else, life for Mack and the Pepsi-Cola Company might have been a little easier during World War II. (In a stirring insight that would have implications for both soda giants, Willkie wrote, "He who wins the war, must maintain the peace.")

The war came at a time of very impressive growth for the company. Profits topped $9 million, and the country was saturated with 469 bottlers. Yet, unlike Woodruff, Mack was unable to turn World War II into a marketing bonanza. Despite his efforts and occasional histrionics, Mack was able only to build a single frontline bottling plant at Guam. "Coca-Cola just had us smothered like a blanket," observed one Pepsi official. Yet, despite rationing, Pepsi emerged from the war relatively intact. It was now fully national, and had passed Royal Crown Cola, Dr Pepper, and the rest of the industry to become second in sales only to the Coca-Cola Company (Pepsi sold at least a third as many bottles as Coke, but was completely outstripped in soda-fountain sales). Further domestic growth would come through population increases and costly advertising slugfests with the Coca-Cola Company. Major growth opportunities lay in the untapped foreign markets, and with the inevitability of manifest destiny, Pepsi too, spilled past U. S. borders.

Pepsi-Cola was first uncapped abroad in Canada, which soon had over eighty-five bottlers, and then Cuba and London. In 1940, Mack plucked from the Coca-Cola Export Corporation William B. Forsythe, a tireless Canadian assigned the task of developing Pepsi's export operations. With an enthusiasm that flirted with obsession, Forsythe began recruiting foreign bottlers, particularly for those locations where Coca-Cola wasn't yet strong. These included: Latin America, which is still one of Pepsi's strongest overseas markets; the Philippines, where Pepsi today outsells Coke; South Africa; the Middle East, an outstanding soft-drink market because of religious strictures against alcoholic beverages; and soon, the Far East. Forsythe managed the development of fifty-six foreign markets from 1945 to 1950, and export sales jumped 45 percent in 1946, and 70 percent in 1947.

Despite some gains overseas, success for the Pepsi-Cola Company would not come easily. The nickel strategy that played so well to a Depression society was rejected by an upwardly mobile postwar America. Pepsi's popularity among youth, labor, and minorities burdened it with the reputation of being the "poor man's drink." Unlike Coke's "Be Sociable" campaign, Pepsi's advertising fell out of touch with the burgeoning middle class which was more concerned with material improvement than with the penny-pinching ways of an era best forgotten. Mack correctly discerned that Pepsi could compete effectively only by grabbing a firm hold of the take-home market. Yet, "More Bounce to the Ounce" and its successors failed to tell the requisite story of Pepsi-Cola quality, and his quixotic efforts to enter the soda-fountain business, long monopolized by Coke, were a bust.

Worse, Mack was unable to compensate for inflation, which hit Pepsi particularly hard after the war. The rising costs of sugar, labor, and other resources made it unprofitable to sell the 12-ounce bottle for a nickel. Pepsi and its bottlers lacked the immense cash reserves of the Coke empire to ride out the tough times, and slowly but surely, the price of a Pepsi rose to six and then seven cents. Mack's entire marketing and merchandising strategies were rendered obsolete, and his precious jingle had to be revised from "Twice as much for a nickel too," to "Twice as much and better too." To defend the price increases, one 1949 ad asked, "If a 12-ounce bottle of the best cola costs 6¢ . . . What should a 6-ounce bottle cost . . . 3¢?"

Mack's heroic efforts to catch the Coca-Cola Company were doomed. From 1946 to 1949, sales leveled off at $45 million and earnings dropped 70 percent in 1946. Coke outsold Pepsi by a five to one margin at home, and a slightly less devastating four to one abroad. "Soft drinks," a soft-drink official had observed, "are an American institution at a five-cent price," and the Pepsi-Cola Company was sliding toward what looked like a repeat of the post-World I bankruptcy.

CHAPTER SIX

Ice-Cold War

IN 1949, four years after his country defeated fascism in Europe, James A. Farley went against the grain of world opinion in a talk at Glens Falls, N.Y., where he urged U.S. support for Spain's fascist leader, Francisco Franco.

> "We are dealing with a world movement, a syndicate of political criminals who have only one objective, the seizure of power. . . . Communism festers on political and economic unrest. The greatest enemy of communism is peace and prosperity. We, in America, have the capacity to bring both to the world. We must provide the leadership."

The Cold War was a struggle of cultures, lifestyles, and institutions. America's ever-hungry consumer and banking free enterprise was pitted against the iron-fisted, deterministic bureaucracy of Soviet socialism. Creeping Communism versus Crawling Capitalism. From the Western point of view, Stalin was certainly a reprehensible demagogue who rode roughshod over Russia. On the other hand, Stalin feared America's reconstruction of Europe and Japan in its own image. He saw the long arm of American imperialism setting up shop precariously close to the homeland. Shortly after World War II, acute paranoia gripped both sides, and what Winston Churchill called "the iron curtain" was drawn.

Americans recoiled from the communist vision of the collapse of capitalism. Communist goals were made apparent at Yalta, in 1945, when Joseph Stalin fought for Soviet hegemony in Eastern Europe, and was fully realized in 1948 with the communist coup in Czechoslovakia and the blockade of West Berlin. A year later, Russia tested its first atomic bomb and communists seized control of China's mainland, an important component of America's Pacific frontier. American policy makers later saw Nikita Khrushchev's vow, "We will bury you," as a chilling summary of Soviet foreign policy. Communist expansion became the prototypal menace around which to unify the Allied countries, and fears of communist totalitarianism rendered America's consumer lifestyle all the more alluring. Consequently, the postwar expansion of America's economic influence took on a pious righteousness.

It was this very expansion that distressed Russian and European communists, who accurately perceived that within the capitalist system growth was an urgent necessity. America's economic expansion, in full swing by the beginning of the century, was greatly accelerated by World War II. The conflict gave America a sinewy presence throughout the world, and rendered it the economic colossus to

74

which damaged countries appealed. The postwar world was a laboratory-perfect environment in which a growth-based economy could flourish. Moreover, this calling was encouraged by American foreign policy. The national interest, as defined by the State Department and the Council on Foreign Relations, was in a one-world corporate economy ruled by the emerging multinational corporations and administered by institutions such as the International Monetary Fund and the World Bank. As seen from Moscow, the Marshall Plan was an overt step toward turning Europe into an American subsidiary.

The advance scout of this corporate hegemony, the very symbol, in communists' eyes, of the decadent American way was the Coca-Cola Company.

Communists and leftists came to associate the West with the American flag and a world ankle-deep in Coca-Cola. Coke was a brilliant though obvious lynchpin, for along with its corporate pedigree, it was as American as baseball and pervasive as the dollar bill. Coke was more widespread than ever after the war, demonstrating again in the eyes of the communists that American capitalism thrives on conflict. To prove how widespread it was, a company brochure once proclaimed, "When you don't see a Cola-Cola sign, you have passed the borders of civilization." The communists agreed with Woodruff that within every bottle dwelled "the essence of capitalism."

As it had during World War II, Coke defended America's honor and propagated the values that shed greatness on both company and country. Although the Coca-Cola Company's wartime struggle could be seen as self-serving, its interests and those of the country had long been intertwined. Communists correctly identified one with the other, and concluded both shared strong anti-communist leanings. Any doubt of the company's antipathy toward them would soon be demolished by Big Jim Farley.

Farley and Woodruff were staunch anti-communists steeped in orthodox, big bank, establishment thinking. The crusading fervor of the Cold War suited them well. They saw America as a bulwark of freedom; consequently, the overseas proliferation of Coke was more than good business—it was their burden. After a three-month global tour in 1946 for the Coca-Cola Export Corporation, Farley boldly declared in messianic tones then typical of American leaders that the peoples of Europe, Asia, and Africa "look to the American nation to lead them out of difficulties. They look to us for loans, for raw materials, and assistance. There isn't any doubt of the affection of the people of these nations for the American people. I don't think they can get out of their difficulties without our help." He was more heated a year later: "Every day, we read in the press of those who would incite class conflict, substitute foreign ideologies for our American way of life, outlaw God and inject atheism, banish free enterprise and establish totalitarianism." By 1950, he was strident. At a podium shared with Secretary of State John Foster Dulles, who, with brother Allen, director of the C.I.A., was a bedrock of anticommunism, Farley warned: "We find ourselves in danger from an enemy more subtle, more ruthless, more fanatic than any we have ever faced. The time has come for Americans to challenge the aggressive, godless, and treasonable practices of totalitarian communism. If we have reached danger and crisis it is because the masters of the Politburo have exhausted our patience and our hope that any moral and ethical relations between our nations can be possible under present conditions." In 1953, Farley headed a fund-raising drive for the "Crusade for Freedom" under the chairmanship of Henry Ford II. All donations supported Radio Free Europe and Radio Free Asia, the CIA-connected voices of big business's anticommunism.

The Coca-Cola Company was well prepared for the Cold War. In the absence of any actual conflict, the struggle was fought with propaganda, a wartime tactic not unlike conventional advertising. Both relied on images, slogans, and repetition to win over converts, and neither was dependent upon logic, nor for that matter, truth. The Coca-Cola Company was the virtual paragon of persuasion whose abilities to win over hearts and minds with such a simple product awed even its reddest critics.

For more than ten tough years, the Coca-Cola Company battled anti-American sentiments to make the world safe for Coke consumption. As in World War II, Europe was the primary theater, a situation which greatly annoyed the Yankee leaders who now saw the continent as America's protectorate. Powerful communist parties clashed head-on with American interests in general, and Coca-Cola in particular, sometimes with ludicrous results.

In Belgium, communists insisted Coke drinking led to fascism. Austrian communists claimed the local Coke bottling plant was really an atomic bomb factory in drag. A Viennese newspaper said, "Ten bottles will make the user a helpless slave of Coca Cola for life." One leftist newspaper likened the drinking of Coke to "sucking the leg of a recently massaged athlete." A Polish newspaper said: "The success of Coca-Cola is based on habit becoming addiction. . . . Thousands of agents of the company work in even the smallest localities of Coca-Colonialized countries, working at the same time for American espionage." (However, the Polish temperance movement, more disturbed over the country's alcohol consumption, declared, "The most imperialistic Coca-Cola is preferable to the ideologically purest Vodka.") Leaflets were distributed in West Germany with the Coca-Cola trademark and "Mach Mal Pause" (Take a Break) on the cover. Inside they said, "The new Coca-Cola family-size bottle is not to be the subject of our deliberations. It is certainly not our habit to make propaganda for this American dope beverage."

The attacks on Coke within Italy were particularly vitriolic. The headline of one newspaper read, "Drinks Coca-Cola and Dies." After Farley and four Cokemen met with Pope Pius XII, the communists equated Coca-Cola with Catholicism. They suggested the drink should be substituted for the sacramental wine and "Coke" should replace "Amen" at all services. Even the Italian fascists took swipes as one publication found Coke "halfway between the sweetish taste of coconuts and the taste of a damp rag for cleaning floors." (The German fascists, not to be outdone, published a pamphlet entitled, "Coca Cola, Karl Marx, and the imbecility of the masses.") All to no avail as five bottling plants were in operation in Italy by 1949. Said one dejected Red, "Yesterday I went to my favorite wineshop and found three people there. All were drinking Coca-Cola. The humiliation of it!"

Coke's roughest going occurred when local wine, beer, and soft-drink makers, threatened by Coke's intrusions onto their turf, teamed up with the politicos. Danish beer manufacturers were able to stem the brown tide in their country until 1959, for example, and Coke was even barred from the tiny Fiji Islands by local soft-drink interests. However, the most intense and controversial situation was in France, where even the levelheaded Farley blew his cork.

Fearing a big loss of business because of Coke's burgeoning sales, the powerful French winegrowers allied with the communists against Coca-Cola. The communists wanted to halt the advance of "Coca-Colonialism," and particularly resented Coke's 1946 hiring of a staunch anti-communist, Alexander Makinsky, to serve as a company lobbyist. Living in Paris at the time, Makinsky was a French-educated, naturalized American of White Russian* background. Makinsky was a suave, influential man accustomed to traveling in the highest ranks of European society. After seventeen years with the Rockefeller Foundation, he became "L'Ambassadeur du Coca-Cola." As if Farley's posture weren't already enough, the French left regarded Coke's new troubleshooter as representative of Coke's alignment with Yankee big business.

The attack on Coke was two-pronged. In late 1949, a court suit was introduced arguing that Coca-Cola should be barred on the grounds that it contained phosphoric acid which is harmful to the health of Frenchmen. At the same time, a bill was introduced in France's National Assembly (akin to the U.S. House of Representatives) which called for an outright ban on Coke. When it failed to gather enough votes, another bill was introduced, aimed specifically at Coke, which empowered the minister of health to regulate all drinks that contained vegetable matter. (This strategy had successfully banned Coke from Portugal.) This second bill gathered a good head of steam among the French, and was even endorsed by the prestigious *Le Monde* which declared, "The moral landscape of France is at stake."

When the bill passed in the Assembly, Farley saw the proverbial red. "Coca Cola wasn't injurious to the health of the American soldiers who liberated France from the Nazis," he bellowed. He noted that Coke had been consumed in France since 1919 without any deleterious effects, and suggested that the U.S. Congress should "bar French wines as seductive to American morals in retaliation for the political slandering of an American living tradition of refreshment!" Americans were equally outraged. One congressman called it "a calculated affront to the people of this country" and suggested the French could use a good belch. Another stated he and his friends would boycott French salad dressing. One newspaper called for the banning of French perfume in America and an-

---

* White Russians, the aristocracy that fled Russia when the communists seized power, were among the most notorious anti-communists in the world.

other said, "What further proof do we need that the Reds are heartless monsters with a diabolical plot to overthrow the world and all of the glorious traditions therein?" One columnist summed up the situation nicely: "You can't spread the doctrines of Marx among people who drink Coca-Cola. It's just that simple. The dark principles of revolution and a rising proletariat may be expounded over a bottle of vodka on a scarred table, or even a bottle of brandy; but it is of course utterly fantastic to imagine two men stepping up to a soda fountain and ordering a couple of Cokes in which to toast the downfall of their capitalist oppressors."

In typical fashion the Coca-Cola Company resolved the French scandal by quietly flexing its muscles. Farley met with Henri Bonnet, France's ambassador to the U.S., and David Bruce, his American counterpart, convened with French officials. This diplomatic summit paid off when the Council of the Republic, France's equivalent of the U.S. Senate, refused to pass the anti-Coke bill. Furthermore, the court case was settled in Coke's favor when the local bottler got a battery of experts to testify that the beverage wasn't harmful to anyone's health. Coke's survival was reportedly assured when the company managed to obtain a photograph of the head of the Communist Party quaffing a Coke at a bar. Coca-Cola had proven too powerful for the French, even when the game was played on their court with their ball. In fact, when a Hungarian communist asked at a U.N. meeting in Geneva shortly after if there was a name more loved throughout the world than Stalin, it was a Frenchman who responded wryly, "Oui, Coca-Cola!"

Coke proceeded to expand its overseas empire, comforted in its conviction that it was morally, politically, and economically right. "As American as Independence Day " boasted a 1946 ad. At their first international conference in Atlantic City in 1948, Coke bottlers were greeted by signs that proclaimed: "When we think of Nazis, we think of the Swastika, when we think of the Japs we think of the Rising Sun (that set), and when we think of Communists we think of the Iron Curtain, BUT when THEY think of democracy they think of Coca-Cola." When asked why everyone was picking on Coke, one executive correctly pointed out, "It's because Coca-Cola is a champion of the profit motive, and wherever it goes, it spreads profits. Everyone who has anything to do with the drink makes money and becomes a member of the bourgeoisie." In messianic tones worthy of Candler, another executive prayed: "May Providence give us the . . . faith . . . to serve those two billion customers who are only waiting for us to bring our product to them." Woodruff was convinced that Coke's antagonists would eventually come around to his way of drinking. "To go into some of these countries," he mused, "takes a lot of patience."

His faith was justified. There was no end to the deluge. Coke weathered the storm with patience, determination, political influence, and lots of money. Sooner or later, Woodruff's brew would be popular in every communist and noncommunist country in Europe. In a spirit of reconciliation, the film capitol of America was already satirizing Farley's bellicose thunderings. Billy Wilder's 1961 film, *One, Two, Three,* starred James Cagney as an energetic, ambitious

Coke executive in charge of the Berlin office at the height of the Cold War. Wilder claimed he was inspired to make the picture during World War II when he saw Coca-Cola trucks advancing with the front lines during the Liberation. The movie came out before the building of the Berlin Wall, and though moderate in tone, it portrays Atlanta in very conservative, if comic colors. In an early sequence, Cagney, who has met with a Russian trade representative, hungrily contemplates a map of the vast Soviet terrain. "Three hundred million thirsty comrades! Volga Bulgars, Cossacks, Ukranians, Outer Mongolians—panting for the Pause That Refreshes." Moments later, he receives a call from the top-level Atlanta executive to whom he has broached the idea.

> CAGNEY: How about the Russian deal? Napoleon blew it, Hitler blew it, but Coca-Cola's gonna pull it off.
> EXEC: Forget it, McNamara, forget it. We are not interested in doing business behind the Iron Curtain.
> CAGNEY: (confused) We're not interested in the Russian market?
> EXEC: I wouldn't touch the Russians with a ten-foot pole. And I don't want anything to do with the Poles either.

From Cold War to World War III, Coke spanned the threshold of East-West conflict, turning up again in *Dr. Strangelove*, Stanley Kubrick's brilliant 1964 satire. In it, a fanatically patriotic major recoils at the prospect of shooting open a Coke vending machine for its change, even though the coins would pay for a call that would avert nuclear war. The dialogue between Keenan Wynn and the late Peter Sellers is worth repeating:

> SELLERS: "Oh blast—still 20 cents short. Operator, hold on, just a second. Colonel, that Coca-Cola machine, I want you to shoot the lock off it; there may be some change in there."
> WYNN: "That's private property."
> SELLERS: "Colonel, can you possibly imagine what is going to happen to you, your way of life and everything when they learn that you have obstructed the telephone call to the President of the United States. Can you imagine? Shoot it off. Shoot with a gun, that's what the bullets are for, you nitwit."
> WYNN: "O.K. I'll get your money to you, but if you don't get the President of the United States on the phone, you know what's going to happen to you."
> SELLERS: "What?"
> WYNN: "You're going to have to answer to the Coca-Cola Company!"

(Sound of shots)

Ironically, Woodruff and his Cokemen had been so preoccupied with communism, they failed to see that their greatest threat was a homegrown product of their dearly beloved free-enterprise system.

CHAPTER SEVEN

The Pepsi-Cola Kid

GLOBAL WAR had brought America out of the Depression, and under Walter Mack, Pepsi began to falter because it was too rooted in its once successful marketing strategies of the thirties. In its darkest hour, whether by luck or shrewdness, Pepsi once again found the right man. Alfred N. Steele, a tough-talking, two-fisted pinstriped warrior grasped the mood of the fifties in much the same way Mack had been attuned to the late thirties and the forties.

Steele was uniquely qualified to lead the Pepsi-Cola Company; he had been educated at the world's greatest soft-drink institution—the Coca-Cola Company. He began his career running a circus, and his showman's flair drew him into advertising. He began with D'Arcy, Coke's ad agency, and with an expertise in marketing and advertising, jumped to a vice-presidency of Coca-Cola. "Steele could talk the horns off a brass bull," said one executive, but his flamboyant ways, uncharacteristic of the company, irritated the staid Robert Woodruff. Steele was isolated from the company mainstream—"no mail, no phone calls, no meetings," recalled one bystander—and his future with Coke had gone flat.

From the other side of the tracks, Mack marked Steele's fall from grace, and offered him $85,000 a year and stock options to forsake Coke for Pepsi. Steele accepted, though during his first quarter with Pepsi the company lost $100,000, while Coca-Cola pulverized the entire industry with a 67 percent stranglehold on the soft-drink market. "When I arrived at Pepsi," Steele observed, "the other vice-presidents figured I had come to liquidate the company." Nothing of the kind. In 1950, as Pepsi neared bankruptcy, Steele demanded complete control. The directors expeditiously bumped Mack upstairs to board chairman and, despite his objections, elected Steele president of the Pepsi-Cola Company. Amid discord with Pepsi's new leadership, Mack resigned several months later.

Al Steele set out to assault a status quo intently preserved by one of America's most gifted corporations. He was up to the task. Steele shone with the dynamism, determination, and keen advertising instincts of the past giants of Pepsi-dom, but thought even bigger. He earnestly sought the day when Pepsi-Cola would outsell Coca-Cola. "Beat Coke," was his war cry, and his ambition was soon infectious.

A Pepsi employee recounted Steele's philosophy toward proper leadership: "Al Steele told me that the whole trick in hiring executives is to find a good man and turn him into a prick. He said that a good man would be able to stand the course, but if the guy was a prick to begin with, he'd crumble along the way." In this vein, Steele once told some of his executives: "I don't care if they want sweat in goat skins. If that's what they want, half of you start running and the other half get out looking for goats." Accordingly, Steele replaced executive deadwood with new faces. Some of them were fresh from the war—young, ambitious, full of optimism—and others, like Steele, defected from Coke in search of quicker advancement. One loyal Cokeman refused to leave, saying: "It would be like leaving the Lord to go to the Devil."

Steele then polished what had become an inefficient and lackluster operation. Pepsi's management under the Guth and Mack regimes had been top-heavy and concentrated in New York where it frequently lost touch with other areas of the country. Steele decentralized leadership by dividing up the country into eight districts and assigning responsibility for each district to divisional vice-presidents. He altered the formula to make Pepsi less sweet, improved quality control, and standardized Pepsi's truck fleet, logo, and signs. A packaging experiment with cans, begun by Mack, was stopped, and many of the company's unprofitable sidelines were liquidated, such as the metal shops that made Pepsi's bottle caps. The Cuban sugar plantation was sold for $6 million, twice what Pepsi had paid for it, which, when added to a $5 million line of credit with some banks, improved the company's weak cash position. To free himself for the more far-reaching tasks at hand, Steele made Herbert Barnett, a veteran attorney of Pepsi's law firm, chief administrator of his policies. Barnett's services with the company dated back to the Loft days, and it was he who uncovered Guth's perfidious Noxie-Cola scheme in Canada.

Steele's product suffered from a worn image created by an outdated advertising strategy. Coca-Cola was the darling of the ever-expanding middle class, while Pepsi was a favorite of the downtrodden who couldn't afford to sacrifice Pepsi's extra ounces for Coke's prestige. Nevertheless, Steele recognized that this same middle class which shunned Pepsi was a unique market, preferring sprawling suburbs to cities, large supermarkets to the corner store, and quaffing its soda at home rather than at the fountains. Soon, take-home sales would outstrip on-premise consumption at soda fountains and vending machines—outlets virtually monopolized by Coke. Thus, Steele set his sights on getting Pepsi into America's living rooms. Pepsi's larger bottle could better exploit take-home sales, prompting Steele to offer still larger flasks and redesign Pepsi's standard 12-ounce bottle. Mack's bottle was fine for the forties, with its ruggedly handsome straight sides and big block lettering. Steele's new creation was dressier and sleeker, and was cast with an elegant swirl pattern and a baked-on label with subdued lettering that replaced the old glue-on paper label.

Steele revamped his advertising as he did his bottle, to reflect the values of the social classes he wished to reach. He convinced his bottlers to invest more heavily in advertising, and by 1955, Pepsi's annual ad budget, including the bottlers' share, was $14 million (the industry total was $80 million, an estimated 10 to 15 percent of which was earmarked for the new medium of television). Pepsi-Cola's new advertising campaign embraced the bourgeois visions of a consumer-oriented middle class. "Be Sociable," ads urged, "with Light Refreshment."

Pepsi was cast as a beverage for all occasions, and its ads stressed recreation and a tony sociability. By 1958, Pepsi had saturated a thousand radio stations with a half million commercial minutes of the "Be Sociable" campaign.

Success had taken the fizz out of some prosperous bottlers, particularly those within large metropolitan markets, and the company bought out some of these in urban terrains like New York, Philadelphia, Houston, and St. Louis to take the fight directly to Coke. Other bottlers were persuaded to increase their investment in advertising and intensify their marketing efforts. During the first five years of Steele's leadership, the company set its own example by investing $38 million in new plants and equipment. "You can conserve yourself into bankruptcy," said Steele, "or you can spend your way to prosperity."

By 1955, the results were nothing short of spectacular. Within five years, sales had increased 112 percent, as opposed to a 29 percent gain for the entire industry, and the company owned 120 plants in over 50 countries. In 1952, Pepsi pioneered the "co-franchisement arrangement" with Schweppes, Ltd. of England, in which Schweppes would bottle and market Pepsi in England while the Pepsi-Cola Company would distribute Schweppes products in America. The Schweppes line, including quinine water and ginger ale, would give Pepsi's domestic bottlers an expanded line of products while overseas the use of existing distribution networks would expedite foreign growth.

Maneuvering in foreign waters, however, was much trickier than a domestic swim, and Pepsi was learning, like many other budding multinationals, that doing business abroad brought a host of problems which were best resolved by political means. Tariffs, currency, an unpredictable sugar market, nationalism, recalcitrant governments, shifting cultures, and political and economic upheavals of all kinds confronted any company doing business abroad. To stay competitive, political alliances had become a necessity.

Presidential conventions became a favorite ground for recruiting friends. Political palates needed refreshing, especially if the gullet belonged to someone who could provide a favorable trade agreement or sugar legislation. Politicians and convention delegates are the highly sought "sociables"—the business leaders, opinion makers, the influential of any community. Indeed, the political arena was the area where Pepsi lacked the weight that from time to time helped secure and retain Coke's preeminent status.

Although Coke traditionally made friends within the Democratic Party and Pepsi was seeking its allies among the Republicans, the conventions themselves were wide open affairs where everyone was desirable game. Mack distributed gratis 30,000 bottles of Pepsi at the 1948 convention in Philadelphia, though the real race between Coke and Pepsi for delegates' attention began during the conventions of 1952. From then on, every Republican and Democratic convention would be awash with free Coke and Pepsi. The competition was fierce and an industry veteran explained: "Coca-Cola just set up booths and the vending machines. Pepsi went in for stunts and other things like checking a horse into the lobby of the Hilton Hotel, getting girls into bathing suits, anything to get the attention of the public a bit more than Coke." At the 1956 Democratic Convention, for example, both companies sought supporters with a febrile pitch worthy of the delegates themselves. Young ladies dispensed drinks from Pepsi stands while Coke gave away 4,000 coolers crammed with its finest. It set up a special trailer to provide delegates easy access to life's amenable pauses—a shower, shave, liquor, and, of course, Coca-Cola. Four years later, Pepsi gave away 120,-000 drinks to delegates, their friends, the press, and everyone else attending the Republican Convention in Los Angeles. Again, attractive women staffed scores of refreshment booths, and Pepsi sponsored a "quiet room" where VIPs could get away from the hustle and bustle of kingmaking. The Coca-Cola Company gave away another 4,500 coolers, packed with fruits, wine, and, of course, the Democratic Party's favorite soft drink.

The largesse of both companies at presidential conventions was boundless, yet their overt pandering to the political community went unchallenged. The soft-drink titans enjoyed carefully polished images as benign, nonstrategic, consumer-oriented companies, and as a part of the national consciousness were allowed to take greater liberties with their promotional techniques. What was taboo for General Motors, ITT., or General Dynamics was all part of the game for Coke and Pepsi. Said the veteran: "I mean, what the hell is U.S. Steel going to give away? . . . Coke and Pepsi are giving away a nickel bottle of belly wash."

Pepsi's most flagrant political coupling at the time began in 1947 with Senator Joe McCarthy who, like Pepsi, was aggressive and ambitious. Both assailed the establishment from within without really being a part of it. Their relationship began when the fledgling Wisconsin senator was befriended by Russell Arundel, a Pepsi-Cola lobbyist and bottler. It wasn't McCarthy's Cold War politics that attracted Pepsi so much as his seat on the sugar subcommittee of the Senate Banking Committee.

The two men met through a representative of Allied Molasses, a firm that had illegally sold Pepsi a million and a half gallons of sugar cane syrup. McCarthy took an interest in Pepsi and its desperate need for additional sugar stemming from the war-time rationing still in effect.

Arundel was an extravagant man who was rumored to have profited handsomely from bootleg liquor that passed near his island retreat of Baldonia off the coast of Nova Scotia. Years later, he fashioned himself as the "Prince of Outer Baldonia" and wined and dined the keepers of power. The *Boston Herald* once called one of his parties, attended by President Harry Truman, a "two-day frolic which made the Biblical feast of Belshazzar look like a White Tower feed." A man of considerable influence, Arundel was a major figure at the lucrative Pepsi-Cola Bottling Company of Long Island. Through Arundel, McCarthy met Mack, and the senator began making appearances at Pepsi-Cola functions in Washington.

Soon, McCarthy began attacking sugar rationing with a vengeance, and Pepsi had its first spokesman in the U.S. Senate. Although many senators labored discreetly against rationing, McCarthy's crusade was so vitriolic that he became known on Capitol Hill as the "Pepsi-Cola Kid."

McCarthy's apparent quid pro quo was temporary relief from a strapping $170,000 debt. Arundel endorsed a $20,000 note against that debt, and there were no visible ill feelings when McCarthy apparently defaulted. Furthermore, Arundel, a Washington lobbyist for some influential interests, advised the senator to participate with Chinese Nationalists in a major soybean speculation that reaped $30 million by anticipating the outbreak of the Korean War.*

The gambit worked, although not without some hitches. McCarthy has been credited with ending sugar rationing in October 1947, six months before the government schedule. However, his vendetta for Pepsi came to the attention of the Senate Privileges and Elections Subcommittee, which was investigating alleged misuses of funds and influence peddling by McCarthy. Their report, issued in the beginning of 1953, said: "McCarthy's acceptance of the $20,000 favor from the Washington representative of the Pepsi-Cola Company at the very time he was attacking the government for its manner of handling sugar control makes it difficult to determine whether Senator McCarthy was working for the best interests of the government as he saw it or for the Pepsi-Cola Company." The report and a subsequent seven-month Justice Department investigation found McCarthy's shenanigans questionable, but not "technically" outside the law. When queried about these and other dubious activities, McCarthy said, "I don't answer charges, I make them." When cornered by disturbed shareholders at the company's annual meeting, Steele denied the company had approved the loan or was guilty of any corporate wrongdoing.

Steele frequently remarked that Pepsi's success was greatly due to the lassitudes of the Coca-Cola Company. For half a century, Coke had no real competition. It had all but a monopoly on the industry, and had grown fat and arrogant. Its position seemed impregnable as it disdainfully swatted away the other colas like a cow shooing flies. It was difficult for Coke even to admit it had competitors, let alone dignify them with a response. But the upstart Pepsi-Cola was something else. Leaner and meaner, it was now a dynamo whose relatively smaller size enabled it to move quickly and precisely through the marketplace. Pepsi no longer reacted to the strategies of King Coke, but had taken the offensive with a fanatic determination. With its share of the market slipping, by the mid-fifties Coke was in trouble for the first time in its history.

---

* Peter Dale Scott, *The War Conspiracy* (New York: Bobbs Merrill, 1972), p. 196. cf. *The New York Times*, July 6, 1951, p. 9; June 9, 1951 p. 6; I.F. Stone, *The Hidden History of the Korean War* (New York: Monthly Review Press, 1969)

CHAPTER EIGHT

Colas in Collision

"IN 1954," said a senior vice-president of the Coca-Cola Company, "we rolled up our sleeves and went to work." Sales had slumped $8 million to $243 million, and profits shrank 8 percent. Meanwhile, Pepsi's sales rose 12 percent to $74.2 million and profits jumped almost 15 percent. Pepsi was "coming up like a scalded cat," remarked one Cokeman, and Coca-Cola's halcyon days were over.

Coke's problem was obvious. Aside from the fountain glass, the only way to buy a Coke since 1916 was in the small 6½-ounce bottle. Observing the impact of Pepsi's larger bottle, one Coke executive conceded, "The consumer not only would accept the larger bottle, but was out looking for it." Thus, Coke's faith in its 6½-ounce bottle had to be reconsidered, a task that was quite painful for Woodruff and his minions.

Their petite, wasp-waisted bottle was as outstanding as the liquid it contained. No other container in history was as closely identified with its product as their bottle. With over six billion manufactured, and a billion still in existence at the time, the bottle was as much a trademark for Coca-Cola as the famous red and white script. Including refills, the 6½-ouncer had delivered an estimated 220 billion Cokes since its creation! The Georgia green beauty ranked with the flag, the baseball, and the hot dog as definitive symbols of the American way, a truly superlative achievement for such a simple vessel. "To put Coca-Cola into another dimension," said one loyalist, "was almost heresy." Ed Forio said it more vividly: "Bringing out another bottle was like being unfaithful to your wife."

Convincing the bottlers proved to be difficult. Coke's bottling network, once the tendons of its economic muscle, was now an obstacle. Years of fat times and the "Ma and Pa" family approach to franchising had created an inbred, paunchy, and provincial lot bereft of new blood and ideas, and rebellious against anything that would complicate their lives. Like the parent company, which had thrived on one product and one package since time immemorial, they were traumatized by the prospects of their precious fluid being embraced by anything alien. Commenting on the habits ingrained by success, a Coke executive said: "Their grandfathers hewed this thing out of the pristine wilderness, but the second generation was raised on the Stutz Bearcat and the yacht. The third generation, even further removed from pioneer days, found it hard to accept what was happening." He added, "By contrast, the Pepsi bottler was lean and hungry, and just plain poor."

In 1955, after a belated consent from Robert Woodruff, Coca-Cola introduced sleek 10- and 12-ounce bottles, followed by a bulbous 26-ouncer aimed directly at the take-home market. As Pepsi made inroads into the domestic market and Coke's share declined to 50 percent, Coke's bottlers gradually relented and marketed the larger containers.

For the conservative one-product company, the new containers represented diversification as real as if it had decided to market lingerie. Coke was merely following Pepsi's lead, but with typical over-exuberance one Atlanta executive asserted that the event was "the biggest upheaval in our industry's history." Said a bottler, "The old giant had turned over and gotten up on its feet. You don't sit by and watch other people take away the business you spent fifty years building up. We want to recapture what we lost in the take-home market. We'll do almost anything to do that."

They almost did. The Coca-Cola Company has spent hundreds of millions of dollars to make its product the best advertised and most familiar in history. The age-old slogan, "The Pause that Refreshes" is a virtual synonym for Coca-Cola. The mastermind of Coke's slick image was the venerable Archie Lee, Woodruff's close friend and bulwark of D'Arcy, Inc., Coke's ad agency for nearly fifty years. With only an astronomical advertising budget behind him, Lee took a nonessential brown liquid and convinced generation after generation throughout the world that it was useful for their well-being. Since there was no patent reason to buy Coke, advertising didn't reason with the consumer. Except for a pleasant taste and an ephemeral caffeine buzz, Coca-Cola didn't nourish, intoxicate, or really quench thirst. Oceans of Coke have been sold by simply identifying it to the point of saturation with cherished values and institutions, and later, with coveted lifestyles. Image had totally triumphed over content.

In 1951, when Coke's advertising had to respond to Pepsi-Cola's gains, Archie Lee died. D'Arcy's campaigns without the wizard were soft and rudderless. The 1953 theme, "The Refreshment of Friends," was mild and without social impact. "Drive Safely—Drive Refreshed" (1953), "Have a Coke and Be Happy" (1954), "America's Preferred Taste" (1955), or "Almost Everyone Appreciates the Best" (1955) were not among Coke's more memorable slogans. Seeking a greater intimacy with the American consumer, the Coca-Cola Company began perhaps the largest mass psychoanalysis ever performed on a society. The company probed, quantified, and catalogued every behavioral nuance of the soft-drink-buying public. Once a product of Archie Lee's mind, advertising became the visual and linguistic expression of exhaustive research and statistical analysis. Teams of psychiatrists, psychologists, clinical sociologists, and social anthropologists tracked the motivational impulses of the American consumer. Every one of the company's 1,600,000 retail outlets was scrutinized as were 21,-000 motorists who stopped at three hundred gas stations. Fifty-three thousand housewives were polled for every little facet of their grocery shopping routine. "There is no question you could ask about beverage consumption that we can't answer," boasted a Coke researcher. The old self-certainty was coming back.

This passion for research, every bit as new and momentous as its packaging changes, led Coke to part with D'Arcy in 1955. The account went to McCann-Erickson, a worldwide firm that was already doing some advertising for Coke Export. Coca-Cola's need for an agency with global punch was apparent; by 1957, 60 million Cokes were consumed daily in 105 countries. The new agency promised more aggressive advertising, and would, in the words of the Coca-Cola Company, "better integrate international and domestic campaigns."

At first, they proceeded cautiously. A Coke executive explained: "We were probing the perimeter, trying to find the enemy's strengths." In 1957, they launched a lackluster campaign that boasted of Coke's good breeding and universality. Intended to exploit the peace and tranquillity of the Eisenhower years, its themes were an exaggerated expression of Coke's traditional motif, in that ads depicted highbrow types saddled up for a fox hunt or in distant settings like Venice, the Great Pyramids, or the Taj Mahal. The campaign overshot its mark. It was too swank and un-American to speak to the average consumer who wanted to be assured that ordinary Main Street folk drink Coke. The same executive elaborated: "The fancy artwork looked as if it might have been right for MacGregor shirts, but not for Coke. The bottlers were telling us, 'You can sell all the Coke you want in Pakistan; we want to sell it in Punkin Center.' " That year, Pepsi enjoyed its biggest sales increase in over a decade and McCann-Erickson retired to the drawing board.

The agency returned with "Be Really Refreshed," a pushy theme implying that another cola lurked out there in consumerland, a fool's cola, that wasn't as refreshing. The public bought the theme and Coke's sales rose 10 percent from 1958 to 1959. In 1960, the Atlanta giant began to bear down when it launched "No Wonder Coke Refreshes Best." By using comparatives and superlatives in its advertising, Coke was shedding its musty traditions and admitting for the first time in over a generation that it had competition. To quote Alvin Toffler from *Fortune* magazine, "An era of aloof grandeur had ended."

To keep its image free of controversy that could in any way inhibit its appeal, Coca-Cola made sure that every slogan, picture, and model in its ads, as well as all of its public activities, created an overriding impression of wholesomeness and the American way. Yet the American society was rapidly changing, and the Coca-Cola Company could no longer afford the luxury of ignoring certain social and political realities. For example, during the civil rights movement of the early fifties, blacks began boycotting Coca-Cola after a South Carolina bottler joined the local White Citizen's Council in protesting the Supreme Court's order to integrate schools. Soon rumors erupted that claimed the parent company also gave a sizeable donation to the racist organization, and segregationists began counter-rumors alleging the donation was really to the NAACP.* One exasperated vice-president complained, "Our problem is to walk a very fine line and be friends with everybody. . . . I've heard the phrase 'Stand up and be counted' for so long from both sides that I'm sick of it. Sure, we want to stand up and be counted, but on both sides of the fence. For God's sake, why won't they let us

---

* National Association for the Advancement of Colored People

go on selling a delicious and refreshing beverage to anybody who's got a gullet he can pour it down?"

Such naiveté was short-lived.

Meanwhile, Pepsi-Cola's relations with Joe McCarthy broke the lock Coke had held on top-drawer politicking and the natural reaction in Atlanta was to redouble its efforts in that direction. Jim Farley had served the company well in this regard. He provided Coke access to the Democratic Party and opened doors abroad. Of Farley's milieu, Newsweek observed in 1958: "He has kept up his ties with an army of political friends across the nation. At every Democratic National Convention, one of the spectacles has been the passage of that towering figure across a hotel lobby shaking hands, calling out names, and graciously accepting homage from those who cluttered about him."

Covering his other flank, Woodruff sought allies within the Republican Party, particularly Eisenhower who had been an apostle of Coke since World War II. Woodruff even broke with Georgian Democratic tradition to campaign for Eisenhower's presidency in 1952, sporting "I Like Ike" ties. (That year, Eisenhower came closer to winning in Atlanta than any other Republican presidential candidate in twenty years.) E. J. Kahn reported that when the President was offered a Pepsi at a reception for campaign workers in 1956, he refused and requested a Coke instead, claiming he was a Coke stockholder. President Eisenhower frequently visited Woodruff's plantation to hunt and play golf and the Georgian was an occasional guest at the White House.

Eisenhower stood on the very bedrock of the Republican Party establishment. He was mainstream America, from Wall Street to the farms. As with Coke, his politics were moderate, his image paternal, and his style unassuming. And like Coke, he emerged from the war a hero. Nowhere were the differences between the Coca-Cola Company and the Pepsi-Cola Company better manifested than in their respective political alliances.

Because Coca-Cola had a secure constituency within the orthodox political establishment, Pepsi had to court up-and-coming stallions like McCarthy, and later, Richard Nixon, in the hope they would develop a national following and some day control the reins of power.

McCarthy represented the upstart reactionary wing of the Republican Party. Like Pepsi, he sought to increase his stature and unnerve his opponents with ambitious assaults on the status quo. He forcefully challenged the powers-that-be, though he possessed neither the breeding nor the discretion of his adversaries. McCarthy earned the nickname "Tail Gunner Joe" by working a machine gun in a bomber during the war.

By the middle of Eisenhower's first term, Coca-Cola had become a client of a public relations firm headed by William Robinson, one of Ike's closest friends.* In 1955, Woodruff went one step better and made Robinson president of the

---

* Kahn recalls an anecdote concerning Robinson's hard-bitten partner, Steve Hannagan. After encountering a team of spirited Coca-Cola men, Hannagan reported back to Woodruff visibly shaken: "These boys are beyond me," he exclaimed. "They believe in the Holy Grail!"

Coca-Cola Company. His alleged strategy was to use the tough ex-news-paperman to cajole his bottlers into peddling the larger bottles.

Yet Robinson mingled with the mighty better than he did with the Coca-Cola family. A director of NBC and a former publisher of the *New York Herald-Tribune*, Robinson helped Eisenhower prepare his war memoirs, organized the powerful Citizens for Eisenhower, and was the President's favorite bridge and golf partner. He always kept his clubs nearby ready at a moment's notice should the Oval Office beckon.

Robinson's leadership violated a long-standing Coke tradition that management emerge from within the company. In addition, his limited experience in the industry made many loyalists within the Coke family distrust him. "Robinson was an all-right fella," commented one vice-president, "but he tried to do things too fast sometimes before he really understood the business." Rather than motivating the bottlers, Robinson alienated them, and consequently, sales and company morale suffered. "Woodruff sensed this," said an observer. "He could look at the figures and at the advertising and wonder what he had gotten himself into."

Taking no chances, Woodruff promoted Robinson to chair the board of directors where he could still be useful, and in 1958 installed Lee Talley in his place (Woodruff himself had officially left the company's management, although as patriarch and largest stockholder, he still made all the major policy decisions. He was known in the Coke hierarchy as the "Consensus.") Talley, the son of an Alabama minister and "a blooded member of Coca-Cola," had been with the company since 1923 when his main task as a soda-fountain salesman had been putting decals on store windows. He rose steadily through the ranks, and by 1954 was president of Coke's export operations. After Robinson's tough newspaperman approach, Talley's soft "old boy" appeal was perfect. One Cokeman said, "Now Lee Talley, he put the company right again. He saved the situation. The bottlers felt that there was a Cokeman at the top in Atlanta again."

While Coca-Cola regained its composure, Pepsi had become an industry phenomenon for the second time in its history. Sales tripled from 1950 to 1958 (the industry as a whole increased only 30 percent), and profits soared from $1.6 million to $11.5 million during the same period. Whereas Coke management referred to Pepsi only as the "imitator" during the forties, it now perceived Pepsi as the "competition" or, more appropriately, the "enemy."

Steele, elected chairman of the board in 1955, incessantly urged his bottlers to escalate the advertising war. The bottlers responded so well that by 1959 they reportedly contributed an unusually high two-thirds of Pepsi's $30 million annual advertising budget. Advertising continued to stress quality and social interaction rather than value, and sought to build a new constituency by emphasizing the present and modernity in contrast to the more nostalgic themes of Coca-Cola. In effect, Coke is fine for the geriatric crowd; Pepsi is for "today's" people. When Coke finally introduced the larger bottles, one Pepsi ad smugly read:

"Now another well-known Cola is bringing out a big bottle. This is gratifying to us. . . . It's fun to be followed—to be recognized as the leader."*

As the popularity of the neighborhood soda fountain waned, the popularity of vending machines, which afforded optimum convenience, increased. The Pepsi-Cola Company persuaded its bottlers to invest $15 million annually into vending machines, and to sweeten the pill, Barnett arranged some clever company-guaranteed financing. By 1959, sales via vending machines doubled to account for 11 percent of the company's business. To exploit the machines' multiflavored selection, both Coke and Pepsi introduced new lines of soft drinks. "Why should we allow other soft-drink producers to hitch free rides on our vending machines?" asked a Pepsi executive. By 1960, Pepsi wheeled out its Patio line, and Coke brought its five-flavor Fanta series out of mothballs. For the first time, neither company was a one-product firm.†

Overseas growth had become torrid by the fifties. Because both colas were inexpensive, nonstrategic goods that addressed a universal affliction—thirst—they were consumer products with a true global reach. For the embattled cola powers, the entire planet, with the temporary exception of the communist countries, was a vast frontier waiting to be civilized by soft drinks.

When it was the unchallenged leader, the Coca-Cola Company was content to develop international markets at a deliberate pace. However, once Pepsi established itself on the home front, it began to chart its own foreign expansion. Coke's monumental head start in the Allied countries didn't carry over to the bush of Brazil or the sands of the Saharas. Like the superpowers, the Pepsi-Cola Company and the Coca-Cola Company raced to carve up their own spheres of influence throughout the world. Supernation or supercola, the first into a host country is the first to begin mustering popular loyalty.

Onward marched legions of bottles. Never before had such territory been so painlessly and quickly conquered. As we shall see in Chapter 13, it is difficult to conceive of any other product that lends itself as eagerly to blanket penetration of the earth. In 1959, Coke added 30 new foreign bottling plants, bringing its overseas roster to 647. By 1960, Pepsi had 237 plants in 86 countries, whereas a decade earlier, it had only 67 plants in 31 countries. Foreign sales now accounted for half the company's total revenue.

At home or abroad, Steele was a marketing genius who promoted Pepsi with

---

* Clearly, this wasn't always the case. For example, there's the Baffling Bottle Battle of 1957. That year, Pepsi set out to market a new bottle in England. But Coke sued, claiming it too closely resembled its own classic. Two years later, a top secret settlement was reached. Apparently, the disputed bottle was never released, although some soft-drink memorabiliophiles disagree and have sought the mysterious Coke-look-alike ever since.

† Although the Pepsi-Cola Company would have been peddling beer in 1958 had Steele had his way. The founding family of the Pabst Brewing Company called in Steele to help them reshuffle the company, which had been steadily losing money. After Steele demanded directorships for himself and several colleagues, including the president of a holding company for a number of Pepsi franchises, he began discussions with Pabst's management for a possible merger with the Pepsi-Cola Company. According to The New York Times, the family frowned upon Steele's back-door dealings (referring to his faction as the "New York group"), and the merger plans dissolved.

unequaled vitality and singlemindedness. Robert Windt, a former Pepsi public relations man, describes Steele's approach: "Every time a Pepsi bottler did anything in terms of an expansion, it became a 'plant opening.' Hell, the guy could have put a new garage onto his plant and there'd be a ribbon-cutting, star-spangled-banner ceremony. The size of the opening, of course, would determine how much of an effort would be put behind it. The local bottler would be king for a day. And if he was smart, he had specials in the supermarkets so he could really wrap it up. By the time the week was over, there was nobody in that market area who didn't know that there was a spanking-new, clean Pepsi-Cola plant that was putting money into the community and getting jobs. Even for the blessing of the plant, there would be a rabbi or a priest. I mean we pulled out every single stop."

In 1955, Steele outdid himself. He married film idol Joan Crawford (who ironically had been featured in some Coke ads in 1933). Crawford relished the challenge of being the company's first lady and championed Pepsi with a professionalism that dazzled bottlers and stockholders alike. She complemented the Pepsi-Cola Company, whose loud and showy style was akin to the make-believe, tinsel, and glamor of the movie industry of the fifties. Says Windt, who was her Pepsi advance man from 1959 to 1965, "She was Mrs. Industrial Executive. She played the part magnificently. This was, frankly, her final role . . ."

Windt recounts the nuances of a public relations event with Mrs. Steele: "I'd go out in advance of a plant opening and spend a day or two getting the press lined up. [When] we set up a press conference, we wouldn't invite the movie guy from [the local paper], we'd invite the business editor. . . . You know damn well that the movie guy would show up [also]. Crawford would call me the day before and ask 'What's the weather out there?' and I'd say , 'Baby, bring your mink coat, it's cold. . . .' The plane would land and I'd have all the photographers there, and I'd run up the steps and would say, 'Joan, the guy at the foot of the stairs with the white shirt—John Doe—his wife's name is Nancy, he met her in Cleveland. . . .' She would come down and I'd say an introduction. Joan would say, 'Oh, you don't have to introduce me. Nancy, how well you look. . . .' These bottlers would just flip."

Crawford would draw bottlers from an entire region for a Pepsi event. As in a chain reaction, they would be swept away in the glamor, go home, and often borrow enough money for a new facility to stage their own prestigious opening. It was the stuff of dreams toward which few were immune. Windt recounts an afternoon with Steele and Crawford in Washington, D.C.: "At that time, we were friendly with Castro and he was in Washington to appear before some Senate committee. We came out of the Senate Office Building and just as we came down the stairs, an entourage of open cars pulled up. There was Castro with the uniform . . . all of a sudden, he does a double take because he recognized Crawford. Steele was a pretty smart guy and he said—sort of under his breath—'Wave at the son of a bitch, Honey, he'll cream in his pants. . . .' She did, and I'll never forget Castro's expression."

When Coke was beginning its comeback in the spring of 1959, Steele embarked on his most flamboyant gimmick yet—a $200,000 Hollywood-like spectacle called Adorama. It was a frantic, gray-flannel circus intended to generate enthusiasm among bottlers and potential investors. Again, Windt was in the thick of things: "Adorama was a big pep meeting that went into all of these cities . . . bringing in all the surrounding bottlers . . . and talked about all the joys and importance of advertising as a kind of investment. It started in San Francisco and ended in Washington. You had the experts, the ad manager, the marketing services guy, the promotion guy, Steele, Barnett . . . and Crawford. The only thing you didn't have was the pompom girls. . . . It was the goddamndest thing I'd ever seen."

On April 17, 1959, the grueling tour ended in Washington. That day, Steele was inaugurated as the new national chairman of the multiple sclerosis campaign. After the obligatory speeches, the outgoing chairman, Senator John F. Kennedy, approached Joan Crawford and said, "Miss Crawford, if I can't introduce you to my secretaries, they'll never type another letter for me again." She agreed and the group journeyed to Kennedy's office where the last photos of Steele alive were taken with the promising young senator from Massachusetts.

Alfred Steele died the following day. The strain of Adorama's ten-week tour was too great for even his stout constitution. His death was an unexpected blow to Pepsi, although he left it in good shape with nearly 30 percent of soft-drink sales nationally. Under his brazen leadership, Pepsi closed the cola gap and was outsold by Coke by a 2.5:1 margin as opposed to 5:1 a decade earlier. His replacement was Herbert Barnett, a competent but colorless man who lacked Steele's dynamic leadership qualities. Yet the gentlemen from Atlanta were wrong if they thought Pepsi's growth would level off. Under Barnett, Pepsi was only getting its second wind, and at a famous event in Moscow, Pepsi heralded a new era not only for the industry, but the entire world.

Steele had learned of a unique trade fair, the American International Exposition, being planned for Moscow. Sponsored by the State Department and the U.S. Information Agency, the show was a display of the consumer might of the United States before a Russian people weary of Stalin's heavy industrialization. Steele suggested to the State Department that the exhibit include a portable soft-drink plant. Said a bystander, "On one side they would make Coke and on the other side Pepsi, and then have the two companies knock each other's brains out with their promotions and their political deals to show the Russians how free enterprise operates. It was a hell of an idea."

Indeed, the concept was vintage Steele, but he died six months before the event. Coke declined the invitation, apparently because it was still smarting from Cold War abuses and perhaps because it did not want to humble itself by appearing side by side with Pepsi.

The idea was kept alive by Donald Kendall, a Steele protégé and head of Pepsi's overseas operations. Despite some opposition within the company, Kendall persevered and in October of 1959 Pepsi-Cola was one of two hundred American companies and the only soft drink represented in Moscow. Coke lobbyist, Prince Alexander Makinsky, traveled with the entourage. He reportedly talked to some Russian officials for Coke, but was upstaged by Kendall. The stage was thus set for a once-in-a-lifetime promotional sensation.

"My one purpose was to get a bottle of Pepsi in the hands of Khrushchev," recalled Kendall. He arranged for Vice-President Richard Nixon to steer Russian Premier Nikita Khrushchev to the Pepsi booth. "Don't worry, I'll bring him by," assured Nixon.

And that he did on a muggy Moscow afternoon that made history while offering luster to more than one American product and opportunity to a handful of budding executives. Khrushchev and Nixon locked horns in the now famous Kitchen Debate arranged by public relations wizard Tex McCrary and assistant William Safire on behalf of McCrary's client, Macy's department store.* The debate became the focus of Nixon's prime campaign poster a year later, largely due to the efforts of Safire. It was shot by photojournalist Elliot Erwitt, who recalls how the two adversaries fell into a heated, if somewhat contrived exchange that set the stage for a rapprochement later in the afternoon over Pepsi. "It was ridiculous. Nixon was saying, 'We're richer than you are' and Khrushchev would say 'We are catching up and we will surpass you.' That was the level of the debate." It soon appeared as though Nixon was grandstanding for the press. "At one point Nixon was getting so irritating that I thought I heard Khrushchev say (in Russian) 'Go fuck my grandmother.' I quickly looked up to see if anybody else had got it and caught the eye of Harrison Salisbury of the *Times*—one of the few Westerners there who spoke Russian. He got it."

Shedding this combative mood, Nixon later ushered Khrushchev over to the Pepsi booth where, under the intent gaze of international publicity, he and Kendall prodded the Russian leader to sample a Pepsi that was bottled in New York. Then, in a clever, subtle move, Kendall handed Khrushchev a bottle of Pepsi made on site at the Exposition. Though there was no difference between the two, the premier, of course, preferred the one made on Russian soil and requested another, as Kendall knew he would. Reportedly, he quaffed a total of seven Pepsis. "It was a warm day," said Kendall, with a wink.

Pepsi became an instant hit with the Russians. Photos swarmed the world of the feisty leader of the communist bloc—the scourge of Coca-Cola—consuming an American soft drink, the very symbol of the decadent bourgeoisie. In orchestrating one of history's more outrageous episodes, Kendall had boldly anticipated a new era of East/West reconciliation, and ensured his future leadership of the Pepsi-Cola Company. Though self-serving, his act was certainly courageous in light of the times. It did have one unheralded effect: it cemented a bond between Kendall and Richard Nixon. Together, they would wheel and deal through the White House, Russia, and beyond.

---

* Safire went on to become Nixon's speechwriter after working on his presidential campaign the following year while McCrary built on Republican ties sown years earlier when he staged an Eisenhower rally at New York's Madison Square Garden.

CHAPTER NINE

The Poetry of Profit

OF ALL THE SUPERLATIVES to which Coke and Pepsi can lay claim, those regarding the power and influence of their advertising are preeminent. By 1900, Coca-Cola was the best-known product in the land. By 1913, Coca-Cola had distributed enough novelties in one year to supply one to every man, woman, and child who had settled in the continental United States since 1650. Coke has long been the world's most advertised product, and Pepsi is never far behind.

The figures, the superlatives, and the reams of articles in marketing and communications journals, business and popular periodicals all confirm what one could not miss in a single stretch in front of the television on any day of the year: advertising is crucial—in fact, the very crux of the war between Coke and Pepsi. All their battles for political influence are but a prologue to the final campaign—the front line of the struggle— that rages most visibly before the consumers. This battle is all the more intense in a market where the products themselves are virtually indistinguishable, where packaging methods closely follow one another, where fluctuations in disposable income do not drastically alter consumption, and where tastes remain fairly constant. Aside from the diversity of advertising media, the only real variable in this mix was the consumer's experience; and ever since the first ads stressed their medicinal benefits, Coke and Pepsi have sung their praises in voices and images which seek to interpret that experience.

This interpretive mission led the ads into an arena far deeper and more encompassing than what is commonly understood to be the normal province of advertising. Rather than merely repeating a message about the product in the hope of converting the nonuser into a faithful user, the advertisers pursued an avenue that identified their respective products with what they saw to be the dominant values and attitudes among consumers. The ads became the medium not only for the surface message—"Coke Adds Life," "Have A Pepsi Day"— but for the ulterior exchange of the consumer's money for soft drinks and the values associated with them. As two of the prime consumer products in modern civilization, Coke and Pepsi have come to epitomize perhaps the central feature of all advertising, which is to provide the forum for placing social values and attitudes on a plane with material ones—be they goods, services, or money. This uniform plane created by advertising is nothing more than a "mental avenue" where words and images freely mix with other mental functions en route to their final destination—the moment of purchase—where the exchange of values is completed.

The social values naturally vary from period to period. William Sharp, current vice-president for advertising at Coca-Cola, recently wrote: "Trying to keep step with each generation and era has been an important factor in advertising for Coke. It strives not to be too far behind or too far ahead of its time; the product has always been positioned for what it was in any era." This strategic positioning of the product to maximize its acceptance has thus always been a conscious objective, the pursuit of which moved the product toward the center of social life.

The social landscape and emotional climate of the Reconstruction South provide some clear initial illustrations. As discussed in Chapter 1, Methodist revivalism in the South, which was financed in no small part by Coca-Cola's first president, Asa Candler, and led by his brother Warren, was rooted in the prevailing mood of gloom and despair following the defeat in the Civil War. First as a medicine, and then as a soft drink, Coca-Cola was depicted in ads that spoke to the people's burdens, much as a physical or spiritual healer would do. "Coca-Cola revives and sustains," "Satisfies the thirsty and helps the weary," "Pure and healthful," the "Heart's Desire"—these are but a few of the dozens of slogans that communicated this theme. On a more concrete level, Coca-Cola was able to offer itself as a clean, wholesome, and temperate alternative to alcohol, whose abuse was one of the prime symptoms of the widespread hopelessness of the period as well as the driving force behind the marriage of revivalism and prohibition.

Relying on images as well as words, Coca-Cola's first ads were no less successful in mediating the emotional conflicts within Southern society at this time. The vigorous market that exists today among collectors of Coca-Cola memorabilia attests to the artistic value placed on these relics of bygone times. What may be less understood, perhaps, is that when they first appeared, these ads' initial appeal was to a pervasive yearning for bygone times that was every bit as widespread as the thriving religiosity of that era. With the dawn of the New South, the cult of the Old South arose to bolster Southern pride and preserve the soul of cherished Southern ideals. As the following examples demonstrate, the conflict between the old and the new was a central feature in the ads, many of whose images comprise a gallery of Southern icons.

In a calendar poster from 1898, a young girl in proper Victorian garb sits beside a tiny antique table delicately sipping Coca-Cola from a small glass. Other ads present women of all ages standing or sitting beside oval picture frames, antique tables, and arras which are adorned with the flourishing Coca-Cola logo. The icon of the Old South invoked here is, of course, that of Southern womanhood. Once the center of plantation life, she became a symbol by which Southern whites reasserted their superior virtue as well as racial superiority, and her elevation above black males became even more of a necessity in Coca-Cola's era than during slavery. "She was the South's Palladium ... this shield-bearing Athena" wrote W. J. Cash. "At the last, I verily believe, the ranks of the Confederacy went rolling into battle in the misty conviction that it was wholly for her that they fought." A fitting homage to Southern womanhood, the oldest

Coca-Cola tray known to exist is a circular portrait of a lady rimmed with designs of classical wreaths whose caption could well have included the toastmaster's words on Georgia's centennial anniversary: "Woman—the center and circumference, diameter and periphery, sine, secant, and tangent of all our affections." The ethereal outlines of her figure, the golden locks and the almost classic Greek manner in which the drink of Coke rests in her palm like some Olympian potion are all poignant features.

Given these sentiments, Southerners of the widest possible range would have been attracted to Coca-Cola. Few, if any, would have been more than half-conscious of the underlying attraction, and there is some real question whether even Candler or his colleagues at the Massengale Agency were entirely cognizant of what they were doing. By presenting certain women on the most abstract level—a queen or an Olympian goddess—the ads identified the product with something otherwise unattainable and completely detached. Slightly less abstract ads depicted all the "beautiful people" found in the "high" art of the period—the elegant Victorian ladies and upright gentlemen lolling in sylvan repose beneath parasols, beside horse and buggy amid splendid surroundings—drinking Coca-Cola. Often, they clasp thin-stemmed glasses with a delicate gentility that leaves the pinky and ring fingers dangling free in a kind of lingering, aristocratic poise. One such ad depicts two couples engaged in just such a posture seated in their automobile, the fruit of progress, parked on some meandering country road before a sprawling pagoda restaurant complete with white plantation columns and a Coca-Cola sign. This ad perfectly positioned Coca-Cola to bridge the chasm between the vanishing pastorale Southern ideal and the otherwise drab, industrial alternative. Along with the other ads, it catered to the Southerner's age-old taste for flamboyant, unreal fantasy and eased the inexorable crossing into modernity where the legendary dream of the Southern heart survived—in a bottle of Coke. Within Coke's ads, the indomitable hedonism of the Southern character was easily transposed into leisure; or in the modern context, consumption.

In the 1910s, Coke cemented its new relationship with the D'Arcy Agency. Continuity of theme was maintained, as explained by Pat Watters: "Pleasant people in pleasant places doing pleasant things as a pleasant nation went pleasantly on its course." A trace of the South's aristocratic legend meshed with the aspirations of a rising white middle class are offered in an ad showing two gentlemen riding in a fine Pullman coach while a black waiter in white uniform pours Coca-Cola for them. The caption points out that consumers could have the same amenities "at your club." A modern, informal elegance characterized other ads showing men and women indulging in the pastimes of the wealthy—golf, tennis, and resort swimming.

Coke continued the vicarious appeal of "beautiful people" right through the twenties—fine ladies and gentlemen in furs and topcoats, or dancing in nightclubs. The slogans meanwhile put the product as well as the users on a somewhat lofty pedestal: "It had to be good to get where it is." Occasionally, the ads would show these "beautiful" users without the product and, at other times, the product without the user. This flexibility afforded all kinds of spatial and compositional arrangements within any given ad: As a pioneer in advertising in the twentieth century, Coke was hence the mediator par excellence, not only in social values, but in a perceptual sense, as well.

Perhaps no presentation was more commanding than the continued use of beautiful women. During the twenties and thirties, Coca-Cola sustained the popular trend by using attractive unknowns as well as celebrities in its posters and periodical advertising. From actress Hilda Clark to Jean Harlow and Joan Crawford (who, like her husband Alfred Steele, came to Pepsi-Cola after a relationship with Coke), well-known female personalities took part in the dominant campaigns of the era. The unknowns, too, appeared in dozens of settings, decked in white lace and bonnets, at a baseball game, clasping a Coke in one hand and a rose in the other, sitting on a boardwalk beneath a parasol, daintily sipping Coke from a glass poised against the ocean background, or on the beach in a bathing suit, with a hand reaching into the frame to pass her a Coke. Even some of the earliest ads included rather enticing slogans, such as: "Nothing is so suggestive of Coca-Cola's own pure deliciousness as the picture of a beautiful, sweet, wholesome, womanly woman." According to Robert Woodruff's guidelines, the women should be beautiful and sexy, but not flagrantly so. Like Candler before him, Woodruff permitted those that portrayed only "Clean American," thus assuring that the purity and other attributes embodied by the women became integrally associated with the product.

From 1930 until well after 1950, Coca-Cola conducted a continuous campaign every Christmas using Santa Claus. This was one of the company's most remarkable campaigns, for it shaped and finally fixed the nation's perception of Santa out of an otherwise vague legend of Saint Nicholas, which was based on an actual person of the same name who lived in Asia Minor around 300 A.D. A generous man, he became the patron saint of children in many countries, and was honored each year with a special day that eventually became Christmas Day. His legend was brought to America by the Dutch colonists where it underwent all kinds of refinements among various groups: the Scandinavians gave him his sleigh and reindeer, the Dutch his pipe and practice of coming through chimneys, and other groups added the fur-trimmed clothes and his home at the North Pole. Santa was being rendered in a wide range of sizes, from the elf in " 'Twas the Night before Christmas" to an average-size human, and the color of his clothes was always changing.

According to Coca-Cola historian Cecil Munsey, it took the Coca-Cola Company to resolve forever the recurring confusion over his portliness and his dress. In 1930, Coke produced a magazine ad featuring a "realistic" version of Santa Claus, followed in 1931 by a commissioned portrait by artist Haddon Sundblom which heightened the "symbolic" element. The result, says Munsey, was "probably the most common conception of Santa Claus" portrayed since then with a long red coat with white fur trim—Coca-Cola's colors—red trousers, high boots, and a large leather belt with the brass buckle. The white hair and flowing beard were incorporated from other portraits.

Although complete and meaningful entities in themselves, the Santa ads used new and different slogans which repeated the central idea of each concurrent campaign. In accord with Coke's traditional style, the ads pictured a user who was the direct opposite of the literal, concrete user—an unattainable, sanctified personage selected, in this case, from ancient legend. In addition to his human shape and his warmth, his one other trait with which viewers could identify was his unabiding love for Coca-Cola. This everyday, earthy taste in the otherwise lofty Santa gave viewers what Sundblom strove for in attempting to mix the realistic with the symbolic—a figure with one hand grasping toys and Rudolph's reins, and the other a bottle of Coke. Considering the persistence of the legends of the Old South that hovered over the surface of Coke's ads back in the 1890s, it seems appropriate to wonder at the appearance of an even older legend in the far more modern ads of the 1930s and 1940s, ads that were woven into the framework of every campaign for twenty-five years. Is there, in fact, an underlying legend or legends which unify the whole structure of Coca-Cola advertising?

In *Hidden Myth,* an insightful exploration of advertising, Varda Leymore explains that advertising creates a continuity of words and images like any other system of communication and, as such, utilizes something very basic in the human makeup.* Some of these words and images pertain to the product, others to the users and the social values they portray. The overwhelming lure of advertising is predicated on exactly this convergence of goods and values within a common system of images. As has been shown, Coca-Cola's advertising pushes the consumer to identify the product with the metaphorical power of the invoked value, thus bonding the two symbolically in the mind. From the 1890s to the 1940s, from ancient Saint Nicholas to Coke's Santa Claus, each age had its own cherished symbols, its own legends, values, and ideals. Thus, if there is an underlying common factor uniting all of Coke's advertising, it is not in any special legend or symbol, but in the symbolic function of the mind itself. As such, it would apply equally to Pepsi's advertising or, as Leymore attempts to show, to all advertising. (Coca-Cola is but one example, though an especially good one since it led the patent-medicine industry which, in turn, says Cecil Munsey, was one of the first consumer industries in the United States to advertise on any scale.)

Thus far, each individual ad discussed has been a meaningful entity in itself. When, however, the individual ads of a campaign are considered together, the meaning of any isolated one can and often does play a very different role, a role which is virtually hidden when the ad is viewed by itself. This new role proves to be the significant one in terms of any common denominator tieing the ads together. The self-evident fact that any campaign presents persistent repetitions of the same slogan or theme is a glaring hint that the underlying message, if there is

* Varda Leymore, *Hidden Myth* (London: Heinemann, 1975). p. vii-x

one, can be culled only by looking at the ads as a group. It is the cumulative impact of *all* the ads in a given campaign that communicates this message.

But what form would the message take? Quite obviously, every product purchase requires the exercise of choice, both in the decision to buy as well as in the selection of a brand. On a more general level, the old saying that something is "the lesser of two evils" or a "happy medium" reflects the common-sense, everyday fact that all of life involves a continuous series of choices. In fact, anthropologists, linguists, and others have argued that the essential activity of the human mind is this selective one that deals with opposing choices or, more simply, opposing forces. The form of the message thus conforms to the choice of whether or not to buy a particular product. Every attribute claimed for the product in a given campaign conforms to this structural premise of oppositions. This premise includes all the dynamics within the campaign, and is consequently a complete and exhaustive statement about the product. Finally, because all this structuring is basic to all communication, the advertisers develop naturally whatever structure the ads have.* They are no more aware of its presence than the viewers, a fact underscored by the remarkable consistency of the message within campaigns whose individual ads bear little surface resemblance to one another.

Communicating within this structure, Coke and Pepsi's ads reiterate the far-reaching and basic dilemmas of the human condition—happiness versus misery, life versus death, we versus they—and offers a solution to them; namely, consuming the respective product. By consuming Coke and Pepsi, the consumer simultaneously buys and consumes the image or attributes associated with them, an image which carries the promise of happiness, life, and belonging rather than misery, death, and alienation. Drawing on renowned French anthropologist Claude Lévi-Strauss, Leymore points out that advertising offers drastically different solutions to the same basic dilemmas addressed by ancient mythology. Even more important than addressing identical themes, advertising operates on identical principles. Despite their differences, the similarities suggest that advertising is a "myth in modern disguise," albeit in a degraded, less-developed form.†

Advertising is best known as a supporter of popular values, a reenforcer of accepted modes of behavior. "Myths," writes Leymore, "reenforce accepted behavior by scanning all the alternative solutions and 'proving' that the one which predominates is, in any society, in given circumstances, the best. As such, the myth is precisely like advertising—a conservative force. ... Over and beyond this, advertising simultaneously provokes anxiety and ... [like a myth] acts as an

---

* Ever since the publication of Vance Packard's *The Hidden Persuaders*, it has been a well-known fact that advertisers consciously deploy certain symbols to heighten the impact on the viewer. Appearing in selected ads in the campaign, these symbols—a tree or some intentional phallic innuendo—make up only a part of the structure, which is an all-inclusive common denominator that runs through every ad in the campaign, and includes the widely hidden persuasion of the advertisers right in with the mundane, unhidden surface claims about the product. In short, the use of symbols is often quite conscious while the existence of an underlying structure, which relates them to all the other elements in the entire campaign, is not.

† *Hidden Myth*, p. ix

anxiety-reducing mechanism. . . . No society exists without some form of myth. Once this is realized, it is not very surprising that a society which is based on the economy of mass production and mass consumption will evolve its own myth in the form of the commercial. Like myth, it touches on every facet of life, and as a myth it makes use of the fabulous in its application to the mundane. Yet in neither [case] do people stop and say, 'but this is impossible.' "*

Before the arrival of Pepsi nationally in 1940, Coca-Cola's campaigns can be broken down into three basic periods: the pre-Massengale era, from the origins of Coke until 1906, when the account was given to the W. C. D'Arcy Agency ; from 1906 until the Candlers sold the company; and from 1920 until the outbreak of World War II, when Archie Lee designed so many of Coke's memorable ads. The literally hundreds of surface messages that appear in this span can be broken down into six fundamental messages.

The central message of the earliest era derives from slogans such as "Exhilarating, Invigorating," "Restores Energy," "Coca-Cola revives and sustains." The central theme is one of life versus death, and it was contained in at least sixteen different ads (which appeared probably hundreds of times), fully twice the number of the next most frequently used message: happiness vs. misery.†
With a good deal of overlap, the surface emphasis was on charm, delight, and gratification, in slogans like "Coca-Cola is a delightful, palatable, healthful beverage" and "Coca-Cola satisfies." The equivalence of these two themes may seem obvious at first, but it was by no means obvious to Asa Candler or the consumers in his market. Far from appearing synonymous with each other, these ads represented a profound ambiguity on Candler's part between selling Coca-Cola as a medicine and as a soft drink. Despite the prevailing ambiguity, the deeper message seems to have had a life of its own.

While these messages prevailed after the arrival of D'Arcy, two new themes also manifest themselves dramatically between 1907 and 1919. One of these derives from one of the deepest and oldest dilemmas known to man: the distinction between we versus they, the in-group and the out-group. Leymore writes, "The separation between 'we' and 'they' operates on all levels of expression—cosmology, marriage rules, religious affiliations, class distinctions, organizational hierarchies, political movements." A humorous strain of this message turns up in Coke's pointed defenses against imitators. "Nicknames encourage substitutions," "Demand the genuine—refuse substitutes," "Get what you ask for and see that you get it," and the elegant, "Coca-Cola is the perfect answer to thirst that no imitation can satisfy." The same opposition of in and out was contained in ads that expressed the general idea that Coke was "the standard beverage"—

* ibid., p. 156
† The underlying message of any campaign is bound to be broad and remarkably simple—so simple, in fact, that uncovering it involves the tedious task of culling the advertisements in the campaign for *all* the attributes and claims about the product and then removing the redundant ones. The result is a non-repetitive list of attributes. This list is then partitioned so that each attribute is associated with its structural opposite, which is either explicitly present in the ad or logically derived. This aggregate set of oppositions is then reduced to its broadest common denominator, which is the underlying message.

"Universally popular, always reliable, tested by time, and proved good." Coke was safe; in other words, Coke was accepted. "The glass that answers the call of millions," "The great national drink" as well as "The national beverage—and yours" identified Coca-Cola with America at a time of heightening nativist sentiment in the face of massive immigration during World War I and the onset of the Red Scare. Under these conditions, the we/they message would be quite effective since "they" represents everything outside the familiar circle, including "demons, ghosts, and foreigners." Between 1908 and 1919, the theme turned up in at least twenty different ads, but in only five between 1891 and 1905.

The second theme developed in this era, first appearing in a single representation in 1904, was the classic opposition of soul and body. The ads that refer to Coca-Cola as the "Great temperance beverage" hearken to the prevalent repugnance to alcohol expressed by the prohibitionists. Within this campaign are other ads which stress desirable qualities that have an even more pronounced role in human life: "Pure and wholesome," "Heart's desire," "A natural drink that answers natural thirst," "It's clean and pure, that's sure." Coca-Cola's historic ties to Methodism came to full flower around 1906; a time when the soul/body theme was being promulgated simultaneously in Coke's advertising as well as in the pulpit, and the more traditional channels. Between 1907 and 1919, the year after the arrival of national Prohibition, the soul/body theme appeared in at least seven different Coke ads versus only one in the earlier period. Because of Coke's Methodist connection, the mythic place of the soul/body message in Coca-Cola advertising is more apparent and helps to illuminate the other less obvious message—in/out—to which it is integrally tied.

Unless connected by other messages that give them their own internal dynamic, these analogies are only pieces of an incomplete puzzle. Between 1920 and 1940, two other messages touched on in earlier campaigns emerge more fully as the pieces which tie the structure together. The claim of total availability is one of the proudest features of the product first proclaimed in such slogans as "Sold Everywhere—5¢" and the mellifluous "Flows from every fountain." The promised-land tone of this 1905 ad was echoed nine times between 1920 and 1940 in such upbeat phrases as "All trails lead to ice-cold Coca-Cola," and "Around the corner from anywhere." The message here—abundance/scarcity—draws a direct line between convenience, Coca-Cola's omnipresence and its bounteous abundant nature on the one hand, and lack of Coke, and inconvenience amounting to scarcity and barrenness on the other. This edenic condition of abundance mediates the conflict between soul and body, and analogously, between we/they. Appearing in at least nine different ads between 1920 and 1940 versus three between 1907 and 1919, the new message served as the cross brace which strengthened the entire structure.

The sixth message, manifested in perhaps the most famous of all Coke slogans, endows the entire network with a meaningful internal logic that leaves no element unrelated. The slogan, of course, was "The Pause That Refreshes," and the underlying message is that of eternal time versus historical or finite time. The slogan was the creation of Archie Lee, who embellished a message that had appeared only once prior to his arrival in 1921. Between 1920 and 1940, the message turned up in at least twenty-six separate ads whose cumulative number of appearances must have been in the thousands. In addition, to the endless permutations of "The Pause," the message was conveyed in ads with slogans like "Through all the years since 1886," "Makes a little moment long enough for a big rest," and "It's part of the game to take time out." The Santa campaign alone used it four of the first ten years, including 1930's "The busiest man in the world comes up smiling after the Pause That Refreshes." Eternal time properly belongs to deities and ageless figures like Santa Claus, the Prophet Elijah, and Jesus, as well as to primitive tribal and agricultural rituals that reenact the saga of creation, birth, death, and regeneration. Eternal time is sacred and prehistoric, while finite time is historical, natural, and profane. In Biblical terms, this coincides with the fall from grace, expulsion from the Garden of Eden, and the advent of misery and death. The ads convey the message that in drinking Coca-Cola the march of time pauses, indeed, stops, and the consumer can actually enter the timeless realm where eternal life and happiness reign.

Whether one looks at a single campaign or at the entire forty-year sweep of these ads, the fundamental themes are reiterated in such a way that each ad offers fragmentary portions of the message, which are then seized on by the other ads and further refined and embellished until the message becomes totally clear. In the Santa campaigns, for example, the stereotyping of his body as fat and round harmonizes with his jolly soul. The slogan given by a smiling Santa, "Give and take say I," suggests an abundance signified by a whole freezer full of Coca-Cola. In the picture of the 1930 ad, Santa's belly protrudes into a circle of wreath-bearing children within a crowded store stocked full of merchandise. The fullness of the environment seems infinite as the pillars of the store practically disappear in the horizon line of the picture. The slogans—"It had to be good to get where it is," and "Nine million a day "—convey the in/out message, which is further resolved within Santa's abundant personage.

These two messages continue in tandem in the campaigns of the forties. The in/out motif was especially prominent, rising from at least twelve executions between 1920 and 1939 to at least thirty-four the following decade. Certainly World War II was a heavy influence, especially evident in slogans like "Coca-Cola helps show the world the friendliness of American ways," "Universal symbol of the American way of life," "As American as Independence Day." Aside from an anxiety over America's uncertain place in the postwar world, the ads also addressed the insecurities of an expanding middle class hungry for acceptance and belonging. "Friendliness and Coca-Cola go together like bread and butter," "The quality of Coca-Cola is a quality you can trust," and "Everybody's Club."

The most important development of the forties, however, was the arrival of national prominence for Pepsi-Cola. The 12-ounces-for-a-nickel strategy had given Pepsi substance; Mack's innovative, sometimes brilliant, advertising gave it form and soon the company advanced into a vaguely competitive stance against Coke. "The best is always the better buy," "The only thing like Coca-

Cola is Coca-Cola itself" are clear signs that, even with its wartime advantage, the dominant brand was feeling the pressure of the challenger's gains.

Yet, as we have seen in Chapter 5, rising costs and the onset of middle-class values doomed the nickel Pepsi, while the demographics of its consumers revealed it to be the "poor man's drink"—the social equivalent of the outsider. While Mack greatly improved Pepsi's national presence, he couldn't improve its stature, and Pepsi's acceptance had deteriorated by the beginning of the fifties.

It would take a former Cokeman, Al Steele, to zero in on the quality theme for the home market. No longer the drink for the downtrodden, Pepsi was casting its product—now in still larger bottles ranging from twelve to twenty-six ounces—as the recreational refreshment for almost any occasion. This campaign effectively undermined the snob effect which had so long moved consumers to drink Coke solely to disassociate themselves from the common herd. Oddly enough, at this time Coke found itself moving in the opposite direction. With such slogans as "Almost everyone appreciates the best," "The most asked-for soft drink in the world," Coke willingly surrendered some of its prestige for the sake of riding on the bandwagon. As Coke and Pepsi became more competitive, their advertising oscillated more freely between snob appeal and mob appeal.

Yet this was a period of intense internal change at both companies, and neither would be comfortable with this unstructured situation for long. The search for surer footing in their advertising was a powerful impulse behind the dramatic changes of the period. In December 1955, Pepsi switched its account to Kenyon and Eckhardt from Biow-Beirn-Toigo who had replaced Newell-Emmett back in 1948. The lackluster performance at D'Arcy was largely due to the 1951 death of Archie Lee, and in 1956, Coke decided to integrate its domestic and international advertising with McCann-Erickson, the agency that had handled its international promotions for years. As the companies moved into television in a major way, their advertising would never again rest on the intuitions of one man, like Mack or Lee, or even of a small group. The mammoth consumer market research undertaken by Coke in the final days of the D'Arcy era—said by some to be the largest of its kind ever performed—provided the company with its major boost into the modern world of motivational research and market analysis. Pepsi was not far behind, as the two swept headlong toward cola Armageddon armed to the gills with their formidable and sophisticated computational tools.

A lot had changed since Candler and Brabham first stamped the logos on their dark tonics. Colas soon begat colors and flavors galore—the soft drink became a part of living. With its absolute dominance no longer a law of life, the Atlantan drink was cast afloat in a well-traveled sea of soda makers, each one more willing than the next to rule the waters that cooled the thirsty throngs. Pepsi was proving that more than one could play this game, and that the rules made allowance for dividing the pie among however many players could cut it. Besides being crowded, and maybe even because of it, the world was growing a little more uncertain, a little more anxious, a little more accepting of the message these mariners bore with their bottles, their slogans, and their songs.

PART TWO

CHAPTER TEN

Through a Cola Darkly

O N NOVEMBER 20, 1963, the head of Batten, Barton, Durstine & Osborne, Pepsi-Cola's ad agency since 1960, was addressing the Dallas convention of the American Bottlers of Carbonated Beverages. Suddenly he was interrupted by a whispered message which made him abruptly leave the podium—and on stage strutted Vice-President Lyndon Johnson. To the hushed crowd, Johnson began with a snap analysis of the American economy: "One way we think . . . to boost the productivity is to increase consumer spending. . . . We think they could buy more soft drinks." The audience expected kind words from the vice-president, but not the sticky sweet homage they received.

"The bottlers," continued Johnson, "get up at daylight and work till midnight, and develop stomach ulcers to keep those trucks going and keep that production up." He lauded the entire industry, down to "the man who mans the trucks, who puts the caps on the bottles, who loads the cases . . . and enjoys the highest standard of living of any human being anywhere in the world."

After Johnson's speech, the first speaker was given a standing ovation when he resumed with "Now that the commercial is over . . . "

In a typically heavy-handed manner, Johnson was simply soliciting the support of an industry which had arrived during the fifties from the backwaters to become one of the most competitive and growth-motivated sectors of the American economy. The soft-drink phenomenon had become a corporate free-for-all. Gone were the days when a single product, single container behemoth jousted with regional firms for a steadily expanding market. The postwar baby boom and a Camelot-enhanced prosperity produced a consumer class voracious for new products to complement leisure-minded lifestyles. The proliferation of television, responsible for $43 million of the industry's record $166 million ad budget in 1963, provided a new intimacy and greater leverage with the consumer. New money from outside the industry accelerated marketing, managerial, and technological innovations, and the number of American bottling plants overseas had doubled to nearly a thousand.

The frontiers of the American market had been conquered, and henceforth domestic growth would come by priming the market with new products and using new ways to market the old ones. The need for a complete soft-drink line was underscored by the widespread acceptance of the multiple-flavor vending machine and the triple-drink fountain dispenser. By 1962, diet sodas accounted for 3 percent of the industry's gross, and within a year, all major manufacturers would boast of a diet cola. To avoid being outflanked by competitors, each manufacturer introduced a spate of new containers intended to make soft-drink consumption as convenient as possible. The most noticeable trend was nonreturnable bottles and cans, the latter particularly after the introduction of the easy opening flip-top in 1962. All told, bottlers invested $70 million for new bottling and dispensing equipment in 1963, prompting some observers to ask if too much emphasis was being placed on the package rather than the product.

Such lofty questions took a back seat to the nuts-and-bolts realities of the day. For example, conventioneers were undoubtedly discussing the rising costs of soft drinks and the loss of cheap Cuban sugar due to the American embargo of Cuba.

Amid diversification and a rash of acquisitions within the industry, the bottlers were also talking about the board room struggles at Pepsi and the election just two months earlier of Pepsi's new president, Donald M. Kendall.

Al Steele's sudden death had left Pepsi leaderless. Barnett continued to handle the daily chores of running the company, but he was a helmsman, not a captain. Lacking Steele's attention-grabbing style, he was more content in executive suites than the spotlight.

Steele's widow heeded the call. Joan Crawford replaced her husband on the board of directors, though one ex-Pepsi executive contends she took the position without pay to work off a debt Steele had run up as president. Nevertheless, she remained the company's first lady and champion—Pepsi's dearest—and was so effective that an entire generation came to associate her with Pepsi-Cola.

Crawford's reign as a premier personality was challenged by Kendall, the highly aspiring young buck who led Pepsi's overseas operations. The struggle between actress and executive was bitter and well publicized (she occasionally referred to him as "fang"). Crawford loathed Kendall's ambition and complained that he used the foreign operations to steal her husband's thunder. On the other hand, Kendall was upset by his subservient status before her, and resented the popular notion that Pepsi-Cola was "Joan Crawford's company." Robert Scheer recounts one particularly telling episode in *Esquire* magazine: Once, Kendall had dutifully escorted Crawford to the Stork Club. She spied Ernest Hemingway at another table and, wanting to meet him, dispatched Kendall to fetch the author. "Mr. Hemingway, Miss Crawford would like to talk to you," said Kendall. According to Scheer, "Hemingway roared out for the benefit of the attendant and gossipy patrons, 'Tell her to bring her ass over here if she wants to meet me.'" Unable to respond, Kendall simply retreated to his table with his tail between his legs.

After Steele's death, Pepsi had lost some of the momentum that had characterized his reign. Its share of the market was stagnant and the bottlers were growing restless. Consequently, managerial skills and business acumen prevailed over glamor and stage dust. Crawford was relegated to the supporting cast and Kendall took center stage.

A big, bluff, fast-talking outdoorsman who barreled his way to the top, Kendall ranks as history's greatest Pepsi-Cola salesman. The son of a Washington

State dairy farmer, he was moderately educated at Western Kentucky State College where he starred as a tackle on the football team. During World War II, he joined the Navy and was twice awarded the Distinguished Flying Cross. In 1945, he married the daughter of his base commander, Vice Admiral Edward Orrick McDonnell, a general partner of Hornblower & Weeks, the renowned investment firm, as well as a director of Hertz, Pan Am, and Pepsi-Cola. The admiral took a shine to his ambitious son-in-law, and according to Walter Mack, asked Mack to find Kendall a spot in the fast-growing Pepsi-Cola Company. In 1947, Kendall was given a forty-dollar-a-week job selling fountain syrup in New York City, and through toughness, determination, and perhaps a guardian angel, rose through the ranks.

Kendall soon came to the attention of Steele. Said an observer, "Steele recognized that the company needed a swinging salesman to talk to theater owners, circus owners—you name it—and Kendall was the guy. Kendall could travel all day, screw all night, drink all night, stay out all night with those bums, but would come and bring in the business."

He became a sales manager, then an assistant national sales manager in 1951, vice-president in charge of sales in 1952, and vice-president in charge of marketing in 1956, which included responsibility for all sales, advertising, and promotions.

As head of Pepsi's national accounts division, Kendall had landed an important concession at Disneyland, apparently through his close friendship with C. V. Wood, Jr. An engineer with a flair for business, Wood had been one of the prominent figures at Stanford Research Institute, and became involved with the Disney organization when the plans for the now legendary amusement park were first formulated. Like Kendall, Wood was talented and aspiring, and was allegedly so involved in arranging the financing for Disneyland, and then designing, building, and actually running it for a year after its 1955 opening that he saw no reason why he shouldn't have a bigger stake. Having helped Pepsi win the concession, said one admirer, he "damn near won" in his legal efforts to change the name of the park to "Woodyland."

Steele decided that Kendall's tenacity could be best used overseas, and in 1957, after only ten years with the company, Kendall was made president of Pepsi-Cola International. Kendall charted his career well, for ambition was best vented in the breakneck pace of foreign expansion. He shared the obsession for Pepsi's growth that had come to characterize Pepsi's leadership. Under his leadership, Pepsi's overseas business tripled and profits increased fivefold, accounting for 30 percent and 40 percent respectively of the company total. Even as he flew to the convention in Dallas, Kendall was preparing to astound many by soon announcing that Pepsi was negotiating an entry behind the Iron Curtain.

Impressive as Kendall's performance was, the seminal event of his career had been the American Exposition in Moscow four years earlier. His triumph there came by courtesy of the Pepsi attorney, now at his side in Dallas, former Vice-President Richard M. Nixon. Although failure could have ended his career,

Kendall's gambit worked spectacularly. Management and stockholders correctly reasoned that if Don Kendall can convince the leader of the communist world to drink Pepsi he could convince anyone.

By 1963, on the other hand, Nixon's career was falling apart, and with Adlai Stevenson, he seemed headed for those pastures reserved for the "also rans" or politically maimed. A pillar of the Cold War, Nixon had espoused a fierce anti-communism that sparked his leap into California congressional politics in the mid-forties. As a vocal member of the House Un-American Activities Committee, he worked energetically alongside Joe McCarthy during the witch hunts, and inherited the mantle as one of America's most powerful and outspoken demagogues when the "Pepsi-Cola Kid" finally went flat. His virulent anticommunism and exaggerated defense of America's worldwide presence stroked Cold War proponents and earned him a spot on the 1952 Republican ticket with Eisenhower. Nixon survived a turbulent, sometimes traumatic vice-presidency, and was odds-on favorite to beat Joe Kennedy's son in the 1960 election.

Alongside Kennedy's confident idealism, Nixon appeared uncomfortable, intractable, and paranoid. The New Frontier was a liberal anticommunism—beside which Nixon's rearguard conservatism seemed ill-tempered and starkly isolationist. Nixon lay exposed as the very embodiment of America's dark fears of mediocrity and failure, and he couldn't appear quite as trustworthy with the future as young Jack.

Fighting for his political life, Nixon regrouped his forces and ran for the governorship of California in 1962. Again, he embraced shotgun subtlety and a Draconian world view to market himself as the new hero of prosperity. Again he lost, this time to Pat Brown. The humiliation of a former vice-president, just two years removed from his office, losing the governorship of his own state was too much. To the delight of intellectuals and libertarians throughout the land, Nixon, in one of his less prophetic moments, vowed to the mass media after the election, "You won't have Nixon to kick around anymore."

The tandem rejection of Richard Nixon was rooted in the new internationalism that was taking hold in the sixties and would flower in the seventies. Nixon didn't yet understand that the thawing of the Cold War was by design, not historical inevitability. Unlike Kendall, he failed to grasp the crucial meaning of that first Pepsi in Moscow back in 1959—that the global realpolitik was shifting to the point where communist countries best served American interests as markets rather than adversaries. As we shall see, it was by no accident that within a few years this same man would rise and lead the country to détente and the recognition of China. There *was* a "new" Nixon in 1968, though the difference was too subtle to appreciate then, and a key architect of his reeducation and comeback would be Donald Kendall.

Shattered by his 1962 loss, Nixon was faced with the difficult task of putting his life back together. Even in defeat, Nixon was a valuable commodity, well schooled in the alleys of political life, a fact appreciated by such friends as Kendall and the head of Warner-Lambert, the pharmaceutical giant, Elmer Bobst, who regularly spent Christmas with the Nixons and was known by them as "Uncle Elmer." Bobst advised Nixon to begin anew in New York, and Kendall sweetened the suggestion by offering Nixon his previous job—the strategically important leadership of Pepsi International. Preferring to practice law, Nixon declined, and Bobst arranged for the former vice-president to join the once prestigious but faltering Manhattan law firm of Mudge, Rose, Baldwin, and Todd. After indications that some new legal accounts would be available, the firm agreed to hire Nixon in June 1963 for a reported $150,000 salary, beginning within six months of his passing the New York bar. Despite his extremely limited legal experience, Nixon would now bask in an air of established influence and visibility, for there were more than a few clients who would pay to be able to quip, "As my lawyer, Richard Nixon, says, ..." Soon known as Nixon, Mudge, Rose, Guthrie, and Alexander, the firm profited handsomely from its new accounts, one of which was Pepsi International. In a perspicacious stroke, Kendall paid a debt he had incurred in Moscow four years before, and invested in Nixon's fortunes. Yet Kendall might well have bought in with an insider's knowledge of some of the former vice-president's hidden assets.

Kendall would have gotten his clearest impression of these assets from the Caribbean involvements of Nixon and others within the Pepsi circle like Wallace Groves, Walter Mack's former partner at Phoenix Securities. The one-time stock-fraud felon and "Boy Wonder of Wall Street," Groves undertook several ventures in the mid-fifties, including Grand Bahama Development Company and Grand Bahama Port Authority. Through the largess of Bahamian government officials, the latter had been able to acquire over half of Grand Bahama Island since 1955 at the irresistible price of one British pound ($2.80) per acre.*

In 1964, Groves's Grand Bahama Development Company opened the 250-room Lucayan Beach Hotel whose casino soon retained the age-old expertise of Meyer Lansky, recognized by most authorities as a premier force in the National Crime Syndicate since the end of World War II.† Groves's casino was completely managed and run by Lansky associates or those of other crime chieftains like Dutch Schultz, who had tried to bribe Walter Mack a quarter-century before. Later that year, the revelation of the Lansky influence resulted in massive turnovers at the Lucayan, but the criminal presence was to endure at Groves's other smaller gambling haunts.

Lansky's interest in the Bahamas grew directly from his expulsion from Cuba where he had operated successfully since 1937.‡ The paths of Nixon and Lansky crossed more than once during the ensuing years. Fresh out of Duke University Law School in 1940, Nixon set up law practice in Whittier, California where he met Bugsy Siegel, Lansky's renowned West Coast partner. Soon after, he made

* Ed Reid, *The Grim Reapers* (Chicago: Henry Regnery and Co., 1969). p. 105
† ibid., p. 109–18
‡ This was the year Lansky opened the splendid Hotel Nacional in Havana. To protect his investment, he forged a close alliance with Cuban dictator Fulgencio Batista, which opened the gates for a rash of gambling, drug, and prostitution rings instrumental in fueling the sentiments that led to the rise of Castro.

a trip to Havana to explore "the possibilities of establishing law or business connections."* Much more significantly, Lansky actually met Nixon some years later in Miami, and again in Havana in the early fifties just before Nixon was to undertake his bid for the vice-presidency.† Nixon was then traveling with Lansky's friend, Dana C. Smith, whose heavy gambling losses created problems for him with a Syndicate-linked casino operator. Lansky was reportedly quite impressed with the way Nixon, then a California senator, tried to get the State Department to mediate on Smith's behalf.‡

With the rise of Castro, Lansky got in touch with Dana Smith and Senator George Smathers of Florida, a close friend of Nixon, in the earnest hope of initiating plans to do away with Fidel. Both the 1961 Bay of Pigs invasion, which Nixon helped design while still vice-president, and the subsequent CIA-Mafia plots to assassinate Castro all failed, and Lansky had to find other waters in which to swim. Among others, Wallace Groves, himself a CIA operative from 1965 to 1972, and Groves's Lucayan Beach Casino would be his vessels to the Bahamas.§

Groves's ventures also attracted attention at Pepsi. In 1959, William Leader, Jr., president of the Pepsi-Cola Bottling Company of Fairfield, Connecticut, sent out feelers to the Port Authority for exclusive rights to bottle soft drinks in the area.

Formerly export sales manager of the parent Pepsi-Cola, Leader had visited the Bahamas on company business during the forties. After a stint at Pepsi International, Leader came to the Fairfield franchise and rekindled his interest in the Bahamas after learning of the developments there. The Port Authority granted him bottling rights, and his plant opened in 1962.||

One of Groves's original partners in the 1955 creation of Grand Bahama Port Authority was Charles Allen, Jr.,who also joined the Pepsi-Cola board in early September of that year. A man once rumored to have helped bring Steele over to Pepsi from Coke, Allen was senior partner of Allen & Company, perhaps Wall Street's foremost venture capital investment firm. It took a 25 percent interest in Groves's venture, and in October purchased a $3 million holding from a company owning the Pepsi franchise in Los Angeles.# (Within two years, that company had been reorganized into a holding company—Pepsi United Bottlers—that was involved in banking as well as two other domestic bottling operations and a Mexican subsidiary which made it the largest independent Pepsi-Cola bottling firm in the world. Its board included such notables as Edgar Bronfman,

---

* Earl Mazo, *Richard Nixon* (New York: Harper, 1959), p. 35
† Hank Messick, *Lansky* (New York: G. P. Putnam's Sons, 1971). p. 187–190. Dennis Eisenberg, Uri Dan, Ely Landau, *Meyer Lansky: Mogul of the Mob* (New York: Paddington Press, 1979). p. 258
‡ Messick, ibid., p. 189–90
§ *Wall Street Journal*, April 18, 1980, p. 30. "A December 30, 1965 Covert Security Approval issued by the CIA's Office of Security, marked 'Secret,' says Mr. Groves 'will be used as an adviser and possible officer for one (of the CIA's) Project entities . . .' "
|| *Beverage Industry* (formerly *Bottling Industry*), November 13, 1962, p. 18
Messick, op. cit., p. 226; *Moody's Industrial Manual*, 1963. p. 2381

of Seagram's; Bernard Relin, the former chairman of Blair Holdings, Pepsi United's corporate predecessor.)

Another Pepsi United director was Greg Bautzer, the Hollywood attorney for billionaire Howard Hughes during the period when the reclusive billionaire was buying heavily into the mob-backed casinos in Las Vegas.

Perhaps history's wealthiest high-school dropout, Allen's unassuming manners, reclusiveness, and a flair for far-flung and bold financial deals rendered him a folk hero on Wall Street and one of the very richest men in the history of American finance. In 1964, he purchased a major interest in Seven Arts Productions, Ltd., a Canadian company (where Pepsi United's Greg Bautzer was also a director) from "Uncle" Lou Chesler, the Toronto financier who had invested some $12 million in Groves's venture since becoming his partner in 1960.* A fast-talking securities and real-estate mogul, Chesler was facing an uprising from stockholders incensed over revelations that he tied himself and Seven Arts funds into Lansky-related operations in the Bahamas. Content that Allen would avoid such maneuvers, the distraught investors ignored his equally conspicuous ties to Groves, which increased dramatically over the years.†

Groves and Chesler would soon have a falling out, but both their careers showed marked similarities nonetheless. Each had been weaned in the securities business, stalking small ailing companies with big potential; each had been directly implicated in dealing in stolen and fraudulent securities; and each had excelled in real estate development. A partner with Lansky in Canadian mining ventures, Chesler was associated with two of Lansky's top officers in Florida's largest real estate outfit—General Development Corporation—and was directly involved with two other companies from which Nixon profited handsomely.‡ One, Major Reality, considered by law enforcement authorities to be Lansky's primary Florida real estate front, arranged a 1962 deal which netted Nixon well over $185,000. The other, Cape Florida Development, owned by a Syndicate-linked figure close to Chesler whom the Secret Service urged Nixon to avoid, sold him choice Key Biscayne property on which he made $100,000 profit.§ The Florida White House eventually sat on a parcel of this property. One of the

* Reid, op. cit., p. 106–07

† Once known as the King of Grand Bahama, Groves lost his political power base in the Bahamian government during the mid-sixties, and was subsequently forced out of a major casino development on Paradise Island. He needed new financial muscle, and Charlie Allen provided it in 1969 when an Allen-controlled company bought up over 90 percent of the shares of the Port Authority, and its casino subsidiary (including the 25 percent already held by Allen interests.) In 1970, a new entity was formed, Intercontinental Diversified. Its stock was traded publicly, representing what Hank Messick called "the final refinement of Lansky's master plan." In hooking up with Allen, "Groves was attempting to arrange for his kingdom to be annexed by that mysterious empire of international finance where Meyer Lansky had so long been powerful." See Messick, Lansky, op cit., p. 248. Also Hank Messick, Syndicate Abroad (New York: Macmillan, 1969). p. 221–24

‡ Messick, Lansky, op. cit., p. 228; Steve Weissman (ed.), Big Brother and the Holding Company (Palo Alto, California, Ramparts Press, 1974). p. 270

§ J. Anthony Lukas, Nightmare (New York: Bantam, 1977). p. 490. Jeff Gerth, "The Miami Connection" in Steve Weissman (ed.) Big Brother and the Holding Company, op. cit., p. 268. North American Congress on Latin America, Latin America & Empire Report, October, 1972, p.

houses on the President's compound belonged to Robert Abplanalp, a millionaire friend of Nixon who held a ninety-nine-year lease on a Bahamian island and
mansion that Nixon often used as a presidential retreat. Abplanalp first acquired
the house in 1966 from Russell Arundel, Pepsi's lobbyist-at-large in the days of
"Tail Gunner" Joe McCarthy, who with his two sons, was the controlling force
of Pepsi-Cola Bottling Co. of Long Island.*

Though he had been stripped of political office, Nixon thus remained close to
his traditional power base where highly influential organized crime interests
converged with legitimate business capital, primarily in the areas of tourism, real
estate, and related consumer services. Because of his association with Allen and
Edward Orrick McDonnell, among others, Kendall recognized Nixon's potential to operate effectively in the international sphere, where the struggle for markets between Coke and Pepsi rendered the ideological struggle between East and
West obsolete. To prevail in his corporate struggle, Kendall was doing what he
could to minimize the geopolitical barriers to trade. For Nixon, the opportunity
to travel the world while representing prestigious corporate clients like Pepsi was
invaluable, for on their name he could rebuild his own political stature while
shaping the dialogue that could significantly affect American foreign policy.

Between 1963 and 1967, while his real estate interests prospered at home,
Nixon toured Europe and Asia as Pepsi's attorney where bottle-plant openings
and luncheons in scores of countries allowed him to meet national leaders, industrialists, and vocal special interests. In Rome, he sipped a Pepsi at the airport
while giving reporters his predictions on the upcoming June 1964 Republican
presidential primary back home in California. Nixon called on the president of
Pakistan and then Lebanon where he stayed in the Beirut home of the head of
the local Pepsi bottling plant. During an interview there, he repeated that he
would accept the nomination "if the party leaders ask me to run." As the local
T.V. cameras rolled, a waiter reached into view to turn a Pepsi bottle at his
elbow so that the label showed.† He delivered a major address in Bangkok and
then went on to Saigon where he met with Ambassador Henry Cabot Lodge, his
running mate in 1960. General William Westmoreland and top South Vietnamese leaders were also there, and on his return to New York, Nixon called for
a rapid escalation of the Vietnam War. The would-be candidate's high-profile
performances were an easy target even for Lyndon Johnson, who was able to enhance the illusion of his being a dove by contrasting himself to the hawkish
Nixon at a 1964 pre-campaign rally. "One of my friends that drinks Pepsi-
Cola—a former vice-president—went out to Vietnam and said we ought to have
a little more war. Well, we won't."‡

While he was agitating for greater U.S. involvement in the conflict, Pepsi
business had brought Nixon into more intimate contact with established right-
wing elements in Southeast Asia already embroiled in war. Indeed, some mem-

---

* *Miami Herald*, June 4, 1973
† Jules Witcover, *The Resurrection of Richard Nixon* (New York: Putnam, 1970). p. 76
‡ Alfred Steinberg, *Sam Johnson's Boy* (New York: Macmillan, 1968). p. 663

bers of the Pepsi family had been hard at work in Indochina for some time prior to Nixon's travels there. Russell Arundel's son, Arthur, was a high-ranking member of General Lansdale's Saigon Military Mission in 1954. A specialist in psychological warfare and propaganda techniques, Arundel was mentioned more than once in *The Pentagon Papers* for his extreme effectiveness in disrupting the communists and the peasant populations. Moreover, ". . . under the guidance of Captain Arundel, a Thomas Paine type series of essays on Vietnamese patriotism against the Communist Vietminh . . . were circulated among influential groups in Vietnam . . . [and] earned front-page editorials in the leading newspaper in Saigon."*

Years later, with Captain Arundel safely back at Pepsi-Cola in Long Island City, the Saigon franchise allegedly included Madame Cao Van Vien, whose husband, a general in the South Vietnamese Army, addressed the World Anti-Communist League in 1969. Just as in the Caribbean, business in this region visibly merged the overworld of government and corporation with the underworld of illicit dealings, chiefly in the form of narcotics. One of the largest heroin operations in all of Southeast Asia was run by a Pepsi-Cola bottler in Vientiane, Laos where the CIA's proprietary Air America delivered opium grown in the hills. The bottler, Huu Tim Heng, was a Chinese financier who formed the major link between the self-proclaimed Laotian opium king, U.S. government-backed General Ouane Rattikone and his South Vietnamese counterpart, former Premier Ky.† The franchise itself had as its official president the son of the Laotian prime minister, whose esteemed presence qualified the venture for generous support from the U.S. Agency for International Development despite the fact that it never bottled a single Pepsi in five years of start-stop construction. It was used instead as a cover for purchases of chemicals vital to the processing of heroin as well as for large financial transactions.

Meanwhile, the Taiwan franchise was held by the family interests of Madame Chiang Kai-shek and her brother, T. V. Soong. The Madame's paintings adorned Nixon's New York apartment, and Nixon, a long-time ally of Chiang's, stayed with him in Taiwan where the agenda called for both business and politics.‡ T.V. Soong had been Chiang's ambassador to the United States during the forties, and was said to have had over $47 million in U.S. holdings as a result of his control of the postwar Chinese Lend-Lease program. Soong was ostensibly one of the bankrollers of Civil Air Transport (CAT), the forerunner of Air America established in the late forties during the Chinese Revolution to conduct relief flights and military airlifts to Chiang's Chinese nationalists.§ Indeed,

---

* *The Pentagon Papers*, published by *The New York Times*, ed. and assembled by Neil Sheehan (New York: Quadrangle, 1971). p. 58-63
    † Alfred W. McCoy , *The Politics of Heroin in Southeast Asia* (New York: Harper, 1972). p. 186
    ‡ Jack Anderson, *The Washington Post*, December 31, 1972. p. C 7. Jules Witcover, op. cit., p. 77. Earl Mazo, op. cit., p. 291
    § Soong's career cited in Peter Dale Scott, op. cit., p. 7. cf. *San Francisco Chronicle*, April 2, 1970, p. 31. W.T. Wertenbaker, "The China Lobby," *Reporter*, April 15, 1952, p. 9-10

Soong was a financial hub of the infamous China Lobby in Washington which, like CAT, strengthened its ties to Chiang after his expulsion from mainland China at a time when Truman and the State Department were preparing to recognize the Chinese communists. (The lobby was threatened by a congressional inquiry expected to probe the soybean speculation involving Pepsi's Russell Arundel and Joe McCarthy. See Chapter 7.)*

While the China Lobby vocalized its opposition to recognition, Soong's CAT undertook covert operations, acting as a CIA contractor in Burma, Korea, and later in the fifties, Laos. As the largest CIA proprietary in Asia, CAT successor Air America supported the heroin suppliers and their entrenched secret societies because they provided a socio-military network undermining Chinese communist influence, especially among the middle classes.† While narcotics continued to be an important factor in the activities of the China Lobby—"prominent Americans have participated in and profited from these transactions"—Air America continued its actions which "were in fact leading our country into war in Southeast Asia."‡

This self-ordained policy of government proprietaries was largely a consequence of their serving primarily private (as opposed to national) interests that came together in a confluence of war lobbies, organized crime, and corporations. Pepsi's foreign franchisees were not the only relevant illustration. A long-time Air America director and a coterie of wealthy Thai investors were associated with Lou Chesler both through the board of Seven Arts and his General Development Corporation.§

All his traveling and hell-bent adventurism moved Nixon closer to the White House. Pepsi, too, was gaining fantastic momentum. Both candidate and corporation were underdogs—runners-up playing catch-up ball—pulling as many strings as they could. Even before the Kendall era, Pepsi, of course, had some pronounced ties to Wall Street. Charles Allen, for instance, held an interest in United Cigar and Whelan Drug Stores, which were early clients of Phoenix Securities, the Mack-Groves investment company that bailed Pepsi out of the Guth era. Edward Orrick McDonnell of the Wall Street investment house of Hornblower-Weeks, later a Mudge-Rose client, joined Pepsi's board in the early fifties and brought with him a modicum of mainstream influence as a director of the establishment giant, Pan Am.

McDonnell was the first in a long succession of Pepsi directors to sit on the board of Pan Am, whose meteoric rise in the sixties was also enhanced by friends from Wall Street and Washington. In fact, the so-called Pan Am lobby in the Senate drew heavily from the China Lobby, and the airline's staggering profits in the decade sprang from its monopoly of Indochina's commercial service, which

* Scott, ibid., p. 7, 195-96. cf. *Time*, October 15, 1951, p. 23
† Scott, op. cit., p. 201
‡ China Lobby discussed in Ross Y. Koen, *The China Lobby in American Politics* (New York: Macmillan, 1960). p. ix. Scott, ibid, p. 20.
§ Scott, op. cit., p. 210-11

was opened with U.S. government assistance during a CAT airlift at the fateful battle of Dienbienphu in 1953. Pan Am later participated in lucrative airlifts for CAT in Laos and supplied the top operating personnel for Air America.*

While Coke's firmer ties with big-business banks like Morgan Guaranty put it at the forefront of power and influence well before World War II, Pepsi's milieu remained a secondary one. A key banking connection at this time appears to have been with Marine Midland Trust Company, in New York, a subsidiary of the Marine Midland Corporation. Two Pepsi director's served on the board of Marine Midland Trust, including James Gillespie Blaine, chairman of the bank from 1930 to 1954 and then a director of the holding company in addition to his directorship of the bank. He was joined on the bank's board by David G. Baird, head of three family foundations which, according to the House Select Committee on Small Business in 1963, "repeatedly violated Treasury regulations" by acting as unregulated tax-free security dealers on behalf of a host of figures, including Lou Chesler and Seven Arts Productions.† A prime player in the formation of numerous movie and television deals, the Baird foundations transgressed Treasury regulations in at least one major transaction involving Allen & Company, the 1956 purchase of $22 million worth of Warner Brothers stock.‡ David Baird was then acting on behalf of Boston financier Serge Semenenko, the "mystery man of the banking world," according to the The New York Times, as well as the "power behind the financing of the film industry."§ Just as notable, however, was Semenenko's less visible role as a banker of the Bahamian development of Lou Chesler and Meyer Lansky .||

Through its orientation toward Marine Midland and the parade of figures extending from Mack to Allen, Pepsi had a financial base which, like Nixon's political base, lay outside the citadels of establishment power. The point, of course, was to change that, which was the purpose of the Kendall-Nixon alliance. Nixon had lost the 1960 election because his own secondary ties to regional interests in the Southwest and Florida were not fully trusted by the powerful New York financial groups headed by the Rockefellers and the Morgans. These interests were displeased after their support of him for vice-president in 1952 failed to strengthen their own position in these regional groupings. But the resurrection of Nixon, triggered in good measure by Kendall, brought him closer to the fold where he could expand his base with the prime movers while retaining the ties which had made him so effective in the past. The debut of Nixon before the Pepsi bottlers at the Dallas soft-drink convention was really the least of the reasons for the pair's presence in Dallas. The trip played a crucial role in Pepsi's

---

* Scott, op. cit., p. 198-99
† U.S. Cong., House Select Committee on Small Business, *Tax Exempt Foundations and Charitable Trusts: Their Impact on Our Economy* , 2nd Installment, Subcommittee Chairman's Report to Subcommittee No. 1, 88th Congress, October 16, 1963. p. 53. *The New York Times*, October 20, 1963, p. 77
‡ *Tax-Exempt Foundations*, ibid., p. 22, 40
§ *The New York Times*, July 2, 1950
|| Messick, *Syndicate Abroad*, op. cit., p. 69

development and launched its leadership into a far-flung political orbit. Coke's belated but extensive diversification in the late fifties and early sixties increased the tremendous pressure on Pepsi to widen its own base of operations. Lacking the capital for wholesale internal expansion or outside acquisitions, Pepsi opted for a merger. Since rumblings of a Pepsi takeover by CBS and others had already been heard in the marketplace, Kendall moved quickly to protect the company's autonomy and his newly acquired presidency.

In 1965, he succeeded brilliantly when Pepsi merged with the Frito-Lay Company of Dallas, a manufacturer of potato chips and snack foods with 1964 sales of $184 million and earnings of $7.8 million. "Potato chips make you thirsty; Pepsi satisfies thirst," chimed Kendall. The directors of the Dallas concern saw just as clearly that Pepsi's international network was ideally suited for their products, and a marriage was consummated. Both companies coalesced into divisions within a corporate infrastructure called PepsiCo, with a third of the new stock in the hands of (former) Frito-Lay stockholders. PepsiCo's board was comprised of five directors from Frito-Lay and eleven from Pepsi. The deal concentrated a sizeable chunk of the stock in the hands of the directors, providing further protection against a takeover.

The chairman of the new board and the company's largest stockholder was Herman W. Lay, Frito-Lay's patriarch. Lay had founded H. W. Lay & Co., a potato chip concern, in Atlanta some twenty-five years earlier. Lay & Co. moved to Dallas in 1960, merging with the Frito Co., and within four years, had fashioned a flourishing operation with forty-five domestic plants.

The merger also introduced onto PepsiCo's board Robert H. Stewart, III, the president and chief executive officer of the First National Bank of Dallas, of which Lay was a director. Powerful within Texas Republican circles, Stewart once remarked: "I've always been on the conservative side of politics. Some people refer to me as being a little to the right of Louis XIV." Still a director of PepsiCo in 1979, Stewart figured prominently in the developments surrounding the merger.

According to his biography, Nixon had "law business in Dallas on November 22, 1963." (He had been admitted to the New York bar one week earlier.) It is likely that Nixon's trip was connected to Pepsi's purchase of $453,000 of land from the Great Southwest Corporation of Dallas.* On September 18, 1964, Pepsi announced that this land would serve as a site for a new multi-million-dollar Pepsi concentrate plant with which to serve some one hundred Southwestern bottlers currently supplied from distant Louisville, Kentucky.† The presence of Stewart and Toddie Lee Wynne, a director of Stewart's First National Bank of Dallas, on the board of Great Southwest suggests that the Pepsi-Frito-Lay merger was related to this land deal. This transaction marked Pepsi's entrance

---

* Peter Dale Scott, *Crime and Cover-up: The CIA, the Mafia, and the Dallas-Watergate Connection* (Berkeley: Westworks, 1977). p. 37. cf. Arlington, Texas, registry of land titles. The authors wish to give special acknowledgment, in the strongest possible terms, to Professor Peter Dale Scott of U.C. Berkeley, whose ground-breaking research made the heart of this chapter possible.

† *Wall Street Journal*, October 8, 1964, p. 16

into a unique and highly charged corporate network. Its fabric was vast—oil, aerospace, banking, and insurance—and its thread was a web of interlocking directorates whose constituents included some of America's most powerful and politically influential men. The cornerstone of this Texas group, including long-time LBJ backers, could not offset the surprising degree of hostility the politically opportunistic Johnson aroused in Texas voters.*

Johnson's presence on the 1960 Democratic presidential ticket may well have been the factor which allowed Nixon to carry the state, though by the slenderest of margins. After arriving in Dallas with Kendall on November 20 in Pepsi's plane, Nixon exploited Johnson's weakness by predicting that Kennedy would dump him in 1964. Nixon had many reasons for believing that he could vastly strengthen his own political future with this timely foray deep into the heart of Johnson country, and most of them concerned the powers behind the Great Southwest Corporation.

Great Southwest was created in 1960 to develop 6,500 choice acres on the Dallas/Ft. Worth corridor. The land had been purchased from the spacious, million-acre estate of W. T. Waggoner, and its investors included a glittering bipartisan consortium of eastern banking interests and high-flying Texas speculators, including Toddie Lee Wynne and his brother, Bedford, and cousin Angus. The Easterners were organized by Bill Zeckendorf whose real estate concern, Webb & Knapp, one of the largest in the world, invested $6 million. Zeckendorf was certainly no stranger to Pepsi's management. In the early fifties, he served on three different boards with Blair Holdings chairman Virgil Dardi, whose company then owned Pepsi-Cola Bottling Company of Los Angeles. Around that time, Walter Mack, an investor in several Webb & Knapp ventures, tipped Zeckendorf to a massive but floundering public utility, American Superpower, which subsequently became an important vehicle for the financier, whose grandiose schemes knew practically no limits.† In the mid-fifties, for instance, he tried to buy out all the holdings of Howard Hughes with $500 million obtained from Laurence Rockefeller, Pepsi's Charles Allen, and a coterie of other New York financial leviathans.‡ Later in the decade, Zeckendorf sold Havana's magnificent Hotel Nacional, acquired from another owner since the Lansky days, to Edward Orrick McDonnell's associate Juan Trippe, Pan Am's largest stockholder.

By this time, Zeckendorf and Charles Allen were involved in Roosevelt Field in Long Island, a successful industrial development of an airfield which served as a model of what to expect from Great Southwest's enterprise. The development paid off promptly because of the swift decision of certain companies to relocate there. These included Arundel's Pepsi-Cola Bottling Company of Long Island, and American Bosch Arma, a leading defense subcontractor of the early sixties whose board included Allen and Pepsi director G. C. Textor.

* Robert Sherrill, *The Accidental President* (New York: Pyramid 1967). p. 117-18
† William Zeckendorf, *Zeckendorf: An Autobiography* (New York: Holt, Rinehart, Winston, 1970), p. 100
‡ ibid., p. 154-161

In the early sixties, the Baird Foundations violated Treasury regulations by failing to report certain of their transactions with Zeckendorf, just as they did in 1953 when they guaranteed an unsecured $2 million bank loan to him.*

In 1960, the irrepressible Zeckendorf was a major backer of Freedomland, the ill-fated $65 million New York amusement park, designed and built by C.V. Wood, Kendall's close friend and one of the masterminds behind Disneyland when Pepsi won its concessions there. And in 1963, long-time Pepsi director Harry Gould and former Pepsi counsel Frank Levien served with Zeckendorf on the board of Universal American, a company engaged in extensive and highly specialized defense contracting as well as Florida real estate.

Zeckendorf also garnered a Great Southwest investment from Carl M. Loeb, Rhoades & Co., a Wall Street investment concern that likewise engaged in questionable transactions with the Baird Foundations. In 1959, Kendall allegedly participated with a Loeb, Rhoades investment group in a contested takeover of Alaskan Airlines. Members of the syndicate included a long-time associate of the Wynne family as well as the brother of a leading investor in the CIA-backed Air America.†

Like Air America, Alaskan Airlines had participated in the Korean airlift and other military, cargo, and personnel movements, but more important it, too, was influenced by volatile developments in its relationship with Pan Am.‡ Finally, the energetic Zeckendorf also persuaded Rockefeller family interests to participate in Great Southwest with a $3.5 million investment channeled through Rockefeller Center, Inc.

The Easterners and Cowboys were introduced by Great Southwest's midwife, Robert Bernard Anderson, the former manager and attorney for the Waggoner estate who became a limited partner in Loeb, Rhoades and a director of Webb & Knapp, Inc., soon after the founding of Great Southwest. A man with contacts in many walks of life, as illustrated by his acquaintance with Lou Chesler, Anderson epitomized the bipartisan malleability that typifies most special-interest representatives.§ After serving as Eisenhower's secretary of the navy, assistant secretary of defense, and secretary of the treasury—Eisenhower even contemplated putting him on the 1956 ticket in place of Nixon—Anderson

---

* *Tax-Exempt Foundations and Charitable Trusts*, op. cit., p. 58. Beginning with only a half million dollars, the Baird Foundations eventually amassed over $28 million from brokerage activities. Their violations cost them their tax-exempt status and $5.5 million in back taxes, and David Baird was subsequently barred from all future brokerage transactions.

† Walter Sloan and Air America cited in Scott, *The War Conspiracy*, op. cit., p. 196. Alaskan director Joseph Walker, Jr. cited in *World Airline Record*, 6th ed.(Chicago: Roadcap & Associates, 1965). p. 322

‡ *Wall Street Journal*, August 12, 1959, p. 24. *World Airline Record*, ibid., p. 321, 397. The takeover by the Loeb, Rhoades group moved ahead in 1959 when it seemed clear that either Pan Am or Alaskan's chief competitor, Pacific Northern, would acquire the other's routes in Alaska. These talks petered out in the early sixties, and Kendall left Alaskan's board in 1966 after similar talks of a Pan-Am takeover of Alaskan were terminated.

§ Reid, op. cit., p. 106–07

became President Johnson's #1 financial advisor. Both Anderson's top-level entry into politics and his facile movement between parties were insured by his long-time intimacy with Texas oilmen, who were most indebted to Anderson for his role in designing the mandatory oil import quota program. Along with the oil depletion allowance, the quota program was seen by oil domestic producers *and* major importers as a triumphant political coup, and Anderson was rewarded with a $970,000 "royalty" from oil mogul Sid Richardson in which Toddie Lee Wynne was a go-between.*

A fascinating amalgam of interregional financial groupings, Great Southwest was, according to one insider, tightly controlled by the Rockefeller and Wynne families. Rockefeller participation underscored this major eastern banking power's interest in increasing its ties with politically powerful southwestern money, a desire which was concurrent with the moves of Pepsi and Nixon in that direction.

Meanwhile, the Wynne family, the Texas component in Great Southwest, administered to the flow of traffic going the other way, primarily through their long-time, intimate association with the Clint Murchison family, who themselves had been moving some of their massive Texas oil and construction wealth into eastern investments over the last several years. Bedford Wynne, Great Southwest director and senior law partner in the company's firm of Wynne, Jaffee, and Tinsley, was the chief Washington troubleshooter for the Murchison clan. Three Great Southwest directors, including both Wynnes, sat on the boards of two Murchison-owned companies while Clint's son, John, served on the board of the previously mentioned First National Bank of Dallas with Toddie Lee Wynne as well as R. H. Stewart and Herman Lay, who would both soon be part of PepsiCo.

A figure whose immense wealth and influence has cast him as a Texas legend, Clint Murchison was a master at using near tax-free oil money to control other businesses and influence politics, particularly the Kennedy-Johnson administration. According to Jack Anderson, "It was oil millionaire Clint Murchison's associate, Bedford Wynne, who offered to stage a $1,000-a-plate Democratic dinner in January 1963. The dinner raised $500,000, largely from oilmen, to pay off the whopping 1960 Democratic debt. Shortly after the dinner, Clint Murchison's son, John, paid a private 90-minute call on the President . . . and assured fellow oilmen they had nothing to worry about" (concerning the oil depletion allowance). Through Bedford Wynne and another Murchison attorney, the Texas oil mogul was engaged in land development and other speculative enterprises with LBJ's protégé, Bobby Baker, formerly secretary to Johnson when he was Senate majority leader.

Murchison was not without his links to the Pepsi orbit, even before the days of Great Southwest. It was Murchison's money, for instance, that had helped

* Steinberg, op. cit., p. 620. Sherrill, op. cit., p. 236. *San Francisco Chronicle*, July 16, 1970, p. 8

Joe McCarthy defeat his enemies in the Senate in 1950 and 1952. Many of McCarthy's investigators in those days were FBI agents, and according to former FBI agent William Turner, J. Edgar Hoover was "quite simpatico with Texas oil tycoon Clint Murchison, usually spending his annual vacation at a Murchison hotel—the Del Charro—in La Jolla, California."* At the same time, Hoover served on the board of the Hertz Foundation while Pepsi's Edward Orrick McDonnell was a director of Hertz. In 1970, Jack Anderson confirmed that Murchison picked up Hoover's tab ($100-a-day suites) at the same time that some of the nation's most notorious gamblers and racketeers were registered there.† Turner adds that Hoover mingled freely with businessmen who profited directly from syndicate-dominated enterprises. A frequent client of Charles Allen's investment firm, Clint Murchison joined with Allen in buying out the aforementioned investment in Seven Arts Productions from the embattled Lou Chesler.‡ Beginning in the early sixties, Murchison and Nixon were very much involved in a secret and politically sensitive Florida highway construction which would have used public funds and greatly increased the value of one of Nixon's real estate investments. Not long before, Nixon had established his California residence at a choice Los Angeles development built by the Murchisons.§

More than merging regional financial groups, Great Southwest debuted a splendid bipartisan political cast that could well justify Nixon's confident efforts in the Lone Star state. Colonel Henry Crown was a major Democratic contributor and, since late 1959, the major stockholder of the mammoth defense contractor, General Dynamics, in which Great Southwest investor Loeb, Rhoades had a major interest. Known as "the sand and gravel man," the colonel took over General Dynamics after merging it with his Material Service Corporation, a company that thrived for thirty years on illicit construction contracts from corrupt politicians and union officials tied to the Chicago underworld. Serving with Pepsi's Edward Orrick McDonnell on the board of Hertz Corporation, Crown was an associate of David Baird and yet another recipient of the services of the Baird Foundations.|| The "sand and gravel man" seems to have been attracted to soda early in his career, for he sold a whole line of soft drinks to Chicago schools at prices higher than those paid by taverns.#

Great Southwest was thus a corridor of power, shaped in the mold of Nixon's own career. It merged established capital, including oil and defense interests,

* William Turner, *Hoover's FBI: The Men and the Myth* (Los Angeles: Sherbourne Press, 1970). p. 81
† *San Francisco Chronicle*, December 31, 1970, p. 25
‡ *Wall Street Journal*, July 9, 1964, p. 11; July 24, 1964, p. 11
§ Jeff Gerth, "The Miami Connection," in Weissman, op. cit., p. 270–71
|| *Tax-Exempt Foundations and Charitable Trusts*, op. cit., p. 32. Back in 1954, Baird and Crown were directors of Hilton Hotels with Chesler associate Joseph Binns of Seven Arts. A $100 million acquisition by Hilton was partially financed by Loeb, Rhoades, again illustrating the high degree of cohesion between the forces gathering at Great Southwest.
Demaris, *Captive City* (Secaucus, N.J.: Lyle Stuart, 1969), p. 214–222

with syndicate money, creating a range of contacts with formidable clout. By the time the PepsiCo merger was completed, it had used both in ample measure, despite the fact that the 6,500 acres sprawling between Dallas and Ft. Worth remained undeveloped. As *Forbes* magazine later pointed out, Great Southwest made profits, but they were largely "paper" profits.*

It seems certain, for instance, that the transfusion of assets to Great Southwest contributed to two of the largest bankruptcies in history. William Zeckendorf's Webb & Knapp suffered a pronounced cash shortage, in part because of its investment in the Texas land speculation, and the company was declared bankrupt in 1965.† Even more spectacular was the bankruptcy of the Penn Central Railroad, the largest in history, which a 1972 congressional committee tied to a $52 million investment in Great Southwest.‡ Like Webb & Knapp before it, the Penn Central made the "mistake" of aggravating an acute cash shortage to the point of bankruptcy by tieing up assets in Great Southwest. Subsequently, Charles Hodge, a director of both the railroad and Great Southwest, was convicted on conspiracy charges of having manipulated over $85 million in Pennsylvania's investments to benefit a private investment group—Penphil. With Hodge and Angus Wynne on its board, Penphil seemed to be merely an extension of the Wynne-Rockefeller alliance embodied in Great Southwest, and some of its subsequent moves showed a marked involvement with the Caribbean oil interests of Rockefeller and other principals in Great Southwest which had been seriously disrupted by the rise of Castro.§

Such transactions, combined with other developments on the political front probably help explain why, by 1963, Nelson Rockefeller was identified by Drew Pearson in the *Washington Post* as the "mastermind" behind the concerted "Cuba Lobby" opposition to Kennedy's agreements with the Soviet Union over Cuba. Though the powers and people back of that operation have been receiving increasing attention over the years, there was one company at the time still on the fringe of the Great Southwest domain with an employee who participated perhaps more fully than any other covert operator from the American corporate sector. Robert Geddes Morton, a Pepsi-Cola vice-president who headed the company's bottling operations in Cuba, was the leader of a major compo-

---

* *Forbes*, October 1, 1970, p. 56

† *Esquire*, May, 1963, p. 121

‡ U.S. Congress, House Committee on Banking and Currency, *The Penn Central Failure and the Role of Financial Institutions*, Staff Report, Part I, 91st Congress, 2nd Session, November 2, 1970, p. 5

§ Hodge, Penphil's founder, was a partner at Glore Forgan, a major Wall Street investment house, with William Jackson, Deputy Director of the CIA under Eisenhower and a member of Ike's committee charting covert operations during the Cold War. In July 1963, Penphil purchased almost $200,000 worth of Tropical Gas which marketed natural gas in the Caribbean extracted from Esso's (Rockefeller's) oil fields in Venezuela. Tropical Gas's extensive Cuban holdings had been nationalized by Castro, whose regime thwarted subsidiary, or farm-out agreements with Cuba held by Trans Cuba Oil (John L. Loeb of Loeb, Rhoades) as well as Stanolind, a subsidiary of Rockefeller's Standard Oil of Indiana, which had participated in Toddie Wynne's million-dollar "royalty" to Robert Anderson years earlier.

nent of the anti-Castro underground, and a principal contact in the CIA's invasion plan.*

The political priorities of the forces converging within the Great Southwest were thus far more important than any short-term profits the corporation itself might realize in the real estate business. Cuba was as much a source of concern to the Wynne-Murchison wing of the company as it was to the Rockefeller one. As Peter Dale Scott points out, "The Texas oil interests and the hot money allies of the Syndicate had common interests not only in U.S. real estate but also in the Caribbean: for both sought quick returns on investment in countries under dictatorships (such as Haiti and Nicaragua). This common stake abroad leads to a common lobbying interest in Washington. Thus the Murchisons and their lawyers owned a 30 percent interest in the profits of a meat-packing plant in Haiti-Hampco which made kickback payments to Bobby Baker."† Another top Murchison lobbyist, I. Irving Davidson, made the arrangements for these payments.‡ Like the Wynnes, Davidson was an active LBJ backer, having supported him over Kennedy at the 1960 convention. A registered lobbyist for Haiti and Nicaragua, where the Somozas were backing new Cuban invasion plans in mid-1963, Davidson was also one of Jimmy Hoffa's closest consultants.§ During 1961 and 1962, he received a $7 million loan from the Teamster Pension Fund, while the rest of the Murchison brood, including Bedford Wynne and Thomas Webb, were also involved with Bobby Baker in a land development loan from the fund.|| Clint Murchison himself was directly involved with the Teamster circle through Florida real estate ventures with Jimmy Hoffa.

The Teamsters, though, were involved with Great Southwest backers on a truly massive scale with the pension fund's largest loan until that time—$25 million—to Zeckendorf's failing firm, Webb & Knapp, whose $19-million-plus deficit and $10-million debt defied the wisdom of any loan, and whose weak cash position owed itself to its investment in Great Southwest. The Teamsters Fund, under the direction of Jimmy Hoffa and consultant Allen Dorfman, was well known for the millions it poured into syndicate-run Las Vegas casinos in the early 1960s to finance such figures as Bobby Baker's principal business partner, Ed Levinson of the Fremont Hotel. Meanwhile, another $9.5 million Teamster loan to Ed Levinson and Moe Dalitz of the Cleveland syndicate financed the expansion of the Stardust, whose mortgage, along with that of Dalitz's Desert Inn, was subsequently held by a Murchison insurance company.#

* See Chapter 12: "No One Needs It"

† Scott, unpublished manuscript. cf. Reid, *The Grim Reapers*, op. cit., p. 138–39

‡ Reid, ibid., p. 138–39

§ Peter Dale Scott, *Crime and Cover-up* op. cit., p. 10–11, 16–17

|| Ralph and Estelle James, *Hoffa and the Teamsters* (Princeton, N.J.: Van Nostrand, 1975). p. 275–77

Fortune, May, 1965, p. 191. In 1962, this company, Gulf State Insurance, was purchased by a Dallas insurance giant whose director was a senior vice-president at First National Bank of Dallas. Its directors, Herman Lay and Robert Stewart, later of PepsiCo, also served on the board of Southwestern Life, with Karl Hoblitzelle of the CIA-conduit, Hoblitzelle Foundation.

In the fall of 1963, the myriad connections that bound the Texas group to the affairs of Baker and the Teamsters began to become unglued. In fact, on September 9—the very day that Donald Kendall ascended to the presidency of Pepsi-Cola—a suit was filed accusing Bobby Baker of using political influence to obtain contracts with defense plants for the vending machines of a company he owned with Ed Levinson. Despite cajoling and arm twisting by Johnson to keep the story out of the papers, the *Washington Post* broke it three days later, and within a month, Baker had resigned his post as Senate majority secretary amid mounting pressure from certain senators for an investigation. Baker's first attorney was LBJ's close advisor, Abe Fortas, himself a director of Stewart and Lay's First National Bank of Dallas. When a later controversy engulfed Fortas, he was replaced by Edward Bennett Williams, who had unsuccessfully defended Jimmy Hoffa in a charge of jury tampering. The Senate hearings, begun in October 1963, eventually led to Baker's indictment in 1966 (he began serving a prison term in 1970), but their immediate effect was to threaten Johnson's political future.

Even as President, Johnson was mortified by the implications of the continuing Baker inquiry, as he revealed in House Speaker John McCormack's office in early February 1964. Totally oblivious to the presence of Robert N. Winter-Berger, who reported the following incident in *The Washington Pay-off*, Johnson came to see McCormack in a fit of anguish and temper over Bobby Baker. " 'John, that son of a bitch is going to ruin me. If that cocksucker talks, I'm gonna land in jail!' By the time he had finished these words, he had reached the chair at McCormack's desk, sat down, and buried his face in his hands. . . . When Johnson looked up at McCormack, I could see he was crying . . . 'I practically raised that motherfucker, and now he's gonna make me the first President of the United States to spend the last days of his life behind bars.' He was hysterical . . . 'Tell Nat to get in touch with Bobby Baker as soon as possible—tomorrow, if he can. Tell Nat to tell Bobby that I will give him a million dollars if he takes this rap. Bobby must not talk. I'll see to it that he gets a million-dollar settlement.' " Nat here is Nathan Voloshen, a high-stakes Washington lobbyist who himself pleaded guilty in 1970 to charges of fraud and conspiracy involving government matters. At this time, he was one of Washington's most powerful nonregistered lobbyists whose clients over the years included Pepsi-Cola and General Dynamics.* Voloshen moved as easily between presidents and political parties as he did between clients. On hearing of Voloshen's indictment, then Representative Jerry Ford complained "[U.S. District Attorney] Morgenthau is attacking the establishment . . . I'll never forgive him for this." Whether or not Voloshen ever actually delivered LBJ's message to Baker is not known, but there is a sign of a dramatic change in Baker's attitude between early November 1963 and later hearings. In November, Baker claimed that Lyndon Johnson had set

* Robert N. Winter-Berger, *The Washington Pay-Off* (Secaucus, N.J.: Lyle Stuart, Inc., 1972). p. 179

up a lobbying session for Clint Murchison and himself with then California Governor Edmund Brown, who denied Johnson's role in arranging the meeting. Subsequent to the Johnson call for Voloshen, however, the embattled Baker clung steadfastly to the Fifth Amendment.

The crackdown on Baker threatened not only LBJ, but the Murchisons as well as the Syndicate and the Teamsters, who themselves were coming under intense pressure from Justice Department investigations stemming from Attorney-General Bobby Kennedy's conviction of Hoffa. Bedford Wynne was brought before the Senate Rules Committee to testify about a 1962 payoff to Baker from Murchison's Sweet Water Development, a water desalination project, and a later disclosure revealed the Murchison-to-Baker kickbacks surrounding Hampco. Future PepsiCo director Robert Stewart was also named in the hearings in connection with a $250,000 loan his bank had made to Baker and associates in 1961. And Arthur Arundel of Pepsi-Long Island was a director of D.C. National Bank, which made unusually liberal loans to Baker while serving as an investment vehicle for Baker, Ed Levinson, and other Baker associates.*

Other revelations of the hearings included the claim of Baker associate Don Reynolds that there had been a $100,000 payoff on the award of the billion-dollar contract to General Dynamics to develop an experimental fighter plane known as the TFX. A subcommittee of the Senate Committee on Government Operations looked more closely into this and similar charges, and found, for example, that Johnson's long-time friend, political ally, and fellow Texan, Fred Korth, the secretary of the navy, had used his influence to favor a Texas bank he had formerly headed—the First National Bank of Ft. Worth. This bank was not only part of a consortium that made loans to General Dynamics, but was also linked to the old Waggoner estate of Great Southwest's Robert B. Anderson. And Great Southwest was already involved with General Dynamics, since Loeb, Rhoades, one of its prime investors, was also a major stockholder in the defense concern. Korth's resignation less than a week after Baker's was an obvious blow to Great Southwest, which was already being frustrated on every front by four of Kennedy's principal initiatives— the proposed disposal of the oil depletion allowance, rapprochement with Castro, the calming of the Cold War, and crackdowns on organized crime and the Teamsters. These policies were making a necessity of some of the above-mentioned maneuvers; and, in a sense, Kennedy was evidently locked in conflict with the forces behind his own vice-president.

Thus, when Johnson addressed the bottlers at the Dallas convention, he was a troubled man struggling for his political life. Nixon's bold prediction of his demise on entering his domain was a pragmatic way of sowing a few seeds in the fertile soil of unrest that ran through the Texas group.

History has shown that the unrest was greatly relieved soon after the assassination of President Kennedy on November 22, 1963. That day, *Life* magazine

* Reid, op. cit., p. 132. U.S. Congress, Senate Committee on Rules, Financial or Business Interests of Officers or Employees of the Senate, Report, 88th Congress, 2nd Session, July 8, 1964, p. 46

named Bedford Wynne and Thomas Webb as part of "the Bobby Baker set," but it would be one of the last times they would be subjected to such unwanted publicity. Soon after the assassination, a Justice Department memo declared, "We stopped getting information from the FBI in the Bobby Baker investigation. Within a month, the FBI in the field wouldn't tell us anything. We started running out of gas."* Similarly, the entire momentum of Bobby Kennedy's organized crime crackdown was lost in the face of a widening rift between the attorney general and the new President. The Senate subcommittee looking into the TFX met a similar fate. It closed the November 20 meeting with the resolve "to resume hearings next week," possibly with Fred Korth as a witness, but the hearings were not resumed until Johnson left office six years later. Under Johnson, an operation entitled "2nd Naval Guerrilla" was undertaken to mount a new invasion of Cuba, which was prevented only by the diversion of the forces during the U.S. intervention in the Dominican crisis in 1965.†

Johnson's longest meeting on Sunday, November 24, was with Robert Anderson. *The New York Times* speculated that they discussed the "dollar-and-gold" problem, which was likely since they were two of the most prominent Texas oil lobbyists of the postwar era. The cherished oil depletion allowance rested safely in their hands and, moreover, the new President's "crisis decision" at a meeting earlier that day for a "decisive commitment" in Vietnam conformed to heavy lobbying pressure from big oil and other international companies to escalate the war.‡

---

* *The New York Times*, quoted in William Turner, op. cit., p. 185
† See Chapter 18: "The Raw Thing"
‡ These oil companies, including California Standard, Texaco, and especially Socony Mobil, were not by any means strictly Texan though nearly all might have held farm-out agreements with local oilmen such as Sid Richardson and the Murchisons. Socony Mobil also interlocked with big eastern powers, such as First National City Bank and IBM, both of which had a prominent stake in the Far East.

CHAPTER ELEVEN

No Deposit, High Return

"There are more profits in a barrel of soft drinks than in a barrel of oil."
—*Thornton Bradshaw, president of Atlantic-Richfield,*
after speaking at Harvard University in 1979

IN 1961, Charlie Brower, the president of Batten, Barton, Durstine, and Osborn introduced Pepsi's first ad campaign of the new decade to a bottlers' convention in New Orleans. To their delight, he vowed that the campaign was not only capable of "knocking you off your seats right here into the aisle, but of knocking your fathead competitor off his undeserved pedestal forever!" He delivered a diatribe laced with military rhetoric that whipped his faithful into a frenzy. He called them "veterans in the war against Coca-Cola" and warned that any slackness would be "giving aid and comfort to the enemy." Describing this scene for *Fortune* magazine, Alvin Toffler noted that such warlike language had become part of the Pepsi vernacular: "They speak of 'invading' Coke's markets, of developing new sales 'weapons,' of turning their salesmen into 'shock troops.' Overseas, Pepsi even has a flying squad of salesmen they call their 'Panzer unit.'" One Pepsi official said of the sales force, "The men are taught to go out there and hate!"

By the beginning of the decade, the struggle between Coke and Pepsi was more than just competitive business. Pepsi had come too far at too maniacal a pace ever to be content with second-rate status, and King Coke, its long and renowned history tucked within the curves of every bottle, was far too proud to relinquish first place. Ranted one Coke vice-president, "We will sell more, . . . keep on selling more and more and more. There's no such thing as a saturation point. Drink a Coke and, theoretically, you're ready for the next one in thirty minutes . . . the growth potential is unlimited. Up and down the highways and the byways of this brave new world, men everywhere will never postpone for long their need for refreshment. It's inevitable. Everything's in our favor."

Nevertheless, it was a time of introspection, strife, and dramatic change for both companies. What was once a simple business now featured products and packages of every shape and size, catering to every taste and purpose. More competitive and sophisticated advertising came to dominate the scene. A Pepsi executive declared, "The time has gone when there was only one customer. Today, as our population grows and expands and becomes more sophisticated, we're dealing with a fragmented market. . . . So it's not enough that we develop one approach." The soft-drink community had to make great adjustments, learning

128

in the process that the only traditions worth saving were those essential to sales.

For seventy-five years, the Coca-Cola Company dominated an entire beverage market with one essential strategy: sell one product in one package and make it available *everywhere.* This formula wasn't enough to provide breakneck growth and the company broke with tradition in the late fifties. The competition for every drop of the soft-drink market had become so fierce that Woodruff was reluctantly convinced of the powerful need to diversify into beverage markets of a different kind. "Making all your money on a single product is hardly in keeping with the expansive spirit of the age," a Coke vice-president stated, "There's a time in every business when you should have a broader base."

To the probable dismay of old Candler's ghost, the Atlanta giant finally succumbed to the pressures of competition and acquired the Minute Maid Company through an exchange of stock in 1960. Minute Maid, the country's largest producer of concentrated fruit drinks, had first sold powdered orange juice to the Army during World War II. After the war, it was the first to perfect and market frozen concentrated orange juice, and by the late forties, was a bustling multi-million-dollar concern. In 1963, with profits of $4.6 million on a hefty $99 million in sales, Minute Maid also marketed Snow Crop orange juice, Hi-C Fruit drinks, and instant coffees and teas produced by Tenco, Inc., a recent acquisition. This array of beverages was now tucked within a division of the Coca-Cola Company.*

Coke then proceeded relentlessly to squeeze the orange juice business for profits. Coke brass found that 89 percent of consumers saw orange juice as a healthy breakfast beverage, and this was reflected in the company's advertising. "Minute Maid Orange Juice is better for your health," declared ads; "Colds and Asian flus, ... don't take chances.... Drink plenty of Minute Maid Orange Juice...." "Look at orange juice advertising," requested Benjamin H. Oehlert, Jr., the Coke vice-president now in charge of the Minute Maid division, "it tells mothers to see to it that the kiddies take a four-ounce dose of the stuff at breakfast and forget it. It tells old folks to drink it to prevent colds. People don't like medicine; they don't like to do things that are good for them." Indeed, the advertising of the entire fresh and frozen fruit juice business was low key, aimed at a narrow market, and accurately premised on their products' healthful qualities. Yet, by the early sixties, Coke's competitive instincts had been sharpened to a biting edge, and mere superiority in the breakfast market was not enough. Consequently, Coke recast orange juice as a beverage refreshing throughout the entire day, and thereby greatly expanded its appeal. In the process, its salubrious virtues were played down to avoid alienating the consumer from nutritionally worthless Coke. The decision reflected a careful assessment of priorities since *Time* magazine then noted that an estimated half million Americans drink

---

* Coke also gained the services of Minute Maid director and vice-chairman, William Appleton Coolidge who joined its board. Coolidge comes from an old Boston family that descends from Thomas Jefferson. His father, Thomas Jefferson Coolidge, organized the Old Colony Trust Company and the United Fruit Company, notorious for its interventionism in Latin America. His brother, also Thomas Jefferson Coolidge, was chairman of United Fruit's board from 1938 to 1958.

Coca-Cola rather than orange juice at breakfast. In effect, the Coca-Cola Company decided to market orange juice as a soft drink.

Coke promptly inflated Minute Maid's advertising budget from $2.8 million to $6.2 million and began what was then a hard sell by industry's standards. Advertising became slicker, more sophisticated, and dripped of the Coca-Cola touch. Gone were the traditional notions of eggs, toast, and concern for the public's health. A glass of frosty orange juice now cuddled next to a sandwich, or cheese and crackers. "Naturally fresher—Gloriously Orange! New Minute Maid. . . . Try it Today at Lunchtime. . . ." "The fundamental change that Coca-Cola has brought to Minute Maid's policies," said Oehlert, "was to go from the business of selling orange juice as a breakfast medicine to the business of selling oranges in any and every form the public will take them." For example, several orange soda derivatives were created and management pondered proliferating vending machines stuffed with orange juice. Coke even pushed the varied Hi-C juice line for the consumer who didn't like orange juice. Oehlert justifies, "I've heard people say that God created oranges and nobody can improve on them. But God made many more different kinds of people than he made oranges."

Coke's rapacity stunned the relatively docile citrus industry. The multi-million-dollar promotions of the Florida Citrus Commission, the industry's quasi-official lobby, were considered so tame by Coke's standards that company officials considered withdrawing Minute Maid's support from the commission. To survive, the entire industry finally followed Coke's lead and stiffened its competition. Said a citrus grower at the time, "Anybody who thinks Coca-Cola is a stupid company ought to have his head examined."

Although the Minute Maid deal broadened the vision of the Coca-Cola Company, it also underscored the difficulties of diversification. Operating a global corporation that was leaping into a sundry of competitive markets required extraordinary leadership. The traditional Cokeman, first and foremost a salesman, was reared within the insular world of Coca-Cola and lacked a breadth of skills. Although Lee Talley's old-guard management had energized Coke at a time of dire lethargy, fresh effervescence was needed if Coke was to modernize and find prosperity in the sixties. Thus, in 1962, Lee Talley was elevated to chairman to make way for the tenth president in Coke's seventy-six-year history—John Paul Austin.

Running the Coca-Cola Company was a challenge worthy of Paul Austin. Born the son of a cotton mill executive in LaGrange, Georgia, he was educated in the North at Culver Military Academy and Harvard, where he excelled at crew, and subsequently competed for the 1936 U.S. Olympic team. In 1940, he was graduated from Harvard Law School, and after a brief stint with a New York law firm, joined the Navy and served as a lieutenant commander during the war. He skippered a PT boat in the Pacific and according to the *Wall Street Journal*, also served as an "intelligence officer." At the war's end, Austin returned to New York to practice law. In 1949, he was plucked from the firm of Larkin, Rathbone, & Perry by a Coke executive who convinced him his future lay with soda pop. Meanwhile, the company soon saw that *its* future lay with Austin, and early on, he was carefully groomed for a position of leadership.

He spent a year as a route salesman peddling Coke off of trucks and laboring within a bottling plant to master the ins and outs of Coca-Cola production. Even in his temporary working-class environment, Austin sought to excel: "One achievement I had was that I equaled the case-filling speed of an operator in the Bethlehem, Pa., plant who had been on the job for several years. We had a bet of a cent a bottle who could fill a case the fastest. I won."

In 1950, Austin was transferred to Coke's legal department for several months (where he met his future wife, a Coca-Cola secretary), and then was made assistant to the president of Coca-Cola Export. When Talley became president of Coke Export in 1954, Austin was put in charge of Coke's African operations. After Talley became president of the parent Coca-Cola Company in 1958, Austin was made executive vice-president of Coke Export, and president of Export a year later. In 1961, Austin became Coke's executive vice-president and then president in 1962 at the age of forty-seven.

Talley was Austin's guardian angel. "I've had lots of breaks," revealed Austin, "but the best has been tracking Talley." Indeed, Austin and Talley were a formidable pair (and striking, with the little five-foot, four-inch Talley alongside the husky six-foot, two-inch Austin). Though both were pedigreed Southerners and Cokemen, Talley was an amiable and well-traveled veteran whose seat-of-the-pants knowledge of the world was garnered in the service of a soft drink. Austin, on the other hand, was a well-heeled corporate renaissance man, a professional leader, able to grasp not only one business or industry, but global economics and concepts. "Every racehorse needs a pony walking alongside to keep him from running away before the race starts," said a company director. "Talley is Paul Austin's pony."

Austin marked a new era of leadership for Coca-Cola. He was a manager sitting on a throne long and gloriously held by salesmen. He recognized that Coke now had to wage a secular war for growth rather than a pious crusade for acceptance, and to this end, he adeptly imposed business-school logic onto the folksy Coke realm. Though deeply respectful of Coke's hallowed traditions, Austin was given a long enough leash by Woodruff to experiment boldly when an ancestral way became a hindrance. In a long and overdue change, the old Atlanta giant now wore pinstripes. Exclaimed one Coke executive, "Every good company needs a son-of-a-gun at the top, and we've got ourselves a dandy."

Where Woodruff elevated management to an art, Austin reduced it to a cool, efficient science, complete with its own values and vernacular. Austin's science was the unsentimental reasoning of trend lines, market shares, and committees, the immediate predecessors of computer technology. He virtually reeducated top management and many bottlers into the ways of progressive corporate leadership by sending them to special business courses at Harvard, Stanford, and other exalted institutions. "There are an increasing number of management techniques," he said, "that are spun off from new and different areas, like organizing to put a man on the moon. Business management gets a fallout from those activities and the fallout, in turn, gets talked about in management circles all over the world. You find, very soon, that you can apply a lot of the techniques to your own business."

Soon, legions of bright young executives, many fresh from business school, scurried about the corridors of the Atlanta headquarters, graphs and market surveys in hand, and imbued with a quiet obsession for sales. Religious fervor had given way to a secular passion.

It is tempting to speculate how Austin and Coca-Cola would have fared with the Kennedy administration. Despite his friendship with Eisenhower, Robert Woodruff disliked Vice-President Richard Nixon, and according to Bob Hall, an editor of *Southern Exposure* magazine, he was a personal friend of Joe Kennedy, the President's father. Coke became a favorite of the Kennedy White House because, in keeping with the company's Democratic traditions that predated Franklin Roosevelt, Woodruff supported J.F.K.'s candidacy. Hall claims that Woodruff introduced young Kennedy to Southern leadership during the 1960 campaign, and later declined the new President's offer of the ambassadorship to England. As a Harvard contemporary, Austin was more in step with the new President, and had J.F.K.'s administration endured, he would have undoubtedly marched to the tune of Camelot.

Coke's Democratic ties earned it good standing with Lyndon Johnson, as perhaps did its reliance on certain powerful law firms. Coke has made use of New York's Simpson, Thacher & Bartlett, whose roster included Cyrus Vance, who would become Jimmy Carter's secretary of state, and Edwin Weisl, Sr., a confidante of Johnson. Weisl was a bulwark of New York State Democratic politics and during the 1968 presidential campaign, he worked beside Big Jim Farley as chairman of Johnson's New York election committee amid a struggle between the President and New York Senator Robert F. Kennedy.

Don Kendall was Pepsi's answer to Austin. Both men were great leaders, Kendall perhaps the best in Pepsi's history, who exemplified the new breed of corporate executives spawned in the early sixties. They were ambitious contemporaries, youthful for their stations, and as adept before congressional committees as with stockholders and bottlers. Both were big, impressive, sports-minded men worthy of their products' robust images and comfortable with the loftiest of geopolitical ideas.

Austin and Kendall were also the culmination of two long and grand traditions, and each man came to shape and, therefore, personify the style and character of his company. In the Coke legacy, Austin was a controlled and cerebral man who preferred to steer precise, highly rational courses. Tough and extroverted like his forebears, Kendall conducted his business in bold, sometimes controversial, strokes. Austin, the Harvard-bred Georgian attorney, was all but cast for his role; Kendall, the outspoken syrup salesman, tore to the top by competitive instincts. Austin educated his Cokemen at his alma mater and other Ivy

League institutions; Kendall prepared his boys at the company's new "soft-drink university," the Pepsi-Cola Management Institute in Phoenix. In a reincarnation, Austin could have been a statesman; Kendall, a general. (Through a golden telephone in his Park Avenue office, Kendall constantly communicated with his army of 525 bottlers, all of whom he reportedly knew by first name.) Kendall was a "man's man," a "take-charge" guy who, if socially inferior to Austin, as Pepsi was to Coke, would compensate with more drive and political savvy.

Kendall's rise at Pepsi was marked by turbulence and struggle which became the pretext for his ceaseless efforts to consolidate his power. When he took command, the company was in the throes of a bottler revolt spearheaded by some of the old-boy bottlers because Pepsi announced a drastic price hike in the cost of its concentrate. The bottlers steadfastly refused to bear the full cost of what they saw as lackluster company performance, and consented to pay only half the increase. To strengthen its showing, Pepsi turned to streamlining its marketing operation.

Some of Pepsi's high priests were dismissed, particularly those persistently loyal to Steele like William Durkee, who followed Steele from Coca-Cola. They were replaced by Kendall's people from Pepsi International—his power base—and the company's leadership was reorganized so that his loyalists, a group of hotshots known as the "Whiz Team," ran the company. Under the new policy, said Kendall, all worldwide marketing functions and sales personnel were "unified under one central marketing staff." This "one-world" apparatus carved the planet into zones, or "profit centers." "The future of our business," explained Kendall, "is best served by centralizing responsibility for strategic planning and control, and decentralizing responsibility for area planning and the operational execution of these strategies."

Having weathered an initial storm, Kendall wasted very little time in revealing his strategy to strengthen the company through merger, and several years later achieved this goal splendidly with Frito-Lay. The snack food giant sought the same consumers as Pepsi, and with the same vigor. Frito-Lay's potato chips rode to national prominence on the punchy "You can't eat just one" campaign which featured Bert Lahr and Buddy Hackett. Herman Lay was also a kindred spirit to Kendall. "I think businesmen should take a very vital interest in politics and governmental affairs," he said. "It's necessary to protect their own interest from punitive legislation."

Actually, Pepsi's first acquisition had come a year earlier, in September 1964, when it bought the Tip Corp. of Marion, Va., a small manufacturer of a super-sweet, citrus-based soda called Mountain Dew. Kendall had been impressed with the drink's strength in the Southeast, Coke's backyard, and boldly gambled that the entire nation would take to its unabashedly cornpone image. Commercials appeared as homespun affairs complete with authentic country music scores: "Yahoo, it's Mountain Dew. It'll tickle your innards." Mountain Dew created a very successful splash. Called the "clown prince of the business" for its zany advertising, the heavily sugared drink was implicitly depicted as nonalcoholic moonshine: "Thar's a bang in every bottle o' that good ole Mountain Dew." "It's a product that doesn't take itself seriously," quipped a Pepsi advertising executive, although everything about it was taken seriously by the Pepsi-Cola Company. Though a gaggle of imitators sprouted in its wake, such as White Lightning, Kick, Old Red Eye, Stone Mt. Mist, and a potion called Kickapoo Joy Juice, Mountain Dew was far and away the leader of the hillbilly market it created.

The acquisition strategy was by no means Kendall's exclusively. Lay was reputed to be a genius at this game too, and he brought broad-gauged professional management to Pepsi which complemented its inherent strength in straight-out marketing. In light of the Lay influence, uncertainty was bandied across the financial pages over who acquired whom. Time has removed any initial misgivings, though Kendall, who sprang from the Pepsi tradition of strong-handed, one-man rule, had to reconcile himself to sharing the burden.

With Austin at the helm, Coke set its sights on a new frontier—the coffee market, then the largest-selling beverage. In 1964, less than a year after Lyndon Johnson had become President of the United States, Coke acquired the Duncan Foods Co. of Houston, Texas. The company processed and distributed blended coffees under the names of Maryland Club, Butter-Nut, Fleetwood, and Admiration through the South, the Midwest, and the West. It also processed and marketed Duncan Tea, hot chocolate, and instant coffees.

Founded in 1918, the company was owned and managed by the Duncan family. According to an Atlantan based journalist, part of the company's lure was its president, Charles W. Duncan, Jr., whose managerial skills were held in high esteem by Woodruff. Duncan exchanged his holdings for Coca-Cola stock and immediately became a Coke director. A 1971 estimate valued his Coke stock at $24 million, and his brother, John H., owned another $13 million. Similar to Pepsi's Lay and Stewart, Duncan provided Coke with access, though more limited, to some of the financial institutions of Texas. He sat on the board of the Great Southern Corporation, a Houston-based insurance company whose board included Raymond M. Holliday, a chief executive of Howard Hughes's vast empire. Holliday and Duncan also sat on the board of Texas Commerce Bankshares, Inc. Furthermore, John Duncan was a former president, and current director of Gulf and Western, a massive conglomerate with major sugar interests.

A long-time associate of Charles Duncan and a director of Duncan Foods until the Coke deal was David C. Bintliff, a Houston businessman with extensive oil, financial, agricultural, and real estate investments in the United States and Guatemala. Bintliff was a director with Duncan, and then Duncan's father, of the Bank of the Southwest. Another director was Watergate prosecutor Leon Jaworski. Bintliff perhaps supplied Duncan Foods with Guatemalan coffee, through his reported ties to United States government and business interests and reactionary elements in Guatemala. Guatemalan expert David Tobis claims that one of Bintliff's companies was involved in the CIA's 1954 overthrow of the Arbenz government in Guatemala. A Bintliff partner was Manuel Ralda Ochoa, a reputed Guatemalan rightist with Guatemalan sugar connections. With the Guatemalan ambassador to the U.S., Ochoa owned the farm that was used by the CIA to train Cuban exiles for the ill-fated Bay of Pigs invasion.

Duncan's connections and his family's massive Coke holdings assured him a Coke vice-presidency shortly after the deal, a promotion that foreshadowed privilege and influence reserved only for the most exalted of Coke's inner circle. He became a trustee of Emory University and a director of Southern Railways, a position formerly held by Woodruff himself. He joined the board of the Trust Company of Georgia, which featured such Coke stalwarts as Austin and Hughes Spalding, a partner of the Atlanta-based law firm of King & Spalding, a member of Coca-Cola's finance committee, and a trustee of the Woodruff Foundation. Thus Coke obtained more than just coffee beans with the Duncan merger; it broadened its business as well as its leadership, whose influence now reached into Latin America through Texas financial circles.

While Coke's internal symmetry changed, the company's well-scrubbed image hadn't. "Americans associate Coca-Cola with the flag and motherhood," mused a Coke ad man, "and that's the image we work night and day to maintain. We don't dare use sexy advertising or cheap gimmicks. We avoid association with alcohol and such things; Coca-Cola is an all-family drink for all ages, and we can't afford to offend the sensibilities of any group anywhere. We stand for the very highest quality and finest taste. Clean-cut, upright, the family, Sunday, the girl next door. Wholesomeness. America's best." Although Coke had entered the jet age, its employees were still thoroughly intoxicated with the product's myths. "It's one big happy family," said the wife of a Coke executive. "It must be awful not to have somebody like Coca-Cola to belong to." A senior vice-president confessed, "Coca-Cola is everything I exist for. I live and breathe it. We all do. It's made us what we are."

The son of a large Coca-Cola bottler from Pennsylvania recalls how, on his seventh birthday, he hid in an attic with his buddies to smoke cigarettes and drink Pepsi-Cola. The following day, his father took him for a walk down by the riverside. Man-to-man, he put him on his knee, and said, "Son, Coca-Cola has put the clothes on your back and the food in your belly. Don't ever drink a Pepsi again." And he drank Coke ever after.

Nor had the company's persistent drumbeating for sales changed. Austin thrived on the pressures and complexities of corporate business, and in the finest Coke tradition, pulled, pushed, and prodded Coke leadership and the bottlers for new business. "Every day is like the day before the big game," he exhorted, and in another metaphor, philosophized, "It's analogous to the violin; if the strings are just hanging there, you don't have music. But apply the right amount of tension and a pair of hands that know how to use the instrument, then you really have something."

The company went to great lengths to incite its family. In 1966, some thirty thousand bottlers, route salesmen, and their families in forty cities were treated to a full-length theatrical spectacle called "A Step Ahead." Reminiscent of Steele's Adorama, it featured Broadway performers, original songs, lyrics, and choreography, and depicted the various Coca-Cola interactions in the day of one Henry Baxter, typical route salesman. Privy to the latest promotional tricks, Henry was the ideal salesman, eager to identify his entire life with Coke. It was a Coke commercial for its own people. Several years later, the barons and dukes of Coke's global empire convened for a marketing meeting in Miami Beach where they too were treated to a two-hour stage presentation called, "This Is What's Happening," complete with a full cast, original score, and orchestration. In echoing the activism of the sixties, Austin urged his flock to "recognize and meet every challenge . . . whenever it may occur. It is imperative that we antici-pate and act . . . now!"

By the mid-sixties, the major soft-drink manufacturers viewed the U.S. market as highly segmented. "In other words," Fred Dickson, Coke's marketing direc-tor, asserts, "different people use different soft drinks at different times for differ-ent purposes, so our whole objective is to lay down specialty products, with carefully conceived marketing plans aimed at specific markets. Ideally, we would approach the consumer with the same specificity with which a salesman ap-proaches a contact." The second string Fanta line, largely introduced to fill up flavor slots in vending machines, was successfully moved up into the marketing big leagues. In the early sixties, Coke and Pepsi pitted Sprite and Teem against Seven-Up, a leader of the lemon-lime category which accounted for a sixth of total industry volume. Coke's vice-president of marketing research would later recall, "We sold more Fanta products during the first six months of 1966 than our worldwide sales for the full year 1936. And I thought it was a big company then."

Although diet sodas had been around since the forties, the combination of calcium cyclamates and saccharin finally produced palatable sugar-free soft drinks by 1960. The result was a new and booming soft-drink market and over-night, Diet Rite Cola, made by the Royal Crown Company, seized a whopping 50 percent of it. In 1963, Coke followed Diet Rite's lead with its own diet cola, Tab, and Pepsi provided Patio Diet Cola, and later Diet Pepsi which almost overtook Diet Rite by 1965. That year, Americans consumed approximately ten million pounds of cyclamates and two million pounds of saccharin, mostly through diet sodas, which then comprised a remarkable 15 percent of the mar-ket. The soda industry was undoubtedly pleased that two-thirds of its diet mar-ket consisted of first-time soft-drink consumers, though William C. Munro, Pepsi's vice-president of marketing, was guarded over the ultimate success of diet drinks: "Sugar and caffeine give a lift that diet drinks can't supply."

Meanwhile, Coke officials, disappointed with Tab's third place share of the diet market, fortuitously discovered that the recently acquired Minute Maid had been experimenting with citrus essences to mask the aftertaste of the artificial sweeteners. In 1966, a citrus-based noncola called Fresca was put into production. It was presented in an ad campaign that downplayed its lack of sugar and compared consumption to the refreshing quality of being in a blizzard. In one ad, a shopper reaching for a can on a supermarket shelf is miraculously engulfed by a snowstorm, and in another, card players at a table sip Fresca, indifferent to the snow accumulating about them: "Our writers are marketing winter," confided an ad executive, "and people accept the fantasy." Fresca and its blizzard were a howling success. Although it cut into Tab's sales somewhat, it effectively eroded its competitors' business and acquired many non-soft-drink converts.

Coca-Cola, of course, was a shoo-in in 1967 with 30.4 percent of the market. Pepsi, the perennial runner-up, had 14.3 percent. That year, each American consumed an average of approximately twenty-six gallons of soft drinks, closing in on milk, with thirty-five plus gallons consumed per capita, and coffee, then America's favorite beverage, at thirty-eight gallons.

The simplicity of these products belies the efforts behind them. To place a new soda on the shelves, trends must be examined, sales forecasted, and promotional campaigns created. The product must run a gauntlet of test markets, usually in metropolitan centers, and finally, the bottlers must be impressed enough with its performance to make an investment in the requisite bottles, machinery, delivery trucks, labor, and promotional effort. Even finding a suitable name was a task. The name Sprite is crisp and implies buoyancy and lightness. Teem was originally to be called Duet, but Pepsi preferred an inference to groups rather than couples. The diet sodas were particularly tricky. The Coca-Cola Company couldn't bear to adulterate its pride and joy into a mutation called Diet Coke, and instead opted for Tab, a bare bones, phonetically trim handle. Because of its limited advertising budget, the Pepsi-Cola Company wanted to associate its diet drink with a national brand name and conducted experiments to determine whether such a course would portray Pepsi as too calorie-laden. After much soul-searching by Kendall and his whiz team, Pepsi introduced Diet Pepsi to ride on the coattails of its famous brother. Aided by an overtly sexual and award-winning advertising campaign—"Girls girlwatchers watch drink Diet Pepsi"—Diet Pepsi was soon second in sales.

The new decade offered a multitude of advertising opportunities. Television was, of course, the key, and each company set out to carve its own territory in the market as well as establish its own unique brand image. Coke's ad agency, McCann Erickson, had targeted white, upper middle class drinkers in their late twenties, but Atlanta's profits and sales were not growing nearly as quickly as its rival's.

Nevertheless, Pepsi's marketing strategy and advertising were in a shambles when its account was shifted from Kenyon and Eckhardt to Batten, Barton, Durstine, and Osborn in 1960. In assessing the new account, the managers at B.B.D. & O took the disparity between Pepsi's uninspired advertising and its rising sales as simply another indication of the phenomenal growth of the soft-drink market. They pegged this growth to the postwar baby boom, and decided to go after the youth market unrelentingly. They scrapped the campaign built on "Be Sociable—Enjoy the Light Refreshment" which was the holdover from the ten-year attempt to tell the story of Pepsi quality, and settled instead on a highly musical theme built around the slogan, "Now, it's Pepsi, for those who think young." The company sank $10,250,000 into advertising in 1961 and almost $14 million in 1962, with over 55 percent of it going into television. A B.B.D. & O. vice-president explained that the campaign "designates our giant rival Coca-Cola as a drink for people who are out of step, out of touch, out of date." And a Pepsi executive added, "Teenagers consume soft drinks far in excess of their weight in the population."

Coca-Cola responded in mid-1963 with what a company spokesman termed "the most intensive advertising campaign ever put into effect for any beverage product." Targeted for more radio and television commercials "than have ever before been used for a single product," "Things Go Better with Coke" was a highly disciplined sales pitch that sought to reaffirm the brand's identity not only with the youth market, but with *every* market. It was designed by McCann-Erickson's Bill Backer, whose central role in every Coke campaign since has rightfully earned him a place beside fellow Southerner Archie Lee as the most important advertising figure in Coke's history. As the cornerstone of the company's first unified marketing strategy, the deceptively simple, almost trite, five-word slogan represented two and a half years and millions of dollars of research and motivational analysis. It was conducted, in the words of Austin, on a "one sight, one sound, one sell" basis. An ever-present graphic "signet" depicting the slogan appeared in every commercial and print ad, and an original musical jingle sung by the Kingston Trio gave TV and radio commercials a familiar ring exclusively identified with Coca-Cola. Virtually every facet of the company's marketing—packaging, distribution, public relations, and promotion—was altered to carry the "Things Go Better with Coke" theme.

The new campaign and attendant face-lift were enormously expensive, and coupled with the new brands, swelled Coke's ad budget to $58 million in 1965, and nearly $65 million the following year. In 1964 alone, Coca-Cola and its bottlers bought nearly $26 million of national TV time for commercials, up $10 million from the previous year. This placed the Coke organization fourth on the list of TV advertisers, behind Procter & Gamble, General Foods, and Colgate Palmolive, all of which had more products to advertise (Pepsi and its bottlers were fourteenth on the list at $11 million).

Not to be outdone, Pepsi announced in December 1963, that nearly $36 million would be invested into "Think young," described by Phil Hinerfield, vice-president for advertising, as the "most extensive campaign in the company's history." Schedules were planned for nearly 400 TV stations, 3,000 radio outlets, 1,500 newspapers, and a host of national magazines. During September 1964, midway in the campaign, Pepsi unveiled the seminal slogan of its youth appeal: "Come Alive, You're in the Pepsi Generation," sung by Joannie Sommers. The jingle appeared in a mix of black-and-white and color commercials that facilitated aggressive local advertising by the bottlers. Pepsi also furnished each bottler with a "warbook" of highly competitive ads to meet any special local marketing need.

Pepsi's generation were spirited, unblemished, pre-Vietnam War youths. They had shed, if they ever knew, the worries of the world to frolic in contemporary recreation before the company's eagle-eyed cameras. "This generation wants happiness," said William Munro, "and the soft drink is a fun thing. . . ." Columnists editorialized about it, cartoonists satirized it, and comedians joked about it, but the "Pepsi Generation" had literally become a national idiom. It was perhaps the only advertising campaign ever eulogized by *Time* magazine. Advertising had again identified and articulated a national image, and rendered the language a little fuller, if not richer.

Because Coke's slogans have always centered on the product, Pepsi's advertising tended to emphasize the users of the product. Over the years, this approach was particularly useful in upgrading its image as a second-class product stemming from its nickel-value days. Finally, by 1966, the company and its bottlers felt confident enough of its product's position within the marketplace to focus on the drink's qualities rather than those of its storyboard consumers. In 1966, it did so with "Taste That Beats the Others Cold . . . Pepsi Pours it On." The product—a bottle inevitably encased in ice—was the star of ads, and people became the props, though in the long run, the campaign was unsuccessful.

In late 1969, Coke and Pepsi nearly simultaneously introduced campaigns with a theme novel for both companies—reality. Neither could ignore any longer the country's turbulent social climate as they had all decade long with their idyllic middle-class ad vignettes.

Pepsi continued the initiative of its earlier efforts with a move toward more openly emotional, candid, less frantically paced ads. These were intended not only for the current youth market but also for the original Pepsi generation that now helped make up the sixties' counterculture: "You've Got a Lot to Live, and Pepsi's Got a Lot to Give" was the slogan and together with the dramatic musical score, still ranks among the most powerful of the company's campaigns. William Munro explained candidly that the "tanned, frolicsome, happy-go-lucky people of the 'Pepsi Generation' began to become advertising anachronisms," and commercials "had nothing more profound to say than 'Drink Up America.'" Though it had national recognition, Pepsi's generation had become divided and dishevelled, and the campaign had lost its effectiveness to actually sell soda. The new campaign was a lucid response to the country's anxious, war-torn mood, and was an upbeat expression of, in the words of Pepsi's new president, James B. Somerall (Kendall, still boss, was elected chairman of the board), "the feeling we have that America should be extolled as a good place." At the height of the Vietnam War, it drew attention to America's "new national pastime—living, and making every second count." It was consumerist optimism tackling national bleakness, all couched in what the company called "jubilation" or "gospel rock." The campaign featured the realism of "all kinds of people—

black, white, all kinds, not just people on diving boards." One can transcend the turmoil and despair, the campaign implied, because Pepsi had the "energy to let you live big and a taste that's bigger than life." "We're selling more than Pepsi-Cola," said Somerall, "we hope, too, to sell the premise that America has never failed to keep the promise of a good life in a good land, for those who work for it." "The story of all America—young, old, rich, and poor," as Somerall called the "Live/Give" campaign, struck a vital cord within the public, and over ten thousand viewers reportedly wrote Pepsi in praise of it. Although the company was justifiably proud, the meaning and encouragement that so many citizens could find in soft-drink commercials is as much a statement of America's apprehensive mood at the time as it was on Pepsi's advertising.

Meanwhile, Coke was up to something even more far-reaching. In 1967, Coca-Cola's "Things Go Better with Coke" had evolved into "For the Taste You Never Get Tired of," a product-sell so fierce that magazine ads not only showed sparkling close-ups of the bottle and a glass of Coke, but even the ad's scant background was colored deep Coca-Cola brown. Two years later, in 1969, Coke unleashed the seventy-fifth slogan of its history, "It's the Real Thing." The product of intense introspection and market research, the slogan reflected the deeply felt but ultimately childish conviction that other soft drinks are mere imitations. "It's a fact of life," stated Austin, "that Coke is the original cola." Print ads showed a plastic cup of cola and asked, "Is it or isn't it?" A bold caption simply read, "It's the Real Thing. Coke." "I want to say in a statesmanlike manner that yes, we're being mean," confessed a Coke vice-president as he recalled a now traditional company phobia, "We're building on the work a lot of people have done in the past eighty-three years, and that doesn't call for us to relinquish our place in the market . . . we're not going to be anybody's patsy." As aggressive as this campaign was, it too sought to link Coke with socially redeeming values. In a true sign of the times, happiness was downplayed. "We'll be using it in scenes and situations that show people as they really are," said the company, which acquiesced to pressure from McCann-Erickson to use soft-core rock music.

After years of reacting to continuous initiatives by its rival, Coca-Cola—whose pride and sheer immensity often cast it in a defensive posture—introduced "The Real Thing" as part of a wholesale advertising and public relations blitz. Coke was intent on developing a new look for its product, in part because of its unique dilemma of being too visible. An ad man explained: "The Coca-Cola sign was so well known and so over-all displayed that people could go through a street with, let's say forty or fifty Coca-Cola signs, on windows, doorways, and so forth, and you ask if they had seen a Coca-Cola sign. And they didn't!" Coke's logo was over-advertised and no longer consciously noticeable. The company had been too effective for its own good.

Consequently, Coke performed massive plastic surgery on itself in an effort appropriately dubbed "Project Arden" after Elizabeth Arden cosmetics. The prodigious feat required revamping all of Coke's advertising and packaging with new homogenous visual themes. The new appearance had to be different enough to attract attention, yet instantly recognizable as Coke. A rectangular red and white logo featured an impressionistic rendition of Coke's curvy bottle. Besides vending machines, containers, cases, coolers, and stationery, the logos on every delivery truck in what is the world's second largest truck fleet (after the U.S. Postal Service) had to be replaced, as did the estimated eighteen million Coke signs that littered the earth. "It cost more to put up a sign than to tear one down," lamented Coke's advertising vice-president, "and to be honest, no one knows where all the signs are. We have become part of the environment." Coke's new look took years to perform and the company wouldn't even speculate as to the costs.*

Although the Coca-Cola Company denied that such monumental overhauls were desperate responses to industry pressures, the competition had become formidable. Pepsi was also increasingly assailed by the rest of the pack. For example, Royal Crown Company, whose Royal Crown Cola had 3.6 percent of the soft-drink market in 1969, third among colas, behind Coke's steadily increasing 34 percent and Pepsi's 14 percent, decided to update its barnyard image. The company revitalized its franchise system, 350 bottlers strong, and hired William C. Durkee, the former president of Rival Pet Foods and a veteran of both Coke and Pepsi. The company also retained Wells, Rich, Greene, Inc., a high-powered New York advertising agency. "We're out to kill Coke and Pepsi," declared Mary Wells Lawrence, the agency's head, to the Royal Crown bottlers. "I hope you'll excuse the word, but we're really out for the jugular." She claimed her agency had identified the one big weakness of Coke and Pepsi's advertising: "We took a Pepsi and a Coke commercial, changed the sound track, and you couldn't tell the difference."

Another grim competitor was the Seven-Up Company of St. Louis, whose lemon-lime Seven-Up was the third most popular soft drink in 1969 with 5.8 percent of total sales. Seven-Up had been around since 1929 when it was called "Bib-Label Lithiated Lemon-Lime Soda." Though hawked as a hangover cure "for home and hospital use," it was nevertheless perceived as a mixer for alcoholic drinks. "It modified the wallop," said the company's president, with a wink.

Family-managed and family-owned until 1967, the Seven-Up Company was content with its fraction of the fizz until the sixties, when the colas, and lemon-lime contenders such as Sprite, Teem, Fresca, and Canada Dry's Wink began to sap Seven-Up's sales. To defend its turf, Seven-Up hopped on the marketing bandwagon with "Where the Action Is," an advertising campaign depicting

* One anonymously authored company publication entitled *A New Look for Coca-Cola—A Synopsis of the 70's* even goes so far as to state that Arden was conceived not in the late sixties, as *Business Week* indicates, but back in 1965, less than two years after the last major overhaul. As if sweeping changes are routinely undertaken for their own sake, the pamphlet asserts that the "new look" for Coke was largely a *matter of style* in order to maintain its leadership in the marketplace. Competition is largely downplayed while Coke's relationship to the consuming public is featured as the primary motive for the changes.

Seven-Up in recreational and athletic contexts. When this failed, the company focused on the product rather than consumers with its "Wet and Wild" campaign. That also failed. Seven-Up's dilemma was that too much of the public perceived it as a mixer. "We had always thought of Seven-Up as a soft drink," said the company's marketing vice-president, "but when our customers thought of a soft drink, they thought of colas." Indeed, six out of every ten soft drinks sold in the U.S. were colas, an increase of 10 percent since 1958. Thus, in 1968, the innovative "UnCola" campaign was unveiled, which portrayed Seven-Up as a rebel defiant before the cola establishment. This was a profane notion that appealed to the sensibilities of America's youth, and sales rose 15 percent the following year. Again, the targets had been Coke and Pepsi.

Another phenomenon of the sixties, which contributed greatly to sales and the industry's internal finances was the trend toward nonreturnable containers. Cans, which date back to the fifties and nonreturnable bottles, which go back to the forties, had been tepidly accepted at first by consumers because of their higher costs.

Cans became popular before one-way bottles, partly due to the $9 million promotional efforts of the American Can and Steel Institute in the early sixties.* One industry ad, for instance, pictured a man in a canoe in the wonderfully free act of tossing the used can overboard. The larger supermarket chains' use of one-ways for their private labels put pressure on the soda makers to get into the act. Coke had experimented with cans as early as 1954, and was currently enjoying success with its latest model—the easy-opening can with flip-top ring. By one account, Walter Mack's departure from Pepsi was triggered by the board's disapproval of his initiative in promoting the use of cans.

By 1965, when cans had attained 13.1 percent of soda consumption, the Glass Containers Manufacturer Institute finally mobilized. The following year, the glass lobby spent $7 million to drench consumers in a promotional campaign for one-way bottles. Pepsi-Cola hopped on the bottlewagon with ads that claimed the no-deposit bottles were "made to order for the Pepsi Generation." Preaching to the converted at the Glass Containers Manufacturer Institute, Donald Kendall mixed observations with self-serving analysis: "The consumer has better things to do than to return packages to the store. . . . Often where store pricing includes deposit, she doesn't even know what the deposit is. The same kid who's used to returning the bottle for two cents now won't stop to pick up a penny off the street. With the increase of leisure time many so-called home-consumption packages are consumed away from home, so our package loss is heavy."

After a slow start, by 1966 Coke, too, had fallen into step with the one-way bottle. It used promotional discounts to prod bottlers, frazzled by a decade of new products and packages, and used advertising to seduce the public. "NOW,

---

* Nowhere as bluntly as in Pittsburgh steel mills where posters exhorted workers to "Help sell Steel. Buy soft drinks in convenient cans."

Coca-Cola in bottles you don't bring back," pitched ads, followed by the familiar "No Deposit, No Return." One-way Fresca bottles were claimed to be for "Busy, busy people." Tab's nonreturnable was posed next to an egg with a caption that read: "Two great one-way containers. Ours is brand new." By the end of 1965, Coca-Cola alone was available in five sizes of returnable bottles, three sizes of one-way bottles—each in two different styles—and the twelve-ounce can.

By 1970, 40 percent of all soft-drink containers were nonreturnables and the figure was still rising. More than mere containers, packaging had become a part of the product's sell worthy of its own advertising. The means had become an end.

It had also become mountains of broken glass and flattened rusty cans littering the nation. In 1972, 15.4 billion cans and bottles were discarded, up 262 percent since 1959. According to one 1971 account, an estimated 5 percent of the country's solid waste litter were containers of the Coca-Cola Company. Great exponents of America's convenience culture, Coke and the rest of the industry bore the brunt of the anti-litter backlash. Faced with increasing moves toward deposit legislation, the soda-makers unsuccessfully moved to undo the carefree romance they had pioneered of throwing away the throwaways. Yet neither the new ads nor the clean-up crews they sponsored could surpass bottle legislation in curtailing litter.

While the industry wrestled with litter, Coke was challenged by another crisis, this time on an unexpected flank. In 1970, NBC aired a documentary entitled "Migrant: An NBC White Paper" which exposed the wretched conditions of orange pickers in the Florida groves owned by Coke's Minute Maid. The show was, in effect, a repeat of Edward R. Murrow's exposé, "Harvest of Shame" broadcast in 1960, the year Coke bought Minute Maid.

Indeed, Coke was vulnerable because nothing had changed in the ensuing decade. Workers labored and lived in subhuman conditions for subhuman wages with frequent exposure to highly toxic pesticides. They lacked hot water, medical attention, education, and hope, as their lives and those of their families were virtually controlled by the company. A trained observer later testified that their conditions suggested the "slave quarters of earlier days."

The Coca-Cola Company was mortified that its precious name had been nationally disgraced. Austin insisted that he first confronted the problem two years earlier in 1968 after he read of Cesar Chavez's fight to organize the California grape pickers. He then dispatched J. Lucian Smith, president of Coke's food division, to investigate the company's thirty thousand acres of citrus groves. Smith allegedly reported back that the workers' living conditions "could not in conscience be tolerated by the Coca-Cola Company." Austin's well intentioned response—interviews with the oppressed workers to find out what they really wanted—revealed the characteristic insulation of lofty corporate management from the effects of some of its policies.

To complicate matters, "efforts to suppress 'Migrant,' " reported one observer, "or at least to dilute it, began about a month before the telecast." In a meeting he arranged with NBC producer Reuvan Frank, Luke Smith persuaded him to add a voice-over on the show which touted Coke's plans to improve its employees' lot. Apparently unsatisfied, Coca-Cola moved all of its business over to CBS and ABC several months after the broadcast, prompting charges that Coke tried to wield its advertising dollars like a club to influence the show's content.* The bad publicity fell like a pestilence on dear Atlanta.

Nothing happened in the citrus groves until public pressure forced Congress to intervene shortly after. Senator Walter Mondale's Subcommittee on Migratory Labor decided to probe the matter, forcing Austin and Smith to testify in Washington. Representing the lords of the Coke realm was Joseph Califano, formerly Lyndon Johnson's most important advisor and then a member of Arnold & Porter, a prestigious Washington firm influential within the Democratic Party.†

While serving Johnson, Califano had arranged a meeting between Austin and consumer activist Ralph Nader, who had been critical of Coke's lack of nutrition. Their meeting was a subject of some controversy in 1976 when *The New York Times* reported that William Ruder, of the public relations firm Ruder & Finn, erroneously claimed that he arranged it. In a letter he wrote to an aerosol company that he was trying to solicit, Ruder implied that he could iron out difficulties with environmentalists as he claimed to have done with Nader and Coca-Cola.

Yet not even Coke's heavy artillery could save them from some abuse. One witness accused Coke of a "deliberate, calculated and purposeful attempt to maintain an economic advantage regardless of the cost in human misery." Said another: "I would like to ask Mr. Austin or Mr. Talley how long it took Coke to introduce a new product like Sprite—was that ten years? Or what about new methods—a new can—does it take ten years to develop a new can? I doubt it. Why is it that when it comes to profit, corporations work fast, but when it comes to human conditions, corporations at best plod along?" When the company opened with a fifteen-page statement on its program to "motivate" workers, Mondale interrupted halfway through, declaring that with workers' oppression being what it is, "You can't argue that there is a problem of 'motivation.' The problem is that these workers can't defend themselves." The overflowing crowd in the Senate caucus room burst into tumultuous applause, after which Mondale wryly commented, "I might remind the audience that these hearings are supposed to be lifeless events." When questioned, Smith denied that he brought pressure to bear on NBC, and claimed he simply wanted to inform the producer that the show "did not include important facts necessary to a truthful portrayal." Neither man could explain why the company continued the crass ex-

* Frank Mankiewicz, *Remote Control: Television and the Manipulation of American Life* (New York: New York Times Books, 1978). p. 229
† Abe Fortas, for example, worked for Arnold & Porter until 1975.

ploitation, though Smith revealed that the citrus operation yielded $157 million in sales annually. However, Austin redeemed the day when he acknowledged that the plight of Coke's citrus work force was "deplorable" and offered to help create a National Alliance of Agribusiness to aid minorities in agriculture. He must have appeared a trace gratuitous to the intent audience when he conceded the gravity of an issue that had been recently exposed on national television and was the very subject of the hearings. He was praised nevertheless for his "candor" by Senator Mondale and friendly journals such as *Time* and *Business Week*. Never mind that his pro-minority corporate alliance never materialized.

After the hearings, Coke launched a highly visible, multi-million-dollar effort to improve workers' conditions. Although humanitarian concerns must have been a factor, the company's real concern was its image. "We decided that was not the kind of image Coca-Cola wanted to be associated with," said the vice-president of grove operations. Consequently, each new phase of Coke's program was accompanied by glossy photos, special tours, and other public relations devices. A journalist received a contract for a possible book: "They obviously viewed it as a long-term goodwill investment," he observed. The book was abandoned in favor of a twenty-five-minute film which the company still screens for visitors. Friendly newspapers received personal letters from Smith stating that their "editorial support means much to us." One editor objected to Coke's effusive public relations spigot: "When I see them spending about as much for publicity as they do for actual services, then I have to question their effort."

However, Coke had not acted quickly enough and Austin's original worry materialized. Cesar Chavez dispatched his cousin and others to unionize the Minute Maid workers, and within six weeks they had signed up 76 percent of the work force. "We knew the thing they hate worse than anything is bad publicity," related a United Farm Workers organizer. "We threatened to bring attention to how they were dealing with their workers and to boycott them if necessary. We knew that despite all their publicity about world harmony, they didn't give anything unless they were pushed hard. We played to their weakness, and that's their 'good-guy' image." Indeed, talk of a boycott terrorized the company, and consequently, in early 1972, the new union won what Chavez himself called "the best contract farm workers have gotten anywhere the first time around." Again, Coke made sure that this achievement did not go unheralded, though not all the honors were bestowed by outsiders. Bob Hall notes how the head of a committee of the Anti-Defamation League which commended Austin for his "humanitarianism" was a top executive of Coke's ad agency, McCann-Erickson. Hall later observed that the first five years of improvements for Coke's twelve hundred workers cost $2 million, about what Minute Maid once spent in several weeks to advertise a new product, which it later recalled.

Though Pepsi presumably couldn't help but chortle over Coke's predicaments, it too had difficulties. For example, a huge refinery constructed in 1963 in upstate New York, turned sour, and after a $12 million loss in 1966, Pepsi had to bail out just as it once sold its ill-fated Cuban sugar plantation in the late forties. Another blunder of the mid-sixties was Pepsi's development of Devil Shake to compete against Yoo-Hoo, a somewhat successful milk-based, noncarbonated chocolate drink made by the Yoo-Hoo Chocolate Beverage Corporation of Carlstadt, New Jersey. Pepsi was initially optimistic since a $100,000 in-house study predicted that Devil Shake would outsell Yoo-Hoo by a 5 to 1 margin. Pepsi's expensive homework was incomplete, for the company learned too late that Yoo-Hoo held the rights to a device called the hydrostatic sterilizer which provided the product with the necessary shelf life. Pepsi offered to pay $1 million for the machine but a clumsy start and $5 million loss persuaded it to abandon the muddy tonic.

A government suit against Frito-Lay was more serious. The FTC was concerned that the original merger between Frito and Lay could provide the company with an unfair advantage in the snack food business, and the 1965 merger with Pepsi just aggravated the concern. It was finally resolved in 1968, when PepsiCo agreed to restrict joint Pepsi-Frito-Lay advertising, known in the industry as "piggy-backing." For example, PepsiCo was prevented from buying a minute of TV time at a cheaper rate to run two thirty-second Pepsi and Frito-Lay ads. PepsiCo was also prohibited for a period of ten years from acquiring further beverage and snack food concerns. However, such restraints were mild compared to other possible outcomes, such as a divestment order, and did not greatly interfere with the company's plans.

Kendall saw that he couldn't beat Coke with soft drinks alone. Like many other companies, PepsiCo sought growth during the sixties by "conglomerating" or acquiring a whole range of businesses rather than building them from scratch. Sometimes, the strategy failed to get off the ground, as in the unsuccessful bid to buy a controlling interest in Miller Brewing Co. (Miller Beer) from W. R. Grace & Co. Sometimes it produced indifferent results, as with the purchase of Wilson Sporting Goods from LTV. Sometimes, it worked to perfection, as with Frito-Lay or the Tip Corp. Soon, PepsiCo had developed the machinery to market, in the words of one executive, "anything that goes down the gullet."

Nor were Kendall and Lay afraid to experiment in the non-leisure areas. In 1964, Kendall established the Pepsi-Cola Equipment Corp. to lease vending machines and trucks to bottlers, and its success led to the $54 million purchase of Lease Plan International, a trucking concern. By the end of the decade, Pepsi followed through with the acquisitions of National Trailer Convoy, North American Van Lines, and Chandler Leasing, huge leasers and movers of heavy equipment.

Pepsi thus greeted the sixties as a soft-drink company, and the seventies as a highly diversified conglomerate whose components were sewn together by common policy, leadership, and fiscal control. Amid the rash of acquisitions, the priority of the Pepsi brand was lost, and one former Pepsi executive recalled that the soft-drink division "somehow floundered in the right direction." Together with PepsiCo's new president, Andrall Pearson, a veteran management consultant from the highly touted McKinsey & Co., Kendall plucked Vic Bonomo from California's United Vintners to rebuild the soft-drink division around organization rather than personalities. PepsiCola would enter the new decade on more equal footing with Coke. Compared to Coke's sales of $1.3 billion, its 1969 volume was $940 million—double that of five years before, mostly because of merger.

Though wealthier, Coke was more cautious in its acquisitions, preferring to concentrate on nonalcoholic consumer beverages. It was now the world's largest producer of soft drinks, citrus products, and private label instant coffee and tea. By 1970, Coke had penetrated the last big beverage frontier—water—when it bought Aqua-Chem, a Milwaukee-based manufacturer of water-pollution equipment. With sales of $55.4 million in 1969, Aqua-Chem had installed about half the noncommunist world's water treatment plants and would prove useful in aiding the quality control of bottlers around the world. Its systems ranged from home use to a plant in Tijuana, Mexico, capable of purifying seven million gallons a day: "We could do a system for New York City. It's no problem," said Aqua-Chem's chairman, John C. Cleaver.

Despite Pepsi's advances, Coca-Cola earned $121 million in 1969, twice that of its rival and three times its 1960 earnings on a concurrent sales jump of 250 percent. Coke yielded more profits per investment dollar than Pepsi and was actually able to increase its total share of the market, an impressive feat considering the accelerated rate at which that market was growing. A bumper crop of young people virtually doubled the entire industry's volume during the sixties, and per capita consumption rose nearly 80 percent from 192 eight-ounce containers in 1960 to 344.4 in 1969. Coke's superior profitability was guaranteed by the fact that a handful of soft drinks out of a sprawling array of products accounted for an estimated 78 percent of its sales and 92 percent of its profits.

Coke gracefully exploited the convenience trend during the sixties by evolving its philosophy from a product orientation to a consumer one. "We're not the boss," insisted Austin, "the consumer is. What the consumer wants, the consumer gets." Of course, this view was very much in accordance with the prevailing orthodoxy on consumer sovereignty, but it is far from the whole story. The introduction of the returnable bottle was not so much the product of an express consumer demand as the result of pressure brought on the soda-makers by the aggressive packaging and retail sectors. (See Chapter 19.) The proliferation of brands in the early sixties was rooted in the intense competition between Coke and Pepsi. Marketed generally as fruit flavors, these drinks grew sweeter and sweeter in succession. Did this spiraling sugar spree originate out of any explicit, or even implicit consumer preference, or did it have more to do with the perception that the heavily sugared diets of many Americans accustomed consumers, both biologically and psychologically, to a certain sweetness threshold that new products had to match in order to gain acceptance? Coke and Pepsi were acutely aware that heightened sugar levels were credited with reversing slumping sales in certain product categories (such as breakfast cereals during the late forties) and it is easy to see how sugar escalation became a prime, if not the premier strategy that supposedly made new brands competitive.* Did the ever-growing presence of caffeine in non-cola beverages like Dr Pepper, Mountain Dew, and more recently, Sunkist Orange (all of which are distributed by Coke or Pepsi bottlers) have anything to do with consumer desires? Or was it because the soda-makers saw no reason why the time-honored sugar-caffeine "kick" of the cola drinks couldn't be duplicated in some of their allied brands? Mountain Dew, for instance, has more caffeine per serving than Pepsi. What the consumer gets can thus often have little to do with what the consumer wants or thinks he wants. On the contrary, the consumer tends to accept what is offered which, in turn, is often fashioned by economic pressures within certain intermediate markets like packaging, or by the self-fulfilling anticipation of certain trends.

The promise of consumer sovereignty held out by Austin is indeed the fundamental creed of a market economy. Without it, the system loses the legitimacy of providing goods and services and degenerates purely into the pursuit of private gain. Though the profit motive has long been a pillar of Western civilization, there is a certain distrust of naked materialism even in the American grain. Nineteenth-century entrepreneurs like Asa Candler resolved the conflict somewhat tenuously in a religious calling that sanctioned "earthly wealth" in the name of "heavenly purposes." Because consumption has long since replaced pious restraint as a central canon of social life, Coke, Pepsi, and other modern consumer-oriented companies legitimate the orthodoxy of maximum profits with one of service to pristine, inviolate consumer desires. This orthodoxy is strong enough to equate these desires with the needs of society itself. However pure Candler's calling may have been, the soda-makers' avowed commitment to the sovereign consumer is a self-justifying ideology that finds its purest expression in advertising. As an outside consultant to Coke and a veteran of the food industry indicated, the bulk of research expenditures are not for product development, as the Coke-Pepsi rivalry might first seem to suggest, but rather for advertising which concentrates on creating an image of the product tailored to consumer desires. The consumer gets what he wants—in the ads. Austin's words were illuminated perfectly by Bill Backer, the genius of so many Coke campaigns, when he said, "The product of the Coca-Cola Company is not Coca-Cola—that makes itself. The product of the Coca-Cola Company is advertising."

This important lesson was not lost on Austin. His skilled orchestration of Coke's performance won him the post of board chairman when Talley stepped aside in 1970. In an unprecedented vote of confidence, the directors allowed Austin to remain as president. Practical control of the company was now fully in the hands of the young Georgian and his new breed of managers. He surprised some by choosing Charles Duncan, Jr., a naturalized Coke man from the Dun-

* U.S., Congress, Senate Committee on Nutrition and Human Needs, *Dietary Goals for the United States* (2nd Edition), Committee Print, 95th Congress, 2nd Session, 1977, p. 31

can Foods acquisition, to serve as his number two man in the post of executive vice-president. Woodruff retired to the wings where he still held final say, and his life-long mission of bringing Coca-Cola to the peoples of the world was now inherited by Austin. As spectacular as domestic growth had been, the real soda surge lay abroad. Potential consumers were more impressionable, and the competition often less severe. If the American drinker felt engulfed by the soft-drink explosion, the peasant in Timbuktu would never know what hit him.

CHAPTER TWELVE

"No One Needs It"

NEITHER ALEXANDER, nor Caesar, nor Napoleon could have conceived of empires as far flung as those of PepsiCo and the Coca-Cola Company, the two most pervasive man-made systems in history. Both have penetrated vast areas of the earth's geography right down to its street corners. Since the creation of its foreign department in 1926, Coke's worldwide consumption increased from 6 million drinks a day to over 215 million, spread out over 140 countries. In even less time, Pepsi established more than 500 bottling operations in over 140 countries as well. No one conqueror, religion, or product has ever achieved such ubiquity.

The magnitude of this feat is all the more spectacular considering the banality of its purpose. "The soft drink is not a serious thing," confessed Pepsi's William C. Munro, "no one needs it." Indeed, no one does, but the diversity of Coke and Pepsi customers is the diversity of humanity itself. Every day peasants, tribespeople, suburbanites, presidents, sheiks, kings and queens, literally people of every race, color, creed, and persuasion consume Coke and Pepsi. Utterly superfluous products, Coke and Pepsi thrive in a world bitterly torn by disparate ideologies, values, and visions. Aside from physiological and biological similarities, the human race may not have a more common denominator than these drinks.

The foreign expansion of both companies, particularly Coke, paralleled the general rise of American investments overseas. Until the late nineteenth century, the United States had not been overly concerned with developing an economic presence abroad, primarily because its own vast western frontier provided its economy with the resources and opportunities necessary for dynamic growth. By the twentieth century, the adolescent offspring of its industrial revolution—rapidly growing giants such as Singer, National Cash Register, and General Electric as well as consumer-oriented Coca-Cola—expanded into Europe's industrialized societies in search of new markets. Meanwhile, with the considerable help of a jingoistic American foreign policy, other companies such as United Fruit and Anaconda began to exploit the cheap labor and natural wealth of the less-developed countries of the Caribbean and later, South America.

With its first step into Cuba once the United States ousted the Spanish at the turn of the century, Coke swelled into the United States-propped regimes of Latin America, though it preferred Europe's more affluent markets. By 1929, the company had accumulated sixty-four plants in twenty-eight countries worldwide. On the other hand, Pepsi's foreign exploration, begun in the mid-thirties, concentrated on Latin America. The foreign business of Coke, young Pepsi, and other American corporations developed at a steady and inexorable pace, primarily in Europe and Central and South America, until World War II.

The war established America as the world's preeminent economic power and provided it—and Coke—with a worldwide presence. What emerged from America's postwar reckoning was the "One World" perspective once heralded by Wendell Willkie and Walter Mack. By the late forties, the earth had been so shrunken by transportation and communication advances, and America's presence had become so widespread that its strategists and corporate leadership *had* to think globally. Board chairmen could begin to view the planet realistically as one highly diverse, barely tapped market.

Furthermore, the postwar expansion of Soviet communism provided a moral justification for the proliferation of America's values and products. Although historically America's foreign policy has been responsive to the needs of its economic interests—particularly in Latin America—the two became inextricably bound during the Cold War. "A serious and explicit purpose of our foreign policy," declared President Eisenhower in his 1953 State of the Union message, "[is] the encouragement of a hospitable climate for investment in foreign nations." The essence of all U.S. foreign policy since the Spanish-American War in 1898—the preservation and expansion of the geo-marketplace for American business—was now official. Political and economic might were united to transform the whole world into a marketplace safe for capitalist appropriation.

Throughout the entire century, Coca-Cola had followed the flag, but now it became the worldwide calling card for U.S. business. The installation of Coke bottling plants became a goodwill gesture by countries soliciting U.S. investments. Coke and Pepsi virtually quadrupled the number of countries in which they did business. From 1955 to 1975, for example, the Coca-Cola Company's foreign sales exploded 2,700 percent with a 3,600 percent increase in earnings. Pepsi was not far behind.

In the past, American companies generally exported their products to branch offices overseas which would then arrange for their distribution. However, in an expanding and increasingly complex international economy, United States corporations began to adjust their structural configurations to maximize growth and their investment return. What emerged was a powerful, controversial, and unique phenomenon, which would play a dramatic role in international affairs—the multinational corporation (MNC), so called since 1958. MNCs differed from their progenitors in that their overseas business was conducted by satellite corporations in each key market. Subsidiaries, generally run by nationals, could explore and exploit local markets more efficiently than the parent American firm. With resources available to them far in excess of their own size, subsidiaries could secure a better than even footing against local competition as well. This approach rapidly resulted in vast formations of private capital and assets, some of which now exceed the budgets of most countries. Girdling the earth, MNCs came to figure prominently in an international order once determined solely by geography and sovereign states.

The Coca-Cola Company was perhaps the first consumer-focused multinational because it marketed not only a retail product, but values and even life-styles. It sought to encourage all peoples, regardless of their needs, to find meaning and gratification in the consumption of soft drinks. Nations became markets, each with its own set of attitudes and cultural values, and as in the United States, citizens were seen as consumers. Advertising presented narrow aspects of a peoples' cultural life at the expense of the rest, thus underscoring Robert Scheer's astute observation that multinationals tend to replace real history with illusions created by advertising.

From its beginnings, Coke's universality owes much to the widespread equation of Coca-Cola and American life. During the first half of this century, Coke was very often the first and frequently the only sign of civilization in remote places, and it quickly became this country's emissary into the wilderness, a missionary of charismatic innocence. To the scattered peoples of the world, it became the bottle beautiful of the fruited plain, a sort of Statue of Liberty miniature.

This sacrosanct place that Coke held in the world's imagination was akin to the one it had in the American mind. The general feeling that Coke was America's emissary had a certain truth to it. Coke, after all, was founded by religious men, and taken to heart by people in the religious spirit of those times. Moreover, it was founded in an underdeveloped society—the ravaged landscape of the post-Civil War South—and its role there was not so diferent from its eventual one in foreign lands. The turn-of-the-century missionary work Coke financed abroad was only one among several American influences creating attitudes toward labor and consumption similar to the ones emerging in American life. Whether in America or the frontier reaches of foreign shores, people were increasingly exposed to a work ethic, whose Christian meaning was that salvation lay in a worldly calling. Worldly success and accumulation were signs of a fulfillment of that calling. The point is that consumption was hardly antagonistic to the religious message and was reenforced by other influences within the environment which the religious teaching actively fostered.

In the twentieth century, the work ethic was slowly replaced by materialistic hedonism. If anything, social redemption—social acceptance and self-identity—now lay in consumption rather than work. Glorification of abundance became the justification of the system.

Coca-Cola is virtually the only product that has been equally positioned to take full advantage of both phases of this fundamental transformation in the American values system. More than surviving the passing of the Protestant work ethic in which it was born and nurtured, Coke actually helped engineer its death, and in doing so successfully straddled both halves of what Daniel Bell has called the cultural contradictions of capitalism. That is why Coke has burned itself indelibly into American culture, and why, as America's cultural emissary, it is seen and accepted as a universal concomitant of Americanism around the world. This Christianizing influence was only a phase, and a bygone one at that, in the much larger impact of America's travels abroad. More recently, economic development in underdeveloped countries, frequently signaled by the arrival of Coke, has fostered a similar emphasis on consumption, and an even stronger clash within their traditional value systems. Thus, in accepting Coke and identifying it with America, these peoples anticipate their own history.

The multinational was now a key character in history, although Coke and Pepsi differed from most others in one critical way—the franchise system. Their galaxy of bottlers is not only locally managed but usually locally owned. As in the United States, bottlers were inevitably men who could lend stature and resources to the business. "There just aren't very many guys out there who grew up in the business, or inherited it from their fathers," said Peter K. Warren, head of PepsiCo International. "Most of the international bottlers are people who have made their money in banking, shipbuilding, import-export, mining, or what have you. They tend to be a more diversified group of people from a wide variety of backgrounds." By relying on local investment capital rather than their own, Coke and Pepsi were able to develop markets at a greater pace than their own resources would allow. Local ownership also minimizes the possibility of expropriation by a host government. "It's a franchise business," said Austin. "If they nationalize the assets, they're nationalizing their own people." Furthermore, aided by the company's aggressive marketing formulas, the owner-operated franchise could best fulfill the marketing requirements of not only the urban markets, but even the smallest village, hamlet, or tribe. "He speaks the language," said a Coke official of its overseas bottler, "knows the culture, and understands the local laws." Such decentralization enabled both companies to adapt their sophisticated marketing skills to prevailing cultural institutions. For example, in 1949, at the opening ceremonies of a Coke plant in Bangkok, Buddhist priests toured the facility swabbing gold paint on the bottle-washing machines and the foreheads of the bottlers. Observed Austin, "We're not multinational, we're multilocal."

Producing soft drinks abroad is a formidable task. Once a franchise is found and financed, a bottling plant must be constructed. Local customs and laws have to be examined, and the tactics of competing brands thoroughly understood. The market must be carefully evaluated to determine packaging requirements, distribution patterns, and consumer preferences. The drink must be available at every feasible location to ensure a sale whenever the soft-drink impulse strikes the consumers. Then, a whole support system must be developed, such as a truck fleet and advertising materials. A sales force must be trained and plant managers found to oversee the operation of sophisticated high-speed bottling equipment. Large and steady supplies of cans, bottles, and caps, built to precise specifications, must be developed and quality control procedures established. Every day, torrents of water must be purified and reduced to its most neutral state to avoid any variation with the beverage in other locations. Said Peter K. Warren, in 1977, "We have laboratories around the world where our products are monitored on a regular basis. We also funnel store samples from every country to our labs in New York where we test for purity and uniformity." Each bottler is tightly regulated for conformity to company specifications, and is even instructed how to wash his equipment. After taking everything into account, an advertising strategy must be formulated to saturate the culture with the message. Finally, the product is introduced with a big promotional splash, featuring bands, pretty girls, and local heroes fondling the bottle.

Coke arrived in England as early as 1900, making Europe its first major overseas conquest. Europe was a marketing man's nightmare, a potpourri of cultures and languages all stuffed within a small but varied terrain. Moreover, Europeans already had strong beverage preferences, including tea, beer, wine, and mineral water, that rested on long and vaunted traditions. American traditions, on the other hand, were just then being created by Coca-Cola. Nevertheless, Europeans enjoyed relatively affluent societies with effective communication, transportation, and advertising systems—all the right accoutrements of potential Coca-Cola markets. Slowly but surely, those little red signs began to pop up throughout the continent.

Cultural patterns in Europe have greatly affected soft-drink consumption. The French are still deeply committed to mineral water and wine, which exceeds soft-drink consumption. In addition, the worldwide scourge of Coke and Pepsi—the labelling law—has reared itself. "The law requires us to list our ingredients," said Coke's local marketing manager. "This tends to scare mothers away from buying Coke for their children, since they see that it contains caffeine. How much has this affected sales? It's impossible to measure, but there's certainly been an impact. The emphasis of late has been on the 'health problem' here in France, and it's surely been hurting us."

The West Germans rate with the Dutch as the greatest per capita guzzlers of soft drinks in Western Europe, and in total sales, they easily outstrip the others. The rise of national food chains and American-style supermarkets has benefitted soft drinks, as has the exploitation of outlets like cafeterias and bars (beer is still the favorite beverage of West Germans). Coke products whip those of Pepsico by a four to one margin, though national "health consciousness" has declined the sales of soft drinks in favor of mineral water.

Italy, on the other hand, is one of Europe's worst markets. "This is a country of wine drinkers," said an industry observer. "Italians think that soft drinks are disgusting." The Italian landscape is generally devoid of fast-food chains or supermarkets, and inflation has crippled the economy. The industry's ennui is far-reaching. "The only way for anyone to get reliable data on soft-drink units," said a trade journal editor, "is to count the trucks coming out of the bottling plants."

In 1977, Coke commemorated its fiftieth anniversary in Italy and took its bows in this lackluster market with a multi-media promotional campaign featuring Coke's original 1927 bottle. After widely circulating reproductions of the first Coke advertisement used in Italy, facsimiles of the original straight-sided bottle were manufactured, filled with Coke, and sold along with the normal container. The overall message of this campaign reportedly was: "Coca-Cola in Italy is Italian. It is a collection of small businesses, Italian businesses. The product is produced in Italy, by Italians, in factories built by Italians and is then distributed and consumed by Italians. And it has been so for half a century." The point is, given enough time, Coca-Cola can not only present itelf as native to any culture, it can even inspire a nostalgia, once solely American, for the ghost of Coca-Cola's past.

In 1934, Pepsi opened its first plant in Canada, followed a year later by its first overseas plants in Cuba and the Dominican Republic. However, the company was too underdeveloped and preoccupied with the domestic market to capitalize immediately on the postwar expansion. When it did go abroad, it, of course, preferred countries uninhabited by its rival. Under the potent management of Al Steele, the company grew quickly during the fifties and toward the end of the decade was primed for its charge abroad, led by Donald Kendall. In the spunkiest Pepsi tradition, Kendall began to challenge Coke overseas as Steele had confronted it at home. During his first three years as president of Pepsi International, Kendall made the best of what he had and then some, as the company expanded at the maniacal pace of a new bottling plant every 11.5 days. Where there were some 70 Pepsi bottlers overseas in 1957, there were 278 in 1962.

By the early sixties, Pepsi set out to make up for lost time in Europe. It allied itself with some powerful bottling partners such as England's Schweppes, Europe's only transnational soft-drink producer, and France's Perrier, bottler of mineral water. In 1966, it opened plants in Belgium and Austria, and three years later, Pepsi was available in Scandinavia. Distributed by Heineken in the Netherlands, which shares in Western Europe's highest soda pop consumption per capita, Pepsi currently outsells Coke and continues to grow. Throughout Europe, Pepsi became Coke's main cola rival, though overall Coke still outsells it by an estimated 3:1 margin.

In victory's aftermath, the U.S. gained a solid foothold along the eastern coast of Asia. Japan, the vanquished foe, became of great strategic value for American policymakers, particularly after a popular revolution in 1949 placed the communists in power in China. Chairman Mao Tse-Tung found Coca-Cola inimical to Chinese interests, even though the drink had been in China since 1928, and expelled it with the rest of Western business.

Coke and Pepsi were first introduced to the Japanese by America's occupational army. Although Japan sharply restricted foreign investment and development to safeguard its own institutions, the Coca-Cola Company, always on the heels of foreign policy initiatives, was one of two U.S. companies allowed to establish a 100 percent owned subsidiary there (the other being IBM). Japan was an ideal market—a large culturally consistent population on an undersized island—and Coke, exploiting Japan's recent infatuation with Western culture, soon dominated a healthy soft-drink market. Pepsi, meanwhile, opened its first bottling plant in 1966, and four years later, to promote itself in Asia, sponsored a Pepsi pavilion at Expo '70, Japan's first trade fair.

For many Japanese, however, the Coca-Cola Company had come too far too fast in their homeland. By 1968, after only eight years of national sales, its Japanese franchises sold 2.7 billion bottles of soft drinks, accounting for 50 percent of the market. That year, Coke's unchecked growth was finally protested by the Japanese soft-drink bottlers' association which complained that Coca-Cola had already driven 15 percent of the country's 3,500 soft-drink manufacturers bankrupt. Hundreds of protesters took to the streets of several cities screaming "Smash Coca-Cola imperialism!" Yet Coke was unsentimental about the plight of its victims. "There are plenty of answers to their problems," said a local Coke executive, "but they'll have to find them themselves."

Unaffected as usual by the "noise" about it, the Coca-Cola Company forged ahead relentlessly. By 1975, Coke's share of Japan's $1.5 billion soft-drink market accounted for 7 percent of its worldwide sales. While Coca-Cola easily overcame the political challenges, a more serious dilemma arose—a recession had struck the Japanese market. Between 1973 and 1975, Coke was hurt more than its competition by a general slump in soft-drink sales, and its 70 million case drop was equal to the combined total sales of its two nearest competitors, Pepsi-Cola and a Japanese favorite, Kirin Lemon. Meanwhile, net profits dipped from $40 million to $22.5 million. Other problems arose, such as the thousands of cases of Fanta Grape that were recalled because of a yeast growth. Worse was the morale of some of Coke's bottlers, now seventeen strong. To compensate for declining business, they began to carry Seven-Up and Dr Pepper products.*

With one of its greatest markets floundering, the Coca-Cola Company returned to its roots for solutions, coaxing long-time Cokeman Morton S. Hodgson out of retirement. A veteran steeped in Coke's greatness, he had a love for tough assignments, having once headed a bottling operation in volatile Latin America and subsequently managing all of the U.S. plants directly owned by the company.

In Japan, Hodgson concentrated on Coke rather than the entire roster of company products, beefed up advertising, and improved merchandising. He improved retail distribution and employee training programs, and most important, strengthened relations with the bottlers. "I have found in many years in this business," said Hodgson, "that we tend to get involved with new projects and forget the basic jobs we are supposed to do." With a real Cokeman in charge, the old magic worked. Bottler morale improved as did business. With Coke bottlers accounting for over 60 percent of the country's soda consumption, Japan still ranks as one of Coke's greatest growth markets, helped by Tokyo and Osaka, among two of the very best regional markets in the Coca-Cola world. By 1979, Coke could boast of 430,000 vending machines throughout Japan, 485,-000 coolers, 500 warehouses, and a veritable army of 11,500 salesmen which service over a million Coke outlets at least once every week.

As American influence spread down through Southeast Asia, so did Coke and

* The latter particularly irritated Atlanta because Dr Pepper had developed its U.S. bottling network by latching onto 185 of Coke's 739 domestic bottlers. Coke responded to the Doctor's challenge with its own cherry cola, Mr. Pibb.

Pepsi. When political stability and a hospitable business climate was assured within a country, both companies, fueled by the deepest, most competitive capitalist instincts, frequently led the pack of MNCs seeking opportunities. Asia's markets were particularly vital to Pepsi because here, as in Latin America, it could secure an even start if not a jump on Coke.

Pepsi's entrance into Asia was facilitated by its roving ambassador, Richard Nixon, who argued vociferously that a strong American economic presence was the best defense against communism. Certainly, it was with great delight that he negotiated Pepsi's exclusive franchise in Chiang Kai Shek's Nationalist China. However, the Nixon/Pepsi approach, even with American foreign policy riding shotgun, was eventually helpless before political inevitabilities. In 1963, for example, Pepsi entered Cambodia two years before Coke and moved quickly to outsell local competitors in sales. By 1969, Pepsi was selling 26 million bottles a year (*The New York Times* noted that Pepsi was popular with the country's opium smokers). Yet that year, the United States commenced its secret bombing of Cambodia, escalating the war in Southeast Asia. The ensuing struggle against the Communists dried up business in that country and the Cambodian government commandeered most of Pepsi's 110 trucks, which became a favorite target for Viet Cong rockets. According to *The New York Times,* the word "Pepsi" came to be associated with the pyrotechnics that resulted when a rocket hit a truck loaded with hand grenades, or with cases of warm soda. In need of greater opposition to Communist operations in Cambodia, the United States backed the overthrow of Cambodia's Prince Norodom Sihanouk by the rightist forces of Lon Nol. Yet the new regime lacked a popular base, enabling the Communists finally to seize power in Cambodia. As in much of Indochina, they shut off the spigot for Coke and Pepsi. The last factory in operation in Cambodia's Phnom Penh before the Communists seized control reportedly was a die-hard Pepsi-Cola bottling plant.

In 1973, amid growing skepticism about investments in the region, Pepsi planned a million-dollar bottling plant in Saigon with a well-connected ally of America—Mrs. Cao Van Vien, wife of the chief of staff of the Saigon army. On the other hand, by 1975, only two years after it first entered Laos, Coke perhaps foresaw the end in Vietnam, for it was reportedly the first Western consumer product to withdraw from Saigon. The company claimed the move was to make Vietnam more self-reliant and less dependent on the United States, an uncommonly benign motive for the Coca-Cola Company.

As a means to preserve America's access to Indochina, the Vietnam War was a stupendous foreign policy failure. France's old colonial empire was not to be resurrected, even by the sorcery of American militarism. The war finally differed from other American conflicts because it lacked any real sense of justice, moral righteousness, or conviction. Atlanta must have sensed this vacuum from the very beginning, for Coke seldom conspicuously identified with the Vietnam conflict. Of course, their reticence didn't stop them from consigning millions of cases of Coke to U.S. armed forces, but the patriotism and sentimentality that

Coke inspired among World War II fighting men were scarce in Vietnam. One of the few tales that surfaced described a Marine lieutenant who wrote his wife in 1966 in quest of a quart of Coke. He received it a month later, courtesy of the Saigon bottler, and requested his father to express his "sincere thanks" to the Coca-Cola Company. Such old-fashioned nostalgia could have come straight from the company archives, which apparently were the source for the words of a Coke vice-president who inserted "Vietnam" in his otherwise literal echo of some nameless but inspired corporate forebear who had trumpeted Coke into a more noble battle a quarter century before. "When a soldier in Vietnam has a Coke, it satisfies his need to identify with American tradition and way of life. It reminds him of what he is fighting for." In Vietnam, American history was *not* repeating itself, but Atlanta was, and in a lame, literal, unconvincing fashion whose half-heartedness confirmed the lie.

Along with American foreign policy, Coke and Pepsi fared better in South Korea which like Japan became a key component of America's Pacific frontier. Although it too was extremely protective of its own economy from foreign influence, repressive regimes, climaxed by the Park government and all backed by U.S. military forces, provided a stable growth economy. In 1968, with the relative affluence of Koreans on the rise as well as their appetite for long denied Western consumer goods, Coca-Cola entered South Korea, followed a year later by Pepsi (its 115th country). Employing massive advertising campaigns and innovative distribution systems, the American behemoths soon overwhelmed the local soft-drink industry. Coke and Pepsi so expanded their market that the largest local bottler found himself in the curious position of actually increasing his sales while his percentage of the market dropped. During Coke's first year, for example, the demand for colas doubled while the demand for all soft drinks increased by nearly a third, prompting the company to construct a local concentrate plant and to introduce its other flavors. Meanwhile, the number of local bottlers dropped from eighty-one to fifty, of which only ten would survive.

The Indian subcontinent provided vast markets for American investment, and almost no end of parched throats. Pakistan was offered American aid in exchange for the liberalization of its import policies, and by 1967, Coke, Fanta, Pepsi, Canada Dry, Seven-Up, and many other soft drinks were available in this far-off country. That year, perhaps because he was impressed with this performance, President Lyndon Johnson called his old chum at the Coca-Cola Company, Benjamin Oehlert, and offered him the ambassadorship to Pakistan. After accepting, Oehlert reportedly hung up, turned to his secretary, and queried, "Where the hell is Pakistan?"

After World War II, India freed itself from English rule and became one of the many countries courted by United States interests. Coca-Cola was a successful suitor and in 1950, the cornerstone was laid for the country's first Coke bottling plant. Indian Prime Minister Jawaharlal Nehru, the father of the country's independence, was in attendance sipping a Coke. Business was good despite some initial hostility and by 1953 three more plants were added. In 1958, a concentrate plant was constructed which eventually exported concentrate, sometimes in twenty-ton loads, to many European and Middle East countries.

The few in India who could afford Coke drank it, and even the exalted Dalai Lama, in refuge in India because of the Chinese takeover of Tibet, had once been caught serenely drinking one. Yet India's sizeable consumption posed a certain irony considering that its impoverished masses found Coke, at a cost of one rupee or 11½ cents a bottle, an all too exotic luxury. Moreover, in the face of economic affliction, India's leadership grew increasingly disdainful of the resident MNCs. The country's recent struggle against an earlier form of Western exploitation still haunted many Indians, and the observations made by Gandhi in 1908 of English rule were still applicable sixty-five years later: "They [the English] are not in India because of their strength but because we keep them. . . . We like their commerce, they please us by their subtle methods, and get what they want from us. . . . They wish to convert the whole world into a vast market for their goods." While anti-imperialist sentiments increased, so did Coke's sales, and another eighteen bottling plants were eventually built.

In 1971, Coke was engaged in a heated battle with its chief competitor, a locally produced orange drink called Gold Spot. Meanwhile, Indians were enraged over the continuing supply of American arms to their old enemy, Pakistan, which was trying to suppress the Bengali secession movement in East Pakistan. The looming thunderclouds were unmistakable. Shortly after Indira Gandhi was elected prime minister with a broad Socialist mandate, the anti-American climate focused on the obvious whipping boy—Coca-Cola.* Critics argued that Coca-Cola created a foreign exchange problem by siphoning more money out of the cash-poor Indian economy than it generated indigenously through the operation of the concentrate plant. Coke was particularly draining, said critics, because it controlled too much of the soft-drink market at the expense of the native industry. However, Coke's operations remained healthy and intact during the Gandhi government, and even managed to elude a bill passed in 1973 that called for greater control and ownership of foreign firms by natives of India.

Whatever peace Coca-Cola worked out with Gandhi's Congress Party vanished when its successor, the Janata Party, was elected in 1977. Let by Morarji Desai, the new government immediately renewed its attack on Coke in order to demonstrate its intent to emancipate India economically. In India's lower house of Parliament, the industry minister, Georges Fernandes, a socialist, announced to loud cheers that in accordance with the 1973 act, Coca-Cola must convert 60 percent of its operations, presumably those making concentrate, to Indian ownership as well as turn over its technical know-how.

"The activities of the Coca-Cola Company in India during the last twenty years," he charged, "furnished a classic example of how a multinational corporation operating in a low-priority, high-profit area in a developing country attains runaway growth and, in the absence of alertness on the part of the government, can trifle with the weaker indigenous industry in the process." He asserted that the company had earned $11,500,000 in India presumably over a twenty-

* It is possible that some Indians may have believed that Ambassador Oehlert influenced Nixon's "tilt" toward Pakistan and away from India, thereby fueling their resentment of Coke.

four-year period on an initial investment of $75,000, and exacted a 400 percent profit from its Indian bottlers on the sale of concentrate. "The manufacture of beverages should be Indianized," Fernandes insisted. The Coca-Cola Company agreed to the former demand because 40 percent ownership would still keep its grasp on the market. Yet, by the standards of the government, the transfer of its technology meant divulging 7-X, Coke's secret formula. For nearly a century, one reality remained an inviolate constant—the secret of the Coca-Cola formula. Of course, the company never considered sharing it with the Indians, arguing that the government was confusing proprietary trade secrets with industrial information. Coke's compromise offer that would have withdrawn everything but a liaison office in India for quality control and the protection of the formula was rejected by Fernandes because, he said, it would reduce the concentrate plant to a mere "selling company . . . which would still be under the manufacturing control of the American company." Coke garnished its offer, as one of its representatives pled, "We have the know-how on agrichemicals and we can give our expertise on desalinization of water. I want to tell Indian leaders that our presence will be useful to them." All to no avail.

Despite the efforts by the company and its bottlers, the government squeezed Coca-Cola out of India. The loss was not very traumatic for Atlanta since India's annual Coke consumption of 450 million bottles annually represented less than 1 percent of the company's global sales.

From India's side, the demise of Coke served to inform foreign investors that India's self-interest would come before theirs.

Convinced it can refresh the people as well as employ them without American help—thousands of jobs were lost with Coke's expulsion—the government decided to sell its own brew. It was called "77" to commemorate the year both Indira Gandhi and Coca-Cola were ousted from power. "It's Coca-Cola all right," said one consumer, "minus the zing."

Yet, the Janata Party endorsed the brew as a symbol of its rule, and several years later when it was challenged at the polls by a resurrected Indira Gandhi and her Congress Party, the struggle was dubbed the "Battle of the Bottles." The director of the company that formerly bottled Coke won a Parliament seat on the Congress Party ticket vowing to return Coca-Cola to India.

Coca-Cola has meanwhile joined Scotch whisky, French wine, and German beer as highly prized black market items, and could be had for the asking outside the Taj Mahal. Reportedly, a few bottles of America's bubbliest are guaranteed to swell the status of any host on New Delhi's cocktail circuit. Within a year, King Coke had been reduced from twenty-two proud plants to being smuggled into the country by tourists, bootleggers, and diplomats.

After World War II, Coke moved into the Middle East, a fine market with its hot sandy climate and religious taboos against alcohol. In 1948, Coke began bottling in Egypt and, by 1966, had eighteen bottling plants in most of the Middle Eastern countries. Ethiopia's Haile Selassie was reportedly a fanatic Coke drinker, surpassed only by Egypt's King Farouk. Pepsi, whose arrival in many foreign locales generally lagged behind Coke's by a decade, was in Egypt by 1958. (Doing business abroad posed unique problems. In 1954, a rumor was circulated in Morocco that Coca-Cola was flavored with pig's blood. Within the devout Moslem population, Coke would have been better off laced with strychnine, and it wasn't until the sultan's son publicly ordered a Coke that the drink returned to Allah's good graces.)

Despite both companies' rampant expansionism, one market remained curiously dry—Israel. In 1949, a year after the creation of the Israeli state, a group of businessmen, approved by the Coca-Cola Company, petitioned the new government for permission to bottle Coke in the country. They were refused, reportedly because the fledgling country's foreign exchange couldn't support the import of unessential materials. Neither Coke nor Pepsi was eager to begin business there, partially because of the strife in the area. In 1958, Kendall left a hotel shortly before rioters attacked it and killed some American guests. Conditions were so bad in Lebanon that Kendall once needed a military escort from the airport to his hotel. To render his stay truly unpleasant, he was shot at by a low-flying plane while in the hotel pool.

Actual warfare wasn't as threatening as the politics of the Arab League, a political arm of eventually over twenty Arab countries. Founded in 1945 to promote Arab interests, the League was waging an economic war against Israel by boycotting any foreign firms that did business with it. Since neither Coke nor Pepsi did, they and their bottlers were left in peace. Only occasionally would incidents flare, such as in 1961 when a Coca-Cola bottle apparently bearing Hebrew characters was found in Cairo. A subsequent inquiry revealed that the bottle had come from Ethiopia and the characters were Amharic. However, the manager of the locally owned bottling plant forcefully declared that "The Coca-Cola Company has not and will never allow Israel to bottle Coca-Cola," prompting a spokesman for the Coca-Cola Export Corporation to assure the world that such decisions were hardly made on the bottler level.

In April of 1966, the lack of Coke or Pepsi bottlers in Israel was finally headlined in America. After a fifteen-month investigation, instigated by an Israeli firm which had been refused a Coke franchise, the Anti-Defamation League of B'nai B'rith concluded that Coke had forsaken Israel and acceded to the Arab boycott. Israel's consumption, it noted, approximated Ireland's, which was worthy of three Coke bottling plants. Furthermore, Coke's policy was blatantly inconsistent with "its proclaimed desire for new markets," adding that in the last three years alone, Coke gained ninety new foreign bottlers and began operations in fourteen new countries.

Coke was mortified. "It's the size of the market, not any political considerations . . .," insisted a spokesman. "It has been the judgment of officials of the company that the market in Israel wouldn't support an entire bottling industry." The response was unconvincing and rumblings of a boycott against Coke were heard among American Jews. In New York City, the reaction was more straightforward. Mount Sinai Hospital stopped buying Coke for its cafeteria and Nathan's Famous Hot Dogs emporium on Coney Island, and a theater chain reportedly threatened to do the same. The New York City Human Rights Commission even called for an investigation of Coke. "Of course, it was an economic decision," an Israeli official asserted. "Somebody looked at a map and saw eighty million thirsty Arabs opposed to a couple of million thirsty Israelis and that was that."

Caught in a mushrooming public relations crisis, Coke Export, five days after the Anti-Defamation League's press conference, called on its famous troubleshooter, Jim Farley. He proclaimed that Coke would never never respect the Arab boycott and termed the allegations "unfair and unfounded."

With the whole affair well publicized and threatening to alienate many Americans, Coke quickly reconsidered its position. Eight days after the scandal began, Coke announced that it had granted Israel's first franchise in Tel Aviv. "I want to emphasize," announced Farley, "that all decisions of this kind are constantly under assessment and reassessment." The new franchise owner was Abraham Feinberg, a top executive with the American Bank and Trust Company and the Israel Development Corporation, as well as the former chairman of the Brandeis University board of trustees. Feinberg had led the original consortium that had been rejected by the Israel government in 1949. Coke's decision "delighted" the Anti-Defamation League.

Coke and American Jews may have been pleased, but the Arabs were not. Six months later, just before a conference of the Arab League, Coke placed ads in a prestigious Cairo newspaper touting the quality of its product and its benefits to Arab welfare, and a day before the conference, an advertisement heralded the opening of a new Coke plant in Kuwait, the very site of the meeting. One irony was that Kuwait had a per capita consumption rate nearly double that of the United States. Again, Coke was thwarted when the League voted to ban its products and those of another offender, the Ford Motor Company. Both companies joined Kaiser-Fraser, Zenith Radio, Sears, Roebuck, Alka Seltzer, and some 5,000 other firms on the Arab League's blacklist, which read like a Who's Who of American corporations.

The Coke-Pepsi rivalry was now superimposed upon the Arab-Israeli struggle. After the six-day war in 1967, Israeli troops, as a symbol of victory, replaced a bullet-ridden Pepsi-Cola sign in the captured Syrian Army headquarters on the Golan Heights with a fresh Coca-Cola sign.

Coke was swept into an age-old maelstrom. In what must have been a very painful decision, it was forced to choose between its image at home and a fruitful market abroad. The company was at least comforted by the fact that Japan, Eastern Europe, and other booming markets would relieve some of the sting from the balance sheets. Yet history had taught Coca-Cola leadership that patience and a cooperative foreign policy can help resolve the thorniest problems, and as we shall see in Chapter 17, this is exactly what would begin to happen in the Middle East.

The exploitation of Africa, though potentially lucrative, has been tedious for

American business. The vast cultural differences between Africa and the West have hindered the creation of the Western-style social and economic components necessary for a viable marketplace. Traditional African society lacks both consuming classes and the necessary marketing institutions of Western culture, such as mass media and convertible monetary systems. Societies were too decentralized and languages and dialects too profuse. Seven languages are reportedly needed to get the advertising message across in South Africa—English, Afrikaans, and five tribal tongues. Furthermore, years of oppression under white colonial rule produced a keen sense of nationalism in many areas. In a way, both the oldest and youngest continent, Africa is still experiencing the sudden shifts and volcanic upheavals characteristic of rapidly evolving societies.

Undeterred, Coke entered the continent prior to World War II through South Africa where it established a solid base before spilling northward. Africans have at least one critical quality necessary for Coca-Cola consumption—a deep, year-round thirst—and though local capital was often short, forcing the company frequently to invest its own money in plants, Coca-Cola gradually gained a following. The seriousness with which the company views Africa is demonstrated by the fact that Paul Austin himself had managed Coke's African operations for four years (headquartered in Johannesburg, South Africa) before heading Coke Export.

By the sixties, with company-owned plants in Rhodesia and South Africa, Pepsi was also in full stride in Africa. Realizing that full-scale promotions create a bigger splash than wall posters, Pepsi invested $300,000 in 1960, for example, to send jazz great Louis Armstrong on a tour of Western Africa, with performances in Nigeria, Ghana, Sierra Leone, Liberia, and Senegal. Pepsi's constant message was reportedly the syllogism: "You like Satchmo. Pepsi brings you Satchmo. Therefore, you like Pepsi." (The Pepsi/Armstrong concert was the first time Ghana ever had advance ticket sales.)

Coke has already developed consumer loyalty in Africa. To protect Zaire from Katanganese rebels in 1977, president Mobuto Sese Seko ordered a C-130 cargo plane from the United States, C-rations, and $60,000 worth of Coca-Cola. "You can't expect a soldier to fight on a Cokeless stomach," explained a State Department official. Mobuto sought the Coke from the United States because the local bottling plant did not produce cans, which were easier to distribute to the troops than bottles. Such adulation was perhaps only equaled by the new nation of Bangladesh which reportedly served a Coke-and-meatball dinner at a diplomatic reception.

In 1980, Coke played a curious role in the parliamentary elections for Rhodesia's first black majority rule. A special ink, visible only under ultraviolet light, was stamped onto the hands of voters to prevent them from voting twice. However, the Popular Front of socialist candidate Roberty Mugabe claimed that the invisible ink could be washed off with a dose of Coca-Cola, and accused his opponent, Bishop Muzorewa, of "Coca-Cola vote-rigging" by urging his supporters to use Coke to vote twice. The matter was resolved when the election commissioner demonstrated to reporters that Coca-Cola, in this case poured from two silver-plated ice-buckets, could not remove the ink.

Within any country, an MNC is concerned with its profits, not its host's values or institutions. Although an MNC will sometimes intervene politically when its interests are threatened, it will generally remain indifferent to the nature of the prevailing political rule. Yet such self-serving pragmatism may be shortsighted, particularly within mercurial Third World countries. In 1977, when asked about Africa's political upheavals, Peter K. Warren, president of PepsiCo International, responded: "Every international business learns to cope with a variety of unusual internal forces. And we have always maintained a strict nonpolitical profile. We work with all types of governments and economic situations. We're even surviving quite happily in Uganda." If able to make a profit, Pepsi and other companies could coexist "quite happily" with the brutal excesses of Ugandan dictator Idi Amin. Two years after Warren's remark, Amin was finally overthrown, and the country was in shambles. The economy barely survives, as do many Ugandans, and signs urging "Have a Pepsi Day" dangle in the wind over lifeless shops. In a country where the average monthly pay is less than $85, a Pepsi-Cola, says The New York Times, costs $7.

Another example of tolerance, if not complicity, is South Africa, a major market for Western products, including soft drinks. Many MNCs have been sharply criticized because their South African operations tend to perpetuate the country's apartheid system. For example, it was reported in 1973 that although Pepsi and some other companies gave their black employees in South Africa above-average pay and promotions, they still paid white employees better wages. In 1977, meanwhile, a Coca-Cola executive proclaimed that his company "needn't fear any criticism in South Africa" because its operations employ a majority of "nonwhites." A year later, however, the Coca-Cola Company was chided for failing to cooperate with a Senate Foreign Relations Subcommittee investigation into the role of American subsidiaries in perpetuating South Africa's racist policies. Out of 259 companies surveyed, the Coca-Cola Company was the largest not to cooperate, ignoring three separate requests for information on its pay scales and hiring and promotional policies in the white-ruled country. A company spokesman cited by the Wall Street Journal, claimed that cooperation would necessarily disclose "confidential information." The subcommittee eventually concluded that American subsidiaries in South Africa do contribute to the apartheid system. Through its bottling facilities, three of which are directly backed by Atlanta, Coca-Cola reportedly employs some 8,400 people, making it one of the country's single largest employers. In 1978, some 70 percent of South Africa's market belonged to Coke,* and according to the aforementioned executive, Coke's South African operations could withstand any trade boycott of the country in protest of its racist policies.

Proponents of MNCs argue that they serve as engines of international cooper-

---

* Pepsi's problems were exacerbated when its local bottler, Cadbury-Schweppes, defected to Coca-Cola, causing some erosion of its already feeble market share.

ation and understanding. Nowhere was this better exemplified than with America's soft-drink diplomacy within the Eastern European countries in the mid-sixties. Capitalist philosophy has always defined human freedom and dignity as a derivative of what it held to be the most fundamental freedom—free enterprise, free and competitive access to the marketplace. Thus, the cardinal sin of communism is its denial of the free marketplace in favor of the noncompetitive state-controlled economy. Much of the Cold War animosity lies in the fact that Communist movements, some influenced or manipulated by the Soviet Union, denied Western firms access to a great bulk of Eurasia's population— Eastern Europe and China. Stalin had only to raise the real fear of capitalist imperialism to the level of headstrong paranoia, and the lines were drawn. And as illustrated in Chapter 6, the Communists seized as their symbol of the West the greatest champion of marketplace encroachment, the Coca-Cola Company.

So went the story of East-West relations until the mid-sixties when, for a variety of reasons, the narrow visions of both sides began to crumble before more refined aspirations. By then, Eastern European countries had developed secure industrial societies, and consequently felt less threatened by the West. Indeed, after weary years of Stalinization, many Eastern Europeans sought reform and yearned to complement their meat and potatoes economies with consumer frills. This gradual independence from hard-line Soviet dogma, coupled with the increasing Soviet-Sino rift, undermined the notions of American policy makers that the Communist world was under the absolute rule of the Kremlin and inimical to the ways of the West. Thus, America's draconian foreign policy gave way to the new internationalism of corporate America with its quest for a worldwide grid of markets and distribution.

As early as 1964, Paul Austin, president of a company that had been soundly abused by Communists, could say, "If the Russians really want to come into our market, let them, provided they'll reciprocate by allowing us to go into theirs. . . ." America's foreign policy is a quest for peace—with profits. Therefore, it is not paradoxical but logically consistent that President Johnson could gently encourage trade of "nonessential," i.e. consumer products, with Eastern Europe as he was escalating the war in less developed Vietnam. Communist rule was threatening the free marketplace in Southeast Asia, and cautiously encouraging it in Eastern Europe. It is also consistent, though not without irony, that America's emissaries to Eastern Europe would be Coke and Pepsi. The same American and capitalist qualities that once made Coke anathema in Eastern Europe now made it a *cause célèbre*. After all, what was more eager, more adaptable, more nonessential, and more forgiving than Coca-Cola? "A peaceful relationship is more likely to last if we have mutual trade than if countries do not," declared Austin. "I don't mean to say if Coke is engaged in business that the Cold War will suddenly be eliminated, but to some degree it would be lessened."

In 1965, the Cold War was thawed appreciably by an ice-cold soft drink. The Coca-Cola Company signed an agreement with the government of Bulgaria to construct the first Coca-Cola bottling plant behind the Iron Curtain. Protective of their own industry, which featured Boza, a rye-based soft drink and a liquid called Bulger Cola, the Bulgarians initially intended to sell the Coke to tourists. (Previously Bulgaria, like other Eastern European countries, had been importing Coke, primarily from West Germany, for this purpose.) Indeed, prolonged exposure to such phrases as "Vschko Vyrvi Po Doubre S Coke" (Things Go Better with Coke) eventually provoked the curiosity of the Bulgarians themselves.

The following year, Pepsi announced similar deals for local plants with the Rumanian and Yugoslavian governments, stating it was following the "recent recommendations of President Johnson and the Department of Commerce" for trade in nonstrategic products with Eastern Europe. For Donald Kendall, whose ascendancy at Pepsi was assured by his 1959 performance in Moscow, it was a dream coming true. He was one of the first to perceive the potential markets behind the Iron Curtain, and as we shall see in Chapter 13, he would emerge as one of the country's most vociferous proponents of East-West reconciliation.

In 1971, 170 million bottles of Coke were sold in Hungary, Bulgaria, Yugoslavia, and Czechoslovakia, more than triple the total two years earlier. The demand for both drinks kept existing plants running around the clock and prompted the creation of new ones. The proscription of Coca-Cola during "Stalinist times," explained one Hungarian beverage official, was "the best advertising. . . . Because Coca-Cola was forbidden, everyone wanted it." Only two months after Coke's introduction in Poland, Warsaw's largest store was selling 1,500 bottles a day and a second plant was already being planned. Coke's stature was discussed in one newspaper editorial: "This innocent soft drink, which until recently could be found only in encyclopedias, has found its way into almost every home. For many years, Coca-Cola has had a reputation of being the symbol of American life or of repulsive dollar imperialism. . . . It finally reached Poland not as a sinful thing but as the fruit of peaceful coexistence."

The grandeurs of multinational consumer marketing required multinational advertising. Thus, the campaigns pioneered in the United States by Coca-Cola were expanded to global proportions. To project an image recognizable worldwide, ad campaigns employed concepts applicable nearly everywhere. Advertising was constructed with visions and values fundamental to most cultures and engineered to plug into basic human motivations. Market penetration was facilitated by the fact that the target group, the fourteen- to twenty-nine year crowd, were the main consumers of soft drinks virtually worldwide. The messages were always the same, but adapted for local cultures and languages. By exploiting its American origins, Coke was able to inculcate foreign consumers well enough for it to air some of its TV commercials in English in such countries as Germany and Japan. "Coke is a part of the U.S. lifestyle that people everywhere want to emulate to some degree," said Coke's marketing director. "That's one reason why advertising for Coca-Cola looks alike everywhere in the world." What played in Peoria was now a hit behind the Iron Curtain.

The advertising campaigns of Coke and Pepsi were integrated into their general strategy of centralized management and decentralized execution. Coke Export sometimes worked with local advertising agencies, but Pepsi International relied on one worldwide firm, J. Walter Thompson. For example, footage from a Pepsi commercial shot in Hungary would go into a general pool of film shot in a variety of locations. This catalog of thirteen reels would be distributed to J. Walter Thompson offices throughout the world, which would then snip and cut commercials tailored for their particular markets and needs. One reel featured vignettes designed to cut across all age groups; another showed couples in love; a third contained action and sports clips. Commercials constructed from the action/sports shots, for example, were popular in Hungary and the Middle East, where their optical construction and quick dissolves were appreciated. Campaigns were sometimes prepared for special purposes, such as the wooing of wine drinkers in Spain and France and beer drinkers in Denmark and Australia. One 1970 Danish spot showed a fleshy middle-aged man drinking beer at one end of a park bench and in contrast a young "with-it" couple sipped Pepsi at the other.

Both companies would invest the first several months in a new market introducing the drinks and informing the uninitiated to drink them cold, a practice taken for granted by Americans. Thereafter, the market became fair game for their standard promotional wizardry. For example, in 1972, working with a Warsaw ad agency, Coke surged into Poland in its inimitable way. One ad displayed the universal Coke logo with a caption that read, "Cold . . . Wonderful, Incomparably Refreshing. Demand Coca-Cola where you see this sign." Another that ran in the Communist-controlled press featured a blond model clasping a bottle: "It's already in Warsaw—try it and you'll understand why it's being drunk in the world over 150 million times daily." Besides the conventional campaigns, in newspapers, movie houses,* radio, and television, Coke effectively used more improvisational techniques to institutionalize itself. For example, Hungarians began to see the emcee of a favorite television show keep a bottle of Coke on his desk for the entire hour, or hear a pair of comedians gratuitously mention Coke during their act before a packed house at a Budapest stadium. An official explained that these plugs were paid for with a "lot of Coca-Cola," rather than money.

Soon, most of the Communist countries in Europe were "Coca-colonized." In Warsaw, Budapest, Belgrade, Prague, and other cities, Coke's bright red signs and delivery trucks dotted the landscape. For Coke, nothing was too sacred. In Hungary's May Day parade, a traditional display of national solidarity and anti-American propaganda, a big red truck rolled past the crowds bearing a giant Coca Cola bottle. Along its side was a sign that read "A Jeghideg . . . Az Igazi" which means "Ice Cold . . . It's the Real Thing."

In the end, two soft drinks became American capitalism's pioneers in Eastern

---

* Sixty-second commercial spots were screened before the feature film not only in Eastern Europe, but in many societies, particularly where the cinema is much more accessible to the public than television, such as India, Greece, Malaysia, and Turkey.

Europe. "For decades," boasted Austin, "we've been held up as the standard bearer of U.S. business abroad. If I must say so, we've done a jolly good job." Who's to argue that the world wasn't made a little safer though not necessarily saner once Communist bloc countries grew dependent on the same sugar and flavoring solutions that have bewitched everyone else?

Both companies understood that the logical course of soft-drink diplomacy led to the Kremlin itself. Yet U.S. interaction with the Soviet Union would be carefully orchestrated by Presidential initiative. Due to his disastrous Vietnam War policy, L.B.J. was in no position to commence such a dialogue. Thus, rapprochement would occur through Johnson's successor, who would also decide whose logo would adorn Red Square.

The highly industrialized economies of Eastern Europe did not falter under the weight of Coke and Pepsi. The cash outflow of these operations was not as critical, and because all were state-owned, the indigenous soft-drink industries were not devastated. Furthermore, neither drink was imposed upon populations that were unwitting or unsophisticated. Eastern Europeans were eager for consumer goods and could afford them. However, despite their enthusiasm and professed good intentions, Coke and Pepsi often have a regrettably negative effect on less developed countries and nowhere was this more apparent than in Latin America.

Ever since its colonial days, the United States has laid a special claim on Latin America. First formalized in 1823 as the Monroe Doctrine, it declared America's self-ordained right to unilateral intervention in Latin American affairs. During the nineteenth century, when America's economy had outgrown its internal market, the United States turned to the Caribbean for raw materials and cheap labor upon which its businesses could feast. In the name of peace, prosperity, and local self-determination, American interests began to develop a continent-wide hegemony. Local economies were kept safe and submissive under foreign ownership through the support of iron-fisted regimes, economic and diplomatic pressures, and the threat of military intervention. The close relationship between America's foreign policy and private economic interests was best articulated in the remarkable boast by Major General Smedley Butler of the U.S. Marine Corps: "I helped make Mexico and especially Tampico safe for American oil interests in 1914. I helped make Haiti and Cuba a decent place for the National City Bank boys to collect revenue in. I helped purify Nicaragua for the international banking house of Brown Brothers from 1909 to 1912. I brought light to the Dominican Republic for American sugar interests in 1916. I helped make Honduras 'right' for American fruit companies in 1903. . . ."

Latin America became the breadbasket of the American empire, a relationship that was preserved during the twentieth century. During World War II, Coca-Cola played its part in protecting the regimes from the Axis powers by representing U.S. efforts to befriend and support certain ruling elites, like Brazil's Getulio Vargas. After World War II, European investments, particularly British, declined tremendously, thus making the U.S. the clearly prevailing force in the region. New international institutions, such as the World Bank and the International Monetary Fund helped finance vast social improvements like transportation and utilities. Overseen by the U.S., these institutions pressured client countries to provide free access for foreign investors. Thus, foreign aid became an effective instrument of the American economic system, as U.S. investors were able to diversify their holdings from extra active industries like mining and petroleum to manufacturing and consumer products.

By the late forties, American hegemony was threatened by the specter of Communism. Any threat to the status quo, particularly protests against Yankee imperialism, was perceived by U.S. interests as exclusively communist inspired. For example, mild social reforms implemented by Colonel Jacobo Arbenz Guzmán in Guatemala provoked the United States to brand him a communist, which provided the moral and political justification for his CIA-triggered overthrow in 1954.

Cuba was both the archetype and the nemesis of America's Latin American policy. After the Spanish were ousted in 1898, Washington imposed a constitution upon the Cuban people including a measure called the Platt Amendment which followed the Monroe Doctrine in allowing the U.S. to intervene, militarily if necessary, in the affairs of the island. Thus, a stable environment for American businesses was assured, and the amount of U.S. investments on the island boomed.

For Coca-Cola and other companies, Cuba was the first step toward overseas empires. American interests came to dominate the island's economy and disproportionately shifted it to the production of sugar. Soon, Cuba became the main source of sugar for North America, and undoubtedly, Coca-Cola. For years Cuban society was subjugated by repressive, American-supported regimes as well as religious proselytizing such as Warren Candler's Methodist crusades. Neo-colonial subservience clearly undermined the well-being of most Cubans, and in 1959, a popular revolt led by a young lawyer named Fidel Castro finally overthrew the cruel rule of President Fulgencio Batista. Although he had not initially avowed communism, Castro's strong sense of nationalism and intended social reforms gravely concerned U.S. corporate and political elites. When he began to nationalize American assets, the U.S. responded with economic sanctions and then a blockade in the hope that the economic chaos would topple him. Out of necessity, Castro successfully replaced Western markets and financing with backing from the Soviet Union.

The so-called "loss" of Cuba in 1960 was a blow for the American interests, particularly those dependent on the sugar trade. For the Coca-Cola Company, it also meant the loss of five bottling plants then valued at $2,100,000 and a handsome profit estimated at $300,000. Yet, more than just the loss of business and sugar, Cuba represented a successful challenge to American hegemony and, consequently, a failure of foreign policy. America's rulers realized, and rightly so, that Castro's blend of nationalism and socialism could spread throughout Latin

America by peoples weary of political and economic oppression. Consequently, American interests reacted sharply to the Cuban revolution.

When economic isolation failed to undermine Castro, full-scale military intervention was plotted during the last days of the Eisenhower administration under the scrutiny of Vice-President Richard Nixon in concert with the CIA. Though unenthusiastically received by the Kennedy administration, plans called for repeated guerrilla raids to soften up the island for an invasion by anti-Castro Cubans organized, financed, trained, and equipped by the U.S. government. Despite the prodigious efforts, the attack on Cuba at the Bay of Pigs in April of 1961 was a total failure. The CIA underestimated Castro's charisma and popular support, and 1,178 invaders, most of the Bay of Pigs brigade, were captured by Castro's forces. These men were later ransomed by the U.S. for $62 million, and Coke Export's Jim Farley was one of 52 prestigious Americans who formed an ad hoc committee to raise the funds.

The humiliation of the Bay of Pigs stiffened the resolve of the CIA and certain economic interests, including those of Richard Nixon and organized crime. In a remote section of the University of Miami campus, the CIA developed a small army with which to launch further commando raids to destroy the island's underpinnings such as power stations and sugar refineries. Code-named JM Wave, this campaign was thinly veiled behind a "front" corporation called Zenith Technical Enterprises. Again, Coke took an apparent interest as Lindsay Hopkins, a director of the Coca-Cola Company joined the company's board of directors.*

An aficionado and owner of Indianapolis 500 race cars, which would later be sponsored by the Coca-Cola Company, Hopkins owned a fortune in Miami real estate, and later Bahamian developments. Were it not for the fact that his father had been a director of Coke, he might just as well have wound up at Pepsi. He was an associate of William Pawley in the founding of the Flying Tigers and Civil Air Transport (CAT), the precursor of the CIA's proprietary in Southeast Asia, Air America.† An officer in Hopkins' realty investment interests was president of Sea Supply Corporation, which joined with some of CAT's 1950 airlifts to Chiang Kai-shek's troops.‡ Sea Supply's founder, Paul Helliwell, was a veteran of the "old boy" spy network who regularly bought information with bags of opium during World War II. He was reputed to be one of the paymasters of the Bay of Pigs operation as well as other CIA forays throughout Latin America. His law partner was counsel and director to a company created by Charles Allen and Wallace Groves to succeed the Grand Bahama Authority.§ Whether or not Coke realized it, Hopkins was an important link to the murky network where legitimate business, intelligence operations, and organized crime overlapped.

* Hopkins' father had been a director of Coca-Cola as well as North American Aviation and the Sperry Corporation
    † Scott, *The War Conspiracy*, op. cit., p. 211
    ‡ Scott, ibid., p. 210-211
    § *Wall Street Journal*, April 18, 1980, p. 1. *The New York Times*, November 28, 1976, III:1 (see Chapter 10)

Coke personnel fought on the field as well as from the suites. In 1958, Manuel Orcarberro Rodriguez left the Manzarillo Coca-Cola plant in Cuba where he was general manager to work with Castro's rebel forces in the Escambray Mountains. At that time, many American interests were supporting both Batista and Castro to assure future government cooperation regardless of the victor. In this vein, Rodriguez introduced Castro to American soldier-of-fortune Frank Sturgis. A warrior from the obfuscated world of intelligence and organized crime, Sturgis fought alongside Castro, some say as a spy for stateside interests, and was eventually rewarded with an influential position in Castro's government. After the revolution, Rodriguez returned to his Coke plant, though he found only brief respite from political intrigue. Rodriguez, Sturgis, and other supporters turned bitterly against Castro once he began to rebuff American interests. Sturgis allied himself with the CIA's campaigns, particularly guerrilla raids against the island and plots to assassinate the Cuban premier. For all of his cowboy escapades, he wouldn't reach the public's attention until 1972, when he and a team of anti-Castro veterans known as the White House Plumbers were caught burglarizing the Democratic National Headquarters. Rodriguez too apparently began to scheme against Castro from his Coke plant and was forced eventually to seek refuge in the Brazilian Embassy in Havana before escaping to the U.S. in 1960. Rodriguez then became a leader of Alpha 66, one of the most violent Cuban exile groups whose hatred for Castro was perhaps only equaled by its disdain for President Kennedy. They and others felt betrayed by Kennedy's growing intolerance of the anti-Castro war, particularly after the Missile Crisis of 1962. Undeterred by White House opposition, Alpha 66 (working with the CIA and other reactionary groups) harassed Cuba with such exploits as the shelling of Russian freighters in Cuban waters. Rodriguez headed the Dallas chapter of Alpha 66 which drew the attention of federal investigators for alleged illicit gun purchases and threats against President Kennedy. Alpha 66's threats surfaced during the Warren Commission's probe of Kennedy's murder, but these and other incidents drew only scant attention from authorities.*

Such activities undoubtedly influenced Castro's growing conviction that Coca-Cola was indeed the epitome of U.S. imperialism. To spite Coke, according to one source, he handed over its nationalized plants to the Pepsi-Cola interests still operating in Cuba. Although Pepsi's trucks were allegedly used by Castro and his guerrillas in their major movement out of the Escambray, and sky-writing bi-planes emblazoned "Pepsi-Cola" across lazy Havana skies fifteen years earlier, Castro was wrong if he thought Pepsi's antipathy toward Coke would ever render it an ally of his government.

Robert Geddes Morton, a Pepsi-Cola vice-president who headed the company's bottling operations in Cuba, was the leader of a major component of the anti-Castro underground, and a principal contact in the CIA's invasion plan. A British national and one of the youngest vice-presidents at Pepsi, Morton trav-

* George Michael Evica, *And We Are Mortal* (West Hartford, Connecticut: University of Hartford, 1978) cf. Warren Commission Document 1085

eled freely between Havana, Miami, and New York without ever arousing suspicion. According to a former Ford Foundation fellow who claimed to have met Morton in Brazil in 1969, Morton was able to infiltrate the high naval command, the most aristocratic and pro-American sector of Castro's military, who were going to join the rebel forces once the invasion was launched.* Moreover, Morton, who is alleged by this source to have been part of a CIA plot to assassinate Fidel Castro prior to the invasion, was actually intending to use Pepsi's eight plants (and the disenfranchised Coke operations) as a base of operations for his small band of 107 commandos some of whose maneuvers were to be undertaken in Pepsi-Cola trucks. Because of a Castro infiltrator and the Kennedy administration's delays, Morton was captured, tried, and imprisoned until the British government secured his release in February 1963.

Castro's success threatened American investments throughout Central and South America, and the Kennedy administration responded with the Alliance for Progress, a strategy, critics argued, designed more to impede revolutions than to spark progress. It differed in style if not intent from previous directions in that it sought Latin American prosperity through a "partnership" of U.S. foreign aid and multinationals with native wealth. This collaboration sought to implement "self-help" programs, relying on both Yankee and local resources, to develop viable consumer classes and curb aspiring Castros. Domestic tranquillity would be further assured by continued weapons sales and foreign aid, in exchange for guarantees by host regimes against the nationalization of foreign assets. The gunboat diplomacy of yore, now too heavy-handed, was deemphasized for American sponsored, locally implemented counterinsurgency and counterintelligence programs. In 1963, several years after the rise of Castro, Secretary of Defense Robert McNamara articulated this tactic: "Until about 1960, military assistance programs for Latin America were oriented toward hemispheric defense. As it became clear that there was no threat of significant overt external aggression against Latin America, emphasis shifted to internal security. . . ." "Internal security" here is just a euphemism for the prevention of protests and rebellions.

Coke and Pepsi had a vested interest in this whole process. As manufacturers of mass appeal, nonessential products, they were concerned with social tranquillity and consequently joined other corporations in the pursuit of what is traditionally known as enlightened self-interest. For example, both were members of the nonprofit Council on Latin America, one of several privately sponsored, quasi-official organizations created to enhance the region's stability while improving the image of American business locally. Acknowledged by the U.S. government as the "chief spokesman" for U.S. firms in Latin America, the council was created in 1965 through the merger of several other business associations to serve as a go-between for corporate interests and America's foreign policy apparatus. It was founded and chaired by the chairman of the Chase Manhattan

---

* Morton's participation in the invasion as well as his position with Pepsi were confirmed in a post-invasion memorial to the Bay of Pigs veterans by John Martino in *I Was Castro's Prisoner* (New York: Devin-Adair, 1963). p. 195–201

Bank, David Rockefeller, whose family and bank had tremendous stakes in Latin America. Donald Kendall was a vice-chairman of the council, which had over two hundred corporate members, including Coke Export and Pepsi International. Other members included the colas' respective Latin American advertising agencies, McCann-Erickson and J. Walter Thompson, and other stars within their orbits such as Morgan Guaranty and General Electric on the one hand, and two other companies whose boards Kendall subsequently served—Atlantic Richfield and Pan-Am.

Within context of the Alliance for Progress, it comes as no surprise that within a few years, Pepsi could shift its approach from a desperate guerrilla war in Cuba to a more refined form of interventionism as exemplified by its support of Accion International, frequently referred to as a private Peace Corps. Accion International was modeled after a pilot program called Accion Venezuela. Founded in 1960 by Joseph Blatchford, a young law student who participated in a USIA-sponsored tennis tour of Latin America, the program was a response to Vice-President Richard Nixon's 1958 trip to Venezuela where he was stoned and nearly engulfed by angry anti-American protesters. With the help of Eugene Burdick, author of *The Ugly American,* Blatchford created Accion [Americans for Community Cooperation in Other Nations] as a goodwill vehicle for American business. In Venezuela, generous private interests funded scores of bright, young volunteers who were dispatched to provide technical assistance and self-help programs for rural and urban slums.

Besides hosting the Accion program, Venezuela was perhaps the only country in the hemisphere where Pepsi-Cola outsold Coca-Cola, and by a wide margin. This demonstration of Coke's fallibility was engineered by an aggressive, highly dynamic Pepsi bottler, Diego Cisneros, who parlayed his holdings into a small industrial empire. Assisting him was the PepsiCo international chief for Venezuela and Colombia, Michael Lvoff, a descendant of White Russian aristocracy who was known by at least one observer as "the Count." Like other astute overseas bottlers who share a concern for their societies' purchasing power, the industrious Venezuelan bottler became one of the premier patrons of Accion Venezuela providing money and donating buckets of Pepsi, while the local Coke franchise, a smaller concern, was allegedly "stingy" with Accion.

In 1965, with Accion Venezuela underway, Blatchford and company incorporated Accion International to replicate the program in other Latin American countries. In Brazil, after the 1964 military takeover; in the Dominican Republic following the 1965 uprising; and elsewhere, Accion International enhanced the domestic stability by depoliticizing the barrios and other potentially volatile areas. Don Kendall, who was undoubtedly introduced to Accion in Venezuela, must have appreciated the possibilities of such social intercession in his markets, for he involved himself as the chairman of Accion International's first board of directors. PepsiCo International would become one of Accion's many corporate supporters, contributing right up to the present, even after Kendall stepped down to become an honorary director. Accion would later turn to more sophis-

ticated programs with the creation of small local businesses to assimilate populations into the free enterprise tradition. Said Kendall: "Business grows more in a
social climate of peace, productivity, and human satisfaction. Any investment in
any business that creates this climate is an investment for our own benefit."

Accion appealed to the interventionist instincts of the supporters of Richard
Nixon, including Yankees like the Rockefellers. Other supporters of Accion were
"Uncle" Elmer Bobst's Warner-Lambert Co., and the Atlantic-Richfield Co.
Secretary for Accion was Milton C. Rose, the semi-retired senior partner of
Nixon, Mudge, Rose, PepsiCo International's law firm, as well as a director of
Warner-Lambert and a trustee of the Fairfield Foundation, an alleged conduit
of CIA funds. Other sponsors included the American Institute for Free Labor
(AIFLD), a business, labor, and government coalition created in 1961 to ward
off Communist infiltration into the Latin American labor movement, and the
Ottinger Foundation, both of which have been suspected as CIA conduits. Another contributor was the Creole Foundation, a branch of the Creole Petroleum
Corp. of Venezuela, which is an affiliate of the Rockefellers' Standard Oil. Creole's Cuban refinery was among the first properties nationalized by Cuba, precipitating the falling out between the United States and Castro.

An offshoot of Accion was the Latin American Teaching Fellowship (LATF),
founded in 1966 to upgrade Latin American universities. Also funded by the
Latin American offices of Coke, Pepsi, and other MNCs, LATF sent American,
European, and Japanese professors to the region's schools on fellowship programs. According to an organizer, its corporate supporters chose to pollinate
ideas consistent with their own interests, and occasionally used the program to
finance academics specifically for their own purposes. For example, the
Pepsi/Frito-Lay office in Mexico City funneled money through LATF to import
an industrial psychologist from Purdue who consulted for the company when
not teaching courses at a local university.

Despite some achievements by private sector programs such as Accion and
LATF, the overall success of such programs is questionable since they were intended to serve two often irreconcilable masters: indigenous underdeveloped
populations and U.S. multinational corporations. In spite of bountiful American
aid, grass roots political movements and anti-imperialist rebellions have persisted
in the region.

As custodians of American culture, Coke and Pepsi have long been conspicuous targets for such protests, especially in those societies most polarized by a lack
of political dialogue. In 1974, for example, several of their plants in Mexico were
targeted for terrorist bombs, and one Pepsi plant was actually stormed by political extremists. That year, a Pepsi executive was kidnapped in Buenos Aires.

Coke decided to fight back in 1973 when leftist guerrillas threatened to kidnap the head of Argentina's Coke operations if the company failed to donate
one million dollars to charity. Coke's dilemma was severe, particularly since
Buenos Aires was virtually Coke's single largest regional market worldwide. The
threatened Coke executive hurried to Atlanta to confer with his superiors and a

confidential meeting ensued at the home of Coke International boss Claus Halle, attended by Mitchell Livingston Werbell, III. An acquaintance of Coke's Lindsay Hopkins, who was involved with the war-time intelligence exploits of Paul Helliwell (and those of Watergate burglar E. Howard Hunt), Mitch, as he is known, has served as a consultant on counterinsurgency tactics and a supplier of ultra-sophisticated small arms for the CIA, Third World military regimes, and any other clients with money and a hostility to communism. On his estate in Powder Springs, Georgia, a half hour drive from Atlanta, he runs a school for anti-communist, guerrilla-style warfare and, over the years, has demonstrated an expertise in his craft that earned him the epithet, "Wizard of Whispering Death." Living up to his larger-than-life image, Mitch prefers a simpler title, "The War Lover."

Upon arriving in Argentina with an associate, Mitch ordered all Coca-Cola executives out of the country and carefully combed the local headquarters for bugs and other surveillance devices. As he retells it, he met with local police and intelligence agencies as well as the U.S. ambassador for information and to brief them on his plans. His soda pop mission was considered serious enough for local authorities to provide him with twenty-four-hour bodyguards. He announced to the rebels that Coke wouldn't ransom any kidnapped official for any price, not even "ten cents." Should they persevere, Mitch warned, "We will go after you. We will kill you. We'll go after your wife. We'll kill her. We'll go after your children. We'll kill them . . . your cats, your dogs, your pigs, and chickens." Mitch later says that his threat was somewhat exaggerated. He devised extra security precautions for the Coke personnel and returned to his farm, where he was handsomely rewarded in "Georgia Green," his nickname for money. Though the extortion threats ceased, the rebels possibly chose another tack, as a Coke warehouse and seven other foreign-held properties were bombed one day in 1974.

Coke refuses to comment on its choice of consultant or on his tactics. Mitch has worked for other corporations, though he insists this foray was his only one for Coke. His proximity to Atlanta has exposed him socially to a variety of Coke people, including Lindsay Hopkins. Both men served in the CIA's covert war against Fidel Castro in the late fifties and early sixties where Mitch provided tactical assistance in the field. A former business partner of Mitch's was Bennet Bintliff, the head of the Atlanta-based Zeta Co. which, according to one newspaper account, specialized in "ongoing military activities against communists." Bennet is the nephew of David Bintliff, Charles Duncan's former associate, who though allied with similar right wing causes in Cuba and elsewhere, regards Bennet, in Mitch's words, as the "black sheep of his family."

Showing no partisanship in the cola field, Mitch asserts he was friendly with Pepsi's Al Steele, a kindred spirit of sorts, and some of Pepsi's bottlers. With a chuckle, Mitch recalls that his only direct contact with Pepsi operations came in 1965 when he was hired to help quell a popular uprising in the Dominican Republic. While flying a mission over Santiago, one of his private B-29 bombers mistook the enemy and inadvertently "wiped out" a herd of goats and the local Pepsi-Cola bottling plant. "The War Lover" and his associates were forced to make reparations.

Coca-Cola does not usually resort to hiring swashbuckling mercenaries when difficulties arise abroad. Although Mitch suspects that Coke may have relied on Intertel at one time—a powerful, intrigue-ridden private intelligence agency owned by Resorts International—he claims that Coke "plays it pretty straight" overseas. Yet there is historical irony whenever a Coca-Cola or anyone else uses a Mitch Werbell to cope with revolts: rebels, especially those on the left, frequently act in protest of the self-serving regimes installed and maintained with the creative help of America's Smedley Butlers and Mitch Werbells.

Political terrorism is generally symptomatic of greater social ills. The foreign presence of MNC's is justified by Kendall, Austin, and other proponents who claim they provide the capital and technology, as well as tax revenue, to stimulate a country's industrialization and productivity which, in turn, provide growth. While such is arguably the case within developed nations, it hardly reflects the realities of lesser developed countries where accelerated industrialization and productivity have not always benefitted the public welfare. Investments overseas are useful only if they eventually return more money—ideally substantially more—in the form of profits, fees, dividends, royalties. Despite their short term influxes of investment capital, MNCs frequently drain host economies of capital, an effect that is particularly crippling to poorer countries with balance of payment deficits.* Consequently, to remain solvent, governments are forced to borrow from Western banks, increasing their debt and dependence on foreign institutions. Even when profits are reinvested locally, which is what PepsiCo does with 20 percent of its foreign earnings according to Kendall, the money will eventually be repatriated to the United States for even greater profit. Precautions taken by host countries to protect their money supply only make the route home more circuitous for profits. For example, in Turkey, which sharply curtails the remittances of foreign earnings, Pepsi invests its Turkish earnings in a local glass plant, sells the glass to a third nation, which in turn compensates Pepsi rather than the Turkish plant.

Meanwhile, the Coca-Cola Trading Company sells tomato paste from Turkey, honey from Colombia, cashews from Brazil, pineapple juice from Indonesia, mineral water from Bulgaria, beer from Poland, and a dozen other products. This service is useful when countries, such as those in Eastern Europe, offer only barter for concentrate rather than cash. This approach requires innovative solutions, such as developing a commercial shrimp farm in Mexico, or learning quickly about a variety of businesses. "If you want to learn about oriental rugs," says Jerome Vielehr, former president of Aqua-Chem and now president of Coke's trading company, "go buy an oriental rug. If you want to learn about the

* According to a 1973 United Nations report, the inflow of direct investments into a sample of developing countries from 1965 to 1970 was only 68 percent of the income outflow. For 1970 alone, the countries examined lost $3.7 billion.

beer business, go buy a million cases of beer." In effect, Coke and Pepsi have capitalized on their customers' problems while trying to solve them. In the long run, the companies stand to make a double profit—once on the concentrate, or syrup going into a country, and once on the goods they will sell coming out. "I wouldn't be part of it if it didn't involve profit," declared Vielehr.

The Latin American peasant, living off a subsistence wage, if employed at all, has less reason to regularly buy a Coke or Pepsi than the middle-class youths of North America. Yet, he, his family, and his whole barrio are potential customers just as meaningful to the profit motive as the relatively small Latin American middle and upper classes. As thirst knows no season, it knows no class. Though just two of many MNCs peddling their consumer wares in underdeveloped nations, the Coca-Cola Company and PepsiCo market products in a way that makes everyone, including the poor, believe they are both desirable and affordable in large quantities. With products originally intended for middle classes, Coke and Pepsi have used their formidable powers of persuasion to create faithful consumers out of the poorest people.

In order to sell less than essential goods, a consumerist ideology is overlaid on host cultures, subsuming local values and visions to those of the Western corporations. As applied anywhere else, it is an ideology predicated on material values and larger-than-life images, distorting indigenous cultural identities in the process. "Ours is the first generation," commented a Mexican writer about consumer advertising, "to be foreigners in our own country." Most defenseless are the poor, the unsophisticated, the disenfranchised, who are unable to perceive the sophistry of the equation consumption equals happiness. They are all too willing to be convinced that just for a moment—the duration of a Coca-Cola for example—they can taste a lifestyle they'll never have. As the Church offered the poor redemption in the hereafter, consumerism promises psychic gratification in the here and now. "Consumer democracy," as suggested by the Council on the Americas, an outgrowth of the Council on Latin America, "is more important than political democracy."

What little communication media exist in Latin America have been invoked to propagandize the myths of Western products in local idioms. For as the American consumer giants sought to broaden markets in Latin America, their advertising agencies followed, becoming multinational themselves. By 1971, Coke's McCann-Erickson earned 61 percent of its profits overseas, and Pepsi's J. Walter Thompson 52 percent. Between them, they had 56 percent of the billings in Latin America in 1970. In the four countries where U.S. investments were most concentrated—Argentina, Brazil, Mexico, and Venezuela—54 percent of all major advertising agencies were U.S. owned or affiliated.

Successful advertising mediates beween extremes, even if the mediation is contrived and the extremes grotesquely disparate. In studying the effects of advertising, a Venezuelan professor and consultant on "social communication" for McCann-Erickson and J. Walter Thompson has repeatedly confirmed that the very poor have "lost their perception of class differences . . . but all have access to the same consumer goods." That is, they may be aware of society's enormous inequalities, but this awareness is surpassed by the tantalizing (but he neglects to mention, often futile) sense of its enormous possibilities. In other words, consumer advertising tends to tantalize poor people with the tastes of the good life, thus promoting values that obscure their best interests by providing immediate gratification.

The publication of the I.M.F. and the World Bank, *Finance and Development* (June 1979), reported that one-third of all Latin Americans suffer from malnutrition. Yet, according to a specialist writing in *Advertising Age*,* "The conventional range of ideas about what will minister to the poor man's needs are obsolete. The psychological significance of his spending his money on a transistor radio may be more important than the physical benefit generated by spending the same money for basic foodstuffs." Therein lies the justification for persuading poor people to aspire to Western luxuries like transistor radios, or more affordable gratifications like soft drinks. Poor people always find enough money for a Coke or Pepsi, though the psychological significance and the cultural identification associated with either is an ephemeral satisfaction for the impoverished consumer. As a Coke franchise distracts local capital from socially beneficial purposes, so does a Coke distract a poor man's pennies from needed nutrition.

In Mexico, for example, where malnutrition is an open wound, Coke and Pepsi have met with great success.† They have helped swell total soft-drink consumption to over 12 billion bottles a year, and can boast of more than 115 bottling plants between them. Coca-Cola Export alone owns over 40 percent of the entire Mexican market, and for Pepsi it is the largest market outside of the United States. With relentless advertising and exploitation of the culture, such as the giant Coca-Cola bottle that "dances" for the crowds before bullfights in Mexico City, both companies have created loyal customers even within the poorest classes.‡ "Coca-Cola in every way is Mexican," asserted a local executive. Joaquin Cravioto, noted nutrition specialist, observed that the two products most desired by Mexican peasants after being exposed to advertising are white bread and soft drinks. For many villages, soft drinks have become a status symbol and are frequently served with meals. Nationwide, 74 percent of all Pepsi is consumed at mealtime. In one village of six thousand, where the average daily income ranges from $2.00 to $5.60—high by neighboring standards—four thousand bottles of soft drinks are consumed every day. Writes a Mexican priest of his remote region: "The great majority of people are convinced that soft drinks must be consumed every day. This is mainly due to extensive advertising, especially on the radio which is so widespread in the mountains. . . . In the meantime, in these same villages, natural products such as fruit are consumed less—in some families just once a week. Other families sell their own natural

* September 22, 1969, p. 64

† As have other corporate brethren. According to a 1974 survey by the Mexican government, Gerber sells 80 percent of all baby food, Carnation sells 85 percent of all evaporated milk, and Kellogg sells 95 percent of all cereals.

‡ This and other examples and quotes used in the Mexico/Brazil discussion are from Robert J. Ledogar, *Hungry for Profits* (New York: IDOC, No. America, 1975)

products in order to buy soft drinks." Furthermore, the aforementioned specialist in *Advertising Age* noted: "It has long been known that in the poorest regions of Mexico where soft drinks play a fundamental role in the diet, it is the international brands—Coke and Pepsi—not the local brands which dominate."* Among peoples whose needs are already great, Coke and Pepsi create another need.

Brazil is a case study of the soft-drink experience in Latin America. Although Brazil's soft-drink market has never equaled Mexico's, it has enjoyed a variety of fruit-flavored drinks supplied by a healthy indigenous industry. The most popular flavor was guarana, derived from the chestnut-like seed of the guarana bush found in the Amazon basin. Guarana provided the consumer with a pleasant taste and a little kick from the natural caffeine within the seed. With several national firms and scores of regional ones producing guarana, the industry as a whole cruised along at its own pace until a momentous day in 1942. That year, as detailed in Chapter 4, Coca-Cola entered Brazil through the back door of an American foreign policy initiative designed to keep the region safe from Nazi influence. Coke came with a little influence of its own, and with help from General Getulio Vargas, Brazil's dictator, and Jim Farley, Coke's entry was greased by favorable tax legislation and a law permitting chemical compounds in soft drinks such as phosphoric acid, an essential ingredient of Coke.† With its slick marketing, Coke first took hold in Rio de Janeiro, and then other urban centers.

The arrival of the pushy Yankee brew hardly went unnoticed by the guarana producers. Presumably, they were behind a ban on phosphoric acid issued by the government at São Paulo in 1946. When this failed to stem the tide, the beer and soft-drink trade association lobbied in 1948 for an investigation into Coca-Cola's preferential treatment by the government. It was disclosed, for example, that from 1945 to 1948, Coke's specially lowered tax rate saved it over a million dollars. Two years later, a government study of soft drinks was released. While claiming that none were beneficial to one's health, it stressed the high caffeine content of Coca-Cola, five times that of guarana products and twice that of maté tea, and prompted the director of the study to warn that Coca-Cola, "if consumed to excess, may be damaging, particularly to those with a sensitive organism, like children and teenagers. . . ." He added that "It is necessary to regulate the consumption of soft drinks . . . or even restrict their intake by children and other groups. . . . Furthermore, if the manufacturers go so far as to disobey our food regulations and offer to the ignorant consumer products which are direct health hazards, the problem goes beyond the authority of the scientist and becomes a police case."

Coke's presence was charmed, for the proscription on phosphoric acid quietly

---

* Foreign drinks account for three quarters of all sales. To help the local industry, the government levied huge taxes on foreign soft drinks—as much as 40 percent of the retail price. Ironically, a major benefactor was General Foods' powdered Kool-Aid, until it too was taxed. To ward off further efforts to discourage foreign drinks, Coke began to export Mexican-produced goods in the mid-seventies in order to help the country's balance of payments.

† According to *The New York Times* and *Fortune* magazine, another ingredient of Coca-Cola is a liquid extract of guarana.

vanished from the books in 1952. However, the governor of São Paulo considered Coca-Cola a police case, and in 1955, closed down the local Coke plant citing the same ideas that had precipitated the old 1946 ban. But Coke's demise was not to be. A court ruled in its favor and Coca-Cola continued its relentless pursuit of growth.

For the next several decades, as modernity swept through Brazil, so did Coca-Cola. As soon as the roads were paved, and quite frequently before, Coke spread to Brazil's hinterlands. Its Fanta flavors were successfully introduced to pummel the fruit drinks, and one by one, many of the regional bottlers succumbed to the competition between Coke and the national guarana manufacturers. As soft-drink consumption soared within the booming Brazilian economy, no drink was winning over the pesos of Brazilians as quickly as Coca-Cola. In Brazil, said Donald Keough, then an executive vice-president for Coke, "you have a developed country, a developing country, and an undeveloped country. The only thing that's going to hold back our growth there for the next several decades is going to be a lack of machinery, trucks, and equipment."

Coke's add-and-stir production provided a much greater profit margin than the guarana drinks, allowing for a higher rate of investment in advertising and marketing. Coupled with its incessant promotional techniques, time-tested at the expense of other markets, Coke slowly eroded guarana's share of the market and displaced the traditional beverages such as beer, coffee, juices, and mineral water, particularly at mealtime.

The challenge to Coca-Cola seldom arises from local industry. In fact, throughout the business world, the only private entity capable of competing head-on with a multinational corporation is another multinational, which in the case of Coke is inevitably its worldwide nemesis, Pepsi-Cola. In 1952, two years into Al Steele's reign at the home office, Pepsi pushed into Brazil like a David in search of his Goliath. Sales in neighboring Argentina had leveled off, and in order to maintain its global growth rate, Pepsi entered Brazil along the southern border, established a beachhead, and began to flow throughout the nation.

By 1967, Rio de Janiero was the last fortress of Coke's cola monopoly in Brazil, and Pepsi's largest single untapped market in the non-Communist world. But Coke's Rio franchise was directly owned and operated by Coke International and was so entrenched that Pepsi's eighteen Brazilian bottlers feared to challenge it. Frustrated, the parent company was on the verge of financing its own franchise when Diego Cisneros from Venezuela, where Pepsi owns 60 percent of the market, volunteered for the task. Pepsi rallied its forces and marched into Rio with all the subtlety of a Mardi Gras. A parade, complete with three dance bands, bulging bathing beauties, and a truckload of free Pepsi rolled raucously down Rio's main boulevards. It was followed by two black-tie dinners, a plant opening with the usual pomp, ceremony, and government dignitaries, and ten days of hammering by Pepsi's armored division—Joan Crawford. When the dust had settled and the last bottle cap was cleaned off the streets, Pepsi too had found itself a new growth market.

In Brazil and elsewhere, the prime target of the message is youth. Long-time sales are best achieved by indoctrinating young consumers. "Over 65 percent of the population is under twenty-five years old," explained a Pepsi advertising man in 1974. "A man sixty years old today doesn't like Pepsi or Coke, but the young, they will start drinking now and will never stop, to the end of their lives." At that time, Coke was using a slogan that translated to "This Is It." "It was," claimed a Coke account executive for McCann-Erickson, Brazil's largest ad agency, "our way of saying 'It's the Real Thing.' " Playing catch-up ball, Pepsi was investing a disproportionate amount of money, as much as $2 million for a four-month campaign, into a variation of "The Pepsi Generation." For Brazilians, the theme was presented as "The Pepsi Revolution," ironic considering Brazil's repressive, anti-revolutionary government. Pepsi's ad man explains: "In this country the youth don't have protest channels; the present generation didn't receive any political or social education. So we provide them with a mechanism for protest. It is protest through consumption; the teenager changes from the old-fashioned Coca-Cola and adopts Pepsi, the Pepsi with a young and new image, and he is happy, because he is young and young people drink Pepsi." They planted their seeds well, for according to one nutritional study of children from a variety of economic classes in Rio, Coca-Cola was most popular, followed by Pepsi, Fanta grape and orange, and then guarana, their father's favorite. Furthermore, milk was found to be in disfavor. In effect, political expression had been sublimated for consumerist expression, enabling the young consumer to realize his social identity within the marketplace.

The effect of such logic on the country's dietary patterns is dramatic. By 1979, Brazilians were quaffing fifty-six million bottles of soft drinks a day, making Brazil the world's fifth largest soft-drink market, behind only the United States, West Germany, Mexico, and Japan. With fifty-one franchises, Coke and Fanta control over half of this market, having easily surpassed the guarana drinks whose collective share has declined to 27 percent. Pepsi's share is approaching 10 percent and still growing.

Yet Brazil's per capita consumption for 1978 was only 102 eight-ounce bottles, hardly a saturated market by Coke and Pepsi standards. By contrast, that year, Argentina's consumption was 178, of which 58 percent were Coke products and roughly one-fifth Pepsi; Mexico's consumption was 254, of which nearly half was Coke, and one-fifth Pepsi; and Venezuela's consumption was 279, of which only 14 percent belonged to Coke and nearly 60 percent to Pepsi. Thus, their next phase is to elevate their products from leisure-time beverages to essential ones. For example, they will stress take-home consumption, and try to displace coffee in office buildings and all liquids at every meal. Partly because of the very high illiteracy rate, TV has become an increasingly popular commercial medium reaching down to low-income industrial and agricultural workers and the very poor in shantytowns. They feature old American shows and serials as well as soft-drink advertising, which propagates Western culture. Only by winning over the poorer classes, an inordinately large part of Brazil's population, can Coke and Pepsi reach the 200+ per capita consumption of Mexico. A local Coca-Cola director explains: "High-income people are accustomed to soft drinks already and their preferences are well defined. But the overall rate of consumption is still very low in this country. . . . This is why we keep prices down."

The ironies of marketing nutritionally impotent consumer products to malnutritioned, politically impotent peoples do not go unnoticed. The Interfaith Center on Corporate Responsibility, sponsored by the National Council of Churches, found that many Third World babies were fed their formula from Coke bottles, because baby bottles were too expensive, or that a form of malnutrition in Africa is called the Fanta syndrome because it is related to excessive consumption of soft drinks. Nowhere are the ironies as great as in Brazil. Brazil's 1970 to 1971 grape harvest produced a *surplus* of 200,000 metric tons, yet Fanta's popular grape drink contained no grape juice. The country is also one of the world's larger exporters of orange juice (two buyers were Coke's Snow Crop and Minute Maid), yet Fanta orange and Crush contained hardly any orange juice. A 1970 study conducted in São Paulo revealed that all but upper-class families had vitamin C deficiencies, with those in the poorer class suffering the most serious lack. In fact, the aforementioned study in Rio found many vitamin deficiencies even in the children of the upper classes.

By the mid-sixties, Coke began to ponder its role in human ecology. "We had had discussions," recounted Austin, "about obligations that the company has to . . . let us say, pay its social rent, and discharge its responsibilities. Move from the area of accountability to the balance sheet to accountability in increasing degrees to the public at large. . . . If you make money for fifty thousand shareholders, you've done a very good job, and that's what we're supposed to do, but should you do something more?"

In 1968, after some seventy-five years in the soft-drink business, Coca-Cola introduced its first nutritional beverage. Called Saci, it was a noncarbonated vitamin-fortified, soybean based drink with 3 percent protein by volume. It came in chocolate and caramel flavors. But it was tepidly greeted in its first marketing by the Coke-owned Rio franchise. "I think we missed the track a bit with viscosity," said Austin, implying that it was too much like milk, a beverage his company did much to victimize. Another drinker opined that it "tasted something like chalk."

Coke has experimented with other products. In Surinam, Guyana's neighbor, in early 1971, it began to manufacture an enriched, noncarbonated drink with a fruity flavor. Called Samson, the pasteurized drink was marketed as a soft drink rather than "something that is good for you," apparently because the company was convinced that the latter approach wasn't effective. "Unfortunately," reflected Austin, "people will not do what is good for them just because it's good for them, so it was our aim to create a soft drink which they would buy because of its taste."

In 1978, Samson was introduced in Mexico as Sanson. Because it provides genuine nutrition, Coca-Cola enjoyed the government's blessing in marketing it to poor, undernourished children. "We wanted to get to the marginal classes . . . before those in the higher socioeconomic groups," explained the product's brand manager. "We're using the local media, theaters, radio, inside store advertising and outside store advertising," he continued. Since the test market had no television, some alternative promotions were used, such as door-to-door canvassing. It was plugged as an elixir "For Active Children" and Coke even contracted with a former soccer star for exclusive endorsements because he has "a good image with children." In what is perhaps a marketing man's dream, Coke is trying to persuade the Mexican government to distribute Sanson daily in tablet form to all schoolchildren.

In 1978, Coke announced its newest entry, a noncarbonated drink called Hi-C, a different product from its domestic Hi-C line of fruit drinks. Though it contains no fruit juice, Hi-C comes equipped with twice the recommended daily allowance of vitamin C. With perhaps a bit of overexuberance, one Coke official proclaimed that "There has been a tremendous change in Coke's philosophy. In fact, I see a tendency throughout the industry toward . . . soft drinks with nutritional value."

The effects of these products on world hunger remain to be seen, particularly since they must compete against Coke's other soft drinks which have been perceived by many as part of the problem. Some soft-drink manufacturers are skeptical of any effort at all. "The soft-drink industry is really in the business of producing a refreshing beverage," insisted one soda maker. "If people wanted nutritional beverages, they'd drink more milk. Beverage companies have to decide what business we're in. If it's nutrition, then maybe we should get out into the milk business." Others are skeptical because of the stark realities of the problem. Coke deserves "credit for having an interest in the problem" voiced another soft-drink executive, "but they're not the solution. These problems are rooted in politics and economics, not just nutrition."

Samson was administered to underprivileged, academically slow schoolchildren in Atlanta with provocative results. "When we fed the children this drink every school-day morning for four months," noted Austin, "their learning curves came right up." Truancy declined and classroom attentiveness increased. Indeed, Austin recognized the politics of despair and deprivation. "So what we have is a closed circle of poverty, malnutrition, and brain damage."

Coca-Cola spokespeople insist the company's interest in nutritional drinks stems from business considerations rather than social concerns. And they are correct. Coke would gladly solve the world's hunger problems if it were feasible *and* profitable to do so. Yet its efforts to date have been limited and somewhat clumsy. The company has become so awesomely efficient at convincing throngs that its sugar and caffeine drinks provide some sort of ill-defined yet valuable psychological lift that it has found difficulty in marketing products whose virtues are real, measurable, and useful by many would-be consumers.

Although it did not extend into nutrition, the competition between Coke and Pepsi for Latin America's loose change has occasionally led to excesses. In 1974,

Forbes magazine reported that a Pepsi bottler in Brazil smashed two million Coke bottles and was fined $27,000. His tactic made sense in light of Brazil's serious glass shortage. "You can recover most of the original bottle cost from the customer's deposit," remarked a Coke franchisee, "but you can't replace the bottle." Should the sabotage continue, the judge vowed to levy fines of up to $1 million. Nor could PepsiCo International deny responsibility, for it owned 80 percent of this franchise.

In another case, a Coke bottler won an injunction against a Pepsi distributor who was selling Coke bottles to a glass factory in São Paulo. Some Coke bottlers feared that Pepsi's dirty tricks were nationally organized. "This happens too broadly to seem accidental," said an angry Coke official. In addition, in 1974, both Coke and Pepsi were accused of smashing the bottles of a local Venezualan competitor. His bottles began to disappear at a rate of 20,000 a day and were later found in "bottle cemeteries" on the outskirts of several cities. Despite appeals to the government, no manufacturers were formally charged, and a truce was finally worked out.

Beyond usurpation of the marketplace and an attendant inculcation of consumer values, the subsidiaries of Coke, Pepsi, and other MNC's have intervened within the local political and legal apparatus, covertly if necessary, to eliminate any possible threats to their business environment.

In 1975, for instance, Coke's sales within a region of Brazil began to drop when published reports alleged that two black workers at a local Coke plant drowned in a huge tank of soft-drink syrup. Their bodies were not recovered for twenty-four hours, during which some 10,000 liters of soda were reportedly made from the syrup and subsequently sold to the public. Coca-Cola denied the whole grisly story, but a scandal erupted when the bodies of the workers were later found in nearby cemeteries. The chief labor investigator vowed to ferret out the truth "if it is the last thing I do in life," while the police commissioner asserted that "economic power and pressure don't intimidate me." During the probes, however, concerned parties were allegedly uncooperative and witnesses turned silent. Of three workers who chose to cooperate with the police, one testified only before a preliminary hearing, another was accused of slander and then jailed for alcoholism, and the third was found dead in a ditch, his body mutilated and his fingers and toes burned off by acid.

Neither the labor nor the police investigation determined the fate of the two workers. The labor investigator lost his enthusiasm after an alleged meeting with the president of Coca-Cola's South American operations. The once determined police commissioner closed his probe saying "Nothing happened. All the workers at the [Coca-Cola] factory can turn up dead and I will not take notice." For his efforts, the journalist who broke the story was faced with anonymous death threats and a law suit by Coca-Cola. In the end, the company was fined a small amount for three incidents of excessive working hours and a failure to meet security provisions.

The local stature of franchisees, coupled with the kinship between the U.S.

government, Coke, and later Pepsi, have strengthened the bottling operations' influence with host governments. Cozy relationships with national political forces enable an unscrupulous bottler to ignore legal or ethical constraints, as in Coke's discriminatory South African practices, or Pepsi's heroin-producing plant in Vientiane, Laos. Despite their public posturings, both parent firms appear to tolerate such activities by taking refuge behind their franchise system. Their detachment from a bottler's activities, even if laws or human rights have been violated, is conspicuously inconsistent with the company's obsession with overseeing local production and promotion. While such crass exploitation appears to be the exception with foreign franchises, one example arises that dramatizes the possible abuses of the franchise system abroad.

Coke bottler John C. Trotter is a virulent anti-communist. A Texas attorney with a taste for oil, Trotter believes that communism has infiltrated all of society except for the Catholic Church and the Coca-Cola Company. Trotter's association with Coca-Cola began in 1957 when he assumed control of the Guatemala City franchise, one of three Coke operations in Guatemala. The franchise was originally owned by Mutt Fleming, a fellow Texan who piloted for Pan-Am and also speculated in oil. Upon his death, his widow assigned power of attorney and virtual control of the Coke business to Trotter.

In 1957, Guatemala was still reeling from the overthrow of President Jacobo Arbenz Guzmán three years earlier. The coup was a bare-knuckled intervention by the U.S. government, and the CIA installed a protégé in his place, the first in a line of military-oriented, ultraconservative regimes. In the service of private capital, the ensuing leadership employed whatever means were necessary to crush popular movements, finally earning in the process the present-day opprobrium of being among the worst human rights violators in the Western Hemisphere. One tactic characteristic of most reactionary regimes is the repression of unionism or any organizing among workers. Despite the grossly disproportionate wealth owned by outside interests and a handful of Guatemalans, as little as 2 percent of the entire labor force has been organized. Herein lay the seeds for a confrontation that would render Coca-Cola the national symbol of the country's struggling labor movement.

John Trotter's bottling operations did well under the various regimes. During the sixties he was selling over sixty million bottles a year and dominating the local soft-drink market, while Pepsi remained a distant second. His success was due partly to his company's lack of a union and, some say, his ties to certain political parties, including the right wing Movimiento de Liberacion Nacional once financed by the CIA against Arbenz. The franchise's original union was dismantled in 1954 by the new military government, and an attempt to re-unionize the company failed in 1967 when the chief organizer was kidnapped and later found dead. That year, in the climate of a brutal, newly implemented counterinsurgency program (provoking liberals within the State Department to call for the cessation of all U.S. aid to Guatemala), Guatemalan President Julio Mendez attended the opening of the company's new plant in Guatemala City.

John Trotter continued to run his show and make money, periodically flying in from the states in his private airplane while paying many of his workers as little as $2 a day—until 1975.

Then, Guatemala was wracked with inflation and other economic ills, producing a consequent surge in the labor movement. In turn, such grass-roots political movements were countered by increased government harassment and paramilitary right-wing terrorism. In this setting, a coalition of 178 out of 211 workers at Trotter's Coke plant filed the necessary papers in August 1975 with the government and courts to form a union. They were in pursuit of dignified working conditions, an end to twelve-hour shifts, and an increase of the $2.08 to $2.50 base pay per day. John Trotter had never signed a union contract in his life, and was not about to do so now. The workers' seven-man executive committee was offered $15,000 and residency permits for the U.S. if they desisted from organizing. If there were any substance to the latter offer, it would have to have been made with the cognizance and cooperation of the Guatemalan government and perhaps the U.S. State Department. Upon the committee's refusal, they and the rest of the workers were threatened with dismissal, and the company began to hire new workers at $3.00 per day if they agreed not to join the union. The company was then sliced into thirteen legally separate paper corporations to neutralize collective bargaining.

In February 1976, six months after papers were filed, the struggle escalated. The company petitioned the court to rescind the union request because it claimed to have reached an agreement with the workers. In verification, a document was produced that was signed by 90 workers, all of whom were those recently hired by the company. Despite the obvious fraudulence of the pact, it was accepted by the court and the embryonic union was temporarily aborted. Upon learning of the court's decision, the workers staged a sit-in protest on the plant's property, and in response, the management called in the crack anti-riot military police which began evicting the demonstrators. Amid the many beatings, thirteen workers were seriously injured and the group's executive secretary taken away unconscious. The following day, Trotter fired 150 of the workers, but his action was such a flagrant violation of even Guatemala's minimal labor laws that he was forced to reinstate them. The ruthless confrontation strengthened the workers' resolve and local press coverage elevated the struggle to a national cause célèbre. Coca-Cola was fast on its way to becoming a symbol of political oppression.

The struggle was soon brought to the attention of the Interfaith Center on Corporate Responsibility, a New York-based group which monitors the activities of corporations in which its constituents, a coalition of over 160 Catholic and Protestant orders and groups, have investments. Their portfolio included the Coca-Cola Company and, in the fall of 1976, a stockholders' resolution was filed calling for a company probe into its Guatemala City franchise. In the winter of 1977, the resolution was withdrawn after the parent company agreed to conduct an investigation. A Coke team was dispatched to poke about in Guatemala, and a seven-page report was filed that spring. It accepted at face value Trotter's denials that he underpaid, intimidated, harassed, and abused his workers. It asserted that the division of his company into a deskful of briefcase companies was "legally feasible and acceptable," and that his use of riot police was "a local matter which can only be judged and resolved locally." It concluded that the situation did not "justify the termination of the bottler's agreements."

The religious groups found the report woefully lacking, and when Trotter's antiunion activities continued, they filed another stockholders' resolution in December 1977 calling for Coca-Cola to establish minimum labor standards for its bottlers worldwide. This time, Coke intervened and pressed Trotter to meet with Interfaith representatives in Guatemala. Although representatives of Coca-Cola confided that the company had had previous problems with Trotter and that his political views were "to the right of Attila the Hun," they argued that they were powerless to take direct action against him. However, a meeting was arranged and in February 1978, in the presence of Interfaith representatives and after much negotiation, a pact was finally signed between Trotter and his workers, 94 percent of whom were already union members. Trotter agreed to sign only if the word "union" was nowhere mentioned. An uneasy truce was made.

That summer, government repression was stepped up throughout the country, particularly after the administration of strong man General Romeo Lucas Garcia took office in July. Peasant organizations, labor unions, professional and student groups—anything that could remotely resemble a "popular movement"—were attacked in a reign of terror. Secret terrorist groups, widely suspected of being unofficial arms of the national police and army, tortured and killed scores of people each week during the following months. Unions were heavily targeted in the fear that a true liberation movement might be incubated, and no union had shown greater fortitude in the face of such adversity than that of John Trotter's Coke plant. Coca-Cola was destined to run blood-red in Guatemala.

In October 1978, Israel Marquez, the union's secretary general, was attacked by machine guns as he drove home. Miraculously, he escaped uninjured. In November, Trotter hired armed guards for his plant and three army lieutenants to serve as security and personnel chiefs. Later that month, Trotter allegedly met with Colonel German Chupina Barranona, the Guatemalan national police chief. Described as "one of the principal executors of the Guatemalan repression," he assured Trotter that the union would be destroyed within six months. In December, according to Marquez, Trotter threatened to kill Pedro Quevedo, another union official, and his name was placed on a hit list of the Secret Anti-Communist Army, one of the most feared right-wing death squads. Eights days after the threat, Quevedo, who had been jailed three times for his union activities, was killed by twelve bullets in the face and neck while making deliveries in his Coca-Cola truck. That day, just before the shooting, Trotter ordered his security force to the plant, further indicating to the workers that Trotter had foreknowledge of the assassination. After Quevedo's murder, in the words of a union statement, "a campaign of terror began." The Secret Anti-Communist Army marked the union's entire executive committee for death, an unsuccessful kidnap attempt was made on Marquez, and union officials and workers were intimidated and jailed. Shortly after, a man mistaken for Marquez was murdered and his wife of a month was critically hurt as they left the union leader's house. Marquez had seen enough, and several days later sought asylum for himself and his family in the Venezuelan embassy. While at the embassy, the Secret Anti-Communist Army phoned him to mockingly send its regards.

In protest of this violence, an Interfaith constituent wrote to the Coca-Cola Company in search of answers. It did not respond. When a call was placed to Atlanta, a company spokesman said, "We can't say what, if anything, we are doing about this situation. You can assume what you want to assume." Nonetheless, in February 1979, the union published a statement which affirmed its determination: "To the managers of Coca-Cola: neither with firearms nor warning of your military personnel are you going to destroy our union." The document asserted that Trotter and his lieutenants were the "authors of the repression suffered by the workers of Coca-Cola."

This grim, fantastic drama continued unchecked. In April, after repeated death threats, twenty-eight-year-old Manuel Lopez Balan, Marquez's successor as the union's secretary general, was beaten to death. Like Quevedos, he was killed in his Coca-Cola truck while making deliveries. Two days later, Balan's father was arrested by twenty policemen, and thirteen days later, two labor lawyers were kidnapped. Two weeks later, Balan's successor began receiving threats, such as "Don't be foolish, resign your post. Can't you see, we have the names of all your loved ones. . . . Remember, torture is extremely painful. . . . Are you aware of the different types of torture. . . ?" By the end of this bloody April, he too was jailed by the police.

A third stockholders' resolution was filed and this one survived until the company's annual meeting in May 1979 to become the first nonmanagement resolution ever voted on by Coca-Cola shareholders. Yet the dramatic point of the meeting (traditionally a tranquil affair to assess the year's successes) was an address given by exile Israel Marquez. Before the shareholders—an audience of wealth and pinstripes—Marquez recounted the Guatemalan debacle and urged passage of the resolution which again called for minimum labor standards to be established by the company for its bottlers. He recalled the beatings, threats, murders, bribes, and the shadowy police and military officials in and about Trotter's franchise. "Besides being inhuman, this situation is poor economics," he argued. "The image of Coca-Cola in Guatemala couldn't be worse. In Guatemala, Coca-Cola is referred to as crime. It is the most repressive company operating in the country . . . I ask for your immediate help to stop the bloodshed at the Coca-Cola bottler in Guatemala."

The company's response suggests it was hardly concerned with human dignity. In its prepared statement, Coke management hid behind its franchise system and urged defeat of the resolution. It argued that it had no right to interfere in labor disputes between independent parties and to do so would only complicate bottler/company relations. "This proposal," asserted management, "would be considered by most of the company's independent bottlers to be an improper and unnecessary intrusion by the company into their business affairs." Management did not address the fact that the company already dictated bottlers' production, selling, distribution, and promotional procedures down to the last detail. Equally ignored was the fact that the good name "Coca-Cola" had been badly maligned by this sordid affair and sales had consequently dropped. Whereas in 1974 Coke controlled 58 percent of the Guatemala City market to Pepsi's 37 percent, Trotter admits that those figures were virtually reversed three years later. Critics argued that Trotter's performance represented a clear negligence of his contractual obligations, which called for a maximization of Coke sales. However, despite Marquez's impassioned plea, the stockholders followed management's recommendation, as is usually the case, and soundly defeated the resolution.

The paranoid Trotter sees his union as a monster created by godless communism. Coca-Cola has conducted another investigation, and though the company called it "thorough," neither Trotter nor his plant managers were questioned. The local Pepsi franchise, which allegedly treats its workers much better, continues to prosper at Coke's expense. And the Coca-Cola workers still fear for their lives. As if Coca-Cola hasn't already been dragged through enough bloody mud, a local boycott is being planned, and other groups have taken an interest, such as the National Council of Churches and Amnesty International, winner of the Nobel Peace Prize. A member of an Amnesty delegation to Guatemala, Dan Gallin, head of the International Union of Food and Allied Workers, reported that the Coke franchise "is recognized as an extreme example of repression. . . ." Even Guatemala's labor minister, perhaps fearful that Coca-Cola could become a rallying point for workers nationwide, has begun to lose his patience. "If Coca-Cola doesn't stop repressing its workers, the government isn't going to protect it anymore," he reportedly declared.

What has motivated four years of terrorism is apparent: Trotter's fanatic anti-communism is part of a general war against unions by the Guatemalan ruling class. For Trotter and his allies, the Coca-Cola union is the big domino against which Communist infiltrators push. If allowed to proceed unchecked, they will, says Trotter, work their way northward to threaten his beloved Texas. What motivates the Coca-Cola Company to tolerate such abuses is not so apparent. Undoubtedly, the company would prefer not to meddle in its bottlers' affairs, and at the same time, is renowned for its disdain of bad publicity, and loss of market share. Bob Morris of the Interfaith Center speculates that "if they dip their hands in this one, they have got to dip their hands into 1,400 labor controversies and it would shake the basis for having a franchise relationship as opposed to subsidiaries." In an exclusive interview with journalist Henry Schipper, Trotter claimed that he and Atlanta coordinated public statements concerning Coke's investigations. If true, Coke protected Trotter and misled the public and the media.

It is possible that part of Trotter's leverage stems from his influence not only with the Guatemalan ruling elite, but political forces within America. He was a founding director of the Houston-based Friends of the Americas, a self-help program for Guatemala similar to Accion. Trotter acknowledges that for years the group has worked with the Guatemalan Army's civil pacification efforts in the countryside. More recently, Trotter arranged a Houston meeting between John Connally and Guatemalan businessmen to drum up support for the regime, and in late 1979, he arranged and financed a trip to Guatemala for representatives of the American Security Council, a powerful, right-wing lobby based in Washington, D.C. The team included retired General John Singlaub, who worked on sensitive intelligence assignments with Mitch Werbell during World War II, and David Graham, former head of the Defense Intelligence Agency. They met with the president of Guatemala and other national leaders to urge them to crack down on all opposition to the regime while President Carter was preoccupied with the crisis in Iran and Afghanistan. Afterwards, the former military men journeyed to South Korea to give the embattled leaders there the same advice. Moreover, Trotter is friendly with David Bintliff, Charles Duncan's former business associate, whose own interests in Guatemala have supplied coffee to the Coca-Cola Company.

Atlanta's stake in the Guatemalan economy goes beyond soft drinks. It has controlling interests in several local companies, including Industria de Cafe, S.A., a multimillion dollar coffee concern (which does have a functioning union).

Given their worldwide organizations, neither cola complex can be topped as potential sources of information. Both companies and their bottlers mingle with a nation's political and economic institutions as well as the media networks that shape its culture and public opinion. As far-flung as the State Department, the CIA, or other multinationals may be, none have penetrated the world right down to the neighborhood level. The globe is laced with millions of Coke and Pepsi retailers, each of which is contacted at least once a week by a bottler or company representative. With their seemingly infinite network of arteries and capillaries pumping soda throughout the surface of the planet, the Coca-Cola Company and PepsiCo have the unique potential of being the corporate sector's global nervous system. Just before his death, Al Steele compared the State Department to Pepsi in terms of strategic use to the government. "We think it stinks," he told reporters. "We have a hell of an influence abroad. If we wanted to disseminate information, we could do it faster than any other agency. Yeah, certainly faster than the State Department, and the communists know it."

The bottom-line effects of the super colas' global business are varied. The production of concentrate is not labor intensive, but Coke and Pepsi can provide significant employment locally through the vast bottling infrastructure and neither export jobs from the U.S. Local gains can be offset, however, when the colas pull the plug on indigenous soft-drink industries, particularly those in developing nations. Their franchise systems provide local ownership, but they can distract valuable investment capital from more productive and useful purposes.

Both companies contribute handsomely to America's balance of payments. Of course, the converse is true for host nations, including those whose populations can ill afford soft drinks and other imported consumer items. A strong industrialized nation is better able to export its currency for such items than a poor underdeveloped country, especially since the drastic jump in world oil prices.

The colas will have an even bigger impact on a nation's people than its economy. While more appropriate for developed societies, a mass consumption ideology within lesser developed consumption promotes disorientation, disproportionately rapid urbanization, and hollow expectations. Consumer culture is not the spontaneous expression of an indigenous people, but the artificial and self-serving imposition of the corporate imagination. At its worst, consumerism can displace local traditions and history. It often champions empty calories, and the worldwide presence of Coke and Pepsi only underscores the critical need for nutrition. "No one needs it," but both companies are far more appropriate to societies whose standards of living are well beyond the poverty line.

Neither companies make such distinctions—each will flow to where the opportunities are. In 1976, just under half of PepsiCo's overseas sales were in Latin America, and the company is busily developing this market for its Frito-Lay snack foods. A 1978 study conducted by the European Economic Market found that the most profitable food-type firm in the Western World was the Coca-Cola Company, with PepsiCo not far behind. Underdeveloped nations have underdeveloped soft-drink markets, and the soda makers will sink all but the most resolute in a sticky sea of sweetness. In their quest for sales, Coke and Pepsi are watering the seeds of a worldwide culture, and only time will tell whether its fruits can feed the hungry.

CHAPTER THIRTEEN

The President Who Went Pop

"Growth is the ultimate goal of what one wants to do."   —*Donald Kendall*

THE ELECTION OF Richard Nixon in 1968 was certainly one of the great political comebacks in American history. A remarkable transformation had occurred between his abysmal 1962 defeat in California and the sweet triumph of
his nomination in Miami six years later. Friends, former enemies, columnists—
in fact, most of the American people—thought they detected a "new" Nixon
who had conquered his own inadequacies while banishing the prejudices and
anachronisms of his Cold War foreign policy. Where once he waved the banner
of anti-communism belligerently, Nixon now spoke of "cooperation and collaboration" with the Eastern countries. His self-possession and composure were
enough to persuade the electorate to vote him into office with scarcely an inkling
of the real changes at hand, or the forces behind Nixon that would prosper from
them.

Nixon's pride, of course was Kendall's joy, for Pepsi had landed its man in the
White House. From Wendell Willkie to Joe McCarthy, Pepsi's quests for influence among Republican lawyers and politicians had long been a concomitant of
its struggle with Coke, but it was Kendall who saw most clearly where the quest
ultimately led. His Moscow tryst with Nixon in 1959 had been all too brief, and
whatever secret hopes he cherished of a President within Pepsi's grasp were
dashed in 1960. But Kendall knew more than anyone of the dregs in Pepsi's
past. Twice bankrupt, twice returned from the dead, this company was gifted at
making comebacks. Kendall was the first, and may be the only leader in Pepsi's
turgid history to dare nurture the company's own presidential tender, cultivate
him, even educate him in the far-flung, paradoxical metaphysics of multination-
alism, and then implant him in the White House.

Robert Woodruff had had the vision thirty years earlier, and reaped its fruits
with presidential ties from Roosevelt to Kennedy. Where Coke was discreet and
subdued, Pepsi was bold and forthright. Ike might retreat to Woodruff's Georgian plantation for a little golf but, once he trained his sights on the White
House, Nixon would globetrot on Pepsi's plane, often with Kendall present.
And why not? Nixon was Pepsi's lawyer, and Kendall modeled a whole philosophy of the corporate citizen-in-politics around this one pragmatic fact. In 1968,
he could thus rejoice more openly than Woodruff ever had at the fruits of a
creed he persistently hammered into his minions at PepsiCo.

He saw nothing provocative in Elmer Bobst's campaign contribution of $63,-

250, nor, for that matter, in Robert O. Anderson's of $44,000. Anderson was then chairman of Atlantic Richfield Oil Company, where Kendall sat as a director. (He should not be confused with Robert B. Anderson, the Texas oil figure who participated in the formation of Great Southwest. See Chapter 10.) The dynamics of the lawyer-client relationship on campaign fund-raising were a little more suggestive. For instance, Hornblower & Weeks, where Kendall's former father-in-law and one-time Pepsi director, Edward Orrick McDonnell, had long been a partner, was, like PepsiCo, a Mudge-Rose client and a $22,000 contributor to the 1968 campaign. Maurice Stans, who went on to be Nixon's Secretary of Commerce, had been the GOP's leading fund raiser since 1962. As partner in the New York-based investment house of Glore Forgan, Stans had helped arrange the Penn Central's ill-fated 1963 and 1964 purchases of the stock of the Great Southwest Corporation, the politically influential real estate concern through which Pepsi was initiated into Dallas financial circles.* As a finders' fee for this deal, Stans received 38,000 shares of Great Southwest stock which he still held and reportedly neglected to acknowledge at the time of his confirmation hearings. Meanwhile Stans' deputy director of the 1968 Nixon campaign, Herbert Kalmbach, became Nixon's personal attorney after the election. Kalmbach had worked on Nixon's bid for the California governorship, and from 1964 to 1967 was a vice-president and director of Macco Realty Corporation, a firm acquired by Penn Central and later merged into Great Southwest. By 1969, Kalmbach's California law firm, which he had joined two years earlier, had Great Southwest, Glore Forgan, and Atlantic Richfield for clients.

In the short run, of course, the campaign strategy was all-important, and Nixon's checkered history lent itself quite well to an overwhelming emphasis on image in contrast to issues. His managers shed Nixon's loser image during the primaries by projecting him "above the battle," as one memo put it, by picturing him as though he were already the candidate—lofty, statesmanlike—as though, says Jules Witcover, "he were in a dress rehearsal for the real thing."† Leonard Hall, National Republican chairman during the Eisenhower administration, remarked, "You sell your candidates and your programs the way a business sells its products."‡

The notion had been around, but the Nixon effort took it to new lengths. Public appearances were turned into bonanzas of balloons, bands, and cheerleaders, all under the careful direction of tinsel-town promoters, particularly one from Disneyland. (The Disney touch was not lost once the President took office, for press secretary Ron Ziegler had been a tour guide at Disneyland.) All other exposure would be through subdued, controlled, low-key media presentations which protected the candidate from potentially embarrasing or revealing encounters.

* Stu Bishop, "Stans: He Fixed the Books," North American Congress on Latin America, *Latin America & Empire Report*, November, 1963. p. 25
† Jules Witcover, *The Resurrection of Richard Nixon*, op. cit., p. 367
‡ Joe McGinniss, *The Selling of the President, 1968* (New York: Trident Press, 1969). p. 27

This electronic solution to the crisis of image did not come easily to Nixon at first. Deep down, he was still haunted by old insecurities and had, after all, bungled the 1960 live television debates against Kennedy. Once assured, however, that live debates, press conferences, and public meetings of any kind—all of which together provide a remarkably telling picture of a candidate's views, if not his character—were off the agenda, completely, Nixon wholeheartedly surrendered to the product sell. As standard as the Pepsi bottle, as opaque as Pepsi itself, the candidate declared, "I am not going to barricade myself into a television studio and make this an antiseptic campaign," and then proceeded to do almost exactly that.* Obviously approving of this approach, Kendall is said to have asked a Pepsi vice-president only weeks before the election what he thought of "our boy." Ignoring his shrug, Kendall allegedly exclaimed, "He's not going to blow it this time. No off-the-cuff remarks, no unscheduled appearances."

The preparations for this duo's delicate waltz to the top had been long under way, particularly through their courtship of converging Eastern and Southwestern interests.

In September 1964, Nixon joined the board of Investor Diversified Services (IDS), the largest investment advisor and mutual fund network in the country. The fund was controlled by the Republican-oriented Alleghany Corporation, a major creditor of Great Southwest's William Zeckendorf with strong ties to Pepsi banker David Baird. Alleghany was, in turn, controlled by the Kirby family who, like the Murchisons of Dallas, represented the sort of regional financial wealth to which Nixon most easily appealed. The Kirbys, in fact, had recently triumphed in a bitter struggle with the Murchisons over control of Alleghany and IDS, an episode which underscores the strategic niche Nixon carved for himself in cultivating ties to both these groups. In 1968, Kendall replaced Nixon on the IDS board, and appears to have played a meaningful role: IDS was subsequently the largest stockholder at Atlantic Richfield and the thirteenth largest at PepsiCo.†

Kendall was also an apparent link in another such regional deal, a 1969 oil exploration agreement involving IDS and the Los Angeles-based McCulloch Oil Corporation, whose board he joined shortly after the conclusion of the deal.‡ McCulloch's president was Kendall's long-time friend, C.V. Wood, who had grown even closer to Kendall in the fifteen years since the Disneyland-Pepsi deal. Wood was the godfather to Kendall's first child by his second marriage, which took place in New York over Christmas in 1965. Wood attended the wedding where Nixon played the piano and other luminaries, such as Spyros Skouras, the chairman of 20th-Century Fox, exhibited considerable hospitality over several

---

* Witcover, ibid., p. 374
† Nixon served IDS well as president. After reversing an SEC ruling and allowing IDS to deregister as an investment company and thus avoid government regulations on disclosures and acquisitions, he ordered the Justice Department to support IDS's motion before the SEC to allow financial institutions to join the New York Stock Exchange. He also directed the IRS to allow mutual funds to pursue the $250 billion pension fund market.
‡ *Who's Who in America*, Vol. 36, 1970-71. *Moody's Industrial Manual*, 1978, p. 3705

days of celebrating. Back in the fifties, Skouras had given Pepsi an exclusive concession at a theater chain he managed. He was the point man in the bold gambit of that time to buy out Howard Hughes with William Zeckendorf and Pepsi's director Charles Allen, and was one of the many figures from the world of film to benefit from the illicit services of the Baird Foundations.

Despite the recent failure of Freedomland in which C.V. Wood and Zeckendorf were partners, Wood was eyeing even vaster projects for McCulloch Oil that would require the kind of Washington clout to which Kendall aspired. Arizona land development ranked high on this list, particularly the mid-1960s creation of Lake Havasu City along the Colorado River on the California-Arizona border. Four other Arizona cities were also earmarked by McCulloch and according to one observer, "Whatever he [Wood] wants out of Washington, D.C., he gets. . . . If he wants Route 66 changed in Arizona, he gets it. Nixon became President, and he was gung-ho on the land deals."

In 1968, Robert McCulloch, chairman of McCulloch Oil, bought *the* London Bridge at an auction, and by 1971, a year or so after Kendall had joined the board, C.V. Wood, in another feat of engineering extravagance, had overseen its transport, piece-by-piece, from its ancient bivuoac on the Thames to a dry stretch of land bordering the Colorado River. "You couldn't find two rocks piled on top of each other," said one observer of the once barren desert site, but Wood and McCulloch obtained the rights to divert waters from the man-made Lake Havasu through a channel they built, bringing the cost of relocating the bridge to $10 million. From Lake Havasu to Disney's Fantasy Land, which was itself modeled on the castle of a deranged, nineteenth-century, pseudo-medieval king who longed for an irretrievable past, C.V. Wood had a gut vision of "entertainment for the masses" that was most compatible with his alliance with Kendall and the Pepsi cause. Almost as if he were a company man, Wood got in the habit of frequently saying "Pepsi, please" when in certain social circles, and took his inspiration so far as to breakfast often on piping hot portions of home-made chili and ice-cold Pepsi-Cola.

With Nixon ensconced in the White House, things began to happen for Kendall. There was considerable talk that he was to be appointed Secretary of Commerce, but as one Pepsi executive scoffed, "Why should he?" Kendall was quickly on his way to becoming a prominent leader in domestic business circles and a key booster of international trade, and he felt more strongly than ever that he could be most effective right where he was. Less than a month after the inauguration, Nixon announced that Kendall had been appointed chairman of the National Alliance of Businessmen (NAB), a group set up by Lyndon Johnson to supplement the government's efforts to find jobs for the hard-core unemployed. Kendall succeeded Henry Ford, the Alliance's first president, and within several months the group merged with Plans for Progress, an organization oriented toward unemployed blacks which was headed by an executive of General Dynamics. Although the Alliance expanded its operations from 50 to 131 cities under

Kendall, hard-core unemployment doubled by 1970. It was a knotty problem as well as a politically sensitive one for PepsiCo, which was then under great pressure from the Southern Christian Leadership Conference to hire more blacks and Puerto Ricans in New York and to deposit corporate funds in black-run banks.

No pressure on Pepsi however, could dampen the impression that Kendall himself was undergoing a change similar to the remarkable metamorphosis his influence had helped to create in the President. The change had less to do with personal trait or style—the well-known toughness and abrasiveness remained—than it did with values and attitudes. Kendall was high profile now, higher than he had ever been, and public light demanded public-spirited pronouncements on the responsibilities of business. A new leader in the business community, Kendall sometimes acted as its conscience, occasionally approaching positions worthy of a liberal.

In a May 1969 speech to the National Industrial Board, Kendall spoke of business's vital need to meet rising consumer demand for safety, quality, and service, concluding that "Many [consumer] complaints are justified." As head of NAB, he declared, "One of the basic misconceptions in this area [chronic unemployment] shows up in such comments as 'They're lazy' or 'They're just no good, they don't want to work, they'd rather be on welfare.' That simply is not true." In this view, Kendall approached almost visionary proportions when he proposed worldwide ownership of stock in multinational corporations. Ownership of shares of the parent company would give "local people" a piece of the action around the globe, and would assure them profits whether or not local subsidiaries were lucrative.

In this linking of the haves and the have-nots, Kendall was articulating a dignified and enlightened self-interest. Some of his other appearances early in the Nixon presidency were less auspicious, such as his stormy departure in December 1969 from a three-day White House Conference on Food, Nutrition, and Health because of some critical remarks toward snack foods made by the President's special consultant. There was also PepsiCo's September 1970 participation in sponsoring the rebroadcast of a highly partisan Nixon speech on campus unrest. The speech was aired during the election campaign in areas where the White House was especially interested in Republican victories. The Democratic National Committee demanded that the Justice Department investigate whether PepsiCo and three sponsors headed by Nixon intimates violated a federal law banning corporate contributions to political campaigns. The action was handled for the DNC by its general counsel, Joseph Califano of Arnold & Porter, but the ubiquitous lawyer who had Coke for a client was up against too much. Under Attorney-General Mitchell, the Justice Department promptly ruled that the broadcast was unrelated to the campaigns and therefore legal.

Like its chief executive, PepsiCo began to bask in an air of prosperity as it continued on the course of conglomeration Kendall ordained for it. In a very short time, Pepsi had undergone a complete transformation from a soft-drink operation into a full-fledged conglomerate providing products *and* services.

In keeping with this new consumer orientation, PepsiCo left the city for the suburbs in October 1970, moving to Purchase, New York, a tiny community of private estates and country clubs. The splendid headquarters had its seven-building complex grouped around a central courtyard of imported cobblestone. Unmarred by a single Pepsi sign, the site was adorned with five thousand new trees, six thousand daffodils, a man-made lake harboring flocks of Canadian geese, and a fountain that gushed skyward whenever Kendall pressed a button on his desk.

This corporate bivouac presented quite a different window on the world than the one Kendall peered through as a syrup salesman on the move at the Long Island City plant twenty-five years before. As the architect of Pepsi's new identity as a diversified, consumer-service company, Kendall moved to altitudes well beyond the grasp of even the most prodigious syrup salesman. In a company stacked with specialists, he is the professional generalist par excellence who leaves the running of the machinery to Andrall Pearson while he lays the tracks on which it all will follow. The goal, of course, is growth—the sine qua non of the corporation and the passionate obsession of its managers and salesmen. From marketing to manufacturing, from advertising to sales, these men and women tend to the daily task of maximizing the company's performance. Kendall, on the other hand, must think years ahead, and in global terms, of new and appropriate markets for his charges to develop. The principal requirements for his job are thus a keen eye for acquisitions and a ready hand for politicians. One serves to attain the goal of 10 percent annual growth directly by putting the company in a new market or a related business, the other indirectly through the ineffable mystique of establishing corporate presence. During the sixties, Kendall was frequently at Nixon's side during the public-relations junkets for Pepsi, but after Nixon gave up the law for higher office, the soft-drink executive took up the mantle himself. "You couldn't be as political as Don," quipped Andrall Pearson to *Esquire* journalist Robert Scheer in 1975. "I've never met Ford—I'd say that Don is, by design [political]—he likes to do that and he does it superbly. I'm proud and impressed with the job he does." Scheer reminds us that "Kendall is above all a company man, and understands that were his political activities to have a negative impact on sales, he would simply be out." Pearson noted that the board of directors would be informed of any digression from company targets. "A lot of guys' bonuses are at stake [under an incentive plan that pro rates bonuses according to PepsiCo's growth rate] and they are sure as hell not going to sit around and let somebody, even the chief executive, fuck up their business for them."

As a multinational, PepsiCo calculates its growth on a worldwide basis, and thus all of Kendall's political initiatives are geared to fashioning an international economic system that will serve that corporate growth. Unlike the Cold War, nation-building strategy that sought territorial hegemony by maximizing political or military conflict on a local level, this brand of system building seeks to create an economic hegemony, partly by reducing the political conflicts, both domestically and internationally, that hinder corporate growth. As explored in the previous chapter, these conflicts are rooted ultimately in the central controversies surrounding the multinationals' impact on the economic well-being of the United States and the rest of the world. As Peter Drucker has observed, "The multinational is a problem precisely because its decisions are based on economic rationality and divorced from political sovereignty. . . . It is a problem because political sovereignty and economic reality no longer coincide."*

A key spokesman for the multinationals' sacrosanct growth ethic, Kendall has worked tirelessly to mediate the conflict between these two. His government appearances and public relations statements have doubled as advertising for the multinational corporation and in similar fashion to reduce political values and social considerations onto a single economic plane.

The liberal views he proffered on world stock ownership, for instance, were part of an ongoing debate highlighted by the publication in 1972 of *The Limits to Growth*, a major international study by the renowned Club of Rome which concluded that unlimited economic growth endangered the planet. Striking at the roots of the belief in growth, which underlies modern society much as the faith in industrial progress did during the Enlightenment, the study prompted an international debate which revealed wide agreement among economists with the general direction of the Club's recommendations, if not the strength of them.† Kendall's world stock ownership plans, which would ensure investors of all countries a "piece of the action," was a timely suggestion whose effect would be to dampen the attitudes of doubt or caution about corporate growth fueled by the study.

There is an underlying urgency to this growth crusade that is shared by all the managers of the multinational community and possessed by Kendall in abundance. His worldwide struggle with Coke makes him a fitting spokesman for the group, but he is an actor in a still larger drama who sees the marriage of political policy making to multinational business interests as the sole means of restoring the greatness of America. "We started out after the war with the Marshall Plan," he told the Senate Finance Committee in 1973, ". . . and in many of our trade discussions, foreign policy was the primary motivator of those trade discussions, not our own economic requirements. We have got to get over the Marshall Plan era, and get into creating foreign policy that fits our own economic needs, the same as England is trying to do. We have got to have people in our

---

* Drucker cited in Harry Antonides, *Multinationals and the Peaceable Kingdom* (Toronto: Clarke, Irwin, & Co., 1978). p. 69

† In *An Inquiry into the Human Prospect* (New York: W. W. Norton, 1974) renowned economic historian Robert Heilbroner admonished the growth ethic by declaring that "In place of the long-established encouragement of industrial production must come its careful restrictions and long-term diminution within society. In place of prodigalities of consumption must come new frugal attitudes." Leonard Silk of *The New York Times* (March 13, 1972) warned that "It would be madness to ignore the warning of Dr. D. L. Meadows and his M.I.T. team of the probable collapse within a century of the world system, resulting in massive destruction of natural resources and human life. . . . We urgently need a change in social values—a shift in our goals from increasing the quantity of production to improving the quality of life." cf. D. L. Meadows, *The Limits to Growth* (New York: Universe Books, 1972).

embassies overseas—which the State Department is beginning to do—looking for opportunities for U.S. companies; to notify companies over here that there are opportunities in those countries when government contracts come up . . . to notify them the same as the British do, the same as the Japanese do."*

The urgency: it pushed Kendall and PepsiCo to open five new markets between 1969 and 1971—Korea, Finland, Denmark, Greece, and Poland—and to carry on expansion at breakneck speed. It also spurred the creation of the PepsiCo World Trade & Development Corporation, which helped finance the opening of plants in countries with foreign exchange difficulties. The urgency for national economic growth was felt in the government, as well. Kendall's testimony on the need for political help from Washington drew a ready response from Chairman Abraham Ribicoff (D-Conn.): "I think you can put your finger on the fact that after 1945, geopolitics was the prime concern of American foreign policy, while ecopolitics dominated the policies of our trading partners, certainly Japan and Germany. Now we are waking up to realize that geopolitics is not as important as it once was. Ecopolitics—what happens to the dollar and to our trade—is becoming the dominant factor today in the world."†

Kendall and other chief executives must be concerned not only about their principal American competitors, but also about formidable foreign competitors, especially when they have the support of their governments in tariff legislations, monetary policies, and other fiscal considerations. Along with Coke and the other multinationals, PepsiCo's urgent push to corner markets abroad with local plants is often spurred by trade barriers to U.S. imports which make it impossible to sell there without a direct investment. As Kendall told Senator Ribicoff's committee, "There might be restrictions which, of course, force you to open up in that market. . . . There are *many, many* countries that we operate in overseas where we just would not be there if we had no plants." As other nations have approached and even surpassed America's productivity, the urgency for growth suddenly seems spurred by motives different from the imperialistic ones long attributed to American companies. As Kendall tells it, the push for direct investment abroad has become almost a matter of self-defense that is quite divorced from the unending expansion of American shores once glorified in Manifest Destiny. In the heyday of America's expansion, business and government were seen to be much more divorced. Now, with a weakening balance of payments, the new ecopolitical view espoused by Kendall has been finding ever wider support on Capitol Hill.

With Nixon in the White House, Kendall became a pivotal figure in the emerging order. On January 3, 1969, he was named chairman of the Emergency Committee for American Trade (ECAT), the top lobbying group for multinational companies founded in October 1967 to fight protectionist sentiment originating primarily from the American labor movement. In naming Kendall,

* U.S. Congress, Senate Committee on Finance, *Multinational Corporations*, Hearings, 93rd Congress, 1st session, 1973. p. 107
† ibid., p. 108.

David Rockefeller, one of the committee's founders and an important influence on the Nixon-Kendall alliance, praised the President-elect for understanding the need for world trade. Succeeding IBM's Arthur Watson as ECAT's chairman, Kendall promptly cautioned the labor community that it would be naive not to expect retaliation from foreign trading partners over what they might deem restrictive trade measures. Vowing to fight quotas wherever possible and to push for equal American exports to all markets, Kendall declared, "We will be working with like-minded business groups which recognize that trade barriers in their own countries are injuring American exports."

One of Kendall's first projects as ECAT chairman involved a trip to Japan to urge a speeding up of that country's removal of its import quotas as well as its restrictions on foreign capital investment in its domestic industries. The Japanese hesitation to open up all of their domestic industry to 100 percent foreign ownership might have been due, in part, to its recent experience with Coca-Cola, whereby five hundred soft-drink manufacturers were driven into bankruptcy after Coke entered the country in 1960 (see Chapter 12). Traveling with a large entourage of heads of ECAT-member companies, Kendall emphasized that the group was in no way a spokesman for American policy, but he wanted to impress Japanese business leaders with the pressures building back home for greater protection of American industry.

The pressures in America reached their pinnacle in 1971 and centered on organized labor's protest that, among other things, foreign direct investment results in the export of jobs to low-wage areas, and that American plants abroad generated increased U.S. imports while discouraging exports. Moreover, said an Executive Council Report from the AFL-CIO, "Multinational firms juggle their production, employment, bookkeeping, prices, and taxes from one country to another to meet corporate needs," implying that this maneuvering favored corporate interests to the detriment of the rest of the country. The AFL-CIO organized these considerations and others into a nine-point slate which served as the basis for the famous Burke-Hartke bill, later voted down in the Congress. Perhaps inadvertently, Kendall tipped his attitude toward such attacks in attempting to discard the charge that multinationals invest abroad to avoid U.S. taxes. "I would like to see one big [Pepsi] plant here in the United States where it was all computerized and run by robots and we did not have to do anything but ship it out, but unfortunately, we cannot do that."*

In a different world, perhaps he could. Perhaps PepsiCo could achieve its declared goal of 10 percent compounded growth rate just on what was consumed in the United States if population and income kept growing, or if the industrial or service sectors of the economy kept right on ballooning, if there were simply no limits to growth. Soft-drink executives are infinitely fond of talking about the limitlessness of their business. Coke people, particularly in the domestic division, seem drawn to the homey little adages about their only limits being the

* ibid., p. 105

self-imposed ones—pronouncements that contain healthy portions of a preacher's conviction and pioneer innocence. What could match soda's potential for limitless, infinite growth? The efforts of both these soda-makers to see consumption of their products surpass that of every other liquid, *including water*, attests to their seriousness when it comes to growth. It also attests to their predicament: there are limits, indeed, recognizable ones which they acknowledge each time they undertake any kind of corporate diversification. Still, the creed of incessant growth—and it is very much a creed—clings tenaciously to the corporate mind. Its urgency carries on in a brazen, rhetorical denial of reality, a little like the man who denies his mortal limits. Perhaps, in a different world, Kendall could own an endless domestic market, and be content with his huge plant and his robots. But his harrowing competition with Coke is a fact of this world, and another very real reason for the virtual saturation of the American market and the consequent need to push farther and farther abroad. If not in this market, then perhaps in one that operated differently, Kendall could find what he wanted, dreamt of, cherished—what every loyal soldier of free enterprise admits to wanting when he is really being honest—a monopoly.

To be sure, he had had a taste of it in the government-planned economies of Eastern Europe, just as Coke had. In fact, Kendall increasingly discovered that Coke could eat through the Iron Curtain just as legends asserted it could eat through nails. In mid-1972, Rumania was the only country in Eastern Europe without a Coke plant, but reports indicated that even there negotiations were underway. Kendall must have eyed this opening of the market with an ironic sense of discomfort, for competition defeated a central advantage of operating in Eastern bloc countries. Kendall and the heads of the other multinationals found much that was secure and comfortable in these Eastern climes, and a great deal of it concerned the structural, almost organic, affinities between multinational corporations and state-run economies. As J. Wilczynski observes, "Both are large organizations noted for centralized decision-making, hierarchical levels of authority, and technocratic elements. Both are dominated by materialist (or materialistic) pursuits, both have an essentially international outlook with interests transcending national frontiers, and both are accustomed to 'thinking big' in long-run, cost-benefit terms. Both pursue short-term and long-term economic planning and engage in optimization studies with the aid of electronic computers. On account of anti-monopoly legislation in the West, the multinationals often feel safer in expanding their operations in the East instead."[*]

In return for the corporate comforts the multinationals enjoy in these havens of monopoly, they must totally adjust their methods to the demands of the Socialist hosts, who recognize the predatory effects that foreign direct investment could have on their economies. Placing aside their capitalist measures, Coke and Pepsi as well as their other corporate peers have entered into a variety of other

[*] Josef Wilczynski, *Multinationals and East-West Relations* (Boulder, Col.: Westview Press, 1976). p. 176–83

types of arrangements, including joint ventures, licensing, and subcontracting, which partially involved barter rather than the remitting of hard currencies. These elaborate arrangements protected the Socialist economies, whose leaders shrewdly gained an additional edge by never granting exclusive rights to any of the soft-drink concerns. In short, the monopolies Coke and Pepsi enjoyed in Eastern Europe were quite real, but by no means eternal. Bulgaria and Rumania were recently the only countries left where Coke and Pepsi respectively had exclusivity.

Creeping competition trained Kendall's sights ever eastward toward one of the world's magnificent markets and perhaps the grandest Eden of monopoly. A tantalizing vision of the possible, it was a far-reaching look forward to the vast expanse where Asia met the West and a glimpse of Pepsi's destiny at the summit of a major historical shift. That shift had actually begun before the East-West embrace of the sixties, and Kendall's perspicacity propelled Pepsi's eventual introduction into the place he first nested with his closest political comrade.

Many changes had taken place there since his fateful entente with Khrushchev at the American Exposition in 1959. Every bit as dramatic as those occurring in Eastern Europe, these changes were highlighted by a sweeping turnover in leadership. Khrushchev had wet his lips with Pepsi, and had even taken some bold steps toward a rapprochement with his Western rivals, but his policies were an erratic mixture of Stalin's priority of heavy industry and the more modern view, resisted by party diehards, that consumer goods should be developed to meet the needs of a people bled white by the obsessive whims of a dictator. This debate was very much at the center of his 1953 struggle to capture Stalin's office, and after denouncing the modernizers as rightists, Khrushchev took power and began reforms he had promised to prevent. While he talked of economic rivalry with the West, the government-owned Moscow-Norodny Bank and its Soviet sister in Paris offered capitalist eurodollars to their customers within a year of Stalin's demise. "We will bury you," he bellowed, all the time dazzled by the technological processes used in American industry and agriculture. Irresolute and indecisive, he spouted propaganda that rendered the massive Soviet bureaucracy impervious to his reforms. Far from overtaking the United States, the USSR fell further and further behind, and Khrushchev was replaced in 1964 by the Brezhnev-Kosygin government which downplayed the tired clichés of economic rivalry and began to address the serious problems their country faced.

Rehabilitation from Stalin's economic isolation required an all-out commitment. Because of the extensive emphasis on labor-intensive, heavy industry, the Soviet economy was twenty-five years behind in the light, modern high-technology industries. Massive labor and management inefficiencies in nearly every area of agriculture and industry precipitated long food lines, woefully inadequate housing, and shoddy equipment and unattractive products that were just as unsaleable in the West.

Unhampered by Khrushchev's traditional Communist rhetoric, the Brezhnev government instituted fundamental reforms and a new system of economic incentives. Profit was introduced as a criterion for measuring the performance of an enterprise and investment was decentralized, which was harmonious with the practices of multinational corporations. A high degree of central authority was preserved, but the market was allowed to play a greater role in the determination of prices and production, thus enhancing the role of the consumer. Through all these changes, the USSR and the Soviet bloc were moving into the age of eco-politics, when the dogma of monolithic international communism was breaking up into a host of pluralistic forms. But these internal measures couldn't begin to close the almost unbridgeable gap in technology and capital-intensive industries. Beyond the end of ideological confrontation and the introduction of the profit motive, only Soviet integration into the technology-based global economy could close the gap. More than anything else, it was the Soviet's need for vastly enhanced trade that drove them to seek détente.

With access to markets as well as the benefit of protection of a legal monopoly and strike-proof labor, it isn't hard to see why the West met them more than halfway. Kendall dates his resolve to enter the Soviet market back to the 1959 American Exposition, but serious discussion did not begin until December 1971 when he was in Moscow as part of a United States trade mission. Understandably, Kendall felt that trade meant consumer products as well as heavy technology, and to underscore the point, played a portable radio in the shape of a Pepsi-Cola can to Premier Kosygin just before a Kremlin meeting attended by other Soviet brass. Kosygin laughed aloud and Kendall took swift advantage of the moment to make one of the boldest pitches ever by any Pepsi salesman. Just then, Maurice Stans strode up and cracked to Kosygin, "What's Kendall trying to do, sell you a Pepsi?" Such disarming tactics must have worked their charms, for that very evening, Kosygin approached Kendall at a reception and said, "I understand that you want to trade Pepsi-Cola for vodka."

"Yes, sir," came the reply.

"Well, will you make that a liter-for-liter transaction?"

"Yes, sir, we sure can."* Offering his hand to Kosygin as he had offered that Pepsi to Khrushchev twelve years before, Kendall shook on a deal making his product the first American consumer item to be made and sold in the Soviet Union.

Six months later, Kendall was back in Moscow negotiating the details with the Soviet foreign trade minister. His visit came shortly after the ruling Communist Party moved sharply to curb liquor sales because of the "tremendous harm to the entire Soviet society" caused by alcoholism.† The long-standing anti-alcohol drive, which emphasized the social evils of drinking, was underscored with a new focus on the economic harm of absenteeism and drastically reduced work efficiency and productivity. Because of the gradual depletion of the labor pool, among other things, the internal measures adopted by the Brezh-

* *Time*, November 27, 1972. *PepsiCo Panorama*, Vol. 19, #1—1977. Excerpt of Kendall interview with David Susskind.

† *The New York Times*, June 17, 1972. p. 1

nev regime included a new emphasis on greater production per worker rather than the traditional expansion of the labor force.

When the USSR curbed liquor sales and encouraged soft drinks, pop assumed a role in the Soviet Union parallel to the one it had filled in America nearly a century before. There, too, the end of slavery and the massive shift into wages precipitated a new emphasis on the productivity of individual labor, whether in the cities or on the farm. And just as the Southerners condemned alcoholism for corrupting the marrow of traditional Southern ideals, so the Soviets imposed these new prohibitions amid appeals to public health and the well-being of Soviet society. Just as it had in the New South, and for that matter, many other places in the world, the American soft drink in the Soviet Union was playing a vital role of acculturation with the onset of modern consumerism.

The significance of this role should not be underestimated: even though the backward, agrarian economy was industrialized, the equally old authoritarian tradition endured. Thus, writes historian Vera Micheles Dean, "Russia's experience under Communist rule shows that it is possible for an underdeveloped country to jump over centuries in scientific and economic development with marked success. . . . But this experience also shows that it is far more difficult to jump over centuries of political and social development, which require the slow growth of new values, of new institutions, and new attitudes toward men's relations in society."* Slow, indeed. Pepsi was simply the latest in a long line of Western creations to cross the great threshold into Mother Russia. Some of them, like a professional army, an administrative bureaucracy, or the railroads pertained to the extremely practical side of Western life. Others, such as those under Catherine the Great, were part of a marvelous though deceptively limited cultural enlightenment, complete with the play of ideas and liberal thinking. The alphabet was simplified and French became the language of many Russian intellectuals. Yet Western ideas in the East, whether of Rousseau or Karl Marx, wound up reenforcing the Russians' hostile tendencies.

Will history repeat itself with Pepsi and consumerism? Since the start of the Cold War, Russian antagonism has been complicated by a certain growing ambivalence noted by Western observers, such as Llewellyn Thompson, former U.S. Ambassador to Russia. Highly esteemed by the Soviets, Thompson advised Kendall on their deep-seated inferiority complex and envy of Western prosperity which, more recently, has become nothing short of a lust for quality products. Partly because they had little choice, the Russian leadership chose the expedient path of allowing the culture to modernize but not to Westernize. In fact, one of Pepsi's largest potential markets lies not in the heavily industrialized northern cities or the tourist areas, but among the Moslem population, Russia's largest ethnic minority, whose traditional strictures forbid alcohol consumption. Numbering some thirty-five million, the Moslems occupy much of the Soviet Central

* Vera Micheles Dean, *The Nature of the Non-Western World* (New York: New American Library, 1957). p. 44–45

Asia, close to the Iranian border, a fact which has occasionally led the Soviets to relax their otherwise vigorous anti-religious propaganda aimed as much at the Moslems as any other religious group. In this vein, Pepsi could anticipate some success as a go-between in the clashing worlds of the Koran and the Kremlin.

Meanwhile, Pepsi's ad slogans were tailored to fit the priorities of acculturation. Many of them, for instance, were intended to inform the consumer that Pepsi should be drunk on ice. The results were ads like "A drink of cold Pepsi-Cola will create a good mood and will refresh you." Many of them sounded like a cross between a news release and what Madison Avenue calls "reason why" copy, generally reserved in the West for products far more utilitarian than soda. But at that point soda was consumerism. Pepsi symbolized détente, and was playing a very pragmatic role, both socially and politically.

The deal itself was announced with great fanfare less than two weeks after Nixon's reelection in November 1972. According to the contract concluded with Soviet trade officials, Pepsi was to supply all the technology, engineers, and managerial know-how to install a bottling plant with a three-million-case capacity at Novorossisk, a prime tourist area near the Black Sea. A Soviet trade organization—Sojuzplodoimport—would receive direct shipments of concentrate from which finished Pepsi-Cola was produced, in much the same fashion as domestic franchises. Unlike the domestic operations, however, this was a cooperative venture with Pepsi in partnership with the Soviet government. In keeping with its goal of importing Western resources without opening the economy to the disadvantages of foreign ownership, the Soviets structured the agreement along classic lines that marked every important East-West agreement growing out of detente. Payment would be made on a modified barter basis, with hard currency transfers being related to commodity exchange. The commodity in this case was Russia's premier vodka, Stolichnaya, already distributed in the United States by Monsieur Henri Wines, Ltd., which was acquired by PepsiCo for $26 million several months after Kosygin's 1971 liter-for-liter proposal to Kendall. Russia's dollar purchases of Pepsi-Cola were to be pegged to PepsiCo's dollar purchases of Stolichnaya, and the two figures were to be balanced after five years. Behind a million-dollar ad budget, sales of the high-priced vodka surpassed all expectations, and by 1977, construction had begun on a second plant in the Black Sea region. Plans were underway for three more there, as well as one each in Moscow, Leningrad, and Tallinon in Estonia. Kendall projected ten plants in the near future, and a total of thirty throughout the Soviet Union.

Unaccustomed to the nuances of East-West trade, Pepsi was anxious to avoid the barter arrangement at first, but Kendall changed his strategy when Llewellyn Thompson suggested that he make just such a proposal. An undisputed expert on Soviet affairs, Thompson was well aware of Soviet priorities and the historical importance of counter-purchase, or the modified barter arrangement. The rigorous pursuit of a nonconvertible monetary policy had always been one of the mainstays of Soviet autarky and economic isolation. In the absence of a meaningful monetary vehicle, straightforward barter long remained the principal form of trade with the Soviet Union. Yet this system proved totally inadequate for the massive transfers of Western resources that would speed Russian integration into the world system. Under the counter-purchase aspect of cooperation deals, the Western company, like Pepsi, agrees to take products as part of full payment for its exports to the Soviet Union. This novel feature permitted Eastern governments to continue their currency barriers while Western corporations took a quantum leap out of the containments of simple barter and mere commodity exchanges.* Western governments and private banks which had always financed trade on a limited basis could suddenly overwhelm the East with credits, confident that the products sold in Russia in partnership with a legal monopoly or bought back under counter-purchase would finance the repayments. The credits facilitated the transfer of the Western companies' assets and personnel in return for the benefits and guarantees from the government. The narrow alley of history known as East-West trade was suddenly the two-way vista of detente.

Early press reports of the deal spent more than a little space ruminating on how Kendall's intimacy with the President might have worked to Pepsi's advantage. "Among both Nixon's warmest admirers and among those who tend to be cynical about him," said the *New York Post*, "the President is given almost as much credit for the latest piece of good fortune for Pepsi as for the first" (the 1959 "Kitchen Debate" with Khrushchev). The stir stretched from Washington to Atlanta where a high-level Coca-Cola official grumbled that "there isn't any doubt that Nixon played a role" in Pepsi's coup. "His influence had to come in there somehow," said the executive, though he was unsure exactly how. Coke may well have used its influence to stir up embarrassment over presidential favoritism in Pepsi's Russian deal. During a 1974 hearing before the Senate Banking Committee, Kendall bristled under charges of special interest made by Senator Adlai Stevenson (D-Ill.). A former *New York Post* reporter recollects that Stevenson's own aides once confided that the questioning was inspired by then Coke attorney Joseph Califano, the former top-level Johnson aide. Meanwhile, a highly reputable businessman, mentioned but not named by the *Post*, said he was told by a top Soviet negotiator that President Nixon had privately communicated a request that Pepsi's bid be considered favorably.† A week-long investigation by the *Chicago Sun-Times* produced nothing but cautiously worded statements by a White House spokesman—"It was entirely a private transac-

---

* *Vodka-Cola* by Charles Levinson (London: Gordon & Cremonesi, 1978) provides a detailed description of the financial workings of detente. Samuel Pisar, another expert, elaborates, "You can't have dividends or profit participations. What you can have is a royalty payment for patents or know-how, engineering fees, management fees, interest, selling commissions. . . . There is nothing to prevent you from incorporating a company outside the USSR where the equity is 50–50 held by an American company and a Soviet enterprise. . . . None of this is precluded by Marx or Lenin." *Wall Street Journal*, March 29, 1973

† *New York Post*, December 13, 1972, p. 42. Subsequent revelations have disclosed that this businessman was David Karr, the formerly prominent entrepreneur in East-West trade who recently died in Paris under questionable circumstances. Karr's business contacts were well connected to both political parties, especially the Democrats. See *Fortune*, December 3, 1979, p. 94

tion"—and a Soviet diplomat who said Nixon's friendship with Kendall "didn't hurt" Pepsi's case.

The most heated denials naturally came from Kendall, who termed the businessman's charges "ridiculous" and "baloney." Kendall reacted with similar indignation to prodding by Donald Riegle (R-Mich.) during hearings on detente held by the House Foreign Affairs Committee in 1973. Rankled by Riegle's questions on the extent of his or other Pepsi executives' support for Nixon's re-election, Kendall snapped, "I don't think that this hearing is for that purpose, and I have made that statement on numerous occasions. It is in the public record."

> RIEGLE: Well, I still would like to know what the figure is, but I gather you have some reluctance to tell us.
>
> KENDALL: Yes, Mr. Congressman, because I don't like the connotation you are putting on it.
>
> RIEGLE: Well, I am not sure I am putting any more connotation on it than you are. I don't understand why it has to be a secret number. It would seem to be an open question. . . . And the fact that you are reluctant to indicate what the support level was bothers me, [and] is the kind of thing that adds to cynicism. . . . If someone, for example, is not a friend of the President, or if someone has not contributed large sums of money to the campaign, do they receive exactly the same treatment from the Soviet government with respect to profitable trade relationships? Frankly, I don't know the answer. . . . If you don't see the possible appearance of a special interest relationship here, I am surprised, because there is that appearance. If in fact it is only an appearance, I would like to put it away so that that question does not have to hang there.
>
> KENDALL: It has been put away several times, Mr. Congressman.
>
> RIEGLE: Well, it has not been put away to my satisfaction.

Kendall is the first to admit that Nixon "created the climate of understanding without which such a transaction would have been impossible." The essence of detente, however, is economic cooperation: as an aspect of that cooperation, trade priorities created the political climate of detente, not vice versa. Though there is no smoking gun to confirm the extent of presidential influence on Pepsi's success, the good fortunes befalling still other intimates and former clients of Nixon suggest that that influence was at work across the whole fabric of sensational agreements negotiated early in his second administration.

In September 1973, Kendall traveled to Moscow and then to Yalta where he, too, enjoyed Brezhnev's hospitality. The two men continued the discussions begun in Washington, agreeing that some institutional mechanism was necessary to put the U.S. private sector in touch with the Soviet government. During much of the negotiations, Kendall was assisted by Michael Lvoff, a Russian-speaking Pepsi vice-president directly descended from Leo Tolstoy, whose own life spanned both extremes of the Russian people's ancient conflict over how to relate to the West.

On his return, Kendall held a lengthy meeting with the President at San Clemente, and a month later, the US-USSR Trade and Economic Council was established, with Kendall serving as co-chairman. Fifty-two people served on the board, half of whom were Soviet officials. American members included the heads of major multinationals with a stake in detente, such as Atlantic Richfield, where Kendall served as a director, and General Electric and American Express, whose boards enjoyed the services of Coke's J. Paul Austin.

In 1972, the Coke executive who grumbled over Nixon's involvement in Pepsi's fortunes said that his company would continue its own five-year-long negotiations with the Soviets, but before Nixon's downfall the company had taken significant steps toward an agreement with the Kremlin for the eventual sale of its non-cola beverages. However, Coke was effectively shut out under Republican rule, and as Kendall said on the David Susskind Show in 1977, he hardly felt sorry for them.

Though he vehemently denied charges of presidential favoritism in the Russian deal, Kendall was quick to assert that business as a whole had a special historical mission in détente to ensure world peace and promote international understanding. Through a heightened exchange of technology, products, people, culture, and ideas, it provides more jobs, and improves trade and payments balances which together will create a greater abundance for all. Amid the technological boom and economic mobilization that constituted detente, Kendall's voice was the loudest in pleading the case for consumer products. As the first nonessential consumer item to be admitted, and perhaps even considered by the Soviets for joint venture status, Pepsi was the foremost sign of detente's higher potential. As Kendall told the Congress, "I think that the Pepsi-Cola announcement perhaps got more headlines in the world than anything else involved in detente because, as *The New York Times* said, when they saw a transaction of this nature, they were convinced that the détente was here, that there was a new era."*

Long a symbol of the Cold War, the soft drink was now the symbol of detente, a label Kendall brandished without any sense of paradox in this remarkable turnabout. An historic perspective would require the mention of Coke, something Kendall goes out of his way to avoid, but it would also point up the pertinent truth that détente, like the Cold War before it, was very much a product of the American creed of corporate growth. Coke and Pepsi embodied that creed more than their other corporate peers because growth in the area of competitive, nonessential consumer products cannot be spread over a five- or ten-year period as the auto makers might do. A lost foreign market or the development of inbred consumer preference can be extremely difficult to alter later, so

---

* U.S. Congress, House Committee on Foreign Affairs, *Détente*, Hearings, 93rd Congress, 2nd Session, 1974. p. 103

that in the soft-drink business at least, long-term, drawing-board growth is secondary to the consistent reckoning of growth in the short term.

Consumer pleasure though it is, Pepsi symbolizes an essentially economic detente characterized by more liberal trade and greater economic cooperation. But what of the greater detente, in which it is hoped that trade will be the prologue for heightened exchange between cultures? Here, Pepsi symbolized the export of America's consumer culture. With Pepsi came its advertising, the values and images designed to create a Pepsi generation on a worldwide scale. During detente, the advertising was altered somewhat to account for the political realities of the Eastern markets. As Pepsi's Alan Pottasch, then senior vice-president for creative services, told *Esquire's* Robert Scheer, "We were afraid in the beginning ... that some countries which don't have democracies would oppose the concept of 'Feelin' Free' [Pepsi's U.S. campaign in the early seventies] on the possibility that they would take it only literally. ... If you substitute 'carefree' for the word 'free' you're getting close to what we're really saying—feeling carefree, not feeling free in the sense of breaking the chains that bind you, but feeling free in spirit, and feeling free in thinking and independent enjoyment. So feeling carefree was the best way to explain what we meant in foreign languages and that's what we've done."

Kendall's lobbying activities to liberalize trade relations with the Soviets readily confirm his explicit emphasis on the economic aspects of detente. Two overlapping concerns arising out of these priorities are whether economic detente might not actually conflict with the greater one and, more immediately, whether the whole structure of détente is not a house of cards listing decisively eastward. In the headlong rush into detente, the banks and the multinationals may well have slighted the economic interests of the rest of American society. Credits to the Soviets and bloc countries have more than tripled since 1973, and now range somewhere between $30 and $40 billion. This increase has placed a greater burden on United States capital reserves and, according to Jacques Billy, NATO's chief economist, heightens worries of long-range capital shortage and, hence, greater inflation. The banks and multinationals were initially more than willing to risk that development at home because the financial techniques underlying detente virtually guaranteed that the credits would be repaid. However, because of the haste to exploit a developing market, many in the financial community are no longer so sure what the stakes of that repayment will be. "We have a saying," a Swiss banker notes, "make a small loan, and you have created a debtor; make a large loan, and you have created a partner." The whole question, then, is one of leverage. "I don't want to use the word blackmail," said a European banker deeply involved in loans to the East, "but that's what it could amount to ... if the Soviets were ever to seek 'favors' as conditions of keeping up their repayments. ... It needn't be anything as sinister as the espionage or illegal loans envisioned in the nightmare situations. ... Most likely, the Soviets would seek such commercial favors as the bank pressing its corporate customers [a Coca-Cola or a PepsiCo] to import Soviet goods in order to make repayment possible."* An American banker adds that hanging over every deliberation is the potential threat of default, which could ruin a bank, or in the more extreme scenarios contemplated by NATO officials and U.S. economists, shake the entire financial structure of the West.

With economic détente in this precarious state, what hope is there for the greater one? Soviet spokesmen repeat continuously that detente is exclusively a matter of governments and does not apply to internal social or labor relations. "Peaceful coexistence," as detente is still called in the Soviet Union, is a time-honored strategy going back to the days when Lenin was backed by Armand Hammer. It allows for ideological confrontation right alongside heightened trade. As Secretary Brezhnev reiterated in the 26th Congress of the Communist Party in 1976, "No one should expect that because of the detente Communists will reconcile themselves with capitalist exploitation. . . ."

Pepsi's advertising switch from "free" to "carefree" offers a clue as to the concessions businesses can and perhaps must make in the eastward flow of ideas in order to support the westward flow of profits. But what about the flow of influence in the other direction? "I am concerned," said Senator Stevenson to Kendall during a 1974 hearing on Eximbank credits, "about such possibilities as enormous investments through the Export-Import Bank giving the Soviet Union increased leverage in bargaining on commercial and also non-commercial matters."† Such a huge financial stake abroad could lead to a very conservative attitude in Washington toward anything that might upset the delicate balance. From Guatemala to Iran, from Uganda to Greece, Coke and Pepsi have each been close to authoritarian, repressive regimes, which have never held anything like the leverage the Russians now seem to have. If the companies did little or nothing to liberalize situations where they may have had the opportunity to do so, how will they react under the relentless pressures of economics?

There has been little outward concern about such considerations since the heyday of détente. Détente is a good thing, both in principle and in fact, and whatever the ironies of either man's traditional anti-communism, Kendall and Nixon deserve a measure of credit as architects of the policy. Nevertheless, a cautious perspective on both the degree and speed of the West-to-East transfer of assets, as well as the special interests supporting the policy, is a valid one. At least until the 1980 Soviet invasion of Afghanistan, détente seemed as new and unlimited to Kendall as it ever had. He was consistently fond of talking of the pent-up consumer demand in the Soviet Union, and gave the impression of believing that the old American know-how, new technological magic, and sheer consumer demand might somehow turn the priorities of the Russian leaders toward the West. His overwhelming belief in the power of personal relations to transform history is an endearing quality, but comes off seeming a little simplistic in a person of his considerable experience. "I have never seen a country in all

* *Wall Street Journal,* February 22, 1977, p. 1
† U.S. Congress, Senate Committee on Banking, *Role of the US Export Import Bank in US International Economic Policy,* Hearings, 93rd Congress, 2nd Session, 1974. p. 278

my trips around the world where personal relationships are as important as they are in the Soviet Union," he told the House Foreign Affairs Committee. ". . . I think the more contact we can have, the more we assure that we are going to have this generation of peace. . . ." Elsewhere he remarked to Robert Scheer that "General Secretary Brezhnev is a very warm, very outgoing person, he's an extrovert, not an introvert. I've got some pictures taken in June and you can see it. He's a *warm* person. He's very outspoken. When you talk to General Secretary Brezhnev and he says something, you don't have to wonder what he meant by that, which I like because I'm a direct outspoken person myself. I don't want to think 'what did he really mean?' "*

In the face of the awesome proportions of Soviet communism, Kendall has reached a kind of personal, greater detente of his own, where an altogether sincere exchange of snapshots, hugs, and handshakes awakened that syrupy sensation from the Khrushchev days that perhaps these Russians are not so different from us Americans after all. The Revolution be damned; these Reds have been educated; they want more things; they want a better life. Somehow, in Kendall's eyes, the potent combination of Pepsi for the people and profits for the government would be the perfect prologue to the greater detente that would melt what's left of the Iron Curtain into blow-dryers, steel-belted radials and the West's irrepressible cultural mobility to go with them.

From Harvard economist John Kenneth Galbraith to Zbigniew Brzezinski, President Carter's advisor on national security affairs, many western observers have believed that the processes bringing capitalism and socialism closer together would continue. Either the two systems would converge, adopting each other's positive features and discarding the negative ones, or they would each emerge in parallel by mutating into completely different systems from their originals, but with essential characteristics that were markedly similar. Sharing each other's penchant for science, planning, and bigness, these new systems would exhibit identical technotronic parameters—high productivity, capital intensive and low unit labor costs—which would discard the worst political and economic and authoritarian features and substitute programs maximizing social welfare.

As one whose salesmanship has brought the triumph of the nonessential to nearly every port in the world, Kendall would be out of character if he did not harbor a third vision of some formulated, fast-food utopia that submerged the Communist vessel in the endless sea of consumer gratification and Western predilections. It is a tempting, potentially self-deceptive vision which might encourage the Soviets to keep faith with the capitalist truth that real wealth can be forged by first going into debt. Laden with the imperatives of retiring such debts, Kendall might find himself among those who discover too late that the shoe has really been on the other foot. The greatest danger would then be to succumb to the tendency, however remote it might presently be, to watch while America

---

* *Esquire*, April, 1975, p. 160. In keeping with the spirit of détente, Kendall commissioned a Russian artist to paint his portrait in 1973.

became more like Eastern European countries, where feeling "carefree" was
more appropriate than just "feeling free."

The first great stumbling block to détente arose over concern for political rights
in the USSR. The trade bill before the Congress in 1973 could have codified
détente in historic fashion by granting the Soviet Union the same tariff privileges
then accorded to 130 non-Communist nations as well as some of the satellite
countries in the Eastern bloc. This "most-favored nation" (MFN) status was
seen as vital to the economic logic of detente, since tariffs on some Soviet products could be twice those on comparable French or German imports. In July
1972, Senator Henry Jackson (D-Wash.), a darling of the defense industry and
one of the more vocal anti-Soviet spokesmen, caught wind of Soviet intentions
to impose a discriminatory tax on Jewish emigrés, and introduced an amendment to the trade bill to deny MFN status to any Communist countries enact-
ing such measures. Jackson and co-sponsor Charles Vanik had tremendous support in Congress and among Jewish groups while Kendall lobbied fiercely against
the bill, marshaling the support of dozens of corporation heads who supported
detente. Kissinger and Nixon tried to outflank Jackson with assurances that the
Soviets intended to drop the tax. Jackson stood fast, and Congress wound up
granting the Russian MFN status but only limited credits. Insulted, they rejected the trade agreement completely in early 1975. In a bitter and unusual
press conference called by the US-USSR Trade and Economic Council, Kendall
blamed Congress for allowing other Western nations to get the trade and the
jobs that could have belonged to the United States.

In the extroverted style he so admired in Brezhnev, Kendall called collapse of
the trade agreement only a temporary setback and he has been pressing Congress
ever since to confer MFN status on the Soviets. For all the support in the business community for such a move, Kendall certainly had perhaps the most to
gain. A 1977 study by the U.S. International Trade Commission found that
"the item with the highest tariff difference between MFN and Soviet tariff rate
is distilled alcoholic beverages. . . . About 93 percent of U.S. imports from the
USSR in 1974 came in either duty free or with a very small additional tariff."*

Pepsi's dealings with the Russians aroused resentment among American Jewish groups from the beginning. The Union of Councils for Soviet Jews called for
a boycott of Pepsi's products within a month of the announcement of the Soviet
deal. Though it wasn't joined by the much larger National Conference on Soviet
Jewry, it still had support from American groups, one of whose leaders, a NASA
scientist, remarked, "We wouldn't boycott any firms dealing in necessities. We
want PepsiCo to resist trade with the Soviets until they [the Soviets] act like a
proper member of the civilized community." Feelings ran high when word
leaked out in August 1973 that Kendall was to be honored for his service to the
National Alliance of Businessmen by the American Jewish Committee, the most

* United States International Trade Commission report for House Ways and Means Committee, April 3, 1977. *Probable Impact on U.S. Trade of Granting Most-Favored Nation Treatment to USSR.* p. 1-2, 8-9

prestigious American Jewish organization. The committee acknowledged that the award was no longer appropriate, and Chairman Richard Maass issued a dignified retraction which cited Kendall nonetheless for his domestic civic activities.

Meanwhile, Hadassah, a women's Zionist organization, complained vigorously that Pepsi had no plant in Israel because of its lucrative business in the Arab countries. In 1968, Coke had been boycotted by the Arabs after similar pressure from the American Jewish community forced it to license a franchise in Israel. However, Pepsi was able to convince the Jewish community that it avoided Israel because the market there could not support another major cola. This facile claim seems irrelevant since PepsiCo has never shied from competing in markets a fraction the size of Israel. Israel concurred, apparently to avoid a further erosion of its balance of payments, and Pepsi was able to avoid jeopardizing its lucrative Arab markets.

As much as any business executive in this country, Kendall has consistently been in the front lines of battle where business, politics, and social issues collide. He is a superbly pragmatic executive, whose staunch belief that government should represent business more than regulate it propelled him into a highly charged activism. As head of several international trade missions and business groups, Kendall put his mouth where his money was, and thereby anticipated the powerful business lobbies which besiege Capitol Hill in the 1980s. No one begrudged Kendall his pragmatism, but his genius never spared him the scrutiny of those who drew the line—if they could find it—at opportunism. Kendall made no bones of his friendship with Nixon, but charges of favoritism were an assault on his honor. During the dawn of detente, when Pepsi unveiled its Russian deal and "peace-with-honor" was the watchword of the Nixon Presidency, Kendall became the topic of some whispers in Washington.

Whatever the truth of the Russian deal, there was much that happened during Nixon's first four years that was bad for Pepsi, including the cyclamate ban (see Chapter 16), as well as the government suit against Pepsi's acquisition of Rheingold Breweries or its complaint against the soft-drink industry's franchise system (see Chapter 19). Though none of these pitfalls originated with the White House, there is no evidence of presidential favor to stem the tide. The real dividend in the long-standing alliance lay abroad where, Jack Anderson suggested, many leaders "remembered that he [Nixon] had once traveled for the company. This was enough to give Pepsi an edge with world leaders who thought they might please the White House by keeping Pepsi on tap. It is this psychology more than any nod from the White House that enabled PepsiCo to negotiate a rash of bottling contracts overseas."*

Yet the psychology that created a consensus abroad somehow smelled of conspiracy at home. Whether there was a "smoking gun" or merely a confluence of interests really didn't matter. In the darkness of Watergate, the hounds in the press came out, baying until they drowned out the Republican peers or the Pepsi loyalists still maintaining that Kendall was an honorable man.

*The Washington Post, December 31, 1972. p. C7

CHAPTER FOURTEEN

The Pepsi Papers

IN 1965, the head of Schenley Industries, a major liquor distributor, donated $1 million to set up the J. Edgar Hoover Foundation. Even before he became a close friend of the late FBI Director, Lewis Rosenstiel had enjoyed a healthy working relationship with associates of Meyer Lansky who had distributed Schenley liquor during Prohibition. Rosenstiel further solidified his working ties with Lansky during World War II when he sought Cuban sugar as a base for cane spirits. Despite his questionable associations, Rosenstiel commanded the approbation of Hoover's closest aide, Louis B. Nichols, who was a Schenley vice-president since 1957 and the Hoover Foundation's first president. Its secretary was Cartha "Deke" DeLoach, Nichols' protégé and successor at the Bureau, as Hoover's most loyal servant, and one of the prime candidates to replace him as FBI director. In 1970, DeLoach left the Bureau to become Vice-President for Corporate Affairs at PepsiCo.

For DeLoach, it was the end of a twenty-eight-year stint at the FBI, beginning as a baby-faced messenger and ending as assistant to the director in charge of all investigative activities. He had literally run the FBI on a day-to-day basis, exercising extraordinary authority as Hoover's personal surrogate. Ever the organization man, he developed a loyalty to his boss that would be the envy of any corporate executive. He was a master at protecting his boss's monarchical hold on law enforcement and domestic intelligence from challenges by rival agencies, such as the CIA, the Treasury, or the Pentagon. Even more interesting to Kendall was his absolute dedication to sustaining a Bureau image to the director's liking. As Sanford Ungar explains in FBI, "Every press release was required to begin with Hoover's name and to include at least two other mentions of him; the Director's name also had to appear twice in every script approved by the Bureau for the weekly program about the FBI on NBC radio's weekend 'Monitor' program. Part of the press policy also involved cooperating only with certified FBI 'friends,' and cutting off all contact with reporters, editors, and organization perceived to be 'enemies.' "*

Beyond his sensibilities toward image, DeLoach was a wholly viable political asset with considerable connections both on Capitol Hill and in the Johnson White House. As Hoover's congressional liaison, DeLoach oversaw the Bureau's

---

* Sanford Ungar, FBI (Boston: Little Brown & Co., 1975). p. 284. One such friend of the Bureau named by the Senate Intelligence Committee, Jeremiah O'Leary of the Washington Star, wrote a glowing tribute to DeLoach on his retirement from the Bureau that was inserted in the Congressional Record. June 30, 1970, p. 19113

drafting of letters to friendly members of Congress for use in making statements important to the Bureau or in prying loose documents from other parts of the government. "It was an intricate game, in which DeLoach played a role not unlike that of an outside lobbyist. He kept his track carefully . . . and was especially good . . . , says one former Bureau official, at 'tooting his own horn' in his memos to Hoover about congressional contacts, boasting, for example, about having brandy with Senator Eastland . . ."* [subsequently a great friend of the soft-drink industry].

Kendall clearly appreciated DeLoach's fine balance of pragmatism and discretion. In dealing with Congress, DeLoach had access to the Bureau's elaborate indexing system, which catalogued every reference in FBI files to members of Congress and gave comprehensive details as to the source. Complete with extensive news clippings and other material, these files became part of DeLoach's equipment after joining Kendall when, according to Ungar, he relied on an old protégé at the Bureau to perform name checks on people of interest to PepsiCo.

DeLoach had also been the Bureau's liaison with President Johnson almost from the moment LBJ took office, and as such, developed a degree of involvement and intimacy with the nation's First Family unprecedented in the FBI. Though not as much of a force at the Nixon White House, DeLoach was the official Attorney General Mitchell called upon at the Bureau, invariably bypassing the more trenchant Hoover, just as Johnson had done before him. Hoover's heir apparent turned fifty in 1970 with no sign that his boss was ever going to step down voluntarily. And even if he did, there was some talk that DeLoach was growing increasingly wary of long-latent controversies about him that might emerge during the selection and confirmation process.† On top of that, he was in debt, and eager to serve another master who was, perhaps, a bit less jealous than the first. As he later told Robert Scheer, "Don Kendall is a J. Edgar Hoover with heart."

In DeLoach, Kendall got what he sought—a professional liaison par excellence, a discreet operator whose soft-spoken ways concealed a bevy of formidable connections, an unscrupulous enforcer—a cop, after all—capable of drawing on his connections under delicate circumstances while tending to the routine tasks of company security, and finally, a spokesman full of confidence and dedication to the right image. Certainly, Deke was not unique in shifting from law enforcement and government intelligence to industry. Leo Conroy, Director of Corporate Security for Coke, had been a special agent with the FBI for thirty-two years before joining the company in 1974. In fact, hundreds of retired special agents

*Ungar, op. cit., 285-86
† Ungar, op. cit., p. 295. Charges have emerged from a former special agent and other associates that he finagled extra reimbursements for expenses arising out of his Pentagon liaison, and over a twenty-five-year period, extensively double-billed the Bureau and the American Legion, a nongovernment organization friendly to the FBI for which he was also liaison. Moverover, a *Los Angeles Times* piece was written in 1970 which detailed these charges as well as a federal grand jury's scrutiny of DeLoach's relations with a contractor suspected of corrupt practices. The piece never ran, Ungar speculates, because DeLoach decided to leave government service.

have found a home in the private sector protecting against theft of patents and proprietary information, computer penetration or electronic eavesdropping by a competitor as well as the transfer of commercial products in violation of law or contractual agreements, an area that has proven especially troublesome to Coke and Pepsi on the domestic front (see Chapter 19). DeLoach was naturally an expert in such countermeasures as infiltration, intimidation, bugging, and surveillance, and he arrived at PepsiCo fresh from the helm of the Bureau's extensive mid-1960s targeting of radicals, militants, and suspected Communist subversives. With the coming of détente, he managed to dispel three decades of conditioned demonology almost overnight. "I deal with the Soviets on a regular basis . . . but I see that as a broadening of my own thinking and personality and I'm glad to have the opportunity. I have some good friends among the Russians today . . . I admire them . . . I admire their business acumen; I admire their sticktoitiveness; I admire the loyalty they have to their country. In short, I'm having a ball."

Détente itself was warmly received, judging by the reaction of the business community to the second Nixon candidacy. All told, the Committee to Re-elect the President (CREEP) raised some $60 million, the most awesome sum ever compiled for a political campaign. Virtually all of it resulted from the joint efforts of Herbert Kalmbach and Maurice Stans. Kalmbach had been intimately involved in Nixon's 1960 and 1968 presidential bids, and in preparing himself for 1972, Kalmbach insisted, "I never want to be outspent again." He was the chief fund raiser until February 1972, when he became second to Stans, CREEP's official finance chairman. In 1970, they had presided over the "Town House Project," a secret $3.9 million fund for the congressional elections, to which Kendall pledged $250,000.* A second secret fund, totalling over $1 million, left over from 1968, got Stans and Kalmbach off to a running start in 1972. Here again, familiar names dot the landscape, often on the wrong side of the law. Political contributions out of corporate funds were strictly forbidden, requiring contributions of this kind to be made through corporate executives. PepsiCo gave $100,-000 in this fashion while Salomon Brothers kicked in $117,000. Hornblower-Weeks (and its new merged firm, Hemphill-Noyes) acted as brokers for over $300,000 worth of stock owned by CREEP. Braniff Airways, whose board included Robert Stewart of PepsiCo, gave $40,000 illegally, and was charged by the Civil Aeronautics Board with diverting over $640,000 into a secret political fund.† Meanwhile, Occidental's Armand Hammer channeled $7,000 directly to the Nixon campaign and funneled another $54,000 through an Occidental senior executive vice-president, who was later fined $1,000 for concealing the source of the contribution. Hammer received a year's probation and was fined $3,000 for making illegal campaign contributions. Stans himself was fined $5,000 after pleading guilty to five charges of violating campaign finance laws.

* J. Anthony Lukas, *Nightmare* (New York: Bantam, 1977). p. 151
† ibid., p. 172-73

None of these contributions was as significant or ill-fated as the $100,000 given by Howard Hughes in two installments in 1969 and 1970. The gift was arranged at the suggestion of Bebe Rebozo by two of Hughes's top men. One was Richard Danner, an ex-FBI man who had been present in Miami in 1952 when Nixon and Rebozo were first introduced.* Now a Washington attorney working as Hughes's liaison to the Nixon administration, Danner assisted Robert Maheu, another former FBI special agent and chief of Hughes' Nevada operations, in arranging the gift.

Maheu had gone to work for Hughes in the 1950s, and had handled his massive purchases of Las Vegas casinos in the 1960s from identified organized crime persons close to Jimmy Hoffa and the Teamsters. The Murchison empire, whose domain Pepsi and Nixon entered in 1963, had profited both politically and financially from its Teamster connections. In his ongoing activities for Howard Hughes, Maheu had recurring meetings with Thomas Webb, the Murchison attorney and associate of Great Southwest's Bedford Wynne.† Richard Danner saw even more of the Murchison circle between 1968 and 1973, meeting with such key figures as I. Irving Davidson and Clint Murchison, Jr. As we saw earlier, Hughes's Hollywood attorney throughout this period, Greg Bautzer, was director of Seven Arts with Clint Murchison and Pepsi's Charles Allen, and was himself a director of Pepsi United Bottlers in the early sixties.

Pepsi was one of Nixon's staunchest allies, yet these connections to Hughes moved it closer to the center of the crisis that finally sunk the President. Though so auspicious in its beginnings, that $100,000 contribution appears to have led almost directly to the Watergate break-in and Nixon's precipitous decline.‡ The benevolent air surrounding the gift quickly evaporated in 1970 when Hughes and Maheu had their famous falling out. The loyal lieutenant was summarily fired and banished from all of Hughes's properties, but not before he gathered up a slew of memos that had passed back and forth between the two of them over the years. Those memos found their way into the safe of Maheu's ally Hank Greenspun, Las Vegas's leading newspaper man and an associate of Jack Anderson. The White House was terrified that those memos could indeed "sink Nixon," as Greenspun hinted, and when innuendos about them began to turn up in Jack Anderson's column in January 1971, the White House made plans to break into Greenspun's safe.

Enter CREEP's general counsel, G. Gordon Liddy, flashing his Gemstone plan for White House counterintelligence and break-ins. With him comes E. Howard Hunt, the retired sleuth of the CIA whose firsthand flights of skulduggery spanning a twenty-three-year career became the basis for forty-six novels of the adventure, intrigue, and moral ambiguity in the life of a spy. A specialist in "dirty tricks," he had been chief of political action in the 1954 overthrow of the Arbenz government in Guatemala and, like Pepsi's Robert Geddes Morton, had

---

* Messick, *Lansky*, op. cit., p. 189
† Peter Dale Scott, *Crime and Cover-Up*, op. cit., p. 38
‡ Two highly respected observers of Watergate advance this view. See J. Anthony Lukas, op. cit., and Carl Oglesby, *The Yankee and Cowboy War* (New York: Berkeley, 1977)

played a key role in the Bay of Pigs operation. Written off in the late sixties by the CIA as a has-been, he was reportedly saddled with increasingly pedestrian assignments and yearned for a return to action. He certainly found it at the Robert R. Mullen Co., a Washington-based public relations firm that became a focus of the Watergate investigation. In coming to the Mullen Company in April 1970, Hunt was aware that the firm had acted as a CIA front in the sixties, providing cover for a variety of people performing services for the agency overseas. In 1971, Robert Fillet, formerly of PepsiCo's Division of Retail Planning and the son of a celebrated Pepsi salesman from the Al Steele era, was allegedly employed at the Chinese Chamber of Commerce, a Mullen subsidiary dedicated to the advancement of East-West trade. It is not known just how Fillet came in contact with the Mullen Company or what he actually did for them while there, but the activities of Pepsi's management overlapped with those of the Mullen Company going back to at least 1959.

The United States Information Agency, which had helped assemble the American Exposition in Moscow, was a one-time Mullen client, and the famous photographs of Kendall, Nixon, and Khrushchev sipping Pepsi appeared in a 1962 authorized, in-house biography of Pepsi, courtesy of the Mullen Company.* Hunt's acquaintance with Mullen dated back to the forties when Mullen was a director of information for the Marshall Plan in Paris. As public relations director for Citizens for Eisenhower in 1952, Mullen became acquainted with Nixon and later met several high-ranking CIA officials (including Richard Helms, who admitted while CIA director that "Mr. Mullen did us the patriotic favor of allowing us to put up some of our agents abroad under his company). He set up the Mullen Company in 1956 and gathered clients through his strong connections in government and the Republican Party. He got a big boost from a prominent Republican, Samuel W. Meek, board chairman of J. Walter Thompson, Pepsi's agency for international markets, and joint Mullen-Thompson offices were set up in Paris, London, and Tokyo. Meek was a member in the early sixties of the Cuban Freedom Committee, a CIA-propaganda outlet founded just prior to the Bay of Pigs invasion with $2 million in agency funds. A CIA memo cited by J. Anthony Lukas in *Nightmare* reported that Robert Mullen was "instrumental in the formation" of the committee.† At JWT, Meek personally handled the prestigious Pan Am account whose board has included a succession of Pepsi luminaries, including Kendall, who lived near Meek in the wealthy New York suburb of Greenwich, Connecticut. Another Mullen client during the Nixon years was the Department of Health, Education, and Welfare. Its secretary between 1968 and 1972 was Robert H. Finch, an old Nixon-Kalmbach associate from California who was also a key campaign director and presidential counselor in areas such as domestic intelligence.‡ His successor at

---

* Milward Martin, *Twelve Full Ounces* (New York: Holt, Rinehart, Winston). p. 110
† J. Anthony Lukas, op. cit., p. 52-53. Another alleged committee member was Dallas Republican Party Chairman Peter O'Donnell (see Chapter 10).
‡ ibid., p. 43

HEW in 1972, Casper Weinberger, subsequently became a director of PepsiCo. Another Mullen client, the Pullman Company, had a major stake in détente.

Kendall stuck by Nixon throughout the ordeal of the Watergate investigation, though in surveying the sprawling middle classes Nixon had dubbed the "silent majority," Pepsi marketing people were ironically accurate when they sensed that things were not quite right for a scheduled ad campaign based on the slogan "smilin' majority."* As time wore on and the Oval Office tapes unraveled, Kendall was beset by a growing disenchantment, more because of the White House's clumsy handling of the issue surrounding the tapes than what was on them. In November 1973, Kendall said in an interview that the two missing Watergate tapes "created doubts in people's mind" about the President's credibility, but he felt nevertheless that Nixon still enjoyed the support of the business community. "I don't know of anybody who's better equipped to run the country than Nixon," Kendall declared. Two weeks later, he was caught in somewhat of a "dirty trick" himself when he erroneously told prestigious Democrats that former Secretary of State Dean Rusk and Ladybird Johnson agreed to sign an ad calling for the patriotic necessity of "preserving this nation." Rusk acknowledged receiving a copy of the ad under conditions of extreme secrecy, but both he and Mrs. Johnson, who had never seen the ad, indicated they had no intention of signing it. Warning against the "weakening of America" and "surrendering to mob rule," the ad sought to convert Nixon's crisis into a replica of Johnson's predicament four years before when he was besieged by antiwar demonstrators. It was one more way in which the Kendall-Nixon duo went to the well of Johnson Democrats to shore up political clout, but as Evans and Novak wrote, "Republicans who know and still admire Mr. Nixon were aghast that Kendall was given a role in the ad campaign. With Don Kendall's debts to Nixon, and Nixon's obligations to Kendall well known, one pro-Republican told us, 'using Kendall to get signatures is incredibly stupid'. . . . If the real issue were saving the Presidency and not Richard M. Nixon, far more objective sponsorship than Don Kendall would have been at hand."†

As much as Nixon and Kendall courted LBJ's political supporters over the years, it was a message from Johnson conveyed through Kendall that ultimately led to Nixon's downfall. Sometime early in the Nixon presidency, Kendall passed a message from LBJ recommending that Nixon install a taping system in the White House since his predecessor had found the recordings "exceedingly valuable in preparing his memoirs."‡ Nixon followed the advice, of course, and his use of them was far more extensive and complex. Herman Schaeffer, a Pepsi vice-president who traveled with Nixon in the sixties, believed that Nixon may well have had an obsession with tapes that was part of a larger pattern of self-destructiveness. Recalling a sensitive Pepsi overture to Egypt in the wake of Coke's

* A "smilin' majority" campaign posed legal problems since Pepsi was not in the majority in terms of sales.
† *Washington Post*, January 9, 1974
‡ Lukas, op. cit., p. 507

expulsion from the Arab countries, Schaeffer told Robert Scheer, "When we first went into some room at the Nile Hilton, he said, 'Now let's get off in a corner someplace and make sure we're not bugged because we're gonna talk about what you want me to do tomorrow when I see such and such and what I'm supposed to tell him.' "

His fear of being heard undoubtedly gave rise to a corresponding sensitivity over what was said, when, and to whom, and it does seem ironic that Kendall, the outspoken man who never wanted to wonder what a person meant, was so drawn to a protected shadowy figure whose most famous nickname—Tricky Dick—referred to his frequent compulsion to say the opposite of what he intended. The apparent irony vanishes, however, in the likelihood that the seemingly paranoid Nixon was all too aware of *Pepsi's* alleged long-time use of extensive in-house surveillance, which surfaced—like that of Nixon—from an otherwise friendly witness at a confidential 1973 proceeding. According to a source close to PepsiCo, a young witness testifying at a labor arbitration acknowledged under cross examination that the company had security people join the Teamsters Local in the early seventies "to find out what was going on." This covert activity would undoubtedly have been the assignment of J. Edgar Hoover's former heavy, Deke DeLoach. However, the very skills which drew him to Kendall's attention later became a source of concern to Nixon, who harbored suspicions of having been bugged by this LBJ intimate during the 1968 campaign.

At this time Johnson became certain that Nixon was trying to snarl the Paris peace talks by hinting that if Hanoi held out until election day, they would get a better deal from Nixon if he were elected. Enraged, Johnson directed the FBI to examine the phone records of Nixon's suspected go-betweens, including running mate Spiro Agnew. As President, Nixon learned of this operation from Hoover and, although no evidence of wiretapping ever turned up, Nixon told an aide, "We were bugged in '68 . . . Hoover told me, and he also told Mitchell personally that this had happened. . . ."[*] In the futile attempt to justify his bugging of Watergate, Nixon resolved to get this story out. DeLoach would probably have been the key man of the 1968 mission, just as he had headed a twelve-man surveillance team of FBI agents at the 1964 Democratic National Convention which gathered information on Martin Luther King, Jr., and other suspected Kennedy loyalists. In a memo, the Nixon White House contemplated pressuring him through Kendall. "Mitchell should probably have Kendall call DeLoach in and say that if this project turns up anything that DeLoach hasn't covered with us, he [Kendall] will, of course, have to fire him."[†] Mitchell called DeLoach, who let him review the files on the 1968 operation, but nothing ever came of it. Nixon, of course, was destroyed by the magnetic magic he thought would protect him from his enemies and immortalize him for history. Kendall was one of

[*] ibid., op. cit., p. 385
[†] ibid., p. 386

the last to jump ship, landing in the lifeboat of Gerald Ford, whose leadership capabilites he was praising within hours of the resignation.

One of the lesser known operations of the White House plumbers was a break-in at the Chilean embassy in Washington only a month before the ill-fated one at the Watergate. In the quiet, predawn hours of May 14, 1972, Frank Sturgis, Bernard Barker, and the others rummaged through the files, their gloved hands searching for documents and secret communications concerning the 1973 overthrow of Chilean President Salvador Allende, one of the most sensitive and sordid chapters of foreign intrigue in modern American history.* Though International Telephone and Telegraph (ITT) has long been associated with this political upheaval, PepsiCo, too, was involved. As he did elsewhere, Kendall sought to protect Pepsi's interests in Chile, in part by encouraging direct intervention in Chilean affairs.

Chile's Socialist President Salvador Allende, elected by a popular majority on September 4, 1970 and violently overthrown three years later, aroused the fear of another Castro as did no other political figure in the West. In the previous Chilean presidential elections in 1964, major intervention by the CIA and the State Department helped to defeat Allende and elect Christian Democrat Eduardo Frei. "U.S. government intervention in 1964 was blatant and obscene," said one strategically placed intelligence officer quoted in *The Washington Post.*† The CIA used that far-reaching covert program, costing some $3 million, to perfect some of the techniques it would use against Allende again between 1970 and 1973.‡ Meanwhile, during the Frei years, Chile received more American aid per capita than any other country in the world except Vietnam. Frei was also the darling of the American business community, which was largely behind David Rockefeller's organization of the Business Group for Latin America, a gathering of thirty-seven leading multinationals which then controlled some 85 percent of American investments in the region. The Business Group was one of the forerunners of the much larger Council on Latin America, whose activities were systematically integrated into the CIA's programs in Chile. During the mid-sixties, it will be remembered, the council ballooned into a powerful business lobby with over two hundred members, including Coca-Cola Export and PepsiCo. Kendall was a vice-chairman of the council in the early seventies when both of the soft-drink giants were joined by the banks, airlines, heavy industrial companies, and ad agencies within their respective spheres. ITT and the copper giants, Anaconda and Kennecott, were also important members whose major holdings in Chile, along with those of the rest of the group, totaled

* North American Congress on Latin America, *Latin America & Empire Report,* July-August, 1974, p. 9
† *The Washington Post,* April 6, 1973
‡ CIA dollars were channeled through the Chilean black market, where the unofficial exchange rate boosted the value up to five times the official rate. *Covert Action in Chile: 1963-73.* Staff Report of the Select Committee to Study Government Operations with Respect to Intelligence. 94th Congress, 1st session, December 18, 1975, p. 1

nearly $1 billion and were backed by some $600 million worth of U.S. government anti-expropriation insurance.*

This huge foreign investment ultimately spelled ruin for Frei's projected reforms, and paved the way directly for Allende. Holding themelves out as a third way somewhere between capitalism and socialism, Frei and the Christian Democrats had promised a lot—redistribution of national income, an end to unemployment and inflation, an attack on monopolies, and increased economic independence. But as Ruy Mauro and others have argued, that billion-dollar foreign investment was highly concentrated in a narrow sector of the Chilean economy dedicated to modern, capital-intensive industries. Luxury goods, durable consumer goods, chemicals, oil, plastics, paper—these industries were more productive and earned higher profits than local capital invested in traditional industries, including mass consumer goods, which employed the vast majority of the population.

Pepsi had a special part to play in this marketing mix. Its manufacture and distribution used a fair amount of sophisticated machinery, and it was thus one of the few, if not the only, *locally* financed consumer product rooted in this *international* flow of capital-intensive technology. As such, Pepsi filled the archetypal role in Chile it shares with Coke around the world: it was the cutting edge of modernizing commerce, able to embrace all sectors of the society even if it represents only the true economic interests of the tiniest one. In Chile, its advertising pushed this tendency to the limit by associating the product with values of consumerism, leisure, recreation, and mobility equally suited to enhancing the sale of the higher-priced luxury goods.

Politically, Frei was tied to this tiny sector of the economy that wanted to foster the entrance of foreign capital and technology and restructure the internal market to increase the purchasing power of the high income groups. The result was that 15 percent of the consumers prospered under policies that produced a recession for the other 85 percent. Salaries fell as prices and unemployment rose, and the working class was suddenly allied with a whole segment of the middle class in growing discontent.

Enter Allende. During his famous interviews with David Frost, Nixon recalled that around mid-1970, an "Italian businessman" met with him in the Oval Office and, according to Nixon, remarked that "if Allende should win the election in Chile, and then you have Castro in Cuba, what you will in effect have in Latin America is a red sandwich and eventually it will all be red." Nixon most certainly agreed, but at the same time was confident that Allende would not win. After all, the CIA had spent $2 million in covert actions in Chile between 1964 and 1969, and was advancing between $800,000 and $1 million to repeat the anti-Allende propaganda effort of 1964 which had equated Allende

---

* According to charges leveled by former U.S. Ambassador to Chile Edward Korry, ITT's subsequent activities against the Allende government amounted to "provocation" which should rightfully have voided the $92.5 million claim they subsequently collected from the U.S. Treasury. *Penthouse*, March 1978, p. 72

with violence, terror, repression, and Russian intervention.* Despite persistent and potentially damaging allegations that the Christian Democrats and other rightist parties were backed by the CIA, the agency conducted a poll only weeks before the election which showed that Allende's opponent, Christian Democrat Jorges Alessandri, would win with 42 percent of the vote. Alessandri was the favorite of the Council on Latin America, some of whose leading lights had met with top State Department officials in April 1970 and offered to funnel at least $500,000 to him through U.S. government channels.† Edward Korry, U.S. Ambassador to Chile, was opposed to this plan and Allende went on to win the election.

Enter the local Pepsi bottler, long-time CIA ally, Augustin Edwards. In a desperation visit to Korry within hours of Allende's triumph, Edwards queried, "Will the United States do anything militarily—directly or indirectly" to stop Allende? Korry was as unhappy as Edwards about the Allende victory, but was opposed to a U.S.-backed coup or anything other than a "Chilean solution" to prevent Allende from taking power. Informed by Korry that the United States intended to abide by the election results, the panic-stricken Edwards left the country, seeking help from Donald Kendall in arranging an audience with President Nixon.

As head of perhaps the richest family in Chile, Edwards had many private holdings over a period of time that intersected with Pepsi's financial bedfellows. His real estate dealings brought him into contact with the Perez Companc family of Argentina, holders of an interest in a Pan Am subsidiary and owners of an oil company controlled by Loeb, Rhoades. Through the Chase Manhattan Bank, the Edwards family had long since achieved the closeness to the Rockefellers more recently achieved by Nixon and Kendall. Edwards was on the board of the Rockefeller-related Deltec Corporation. In the late sixties, he became president of the newly instituted Chilean branch of the International Basic Economy Corporation (IBEC), a special project of the Rockefeller portfolio begun by Nelson in 1947 to combine pursuit of profit with high-minded efforts to develop the economies of backward countries. With huge developments in textiles and food, IBEC was a leader in the consumer goods industries, which was one of the first areas expropriated by Allende's government.‡ In hopes of winning middle-class support, Allende left the luxury sector untouched, but he did nationalize heavily in such basic industries as copper and steel, where Ed-

---

* *Covert Action in Chile: 1963-1973*, op. cit., p. 17-20

† "Inside the Department of Dirty Tricks" by Thomas Powers. *Atlantic*, August 1979. U.S. Ambassador Korry opposed this scheme, and ITT made its own $1 million offer to the CIA, eventually passing $350,000 to candidates opposed to Allende. Subsequent testimony by ITT officials denying the purpose of the $1 million as well as ITT's complicity with the CIA led to perjury indictments. "National security" resulted in suspended sentences and plea bargaining rather than full investigations.

‡ In June 1972, the Allende government bought out Coca-Cola's 51 percent interest in the Chilean bottling operation for $1.5 million. The remaining 49 percent stayed in the hands of private Chilean interests, none of which was as influential or as extensively involved in the Chilean economy as Edwards.

wards had been involved since the fifties, as president of Armco International, the export division of Armco Steel. A major client of John Connally's law firm, with an office in other Latin American countries and in Moscow, this Texas-based international giant also had Rockefeller banking ties. Thus Edwards' presence in 1964 at an anti-Allende strategy session of top multinational executives held at David Rockefeller's Park Avenue office is no more surprising than his subsequent position on the steering committee of the Council on the Americas.

Yet the source of the bulk of Edwards' wealth and a great deal of his influence lay in his family's powerful position at the center of the Chilean press. According to Edward Korry, he was perhaps the largest stockholder in the Lord Cochran Press, which had gotten its start in the early sixties by publishing the Spanish edition of *Reader's Digest,* owned by Nixon's friend and campaign supporter Dewitt Wallace. In 1967, the Edwards group also signed a contract with a subsidiary of the Hearst empire to publish its comics in Chile. Most significant, though, was the Edwards family's century-and-a-half ownership of *El Mercurio,* the most important daily newspaper in the country. *El Mercurio* was the cornerstone of the opposition press pitted against Allende, and as such, was the key to the CIA's ongoing propaganda efforts to discredit Allende in the decade after 1964. More than simply supplying funds, the agency developed "assets" (personnel) on the paper capable of writing or placing articles and editorials favorable to U.S. interests in Chile and around the world. According to the Senate Select Committee on Intelligence, "CIA-inspired editorials began to appear almost daily in *El Mercurio* in the mid-sixties, and after 1968, exerted substantial control over the paper's international news section."*

In the 1970 presidential election, employees of *El Mercurio* enhanced the CIA's propaganda efforts by helping a local agency-backed radio station generate more anti-Allende editorials. The Senate committee's staff report observed that "CIA access to *El Mercurio* had a multiplier effect, since editorials were read throughout the country on various national radio networks. Moreover, *El Mercurio* was one of the most influential Latin American newspapers, particularly in business circles abroad. A project which placed anti-Communist press and radio items was reported in 1970 to reach an audience of well over five million listeners."†

El Mercurio was the hot spot during the electoral campaign, and something close to a bitter personal enmity developed between Edwards and Allende. Impassioned political reportage poured across *El Mercurio's* pages, much of it laced with a lethal seasoning of the CIA's "black" propaganda, or false or misleading information designed to manipulate public opinion and incite action. When candidate Allende protested, says the Senate staff report, "the CIA, through its covert action resources, orchestrated cables of support and protest from foreign newspapers, and a protest statement from an international press association, and world press coverage of the association's protest. In addition, jour-

---

* *Covert Action In Chile,* op. cit., p. 19
† ibid., p. 22

nalists—agents and otherwise—traveled to Chile for on-the-scene reporting."

One such agent, Alvaro Puga, was put on *El Mercurio's* staff in charge of the paper's propaganda campaigns. He was so successful at his job, which included placing stories written at CIA headquarters in Langley, Virginia, that he became a part of the command which eventually directed the coup. Enno Hobbing, who was also reportedly tied to the CIA, was a high-ranking staff member of the Council on Latin America and was earlier in charge of *El Mercurio's* finances.* Like Edwards, Hobbing had spent a part of his life working for Time-Life, Inc., whose coverage of Allende was materially altered by special CIA "inside" briefings requested by *Time* magazine.†

Kendall's efforts to exclude himself from all complicity in the origins of the Chilean coup merely reemphasize his involvement. In the wake of his unsatisfactory meeting with Korry in Santiago, Edwards fled Chile within a week of Allende's September 4 election, and according to Thomas Powers, besieged Kendall on his arrival in the United States with tales of the disaster that lay ahead, should Allende be allowed to take office.‡ Making no reference to what must have been a torrid encounter with Edwards, Kendall stated in a subsequent press interview merely that "Nixon called me on a Sunday at the house regarding something else, and I told him Augustin Edwards was here. . . He (Mr. Nixon) said, 'I want you to get him together with Kissinger and Mitchell,' and that's all I did."§

Not quite. In addition to "getting him together with Kissinger and Mitchell," Kendall also attended Edwards' breakfast with these officials on September 15, just as he attended Edwards' audience with CIA Director Richard Helms in a Washington hotel later that morning. Furthermore, a 1975 interim report of the Senate Intelligence Committee stated that it was Kendall and *not* Nixon who initiated the request to meet with the high administration officials.|| According to Thomas Powers, Kendall knew Helms fairly well, having seen him at Washington meetings on four or five occasions a year. As a result, Helms was probably

---

* North American Congress on Latin America, *Latin America & Empire Report*, July-August, 1974, p. 19

† Edwards' ties to Time-Life were mentioned in a *New York Times* piece on November 7, 1966 (p. 18:5), while Hobbing's were reported in NACLA Vol. VIII, #6, July-August, 1974. According to the Senate staff report, a *Time* correspondent in Chile "apparently had accepted Allende's protestations of moderation and constitutionality at face value. Briefings requested by *Time* and provided by the CIA in Washington resulted in a change in the basic thrust of the *Time* story on Allende's September 4 victory and in the timing of that story" (p. 25). Although he was doubtless far removed from these specific occurrences, Kendall was no stranger to the Time-Life circle himself. According to the *New York Times* (April 18, 1971), his hometown of Greenwich, Connecticut was known as Time-Ville, with such residents as the late Henry R. Luce, *Time's* founder, as well as Samuel Meek, one of the original Time-Life investors and long-time former board member. In all, some forty executives of this media conglomerate hailed from Greenwich, including James Linen, an associate of Kendall's through their newly held directorships at Pan Am.

‡ Powers, *op. cit.*, p. 47

§ *The New York Times*, July 25, 1976

|| U.S. Senate, Select Committee to Study Government Operations with Respect to Intelligence Activities, *Alleged Assassination Plots Involving Foreign Leaders:* Interim Report, 94th Congress, 1st Session, 1975, p. 228. "That morning, at the request of Donald Kendall, president of Pepsi-Cola, Henry Kissinger and John Mitchell had met for breakfast with Kendall and Edwards."

aware of just how close Nixon and Kendall were, which tends to add credence to his testimony that Nixon's resolve to act was sealed by the impassioned plea for CIA help from the men of PepsiCo.*

At a meeting with his officials that very afternoon, the President enumerated the dangers as he saw them, vowed that his administration would not "cave in at the edges," and directed Helms to exhaust every possible means to abort Allende's upcoming confirmation in the Chilean Congress. The result was the ultra-secret Track II plan, whose existence was never even discussed by the "40 Committee," a sub-cabinet-level body of the Executive mandated to review all proposals for major covert actions. No coordination was to occur with the Defense or State Department. Its existence was also withheld from the embassy in Chile, including Ambassador Korry, who was no longer trusted since his rebuff of Edwards' proposal for military intervention only ten days before. In fact, Korry and the 40 Committee were then preoccupied with Track I, a covert operation thrown together between two hurried meetings on September 8 and 14 which sought to block Allende with a "Chilean solution." Track I called for an economic blockade as well as political and black propaganda activities and a $250,000 contingency fund to induce the Chilean Congress to reject Allende. It was more acceptable to many who sought to work within the Chilean Constitution. Track II, though, called for the CIA to play a direct role in organizing a military coup d'etat in Chile before the scheduled confirmation on October 24. It was known only to a small group of individuals in the CIA, and the White House, as well as their contacts in the Chilean military, some of whom were actively involved in the disorganized, last-minute attempt of October 22 which culminated in the shooting of General Rene Schneider, commander in chief of the army.†

Allende acceded to the presidency on October 24, but Nixon's extraordinary instructions, revealed in Helms's notes of September 15, set the tone for operations over the next three years: "*One* in *ten* chance, perhaps, but save Chile. . . . not concerned with risks involved. $10,000,000 available, more if necessary. . . . Make the economy scream. . . .*"

As Helms later testified: "If I ever carried a marshal's baton in my knapsack out of the Oval Ofice, it was that day."

Almost three years later to the day, Allende was shot and his government swept out of office by a military junta which destroyed the institutions of parliamentary government, unleashed a savage repression against peasants, workers, and union leaders, and suppressed elemental liberties in a reign of terror in which thousands died. Of the $8 million spent between 1970 and 1973 for covert operations, the CIA allotted $1.5 million in support of *El Mercurio* based on reports that the Chilean government was trying to close the Edwards chain. "In fact," wrote the Senate staff report, "the press remained free throughout the Al-

* ibid., p. 228n
† "The CIA had been in touch with that group of plotters but a week earlier had withdrawn its support for the groups's specific plans." *Covert Action in Chile,* op cit., p. 11. The agency's withdrawal was apparently prompted by the estimation that it was too late to stop Allende.

lende period, despite attempts to harass and financially damage opposition media." Even though *El Mercurio* was the prime target of Allende's threats and pressure, especially before the election, it still managed to maintain its independence throughout the first year of his presidency. The bitter conflict between *El Mercurio* and Allende actually seemed to subside during this period. Though he retained ownership, Edwards stepped down as publisher of the paper in late 1970 in a move which the paper denied had anything to do with government pressure. Several months later, sudden and alarming field reports of government harassment, which were at variance with the CIA's own analysis, prompted a $700,000 cash transfusion to *El Mercurio*, voted by the 40 Committee. These exaggerated reports originated primarily with the Inter-American Press Association (IAPA), which had been widely circulating these and similar reports among its members since 1970. Augustin Edwards was president of the organization until 1972, when he was replaced by *El Mercurio* official Ren Espejo.*

CIA's own documents indicate that its efforts involving *El Mercurio* played a significant role in setting the stage for the military coup of September 11, 1973. *Psychological Warfare and Media Operations in Chile, 1970-73*, a doctoral dissertation by Fred Simon Landis, presents a chilling picture of covert media operations utilized in *El Mercurio* which dwarfs even the most compelling charges made against the deleterious effects of advertising on the ingenuous citizens in less developed countries. Aside from the fabrication of news or headlines escalating false charges, there was metaphorical association and misleading juxtaposition between photos and headlines which dealt with different stories, use of coined words and invented acronyms in order to more easily manipulate public opinion concerning complex issues, and headlines from other countries timed in order to further a propaganda theme. After the March 1973 elections, there was a marked shift from a fear campaign targeted at middle-class women to a hate campaign targeted at the military, intended to provoke an immediate coup. Landis also charges that *El Mercurio* was used directly in anti-Allende operations through the "laundering" of black propaganda and the communication of concealed and open codes imparting directives to opposition leaders.†

* Ink runs thick as blood among IAPA members which included the Hearst and Knight newspaper chains. The *Miami Herald* published a very friendly piece on Edwards only days after his fateful round of Washington meetings. Apparently unaware of the CIA's two-year domination of *El Mercurio's* international news section, the *Herald* declared that "*Mercurio* is also unique in that it attempts to offer a fairly balanced report of news from abroad." More ironically, the *Herald* brushed aside intimations by Edwards' enemies that he had fled the country in fear, preferring instead to print the more rational explanation offered by his colleagues that he wanted "to avoid efforts to link him with any possible coup efforts in coming days." *Miami Herald*, September 20, 1970

† Landis's conclusions were reportedly based on prodigious research, including interviews before the coup with reporters and editors of Chile's major newspapers and with Chilean government officials as well as after the coup with military officers who led the overthrow. There was also systematic study of documents and books seized by the military and intended for destruction as well as information supplied by former CIA officers. A detailed content analysis of *El Mercurio* was also undertaken. (Dissertation written for Department of Political Science, University of Illinois at Urbana-Champaign, 1975.)

Edwards, whom Kendall appointed as a vice-president with PepsiCo's food division during his exile, returned to Santiago in the aftermath of the coup to enjoy the fruits of what he had reaped. *El Mercurio* now enjoyed unparalleled influence in the new military junta headed by General Augusto Pinochet. Fernando Leniz, *El Mercurio's* ex-president, became a high-ranking political adviser in the Pinochet government. Herman Cubillos, appointed Pinochet's foreign minister in 1978, had risen through the ranks of *El Mercurio* during the Allende years. During the perjury trial of a former ITT official who had participated with *El Mercurio* in the efforts to block Allende, Cubillos was named as a "principal" CIA operative during the Allende presidency.* Another close Edwards associate, Orlando Szenz, head of the Chilean Manufacturers Association, was a top-ranking figure of Patria Y Libertad, a right-wing paramilitary group backed by the CIA that fomented strikes, sabotage, terrorist acts, and propaganda leading up to the 1973 coup. Thereafter, it concentrated on counterinsurgency, but its name surfaced again when one of its members, an American living in Chile named Michael Townley, turned states' evidence in the dramatic and tragic 1976 assassination of Orlando Letelier, who had been Allende's ambassador to the United States.

Since the coup, Letelier, who had been living in Washington, remained perhaps the most vocal critic of Pinochet's brutal, repressive regime. He was by no means alone in this conviction, and as American officials and public opinion turned increasingly against the junta, Pinochet sought and found expert public relations help from J. Walter Thompson as well as Adolf Yankelevich, a former chief of public relations for McCann-Erickson's Chilean subsidiary. Yankelevich became the junta's New York-based press attaché, but JWT called the deal off, presumably because of mounting anti-junta sentiment.

Chile's rulers bitterly resented Letelier, whom they saw as the prime cause of their sagging image, and ordered his assassination, which Townley carried out in Washington on September 21, 1976 with the help of Cuban exiles. Townley himself had had several contacts with the CIA, and was widely suspected in Chile of being directly connected with the agency. Within two weeks of the killing, CIA Director George Bush, a Ford appointee, personally met with key Justice Department officials to aid in the federal investigation already underway. In 1972 while Edwards was a PepsiCo vice-president, Bush sat on the board of First International Bancshares, a newly formed Texas bank holding company whose politically powerful board included Herman Lay and Robert Stewart of PepsiCo. Bush's unsuccessful 1970 bid for the Senate had also benefitted substantially from the secret Town House fund to which Kendall had pledged a quarter million dollars.† Edwards, of course, returned to Chile the following year where he was very close to the junta, and the CIA, under Bush, treated the junta kindly by discounting as distorted and exaggerated the repeated, widespread al-

* *New York Post*, November 11, 1978
† *Los Angeles Times*, February 7, 1980. p. 1; February 8, 1980. p. 1

legations of political repression, torture, and imprisonment.* Whatever Bush's impact on the Letelier inquiry, the *Washington Post* promptly commented that "the CIA's role in the investigation poses sensitive ethical and legal questions. . . . The CIA was involved in efforts to overthrow . . . Allende . . . the investigation may turn up sensitive information that the CIA may want to keep secret for 'national security' reasons . . ." No direct evidence linking the CIA to the killing emerged, though some tantalizing leads developed and the question became a burning issue in the weeks leading up to the trial of Townley and the Cubans.

Appalling as it may seem, Kendall viewed the overthrow of the Allende government in Chile as the most demonstrative illustration that detente worked. Allende waved the red banners, just as Castro had a decade before, but in this case, Pepsi got Chile back. The difference, of course, was the role played by the Russians, who rejected Allende's request for $500 million in aid in November 1972. In the embryonic stages of detente between 1970 and 1972, Russian technicians surveyed the copper mines where U.S. interests were being nationalized. But after the detente of mid-1972, the Russians turned a deaf ear, advising Allende to make his peace with the United States. Kendall explained his view in an address to the Sales Executive Club of New York at the Waldorf-Astoria. Flanked by high Soviet trade officials and other top brass from Coca-Cola, Kendall declared, "In Chile you had an elected government that was elected Communist, and I think that anybody who knows the power of the Soviet Union knows that, if they wanted to maintain that government in Chile, that Allende would probably still be there today. But I think this is a sign of change in their policy that did not occur at the time of Cuba, and you know the results of that."

The Russians at the meeting nodded their assent. "I enjoyed his speech," one of them told Robert Scheer. "I think it was a really good representation of the view on Soviet-American trade . . ." But did he find the remarks on Chile and detente objectionable? "No, I think he is right in general." Certainly, there was precedent for Kendall's provocative angle on Russian-American cooperation. In May 1972, Nixon had consulted with the Russians only hours before going on television to announce the mining of the Haiphong Harbor just to be sure they wouldn't cancel the Moscow summit later that month to inaugurate detente. Even before the ink was dry, detente had come to signify an era not so much of peace and nonintervention as limited war and cointervention, or, at least, intervention with permission. It was a satisfactory compromise, and maybe even a necessary condition of avoiding misunderstandings in the developing world. Crises were going to emerge there and detente extended to both parties a maximum of economic advantage and political hegemony.

At home, meanwhile, Kendall would seek to maximize the kind of monopoly advantage he had won in detente through his hands-on political partnerships by invoking the hands-off tradition of American free enterprise. In endorsing

* *Washington Post*, October 9, 1976

Gerald Ford for President in 1976, PepsiCo issued a statement illustrative of how selectively applied the whole concept of free enterprise had become in the contemporary climate. Criticizing the Carter promise (hardly acted on) to "promote competition" in industries which are led by a few large companies, the statement complimented Ford on his perception that such actions are government-sponsored "punishments" for efficient economic operations. Whether or not such efficient operations pass their savings on to the consumer, the statement illustrates the attempt by allies in business and government to make those statesmen who promote competition appear as meddlesome, punitive, and oppressive as Communist regimes.

CHAPTER FIFTEEN

To Have and to Have More

IN LATE 1959, the American Bottlers of Carbonated Beverages was considering the creation of an industry-wide institutional soft-drink advertising program to address certain common interests in the bottling community. At their annual convention in St. Louis, they listened to an address from Senator John Sparkman, a Democrat from Alabama, who exhorted that "there is nothing I should rather see than for your industry to embark upon a promotional effort which should carry in to every single home in this country a hard-hitting message on the social values that are contained in a soft-drink bottle . . . it seems obvious to me that one way to combat . . . antisocial behavior in general—regardless of the age groups involved—and at the same time to strengthen the moral fabric of our society would be to encourage the greatest possible consumption of soft drinks."

Strained as it might seem, out of context, the senator's awkwardly dramatic equation of consumption with morality was simply a Southern politician's inflated acknowledgment of a theme dear to his audience. As contributing partners with a definite say in the advertising enterprise, the bottlers were well aware of the power of advertising to transform their soda into the image of something important and powerful enough to influence wider social values and behavior. Whether or not it ever materialized, the joint promotional program that Sparkman was endorsing could hardly have surpassed what Coca-Cola, and later Pepsi, accomplished on their own. Well before the days of Archie Lee, Coca-Cola's advertising was putting across the "hard-hitting message" on social values that the senator envisioned, but in a subtler, more careful way. The heated competition between Coke and Pepsi in the television era merely refined advertising's role as a mediator between cultural values and soft-drink consumption. The senator was certainly no better schooled in the subtleties of advertising's impact than any of his audience. However, his remarks on the faltering "moral fabric" indicated at least an intuitive recognition that an important by-product of effective advertising was that it rechanneled potentially disruptive anxieties into socially acceptable patterns of behavior.

In the visibly spreading struggle for ever higher market share, Coke and Pepsi were on a grease pole, climbing over each other only to slip back a little as the other came up at the rear. It was a game of constant punch and counterpunch, in which the leader was faced with a relentless, almost inevitable attrition. "We had some serious problems," said one Coke executive, referring to the early sixties, "one of them being that Coke did not recognize that it indeed has aggressive competitors who are talented. We finally got off our duff and decided that it

231

was a competitive world after all." This obvious overconfidence was acknowledged too late to forestall Pepsi's drive. Pepsi was successfully claiming its own
piece of the market, and then honing an ad style sharp enough to defend that
turf as if it were precious sovereign soil. Both companies were after the "heavy
users"—those who put down a six-pack or more per day, and the unabashed
hard sell had to go well beyond any normal reasons people might have for drinking a beverage—thirst, taste, and refreshment. Coke's ads, which didn't target
the heavy users until later in the sixties, had dwelled on these product attributes
since the drink had been invented. Arising from the patent medicine industry
that spawned modern advertising, the psychic and social anxieties prevalent in
Coke's background put the company at the forefront of advertising's salient tendency to implant social values within the selling message.

Pepsi was playing the game by 1960, when the company moved its account
from Kenyon and Eckhardt. The agency had promoted the message of Pepsi
quality to reap some of the prestige which Coke seemed ready to surrender. This
trade of mob appeal for snob appeal seemed perfect during the fifties, especially
since the prevailing social values automatically doomed the lowest-priced brand
to a permanent second place. Steele agreed with this approach and wholeheartedly approved "The Sociables" campaign. These ads pictured a vague and confusing mixture of older people and young adults immersed in exclusive country-
club settings. The campaign was soon seen as a flop—history has not altered
that judgment—and after only four years, the Pepsi account went to BBD&O
where it has remained ever since. The new custodians sought a broader base for
Pepsi, and quickly saw that in K&E's haste to discard the labor and minority
markets which were holding Pepsi back from middle-class acceptance, Steele
and company were throwing out the one piece of virgin territory Pepsi could
truly claim as its own—the youth market.

It was so obvious. McCann-Erickson's early television campaigns for Coke included a flat, lackluster effort featuring Anita Bryant as spokeswoman. Backed
by a monotonous chorus of studio voices, forever repeating "Only Coca-Cola
gives you that refreshing new feeling" to music that would have been discarded
by Lawrence Welk, Bryant swilled Coke as she smiled and swayed her way
across miles of beaches and acres of tennis courts, surrounded exclusively by
white, middle-class adults in their late twenties or early thirties. Though they
were younger, freer, and more informal than the users of a decade before, they
were still shown dressed glamorously, almost lavishly, for simple barbecues that
followed the day's recreation. Moreover these commercials never showed Coke
being drunk alone or in odd-numbered groups but rather by several couples of
marriageable age who seldom appeared married. With Bryant's stress on a taste
that was "never too sweet" and the feature that a Coke had fewer calories than
half a grapefruit, Coke's appeal was still circumscribed by the parameters of the
adult market.

Pepsi found the opening and went after it without compromise, not only
speaking directly to its prime prospects, but to shared values which that segment

had in common with the rest of society. "Now, it's Pepsi for those who Think Young," garnered those with a young outlook as well as those who were young. Far from being anything new, the pronounced emphasis on youth had been an American tradition well before Mark Twain immortalized it in *Huckleberry Finn*.

The slogan in the ads was accomplished by lyrics in the jingle and voice-over copy which hailed Pepsi as not only "light," "sparkling," "lively"—the eternal attributes of youth—but also as "new," "modern," and "right." The emphasis on the new and the modern was carried forward in the "Pepsi Generation." "Think young, think straight, think right up to date"—and both campaigns characterized Pepsi people as having a "zest for life." "People who think young set their sights for lively living, and light, bracing clean-tasting refreshment." "Famous regular Pepsi with the bold, clean taste—the modern kind of energy that livens up your taste while it cools down your thirst. . . ." Thus, at the dawn of the sixties, Pepsi was wedding the tradition of youth to the spirit of the New Frontier, of prosperous abundance, of progress, of bigness, of technological power amid a resolve that that power was not only "modern" but "right." The "Pepsi Generation" positioned the product for the present and the future.

In the midst of "Think young," Coke debuted its "Things Go Better with Coke" which, true to company tradition, was targeted for a much broader market. Bill Backer, who had recently joined McCann-Erickson and was destined to become the TV era's counterpart to Archie Lee recalls that Coke was always unwilling to target a whole campaign toward youth, preferring to allocate about 30 percent of its ad budget to the youth market. But he feels Atlanta may have erred in resisting the agency's pressure to make the whole campaign younger. "They never could quite grasp that the kid who thought it was a young, hip drink while listening to radio at 5 P.M. or Dick Clark and then seeing it treated as an all-purpose, family drink at 9 P.M. would emerge with a cloudier image of Coke than Pepsi, which was willing to put its major money against a target audience—youth."

Pepsi began to have an impact soon after the 1961 debut of "Think young," and when it raised the curtain on the "Pepsi Generation," Atlanta's nerves went ice cold. Bill Backer remembers how Coke suddenly wanted to drop "Things Go Better" barely six months into the campaign. Cavalier, gentlemanly Coke wasn't quite used to fighting it out in the clinch, but Backer was nevertheless appalled at such jitters. " 'My God,' I told them, 'it took us nearly two years to introduce this campaign and get it sold; we can't drop it now.' " Instead, he suggested shifting the music to a pop-rock idiom in selected radio youth markets, and was again startled at how Coke clung all the more stubbornly to its stuffy, upright traditions.

"Rock music was considered dirty and low class," Backer said, referring to this condescending attitude of the late fifties. "And I went to the company and said, 'You know, people don't ever consistently listen to something that they think is low class. They may go to a porn movie here or there, but they think the music of their culture is o.k!" He well remembers the thick, heavy silence of those meetings with the Coke leadership during the early sixties when he desperately tried to dispel the fears born of that ancient, inbred prudery that suffused so much of Coca-Cola. " 'Forget the aberrations of Elvis Presley screwing the microphone and those kinds of sensationalism,' " he urged them. " 'The music is a music of a class of people, and if you want to sell to those people, then talk in their music. You're not going to lose the rest of the audience—they're not going to know you're in it.' "

Coke wouldn't hear of going on television with pop or rock, but Backer was given a cautious o.k. to go ahead with plans for a subcampaign for the youth radio market. He prepared a jingle to show Coke executives how it would sound with a slight pop treatment, using John Bubbles, a swing singer who "represented the old folks" and the Shirelles, a top-40 group of black female vocalists "who were very hot." Bubbles gave the lyrics a smooth, mellow treatment while the Shirelles sang rhythmic backround during the pauses. "I wanna tell you—when they heard that 'be-do, be-do' from black girls singing along, the atmosphere in the room was—you couldn't believe it. As it turned out, McCann was more scared than 'old' Fred Dixon (then the advertising manager), who was willing. 'As long as you keep it on radio, it's all right with me. 'Cause Mr. Woodruff doesn't own a radio, and if he does, he's not gonna be listening to those stations. If this is what the kids are listenin' to, it's all right by me.' "

When Coke aired the jingle, thousands of listeners wrote the company in praise of Bubble's fluid voice and the Shireles' soaring topnotes. Backer suspects the ad's impact was all the greater because it was the first ever to use prominent pop-rock singers. He followed with wave after wave of saucy ads that featured some of America's greatest pop and rock groups, garnering every radio award for five years running. Roy Orbison, Diana Ross and the Supremes, the Four Seasons, The 5th Dimension, the Coasters, and many others belted out lyrics written by Backer or his collaborators. Occasionally, Backer teamed with the artists themselves like Ray Charles, or with other creative people brought in by McCann-Erickson. Neil Diamond was the only performer in all those years who wrote his own ads. As Backer explains, "He was the only one who had the discipline to write to a point. He understood the assignment, brought those things back, and they were right."

The best of Backer and his pop artists never made it onto television until the very end of "Things Go Better with Coke" in the late sixties. Yet for all of Coke's discretion, the television ads up until then were full of bare legs, puckered lips, and risqué innuendos that surpassed practically anything in Pepsi's ads. How could pop music appear so low and dirty while, at the same time, many of the things sung about in those radio ads were all but acted out in many of the TV entries and pointedly suggested in many others? Robert Woodruff himself, who succeeded Candler as the guardian of Coca-Cola's chastity, pioneered the company's use of calendar girls in swim suits thirty years earlier. Woodruff personally reviewed the pose and picture of every model appearing

beside the Coke logo to be sure they conveyed the right blend of wholesomeness, cleanliness, and womanliness. Woodruff was a pious Southern gentleman,
and along with the rest of the Coke leadership, balanced his protective reverence
for Southern belles with a certain resistance or even fear of black culture. Psychologically, it was far easier for Coke to bring the aplomb, carriage, and dignity
of those early poster girls to life in 1960's beaches and backyards than it was to
incorporate a few bars of pop and rock music, much of whose roots lay in black
culture.

Not every campaign of the sixties was so decidedly affected by social values
and mores, but those of the late sixties and seventies were more so. The political
trauma of the Vietnam War was accompanied by rapid social dislocation as well
as the first signs of inflation and economic hardship. The simple ease suffusing
"Things Go Better With Coke" was replaced by a hard-edged *cinéma-vérité* approach that used the same slogan in a completely different context. The new
emphasis shifted clearly from pleasure to the grind where the effort was to keep
the human mechanism operating at peak efficiency. "These are people who
think of themselves as expending a lot of energy," said vice-president Richard
Harvey. "[Drinking] all around the day, at 11, at 2, at 4, before dinner and so
on, drinking five or six Cokes throughout the day. . . . They are restless people
who don't look upon Coca-Cola as a reward, but as a means of getting a job
done."* The impression given by the ads was of a machine America where the
work never stops, and the central theme was no longer that Coke was a pause or
a break, but rather an instrumental element of work, of sheer functioning.

Pinpointing the social values to be exploited in a given campaign has never
been a simple matter. They must be widely shared, and contemporary, and yet
not addressed by a competitor's campaign.

According to a former vice-president at BBD&O, the agency had developed a
central philosophy of advertising which it applied assiduously toward the Pepsi
account. The key was to identify and study the prime prospects in the closest
detail, specifically to discern how their expectations toward the product in general—in this case, cola—as well as toward life, are going unfulfilled. The trick is
then to find something to say about cola that resolves the discrepancies, and
then to present it in a way that breaks down the boredom barrier and the natural
resistance to the inflow of messages from an estimated two hundred or more ads
which bombard everyone in America daily. "The only way to sell a product,"
says another former vice-president for the Pepsi account at BBD&O, "is to solve
a consumer's problem. It's not just thirst, but the thirst for life, not just taste,
but the desire for refreshment. When we sell Pepsi-Cola, we're solving a psychological problem which is that everyone wants to feel good about themselves,
everybody wants to feel part of a special thing, everyone wants to have a good
day." He likens Pepsi and soft drinks in general to certain kinds of apparel which
serve no utilitarian purpose but which nevertheless make a statement about how

* *Advertising Age*, October 17, 1966, p. 65

a person feels. The "problem" is not the physical sensation of thirst or taste, which is secondary to more pressing metaphysical concerns. "People say 'that is hucksterism,' but that, my friends, is selling."

In this vein, Pepsi's ads virtually always emphasize the literal user, usually young people engaged in vigorous, sometimes dangerous, activity. By targeting a more specific group than Coke does, Pepsi feels it has the flexibility to produce ads that reflect a more concrete realism.

Under McCann-Erickson's Bill Backer, creator of every Coke campaign since the early sixties, Coke slogans circumvented the consumers' "problems" in favor of a grand "promise of reward" stemming from the product. The historic "Pause that Refreshes," as well as Backer's creations, "It's the Real Thing," and "Coke Adds Life," all obviously give center stage to a core promise tied directly to the product. "Things Go Better with Coke" is, for Backer, the archetypal distillation of a product promise. Much of the research impetus behind the slogan came from the company's own intimacy with Southern tastes, just as Backer's own upbringing in Dixie helped groom him for the twenty-year stewardship of Coke's advertising. "Southerners think of colas as something that just makes the moment a little bit brighter. 'Things Go Better with Coke' is the definitive battle cry for all colas. It is why colas exist—to make the moment just a little bit brighter."

Coke, of course, traded its Southern provincialism long ago for an earnest appeal to every man, woman, and child on the face of the earth. With a target that wide, Coca-Cola naturally gravitated toward slogans that highlighted the product rather than some impossibly amorphous collection of consumers.

In fact, the opposing emphasis on user or product has been the focus of a long-standing debate at both companies. Each thinks it sees the flaws in the other's approach, and tries to maximize its own flexibility to take advantage of the opening. From time to time, Pepsi's search for dominance in the take-home market has led it to make ads that speak to the housewife, the prime purchasing agent for the home, rather than the literal, and in this case, youthful consumer. Likewise, Coke feels the product emphasis of its slogan frees it to pursue the consumer in its actual executions. "In the biggest Coke commercial of all time," says Backer, referring to the classic "I'd like to buy the world a Coke" by the New Seekers, "nobody drank the product at all."

In the seventies, both Coke and Pepsi have gone into more complete, narrative kinds of commercials. Coke ads generally invoked a more abstract idiom of traditions or institutions with which everyone could identify. Their focus was the preservation of the past, nostalgia. Coke was Americana, but Pepsi was America, the now and the future. Pepsi felt this emphasis on immediacy was part of its larger one on the user, and allowed it to strike a much more emotional chord. "If your advertising can make the consumer feel special and feel good, why won't he take the product that talks to him in a way that says, 'You're special, you're good' rather than the one that says 'I'm special, I'm it, I'm the Real Thing—buy me.'" Pepsi's emphasis on the literal user has occasionally prompted it to cast the extras for its commercials on location and even to replace performers already cast for central roles with crew members, townspeople, and other nonactors who seemed to exude the real-life, you-are-there quality which Pepsi is dedicated to capturing.

Coke's Backer observed that Pepsi's intent is to show what the product can do for the consumer socially. As a result, their executions more frequently depict people guzzling the product than Coke's ads do. In fact, Coke ads going back to the early sixties occasionally showed no people at all—simply the image of that frosty, Georgia-green bottle poised in a Colorado creek or beside a roaring fire in the dead of winter. In the Real Thing, actual interaction was sometimes between people and their Coke rather than one another. Owing to its confident position of leadership, Coke has often been successful in establishing a mood of relaxation and ease that makes a ready contrast to the more frenetic emotional action of Pepsi's ads. In earlier campaigns, on the other hand, this practice of putting the product on the pedestal made for some comic, but sometimes contrived executions. For example, at a party in an ad for "Things . . . ," several men were unsuccessful in getting a young lady to dance. Another came up, offered her a Coke, and stood by bewildered as she danced off, bottle in hand, into the party without him or anyone else. Another showed a couple attempting to transplant a heavy tree, but despite the labor, the woman is determined to keep one hand free to carry a bulky, six-pack of Coke. Others showed novice skiers, who could barely stand up, poised high on the slopes with their poles and their bottles, and yet another depicted a man getting his finger stuck in a bowling ball. Even in the highly acclaimed "Real Thing," there were occasional lapses, such as when a young couple jitterbug through New Orleans on a Saturday night, only to be spotted by a much older couple, possibly their parents, who join them in a frolicking dance.

Meanwhile, says a veteran of BBD&O, "Pepsi showed people in situations that they wanted to see themselves in. . . . Nobody wants to sit and watch a bottle of Pepsi being poured or a bottle of Coke sitting in a stream—it's dull. So what did we do? We said, 'Do your own thing. Join the Pepsi People feelin' free; Think young; live life to the fullest'. . . . We try to make people laugh, we try to make them cry, and sometimes we do it all at once. It's very difficult for us to get that realism that makes you feel like you are there. We'll shoot ten thousand feet of film to get ninety feet—just ninety feet—tens of thousands of dollars to get that moment that says 'Holy smokes' . . . and when you get it, people say, 'I like you, and I like your product . . . I must be a Pepsi person.' . . . Coke will probably disagree, and say there is no difference, and it is that difference that is making us grow."

In developing their competing ad strategies, Coke and Pepsi each went after their own piece of the rock, claiming a different segment of the market, a different place on the spectrum of social values, and evolving a markedly different look to their ads. All of these factors belong to the surface aspects of the commercials. The statements by the various company executives that characterized them as "relevant," or "in tune with the times," demonstrate that the implicit messages expressing this or that trend were primarily conscious decisions by the advertisers. As mentioned above, advertising's overwhelming power begins with this deliberate superimposition of values onto goods, which confers on the advertised product the metaphorical power of the invoked value, thus creating a symbol.

The long-standing controversy over advertising surrounds precisely this issue of conscious, deliberate exploitation of the consumer by the advertiser. From Vance Packard to Ralph Nader, and at countless other junctures in between, advertising has been excoriated for a host of sins. It tempts the consumer to buy unnecessary things and encourages superfluous wants. It leads people to compete excessively and to misdirect their energies. It manipulates human frailty in the interests of human profit. Though they reject the interpretations, the advertisers themselves have been all but admitting many of the critics' factual charges for years.

For example, in 1959, Coca-Cola actually invited the press to a demonstration of its marvelous new technique of "subliminal" advertising in which single film frames saying "Buy Coca-Cola" were spliced into feature-length films playing in local theaters around the East. The theory was that the viewer would never notice the frames flickering by, but would nevertheless be overcome with an unconscious desire to walk into the lobby and buy a Coke. Fifteen years later, Wilson Brian Key created a minor sensation with his book, *Subliminal Seduction*, in which he catalogued a litany of instances where advertisers airbrushed images of skulls and sensuous female forms into their ads, again assuming that the hidden lure of sex or death might create an unconscious attraction among consumers for the products.

Denying the effectiveness of cheap gimmicks or pseudo-psychological tricks, a recent BBD&O person admitted that the agency would "use any kind of persuasion method it could to tell you what you wanted to hear, and it would do a lot of research to find out what that was." The advertisers choose to see themselves as satisfiers of the consumer's deeper desires rather than as manipulators of artificial ones. Coke and Pepsi deliberately put these images across, but the consumers, they insist, often *just as deliberately* use the advertised products as badges to make statements about themselves. "So," says the agency veteran, "there is a constant matching of the product's imagery with people's desires." Guilty as charged? Not at all, reply the advertisers.

They point with assurance to the work of distinguished psychologists, such as Ernest Dichter, who was brought in to BBD&O for brief consultation during the preparation of Pepsi's Live-Give campaign. Dichter was the premier practitioner of "motivational research," a prominent marketing research method of the fifties, solidly rooted in Freudian theory. Working with small groups of subjects toward qualitative conclusions, Dichter explored the consumer's symbolic affinities with every conceivable kind of product, from soups to furs, from soft drinks to life insurance. He demonstrated that these symbolic ties are strong—so strong, in fact, that it is "The Burden of the Good Life" (a chapter heading in one of his books) for modern man to unlock and explore his mystifying attraction for "things," and in uncovering the "soul" which he finds in products, he will uncover his own.

Just as the post-Freudian behavioral and experimental psychologists attempted to quantify their conclusions by creating personality inventory tests to catalogue people by types, so Dichter's heirs left the small and the qualitative for the big and the quantitative. In fact, the huge, nationally projectible market segmentation studies run by Pepsi and BBD&O, which tried to discover the consumer's "problems" and "discrepancies," grew naturally out of the kind of work Dichter specialized in a decade before.

The method now in vogue signifies a return to the small and the qualitative in the form of "focus group interviews" where consumers simply report on their various preferences and benefits of the product without any attempt by the researcher to probe into the mind. In adopting the least meddlesome posture possible, the advertisers increasingly find the consumers talking back to them in the language of the advertising campaigns that have been constantly bombarding them since birth. Cigarettes should have "smooth taste," detergents should be "whiter and brighter," and soft drinks should be "refreshing." In short, consumers have been so manipulated, so shaped by the persistent hammer of repetition that the advertisers themselves are finding it increasingly difficult to get a fresh and accurate picture of them. This echo tendency, also known as "noise," is fine with the advertisers as long as it is they who are generating it. But when the consumers quite naturally absorb it to the point where they cannot respond otherwise, the advertising effort itself becomes trapped in its own noise.

In a private talk during the Live-Give era, BBD&O president Tom Dylan alerted Pepsi-Cola's top management to the prospect that an entire industry could become dominated by an ever regressive cycle of tracking the consumer, who is simply repeating earlier ads verbatim. Dylan was more accurate than he anticipated, for even the creative talent of the people behind some of Pepsi's own ads was showing the first signs of being lost in this bottomless chamber of echoes. Alan Pottasch, for instance, Pepsi's senior vice-president for creative affairs, promoted the "Have a Pepsi Day" campaign as if he were auditioning for it. "Pepsi has a front seat on what's happening in this country—fun. Fun is with us—it is a regular part of life, and it's foremost in the hearts and minds of Americans." For all his reasoned probing of the consumer psyche, Dichter himself never seems to have asked how it happened that soft drinks came to be associated with "lightness" or soups came to be seen as "a potent magic that satisfies not only the hunger of the body, but the yearnings of the soul." A brilliant researcher, he studied soups in "legends, fairytales—the far-off history of the human race" finding that soups were cast as a "witches brew, the love potion . . . we can almost say soup is orgiastic," but he never suggests that perhaps these entrenched symbolic associations with soup in the minds of his subjects got there not so much from direct contact with the "far-off history" as from the representation of that history in prior advertising campaigns about soup. A little like Christopher Columbus, Dichter thought his explorations had led him to a long-sought exotic place of secrets, the far-off mystery—the mind's Orient—when, in fact, he had found simply America, the land of consumption, whose natives talked back to him in the idiom of the "new world"—advertising campaigns—rather than the ancient, untrammeled soil whose shores he thought he had reached.

Serving a host of corporate advertisers as clients, Dichter was the most skilled navigator of his day through the topography of the consumer mentality, yet even he seems to have fallen prey to that blind spot at which Dylan hinted. But beyond the "noise," the redundancy, and the sheer obliviousness of the advertisers, a message gets through. One of the top researchers at Coke's McCann-Erickson wrote an entire book* based on the simple assumption that, in products where no major purchase decision is involved, advertising can have a direct impact on behavior, totally bypassing thoughts, attitudes, social values, and all the other criteria advertisers often use to evaluate campaigns. Though there is little recall of the slogan here and only a faint awareness of the commercials, something miraculous happens at the moment of purchase—all the ads come home to roost, stimulated by the product on the shelf.

If it were possible to freeze that moment of purchase—if only long enough to see the light and trace it back to its source—where would it lead? In the electronic age, it is impossible to keep things from speeding up, much less stopping them. Television relies on incessant movement and change, where recall and perception are both infinitely more fleeting than in print ads. There, theme and copy are fixed in one setting only, and tend to reflect each other very closely. TV has a rounded appeal to the senses—visual, verbal, written—and the temporal dimension captivates the viewer, who must watch the commercial caught in the pause between the influence and expectation of successive images.

If the images cannot be stopped, they can be replayed over and over again. Behind the ceaseless repetitions of advertising campaigns lies an intrinsic coherence. "For a campaign to be meaningful," Varda Leymore reminds us, "it must have a structure. Were it not for the structural resolution, the advertisements would remain ambiguous . . . their meaning will elude the consumer as well as the advertiser." As mentioned earlier, the structural message is virtually never communicated as a result of any individual ad, but rather through the cumulative impact of all the ads within a campaign. Though many different symbolic associations might be put in by the advertisers, the relationship they bear to one another—the structure—is present throughout. That presence is felt as a conflict of opposing forces which is resolved, of course, through consumption of the product.

The print ads during Coke's first forty years appeared when Coke was the

---

* Herb Krugman, *The Low-Involvement Hypothesis*

dominant brand, but the TV commercials were made at a time when the companies were keenly competitive, each one supplying certain fragments of the puzzle which together form one integral symbolic network. As competing brands, Coke and Pepsi thus produce the necessary structure *collectively*, despite the fierce competition between the companies and the strikingly different styles of their ads. Both sides appear oblivious to this shared symbolic system, yet the campaign which most favorably resolves the conflict of opposing forces represented within that system is generally the most effective.

Two examples are evident throughout the prominent campaigns of the sixties. Pepsi, of course, inaugurated the era with "Now, it's Pepsi, for those who think young." The campaign focused on people with a "zest for life" and "lively living." "Home life is lively in modern families when light, bracing refreshment is always right at home." The jingle to the tune of Duke Ellington's hit "Makin' Whoopee," reiterated the theme of Pepsi as "modern" as well as young and lively.

While a cola commercial with the action taking place at night is a rarity today, part of the "liveliness" of that period was captured in couples going to a bar and ordering Pepsi-Cola. In one such ad, the man is the smooth, capable one who knows the bartender and sees that he and his date receive proper service. The ad is lit in a way that contrasts their bright, young faces with a surrounding perimeter of dark shadows, and on the line "They choose the right one, the modern light one" the man's smiling face is cast against the silhouette of a much older man who is smoking and drinking a clear liquid on ice, presumably alcohol. Wearing his Fedora hat, the man in the shadow cuts an image that is anything but young and modern.

Coming out shortly after Coke's major thrust of 1963, "Come Alive—You're in the Pepsi Generation" developed all the earlier trends. Not only modern, young and "clean," Pepsi was now "bold" and "bracing," full of a "new kind of living" for those "active, lively people" with a "thirst for living." The jingle reenforced the positioning of Pepsi for the "now" as well as the hereafter by telling people to "Come Alive," and "drink right up today." One of these ads showed a couple riding across a dusty, deserted road on a motorcycle. As the jingle plays, the man points to a helicopter flying toward them. The 'copter moves in for the wilderness rendezvous, and they pull over and see that a vending machine full of Pepsi-Cola is dangling from the chopper. In a more famous commercial from the same campaign, a couple in a convertible sped down a straightaway and brush-country flats, and suddenly splashed dead-on into a lake, setting off a huge burst of white spray that fills the screen. As it turns out, the car is an aquamobile, which is just as comfortable in the water as on the road. In both ads, "modern" technology itself, sparkling and bold, is subduing not only the dry wilderness terrain, but natural water, as well. The naturalness of water, including beach scenes and surfing, was part of the Pepsi imagery, but in the metaphorical sense, this idea of nature was being set in opposition to that of culture, as embodied in modern, male-operated technology. Modernity, leisure, sparkling technology, and newness were exalted over nature, which was pictured as dry, even barren, full of hardships and lacking in contemporary conveniences. Pepsi's central image—that of youth, with its sparkling cleanliness and lively activeness—was nothing more than an adjunct to the underlying symbolism of culture. Even the image of Pepsi's coldness avoids the quality's negative connotation—lack of warmth, harshness, even death—through an association with sparkling, clean technology rendered as "modern energy" that "livens the taste while it cools the thirst." The transformation of coldness into a wholly positive psychological force is completed with images of vibrating warmth. In one commercial, a couple in a modern house go through seductive glances and gestures, and the final, male-oriented image is of a Pepsi bottle jutting at a suggestive angle from a huge bucket of ice.

In 1963, Coca-Cola unveiled its "Things Go Better with Coke" theme in a massive marketing effort to reassert the identity of the product. "We took the definitive raison d'etre for all colas and made it the Coke raison d'etre," recounts Bill Backer. "In a competitive situation, you could say 'better' meant better than Pepsi, but it didn't have to be taken that way at all. If there never were a Pepsi-Cola, if Coke were the only soft drink out there, 'Things Go Better with Coke' was still a helluva campaign."

Ah, but there *was* a Pepsi-Cola out there, and when it unveiled its "Pepsi Generation" slogan, Coke was suddenly so flushed with competitive panic it was ready to go back to the drawing boards. But Backer, who saw infinite possibilities in the new creation, argued forcefully for its preservation and rolled out the pop artists for the radio youth markets. Pepsi's presence made "Things" stand out as a bold, decisive, counter-punch. Every line of the jingle was shot through with comparative and superlative references to Coca-Cola's quality. The idea, like the company's inimitably broad definition of its market, remained very general, allowing for many different kinds of executions.

Within "Things," Coca-Cola conducted a whole range of subcampaigns, all of which relied on symbolic associations to get the underlying message across, perhaps even more than Pepsi did in its ads. To be sure, some of the ads supplemented the jingle with talking which generally reiterated the central theme of refreshment alongside the notion of coldness: "Right now, when it's hot, why not let an ice-cold Coca-Cola make things go better for you. Mmmm . . . cold, refreshing—never too sweet—Food, fun, and people all need the spirited taste of Coca-Cola to help beat the heat. . . ."

In many of these ads, the "heat" is that of the beach, where Coke's cold and refreshing quality is equated with the ocean—so much so that the expansive atmosphere of water becomes a symbol not only of Coke's coldness, but also of its naturalness. Nature redeems ice-cold Coca-Cola from the primary association of coldness—death. The link of coldness and Coke is made so often and with so much more force than it is with Pepsi that the redeeming identification with nature must be thoroughgoing and complete.*

* The identification of Coke with explicit, literal representations of nature had been prominent in Coke's earlier campaigns. In "Things," however, the images of nature were much more symbolic and metaphorical, and their effects were consequently much more subtle.

Nature takes the form not only of clean, blue ocean, but of fine, shapely women. Where the Pepsi commercials of the era subtly featured the centrality of men, the corresponding Coke campaign clearly made women the prime agent of much of the coupling that occurred. The beach ads repeatedly fixed on women in horizontal positions as the men moved in and out of the picture. One ad mentioned "fun," and simultaneously showed a blond woman on her stomach lifting her head from the sand to look up between the legs of a man reaching down to hand her a Coke. Another one, taking place at a lake, shows a man swimming out with an opened bottle of Coke to a raft where he hands it to a young lady. As the announcer says "to beat the heat," she sips while boldly fondling the bottle with her tongue and lips.

The ads of snowbound winter and skiing fun repeat the same basic symbolic interactions. In near blizzard conditions, two couples stand by a deserted country road, feverishly drinking Coke as they wait for a bus. Following their trip to the mountains the commercial focuses on the cute, blond ladies who leap off the bus as a pair, downing more Coca-Cola, while the men are left to the periphery of the picture to carry the skis and the poles. Elsewhere, a man opens his refrigerator and reaches for a Coke, only to encounter the picture of a smiling woman clad in a single-piece bathing suit standing in the middle of the snow, waving at him.

As blatant and seemingly intentional as some of these innuendos might be, the over-all consistency with which Coke and Pepsi adopt opposing postures in the same network of symbols underscores the unconscious or inadvertently collaborative dimension in the creation of the otherwise competitive campaigns.

Where Coke is nature and female-centered, Pepsi is culture and male-centered. Bill Backer agrees that nature was the vehicle he used in "Things Go Better with Coke" to convey the "refreshing, appetizing, healthy" association with the product. "Nature has been Coca-Cola's turf over the years. Coke has not been machine-oriented in its ads." There is no question in these campaigns that Coke and Pepsi each represented an opposing sex, but determining which is which is difficult without having access to *all* the ads in both campaigns. Backer points out that research at the time definitely indicated that more people perceived Coke as male. Dr. Roy Stout elaborates that ads like Coke's which portray women either serving or luring men will frequently prompt viewers to project the male characteristic onto the product, even though females dominate the action.

In 1966, when "Things" was in full swing, Pepsi followed the "Pepsi Generation" with "Taste that Beats the Others Cold, Pepsi pours it on." The coldness here is Pepsi's kind of coldness—a technological one, where the "cold turns on that Pepsi drive" as if it were a machine-tooled feature on a custom car. Pepsi's got a special taste which endows it with a masculine strength that "beats the others cold." Pepsi generates its own machine energy proclaimed in the predominantly all-male group of voices, which practically shouts how "Pepsi pours it on."

The commercial reiterated the theme that Pepsi epitomizes modernity and culture, and that its coldness contains the sleek, sparkling quality of technological precision. "Pepsi-Cola's objective is to preempt 'coldness' in the soft-drink business," said advertising vice-president Phil Hinerfield. "When the consumers want a really cold drink, the one we want them to think of automatically is Pepsi-Cola." The specific theme is reiterated in images which show the product in an ice-encased container in the middle of a modern living room as well as in other ice-embedded dispensers in a variety of environments.

Though sales were not bad during this period, BBD&O saw this campaign as a regression away from Pepsi's emphasis on the user. Yet there could well have been other reasons why "Taste . . ." was not more successful. Pepsi's stress on coldness was a bold attempt to take over the competition's prime turf. To succeed in getting the message across, the commercials would have had to offer a more favorable resolution of the underlying themes than those of Coke, with their images of nature, and warm, feminine life. Pepsi commercials employed quick cuts in a frenetic, modern montage of people drinking the product after intense and dangerous—that is, masculine—activities such as treetopping and—the "Pepsi drive"—race-car driving.* It was not people that were warm so much as the friction or torque of "Pepsi drive." The ad was casting the "cold" machine as the crucial link to life and regeneration. By and large, the campaign failed to transform the attribute into one signifying warmth and produced instead a message that was psychically and emotionally less agreeable than that conveyed in Coke's complementary campaign.

Coke ran into precisely the same problem with its subcampaign to "Things Go Better with Coke" where consumers are shown in grueling routines. While Pepsi may have been "right," "new," and "modern" back in 1961, in these more trying times Coke was presented as the octane in human fuel. Gone was the Kingston Trio's cheery musical accompaniment, replaced by a straight-talking announcer whose voice follows consumers on their daily routines with the grim matter-of-factness of Dragnet's Joe Friday. A teacher graduate student is on her feet teaching all day, standing through interminable bus rides to and from work and, before trudging on to evening classes, standing while downing a Coke and a hot dog. A truck driver rigging from Chicago to Dade City drinks Coke en route and on breaks. A hundred times a year, he does this run. ". . . the grind, the stress, the dust . . . and only seven stops along the way. . . . That means a lot of Coke."

The timing of the ads and the hard-selling, documentary tone suggest that they were intended to respond to Pepsi's "Taste That Beats the Others Cold." After all, Pepsi announced that it was going after "coldness," in effect changing its emphasis to a strong product orientation very much like the one that had pre-

---

* The car imagery in the ad is a most amusing coincidence since Pepsi was one of the companies outside the sports car industry to be financing race-car driving at this time, and Kendall was himself a director of Daytona International speedway. Meanwhile, Coke director Lindsay Hopkins' racers at the Indy 500 received backing from Sprite.

occupied Coke over the years. Coke just as deliberately responded with a decisive shift to people, hoping to surpass anything Pepsi had ever done in its portrayals of the users of its product. Coke went out to capture the literal, concrete users, going so far as to give their addresses and encouraging viewers to write and ask them if "Things go better with Coke after Coke" is just another slogan. Coke was forgetting Americana to go after America. To be sure, the documentary, word-of-mouth quality they sought captured the stark mood of the times—so well, in fact, that there lingers a crass, uneasy feeling about the campaign, a grating dreariness which even the promise of Coke could not penetrate. This unCoke-like quality resulting from the stylistic change was no more intended than the shortcomings of Pepsi's concurrent campaign. But is it just a coincidence that neither campaign was particularly well received nor ran for very long, or that these problems should befall them simultaneously? What happened, it seems, is that Pepsi quite deliberately moved to encroach on Coke's surface quality of "coldness." This quality was intimately tied to the underlying dynamic of nature/culture, and the move inadvertently rattled that structure, precipitating an otherwise inexplicable reaction where Coke simply surrendered its familiar thematic emphasis on nature and groped for a corresponding one on culture. Neither campaign could handle the competitor's theme gracefully. What was shiny, sparkling, and new in Pepsi's hands thus became somber, tawdry, and wholly inappropriate in Coke's subcampaigns.

The atmosphere brewing between Purchase, Atlanta, and their respective agencies during the sixties undoubtedly contributed to this fiasco. As Backer points out, "Both companies, particularly Coke, would have been much better off if they had never looked at each other's commercials." Backer recalls responding to a casual query some years ago from Paul Foley, the head of Interpublic, McCann-Erickson's parent company, on how the Coke campaign was going. Shaking his head, Backer answered, "I haven't the slightest idea of what they want."

"I'll tell you want they want," Foley immediatelly offered. "They want what Pepsi's doing."

The situation became more apparent for Backer when he learned from an associate at BBD&O of Monday morning meetings between executives from Pepsi and the agency to huddle over the latest Coke commercials. " 'Goddammit,' " the Pepsi men were quoted as saying, " 'that's what we need more of.' " Sure enough, Backer soon found himself at meetings with Coke management to air their desires to be more like Pepsi. After a struggle, Backer would give in. "In the final analysis, you lose. The client is always right when he's got that amount of millions to spread." As an indication of what he was up against, Backer pointed out how "Coke thought that Pepsi's 'Taste that Beats the Others Cold' was a super, hard-hitting campaign. I didn't. . . . Had Pepsi kept on running it, Coke would have been in great shape. Pepsi found out how bad it was earlier, but Coke never could understand why Pepsi dropped it."

In 1969, Pepsi's most powerful and perhaps most successful campaign—

"You Got A Lot to Live, and Pepsi's Got A Lot to Give"—emerged during the deepest cultural crisis in memory. While the economic scarcity and hardships which came home to roost in the late seventies were not as much of a factor then, America's unprecedented prosperity was felt by many to be the product of a technocratic system which was unleashing the terrifying horrors of wholesale war in Vietnam while threatening the destruction of the natural and social environment at home. Just as it had done seventy-five years before, Coca-Cola, and now Pepsi-Cola, sprang into action against cultural despair. The fact that the current version was prompting radical rather than conservative sentiments required only a slight modification in the sales pitch.

More emotional, more physical, and more intimate than any of its previous campaigns, Pepsi's "Live-Give" explored the images and settings of a maturing "Pepsi Generation." The conscious emphasis was still on the young user, but the modernistic, technological dimension of mobilely active youth was downplayed in favor of warm, tactile, physically active youth. No talking whatsoever occurred, so that the entire message was delivered in the highly orchestrated, vocally dramatic jingle. "You Got A Lot to Live and Pepsi's Got A Lot to Give" addressed the wide range of consumer problems far beyond expectations. "I was never involved in anything like it before or after," says a former BBD&O executive. "Priests, ministers, rabbis, writing or calling in comments, such as 'Every day we turn on that television and all we can hear are horrible things about America, horrible things about life, and horrible things about war, and you people are saying something different! A couple of people called who said they were on the verge of committing suicide until they saw the Pepsi-Cola commercials."

The lyrics for the jingle were written by Joe Brooks, author of the fantastically successful 1976 commercial hit, "You Light Up My Life."

The words so jolted BBD&O that a highly uncharacteristic decision was made to bypass all but the most minimal testing procedures. Within six weeks of the first airing, the reactions confirmed that their instincts had been right.

Pepsi helps—it supplies, "it has a lot to give"; it signifies not only physical quantity, but also the aura of abundance, the provider. Pepsi helps "those who like to live . . . come alive"; that is, Pepsi gives life to those who have the right attitude, it helps those who help themselves. All of these elements appear in the first four lines of Live-Give's jingle, and again in the chorus, and signify quite clearly that the choice between Pepsi and something else is the choice between living and something else. The last line of the jingle reiterates a theme in the first line that living is not simply something people do, but something that they are; that is, living is a "way " to which people "belong," just as the Pepsi Generation is a group to which people belong, and because it is "coming at you," it is a group to which you belong. The underlying messages, then, are between living and not living—life/death—as well as belonging and not belonging—in/out.

The same themes continued in Live-Give's successor, "Join the Pepsi People—Feelin' Free." The jingle tells us that feeling free is pervasive, and is felt by the select group of Pepsi drinkers as both a freedom to choose and to express oneself, and a thirst, a need to live. Pepsi not only satisfies that thirst, but reduces any potential conflict inherent in "you be you, and I'll be me." The Pepsi people are here and there is nothing to do but to join the group.

Coca-Cola, too, addressed the feeling of futility prominent in the Nixon years with "It's the Real Thing." Coke was being positioned for a message that would make people feel more together with others as well as themselves. Aside from the "Look-Up America" series that followed Watergate, its emphasis was truly global, and its marketing strategy reflected an orientation to a much broader market than Pepsi was reaching.

The campaign took longer to prepare, and was far more costly because of the diversity in style and sheer number of executions. Coke employed not only a central jingle, but extensive voice-over narration as well as numerous musical renditions written by Backer and sung by different artists in a host of popular forms, including the ballad, country and Western, rhythm and blues, and soul. The voices and lyrics sound authentic, and except for an occasional phrase from the central jingle and the more noticeable repetition of "It's the Real Thing" at the conclusion of each, it is difficult to tell many of these from popular radio tunes. Not only does the jingle manifest the same underlying themes as Pepsi's campaign, but, remarkably, the musical renditions all reflect the basic message of life/death and in/out developed in Pepsi's campaign.

"The Real Thing" was a coincidental repeat of a World War II billboard announcing "Here's the Real Thing." It owed its much grander success in 1969 to a host of factors, including Coke's recently celebrated 75th anniversary and the then secret Project Arden, the overhaul of Coke's entire corporate image and logo. Having gathered en masse for the first time in history to commemorate the 75th anniversary, the bottlers joined Atlanta in calling for a new campaign. Bill Backer, who was still very partial to the product promise and flexibility offered by "Things Go Better" began to cast about for an idea. "I thought this was a good time to present a calling card. . . . Research showed that young people were asking which came first—Coke or Pepsi"—a question that would all but anger any Coke-respecting person. Competition had never been entirely separate from imitation in Coke's view, and "The Real Thing" loudly proclaimed the authenticity of Coca-Cola. "It was a great thing to point out in those times, when so much was coming up phony. Right after it broke, there was the scare over cyclamates [synthetic sweeteners used in diet soda prior to a 1969 FDA ban], and people were railing about preservatives. Here was a basic 75-year-old product that could stand up and say 'We haven't changed.' The times were lucky for 'It's the Real Thing.' "

The Real Thing is in one's mind, a knowledge, a certainty, a security that "you're hoping to find," and which the whole world seeks along with you—not only those with a certain attitude about living, as with Pepsi. All people want to find "life's good things"—"real life," a taste of life, all of which they can find uniquely in Coca-Cola, now and forever. By itself, the jingle imparts a feeling of awesome, faceless security. While people hope, and the whole world wants, Coke simply is an absolute, titanic, all-powerful Thing (The *Thing* that Refreshes) that imparts the certainty and inner security it totally possesses.

In/out is then an overpowering theme, and it is fully developed in the musical renditions. One of the biggest Coke ads of all time, "I'd Like to Buy the World a Coke" by the New Seekers, embodies it perfectly. Security and belonging are here in the image of home, the warmth of furnishings, a world that is singing in harmony, together rather than asunder, drinking Coke for company.

Another musical ad, "It Really Makes Me Happy Knowing I'm that Country Girl," is an ode to the security inherent in simple living and equates the home-cooked meals, shade from the sun, and Coke on ice as the real things which give the singer security. In this ad as in all the other song ads, romantic love, coupling, having children, living simply in nature, and drinking Coke are all facets of security and belonging. Coke's ice coldness is made warm by couples—metaphorically "we"—who share Coca-Cola. "If you're thirsty and down, I'll bring you Coke and some ice—For you and for me, it's the Real Things in life—I'd do it for you, 'Cause you'd do it for me."

"Loving Her Enough" depicts a high-school trip to the Lincoln Memorial. As the ballad evolves, the camera pans across the wonderstruck eyes of the students as they fix on Lincoln's eternal gaze, and the image partially dissolves to the unmistakable script of the Preamble to the Constitution. The balladeer sings sentimentally as the image dissolves to the group sitting on a green lawn in a circle around their teacher, all drinking Coke. A tight shot of Lincoln's face appears as "the Real Thing" refrain is sung briefly. The romance here is for America, personified as a feminine lover who has been wronged by those "guilty of not loving her enough" (presumably during the social unrest of the sixties). The price is exile from the kingdom of her beauty. Sipping Coke "in the shade of her touch," however, the sinner reenters the sacred realm of her grace.

While both advertisers in a competitive campaign contribute to the message, the brand whose campaign resolves the message most favorably should enjoy a proportionately greater market share, all other things being equal. Aside from we/they, the other message—life/death—is present, as it must be, in "The Real Thing," but it did not begin to appear as clearly as in the Pepsi campaign until at least 1973 when "I Was Raised on Country Sunshine" was aired nationally and won the Clio Award for best commercial in the soft-drink category. The ad shows a girl in city clothes returning home to a reunion with her family at their country farm. While there is plenty of security in this setting, the girl sings mainly of the excitement and "joy that the bluebirds bring." Romantic love is an interference in the transcendental experience of life found in the simplicity of nature. "You love me and it's inviting, to go where life is more exciting, but I was raised on country sunshine."

As good as "Country Sunshine" was, the main group of ads contributing to this message appeared in the "Look-Up, America" series, which ran as a subcampaign with the Real Thing from 1974 to 1976. In one of the most eloquent entries of this series, the narrator talks of the "surf at Big Sur, pounding the rocks into the shape of dreams, the random energy of the Big Apple on a Saturday night, Iowa farmers, harvesting the land." In other words, the primordial source of all natural life mystically creates a world etched with dreams which are found, the jingle reminds us, "in the back of your mind." City and country are both part of the rhythm of life, but the full cycle of life *and decay* is expressed in the "harvest" of nature, which itself is bounded by the "smell of home-made bread," the staff of life. In the midst of this life, there is Coca-Cola refreshing the thirsty while cheering the disheartened. The jingle reenforces that message, advising viewers to "let in the sunnyside of living, to live life refreshed." The narrator in all of these ads assumes that a lasting depression grips the viewers, and advises them to "have a Coke, and start looking up." Images of American culture and youth repeat the we/they message in the idea that Coca-Cola, "the drink with the taste that won over the entire world" belongs to America, which has more of the "real things than any other place on the planet."

The central themes are thus well developed after 1973, but prior to that time there are many indications that Pepsi's campaign was the more effective. Though the ads which ran exclusively with "It's the Real Thing" were sprawling with images of breadbasket farmland, and dozens of unaccompanied women strolling in grass—clear symbols of regeneration and the life cycle—the jingle itself does not reenforce them. It positions Coke as the "Real Thing" *opposite* a world whose wants remain unsatisfied. Coke is real, unusual, the world's ideal; it has "real life." People, meanwhile, search for real life, find it in Coca-Cola, but instead of having "the Real Thing" return to a state of want, of searching. "What the world *wants* today is the Real Thing." The line emphasizing what the world wants instead of what it has is crucial because it is the *only* line of the jingle that is repeated in nearly every musical rendition of the campaign. By making Coke appear to be *in* the world, but not entirely of it, the campaign does not fully resolve the in/out (we/they) theme. Viewed as structural opposites which come together to make the whole, Pepsi was "in" while Coke signified "out."

While this is only one interpretation, reactions from various sources generally tend to corroborate that, at least in the initial stages, Pepsi's message was getting through better than Coke's despite the diversity, sophistication, and dollars tied up in Coke's effort. A BBD&O source claims that after the first six weeks, 30 percent of a given sample were able to identify the slogan while only 18 percent could do so with Coke's.

Bill Backer's own reactions add a further corroboration. "I tell you right now, and you can print this," he said, referring to the replacement of "Things Go Better with Coke" with "The Real Thing," "that company would have been better off today if they had never changed that campaign. I could have kept it alive for fifty years! It's the *basic* human promise. What *more* can a drink do for you? You can dramatize it in a million ways. . . . 'The Real Thing' was never as strong a promise. It's about the product, but not so direct as 'Things Go Better with Coke' or 'Pepsi's Got A Lot to Give.' Those are real promises of reward. You had to execute 'The Real Thing' into a reward." In Backer's eyes, Live-Give "was the only Pepsi campaign to go at it like Coke has gone at it. 'Pepsi's Got A Lot to Give'—now *that's* a product promise. If I had had "Pepsi's Got A Lot to Give," I would not have dropped that campaign as quick as they did to go to 'Pepsi people, feelin' free.' . . . Undoubtedly, it was little people playing politics in the company. That's not the agency. The agency doesn't want to launch a new campaign if it's a sensible agency." Backer suspected the problem in Purchase was typical in some way of many large companies, but Atlanta was the scene he knew best. "If you're gonna get ahead, you've got to make your mark. A new ad manager can't ride along on what's going on." During the late sixties, Backer was frustrated by a virtual revolving door of ad managers, some of whom he claims totally altered the target and strategy of entire campaigns in midstream. Backer believes these reversals accounted as much for Pepsi's advertising successes in the seventies as anything Purchase was putting out on its own.

All, perhaps, except for one area. Between 1975 and 1976, a chapter was begun which poignantly illustrated how the rivalry could undermine the delicate balance on which the advertising rests. Though Pepsi's national market was healthy at that time, it was faced with certain unusually depressed regional markets, primarily in the South, where it was far behind Coke. After some research, Pepsi discovered that it had no image—good or bad—in the region. "Our share of mind," said Peter Reader, ad manager for Pepsi-Cola, "was lower than our share of market." Further research by a local Dallas agent commissioned by Pepsi turned up an even more startling conclusion. In blind taste tests, more people preferred Pepsi than Coke. A writer at the agency worked up a campaign based on the tests entitled "The Pepsi Challenge." (The writer, D. L. Coburn, was well versed in the dialect of competition; his Pulitzer Prize-winning Broadway play, *The Gin Game* dealt heavily with this theme.)

The taste war precipitated a price war in many markets which drove other soft-drink products off the retail shelves and put numerous bottlers of local brands out of business completely. Bottlers of both companies, especially Coke, expressed discontent with comparative ads, describing them as "ludicrous," "confusing," and even "cheap."

These sentiments were echoed by more or less neutral observers throughout the advertising community. An executive at J. Walter Thompson, Arnold Grisman, pointed out that the consumer's reaction to a public ad war is likely to be "a plague on both your houses." More than loyalty to a particular brand, the ad war threatened to disrupt the positive emotions attendant on loyalty to *any* brand within the cola category. By pitting negative counterclaims against one another, comparative advertisements allow negative emotions in the consumer to surface.* "Customers of the product being unfavorably compared," says

---

* Peter Reader had worked on comparative campaigns before, such as Avis *vs.* Hertz, and SOS *vs.* Brillo. Yet these are clearly paired in a straightforward fashion. Used in this way, comparative advertising can resolve rather than arouse anxiety.

Grisman, "react by intensifying their commitment to their familiar brand." Far from brand loyalty, this response is a defensive hostility rooted in deeper emotions which the normal advertising would circumvent. Comparative advertising unleashes a boomerang effect that simultaneously denigrates the image of the brand while it disrupts the psychic disposition toward all soft-drink products. The taste tests confirm what the companies have known all along: the public's taste is fickle, and the real differences between Coke and Pepsi lie not in the products, but in the images propagated in their advertising. On the other hand, the use of the tests in commercials revealed that the companies have scarcely suspected that their competition within the advertising realm is, at bottom, a grand collaboration in advertising's pervasive myth-making power, a power, Leymore concludes, that can get stronger the more anxious, confused, and uncertain modern society becomes.

CHAPTER SIXTEEN

Crime and Nourishment

FOR ALL ITS INTENSITY, the war of the soda giants is a feud among siblings. Coke and Pepsi share the same cultural roots, spawned similar systems of distribution and, later, product lines, underwent similar patterns of diversification, consistently groped for parallel political and financial alliances, and in every measure aspired to a similar brand of global universality. Where the companies are siblings, though, the colas are twins—they look the same, they taste the same, and they bubble into foam the same. As much as anything else, the twins' most plentiful ingredient after water—sugar—is one area of intense common interest.

Sugar has long been second nature to Americans, who were sweetening their palates well before Coke arrived. In 1889, for instance, when Americans drank the equivalent of only 6.6 twelve-ounce containers of any brand of soft drink— probably less than half a pound of sugar—they still managed to consume almost fifty pounds of the sweetener, largely through personal household use. In the twentieth century, the dramatic increase in per capita intake was accompanied by a marked shift in the manner of consumption. By the early seventies, Americans were consuming, on the average, one hundred pounds of refined sugar annually, but household use had dropped to half of what it had been early in the century.* The difference was more than covered by the fantastic increase in consumption—from twenty to seventy pounds—through processed foods and soft drinks. This phenomenon was directly traceable to the efforts of soft-drink and food manufacturers to create new products with a competitive edge. While colorings, dyes, and preservatives enhanced appearance of new products and lengthened shelf life, they seldom helped and sometimes hindered taste appeal. Under these conditions, sugar became the soldier in the escalating war to protect market shares, and both the primary choice and last resort of product innovation.

Among Coca-Cola's brands, Coke contains less sugar than Mr. Pibb, Fanta Orange, Grape, and Root Beer, and about the same amount as Sprite. Only Teem contains less sugar than Pepsi, while Mountain Dew, Patio Root Beer, Orange, and Grape are all sweeter. As of mid-1976, according to the companies, Pepsi contained about 10 percent more sugar than Coke. Sprite, appearing the year after Teem, contains slightly more sugar, while Mountain Dew, acquired by

---

* This total includes sugar processed from cane and beets. If corn sweeteners are included, the figure is over 125 pounds.

Pepsi after the invention of Sprite, has over 20 percent more sugar than Sprite. (Recently, Coke introduced its heavily sugared Mello Yello to compete with Mountain Dew in the so-called citrus category.) Patio and Fanta both appeared in 1960, and the Patio flavors averaged about 8 percent higher in sugar content.

With beverages now comprising the largest single industrial use of refined sugar, Coke and Pepsi were quite naturally interested in the Senate Select Committee on Nutrition, established in 1968 under Chairman George McGovern (D–S.D.) to look at hunger in America. This committee held an ambitious series of hearings in the mid-seventies on the relationship of diet to killer diseases sweeping America—stroke, heart disease, obesity, diabetes, cancer, and hypertension. The conclusions from these hearings, reported in *Dietary Goals for the United States*, were so provocative that they had to be watered down under intense pressure from industries besides soft drinks and restated in a second edition in December 1977. Recommendations to reduce consumption of meat, milk, eggs, butter, and other products high in salt, fat, or sugar drew sharp and often self-serving reactions from the appropriate corners, but scarcely a whimper from Coke or Pepsi.

This silence was based on prudence, for the siblings were now confronted by a common, potentially threatening force that could, under certain circumstances, pyramid into an untenable, anti-soda backlash. From the cocaine craze to the caffeine crusade, Coke had seen it all before—the volatile mixture of public sentiment and political advocacy. Coke had learned from long experience that it was the mixture that was dangerous, and that neither an unorganized public nor government scrutiny were, by themselves, causes for much concern. Executives at both companies recognized that Americans, like most people, were creatures of habit who carried childhood patterns right into middle age. It would take more than a Senate proceeding to change all that. Still, from Atlanta and Purchase, they watched and, occasionally, they stirred in their seats.

During one of the hearings, Senator McGovern put a leading question on the relationship between sugar consumption and diabetes to Dr. G. D. Campbell, a South African expert on the disease. "Doctor," he began, "in terms of the sugar intake, where do you put the kind of soft drinks that we consume in this country . . . on the scale, in terms of offenders? Are they major offenders, major problems?" Dr. Campbell responded, "I must declare an interest here, because I am actually in the employ of Coca-Cola as a consultant in synthetic sweeteners (e.g. cyclamates and saccharin). I would hate to prejudice my very pleasurable association with this company, . . . but I think that the soft drinks are the biggest villains of all because they are the thing that starts the children off. . . . Too many children are drinking a liter of sugar-sweetened Coca-Cola a day."* Coming at the end of his lengthy testimony that outlined definite links between dispropor-

---

* U.S. Congress, Senate Committee on Nutrition and Human Needs, *Nutrition and Disease*, Hearings, Pt. II ("Sugar in Diet, Diabetes, and Heart Disease") 93rd Congress, 1st Session, 1973. p. 223-24

tionate consumption of refined carbohydrates—especially sugar—and diabetes, Campbell's strongly worded conviction was anything but a bombshell.* With a known diabetic population in the U.S. of about six million growing at some 6 percent a year, and coronary heart disease, which is statistically linked to both diabetes and obesity, the number one killer in America, McGovern and his colleagues paid close heed to Campbell and other experts. On the other hand, several medical specialists were not nearly so concerned about refined carbohydrate consumption. One such person, Dr. Fred Stare, chairman of Harvard's Department of Nutrition, was partially funded by Coca-Cola in the early sixties.† Stare received much larger grants over a twenty-five-year period from such non-profit channels as the Nutrition Foundation and the Sugar Research Foundation, whose directors and funding have also come from Coke during this time.‡

A good part of Stare's career has been devoted to battling anti-sugar sensationalism, built up, he says, in a paper delivered to the Senate committee, "of food faddists, consumerists, popular writers, special interests antagonistic to sugar, and even a few individuals with good training in nutrition but with no qualifications in medicine or dentistry." While failing to acknowledge his own "special interest" that would make him friendly to sugar, Stare commenced his argument by impugning the credentials of those with whom he disagrees, such as Dr. Campbell. "Sugar is an important nutrient and good in the U.S. diet, when used in moderation," he declared; those who attack it as a non-nutrient are playing with semantics, since any substance that supplies calories—however empty they may be—is still a nutrient. The colossal effort, by Stare and other doctors who testified, to classify refined sugar as a nutrient in a category with unrefined carbohydrates was and remains the crucial defense against the "sensational" charges which, the committee acknowledged, were valid. They were thus not picking on soft drinks per se when they agreed with Coke's Dr. Campbell that the sodas were indeed the contemporary "villains" in the sugar scenario.

In their final recommendations published in *Dietary Goals*, the committee proposed that consumption of refined sugar be cut from 20 percent of total caloric intake to 10 percent (or 250 mgs. per day, based on an estimated average intake of twenty-five hundred calories), a level slightly below that of the early 1900s. As the prime means of achieving that reduction, they recommended a drastic cutback in soft-drink consumption, which had doubled in the United

---

* According to Dr. Campell and a preponderance of other experts, the difference between raw and refined carbohydrates—be they grains, fruits, breads, or sugars—can be crucial. Refined sugar, produced by multiple chemical processing of the juice of the sugarcane or beet, effectively removes all the fiber and protein which comprise some 90 percent of the natural plant. Thus, over two thousand cane-cutters that Campbell observed could eat up to six thousand calories a day and chew large quantities of raw sugarcane without a single one developing diabetes. Likewise, Jewish immigrants to Israel from Yemen and Kurdistan observed by another witness at the hearings had a very low incidence of diabetes and heart attacks until they consumed for several years a Western diet high in refined carbohydrates.

† *Harvard University Treasurer's Report*, 1961, 1962
‡ ibid., 1955–1976

States between 1960 and 1975, rising from 13.6 gallons per capita per year to 27.6 gallons. This translates into approximately 294 twelve-ounce containers, or about 23.6 pounds of refined sugar a year versus 11.3 pounds in 1960. Between them, the twins owned approximately 43 percent of this market. On a per capita basis about 12.2 pounds a year were from the consumption of Coke and Pepsi alone. This figure is slightly over the level supplied *by the entire industry* in 1960 while all of the siblings' other brands supplied about 2.1 pounds per capita in 1975.* All told, Coke and Pepsi products supplied some 60 percent of the sugar in the soft-drink category. While over-all sugar consumption, including household use, climbed some 25 percent since the turn of the century; its consumption through soft-drinks has shot up nearly 700 percent during the same period. The committee was unequivocal in its conclusion that "total elimination of soft-drinks from the diet, for many people, would being at least half the recommended reduction of consumption of sugars."

No product category was singled out more forcefully by the committee for its harmfulness. Meat and dairy people, for example, could claim definite benefits from their foods. Soft drinks, on the other hand, held a disproportionately high place in the American dietary scheme in relation to what they contributed nutritionally, and the siblings, whose interests were rarely so allied, had to move quietly to offset possible wider effects from the committee's damning commentary. Fortunately for them, there were many health professionals they could cite, who voiced opinions closer to those of Dr. Stare, including the American Medical Association, which declared the committee's goals to be "inappropriate," based on "insufficient data," and fraught with the "potential for harmful effects from a radical, long-term dietary change."

To neutralize the threat to soft drinks, Coke prudently reemphasized an old stance that begs the nutritional debate completely. "No nutrient claims are made for Coca-Cola or the other soft drinks marketed by this company. Since human beings need both physical and psychological refreshment, there is a place in a balanced diet for soft drinks and simple pleasures." Pepsi, likewise, was quick to strike this chord of "psychological refreshment." It is an attribute evident in virtually every advertisement the siblings produce and, after the patent medicine phase, one of the founding philosophies on which both companies were built. Once advertised as "healthful beverages" that "revive and sustain," the twins must now be defended in narrowly worded medical and legalistic refinements of questionable logic.

Responding, as Coke did, to queries from the Interfaith Center for Corporate Responsibility, an ecumenical, church-sponsored agency in New York City, PepsiCo president Andrall Pearson wrote, "While we support the establishment

---

* In 1977, consumption of Coke hit 103 twelve-ounce cans per capita while Pepsi was 66.5. Those 169 cans supplied about 14.2 pounds of sugar while consumption of their other brands brought the over-all total sugar consumption from the siblings' sugared products to about 17.1 pounds. Calculations made on the basis of volume figures supplied by *Beverage Industry Annual Manual*, 1977-78, p. 24, 30. Figures on sugar content supplied by each company.

of sound nutritional goals, we believe that such goals should serve as guidelines to health professionals, food producers and processors, and to better food selection . . . but not as a yardstick against which to measure individual food products, or any given company's product line." Because "food products can and do have reason for being other than the nature and level of their nutrition contributions," the "yardstick" of nutrition cannot be the final criterion for a given product's inclusion in the diet. But what about when it comes to evaluating an entire industry, such as soft drinks or snack foods? By Pepsi's logic, the yardstick of nutrition could no more be applied to an entire industry than to a single company's product line. Indeed, the entire industry fostered the spiraling sugar race, which resulted in the generic similarity that presently exists among soft-drink products. The siblings and their many cousins both in soft drinks and processed foods can now cash in on that uniformity by rightfully asserting the awkwardness of singling out individual products for particular attention. Sweeping recommendations to develop public understanding about nutrition must begin by addressing entire industries, or food categories, rather than individual companies or brands, and that is precisely what the Senate committee recommended in the final edition of its report. In fact, the aforementioned Nutrition Foundation, whose "Commentary on the Dietary Goals" was endorsed by PepsiCo, recommended a comprehensive monitoring of food quality by product categories.

The siblings' evasion of the nutritional question under the banner of "psychological refreshment" rests on the assumption that sugar, though an empty food, poses no harm to the human body. PepsiCo's Pearson comments that "Products that provide primarily refreshment and pleasure make a valid and constructive contribution to the total human eating experience, both physically and psychologically, *when used as supplements to rather than replacements for food of higher nutrition content.*" (Emphasis added.) Even if science were to find that sugar does not promote any degenerative diseases, there is no way soft drinks could be classified merely as "supplements" to foods of higher nutrition content, given the present levels of consumption. With 1976 per capita consumption over a third higher than that of milk and nearly six times that of juices, they have all but dominated the liquid category.

In their relation to food, the picture is even more ambiguous. The siblings' trade group, the National Soft-Drink Association, asserts in its publication, "Liquids for Living," that "carbonated soft drinks actually aid digestion and thus stimulate the appetite." Yet this practice can just as easily contribute to excessive caloric intake and eventual obesity, especially since trends suggest that other foods happened to be processed foods. Meanwhile, the sugar industry offered dietary hints urging chubby people to "have a soft drink before your main meal . . ." because "you can spoil your appetite by eating something with sugar." Should this advice become standard practice, soft drinks would replace all foods of any kind in the diet. In fact, according to a top analyst at the Department of Agriculture, "Beverages have become one of the core foods of the American diet," well on their way to replacing water. Between 1968 and 1976, per capita water consumption dropped by a quarter, from 64 gallons a year to about 46 while soft drinks jumped from 24.8 gallons to 34.2, or 38 percent.

Whatever the weaknesses or inconsistencies of the companies' defense of their products, their responses have been placid, even meek, in proportion to the vast interest they share in the issue's outcome. If anything, the companies have been conspicuously calm, expressing themselves primarily through the National Soft-Drink Association or favorable medical channels. Their discretion was a response to a growing struggle within the federal establishment over what the proper American diet should be. That struggle could easily merge with mounting public concern over the same question, and thereby sweep the siblings from their lofty stations in American life to a defensive, embattled stance.

The lines of that struggle were drawn after the publication of *Dietary Goals* when Congress, appalled by the rising cost of health care, turned to prevention to ensure the nation's health. The diet-disease link was a natural place to begin, but the controversy engendered by the Senate's report will be settled by two agencies with conflicting political orientations and widely differing philosophies. One agency is the U.S. Department of Agriculture (USDA), the source of conventional wisdom about what the American diet should be. Seeking to ensure that the farm sector produces healthy food, USDA has become the strongest advocate of the prevention approach extolled by Congress. On the other side sat the huge bureaucratic behemoth, the Department of Health, Education, and Welfare, and its principal subdivision in disease research, the National Institutes of Health (NIH). NIH is filled with researchers, doctors, and health officials whose emphasis on the biochemistry of disease made them skeptical of the diet-disease link. For the most part, they agreed with the AMA that it would be better to tell the public nothing in regard to dietary guidelines than recommend drastic but possibly harmful changes. Coke and Pepsi, of course, preferred this brand of skepticism, which was no doubt shared by some of the top and middle-level brass at HEW in recent years. Joseph Califano, Carter's Secretary of HEW until the massive cabinet resignations of 1979, frequently represented Coke while at both Arnold & Porter and, later, Williams, Connally, and Califano. Casper Weinberger, appointed Secretary of HEW by Nixon in 1973, joined the PepsiCo board in 1976. George Lythcotte, director of the Health Services Administration at HEW during the Carter era, represented the public on the otherwise heavily business-oriented board of the Nutrition Foundation with J. Paul Austin. In 1960, apparently at the bidding of Senator Talmadge of Georgia, President Kennedy nominated Boisefeuillet Jones, a prime administrator of some of the Woodruff Family foundations and formerly a prominent health consultant at Emory University to be Special Assistant on Health and Medical Affairs at HEW.*

According to William Broad of *Science* magazine, the head-bucking between the two agencies began right after the publication of *Dietary Goals*, when Con-

* Charles Candler, *Asa Griggs Candler* (Atlanta: Emory University, 1950), p. x

gress suddenly accorded USDA the status of "lead agency" in diet and disease prevention. For the first time in any year, the Farm Bill of 1977 spoke not only of rice, wheat, potatoes, and tariffs, but of disease as well and called for a more "natural" diet. Putting precious little stock in this approach, HEW and NIH were not about to sit and watch Congress appropriate millions of dollars in research funds in the disease area to another government agency.

As the Carter White House moved to maintain the status quo, Califano and Agriculture Secretary Robert Bergland, who hailed from sugar-beet rich Montana, signed a letter of agreement: HEW would keep the whole operation. Intense lobbying ensued on both sides, and without the support of Bergland, the USDA people were starting to cave in. Senator Hubert Humphrey, himelf in the throes of a losing battle with cancer, apparently decided the issue of lead agency in a Senate conference. "HEW has avoided the area of prevention like the plague," he snapped, "and it's about time that USDA moves in. It's going to take this aspect of the nutrition program whether it wants to or not."

Off and running on a radical revision of the American diet, USDA people were dubbed by one prominent nutrition editor as "the barefoot boys of nutrition. . . . Now, they're the activists, new-age neo-naturalists and they have an issue. On the level of popular ideology, HEW just can't compete." For many at USDA who are, says one Agriculture official, "worlds apart" from those at HEW "when it comes . . . to the values they bring to their jobs," the facts are already in. The task at hand for the eighties is to translate *Dietary Goals* into a meaningful program that weds affirmative government action to consumer behavior and awareness. This is the effort that Coke and Pepsi fear, but it is truly a monumental one requiring market research and analysis, consumer psychology, and statistical techniques every bit as accurate and far-reaching as those employed by the companies themselves. Using weekly shopping-basket and home consumption monitoring as well as an elaborate overview of national food inventories, including regular checks of what is stocked in the warehouses and then what is sold (known as "disappearance data"), the "barefoot boys of nutrition" see themselves locked in a race to penetrate the companies' own markets with a fundamentally opposite message—drink fewer soft drinks.

Dr. Louise Light of USDA confirms the findings expressed in *Dietary Goals*. "There is no question from the national food supply data we have that a very heavy load of sugar incrementally added to our diets year by year is coming from sodas." Moreover, says Dr. Light, the enormously high per capita consumption—some 359 twelve-ounce cans in 1977—conceals the fact that the preponderance of this consumption is occurring within a very small group of heavy users.

As if on a rescue mission, Light declares, "We've got to identify those folks . . . and I hope with our nationwide survey we will be able to pick them out for the first time."

A 1979 publication by the National Center for Health Statistics offers a few hints based on data gathered between 1971 and 1974. Per capita consumption of sugar-sweetened soft drinks in twelve-ounce containers for those years averaged about 275.5 cans. Yet nearly half the black population and a third of the white population topped this range with one or more drinks per day, while 20 percent of the blacks and about 12 percent of the whites were heavy users, consuming from two to four drinks a day.* This represents nearly four times the national per capita soft-drink consumption, or a staggering 93 pounds of sugar annually. By far the greatest number of these heavy consumers belonged to the 18 to 44 age group, where 6 percent of the populace managed to swallow close to 25 percent of the total. Although whites claimed the greatest numbers, the proportion of heavy users among blacks was twice what it was among whites, largely because of the percentage of black heavy users below the poverty line. Poor black males comprised the highest proportion of heavy users within any group—an astounding 41 percent. Still, in this study, income was not as good an indicator of heavy-user tendencies as race or sex, but for the purposes of the companies' marketing strategies, none of them could touch age as the single best avenue to the soft-drink guzzler.

But for Dr. Light and "the barefoot boys," picking out these hardened soft drinkers will be a small breakthrough compared with actually getting across the message that they simply must cut back. For one thing, it will require an ingenious means of neutralizing the overwhelming influence of advertising which, within the youth market, has targeted lifestyle rather than sex, race, or income as the primary focus of their pitch. "We have a population segmented by lifestyle . . . where we didn't have it twenty years ago," says Dr. Light. The effect of the companies' targeted campaigning is compounded by life-long consumption habits that are engendered in early childhood. Where per capita consumption in the under-12 age group is up over 55 percent in the last decade, Coke executives maintain that consumption by both this group and the 13 to 17-year-old group will not abate as they enter the 25 to 44-year category in the eighties and nineties. This prediction seems accurate, since per capita consumption by the 25 to 44-year-old group, which includes drinkers from the postwar baby-boom years, is greater now than when many of these same consumers belonged to the 18 to 24 group in 1966.

While Pepsi tends to stress the continued importance of this aging "youth" market, Coke continues to tell the story of soft-drink demographics in sweeping terms. A company spokesperson recently told *Beverage Industry* that its market strategy is not aimed at any particular demographic segment, but rather tries "to appeal to everyone who might be thirsty, who wants a refreshing beverage . . . We don't feel that age has a whole lot to do with the way we market our product. . . . We give a youthful flavor to our advertising simply because everybody likes to feel youthful."

Occasionally, two departments within the same company will manifest the

---

* Some of the available statistics included powdered sugared drinks, such as Kool-Aid, which held about 1 percent of the total during these years.

same tension in their over-all positioning of the product. Public relations people sometimes seem willing to contradict the explicit statements of advertising executives, who maintain that the marketing effort *does* indeed include the targeting of segments likely to contain the largest number of heavy users. In doing so, P.R. spokesmen prefer to paint a picture of consumption as an activity of the *total* population rather than any narrow group, however it be defined. Such renditions reenforce over-all public acceptance of soft drinks as an integral part of the social fabric. By playing up the idea that people in all walks of life consume soft drinks in generous quantities and playing down the activities of the marketing departments, which know better, the companies can minimize the ultimate effectiveness of the government's attempts to rescue the soda-logged consumers who are the core of their market.

"Those are the people we have to reach with information and education," affirms Dr. Light, "but the problem is that knots in the system constrain us—which is interesting, politically. How come, if we want to say something to the public, we either have to go to government electronic media, or we have to put out a publication through GPO [Government Printing Office] where no one finds it? The media is a matter of access."

Pitted against the leviathan media apparatus of the companies and the entrenched habits of the heavy users, Light and her cohorts at USDA feel they pose little threat to the siblings' secure status. "Frankly," she says, "I don't think they're worried. . . . They've got this enormous habit going, and I don't think they see these guidelines as affecting their consumers."

Though the companies watched blithely from afar, they reacted noticeably when the government moved in. In 1977, the Congress amended the Child Nutrition Act of 1966 to regulate the sale of foods sold in competition with federally subsidized school meals under the National School Lunch Program. From snack counters and vending machines to a la carte lunch lines, a healthy traffic existed in items like soups, sandwiches, fruit, candies, chips, and soft drinks. Under the mandate of Congress, the USDA, which administered the lunch program, was directed to prepare a list of the least nutritious foods and restrict their sale until after the last lunch period. A similar rule instituted in 1970 was overturned in 1972 by a massive food industry outcry. Keenly aware of both the need for local self-determination and the role competitive foods play in adding to school revenues, Congress sought to "regulate only those foods that do not make a positive nutritional contribution." In addition, no outright ban was proposed, but rather a restriction during certain hours of the school day in order to preserve the nutritional integrity of the federally subsidized program.

The Department of Agriculture went to considerable lengths to come up with its list of non-nutritious foods to be covered by the new rule. A review of the general nutritional status of children revealed that overconsumption of calories existed right alongside an inadequate intake of certain key nutrients like Vitamins A and C, iron, and niacin. Excessive intake of calories was suggested in studies that found that 9 to 39 percent of adolescents were obese, and that the pattern, begun in childhood, was often predicated on parental obesity.* The department reasoned that an additional responsibility fell to the schools to try to mitigate a problem begun in the home. In pinpointing the source of all these excess calories, the department relied on one astounding study which concluded that snacks contributed about a third of children's daily calories on the average— more than any single meal—and that for about a third of the children, snacks contributed between 40 and 70 percent of the calories, sometimes replacing meals. Without the vital nutrients that meals provide, children were taking in 20 percent of their calories from sugar and nearly 60 percent of their sugar from snacks, principally candy and soft drinks which were consumed more frequently by those aged 1 to 17 than any other group.† In selecting the foods that it would regulate—including candy, soft drinks, frozen desserts, and chewing gum—the department concluded that snacks had to contain nutrients as well as calories if children's diets were to be adequate.

Public reaction ran high in support of the Department's proposals. Some organizations, such as the American Heart Association, indicated that the rule did not go far enough, either in the foods included or in the strictures placed on them, and that it was counterproductive to teach good eating habits in the classroom while allowing the sale of non-nutritious foods in the corridors.

On the other hand, from letters to lobbying, Coke, Pepsi, and their bottlers mounted a counter campaign built on three basic arguments:

1. *Enlightenment, or the Freedom Theorem.* Bottlers from all over the country echoed the ringing manifesto of the Coke bottler from Rhinelander, Wisconsin who declared that "candy, soft drinks, and snacks are part of *real life*, just as is a nutritious balanced diet already provided by schools. Freedom of choice is also part of real life. Prisoners are deprived of such freedom, and all too often so deprived is John Q. Public and his kids through actions of bureaucrats and regulators like yourself—who profess to 'know best' for all the rest of us who pay for your services and for the operation of our local schools through local *and* state *and* federal taxes." The NSDA, which was planning litigation anticipating the 1980 institution of the rule, argued that schools had become "prisoner-of-war camps or a collection of children organized for the purpose of carrying out government mandates on food or diet." Moreover, "taste dictates personal choice" which "is one of the most fundamental and basic freedoms of citizenship." Many other reactions by bottlers hammered at the idea that parents were in the best position to judge what was best for their children.

2. *Enhancement, or the Pleasure Theorem.* Many bottlers also struck a chord sounded by the Coke bottler from Milwaukee who intoned, "Indeed, a soft drink complements and enchances the meal with which it is consumed, and often makes what might be considered insipid a satisfying experience." The NSDA reiterated this idea, arguing that because of the poor quality of federally

* U.S. Department of Agriculture, Food & Nutrition Service, *National School Lunch Program and School Breakfast Program*, July 1979, p. 15
† ibid., p. 16

funded meals, "the presence of soft drinks in schools contributes to whatever success the federal school lunch program wishes to claim."

3. *Entrenchment, or the Habit Theorem.* PepsiCo responded that "Certain foods, soft drinks among them, are such frequent accompaniments to meals consumed by children at home that they are likely to stimulate the consumption of school-provided lunches by creating a context the child has learned to expect. The primary training ground for children's nutritional habits is the home. . . . By establishing a meal format which is drastically different from what children expect, the program dooms itself to defeat." The habit is apparently so strong that children will not only decrease or cease their consumption of the meals altogether, but will leave the school grounds to procure what they're used to having.

Most of the Coke bottlers' comments read as if the Agriculture Department were proposing a total ban rather than restriction of sales between certain hours. In fact, the comments of the Coke bottlers are uniform in enough respects to suggest that Coca-Cola mobilized the bottlers with a high degree of centralized coordination. This tactic has frequently been used by Coke when threatened by legislation or regulation. The hope is that the apparent absence of a comment from Atlanta combined with so much grassroots protest from the bottlers will convey the feeling of strong public response.

Yet USDA was hardly swayed by Coke's low-profile techniques, or similar ones employed by the Detroit Coke bottler, for instance, who declared that "many of these voices who have spoken against the banning of competitive foods have no vested interest in the matter other than freedom of choice." On inquiring into the public hearings held in the Detroit area, USDA officials discovered that at least one statement by a school official opposed to the ruling was read into the record by a man who failed to identify himself as an employee of the bottler. And in Tennessee, at least one statement opposing the rule was taken from a person whose expenses had been paid by the local bottler.

Such measures reflect the alarm aroused within the industry by the government action. "At stake in these actions and others which are sure to follow" editorialized one industry journal, "is the protection of the soft-drink product image, and its place in the American pattern of food and beverage consumption." Coca-Cola, too, was none too pleased at the censure it received from its own Dr. Campbell at the Senate Nutrition Committee's hearings. Within days of Dr. Campbell's remark that the soft drinks "are the biggest villains of all . . . because they are the things that start the children off," the committee received a communiqué from him: "Tell Senator McGovern that Coca-Cola and I have parted with animus. It is difficult to be honest, and be a food consultant at the same time."*

Public reaction over sugar has never approached anything like the panic that engulfed Coke during the turn-of-the-century cocaine crisis, nor is it likely that it

* *Nutrition and Disease, Part II op. cit.,* p. 223

soon will, given the prevailing habits of consumption. But the two white powders have a good deal more in common than the chemical capacity to give their users a swift lift. Pepsi never contained cocaine, yet, like Coke, it was initially marketed as a medicine rather than a refreshment and it promised many of the same benefits that Coke did. Like cocaine, sugar has evolved in a similar though grander progression moving from wonder drug and esoteric luxury to the pleasure of the masses.

Unrefined "sweet cane" and "honey without bees" dates back to the Greeks and Romans, and appears in ancient Indian, Chinese, and Polynesian legends. Sugar was first cultivated and refined by the Persians in 600 A.D. As Islamic conquerors spread it throughout the Near East, sugar passed from exclusive imperial use into heavy popular demand at the height of the Turkish Empire, and was brought to Europe in quantity by the returning Crusaders. In America, sugar has been standard fare in the diet since the drafting of the Constitution, and was imported for mass consumption throughout the nineteenth century when industrial technology facilitated its refinement. During the Civil War, it was a favorite condiment of soldiers, particularly in condensed milk. Diabetes made its first appearance at this time, and was being treated with the same opium derivatives that became the forerunners of the patent-medicine industry.

Like cocaine, opium passed from imperial wonder drug to popular usage, and thence to verboten, but its derivatives, including morphine and heroin, were hailed as the "new" wonder drugs and nonaddictive pain killers. By the time Coca-Cola was born, morphine's addictiveness was well known, and it was only a little more than a decade before cocaine traveled the same cycle, finally joining morphine and alcohol as "the third scourge of the human race." Do the ill-fated careers of these derivatives suggest a like destiny for sugar? If so, the Senate Committee's branding of soft drinks as the prime contributors to excessive sugar intake reads like the curtain rise for the final act.

Yet both soft-drink leaders seem complacent, barely stirring in their seats. For having sat through the first act, they saw that cocaine was outlawed, not because of valid scientific evidence of its addictiveness—Freud and other researchers constantly claimed otherwise—but because of the manipulation of public paranoia by a well-concealed coterie of vested interests bent on curbing the patent-medicine industry. Likewise, public sentiment and established habits and practices will hold sway in the otherwise modern, scientific debate over sugar, and the companies have nothing to fear from government regulation in this regard as long as they can lay unmitigated claim to the special province they call "psychological refreshment."

More than a catch phrase to win the support of consumers and neutralize the consumer-advocates, this idea of psychic and spiritual refreshment goes back to the very roots of the colas' appeal. The Victorian morality of the age spurned alcohol and helped the spread of Coke and, for a while, cocaine. Through it all, Coke remained that dark and bubbling novelty for those mischievous ones who wanted to mix their tonic with a little extra indulgence. By spiking their Coca-Cola with alcohol or cocaine, many pleasure-loving Southerners practiced a furtive brand of secrecy which strangely mirrored the Candlers' own elaborate cultic rituals to conceal the precise makeup of their Merchandise 7X, itself an artful blend of flavors and oils designed to hide the bitter aftertaste of the coca and the kola extracts. The essential nature of the drink was true to its color—dark, mysterious, opaque. To this day, scarcely anyone in America has drunk of this sweet soda nectar and not encountered the inevitable tales of the closely held formula—"the best-kept industrial secret in the free world"—and of Coca-Cola's power to dissolve everything from baby's teeth to rusty nails while never failing as an effective douche.*

A surprising number of these tales originated from litigation and official investigations beginning with the Pure Food Laws of the early 1900s. In 1951, a doctor responsible for the Navy's nutritional research during World War II testified before a congressional committee that the Navy conducted an investigation into cola beverages after learning how much money its recruits were spending on Coca-Cola. "I was amazed to learn," the doctor testified, "that the beverage contained substantial amounts of phosphoric acid. . . . At the Naval Medical Research Institute, we put human teeth in a cola beverage and found they softened and started to dissolve within a short period. The acidity of cola beverages is about the same as vinegar. The sugar content masks the acidity, and children little realize they are drinking this strange mixture of phosphoric acid, sugar, caffeine, coloring, and flavoring matter." A congressman inquired whether the doctor had made any tests of the effect of cola beverages on metal and iron, adding "A friend of mine told me once that he dropped three ten-penny nails into one of the cola bottles, and in forty-eight hours the nails had completely dissolved."

"Sure," the doctor replied, "phosphoric acid would dissolve iron or limestone . . . it would erode the steps [of the Capitol] coming up here. . . . Try it."†

The entire debate surrounding caffeine, beginning with the celebrated 1909 case, "The U.S. vs. Forty Barrels and Twenty Kegs of Coca-Cola," hinged on the question of caffeine and Coke's essence. Was the substance an additive, as the government contended, or was it "an essential ingredient" as Coke's lawyers maintained? The Supreme Court upheld the government, which never enforced the decision, and there the matter stood for sixty years until the American Bottlers of Carbonated Beverages petitioned the FDA in the so-called "Coca-Cola" amendment to create a new "standard of identity" [requisite ingredients] for soda water.‡ The standard of identity granted by the FDA didn't require the beverage maker to identify any of the essential ingredients on the label—in-

---

* There are couples who swear to having used a Coca-Cola douche for years as their preferred form of birth control, and at least one man interviewed claimed that his wife became pregnant when they used Pepsi. Needless to say, such practices are less than reliable, and should be avoided.
† William Dufty, *Sugar Blues* (New York: Warner Books, 1975). p. 177-78
‡ Cola drinks were included in the standard of identity as one category of soda water.

cluding water, sugar, phosphoric acid, caramel, and caffeine—since these were now mandatory for all drinks calling themselves colas. It also explicitly excluded Vitamin C, thiamin, and other such fortifiers on the theory that they might encourage even greater soft-drink consumption. Even though most colas contained caffeine beyond that present in the kola nut extract, the FDA concluded that to require an indication on the label of such additional caffeine would mislead consumers with the impression that a cola drink without such labeling contained no caffeine. Under these circumstances, the standard of identity requested by the industry acted as a license for concealment, and reenforced with legal sanction the already powerful aura of the secret essence.

Recently, the question of caffeine's health effects has surfaced once again, and evidence tends to confirm some of the bleaker views. In 1972 Dr. Murray Jarvick, Professor of Pharmacology at New York's Albert Einstein College of Medicine, partially anticipated later studies linking caffeine and breast cancer when he told the *Wall Street Journal* that caffeine "may play a role in death from cancer or heart stoppage." In mid-1978, the Federation of American Societies for Experimental Biology recommended that caffeine be removed from the GRAS (Generally Recognized As Safe) list of food ingredients, which the FDA oversees as part of the Food, Drug, and Cosmetic Act of 1938. "At current levels of consumption of cola-type beverages," the Federation declared, "the doses of caffeine can approximate that known to induce such pharmacological effects as central nervous system stimulation."

Yet the caffeine-sugar combination found in colas seems capable of creating its own unique combination of symptoms. Dr. Jarvick commented, "Although caffeinated soft drinks provide a lift that refreshes and fights fatigue fairly well, they produce a tremor, insomnia, gastrointestinal disorder and possible cellular damage to the drinker or unborn fetus." Indeed, FDA-sponsored animal tests have shown that caffeine can cause birth defects, a finding corroborated in fourteen separate animal studies cited by the Center for Science in the Public Interest, the Washington-based public interest group.

Meanwhile, Dr. David Hoffman of the Center for Health Behavior and Nutrition in Beverly Hills has had a thriving practice in recent years treating "colaholics" who drink from twenty-four to thirty-six cans of cola a day. He approaches his patients as addicts, and adds, "It's not easy. It's actually more difficult than stopping smoking or giving up alcohol because cola is a much stronger physiological dependence."

In early 1980, the FDA showed clear signs of taking even stronger action than removing caffeine from the GRAS list. A complete ban on its use in food has received some consideration, but a top priority is a change in the soda water standard to allow it to be an optional rather than mandatory ingredient. Cola manufacturers would then either have to drop it from their products or include it on their labels, which many of the major brands already do. Even if the sodamakers added no caffeine to the beverages, however, cola is naturally caffeinated. Though the levels are only a fraction of those in tea or coffee, it is quite possible that some kind of warning would have to appear on the label. Such a declaration would indeed cast an unwanted shadow across the noble logos of Coke and Pepsi, and be seen from every cola capitol in America as a blight on this revered industry. "Anyway we go, we're going to end up in court," said Tom Brown, a top official in FDA's Division of Foods, "with cola makers probably leading the battle."

Because of Coke's legal problems over caffeine early in the century, the Atlanta giant has long led the industry in its wariness over disclosing its main ingredients. The FDA's creation of the standard of identity legitimized this practice, but under increasing pressure from consumer groups, Coke relented in the early seventies, and was followed by Pepsi in listing the mandatory ingredients included under the standard of identity. Both companies expanded the policy to include all their brands, but in no way approached a full disclosure of many of the more exotic ingredients, such as ammoniated glycyrrhizine, sodium metabisulfite, methylcellulose, and more than seventy-five others. The real trade secrets were thus preserved. So, says the *Wall Street Journal*, were the legends of secrecy, strengthened over the years by "the cola makers themselves who love to point out how their 'secret formulas,' known to a few trusted hands are locked away in safe deposit vaults," which, in Coke's case, can be opened only by a vote of the board of directors.

With each company having literally dozens of concentrate plants around the world that manufacture syrup for the various bottlers, it is tempting to wonder how the "secret" could ever have been kept in the first place, or whether it's such a secret after all. "You bet it is," assures Harry Korab, technical director of the National Soft Drink Association, who indicated that all the soft-drink manufacturers take elaborate security precautions when it comes to protecting their formulas. Often, these measures include dispatching one or more couriers from the respective companies armed with the proprietary traces of their secret soda bounty to the various concentrate plants around the world.

But couldn't any laboratory simply analyze a sample of any of these drinks, and thereby fathom the mystery fueling the cola legends? Over the years, many attempts have been made by outsiders to discover the formula, but there has never been a precise breakthrough. According to Korab and other qualified chemists, the root of this impenetrability lies in the high number of natural oils, flavors, and extracts which are present in the formulas for Coke and Pepsi. These might include cinnamon, nutmeg, vanilla, lavender, lime juice, citrus oils and, in Coke's case, the fluid extract of guarana, which comes from the seed of a Brazilian tree. Unlike the inorganic or synthetic chemicals also present, these organic compounds are practically impossible to detect in their precise proportions. The secrets of Coke and Pepsi are thus bound up in nature. As if born of some ancient, esoteric knowledge, these ingredients have a natural alchemy.

Coke and Pepsi have been on their guard with the growing concern over sugar, but they bared their knuckles at the regulatory furor surrounding synthetic sweeteners. With at least 8 percent of their total sales in diet drinks, the companies have flung themselves into a wide-ranging debate on the medical and social issues raised by cyclamates and saccharin. The sudden, total, and outright ban on cyclamates in October 1969 sent shock waves through the industry. Six months before, when the FDA announced that foods and drinks containing cyclamates must carry prominent warnings against overconsumption, a spokesman for PepsiCo shrugged off the order, commenting "It's just a labeling change" while Coca-Cola called the move "sound." Their tune changed with the ban, however, as estimates of its cost to the industry reached as high as $359 million. Tax write-offs and sales of foreign inventories brought the figure down, and within a year and a half, the companies were on Capitol Hill pushing for a bill co-sponsored by thirty-four congressmen that would have awarded $3.1 million in damages to Coke, $2.5 million to Pepsi, and tens of thousands of dollars to each of the 2,250 bottlers for the alleged losses. Even though no one in industry was asserting the government had done anything wrong, the bill would have reimbursed the users which included other industries (such as fruit packers) that used only half of what the soft-drink industry did. Nevertheless, there were clear signs that the siblings were not nearly as surprised as they appeared to be by the ban. Coke and Pepsi had cyclamate-free versions of Tab and Diet Pepsi ready within days of the ban, and by early November, the new Diet Pepsi was already available in 50 percent of the country. Opponents of the bill, such as House Judiciary Chairman Emanuel Celler, linked this readiness to the industry's awareness of decade-old warnings about the unrestricted use of cyclamates from both the FDA and the National Academy of Sciences. A nutritionist for the Senate Select Committee on Nutrition declared, "Why should we expect the American government to reward the private enterprise system for having been sloppy in its self-regulatory procedures, nonsupportive of the FDA, and careless of the public's health?" All too aware of the bill's political sensitivity, its supporters, which included the Nixon administration, worked to move it through Congress with a minimum of public attention, but it was eventually defeated.

Indeed, the last thing the companies wanted at this stage was attention, for as with cocaine sixty years before, it was the public's mood far more than scientific evidence that led to the banning of cyclamates. Following the cranberry and mushroom scares of the early 1960s, that mood was grounded in a pronounced fear centered on the diet-disease link. "It is highly unlikely," wrote Fred Stare and Elizabeth Whelan in Panic in the Pantry, "that cyclamates would have been banished as quickly as they were if there had not been a widespread, intense, and immediate specter of cancer."* Some business groups, like Sugar Information, Inc. and the Sugar Research Foundation, were at odds with the siblings on this question. They funded a half million dollars of cyclamate experiments in search of damning evidence while conducting lengthy ad campaigns that dubbed the diet drinks "synthacolas." Later denounced by scientists

---

* Elizabeth Whelan and Fred Stare, Panic in the Pantry (New York: Atheneum, 1975)

and administrators both in industry and government, the outright banning of cyclamates brought sharp reaction from one team of government-employed researchers in Wisconsin who wrote that "political or economic pressures caused [the FDA and the Secretary of HEW] to bypass the established scientific evaluation procedures."* Such pressure could not have averted the ban, as Jack Anderson reported. Kendall was the first business man to reach then Secretary Robert Finch, himself a long-time Nixon adviser who had no choice under existing law other than to impose a ban. "With typical good humor, Kendall strode into Finch's office carrying a canvas bag. Pretending there was a bomb in the bag, he shoved it under Finch's desk. 'Is this where he sits?' demanded Kendall mischievously. 'I don't want to miss him the way they did Hitler.' "† Many consumers, however, were apparently gratified by the government's sensitivity, said one editorial, in "protecting man from some of his most ingenious chemical creations."

To be sure, the literal, air-tight wording of the Delaney Amendment to the Food, Drug, and Cosmetic Act of 1938 had something to do with the ban. Passed in 1958, the amendment simply prohibited the use in food of any ingredient found to cause cancer in man or animal after appropriate scientific tests. Coke and Pepsi quickly realized, however, that factors beyond science could well influence official acceptance of scientific findings, and that their own fortunes were inextricably linked to social forces and shifting public opinion.

With cyclamates gone, there was only one synthetic sweetener left—saccharin—and Coke and Pepsi soon found that the public was clinging to it as dearly as they were. Saccharin, indeed, was as old as Coke, having first been used in the 1880s as an antiseptic and food preservative. Diabetics began using it as a sweetener at that time, and the canning industry followed suit some twenty years later. The clashing emotions in the contemporary saccharin debate, caught somewhere between science, profits, and political freedom, were evident years earlier in a pointed White House encounter between Teddy Roosevelt and Coke's old nemesis, Dr. Harvey Wiley, who reported the incident in his book, *The History of a Crime Against the Food Law*.‡ As head of the Bureau of Chemistry under the newly passed Food and Drug Act, Wiley had been summoned to the President's office to answer complaints of food processors whose operations had been strapped by Wiley's vigilant policies. One of them was a clever New York attorney who, knowing of Roosevelt's heavy personal use of saccharin, outsmarted the zealous Wiley by making a bald political play for presidential favor. Unaware of the President's preferences for saccharin, the outraged Wiley took the bait, and launched a searing attack on saccharin and the food industry's deceptive labeling.

Roosevelt was suddenly incensed. "Are you telling me that saccharin is injurious to health?"

* *Science*, November 7, 1969, p.685
† Jack Anderson, *The Washington Post*, December 31, 1972, p. C7
‡ Cited in Chapter 1.

"Yes, Mr. President, I do tell you that."

"Dr. Rixey gives it to me every day."

Realizing he had overstepped his bounds, Wiley quickly tried to cover his tracks. "Mr. President," he slowly replied, "he probably thinks you may be threatened with diabetes."

"Anyone who says saccharin is injurious to health is an idiot," snapped Roosevelt. The meeting promptly broke up and Wiley, who never saw the President again, dates the slack enforcement of the Pure Food and Drug Act to that incident, which occurred only several months after the law was passed.

Indeed, the FDA's 1977 announcement of a proposed ban on saccharin triggered congressional intervention almost as swiftly as a President reacted nearly seventy years before. Consumers voiced their anger, and promptly rushed out to buy up all available supplies of diet soft drinks. No one, least of all the soda makers, was placated by the agency's intention to keep saccharin as an over-the-counter item or table-top sweetener. Aside from the controversial Canadian rat study that prompted the FDA move, a number of other cancer-positive studies were completed in the early seventies. "Some of those studies were less than perfect by today's standards," said the Washington-based Health Research Group at an FDA saccharin hearing in 1977. "Nevertheless, the consistency of the findings should have compelled a saccharin ban years ago. . . . In some studies, the effect occurs at low doses as well as high. In two FDA studies, for example, cancers were seen at the equivalent of 1.6 bottles of diet soda per day."

Opponents of the saccharin ban urged the public to reject the recent Canadian rat study because the tumors were quite possibly the by-product of stress arising from the massive dosages.* Nevertheless, Dr. Robert Hoover, co-author of a major on-going saccharin study by the National Cancer Institute (NCI), says that the preponderance of the evidence in a variety of studies "has confirmed the capacity of saccharin itself to initiate cancer, although with less potency than most other carcinogens."† Among rats, that capacity is most pronounced "when the mother is exposed to high doses before pregnancy and the offspring are exposed in utero (prior to birth) and throughout their lives. It also appears that high doses of saccharin can markedly promote or enhance the potential of other carcinogens in rats."

Is saccharin a human carcinogen? Recent studies have exonerated the sweetener from inducing any epidemic of bladder cancer in this country, but the massive NCI study has detected evidence of heightened risks among heavy cigarette smokers and certain other groups. Though the findings here are thus far

---

* Dr. William Havender explains that high dosages are normal procedures in cancer tests. ". . . a substance capable of causing some 2 million cases of cancer in the United States (an incidence of 1 percent in a population of 200 million) might well go undetected if it were tested only at doses that simulated human usage . . . the test's sensitivity can be magnified by using very high dosages and in fact, the normal practice is to include the highest dose that will not poison the animals to death (the maximum tolerated dose, or MTD) in order to make the test as sensitive as possible." *Regulation*, March/April, 1979. p. 18

† "Saccharin—Bitter Aftertaste," *The New England Journal of Medicine*, March 6, 1980. p. 573-75

inconclusive, Dr. Hoover continues, "the general patterns of use of artificial sweeteners in this country are troublesome. The heaviest use is by women in the child-bearing years. There has also been an increase in use among children who are receiving much higher doses (per kilogram of bodyweight) than adults. Although very few people at the age when bladder cancer is likely to occur drink two or more dietetic drinks daily, many young adults drink four or more."

While the scientific disagreement over saccharin has been intense, the policy debate over what should be done about it is more so, pitting those that would err on the side of caution against those that insist on proven *human* health risks before supporting a ban. Responding to the massive public outcry after the FDA's 1977 announcement, Congress voted an eighteen-month moratorium on the ban, which was renewed for two more years in July 1979.

Though sticklers for proof of risk, opponents of an outright ban (including drugstore sales) or even removal from the food supply settle for less than scientific conclusiveness on saccharin's alleged benefits. Many experts on both sides of the controversy agree that virtually no studies have demonstrated any health benefits of saccharin in preventing obesity or contributing to weight loss or fewer heart attacks among diabetics. To be sure, there are widespread psychological benefits perceived by doctor and patient alike in the management of certain medical problems, but as a 1978 *New York Times* editorial suggested, the specter of more demonstrable risks has shifted some of the onus back to the pro-saccharin forces.

Coca-Cola is the largest single contributor to the Calorie Control Council (CCC), an Atlanta-based association of dietary food and beverage makers which has sought to steer the debate by funding a wide array of marketing surveys and lobbying efforts. The CCC has been cited for frequently quoting medical authorities out of context by an aide to Senator Edward Kennedy, whose Senate Subcommittee on Health and Scientific Research has jurisdiction over the saccharin issue in the Senate. This allegation was reiterated in a pointed letter to CCC president Robert Kellen from the FDA's Associate Commissioner for Public Affairs. The letter concerned the "lack of balance" and "misimpressions" created in the public mind by a 1979 brochure circulated by the Council just prior to a crucial congressional vote to extend the moratorium on the FDA ban. The letter drew a five-page response from the CCC, some of which berated the FDA official for his lack of awareness of the subject as well as his partisanship in seeking to criticize a responsible industry group for expressing its view. But a scathing attack on the CCC emerged in another letter to Kellen from Cornell University Professor T. Colin Campbell, a dissenting member of a National Academy of Sciences Panel (NAS) which cleared the way for federal approval of saccharin. "I consider your pamphlet to be equivalent to nothing more than selling a product without concern for moral principles. . . . Although the . . . pamphlet recklessly distorts the scientific statement of (NAS) Panel I—and that is serious enough—I am deeply troubled by the fact that you believe you can get away with it. I have since taken the opportunity in talks before various nutrition and health educators to hand out and discuss your pamphlet together with an Executive Summary of the Panel I Report to illustrate how seriously unresponsible an industry group can become. It's a marvelous case study of how an advocacy position with a blatant disregard for carefully considered scientific findings can still be effective simply by having the resources to reach enough people."

At least one of the scientific bodies cited by CCC—the American Council of Science and Health (ACSH)—has Coca-Cola's old ally, Dr. Fred Stare, on its board. The ACSH has certainly been among the kindest of any scientific group toward saccharin, advocating its free and untrammeled use without so much as the special warning label now in use. Stare's group reached notably less cautious conclusions than NAS, even though both groups analyzed precisely the same data.

In opposing the proposed saccharin ban, CCC president Robert Kellen has played heavily on the freedom of choice angle. "The American people have left no doubt about their desires; they want and need saccharin." While erroneously implying that the proposed action would totally ban saccharin, Kellen is suggesting that the greatest freedom of choice exists in the present arrangement, which offers consumers either a high-sugar drink containing from 140 to 200 calories or a diet drink containing about 100 milligrams of saccharin. In Canada, where saccharin has been banned from the food supply, Canadians have a choice between fully sugared sodas, reduced caloried drinks sweetened with sugar or, more recently, fructose (such as Pepsi Light), and diet drinks to which they add one or two 15-milligram saccharin tablets as they would to a cup of coffee. The Canadian experience is instructive in that none of the bleak scenarios circulated by the CCC in the United States with regard to spreading incidence of diabetes and heart attacks was confirmed. On the contrary, two Canadian experts contacted by Sydney Wolfe of the Public Citizen's Health Research Group attested to the lack of any known adverse medical consequences resulting from the saccharin ban. Moreover, both doctors indicated that "the furor in Canada was considerably lessened by the absence of a Calorie Control Council campaign" which, alleges Wolfe, "inflamed" thousands of consumers and doctors into protesting the saccharin ban.

From the very start, the soft-drink industry and the CCC made it clear that any action against saccharin would be vigorously resisted. As far as Coke and Pepsi were concerned, the clearest reason for their stance, aside from any consideration of the scientific issues, was money. The price of sugar is many times that of an equivalent amount of saccharin and, during the 1974 era of soaring sugar prices, both Coke and Pepsi were able to make tremendous profits by pricing their diet drinks on a par with sugar-sweetened ones. Most of their bottlers enthusiastically supported this practice, both because so-called "level pricing" was simpler and because they desperately needed to offset the profit squeeze of high-priced sugar with a handsome margin on the diet line. According to the *Washington Post*, Pepsi was actually attempting to justify the policy by erroneously asserting that the price of saccharin rose with that of sugar, but in general, the practice was defended with the claim that the prices represented an average and that without level pricing, the cost of sugared drinks would be much higher. This practice of averaging has been "going on for years," according to NSDA president Tom Baker. Nevertheless, as early as 1970, this practice was vociferously denounced by J. Paul Austin himself in a lengthy letter to the secretary of HEW in which he outlined Coca-Cola's opposition to products which combine sugar and synthetic sweeteners. ". . . it should be recognized that some manufacturers may attempt to combine sweeteners simply as an economy move. It is well known that sugar is an expensive sweetener, especially when compared to saccharin; and adoption of the proposed policy is an invitation to unethical manufacturers to cut costs by the substitution of saccharin, in whole or in part, for sugar. . . . This adulteration," he concluded, "will in all likelihood not result in any cost reduction at the retail level." Even as he warned against scalawags, Austin accurately prophesied the future pricing practices of the industry he led.

CHAPTER SEVENTEEN

The Syrup of '76

"This is a big business. We're not just fooling around with it." —J. Paul Austin

WHEN JIMMY CARTER'S QUEST for the White House began, he was a politician without a base, a populist in need of a constituency. Yet between 1975 and November of 1976, something seemingly miraculous happened to the former governor of Georgia. He defeated a long-time mainstay of the Republican Party, an incumbent at that, to become the thirty-ninth President of the United States.

Carter's strength lay not in the public's recognition of his platform, but in its perception of him. In a time of national despair, he was seen as the "un" politician, who dared to challenge the Washington establishment. "His basic strategy consists of handshaking and street cornering his way into familiarity," touted Time magazine.

This image, however, does not accurately reflect the man. Not that Jimmy Carter isn't a homespun, albeit sophisticated ex-peanut farmer, who undoubtedly feels more comfortable in jeans than in a suit. Yet his popular style was carefully enhanced and packaged in much the same way Coke is marketed as the "Real Thing." Like Coke, behind the simple, spit-clean, ma and pa appearance was ultrasophisticated machinery. Much the same political forces and media techniques that have helped to institutionalize Coke elected Jimmy Carter. Indeed, the Coca-Cola Company was behind both of Georgia's most famous products.

In 1962, Jimmy Carter, a thirty-seven-year-old peanut farmer, narrowly lost the Democratic primary for the Georgia State Senate. Convinced that the ballot box had been stuffed, Carter turned for advice to old family friend Griffin Bell, a partner of the prestigious Atlanta law firm, King & Spalding. Bell referred him to an associate at the firm, Charles Kirbo, who proceeded to prove in court that his client had been defrauded. Carter was declared the primary's winner and he went on to win the general election, his first political victory.

"Going to see Charles Kirbo," Carter would later say, "was probably one of the smartest things I ever did in my life." A partner in King & Spalding (K&S), Georgia's premier law firm, Kirbo became one of Carter's closest friends and advisors, providing the latter with entree into the state's highet ruling circles. Long intimate with the state's political affairs, K&S listed as clients: General Motors, which has a large assembly plant in Atlanta; Rich's, the South's oldest and largest department store; Cox Enterprises, owner of virtually all of Atlanta's major radio and television stations and newspapers; Southern Railways, one of the nation's largest; the Trust Co. of Georgia, whose building houses the offices of King & Spalding; and, since the 1920s, the Coca-Cola Company. According to Calvin Trillin in *The New Yorker*, "The firm's primary mission from the start may have been to keep the world safe for Coca-Cola."

It was into this circuit that Kirbo plugged the peanut farmer. Carter won reelection in 1964, but lost the state's gubernatorial election in 1966. The loss marshaled his spirits; soon after, he was reborn a Christian, and he continued to pay his political dues and accumulate a loyal following. When he decided to run again in 1970, Carter's team included such local stars as: Atlanta attorney Robert Lipschultz; Gerald Rafshoon, owner of an Atlanta advertising agency; aspiring banker Bert Lance, a big Carter supporter; University of Georgia graduate Hamilton Jordan; and a political science graduate fresh from Emory University, Jody Powell. This was also the time that the Coca-Cola Company provided its first perceptible endorsement of Carter when its executives contributed $4,000 to his campaign. Kirbo had introduced Carter to Austin, and although it has been reported that Austin supported his opponent, former governor Carl Sanders, the *Atlanta Constitution* claimed that Austin contributed $2,500 to Carter's campaign. Clearly, the company was still hedging its bets, for its support was a pittance compared to Carter's largest contribution—$26,500 from the chairwoman of Cox Broadcasting Co. With the help of a small community of wealthy Georgian bankers, lawyers, and business executives who provided half of his campaign chest, Jimmy Carter became the governor of Georgia.

Coke's backing of Carter is not surprising considering the company's traditional ties to the state's political hierarchy. It is reported that the company customarily wines and dines the Georgian House Speaker and the committee chairmen on the opening day of each legislative session. Carter's warmth toward Coke is even less surprising. His state was virtually the multinational's backyard, and survival within its fences, let alone beyond them, was eminently facilitated with Coke's approbation.

Carter gave promise of being more than just a state governor, a fact that aroused the interest of Coke and its allies in the Eastern establishment. Though progressive by Georgia's strife-ridden standards, Carter's politics were seen by most as moderate and centrist. His Kennedyesque shock of hair, quick-draw sunburst smile, and soft-spoken style gave him an air of "newness" and of-the-people credibility. His espousal of Christian doctrine gave him the appearance of humility: "I spend much time in prayer on my knees in the back room of the governor's office." Above all, he was sensitive to the priorities of the business sector. Carter was accurately proclaimed as the embodiment of the New South on the cover of *Time* magazine in May of 1971. His was the rhetoric of reconciliation and cooperation, and its reward was political office.

Austin and Carter struck up a friendship after the election. Carter turned for counsel to the soft-drink executive, who would sometimes conduct prayer breakfasts at the governor's mansion. During his term, Carter frequently rejected transportation provided by the state in favor of free travel aboard Coca-Cola's aircraft. Carter flew on state business to and from Washington, the annual Southern Governors' Conference, and other destinations, prompting one Coke executive to assure the public that it is a service the company has provided to all the state's governors for decades. When Carter traveled to Europe and Japan to drum up business for Georgia, he was greeted and escorted at each stop by local Coke executives who undoubtedly provided some useful introductions.

In 1973, Carter was admitted to the Big Time when he was asked by David Rockefeller to join a most select club—the Trilateral Commission. Founded that year by Rockefeller upon the suggestion of political scientist and advisor Zbigniew Brzezinski, the commission sought to strengthen America's alliance with Europe and Japan. With an ever-weakening trade balance, the United States needed to position itself to be more competitive with respect to these allies and the rest of the world order. The stature of the commission's ranks is awesome. Functioning as both a think tank and a roundtable, the membership, which numbers approximately two hundred, is the very top-of-the-bottle cream of American, European, and Japanese leadership. From the United States came such political leaders as Senator Walter Mondale; labor leaders like Lane Kirkland, secretary/treasurer of the AFL-CIO and now its president; such academicians as Harold Brown, president of the California Institute of Technology; opinion makers including Hedley Donovan, editor-in-chief of Time, Inc.; such bankers as Rockefeller and Alden W. Clausen, president of the Bank of America; Wall Street financiers like George W. Ball, a senior partner at Lehman Brothers; captains of industry like W. Michael Blumenthal, chairman of the Bendix Corp.; attorneys such as Cyrus Vance, partner of Simpson, Thacher & Bartlett, whose clients include the Coca-Cola Company; and a high priest of multinational consumerism, Coke's chairman, J. Paul Austin. Those from Europe and Japan are equally lofty. To round off the commission's membership, it was decided that a Southern governor was needed, and with the help of Austin, Jimmy Carter was barely picked over Florida's Reubin Askew. In one swift and unheralded stroke, the commission propelled the rural populist from his Peachtree State to the Olympian realms of global wealth and power.

"After every major war in this century," said C. Fred Bergsten, economist and Trilateralist, "Americans sought a new world order. Wilson pushed the League of Nations; Roosevelt and Truman constructed the U.S.–Bretton Woods system; and now, after Vietnam . . . the Trilateral plan."* The "plan" is to integrate national economies into an international matrix which would be preserved not by a balance of powers approach, which implies conflict and tense stalemates, but a rational, economically viable world order. In the process, national sovereignty would be eroded by supranational interdependence. Despite the commission's cabalistic appearance, its short-term goals are hardly extreme or sinister. It has favored a reduction of arms sales, further conservation of energy,

---

* Jeremiah Novak, "The Trilateral Connection," *The Atlantic,* July, 1977, pp. 57–59

greater assistance for poor nations, and an expansion of the international financial institutions. But the overriding concerns of the Trilateral Commission's new world order are economic homogeneity and stability. In short, the hospitable business climate. One controversial position paper entitled the "Crisis of Democracy," reads in part: "The vulnerability of democratic government in the United States comes not primarily from external threats ... nor from internal subversion ... but rather from the internal dynamics of democracy itself in a highly educated, mobilized and participant society.... Al Smith once remarked, 'The only cure for the evils of democracy is more democracy.' Our analysis suggests that applying that cure at present could well be adding fuel to the flames. Needed instead is a greater degree of moderation in democracy." The author goes on to assure the members that "Democracy is only one way of constituting authority, and it is not a universally applicable one. In many situations, the claims of expertise, seniority, experience, and special talent may override the claims of democracy as a way of constituting authority."

Some see Jimmy Carter's relationship with the Trilateral Commission as nothing but a well-publicized fling! Others perceived it as a marriage. Besides the Trilateralism of the President and his administration, the emergence of two Trilaterialists as serious presidential contenders in 1980, Republicans John Anderson and George Bush (who had resigned in 1978), has fueled the controversy surrounding the commission. Should the Trilateralists prevail, believes one critic, "We will have a new supernational community dominated by the multinational corporations." Even conservatives like Ronald Reagan and John Connally have denounced the commission. In search of the throne, nevertheless, Jimmy Carter cavorted with the king makers. An active member, he had lobbied for himself both in and out of the commission, and he became a careful student of the global realpolitick, tutored by Brzezinski himself.

Despite his lack of a national following, Carter was able to convince many that as a synthesis of the Industrial North and the New South, he possessed "electability." Said one Carter associate, "David Rockefeller and Zbig [Brzezinski] have both agreed that Carter is the ideal politician to build on." Carter long believed that the world was ready for him; now he was ready for the world. In December of 1974, just before his term as governor was over, Jimmy Carter declared himself a candidate for the U.S. Presidency.

With the crack of the gun, Carter's Georgian team began paving the route to the White House. Almost immediately, the Coca-Cola Company seeded the fledgling crusade with $3,000; again not much considering it gave $5,000 to President Ford and various amounts to most of the top-seeded candidates, including a contribution to Senator Edward Kennedy's senatorial campaign. After Carter won the Democratic nomination, many of the company's directors and chief executives, with the exception of president Luke Smith, a Republican, began to open their wallets. It is impossible to determine how much money Coke gave in total, particularly because limits on campaign gifts resulted in an avalanche of small checks from all sectors, yet it is known that many executives of the Trust Company of Georgia as well as some prominent bottlers chipped into Carter's coffers. With a nationwide distribution and bottling network, the potential of a Coca-Cola lobby is tremendous.

PepsiCo, true to its Republican tradition, supported President Ford. No sooner had Nixon resigned than Don Kendall was chumming with Ford, and his company was one of only four major firms to endorse the Republican formally. In one of its quarterly communications to the shareholders, PepsiCo offered an analysis entitled "Ford vs. Carter: PepsiCo's Opinion," which argued the classic Republican line—lower taxes, less government, less spending, and less regulation, implying in the process that big business is the proper custodian of the public good. The statement was pure Kendall, right down to its concluding assertion that PepsiCo "has not only a legal and moral right but a positive obligation to make its position clear."

Coke's long and glorious reign as the Presidential Pause had been ended by a politician deeply indebted to its competitor. For Coke, steeped in the South's democratic traditions, both Nixon and his cola patron were crass upstarts. Carter provided the opportunity to return the throne to its rightful owners. In his support for the peanut farmer, Austin was lobbying for the Democratic heritage, as well as representing Coca-Cola and the tight Atlantan community from which Carter came.

With both his Trilateral and Coca-Cola connections, Austin was in an excellent position to sell Jimmy Carter to businessmen, and that he did, perhaps better than anyone else. One financial journal wrote that "the influential Austin has spent most of the last year [1976] allaying businessmen's fears about a Carter administration." For example, a week after Carter's Democratic nomination, Austin co-hosted a luncheon at Manhattan's swank "21" Club to introduce the candidate to corporate leaders. Sponsored by Edgar Bronfman, chairman of the Seagram Company and a former director of Pepsi United Bottlers; Henry Ford II, president of the Ford Motor Company; and the Non-Partisan Committee for Good Government, a political funding arm of the Coca-Cola Company, the gathering featured fifty-two business leaders, including Pan Am's chairman, William T. Seawell, and fellow Trilateralist W. Michael Blumenthal. Outside the restaurant's private dining room, Carter was a populist farmer and political "outsider"; inside he was a former businessman strongly in favor of free enterprise and multinational corporations. After an introduction by Austin, Carter assured his audience that he "never had a goal for government to dominate business," and would "continue and strengthen if possible American involvement in foreign countries and vice versa." "I'll depend very heavily on business leaders to help me in government," he continued. "I've had a very good relationship with the business leaders of Georgia."

With assistance from Austin, Kirbo, and others, Carter navigated surprisingly well through corporate America, and found the backing with which to win over the rest of the country. For twenty-five years, presidential candidates of both political persuasions have used the media to project vote-getting images. The

Nixon machine had honed the technique into a science, but the campaign of the little farmer from the little farm town in Georgia perfected the art.

With the help of Gerald Rafshoon and his computer technology, space-age marketing analyses, and a $10,500,000 advertising budget, Jimmy Carter's campaign was essentially a dialogue between consumer and product. During the race, his carefully crafted image assumed almost heroic proportions. Television ads showed Carter close to the earth strolling pensively with open collar and brow as furrowed as Georgian fields, or Carter flashing his pearly-white smile before adoring common folk. Ignored were the issues and the problems of running the country as if they would somehow work themselves out. "I told him not to run his campaign on an intellectual approach to issues, but on a restoration of confidence in government. I thought people would buy that," said Kirbo. "They were worn out on issues."

Carter represented not an ideological position as much as the ideal of a new and sinless America. Like the social forces once fueling the New South, Jimmy Carter reflected the symbols and illusions of hope to a despondent nation. As the New South arose from war, so shall America rise from turpitude. He reduced political debate into a simple structure of good versus evil, positioning himself as the American apotheosis of the righteous.

Although Carter's entire media campaign appears to have been influenced by the Coca-Cola style, when Carter began to lose ground, the candidate again appealed directly to Coke's wizardry.* Several weeks before the election, Jimmy Carter stepped into a former Pentacostal Church in Manhattan seeking added life for his image. The church had been converted into studios for advertising man Tony Schwartz, creator of over 300 Coca-Cola commercials, who was called on by the Carter campaign to produce a series of television spots.

A master of images, Schwartz had worked for every Democratic presidential nominee since 1964. He claims that voters are best persuaded by commercials because radio and television "are emotional media, the effect is the important thing . . . I don't do the type of spot where you follow the candidate around; I don't do *cinéma vérité*, I do head-on spots and symbolic spots." His most brilliant and certainly most controversial example of such persuasion was a TV ad he made for President Lyndon Johnson's 1964 presidential campaign against Sen. Barry Goldwater. It begins with a little girl in a field counting petals on a daisy. When she reaches ten, the picture freezes, a voice-over counts back down to zero, and a nuclear explosion flashes on the screen. The Johnson's voice says, "These are the stakes, to make a world in which all God's children can live, or go into the darkness. Either we must love each other or we must die." The screen goes black, and white lettering appears: "On November 3, Vote for President Johnson." Without mentioning Goldwater by name, Schwartz dramatized

---

* According to the *Nation*, Carter, on one of his trips to New York City, surreptitiously slipped into McCann-Erickson's offices to confer with senior executives from the agency and its parent, Interpublic.

his hawkish stance and rendered Johnson as the candidate for all of God's children.

Schwartz's ads were a departure from Rafshoon's semi-documentary style in that Carter was filmed close up speaking directly into the camera. "I felt that nowhere had he been speaking directly into your home," Schwartz explained. "He'd always been photographed speaking to someone else. Secondly, I felt he hadn't looked presidential, hadn't been in a suit. And people, especially in major cities, wanted to feel this was a man of stature. Until I came into the campaign, they were using TV as a window on the world rather than a door into your home. I put him into a one-to-one relationship with you as a voter." The Rafshoon ads identified Jimmy Carter with the voter, much as Pepsi's ads sought to identify users with their "Generation." The new ones, on the other hand, peddled the product directly. It was the Coca-Cola equivalent of the hard sell and some have credited it with assuring Carter's victory.

"A voter wants the candidate to talk to him, not at him," Schwartz once philosophized; "to use the medium not as a large public address system, but rather as a private undress system." What Carter bared was not his solutions to the country's problems, but his empathy, his concern for them. "I'm Jimmy Carter," he begins a commercial on inflation, "the problem isn't 6½ percent inflation. That's just something written on a piece of paper. The problem is how can a family pay those grocery bills and keep up with the mortgage and the taxes and pay for a college education when the time comes . . ." In another aimed at senior citizens, he asks the right questions but offers no answers: "Isn't it bad enough that older people are the worst victims, the easiest victims of hoodlums and criminals? Must they also be victimized by their own government in Washington? How could anyone serve in the White House without wanting to help them?" Schwartz insists, "People cannot identify with answers to problems because they have no experience of them, but people can identify with a man's feelings about things they have experienced."

"Whether Coke or Carter," asserts Schwartz, "we appeal to an attitude in the consumer or the voter. We don't try to convey a point of view, but a montage of images and sounds that leaves the viewer with a positive attitude toward the product regardless of his perspective." Schwartz sought to spiritualize both items, rendering each with a public esteem beyond what its actual realities alone would merit. Carter was indeed the "Cause that Refreshes," and a vote for him was simply a vote for a consumer gratification he called "good government." Time has cast doubt as to whether great products make great presidents.

Never were the corporate styles of Coke and Pepsi better reflected than in the differing character of their political alliances. Just as Nixon often resorted to partisan and ideological divisiveness, Pepsi has been known to train its sales staff to "go out there and hate the competition."

Pepsi, like Nixon and later Ford, sought to identify with the consumers, the "silent majority." Carter, like Coke, focussed on the product, the "Real Thing." Nixon was America. Carter was Americana. Carter's reputation for reconcilia-

tion and playing upon images was well complemented by the use of Coke's
Tony Schwartz, just as his emphasis on authentic leadership "as good as the
people" was reenforced by Coke's untarnished reputation for quality and integrity. The subtleties of marketing and advertising Jimmy Carter, like Coca-Cola,
tended to propel the man and his image toward the center of social life until he
became the whole measure of what society could be and do. Pepsi's decade-long
support of Nixon had forced Coke into an uncharacteristically conspicuous alliance with Carter, and his election was a stunning victory for both the man and
the soda. While Pepsi's ties to Nixon revolved around one man, Donald Kendall, Coke's relationship with Carter was broader and more corporate. Though a
trusted advisor, Austin was not an intimate friend of Carter's. "They're just admirers of each other's abilities," commented Charles Kirbo.

After the election Austin's name was quite expectedly bandied about for a
possible appointment as Secretary of Commerce, just as Kendall's was in 1968.
Though such a position was undoubtedly his for the asking, he chose to maintain a lower profile where he could be more effective. Austin once told reporters: "From the very beginning, I told Jimmy I'd do everything I could to get
him elected—work for him, speak for him, give advice if asked. But I also made
it clear I would never accept any job in the administration."

Austin was instrumental in the assembling of Carter's cabinet, particularly the
business-related positions, and he and Bert Lance organized a meeting with a
handful of business leaders to consult Carter on his selections. Besides Lance
and Austin, included in the meeting was W. Graham Claytor, Jr., a director of
the Morgan Guaranty Trust Co., and chairman of the Southern Railways, some
of whose directors served on Coke's board. Two others involved in the planning
of the administration were Jack Watson of King & Spalding, overseer of the
transitional team between governments, and William Ruder of the public relations firm Ruder & Finn, whose clients include the Coca-Cola Company and
Philip Morris, Inc., the beer and cigarette concern. Lance and Austin were at
least cordial friends and both served with Rosalynn Carter on the "Friendship
Force," a "people to people" group created by Carter to spread goodwill overseas. With both men influential in the casting of the new administration, it is
not surprising that it would be a marriage of Georgians and Trilateralists.

Bert Lance, despite his lack of national stature, was chosen to head the Office
of Management and Budget. He once chided an OMB secretary he'd caught
with a Pepsi on her desk, "You know, ma'am," he reportedly said, "our crowd
drinks a good old Democratic drink, Coke." Trilateralist Cyrus Vance, whose
law firm has represented Coke on occasion, was tapped as Secretary of State.
King & Spalding's Griffin Bell was chosen to be Attorney General. Joseph A.
Califano, Jr., who has personally represented Coke (see Chapter 11), was appointed head of Health, Education and Welfare. Trilateralists W. Michael Blumenthal and Harold Brown were made heads of the Treasury and Defense Departments (Austin was a trustee of CalTech when the latter was president).
Assistant Secretary of the Treasury was Trilateralist Fred Bergsten. Navy Secre-

tary W. Graham Claytor was a Trilateralist as was U.N. Ambassador Andrew Young. Former Coca-Cola president Charles Duncan was appointed Assistant Secretary of Defense. Trilateralist Brzezinski, a director of the Rand Corporation with Energy Secretary James Schlesinger while Austin was Rand's chairman, became Carter's National Security Adviser. Trilateralist Richard Holbrooke assumed the post of Assistant Secretary for East Asia and Pacific Affairs, and Trilateralist Richard N. Cooper became Under Secretary of State for Economic Affairs. Chief negotiator for the SALT talks was Trilateralist Paul Warnke, chief negotiator of the Panama Canal Treaty was Trilateralist Sol Linowitz, and appointed Ambassador to Italy was Trilateralist Richard Gardner. Lest anyone accuse the commission of sexism, Assistant Secretary of State was Trilateralist Lucy W. Jarvis, and an Under Secretary of State was Trilateralist Lucy Benson. Besides the President himself, another Trilateralist was Vice-President Walter Mondale. Trilateralists virtually dominated Carter's foreign policy and national security teams. Meanwhile, the White House staff is so overrun by a tightly knit clan of Georgians, led by Press Secretary Jody Powell and current Chief of Staff Hamilton Jordan, that early on they were semifacetiously labeled by the media as the "Georgia Mafia."*

Despite his campaign pledge, the government of Jimmy Carter was not led by "outsiders" unfamiliar with the Washingtonian ways of dispensing power. No less than five cabinet secretaries, for example, hailed from the administration of Lyndon Johnson. Those who were new—the Georgians—were a tough and shrewd lot and the Trilateralists long held an inside track on worldwide political might. With the possible exception of Carter himself, the man who best bridges both camps is the soft-spoken boss from Coca-Cola, J. Paul Austin. He was an adroit traveler throughout the preserves of Trilateralism and a demure don of the Georgia Mafia. Perhaps one of the first acts of the new administration was the replacement of the Pepsi-Cola machines in the White House with Coca-Cola machines. After years of rule by soft-drink philistines, the White House was again safe for Coca-Cola.

"Now, it's our inning," proclaimed a Coke executive, and after all of its efforts, there were certainly benefits for Coke. Even Pat Watters, a highly sympathetic biographer of Coca-Cola, said, "Obviously, having President Carter for a friend serves Coca-Cola's interest as much as the prestige and power of King and Spalding work upon the lowlier politicians in Georgia." Indeed, an ally in the White House is useful for a worldwide business, though the workings of such alliances are rarely visible, particularly if a member is a public relations crazed firm like Coke. They just go bump in the night. "Coca-Cola is like electrons," opined a congressman. "You know they're there, you can feel them but can't see them." However, Coke, like electrons, leaves tracks. Both tell you where they've been.

---

* Besides Coke, the Trilateral Commission, and Georgia, another thread running through the Carter administration is IBM from whose board sprang Vance, Brown, and Patricia Harris, Secretary of Housing and Urban Development.

For example, there's the matter of Charles Duncan. After the merger between the Coca-Cola Company and Duncan Foods in 1964 (see Chapter 11), Charles Duncan rose through the ranks of the Coca-Cola Company to become president in 1971, second in command only to Chairman Austin. Well endowed with managerial skills and a large bloc of Coke stock, the square-jawed Texan became a director of Coke, the Trust Company of Georgia, replacing former World Bank chief Eugene Black, Southern Railways (having succeeded Woodruff at one time, the railway's largest stockholder), and a trustee of Emory University.* But his influence extended beyond the Coke realm. A member in good standing with the financial and oil axis of Houston, he had been a director of Texas Commerce Bancshares, an $8 billion bank holding company, whose board has included his brother, John H. Duncan, Raymond M. Holliday, a top executive of billionaire Howard Hughes's empire, Allan Shivers, former governor of Texas, and Ladybird Johnson, widow of LBJ. Holliday and Charles Duncan also sat on the board of the Great Southern Corporation. Duncan's father, Charles, Sr., was a director of the Houston-based Bank of the Southwest with Leon Jaworski, former Watergate prosecutor, and B.M. Middlebrook, chairman of Coca-Cola foods division. Duncan's brother is still a top executive with Gulf & Western Industries. While in Atlanta, Duncan came to support Jimmy Carter. "I got to know him in a civic way and a personal way," he said. "We were social friends."

In 1974, however, Duncan resigned his $205,000 a year presidency at Coke. He cited personal reasons and unspecified family business in Houston that required his attention. Details were sketchy and some published reports speculated that his departure was actually rooted in irreconcilable differences between the Texan and Austin. The Coca-Cola watcher for a highly respected national business publication privately speculated that Duncan quit after he lost in an attempt to depose Austin. Duncan had accumulated some support and momentum within the company, and not contented with the presidency, sought the top post of board chairman. Both men were tough, forceful executives, and according to this source, "Coca-Cola wasn't big enough for both of them." Duncan's challenge boiled down to a decision by the board of directors which he lost, allegedly by just one vote. In anticipation of the outcome, Coke's corporate jet was fueled and warmed by the end of the board meeting to spirit Duncan immediately back to Houston. He resigned shortly after and became chairman of Rotan Mosle, a Houston-based holding company whose board included a former director of Duncan Foods. He stayed there until tapped by Carter, and was replaced at Coke by Lucian Smith, head of Coke's domestic soft-drink operations.

Duncan may have lost a battle, but he was still a Cokeman. His bloc of Coke stock, reported by the *Atlanta Constitution* to number 220,825 shares, at the time, second largest family holdings after the Woodruff's, helped extend the affinity, and for a while, he continued his relationships with Coke and some of the

---

* Presumably, Woodruff was interested in the fact that Southern Railways, once the South's largest carrier, was useful for the distribution of Coca-Cola.

aforementioned institutions. "I look forward to a continuing association with the company as a member of its board," he said. Duncan remained a powerful voice within Coke, and despite the alleged internal struggles, the ranks of the Coke family remain closed.

Despite the strict conflict-of-interest guidelines Carter established for his top help, he made an exception with Duncan. Although nominees are reportedly required to divest themselves of stock in any company which does more than $10,-000 of business annually with the Defense Department, Duncan was allowed to retain his Coke stock, reportedly valued at the time at $13.4 million, provided it was put into a blind trust. The exemption was granted, said Carter, because the sale of his stock "would significantly deplete . . . [his] family's assets by reason of the taxes imposed on such a sale." Unreported by the media was the fact that Carter authorized Duncan to "limit . . . [the] discretion" of the fund's trustees to "sell some or all of the stock of the Coca-Cola Company," in effect giving Duncan certain control over his blind trust. *The New York Times* reported that by the summer of 1979, his cache of stock, if unsold, would be worth only $6.3 million because of a drop in the market value.

In addition, Duncan was required to disqualify himself from acting on matters "affecting the financial interests of the Coca-Cola Company." A prevailing sentiment voiced by the press exonerated Carter because Coke's business with the Defense Department was apparently limited to soft drinks. But, the Defense Department's purchase of Coke's Minute Maid orange juice, Snow Crop orange juice, and Taylor wines, a recent Coke acquisition, went largely unnoticed. More significant was the department's patronage of Coke's water purification division, Aqua-Chem. In the year preceding the 1970 acquisition, Aqua-Chem had only $57,000 in Defense Department contracts. Once Aqua-Chem fell within Coke's fold, the figure jumped to $1.5 million, and from 1970 to 1976, Aqua-Chem reportedly secured fifty-four contracts each in excess of $10,000, with one Navy contract in 1975 worth over $3 million. These contracts called for industrial equipment such as boilers, condensers, and water purification systems, all of which were considerably more vital than soft drinks and vending machines.

The only other exemption granted by Carter was to Navy Secretary W. Graham Claytor, who was allowed to keep his Southern Railway stock in a blind trust for the same reason—divestiture would cost him dearly in taxes. The cozy ties between Duncan and Claytor and how both dwelled in Carter's back-home financial nexus were similarly ignored. Duncan was a director of Claytor's Southern Railways until his appointment (he was succeeded by Lucian Smith on the railroad's board, apparently to represent Woodruff's interests), and Claytor sat with Duncan on the board of the Trust Company of Georgia.

Except for minor tiffs over his membership and those of other cabinet members in country clubs that forbade or limited blacks or women* and the disclo-

---

* The others were Bert Lance, Griffin Bell, Michael Blumenthal, Cyrus Vance, and Harold Brown.

sure that he reportedly requested funds for the development of a new nerve gas, Duncan performed well according to the party line and impressed many within the administration. In May 1979, Carter sent him to Morocco for talks with King Hassan II on the Middle East and U.S./Moroccan ties, and two months later he was elevated to Secretary of Energy, replacing the imperious James Schlesinger during what has been called "The Great Cabinet Purge." In an effort to revive the mediocre performance of his government and publicly verify his powers of leadership,* Carter reshuffled much of his top-level management. Among the changes, the independent-minded Califano at HEW was replaced by HUD secretary Patricia Harris, known in Washington as a "twofer" because she was both black and a woman, and Deputy Attorney General Benjamin Civiletti replaced Bell who had decided much earlier to retire from Washington to practice law again in Atlanta. Hamilton Jordan, Carter's top lieutenant of the "Georgia Mafia," became White House Chief of Staff, and Navy Secretary Claytor replaced Duncan at the Defense Department. Aside from his own abilities, Duncan's Georgia connections probably helped him secure the job as energy czar, and his Texas connections will undoubtedly help him keep it. "I have friends in the Texas oil industry," he said, as quoted in Newsweek.

The soft-drink industry, like most others, is dependent upon oil. In 1973, under the Nixon administration, the Department of Energy granted the industry 100 percent priority status in times of gasoline shortage. Soft drinks were classified under "agricultural production," entitling manufacturers and bottlers to allocations equal to their complete needs at the time. For Coke, this remarkable, unnoticed ruling was like the war come home. As the transport of Coke was given top priority on numerous fronts throughout the world, so it was to be at home during the war against scarcity. Coke, Pepsi, the whole lot, were deemed as crucial as food, sanitation, ambulances, and public transportation when gasoline shortages occurred in 1979. However, the industry found some regional energy department offices and some gasoline wholesalers reluctant to provide all of its needs, and the Department of Energy was expected to clarify the ruling on the very day that Duncan was appointed the new energy chief.† Very shortly after, in what was perhaps the department's first act following his appointment, the earlier ruling was reaffirmed, entitling the industry, like the rest of the agricultural sector, to supplies equal to its needs from November 1977, to October 1979.

There were other times when Coca-Cola fared well under the Carter administration. One Carter bill concerning sugar prices was popularly dubbed the "Coca-Cola Amendment" because it so favored the large corporate consumers of sugar (see Chapter 18). When the company and its bottlers sponsored an ex-

---

* Two of Carter's greatest concerns were loyalty and his image, the same qualities long cherished by the Coca-Cola Co. Carter believed some of his starting team were not as faithful to him as they could be. A Carter aide reportedly confided: "Competence is not enough. There has to be loyalty."

† *Beverage Industry,* July 20, 1979

hibit of Japanese art, it was displayed in the National Gallery of Art and attended by the President and Mrs. Carter. In addition, there was the President's highly publicized cruise during the summer of 1979 down the Mississippi River aboard an authentic riverboat. As reported by Jack Anderson, the ship, the *Delta Queen*, was owned by the Coca-Cola Co. of New York. Prior to the President's journey, the vessel had been largely unbooked and losing millions of dollars each year. Afterwards, an executive of the subsidiary that owned the boat claimed, "Sales should be increased for several years to come, since the boat was exposed to people all around the world who had never heard of it before." "You just can't buy that kind of publicity," another official declared with some understatement.*

Coke's global reach was useful for Jimmy Carter just as Pepsi's empire once buoyed Richard Nixon. Besides his support of Carter as governor and then candidate, Austin occasionally served as an unofficial emissary between President Carter and heads of state, circumventing the State Department and other normal diplomatic channels in the process. For instance, in the beginning of 1977, Austin had a long, private discussion with Egyptian president Anwar Sadat. As Austin himself retells it: "At the end of the conversation, I said, 'Do you want this to remain confidential, or do you want me to report directly to my government?'" Sadat had picked his confidants well, and according to Austin, responded, "I'd like very much if you would report it. That's the reason for our conversation." Austin reportedly conveyed the message to the President via Charles Kirbo. As early as 1974, Carter said that ". . . we have our own built-in State Department in the Coca-Cola Company. They provide me ahead of time with . . . penetrating analyses of what the country is, what its problems are, who its leaders are, and when I arrive there, provide me with an introduction to the leaders of that country . . ."†

Overseas, the company's gains were most impressive, suggesting that Coke indeed tapped into the machinery of presidential power it had resourcefully helped construct. Shortly after Carter's election, Portugal, where Coke had been banned for half a century, gave in to the bubbling tide. To increase foreign investments, Portugal's newly seated government of Mario Soares, a moderate socialist, opted for the conventional wisdom and, in late 1976, permitted a Swiss/Portuguese firm to bottle Coke. Very soon thereafter eyebrows were raised when the U.S. provided Portugal with an emergency $300 million loan. Editorialists at home promptly pondered what role Coke played in this U.S. overture to the new Soares government, and in turn, what effect the loan might have had on Coke's admittance. Now more than any time since its Eastern Eu-

---

* The President's loyalty to Coke extended to at least one member of his family. "He said we'd go to a country bar and gallivant," said Billy Carter's physician after making arrangements to visit the President's brother who was undergoing treatment for alcoholism. However, the doctor added that according to Billy, "I could drink the beer . . . he'd stick to Coke."

† Robert W. Turner, *I'll Never Lie to You: Jimmy Carter in His Own Words* (New York: Ballantine, 1976). p. 36

ropean debut during the 1960s, Coke was happily exercising its traditional support of, and dependency on, American foreign policy.

In Latin America, Coke's 240 bottlers have continued to flourish despite much of the region's chronic poverty. Bright stars still include Brazil, Argentina, and Mexico. When Rosalynn Carter visited Mexico to attend the inauguration of President-elect José Portillo, she was escorted by Austin and his wife.

The war in Guatemala between the Coke operation and its workers continues. Congressman Don J. Pease of Ohio took note of the situation in the fall of 1979 and wrote a sharply worded letter to President Carter pleading for his intervention. The White House forwarded the communication to the State Department which responded with a one-page letter to Pease expressing its concern over the matter. Unsatisfied with the one-page reply from the State Department, Pease again wrote the White House urging the President to use his long-standing relationship with Coke to seek a just peace. The brief reply from a White House congressional liaison officer stated only that the U.S. embassy in Guatemala had expressed its dismay, and the State Department had been in contact with Coke officials in Atlanta. Pease finally wrote to chairman Austin. A senior vice-president wrote back with precious few answers. He stressed that local authorities have not pressed any charges, ignoring in the process the many allegations that elements of the Guatemalan government were involved in the Coca-Cola reign of terror. Instead, he assured Pease that Coke will "monitor the situation." Although he never even implies that the franchise may be guilty of egregious acts, including murder, he claimed without explanation that the franchise agreement will not be renewed when it expires in 1981. Coke's decision is a reaction not to human rights violations but a five-country-wide boycott of Coca-Cola in protest of the situation. The boycott has cost Coke millions of dollars and has warranted the utmost attention of Donald Keough himself. However, the political situation in Guatemala has scared off at least one group of investors.

There are indications of a growing awareness that the all-critical social stability of Third World countries so necessary to business interests can no longer be assured by strongman rule. After extended civil protest and strife in Nicaragua, a U.S. arms embargo by the Carter administration helped topple the tyrannical rule of Anastasio Somoza. This was one instance when Coke refreshed a popular movement. As Orcarberro initially fought against Batista twenty years earlier in Cuba, Adolpho Calero, the manager of the country's single large Coca-Cola franchise, was a leader of the Authentic Conservative Party, a part of the anti-Somoza Broad Opposition Front. The dictator had him jailed for his activities with other political activists for a month during the fall of 1978, and later released him in a futile attempt to appease his many opponents. Once Somoza fled the country, the United States unsuccessfully tried to place the Coke manager in the provisional Sandinista government.

When either cola is closely allied with an unpopular ruling class, hostility toward it can run deeper than anti-American protests. Pepsi-Cola had been banned since the sixties by Moslem leaders in Iran because some of the bottlers were members of the Bahai faith, a non-Moslem sect widely suspected of ties to the hated Shah. However, while the Shah ruled, with U.S. support, the ban was only titular and Pepsi flourished. When the Iranian people rose up against the Shah in 1978 and 1979, Pepsi was targeted heavily by the revolutionaries. Three plants were burned, including one in Qom, home of religious leader Ayatollah Khomeini, and PepsiCo reportedly wrote off $8.8 million of its claimed $15 million investment in the last quarter of 1978. Khomeini lifted the ban on Pepsi in the summer of 1979 when the Pepsi facilities came under new ownership, though in the spring of 1980, PepsiCo claimed to have conformed to a general boycott of the country called by Jimmy Carter and ceased shipments of concentrate. Ironically, when the militant students displayed some of their American hostages to assure the world of their well-being, one widely circulated photograh showed a captive with a smile on his face and a big bottle of Coke (a returnable?) in his hand.

Even in relative peace, the soft-drink makers are a part of the international equation. An Egyptian engineer said at an ecumenical conference in the United States, "We have to have your industrial technology, but we can do without your Coke and Sprite plants." Yet in his country, as in all the Arab world, the salient question wasn't whether Egypt could do without Coke; it was whether Coke could do without Egypt.

In 1966, public pressure within the United States coerced Coke into granting a franchise in Israel (see Chapter 11), and in response, the Arab League banned the drink, but allowed Pepsi, which was not bottled in Israel, to remain. Initially Coke got the skinny end of the bottle, but the little Israeli market has matured to approximately $60 million wholesale and some forty-seven plants, exceeded in number only by Syria's plants. Coke, of course, is the dominant brand, and its original fleet of seventeen trucks has mushroomed into an armada of over a hundred, second in size only to the country's postal service. In 1977, Coke was doing so well that Austin was awarded a medal for "his distinguished service to democracy and freedom and his company's outstanding support for the economic well-being of Israel." As appreciated as his efforts were in Israel, Paul Austin still coveted its thirsty neighbors where Coke enjoyed popularity as a black-market item. He and his company bided their time patiently, always on the lookout for an opening in the ban, the tiniest crack through which the forbidden market could be breached. In 1974, they found it.

That year, during negotiations with Secretary of State Henry Kissinger for an interim peace agreement with Israel, Egypt revealed a tentative willingness to stop enforcing the Arab boycott. With the region's largest population but without the region's oil resources, Egypt was economically crippled. As a member of the Arab League, it had agreed to boycott Coca-Cola and other Western firms before the 1967 Middle East war. After the 1973 war, Egypt had to solicit Western investments and aid in order to survive, and in the fall of 1974, Austin dispatched a Coke executive, Sam Ayoub, to Egypt to "just explore the possibilities."

Ayoub is a shrewd, worldly man intimately familiar with the spirit and culture of the Middle East. His strategy was simple and he played it with the toughness and patience of a chess master. By enticing first Egypt and then other Arab countries with offers of Coca-Cola investments, he sought to amass enough of a lobby within the Arab League to get Coke off the blacklist. Through contacts, Ayoub gained the support of Ashraf Marwan, then Foreign Affairs Secretary who was Nasser's son-in-law and a confidant of Sadat's. Marwan then approached Sadat which, says Ayoub, "opened the door for us."

Coke went right to its strengths—agricultural know-how and money. In July 1976, Coke offered the Egyptian government a proposal to form a joint venture to transform fifteen thousand acres of desert into a citrus farm. In the beginning of 1977, Austin met with Sadat in Cairo, and that fall, as a goodwill gesture, Coke kicked in $400,000 to New York's Brooklyn Museum for archeological projects in Egypt. Naturally, Ayoub affirmed that the gift was for "humanitarian" reasons only. By the end of the year, Coke anted up 25 percent of its $5 million commitment to the Ramses Agricultural Co., formed with Egyptian interersts to create the farmlands. In return for its largesse, Coke was granted rights to market its full line of products in Egypt as well as a pledge by the Egyptians to help remove Coke from the boycott. As if to anticipate the outcome of its support within Egypt and other Arab countries, Coke formed a new division, Coca-Cola Middle East, with the able Mr. Ayoub at its helm.

Again Coke greased the machinery of foreign policy. Its acceptance by Egypt further improved Egyptian-American relations, and helped Carter's plans to resolve the Mideast crisis. Coke's entrance also served notice to Western investors that the Egyptian business climate was changing, and that a separate peace with Egypt was possible. Very shortly after, other boycotted corporations consummated deals in Egypt, and the State Department began to sponsor a series of civic conferences nationwide to encourage Arab relations and its foreign policy. In Atlanta, a featured speaker was Sam Ayoub. Ayoub also met with Jordan's King Hussein for similar purposes when the latter visited Atlanta several months earlier. Hussein reportedly invited the Coke executive back to Cokeless Jordan as a guest of his government.

To date, Coca-Cola's investment is the largest under Sadat's "Open Door" policy. Its $5 million contribution to Ramses Agricultural Co. is the beginning of what will be, at a total cost of $50 million, one of the largest citrus orchards in the world. Coke is also reportedly guaranteeing half of the $40 million financing of nine bottling plants throughout the country. It is also investing $9 million for a Coke concentrate plant in Alexandria and $4 million to improve current bottling production, a necessity considering the poor quality control of the local industry.

Egypt is an unusual soft-drink market that is supplied by both private and government-owned firms. The entire industry had been nationalized by Nasser in the sixties, and the two major brands, Pepsi-Cola and a local imitation called Si-Cola, were then bottled by government-owned companies. In 1978, beckoned by Sadat's "Open Door," a private company began to market Seven-Up and a cola by Canada Dry called Sport. The firm, Cairo Beverages, whose largest investor was allegedly the former chief of Saudi Arabian intelligence, was one of the first private, foreign-financed operations to commence under Sadat's new policies. If anything, Sadat may well be closer to Pepsi. His son-in-law is Pepsi's Egyptian representative, while a close personal friend founded a local construction firm which later explored opening Pepsi plants throughout the country.

After twelve years, Coke went on sale again in Egypt in the summer of 1979 accompanied by the company's usual advertising pageantry. Forty Coke billboards sprang up overnight in Cairo, and McCann-Erickson prepared a series of television commercials. Despite the poverty of much of their audience, the ads featured the typical young spirited types who forever enjoy their leisure. Westerners were frequently used in ads because Egyptians were most susceptible to the mystique of Western lifestyles.

Although Coke wasn't officially lifted from the boycott, its hard-won success in Egypt has encouraged the company to deal with each Arab country individually, beginning with the more moderate ones. By 1979, Coke was already available in Egypt, Morocco, Tunisia, Djibouti, Somalia, Mauritania, North Yemen, Algeria, and was making overtures to Saudi Arabia. Although Egypt has lost much of its influence within the Arab world because of its separate peace with Coke, and more recently Israel, Ayoub and other Coke leaders are convinced that all it takes is patience and money. So far, they are right. Despite increased antagonism from officials involved in the Arab League boycott, Coke began studying the entire Persian Gulf region for bottling sites even before it went on sale in Egypt. For example, plans were reportedly drawn for a $10 to $15 million investment in Saudi Arabia once Coke was removed from the ban. Potential investors were Sadaki Kaki, a merchant whose several bottling plants were churning out a concoction called Kaki-Cola, and the Aliriza family, cousins of the Saudi ambassador to the United States. Said Ayoub in 1979, "We are confident that the other countries will open up—we hope within two years."

Another market pursued by Coca-Cola, though much more gingerly, is Cuba. Until the recent challenges to detente, sentiments had been gradually building both in and out of the Carter administration to resume relations with Cuba, particularly since the United States has already established ties with most of the Communist world.

Among many others, the advantage for both countries of such a move is the economic stimulus of renewed trade. Cuba is one of the largest producers of sugar in the world, and had long supplied the bulk of America's sugar before the United States embargoed its products. With Cuba as Coke's first overseas venture, it is not surprising that the world's largest private consumer of sugar has had a deep and abiding interest in Cuban-American relations.

On June 4, 1977, Paul Austin flew to Havana and met with Fidel Castro undoubtedly to discuss that interest. Immediately upon his return, Austin briefed President Carter for thirty minutes in the Oval Office, strongly suggesting that besides his Coke business, Austin again served as an unofficial channel between two heads of state as he had between Carter and Sadat. Neither American will discuss their conversations. (According to Jack Anderson, Kendall was ahead of Austin during the Ford administration in sending out feelers to Castro.)

There are obstacles to a Cuban Coca-Cola franchise apart from the renewed Cold War atmosphere. One is the $1 billion claim by United States citizens and companies on assets that were nationalized by the Cuban revolution. Coke's $27.5 million claim, long written off on its ledgers, should not be an obstacle considering the fortunes the company has gleefully invested to secure other markets. Yet Coke's biggest roadblock may be the Cuban people. Do they want Coca-Cola? Said Fidel Castro on the twentieth anniversary of the Cuban revolution: "Cuba cannot be pressured nor intimidated nor bribed nor bought. Cuba is not China or Egypt."

The Coca-Cola Company is both patient and savvy . After the better part of a century, it has learned well how to cope with the vicissitudes of global commerce. Perhaps no company has been more adroit at penetrating a country's marketplace, particularly considering the triviality of its offerings. Consequently, when Pepsi entered the Soviet Union, Coke was appalled and all the more determined to secure its own deal with Moscow.

Pepsi too had shown patience and savvy in Russia. In 1959, Kendall exploited Coke's ill-advised refusal to attend the Moscow Exposition (see Chapter 8), and in 1973, took advantage of the fact that a former Pepsi attorney was in the White House. Granted, the dollars and cents value of the Russian business will be relatively small for some time to come, the public relations value was nonetheless priceless.

Pepsi consummated the Russian deal nine days after Nixon was reelected. But before his ill-fated second administration was half over, Coke had quietly taken a significant though circuitous step toward getting its product into Soviet markets. In June 1974, Coke and the State Committee for Science and Technology signed an agreement of cooperation on the eve of Nixon's second summit visit to Moscow. Because of Pepsi's exclusive deal with the Russians, Coke's agreement didn't anticipate any exchange of goods, services, or money. However, Austin, who had spent a week of negotiations in Moscow prior to Nixon's arrival, clearly hoped that cooperation would soon include Coke's other soft drinks. The classic formulation of detente—Western technology and resources traded for access to Soviet markets—was very much at play, as the pact covered a far-reaching exchange of scientific and technical information intended to increase the efficiency and quality of Soviet food production.

Coke had a formidable technical arsenal at its disposal. The agreement called for cooperation in developing plants to process protein foods from dairy byproducts and to make various other products from tea and tea waste. Also anticipated was the sharing of scientific and technical information on the manufacture of steam generators, water purification equipment, and pollution abatement equipment as well as water desalinators, which would come through Coke's Aqua-

Chem, already responsible for 75 percent of the world's desalination equipment.

Other parts of the agreement included joint research and experiments in cultivating fruits and vegetables in wasteland areas, swamps, deserts, and other arid zones, as well as hydroponics and advanced farming. In turn, Coke hoped to learn from the Soviets' advanced research in the cultivation of semitropical fruits, but its real desires were manifest. "Obviously," said a company spokesman, "we want to eventually find a basis for commercial arrangements that will generate substantial revenue for the company . . . this agreement is a signal to Soviet officials that this company has technical resources that could prove valuable to them." The clear hint was that "resources in helping to meet the needs of all people in the crucially important sphere of food and nutrition" were available in return for markets to sell nutritionally empty but highly profitable soft drinks. The Soviets took the hint nearly a year later when the original accord was expanded to include the development of manufacturing technology for beverage products.

The presidency of Jimmy Carter undoubtedly enhanced Coca-Cola's leverage. Even in the weeks and months prior to the election, Austin again reportedly made several trips to the Soviet Union, posing enough of a threat to send Kendall scurrying to Moscow himself. Even before Carter took office, however, both companies joined hands in a statement issued by the American Committee on U.S.-U.S.S.R. Relations urging the President-elect to improve Soviet relations, which it asserted had been somewhat neglected under the Ford administration. A year later, in January 1978, Pepsi inched ahead with a momentous announcement of an agreement for five additional plants to match the five it already had in the Soviet Union. Perhaps the most promising of these from a marketing standpoint was slated for the predominantly Moslem industrial boom city of Tashkent, near the Iranian border. The Shah was still in power at the time, and despite Iran's opposition to the Soviets, Pepsi found itself in an increasingly strategic role of supplying a Western cultural influence on the vast and restive Moslem population on both sides of the border. Only two months after Pepsi's announcement, however, Coke unveiled an extension of its 1974 agreement with the Russians that would finally allow it to market soft drinks in the Soviet Union. Because Pepsi still held the exclusive on cola drinks, Coke turned to Fanta orange, and in concert with the Soviet Ministry of Trade, and with Austin present, a bottling plant was dedicated in August 1979. Like Pepsi, Fanta would be sold from street kiosks and pushcarts in Moscow, and a struggle quickly ensued for choice locations on the city's boulevards.

One of the most titanic corporate rivalries of the West was off and running inside Soviet borders, but by all appearances, the Russians were in control, effectively playing the two soda giants against each other. With Pepsi's exclusivity due to run out in 1984, the agreement of rival Coke undoubtedly provided Kendall with some sleepless nights. To date, little progress has been made in constructing any of Pepsi's five new plants, and without real political clout, at least during the Carter presidency, Kendall may be unable to contain the ever-

mounting pressures to unleash Coca-Cola on the Russians. There was some solace when Pepsi began to complement its Stolichnaya vodka with a high quality
Armenian cognac in 1979, but there has been no escaping Austin's shadow. "Ultimately, we have every intention of obtaining full soft-drink distribution in the
Soviet Union," said a Coke spokesman, to which Austin added, "and we're perfectly willing to bide our time with the main product."

Indeed, the "main product" had a successful audition when the Soviets licensed Coca-Cola to be the official soft drink of the 1980 Summer Olympics in
Moscow. The games were an international event deemed beyond the limitations
of Pepsi's exclusive arrangement and, as far as Atlanta was concerned, it was
continuing a tradition of serving the Olympics going back to 1928. As in its previous Olympic outings, Coke undertook lengthy preparations, such as putting
the Olympic logo on its cans, preparing a special $10 million ad campaign to be
aired over NBC's broadcast of the games (a budget second only to the $12 mil-
lion allocated by Philip Morris for Miller Beer), and opening a school in Moscow to teach 500 workers how to dispense an anticipated 19 million drinks. The
first class of trainees quickly pilfered the familiar red and white cups for souve-
nirs, precipitating a shortage. "They'll be there for only two weeks," rationalized
Kendall, but both he and Austin knew that a taste of what had long been denied
would arouse curiosity and heighten its mystique.

But, Coke's march into Russia was thwarted by edict of its chum in the
White House who imposed first a boycott of the games in the wake of the Soviet invasion of Afghanistan, and then a larger series of restrictions on American
trade with the Soviet Union. Carter's policy horrified many corporate executives,
particularly those whose firms had already invested heavily in the games. Many
saw the boycott as a threat to detente and consequently access to an important
marketplace. It was a frustrating irony for Coke which had lost an opportunity
for at least temporary access to the Russian market twenty years before by refusing to participate in the American Exposition in Moscow.

Several months after the President's decision, Atlanta informed the world that
it would accede to the boycott and stop Olympic shipments to the Soviet Union.
However, the company flatly refused to comment on whether Coca-Cola would
be on sale at the games, and acknowledged that "considerable quantities" of
Coke concentrate were sent to Moscow before Atlanta's compliance with the
boycott was announced. It is likely that Coke was sold at the Moscow games,
though not without the fanfare it would have once merited.

At first, PepsiCo conspicuously refrained from revealing its intentions with
regard to the Olympics in particular, and the whole Soviet market in general.* A
spokesperson finally indicated that PepsiCo would comply with the President's
wishes. "After all, we're an American company." Though Pepsi acknowledged
that it too stockpiled an undisclosed amount of concentrate in the Soviet Union,
the interruption of the agreement can only add further delay to the construction

---

* *Miami Herald*, April 25, 1974

of its plants. However, indications are that at least one of the companies is intending to supply its Soviet facilities from a third country while ostensibly conforming to the boycott. Traditionally, Kendall is not sympathetic toward embargoes. In 1974, testifying at hearings about Cuba, he urged the Senate Banking Committee to repeal a law that bans foreign subsidiaries of U.S. companies from selling to countries embargoed by the United States.*

If the soft-drink stakes were high in the Soviet Union, they were off the chart in the People's Republic of China. With a quarter of the world's population, China is the largest nation of thirsty gullets and the world's last major cola frontier. Coke had first tapped into it in 1928, and had four plants in urban centers when the Chinese revolution kicked it and other American firms out of the country in 1949. American-Chinese relations immediately soured and the United States steadfastly supported the former government in exile on the island of Taiwan. As part of its Cold War policy, America sought to "contain" mainland China, and consequently in 1956, Secretary of State John Foster Dulles rejected China's overture to seek a peaceable solution to the Taiwan problem. By the seventies, nearly a decade after the United States had commenced working relations with most other Communist countries. U.S. strategists recognized the political necessity of dealing with China as a foil to Soviet policies as well as its possibilities as an immense marketplace. Concurrently, the Chinese began to perceive the need to modernize and more fully interact with the world community. After twenty years of silent hostilities, both countries realized that neither was a primary threat to the other, and thus, in 1972, President Nixon, the old Cold War warrior, made his historic trip to China and relations were cautiously renewed. Had it not been for a piece of tape on a lock in the Democratic National headquarters, Don Kendall might well have negotiated Pepsi into China during the Nixon regime. However, Nixon was swallowed up by Watergate, and his successor, Gerald Ford, had to contend with the end of the Vietnam War and proving he was electable to the office. According to Jack Anderson, Kendall, like Austin, made exploratory trips to China, but once Carter was elected, presidential preference shifted to his competitor.

By 1978, with the Vietnam War ended, China reacted to the diplomatic embrace of Vietnam with its principal foe, the Soviet Union, by concluding alliances first with the Coca-Cola Company and two days later, with the U.S. government. On December 13, Coke was granted exclusive rights to market its cola in China for an indefinite period. On December 15, the U.S. and China agreed to normalize relations and exchange ambassadors. The Coke deal was a surprise for some who expected China to shy away from consumer goods in favor of industry and technology. But veteran Coke watchers had known that it was only a matter of time. By allowing the standard bearer of American commerce into

---

* Anti-Soviet sentiments in the U.S., whipped up by the Afghanistan invasion, threatened to disrupt the brisk sales of Stolichnaya vodka. "If the Afghanistan thing lasts, it certainly makes the horizon look a lot brighter for us," said a competitor.

their country, the Chinese were notifying the Carter administration and the world that its xenophobic days were officially over.

From pundits to politicians, speculation on the motives and methods behind the deal were rampant. Whether in cynical tones or bemusement, much of it centered on the coziness between Coke and Carter, but few observers had the expertise or inclination to consider the proposition from the Oriental point of view. In this vein, humorist Arthur Hoppe perspicaciously observed that, "The primary motive behind Peking's surprise move was to weaken the power of the Soviet Union and its ally Pepsi. With hundreds of thousands of Pepsi-drinking Russian troops stationed along its western borders, China naturally feared the dominance of either."

The publicity for Coke was tremendous as newspapers throughout the country splashed on their front pages the felicitous translation of Coca-Cola into Chinese—Can Mouth, Can Happy. Austin hailed it as the "beginning of a new era," and for himself, it was a dream uncorked. Said one New York stock analyst: "One of the things Paul Austin wanted to cap his career with was to get Coke into . . . China and Russia and back into the Middle East and India . . . the China deal was a nice way to finish his act, and it will be a tough act to follow." His efforts, according to *Beverage Industry*, climaxed "one of the longest, most hard-nosed struggles ever undertaken by the Atlanta-based international leader." Austin's Coca-Cola must have tasted particularly sweet that day, for after setbacks and a lot of hard work and money, he had finally beaten the masterful Don Kendall at his own game.

Although it closed the deal on December 13, Coke waited nearly a week to announce it formally. In between, President Carter announced the normalization of relations with China. The timing of these events has suggested to some observers something considerably greater than a coincidence. Coke, of course, denies such speculation. "We knew nothing of the Carter agreement," said one Cokeman, "we were surprised and ran to the television set like everybody else." Said Austin, "Traditionally we carry on our own relations. We had no advice from anybody. We have been quietly negotiating with China for the better part of ten years." State Department sources reportedly claimed it was "very unlikely" that plans to normalize relations could have leaked to Coke executives. However, it seems more likely that the State Department or other branches of the government were aware of the China dealings of Coca-Cola and other major companies like Boeing and Pan-American, just as it is likely that Coke, with its long-standing government ties, could be privy to an impending major policy statement that could dramatically impact on its business. The company's claim that the China announcement was postponed for a week because Austin was travelling in Europe rings hollow considering the deal's stature. Coca-Cola has never been a company to delay public relations coups. Is it possible that Coke had advance knowledge of the imminent diplomatic breakthrough and chose to cooperate by delaying its news until just after Carter made his peace with China? Such arrangements need not necessarily have involved the State Department or Coke management, but could have been the result of communications between two long allied chief executives who were acting out of mutual self-interest.

Coca-Cola's rapprochement with the Chinese extended beyond China. Paul Austin was a guest at the White House dinner for Deputy Prime Minister Deng Xiaoping on the latter's historic tour of the United States in January 1979. Coca-Cola, along with Ford Motors, was a co-sponsor of an evening of entertainment for Deng at the Kennedy Center. After Washington, Deng's next stop was Atlanta, where he was honored at a luncheon at the Peachtree Plaza Hotel. Among the guests were Henry Ford 2nd and, of course, Austin. When asked how Coca-Cola fits into China's drive to modernize, a member of the Chinese delegation replied, "This is a very simple matter. We want to have foreign visitors in very great numbers. And these foreign visitors, tourists, want to drink Coca-Cola. They are accustomed to it. As for us Chinese, we prefer our green tea." When Deng was asked about Coke, he replied, "I'd better start getting used to it."

The Sino-Coke pact was hailed throughout the business community, and recouped much of the prestige Coke had lost after Pepsi's Russian deal, particularly since it came only nine months after Coke negotiated Fanta into the Soviet Union. Both deals called for cola exclusivity but Coke's had the advantage that the company would be compensated in cash, not vodka. However, neither deal would amount to much in the short run. Initially, the Chinese sharply limited the sale of Coca-Cola to tourists and the hotels and restaurants that cater to them. When it did go on sale to the Chinese in the spring of 1980, its reception was lukewarm. "You have to get used to it," said one venturesome consumer who claimed that it tasted like medicine. Furthermore, "It's a nation of peasants," remarked a government official. "It's tempting to talk about 900 million Chinese consumers, but 85 percent of them are still on the farm with an annual income of $380 each." Coke executives smile at such reservations, knowing full well their prize drink began with limited access in many countries. Commented one stock analyst, "These are the seeds for the 1980s and 1990s. In the long run, it will be a major shot in the arm."

The charismatic lure possible with soft drinks has manifested itself even in China. The Chinese have begun to advertise their own brand, Lucky Cola, in Shanghai where Westerners are greeted by huge billboards featuring a silhouetted rake with a bottle pursed to his lips. It must be more than just coincidence that Lucky Cola's bottle is shaped much like Coke's famous Georgia Green beauty. In what Coke undoubtedly hopes is a harbinger of things to come, China's first television commercial advertised a Chinese brew called Happiness Cola, and it relied on one of the oldest techniques in the book—the sports endorsement. A popular men's basketball team plugged it on a commercial that punctuated a live broadcast of a women's basketball game in Shanghai. Coke's turn may yet come, since, in the fall of 1979, the Chinese permitted McCann-Erickson and other Western advertising agencies to handle foreign accounts in

China as well as Chinese accounts abroad. According to a McCann-Erickson executive, China offers some forty television stations, professional and trade journals, newspapers, radios, and plenty of billboard space.

The destiny of Chinese society is, of course, in the hands of the Chinese. Yet some of the most sophisticated multinationals in the world will try to beckon them down a particular path. Ulysses-like, the Chinese are determined to steer a course clear of any capitalist pitfalls. There has already been talk of McDonald's restaurants entering China and, as it has often been said, dining on Big Macs and Coke can flatten the politics of the most diehard radical. "The Chinese want to curtail the time taken for eating and cooking," said the president of the McDonald's affiliate in Japan, commenting on imported Westernized lifestyles. Another consideration was provided by the executive director of the Washington-based Center for Science in the Public Interest in a letter to Deputy Premier Deng. "I can think of few American food products," he said, "that are more injurious to health than Coca-Cola. . . . Coca-Cola contains no vitamins, no minerals, no protein . . . only sugar." He asked Deng to reconsider China's decision, arguing that Coke in China is "irrational in terms of both industrial development and health."

On a loftier level, China is an affirmation of Coke's manifest destiny. Less abstractly, it was a dramatic touché against its arch foe. Yet as Coke knew it would someday strut into Moscow, barring global catastrophe, Pepsi knows it will eventually cohabit Peking. Coke's initial shipment—half a million cans and bottles weighing in at 350 tons—was just the first wave to refresh the deep Orient. As Russell Baker observed in *The New York Times* on the heels of the China deal, "The struggle to carbonate man's stomach enters a new stage."

CHAPTER EIGHTEEN

The Raw Thing

FROM FINANCING RELIGIOUS CRUSADES in the twelfth century and fueling the earliest slave trade in the Americas to corrupt Washington lobbying efforts, sugar has a long and turgid history, entrenched as much in politics as it has been in the patterns of consumption. The question, then, of how such two politically oriented and prestigious buyers as Coke and Pepsi actually procure the mass tonnage they require is a provocative one.

The industry itself is divided into several broad areas: the growers, who raise the cane (or, in the Northern climes, beets), and the processors, who extract the juice from the cane and manufacture the raw or tan sugar from it. Often the growers will own the processing operations as well, since the cane spoils easily and must be transported to the mill for crushing within twenty-four hours of reaping. The refining operations are nearly always separately owned, but both sectors are highly centralized.* Although the big refiners often purchase directly from the growers, the contact between them is usually handled by major brokers (who operate on commission only) and operators (who also take holdings without having an immediate buyer), especially when international purchases are involved. In addition, Coke will frequently process its raw sugar under year-long tolling agreements it makes with the big refiners.

Ever since the industrial revolution, sugar production has involved huge amounts of specialized technology, necessitating heavy investments while retaining the need for abundant supplies of cheap labor, especially during the harvest. Both capital and labor intensive, the sugar industry was first introduced into the West Indies by imperialistic Europeans who wanted to export it to North America. It was the basis of the entire economy in many Caribbean islands which, in turn, became prime export markets for the infant American colonies. The cornerstone of the whole system was slavery. Both British and Yankee traders hauled West African blacks to be sold in the Caribbean where they harvested cane to make sugar and molasses.† In America, the molasses often became rum which was sold or used to buy more slaves, many of whom wound up in the Old South. The triangle was complete, but it was only a step along the

---

* *Pacific Basin Reports.* September, 1973. p. 196. The top five sugar companies in 1973 held 52 percent of the refined sugar market, and the top ten accounted for 72 percent. Similarly in beet sugar, three companies controlled half the market.

† "It will be no exaggeration," writes British historian Noel Deerr, "to put the tale and toll of the slave trade at twenty million Africans, of which two-thirds are to be charged against sugar." See Noel Deerr, *The History of Sugar* (London: Chapman and Hall, 1949)

way to the post-colonial stage where the diverse growers and mill owners were consolidated into a worldwide structure of giant sugar companies that coordinated the factors of production and dominated whole governments to ensure the highest rate of return. Except for the recent crisis in oil, no commodity in history has been as influenced by politics nor been as influential on governments as sugar.

The companies each caught a glimpse of the volatility of the sugar economy during World War I: Caleb Brabham and Pepsi-Cola went into bankruptcy, and Coca-Cola was threatened with a similar fate, thanks to Samuel Dobbs's untimely purchase of sugar just before the effects of wartime overproduction in a peacetime economy took hold. Through its successive incarnations, Pepsi tended to react like a frightened government trying to approach self-sufficiency. It made several ill-fated attempts at its own growing, processing, and refining operations over the years, including the Cuban plantation during the forties, the New York state plantation during the sixties, and the Long Island City refinery. This last operation, which was sold in 1974, proved particularly sticky when Pepsi and three other refiners were fined $50,000 each for conspiring to fix cane prices in 1972 and 1973. Coke, on the other hand, has never deviated from the policy set by Asa Candler and maintained by Robert Woodruff of avoiding direct investment in sugar-growing operations, though the company's clout as a buyer surpasses that of almost any major refiner. What Pepsi failed to do through acquisition, Coke has accomplished rather handily by shifting with the tide of the market.

The dominant political control of the sugar market until just after the Depression was the American tariff system, long a source of funds for the U.S. Treasury dating back to the 1790s. During the Depression, sugar prices were the lowest in history, and domestic growers pleaded for the government to restore stability and additional protection, which it did with the Sugar Act of 1934. The act replaced the tariffs with a much more rigid quota system. Between 1934 and 1974, when the Sugar Act expired, nobody was permitted to import, refine, sell, or even grow a pound of sugar in the United States above an amount assigned in a quota. Imports were handled on a country-by-country basis while domestic sugar was governed on a regional basis. Premium payments were made to producers in order to stabilize the domestic price at a level sufficiently above the cheaper world price to ensure ample profits for the domestic growers.

There is no question that the Sugar Act vastly favored the growers over the buyers, who were made to bear the brunt of these massive premium payments (which they simply passed along to the consumer). Yet the Act provided a predictability which was surely welcomed by Coke and Pepsi. After the Cuban revolution in 1959, Eisenhower revoked the Cuban quota, which amounted to three million tons, or 30 percent of American consumption. Other countries were scrambling to grab what they could of the Cuban quota, and hired a bevy of Washington lobbyists at exorbitant fees to pull every available string.

Coke and Pepsi are among the largest customers in a tightly knit but far-reaching market. One supplier in the mid-fifties was the international king of sugar, Julio Lobo, a self-styled Cuban whose stealthful, mysterious manner led to his freely translated nickname—Lone Wolf. Through the Galban Lobo Trading Corporation in Havana, then the largest sugar-trading house in the world, Lobo marketed vast quantities of Cuban sugar and once supplied thousands of tons of primarily Philippine sugar directly to Pepsi during a week in April 1959 when he achieved the unbelievable, almost miraculous, feat of cornering the entire open market on sugar.* A man whose fantastic admiration for Napoleon was manifested in his unsurpassed collection of the general's signed letters, Lobo was then trying to impress the newly arrived Castro with how much one little Cuban could rattle the giant neighbor to the north. In a matter of a few days, Lobo managed to drive up the price by over half a cent a pound.

In 1958, Lobo acquired a prize he had long coveted—the $24.5 million Hershey sugar properties across the bay from Havana. Until recently, these had been owned by Cuban Atlantic, a U.S. company which was then the largest sugar producer in Cuba. Cuban Atlantic's board then included Edgar Bronfman of the Seagram fortune who would later join the board of Pepsi-Cola United Bottlers as well as John L. Loeb and John, Jr. of Carl M. Loeb, Rhoades & Co., the New York bankers who would, over the next year and a half, play such a vital role in the affairs of the Pepsi-linked Great Southwest Corporation (see Chapter 10). The Loebs sought control of Cuban Atlantic about the same time that Lobo did, and the two temporarily joined forces.

Lobo's interests extended into the world of tourism and leisure for, according to Peter Dale Scott, he was a part owner of the syndicate-linked Tropicana Hotel which employed some of the figures later linked to the CIA-Mafia plots against Castro. Lobo shared a common interest with Coke and Pepsi in retaining access to Cuba's abundant sugar supply. The soda-makers' efforts in that direction were evident in their respective roles in anti-Castro activities. Lobo attempted to form a partnership with William Zeckendorf and Cuban president Batista to buy a major Cuban sugar operation only a year before Castro's rise.† His brother Mario was allegedly involved in running arms to anti-Castro forces while another relative, Dr. Martin Giberga, was a former head of Cuban intelligence, apparently under Batista.‡

In 1961, Giberga was associated with I. Irving Davidson, the aforementioned Washington representative of Texas tycoon Clint Murchison, as well as a registered lobbyist for Nicaragua, Haiti, the Dominican Republic, and Ecuadorian sugar interests.§ Davidson is a particularly good example of how some of the more influential lobbyists fit into that community of interest that embraced

---

* *Business Week*, May 9, 1959, p. 34
† Zeckendorf, op. cit., p. 255-61
‡ U.S. Congress, Senate Committee on Foreign Relations, *Activities of Non-diplomatic Representatives of Foreign Principals in the United States, Hearings*, 88th Congress, 1st session, 1963, p. 1644
§ ibid., p. 1525, 1644–45, 1662–63; Scott, *Crime and Cover-Up*, op. cit., p. 9

Lobo and the soft-drink siblings. During the Senate Foreign Relations Committee 1963 investigation into the questionable practices of many of these lobbyists, Senator J. William Fulbright, the chairman, observed, "Where there is sugar, there you will find flies . . . the lobbyists on Capitol Hill working on the sugar bill are thick as flies." During Davidson's own testimony, he commented innocently that Giberga "did a lot of little things for me thereby giving me Cuban intelligence and things that I passed down to the FBI. . . ." He said nothing of the fact that his other employers at the time, the Somoza brothers of Nicaragua, whom he helped by lobbying for arms under joint Nicaraguan-American agreement, were engaged at the time with the CIA in the elaborate plots to assassinate Fidel Castro.* Nor did he mention that the Somozas had paid him over $500,000 in the five-year period from 1955 to 1960. He did elaborate somewhat, however, on his intimacy with the FBI, which was based, among other things, on a long-standing business association with Allen Oakley Hunter, a former FBI agent and U.S. congressman from California who counted Clint Murchison and Richard Nixon among his closest personal friends.† Davidson's effectiveness was grounded in long experience and superb contacts born of his recurring links to the same syndicate-allied elements and their corrupt foreign contacts which Pepsi encountered in its Dallas push. These included the Murchisons, Bobby Baker, Jimmy Hoffa (Davidson boasted that through his close ties to the Teamsters, he could organize twelve thousand workers in the 1960 presidential campaign) as well as the Somozas and the Dominican dictator, Rafael Trujillo.

For thirty years, Trujillo had worked at gaining complete control of the Dominican economy. Cement, paper, wheat and flour, tobacco, the nation's only airline, its leading newspapers, and three radio and television stations all eventually ended up in his hands. But none of these could match the most coveted prize in the Dominican economy—the cane-sugar industry. During the late forties and early fifties, he bought up as many small and moderate-sized mills as he could, constructed a railroad to link them together, and climaxed with the largest economic deal of his reign: the 1957 acquisition of the Dominican subsidiaries of the American-owned West Indies Sugar Company. The company's directors included Henry Crown, who then sat with Edward Orrick McDonnell on the board of the Hertz Foundation.

These acquisitions spurred Trujillo's continuing attempts to enlarge his country's share of the profitable U.S. sugar quota. Though the Dominican Republic received the largest share of Cuba's canceled quota in July 1960, Trujillo was by

    * Davidson in *Non-diplomatic Representatives, Hearings*, p. 1662–63; Somoza plots in *Miami Herald*, July 21, 1963; Tad Szulc, *Compulsive Spy: The Strange Career of E. Howard Hunt* (New York: Viking, 1974) p. 96–97. Also Peter Dale Scott, *Crime and Cover-Up*, op. cit., p. 10
    † *Non-diplomatic Representatives, Hearings*, p. 1528–33. Davidson wanted to involve Hunter, then a general counsel with the Housing and Home Finance Agency, in a U.S.-backed housing project in Nicaragua, endorsed by then Vice-President Nixon that would have paralleled a private real-estate development involving President Somoza and Clint Murchison. The recurring links of this arms and sugar lobbyist furthered the Somoza pattern, described by U.S. government investigators, in which the family actually cemented its ties to organized crime through kickbacks financed with foreign aid from the United States.

then encountering increasing resistance from the United States government to his ruthless drive for monopolistic control of his dominion.

With the rise of Castro and the increased U.S. reliance on Dominican sugar, even his closest allies in Congress and the sugar industry realized that his iron-fisted rule was unable to secure a stable business climate within his country. Two of those who visited Trujillo in a last-ditch, unsuccessful effort to persuade him to abdicate were then intimates of Nixon, if not of his new client, Pepsi. A counter-revolutionary of legendary stature, William Pawley had headed up Pan Am's China subsidiary before World War II and established the forerunner of what later became CIA's Asian proprietary, Air America. He was now a multi-millionaire and rabid anti-Castroite who recruited mercenaries and refugees for the Bay of Pigs as well as other sundry raids on the Havana harbor in which he participated directly. An avid Nixon supporter, Pawley was president of Talisman Sugar Co., which hired Mudge, Rose, Pepsi's law firm, to be its registered sugar lobbyist during this period. He was accompanied on this trip by Nixon's old ally Senator George Smathers, who had a million-dollar interest and direct family ties to the same Lansky Florida real estate fronts that were enriching Nixon during this early period when he was first representing Pepsi.*

With the failure of the Pawley-Smathers mission, the darkness began to close in on Trujillo. Military assistance and arms shipments were summarily withdrawn. On September 1, 1959, a three-count indictment was returned in the District of Columbia against an American-based Trujillo representative, stock manipulator Alexander Guterma, and two associates for violation of the law governing agents of foreign governments. The indictment, which led to a $10,000 fine and an eight-month to two-year prison sentence for Guterma, alleged in part that as president of the Mutual Broadcasting Co., Guterma was paid $750,000—reportedly in cash, which he personally carried from the Dominican Republic in a silk bag—to disseminate propaganda over the airwaves favorable to the Trujillo regime. When he struck his deal with Trujillo, Guterma was deeply in debt as a result of stock manipulations he orchestrated during the mid-fifties involving Virgil Dardi, the former chairman of the company owning Pepsi's Los Angeles franchise, and several members of Moe Dalitz's Desert Inn group. Disenchanted with Guterma's handling of a subsequent scheme involving their own Las Vegas operations, the Teamster-linked Desert Inn Group sought the tax maneuvering of New York attorney Lawrence Wien.† Much like David Baird, an associate whose banking ties put him close to Pepsi management, Wien personally operated a tax-free foundation that later attracted congressional attention for its repeated infringements of Treasury regulations, including one involving a long-time Pepsi counsel.‡ The law was harder on Guterma, whose machinations later saddled him with still other indictments

---

* North American Congress on Latin America, *Latin America & Empire Report*, October, p. 9–10

† Turner, op. cit., p. 193

‡ Tax-Exempt Foundations and Charitable Trusts, op, cit., p. 75–76

that named Dardi and key figures from the Desert Inn as well. Though the mob had exhausted its use for Guterma by this time, some of those in the Pepsi circle had not. Baird and Pepsi director Charles Allen sought his services several years later in connection with a huge Florida real-estate speculation they were undertaking, and with a third partner, helped settle his parole restrictions by advancing him the funds to pay an outstanding $129,000 fine.*

When the Eisenhower administration withdrew Ambassador Joseph Farland from his diplomatic post in May 1960, Trujillo undertook an all-out defense of his cherished quota, which was now threatened with suspension. Trujillo's old allies in the Congress had become disenchanted and the "Great Benefactor," as he was known to his boosters, needed new lobbying muscle. He retained Michael Deane, whose background and business affiliations were of definite interest to his Dominican employers. From 1953 to 1955, Deane had been assistant to the president of the Coca-Cola Export Corporation, and previously special adviser to the U.S. representative in the Economic Cooperation Administration (ECA), the agency most involved with overseeing the implementation of the Marshall Plan† The ECA's ties to the Mutual Security Agency and Deane's earlier service to the Wartime Planning Committee of NATO thus suggest ostensible links to the intelligence community which might well have intrigued his subsequent employers at Coke Export.

Like Coke, Deane had been involved primarily in Democratic politics, which was something of a contrast with the Republican leanings of Trujillo's previous representatives. Deane had been a fund raiser for Adlai Stevenson and a delegate to the 1960 Democratic Natonal Convention only a month before his firm, Michael B. Deane Associates, was hired by Trujillo to restore the 322,000-ton quota. The hope was that his connections within the party would afford him inside contact with the members of the House Agriculture Committee, which set the foreign quotas each time the Sugar Act came up for renewal. Deane and other lobbyists employed by Trujillo confidentially contacted three top officials in the Agriculture Department as well as Representative Harold Cooley, chairman of the House Agriculture Committee and perhaps Trujillo's last, most loyal, and certainly most powerful ally in Congress.‡ In an eleventh-hour move, Cooley blocked legislative sanctions by Eisenhower which had been approved by the Senate, but Eisenhower had the last say by imposing a special punitive tax on Dominican sugar of two cents per pound, and the whole problem fell into the lap of the Kennedy brothers.

---

* Winter-Berger, op. cit., p. 106

† *Non-diplomatic Representatives, Hearings*, op. cit., p. 548–53. Robert Mullen, whose CIA-related public relations firm would later emerge during Watergate, was the director of information for the ECA.

‡ On July 3, 1962, *New York Times* reporter Tad Szulc reported on a series of secret Trujillo files which show the long courtship of Trujillo for the members of the committee dated back to at least 1955, when he invited the entire committee, their families, and staff on an all-expense paid trip to the Dominican Republic. Cooley sent his family, and continued to work hard for Trujillo well after the United States broke diplomatic relations and applied economic sanctions against Trujillo in 1961.

With a Democratic President and a Democratic Congress, Trujillo sensed new possibilities, and his lobbyists surged ahead, contacting some of the top State Department personnel, such as Adolph Berle, Jr., an adviser to presidents since the New Deal and the postwar board chairman of SuCrest, a major East coast refinery. Along with other Trujillo representatives, Michael Deane knew that on the heels of losing Cuba's abundant supply, U.S. leadership would be intent on averting shortages. He realized that in the absence of price stability and predictable supplies, long the rationale for the rigid country-by-country quota system, friendly foreign suppliers stood a good chance of becoming the mainstay of the U.S. sugar program, especially considering the priorities of his former employers. Coca-Cola and the other big importers wanted to avoid enlarging the domestic quota since it would undoubtedly lead to the need for greater government protection and higher sugar costs over the long haul. He saw that the Kennedys, who had been supported by Coke, were intent on seeing that importers indeed had greater access to foreign sugar. More than anything else, he saw that, under the Sugar Act, the redistribution of the three-million-ton Cuban quota was to be worth some $220 million in premiums.* Under these conditions, a resourceful lobbyist with the right ties could do quite well.

True enough, but three years later, Deane found himself under castigation by Senator Fulbright for apparently lying to his Dominican employers as well as for attempting to play off a Democratic President against a Republican one in the final weeks of the Eisenhower administration in order to alter the stated foreign policy of the United States with regard to Trujillo. Congressmen on both sides of the aisle expressed equal dissatisfaction with other lobbyists whose solicitations before Cooley's Committee, which awarded the quotas, earned it the nickname of the "Little State Department."

Indeed, it was well recognized on the Hill as well as at the White House that the quotas were a form of foreign aid, and touched intimately on foreign policy. This fact irked the Kennedys, who were opposed to furthering Trujillo's reign in any fashion. Concerned about foreign policy and apparent attempts by Trujillo lobbyists to bribe members of the House Agriculture Committee, the Kennedys authorized wiretaps on Cooley and others (including quite possibly, Michael Deane) suspected of involvement.† FBI memoranda asserted that the politically inspired surveillance contributed heavily to the administration's successful passage of a bill that deflated the clout of the sugar lobby in Congress. The May 1961 assassination of Trujillo, arranged by his own military officers with American complicity, achieved another foreign policy priority.

The Dominican quota was reinstated in 1962 with over 90 percent of the crop

---

* In order to protect the domestic growers, the world price of $40 a ton was supplemented by the U.S. premium of $70 a ton paid to foreign producers by the importers, and ultimately, consumers. For domestic producers, the premium covered what would otherwise have been losses, but to the foreign producer, the $70 a ton was practically pure profit.

† U.S. Senate, Select Committee to Study Governmental Operations with Respect to Intelligence Activities, Final Report, Book Two, *Intelligence Activities and the Rights of Americans*, 94th Congress, 2nd Session 1976). p. 61, 328–330, 345–46

going to the United States, which was then suffering a tremendous shortage, but the dilemma in the Dominican Republic was not fully resolved with the elimination of Trujillo.* U.S. policymakers, some of whom also happened to be among the most powerful men in the sugar industry, tried unsuccessfully to coalesce the remnants of the Trujillo regime with the urban middle classes. Juan Bosch was elected president in late 1962 with the initial support of both the Kennedy administration and the CIA. Once in power, Bosch attempted to rescind several major sugar contracts negotiated after the fall of Trujillo. Consequently, American support evaporated, including that of the sugar interests, and he was ousted in a bloodless coup in 1963 by right-wing generals who sought to undo his progressive social reforms. Kennedy refused to recognize the new military government, but he, too, was assassinated two months later, and within weeks, Lyndon Johnson installed a new hard-line ambassador. When Bosch nearly succeeded in overthrowing the right-wing generals, Johnson dispatched his most intimate friend and adviser, Abe Fortas, to make it clear to him that despite his popularity, Washington would not support his return to power. Bosch's actions while in office made him appear all too much like Castro, who skillfully used American business to help him into power. Thus, LBJ's express fear of "another Cuba" in the Dominican Republic had an ironic double meaning underscored by his choice of Fortas as the courier of Washington's disapproval. On the one hand, Fortas had earlier been the attorney for Bobby Baker, who continued his associations with Trujillo's old allies by traveling to the Dominican Republic early in the Bosch era in search of hotel gambling concessions on behalf of Nevada underworld gamblers.† In the larger scheme, Fortas was a key link between the Great Southwest-Pepsi network and American sugar interests in the Caribbean. A director and general counsel of Greatamerica Corporation, a Dallas insurance giant then controlled partially by Clint Murchison, Fortas also served on the board of First National Bank of Dallas with PepsiCo directors Robert Stewart and Herman Lay.

Fortas was also a twenty-year director of SuCrest, the third largest East Coast refiner which seems to have had major ties to that element of the Johnson circle which Pepsi and Nixon hoped to penetrate on their foray into Texas. SuCrest's Wall Street counsel was then Stroock & Stroock & Levan, one of whose partners, Max Rabb, was a top Johnson supporter and a director of Seven Arts, the Canadian company in which Pepsi's Charles Allen and Clint Murchison invested heavily in 1964. Its postwar board chairman, Adolph Berle, Jr., was a top Kennedy and Johnson adviser who advocated an all-out commitment at the Bay of Pigs and in 1965, backed the Johnson administration's final decision to send thirty thousand United States Marines into the Dominican Republic, ostensibly to evacuate Americans who, it was later learned, were scarcely threatened.

---

* *Barron's*, May 11, 1964. p. 9. It was in the teeth of this shortage that Pepsi decided to pursue the ill-fated Empire State Sugar in upstate New York. The $22 million operation was to be the first of its kind in the U.S. capable of processing both beet and cane sugar, and would have given Pepsi a sizeable stake in a domestic quota, thus pitting it against Coke's priorities at the time. See Chapter 11.

† Reid, op. cit., p. 136

Other high-ranking Johnson administration officials who played major roles were equally immersed in the sugar sector. OAS ambassador and special envoy to the Dominican Republic, Ellsworth Bunker, was past chairman, president, and a thirty-eight-year director of the second largest East Coast refiner, National Sugar Refining Co. Roving Ambassador W. Averell Harriman, sent to Latin America by Johnson to explain the Dominican intervention, was a limited partner in a prominent New York banking house, Brown Brothers & Harriman, which owned 5 percent of National Sugar at the time.* In 1956, National Sugar bought out the Louisiana refinery and business of Godschaux Sugar from William Zeckendorf, who was later so important to Pepsi's orientation in Dallas. National's Wall Street legal counsel, Cravath, Swaine, and Moore, also represented General Dynamics, whose principal stockholder, Henry Crown, was directly linked to Great Southwest through the investment of the sugar-oriented Loeb interests, and was himself a director of West Indies Sugar until well after its Dominican holdings were bought out by Trujillo.

Coke and Pepsi thus interlocked with the political and corporate apparatus of the sugar sector, which also manifestly influenced developments in the Dominican Republic from the rise of Trujillo to the fall of Bosch. Their good fortune in the aftermath of the intervention was much more apparent. In a much criticized move, the State Department used I. Irving Davidson to contact a potential successor to Bosch, Joaquin Balaguer, a member of the Trujillista coalition who was then living in exile in New York.† On June 1, 1966, with heavy backing from an OAS mission headed by Ellsworth Bunker, Balaguer triumphed in an election over the irrepressible Juan Bosch. The U.S. sugar quota was dramatically increased, and a year later, Gulf and Western Industries completed the major acquisition of South Puerto Rico Sugar (SPRS) from a group of investors closely linked to the Rockefellers. Gulf and Western (G&W), whose president and twelfth largest stockholder, John H. Duncan, was the brother of top Coke executive Charles Duncan, started purchasing shares of SPRS a few months after the intervention. G&W's guiding light, Charles Bludhorn, the architect of the deal, who acquired his initial capital trading sugar and coffee, commented to officers of the Chase Manhattan Bank, a principal G&W creditor, that the company was relying on President Johnson to minimize the political risks of the investment.

In addition to Duncan's ties to Johnson, G&W's own relations with the administration were further cemented on October 22, 1966 when Democratic National committeeman Edwin Weisl, the President's closest friend and confidant in New York State, joined the board of Gulf and Western as a result of the huge conglomerate's acquisition of Paramount Pictures, where he had long been a

---

* Fred Goff and Michael Locker, "The Nationalist Pivot," in Irving Horowitz, ed., *Latin American Radicalism* (New York: Random House, 1969). p. 280-82. Trujillo's old ally, George Smathers, belonged to a law firm representing Atlantic Mutual Life, whose board included Harriman's brother and Ellsworth Bunker.

† Among the most vociferous critics was Senator Wayne Morse, who commented that to use Davidson as an intermediary was a "dirty business at best ..." which "can only cloud the good intentions of the U.S."

director. Weisl was then a law partner with Cyrus Vance at the New York firm of Simpson, Thacher, and Bartlett, one of whose partners, Joel Dolkart, was already general counsel at G&W. Until 1976, Simpson, Thacher, and Bartlett frequently served as Coke's New York counsel. Also known as the "18th partner of Lehman Bros.," Weisl was associated with another Lehman partner, Ellsworth Bunker's brother, Arthur, and served on the board of the Hertz Foundation with still other figures from the sugar world, including United Fruit's Floyd Odlum, and Robert Lehman, as well as Pepsi's Edward Orrick McDonnell, who joined Lehman as a long-time director of Pan Am. Odlum was a very prominent and accomplished industrialist who emerged from the Depression as one of the thirty wealthiest men in America. Like Henry Crown, he was a major figure in Democratic politics, and his Atlas Corporation was a big investor in Crown's General Dynamics as well as a major recipient during the fifties of millions of dollars from the family foundations of Pepsi's important banking connection, David G. Baird.

Meanwhile, Gulf and Western's big move into Dominican sugar a decade later was one of several acquisitions which involved Coca-Cola, and to a lesser degree, Pepsi. In 1968, Pepsi director Harry Gould joined the board of G&W, largely as a result of the latter's acquisition of Universal American Corp., where Gould had been a director with William Zeckendorf. The G&W board was enhanced with a key figure from the worlds of Nixon, Lansky, and Dominican sugar, the former senator from Florida, George A. Smathers.

G&W's experience in the Dominican Republic catapulted the company into a strong posture on the world market. In 1974, when sugar prices soared some 400 percent, sugar production accounted for about 20 percent of the company's $224 million earnings.

Highly confident of G&W's sugar operations, Bludhorn undertook a major expansion in the mid-seventies in the Dominican Republic, Florida, and Hawaii. In Hawaii the company acquired a 22 percent controlling interest in Amfac, itself a billion-dollar conglomerate and the state's largest sugar manufacturer. G&W also bought into Charles Brewer & Sons, another major Hawaiian producer and the state's largest corporate landowner. Brewer and Amfac owned about half of California & Hawaii Sugar Co. (C&H), a huge cooperatively owned refiner in Crockett, California that refines and markets all the sugar produced in Hawaii. One of C&H's largest customers is Coca-Cola.

Through its subsidiaries, Brewer had been active in the Philippines, the most important American supplier since the demise of the Cuban allocation back in 1961. The great family fortunes in the Philippines were founded on sugar and supported flawlessly by President Ferdinand Marcos, whose land and social reforms left the near slave-labor conditions on the plantations virtually untouched.

This climate was particularly hospitable to Pepsi which outsold Coke through its Pepsi Cola Far East Development Company, one of the country's biggest money-makers in the last fifty years. As might be imagined, Pepsi enjoyed an especially cordial relationship with local sugar producers. For example, despite

the apparent opposition of buyer and seller, Pepsi director Don G. Mitchell
served on the board of Corn Products Company, a principal Pepsi supplier
(through its subsidiary, Refined Syrups and Sugars) which purchased virtually all
of its foreign sugar from the Philippines.* In order to reap their share of the
sugar windfall during the reallocation of the Cuban quota, Philippine producers
retained as their lobbyist John O'Donnell, who, back in the fifties, briefly represented a Philippine mining concern, Benguet Consolidated.† Once one of the
largest gold producers in the world, Benguet was perhaps the foundation of the
family fortune of Pepsi's director Charles Allen who, with brother Herbert,
gambled on a one-third interest in the mine when it was in shambles back in the
darkest days of World War II.‡

As a big buyer of local Philippine sugar, Pepsi Far East Development could
well have benefitted from large U.S. quotas since the premiums generated by
these quotas would have helped lower the price of local sugar. Overall, Pepsi
benefitted from cheap sugar in the United States, but its subsidiary in the Philippines gave it a common interest with the sugar industry there. O'Donnell was
charged by Fulbright's Foreign Relations Committee "with deceiving Congress
and with serving as the middleman for Philippine sugar interests in passing out
over $15,000 for 1960 congressional campaigns." Insofar as he served his clients
faithfully, O'Donnell also served the Pepsi subsidiary.

Like Kennedy before him, Jimmy Carter was swept into the sugar chaos as soon
as he entered office. In 1974, the forty-year-old Sugar Act expired. The rigid
country-by-country quota system, which protected domestic growers and maintained stable prices, was effective only in the midst of a sugar glut. In late 1973,
however, the world sugar crop was badly damaged by weather, supplies shrank,
and the unsupported world price soared to sixty-five cents a pound near the end
of 1974, almost eight times the supported American domestic price of a year
and a half earlier. Under these circumstances of scarcity, which were the most
acute in modern history, there was no competition from cheap, foreign sugar.
Along with many consumer organizations and big industrial users who wanted
to hold down prices, Coke actively moved to scuttle the bill as a useless anachro-
nism. The last gasp of decisive support for the growers came from President
Ford, who tripled the duty on sugar without warning in late 1976, putting at
least one major New York sugar broker out of business and winning few friends
in the soft-drink industry.

---

* *Pacific Basin Reports*, September, 1973. p. 196. During the 1960s, Mitchell was joined on
the Corn Products board by Nixon's friend Harold Helm, the chairman of Chemical Bank as well
as a future member of CREEP's Finance Committee with Maurice Stans.

† *Non-diplomatic Representatives, Hearings*, Pt. II, op. cit., p. 197, 199

‡ *The New York Times*, November 28, 1976, III:1. According to the *Times*, Allen and Company swapped its interest in Wallace Groves' Grand Bahama Port Authority in 1969 with Benguet,
receiving $15 million in Benguet stock for its initial $1 million investment fourteen years earlier. As
noted in Chapter 10, this transaction was the first leg of the deal that resurrected Groves as a legitimate force in Bahamian gambling.

Despite higher sweetener costs, Coke's earnings in the third quarter of 1974 were about the same as the year before, reflecting the fact that higher costs were simply passed along to the consumer. In that period of single-digit inflation, sweetener costs were still the number one pressure on soft-drink retail prices, which jumped 26 percent in one year. For the first time in years, Americans were drinking fewer soft drinks. Unlike Pepsi, whose bottlers purchase their sugar directly, Coke purchases some two *billion* pounds a year, and price fluctuations of a single penny could conceivably affect earnings over the course of a year by over $20 million.

The demise of the Sugar Act provided the major users with their first opportunity in years to gain a legislative edge over the domestic growers. Over the last decade, the cost of domestic sugar production had risen steadily while the world price, at least until the 1973 harvest, held its own. Thus the cost of protecting the growers, borne largely by the major users and the consumers, also rose. Yet the frequently shared political interests between seller and buyer, which date back to the heyday of the Sugar Act, largely involved international producers or the largest and most efficient domestic growers. It was a new game now—a head-to-head confrontation—and Coke's powerful rivals on the domestic growers' side were lining up behind their congressional representatives who formed the most powerful lobby in the agricultural sector. Their goal, of course, was a stable market for their sugar at the highest possible price. So acute was the need to find a mechanism to replace the old Sugar Act that both camps were drawn into a classic conflict which raged from the White House to Capitol Hill, from the Justice Department to Agriculture and back again, gathering wind along the way from high-flying Washington lobbyists, grandstanding congressmen, forceful cabinet members, stubborn bureaucrats, and presidential advisers, to say nothing of farmers, labor unions, foreign governments, free-trade advocates—including Donald Kendall—and consumer groups. Complete with a byplay of acrimony, allegations, ineptitude, betrayal, and scandal, the battle raged for two years as both sides marshaled their forces to corral the Congress and court the President.

"This is a big struggle between big and powerful interests," said one congressional aide who witnessed the developments from close range. "And the survival of an industry is at stake." This kind of melodrama was common among the growers and their allies in Congress who were pushing Carter to enact a generous price-support program and to reintroduce restrictive import fees and quotas that would ensure higher prices for the domestically produced sugar. In the opposite corner swaggered Coke and the other titanic sugar users, the processors and refiners, all of whom consistently sought a liberal import policy to keep prices of raw sugar low. Conceding to the growers the necessity for some kind of protection, they favored direct federal subsidies rather than import fees for a simple reason: direct subsidies would be financed by the federal treasury, and would hence help the farmers at the expense of taxpayers without raising the price of sugar. The growers always fought the use of subsidies, since the multi-million dollar payments made them vulnerable to public criticism and aroused fears of legislated limitations. Almost from the beginning, the Carter administration weighed in on the side of the users and the refiners, justifying its stand with a strong philosophic preference for free trade and a politically popular stance aimed at fighting inflation.

On January 25, 1977, in one of his first official acts, President Carter put together a task force on sugar and gave the experts until February 15 to come up with proposals. One such expert, a high-ranking official at Agriculture with long experience in agricultural economics, was later moved to comment, "I soon found out that sugar was the most complex, devilish issue I'd ever dealt with." At the time, the only sugar policy in effect was a meaningless quota well above the actual level of imports and a very low tariff dating back to the eighteenth century. The final recommendations seemed to come out with a policy favorable to the growers. The study called for a quota to limit imports to 4.2 million tons a year, a little over a third of America's total annual consumption of eleven million tons, and price supports in the form of fees and tariffs. The recommended level was set at thirteen to fourteen cents a pound, considerably more than the 10.5 cents (8 percent world price plus 2.5 cents tariff) which Coke and its cousins in the user category were then paying. Carter seemed equally displeased with the recommendation, and chose instead to heed a memo from Treasury Secretary Blumenthal which warned that import restrictions would be "inconsistent with U.S. attempts to liberalize world trade." Blumenthal offered many alternatives in the memo, all of which were presented in language that favored keeping market prices low while supporting producers with a subsidy. Carter must have been told what he wanted to hear, for he not only rejected the proposals of his task force, but similar ones forwarded by the U.S. International Trade Commission. In May 1977, he instituted a program favorable to the users which called for subsidies up to two cents per pound. The growers were doubly pained by this measure, for the amount of the subsidy, they claimed, was wholly inadequate to their needs.

Not surprisingly, the form and figures of the President's plan closely paralleled those publicly endorsed by Coke. John Mount, chief sugar purchaser for Coca-Cola USA and head of the Sugar Users Group, a food industry lobby, later claimed that "any subsequent increase in minimum returns to growers above 13.5 cents should be achieved through direct payments" from the government. Carter defended his subsidy plan as the most beneficial to consumers as well as the one least likely to offend U.S. trading partners, some of whom were members in the International Sugar Agreement, a 1977 multilateral trade arrangement to stabilize world sugar prices.

While the President struggled to hammer his sugar policy into shape, Senator Church and the growers' other allies in Congress were working on a plan that would be tied to the cornerstone of the government's agricultural policy for the coming year, the Farm Bill of 1977. The plan was attached to the bill as an amendment, named for its chief sponsor in the House, E. de la Garza of Texas.

Designed by the growers' leading Washington lobbyist, Horace Godfrey, the de la Garza amendment proposed the growers' long-sought price support program.

Senate and House conferees worked to reconcile differences in the amendment, but the most experienced hands on Capitol Hill knew that the crux would come not in pushing the amendment through Congress, but in making sure that the administration enforced it. Suspicions over the President's willingness to do so, born in his known preference for the subsidy plan, peaked during the bitter legislative struggle over the de la Garza amendment. During one hearing when Agriculture Secretary Robert Bergland was testifying, Senator Russell Long (D-La.) evaluated the current policy, with its anachronistically low tariff and uselessly high quota. "I would call the existing program a Coca-Cola program." His suspicion pyramided when *Time* magazine reported that, days before the Carter administration threatened to veto the entire farm bill unless the Senate conference committee lowered the sugar support price, John Mount had told friends in a Washington bar, "If we cannot prevail in conference, we will just have to call in a few chits and have the President veto the farm bill." After that slip of the tongue, Mount was unavailable for comment to all major media, and Carter aides insisted that the administration was unconcerned about the impact of sugar policy on Coca-Cola. As the debate over the amendment intensified, the growers became impatient and developed what one lobbyist called a "demonology" which attributed the administration's stubborn opposition to their proposals to the long-standing ties between the President and Coca-Cola.

Was there any substance behind these emotion-ridden allegations? One of the government's top sugar experts confirmed that the growers' suspicions were based on more than a need for a scapegoat. "There is no question of the Coca-Cola influence. Nothing is provable, but a President who had as much help from Coca-Cola as he had who did not have some Coca-Cola interests at heart would be a very funny President."

Viewing Carter as anything but a "funny President," Senator Long turned very early to the issue of enforcing the de la Garza amendment, should it be enacted into law. In early August 1977, he was assured by Secretary Bergland that aides would immediately be assigned to implement the amendment. Weeks later, a high-level official at the Agriculture Department complained in a memo that "because we are so shorthanded," he and his aides "have not yet started work on regulations to implement the de la Garza amendment," which was then scheduled to become law on October 1. Secretary Bergland, directly responsible to the White House, essentially agreed that the proper manpower was not available to implement the impending law. Yet this bureaucratic failure was only a prologue to a whole pattern of similar failures, which, taken as a whole, raises the question for some of a deliberate sabotaging by the Carter White House of the grower-sponsored legislation. Jim Leach, a Republican congressman from Iowa, stronghold of the corn growers who were allies of the sugar growers in this issue, remarked that "It looks as though the President of the United States of America refused to implement the law of the land, which is his primary responsibility. Far more involved than basic competence was a considered decision to delay."

The delays concerned not only the implementation of the program but also the establishment of the necessary import restrictions. A top Carter aide as well as colleagues of Representative Leach repeatedly warned the White House that these restrictions were absolutely necessary to prevent floods of foreign sugar from overwhelming the domestic market and defeating the purpose of the law. Yet on October 1, 1977, nothing had been done in either of these areas, nor would there be for some time to come. The presidential proclamation setting the new import fees was not issued until November 11, and evidence indicates that, after the lengthy delays, it was hastily prepared, sometimes passing through important stages of revision at various agencies of the Executive in less than a day.

Once issued, glaring flaws immediately emerged, but none so prominent as the exemption from all fees and increases in the duty until January 1 for sugar already under contract or on the high seas. The staggering implications of what this could ultimately mean to the world's premier sugar buyer was not lost for an instant on John Mount, the burly, bespectacled steward of Coke's huge sugar stocks. His years of service to the company had been spent in purchasing mountains, piles—pyramids—of sugar which eventually found their way into Coke's various soft-drink syrups at the rate of almost six *million* pounds a day. Of course, Mount seldom thought about the present day's usage, but of the thousands of tons he and his crew must contract for weeks and often months in advance. He is buying the raw sugar far ahead of the daily "spot" market, much as the big refiners do, and hedging the price he contracts to pay against what he is selling it for to the bottlers (see Chapter 19). He must also allow for the cost of refining and the import duty, which had been constant for so long at 1.875 cents per pound that it was perhaps the most routine part of the equation.

But now the proclamation of the President from Plains suddenly altered the routine. As Mount arrived at work that Atlanta morning, strolling across Coke's North Street grounds through the candy-smelling breeze, how could he have helped wondering—is this the "chit?" It seemed too fantastic, too perfectly unreal to be anything but a mistake.

Indeed, the presidential proclamation of November 11 was a flawed and far-fetched plan patterned after an ancient clause on the books for forty-five years. It allowed the President to assess a variable fee to importers, dependent on the purchase price, a feature which created a powerful temptation for collusion between American buyers and foreign sellers to avoid payment and split the savings. And the maximum variable fee of 3.3 cents that was supposed to protect the domestic raw price at 13.5 cents wasn't high enough to affect the unusually low price of refined sugar, some of which would begin flowing down from Canada in a matter of weeks.

Nevertheless, Mount concentrated on the Big Flaw that made the others moot—the exemption. His mind must have raced over staggering numbers as he checked his schedule of shipments en route from the big international suppliers like Brazil or the Dominican Republic. Thousands of tons, millions of pounds—exempt until January 1. Anticipating the coming crush, Mount was on his phone to sugar brokers and operators before it could start ringing. His message was terse and decisive—buy heavily on the spot market or for delivery before January 1. Just as quickly, the sugar moguls throughout the American food industry were swept up in this buying spree while foreign producers around the globe caught wind of the Proclamation and hastily diverted sugar bound for other destinations to American ports. "Like everyone else," explained a government sugar expert, "I'm sure they advanced delivery to avoid the duties on sugar they were planning to get in January, February, and March. They're no dummies."

An American lobbyist with a stake in the imposition of the fees told *The New York Times* he frantically called Washington from London "screaming" to anyone in the administration who would listen to close the loophole.* Meanwhile, an avalanche had been unloosed that would dump some two million tons through American customs before the New Year, making December the biggest month ever in U.S. sugar imports. Aside from the $54 million in import fees which were never collected, some $29 million in sugar-support payments were made to ineligible processors.†

What did Coke reap from this fiasco? As might be expected, the company is very loath to discuss any aspect of its sugar acquisitions, much less an episode from which it apparently profited greatly. Using figures from Coke's Annual Report, industry journals, the U.S. International Trade Commission, Drexel-Burnham, a leading Wall Street investment house, and a source at a major New York sugar broker with which Coke does business, it is reasonable to estimate that Coke saved almost $24.3 million in duties and fees in the final two months of 1977. According to these calculations, Coke would have used a little over 300 million pounds from the day of the president's proclamation until the end of the year. The USITC estimates an average saving of a little over 4.3 cents per pound, or a total of just over $13 million.

The $24 million estimate (the saving on a total of 565 million pounds) assumes that Coke would have bought for its future needs as well, and is based on

* *The New York Times*, January 14, 1979, p. 48

† This figure was reached by first estimating how much sugar Coke used during the weeks involved, as follows:

a) Compile Coca-Cola's total sugar volume for the year for its major sugared brands (the company published the amount of sugar in each 8-ounce serving, and total 1977 volume for each brand published in *Beverage Industry Annual Manual, 1977–78*, p. 24)

b) The fourth-quarter percentage of the dollar total for domestic soft drinks sold within U.S. is assumed to be the percentage of domestic total for Coca-Cola's sugar use during the fourth quarter of 1977. It was about 24.7 percent. This figure calculated by breaking down quarterly figures for Coca-Cola's total worldwide dollar volume into quarterly figures for domestic sales of the company's major sugared brands. (Figures for this calculation in *The Coca-Cola Company Annual Report*, 1977, p. 18; *Annual Report* 1978, p. 6, 32–33 varying estimates of Coca-Cola's storage capacity from Wall Street analysts and at least one sugar broker who dealt with the company regularly.

Even taking the lower of these estimates, one might wonder with Mount: was this the "chit?" Internal documents do show that Carter himself followed the sugar market extremely closely in this period, and that a half or even quarter cent change in price often led to numerous presidential memoranda. "The windfall was not a deliberate policy by anybody," insists one of Washington's best-informed sugar watchers. "It was an oversight by people who didn't think out this program. But," he added, "the fact that it was realized there was going to be a windfall and nothing was done about it could perhaps be faulted."

Responding to a direct query from the authors on this question, Coke completely overlooked the crucial issue of the fees, but conceded an impact on the market price of sugar from the surge of imports. "The beneficiaries of these lower prices were consumers. . . . It is well documented that the price we charge bottlers for syrup is based on the market prices of refined sugar. Thus, we had no 'windfall.' "

In actuality, Coke had a *second,* much larger windfall throughout 1978 which grew directly out of the first and resulted from its historic policy of charging the bottlers an average of the "spot" (daily) market price rather than what it actually pays for its sugar. In a February 1980 report, Drexel-Burnham, a leading Wall Street concern, asserted that the surplus tonnage at the end of 1977 lowered Coke's sugar costs during 1978 to an average (including refining) of 17 cents per pound. But, the report continues, under its cost-computing method (which has since been modified somewhat for those bottlers signing the new contract amendment), Coke charged all the bottlers 21 cents per pound, reaping 4 cents or a 25 percent profit on the difference. Based on the figures used in the above estimates as well as on 1978 case volume figures for Coke's sugared brands, this second windfall totaled some $10 million in the opening weeks of 1978, and almost $90 million on the year, or twice what they normally made.* These higher costs to bottlers must be passed along to consumers. The Drexel Report estimates a 1.5 cents per case (192-oz.) change for each 1-cent fluctuation in sweetener price. The bottlers undoubtedly absorbed about 15 percent of this increase themselves, so that in 1978, consumers made Coke's little spree possible by paying about $86 million more than Coke did for its sugar.

Meanwhile, the lobbying and fighting over the real future of sugar continued, since the de la Garza amendment was put into law only as a two-year measure. Throughout 1978, Carter fought two bills that called for price supports up to seventeen cents, claiming that the proposals were too inflationary, and that they protected the most inefficient producers at the expense of the whole market.

---

* Arthur S. Kirsch, *The Soft-Drink Industry: A Review of the Impact of Rising Sweetener Costs* (New York: Drexel-Burnham Lambert, Inc., February 22, 1980), p. 17. Case volume data in *Beverage Industry Annual Manual, 1978-79,* p. 21. The 4-cent differential was also deemed accurate by a leading analyst at Goldman-Sachs, another premier investment concern. Historically, says Kirsch, Coke has made about 2 cents per pound on its sale of sugar to the bottlers.

Despite the coziness of Austin and Carter, this was a position which Donald Kendall had been endorsing since Carter came into office. "The problem," he said in February 1977, "is that the American sugar producers can't produce efficiently, and they want the consumer to pay the bill for their inefficiency. We shouldn't subsidize inefficient industries. . . . We could produce valuable crops at competitive prices for world markets and everyone would be the better for it. . . ." In his familiar free-trade vernacular, Kendall added, "The long term result of protectionism—and that's what we're talking about here—is retaliation against other trade producers and an undermining of our competitive strength."

Kendall can afford to be as outspoken as he is since most of the sugar in Pepsi-Cola is purchased at the bottler level. While Austin might agree with Kendall's premise, he must be far more cautious, since Coke's relations extend to many corners of the domestic market. Coke's interest in a domestic market, however, ceases at the threshold of inefficiency, which includes practically every producer not located in Florida or Hawaii. Domestically, Coke has attempted to buy in the same proportions that U.S. growers contribute to over-all world production. Thus, as one astute Washington observer put it, "If Puerto Rico, Louisiana, and Texas were to go out of business tomorrow, that wouldn't bother Coke at all. It would mean that the likelihood of future government programs asking for a figure three cents above what it would be if we had only Florida and Hawaii would be down the drain. . . . When the sugar users see individual producers—the small farmers, and so on—closing down, that is in their interest. When there finally is legislation, it will be more toward a lower price of sugar than a higher one."

Despite all the signs that the alliance of Coke and Carter heavily influenced the President's resolve to enforce the grower policy when it had become law, Carter's views on sugar were arguably the best for consumers. After all, each penny increase in the supported price of sugar, as advocated by the growers, might have cost $20 million, but it cost the consumers of all sugared products some $224 million. Yet neither Coke nor Carter was able to take full advantage of this fortuitious convergence of public and private interest precisely because of the widespread publicity and Capitol Hill innuendo concerning the ties between them. In August 1979, President Carter finally gave in, and agreed to sponsor new sugar legislation that would support domestic sugar prices at 17 cents a pound, going up to 18.1 cents in 1981, with only half a cent of that amount coming through the subsidy channel long favored by Coke.

By 1980, inflation had pushed the world price of sugar well above the support level. The real irony, though, was that the darkest shadow on the Coke-Carter alliance was cast by an extemporaneous alliance between the sugarcane growers and the corn refiners. Utilized in the soft-drink industry in the form of high fructose corn syrup (HFCS), these corn sweeteners were cleared by Coke and Pepsi for use in all brands but the colas beginning in 1978, and the 50 to 75 percent run-up in refined sugar prices in early 1980 inspired many bottlers to make the switch. Corn refiners invested hundreds of millions of dollars to expand output and compete more fully with the sugar industry. Consequently, they had a major interest in seeing high sugar prices continue, a trend that would have enhanced the competitive position of corn syrup. Like the growers, the corn refiners were behind the de la Garza amendment which would set a market price floor for sugar, and when the Carter administration delayed in its implementation, they moved into the foreground.

In September 1978, they sued the Agriculture Department in Des Moines Federal Court, claiming a "blatant administration refusal to comply with the de la Garza amendment." The little-publicized court action quickly showed some familiar signs of presidential malfeasance. When the issue reached the White House, twenty documents necessary for the preparation of the administration's defense were sent for review from the Department of Agriculture to the White House, where they simply "disappeared" from the desk of the presidential counsel.* A search was later undertaken of all files in the White House, including those of the President himself, but the missing envelope was never found. The White House then attempted to reconstruct the missing documents by culling its central files for all memos relating to sugar. It found twenty-one documents, and claimed executive privilege on seventeen of them. The President believed their release would impair "the free and frank discussions" of issues between himself and his advisers, and would be "injurious to the public interest and to the constitutional doctrine of separation of powers."

Informed of the missing documents in late September 1978, the federal judge hearing the case in Des Moines, termed the situation both "serious and unfortunate." In April 1979, he ruled in favor of the corn refiners, declaring that "the [Agriculture] Secretary's actions were contrary to the clear meaning of the de la Garza amendment." No damages were awarded, but the government appealed the decision, charging that the expiration of the de la Garza amendment renders the entire case moot. The corn refiners contested the appeal with the claim that $210 million dispensed from the government treasury is anything but moot. The appeals court apparently concurred, remanding the case back to the lower court and stating that some awarding of damages is necessary before the appeal can proceed. In addition, the corn refiners have pressed a motion to have the reconstructed White House documents examined to determine whether favoritism was a factor in the administration's handling of sugar policy.

However strong the corn industry's suspicions of presidential patronage toward Atlanta, at least some of the wounds were healed in early 1980 when Coca-Cola announced its historic decision to use HFCS in addition to sugar in its hallowed brand. Prompted primarily by economics, the company had been contemplating such a move probably since the sugar price-run of 1974, but fructose threw off the taste created by the delicately balanced formula. Extended lab work and eighteen months of tests were required to come up with a product which consumers could not distinguish from sugar-sweetened Coke.

This achievement, which altered the famous formula, was vital but expensive.

---

* *San Francisco Examiner*, September 28, 1978, p. 1. Jack Egan, "Executive Privilege: It's the Real Thing," *New York*, December 25, 1978, p. 16-18

It cleared the way for the company to use up to 100 percent fructose, as several industry observers predict they will do rather than its stated limit of up to half.* With the capability to vary the mix at will, Atlanta was in a better competitive position than it had been in years, not only with respect to Pepsi and its other rivals, who were expected to make similar announcements soon, but also in its enhanced ability to play the sugar and corn sectors off against one another. When the announcement hit the major commodities markets, sugar promptly plummeted 1.6 cents a pound while fructose shot up 4 cents a pound. This upward pressure on fructose prices, which could be increased if the other soft-drink companies make similar announcements, will probably never be strong enough to push them above sugar prices. An observer at one major financial publication believes that several large fructose makers even went so far as to promise Coke that they would hold their prices 10 to 15 percent below those of sugar indefinitely.

Atlanta certainly had every reason to expect that they could do it. Industry projections for 1980 consistently put fructose some 20 percent below the cost of refined sugar. Coke's announcement was made at a time when sugar prices were skyrocketing. The move was a boon for Coke bottlers, who were already looking at savings of up to 15 percent on the other brands using fructose. With its company-owned bottlers and huge fountain business, Big Coke, meanwhile, could contemplate long-range savings of $27 million annually, or more if it decided to use a higher percentage of fructose in its premier brand.

Coke's leverage will be enhanced because of the tremendous expansion the corn processors will have to undertake to fulfill its voracious demand. With fructose contributing only half the sweetener in Coca-Cola syrup, estimates of Coke's anticipated needs range from 800 million to 1.2 billion pounds annually, or some 35 percent of the entire corn-refining industry's 1979 output of 3.4 billion pounds. Leaving aside the 500 million pounds Pepsi would require annually should it make a similar move, the corn refiners must now invest millions just to fill the needs of its major customer. In 1980, its sagging production capacity was only able to provide Coke with an estimated 300 million pounds, but the short-range saving of over $9 million moved a company spokesman to declare, "For the time being, we'll take all we can get." Should increased fructose prices ever move the soda giant to reconsider, it is very unlikely that foreign markets already abundant with sugar could ever absorb the excess corn sweeteners. In a very real sense, the corn refiners are willing and eager to become the captive suppliers of the soft-drink industry. This arrangement of many suppliers serving a relatively small number of customers is known in economic parlance as a monopsony, and in this instance, there could be an important political bonus.

During the 1980 grain embargo following the Soviet invasion of Afghanistan,

---

* *Wall Street Journal,* August 3, 1978. "Fructose is also subject to the same health warnings attached to sugar, medical researchers say. Both . . . have been linked to tooth decay and higher levels of triglycerides, fatty substances suspected of being related to heart attacks."

the Carter administration announced plans to promote production of gasahol from grain previously intended for export. According to government sources gasahol plants can be converted overnight for fructose production which would be far more profitable than gasahol at the prices prevailing when the policy was declared. Realizing this coincidence, government analysts were mulling over the prospect that subsidies for gasahol production might well help finance the fructose explosion precipitated by Coca-Cola. In such a case, the connections between Coca-Cola, Jimmy Carter, and Energy Secretary Charles Duncan would then be worthy of even closer scrutiny.

CHAPTER NINETEEN

The Bottler's Apprentice

BY 1900, Coca-Cola was so successful that Asa Candler could afford to scoff at the far-reaching advice of a friend that perhaps another king's fortune could be had if only he could "bottle it." Just home from the Spanish-American War, young Benjamin Franklin Thomas approached Candler with law partner Joseph Whitehead and persuaded him to let them take the risks he was so loath to assume. With J.T. Lupton of Chattanooga putting up the initial capital, the trio set out on a journey that would soon make them the first of a bumper crop of entrepreneurs made rich from bottling. Scarcely anyone in Purchase or anywhere else would dispute the claim that Coke's bottling franchises have produced more millionaires than any similar operation in history. That fact alone is the stuff from which legends are born, a truism which Robert Woodruff perceived from his earliest days at Coke. He saw Coke's future in bottling, and took every opportunity to hail his bottlers as something approaching the Jeffersonian ideal of the independent yeoman cultivating his garden. For many years, there was no competition to sully the landscape, or to push the bottler beyond the cocoon that Woodruff and Coke were spinning for them. In Woodruff's words, the bottler was "the classic embodiment of the free enterprise system," a good Yankee trader to be sure, but his brand of rugged individualism more likely owed itself to the physical obstacles of saturating his market than to the economic one of outdoing a competitor. Consequently, the enterprising Yankee in him was seasoned with a good bit of the free and easy ways of the old Georgia vintage, at least until Pepsi came along in the late forties. The legendary tradition of the "one big happy family" of bottlers was passed down from the beginning and rooted in the rock-bed stability of the franchised territory.

As much as a man's home is his castle, a bottler's franchise is his territory, a protected barony where he reigns as lord and sovereign. For years, he dwelt in the happy, enlightened reciprocity of this arrangement, which had all the blessings of a social contract between a ruler and his subjects. The bottler's world extended not one inch past this sacred sphere which he administered in the steady, reverent pursuit of profits. As one bottler explained at a congressional hearing several years ago, "If Atlanta said the moon came up backwards, it came up backwards." As above, so below. The divine king who set the heavens in order ruled the realm with a benevolent touch, and the subjects became a fat and contented lot.

The 1970s was the decade when this happy balance of forces began to buckle seriously—not enough to make the subjects ever doubt the age-old validity of their heritage, since far too many of them were too wealthy for that—but enough to start questioning whether that heritage applied anymore, and whether, in fact, it wasn't being used by the parent companies as a smokescreen in a master plan that would make them—the loyal subjects—its principal victims.

The independent bottler reflects the pride and plight of the small businessman. His common sense is still his principal weapon in the computer age; his dedicated service in a limited, local market must bend to economic pressures to consolidate into ever larger territories; and his desire for standardization has been virtually uprooted by an endless proliferation of products and packages. To keep pace with these changes, he has made large commitments of capital only to be challenged by medical or scientific research, environmental actions, and a constantly shifting climate of government regulations. Compounded by the already stiff competition, the problems he faces are every bit as big as the profits he makes.

This age of complexity seems to go back at least to the sudden proliferation of new brands back in the late fifties and early sixties. The introduction of Sprite, Tab, and Fanta on the Coke side and Teem, Diet Pepsi, and Mountain Dew in the Pepsi line all came within a two- or three-year span. Of course, a bottler wasn't legally bound to make the necessary investment in equipment to take on these brands, but the parent companies made no attempt to hide their firm disapproval of one who didn't. Far worse, however, was the bottler who elected to take on, say, a Dr Pepper or a Seven-Up. Those who went against the grain were threatened with a variety of sanctions. Meanwhile, the companies each came out with a bevy of "Mickey-Mouse" flavors—Coke's Mello Yello and Sugar Bush, Pepsi's Aspen, Tropic Surf, and Skandi—to keep the bottlers in tow.

Meanwhile, plant expansion and tremendous capital outlays have produced arsenals of bottler hardware—washers, rinsers, carbonating and cooling equipment, cappers, decappers, refrigeration, case washers, bottle and can warmers, syrup mixing systems, boilers, liquid sugar production equipment, as well as coding, inspection, and water treatment equipment. Product diversification created a slew of distribution problems, including out-of-stock conditions on the routes and in the stores, rationing of products, and a high proportion of undelivered goods.

For years, the many advantages bottlers enjoyed over distributors of other food products lay in direct store delivery. More than simply supplying the actual labor of moving the crates onto the premises, this service assured the retailer and bottler that his display and promotional material were properly arranged. Even more important from the bottler's point of view, it ensured his receiving the maximum shelf space or "facings," which the retailer allocated to his products. Shelf space is a top priority and the bottom line to a bottler. A stroll down the soft-drink aisle of any supermarket quickly reveals that a product with forty facings has much more visibility than one with twenty-five. Supermarkets recognize soft drinks as products that draw customers, spur impulse sales, and deliver remarkably high profit margins. The shelf space will always be there for soft drinks, but how it gets divided up among brands is the whole ballgame for the bottler. Even more valuable to the bottler are the huge end-aisle displays of brightly colored scaffold units on which the goods are stacked. Some of these, such as the "Power Tower," exhibit the soft drink with snack foods and other related items in a modular display of massive proportions.

The competition for these end-aisle spots and for total shelf space frequently amounts to all-out war. "In some stores," claims a spokesman for an Erie, Pennsylvania bottling firm, "shelf space goes for so much a foot. The deals are being negotiated with buyers" as well as store owners who are looking for the best deal in a strong buyer's market. A bigger market weapon in the battle are discounts. They take many forms—coupons, off-invoice (immediate price drop), allowances for window and display advertising, free goods with purchase, and so on. Discounts are an aspect of pricing so common in recent years that management consultants, writers, editors, and the bottlers themselves have begun to protest their counterproductive effects. Certainly discounts increase volume, market visibility (including shelf space) and perhaps even market share, but they have been so flagrantly overused that many bottlers are finding out that they are leaders in their territories only because they are all but giving the product away.

"This thing has gotten so ridiculous" a major cola bottler told *Leisure Beverage Insider,* an industry newsletter, in mid-1979. "So a couple of months ago I personally decided to study the situation in our own plant. I carefully checked the printouts on special prices for one month. Good Lord! The total was . . . . well, I'm ashamed to admit how much. But I will say that it was over $100,000. And that was a slow-selling month." (His annual volume was about five million cases.) "So I told my sales manager that he had let this thing get away from him. He wasn't watching it; he and the route managers were taking the easy way out and just discounting everybody." Was this bottler one of those made negligent by too many fat years? He later discovered that in eighteen out of twenty markets, his staff had been giving discounts to tiny two- and three-store chains that didn't even have room for his displays.

This bottler was undoubtedly typical of a whole group of discounters who believe that by dropping price in a whirlwind of wheeling and dealing with the retailers, they can garner a bigger share of the market, which will eventually lead to higher profits. Not so, say the more fiscally minded bottlers, who see the necessity in making a larger margin per case, and are willing to sell fewer cases to do it. They see the push for ever higher market share as a red herring for those who can't afford excessive discounting but still fall into the trap of trying to play like the big boys. Coke bottlers are especially well known in taking their cue from the top, and more than a few have earned reputations as "share mongers" willing to give up profits in a given territory just to see the competition squirm.

Regardless of how they compute that bottom line, many bottlers in the last year or two have come away from their ledger books livid and confused, complaining universally that the discounting rage is a "killer" in their markets. Some are reportedly discussing the matter with their competitors, reminiscent of a much earlier time when rival families, bickering in a territory, settled matters with a minimum of bloodshed—if possible. "We all agree that the situation has got to be brought down to a reasonable level," admits a bottler, "but no one wants to be the first one to start." One who did vowed that, having shed himself of sin, he *would* cast the first stone should the strategy fail. "We've cut way back on discounting and rebates. . . . We're taking a beating, sure. And we may have to go through a bloodbath to stop this thing. . . . I swear I'll drop all my prices and gut the hell out of them. We have the top shares of the market with our three leading labels. . . . We can play the game as rough as it is necessary to put this market back on a normal competitive level."

The battle between Big Coke and Big Pepsi (these appellations widely used in *Leisure Beverage Insider* conveniently distinguish the parent companies from their franchisees) was thus fought in the trenches by their shock troops on the front lines: the bottlers. The combat was not literally hand-to-hand, as it was, say, in the bottle-smashing episodes between Coke and Pepsi bottlers in Venezuela, but neither was it schoolyard play. "We're dominated in our market by what the Coke bottler does," said one bottler. "His prices are too low and he hasn't raised them in a year." Elsewhere, a Coke bottler blames the aggressive efforts of the local Pepsi bottler to increase his share of the take-home market.

Elemental as these sentiments are, bottlers on both sides of the struggle faced a common enemy in the retailers. "Discounting's always bad here," explained a Midwestern Coke bottler. "In our market, the stores take the best deal or we're not in the stores, and then sell our products even lower, as loss leaders.* The dealers aren't making their normal profit here, and neither are the bottlers. That's how deep it is." Elsewhere, explains a bottler, "The stores play us against each other, get the best deal, but don't pass it on to the customers. They put our products at high prices and their own [private label brands] at much below cost. But when the government and consumer advocates bellyache about soaring food costs, the retailers blame the brand-name suppliers, and point out how they are giving the consumers a break with their labels." And to make matters even tougher on the bottlers, the chains are increasingly dictating when they can deliver, down to the day and even the hour.

This pressure from the chains is rooted in the simple fact that they are doubling as retailers *and* competitors marketing their own private label soft drinks. This two-edged attack affords them the freedom to play either role, but often as not they seem to be the competitor. This unfortunate position is underscored by the insistence by some chains that the bottlers deliver their product to the chain's warehouse which will, in turn, distribute the product to the individual branch stores. They allege that, in addition to relieving the problem of congestion, warehousing cuts delivery costs and makes distribution more efficient by

---

* Heavily discounted items used to lure customers into a store on the probability that they will make other purchases while there.

achieving quick saturation. Just as quickly, the bottlers point out, this saturation gives way to a decline in sales and diminishing market shares. Many bottlers had to watch in frustration as store delivery, with its careful attention to detail surrounding shelf arrangement, passed into the hands of those who placed no real priority on seeing that the empty shelves were promptly and properly filled. The resulting loss of sales for the traditionally profitable brands led many bottlers to conclude angrily that the chains are being deliberate in their negligence. Said one prominent editor in the beverage field: "By and large, supermarket managements are so stupid, they wouldn't be able to put a key in a keyhole if it hit them in the face. Soft drinks are a very, very high profit margin product for the supermarkets, and they do everything possible to louse up the sales."

The product and equipment proliferation over the last two decades has spawned corresponding advances in packaging. Coke's diversification from its classic six-and-a-half-ounce bottle represented a departure from the gospel espoused by Woodruff and other Coke leaders. The first change, though the hardest for them, was only the beginning for the bottlers. For example, cans had arrived in the mid-fifties, to become the preferred container by the late seventies, surpassing returnable bottles in 1977 with over 23.3 billion twelve-ounce equivalents, or 36.8 percent of the market. Vending machine sales played a large part in this strong showing. Convenience packaging costs, and consumers are apparently willing to foot the bill when they can afford it. In making a major commitment to the can, a bottler must reckon with the fact that it is basically a single-serving container, and thus could suffer as volume in soft-drink packaging shifts toward larger, multiple-serving containers.

The bottler is thus supplied with a great many options that he must consider, because his competition is inevitably doing so. And it doesn't stop with primary packaging—bottles and cans—but continues into the coating used on the bottles, the closures, the seals, and then into secondary and tertiary packaging, including paper wraps, paper basket carriers, plastic carriers, plastic film (especially for wrapping large bottles), corrugated containers, paperboard, and on and on. Economy and efficiency have taken their place along with attractive unique design as the principal preoccupations of a latter-day bottler, whose apprenticeship lies in the mastery of certain industry truths.

For instance, packaging itself is a very powerful form of advertising which helps identify the product in the marketplace. Though they generate sales for new products, packaging innovations are often used to keep a dying product alive by catering to carefully researched consumer preferences in packaging. For example, Big Pepsi's 1972 reorganization involved a shift away from new product programs to new packaging programs since most of its new products in recent years, like Skandi and Tropic Surf, were virtual failures. Packaged goods experts brought in by Pepsi president John Sculley presided over an avalanche of some forty different packages and helped trigger innovations which led directly to improvement in its share of the take-home market. There is plenty of evidence that consumers have very strong loyalties to a particular kind of package which often surpass their loyalties to a particular brand. "Future consumer packages," wrote Frost and Sullivan, a New York-based marketing research outfit, "will be used as a market segmentation tool, becoming the means to create effective brand identification and give superior product positioning by type and pricing." To implement this future, the parent companies and the marketing departments of the various packaging concerns offer no end of advice and advertising to the franchisees. Even Big Pepsi acknowledged, however, that the proliferation of sizes, prices, and promotions caused some confusion among national accounts that dealt with different bottlers. "You don't market soft drinks anymore, the way we used to, as a refreshing product of quality to enjoy, to share. You market price and packages."

These attitudes are echoed in the retail sector. Said a buyer for a major statewide chain: "The number of bottle sizes, plus the cans and wraparounds coming in and out of the store is a big problem—we have too much variety . . ." Even more than product proliferation, the package boom is a kind of Rube Goldberg bubble conveyor—a highly imaginative, technologically superior maze of designs that does more and more about less and less. The buyer continued: "If all the bottlers agreed to reduce the number of packages across the board . . . the customer wouldn't miss some of the sizes we're offering now."

This buyer was from Maine, one of six states with a mandatory deposit law on all beverage containers. With the debate over mandatory deposit laws commanding headlines in dozens of states and talk of a federal bottling bill already underway, his comments articulate a vital current of industry thought on the economics of convenience packaging. *Leisure Beverage Insider* reports that at the Texas Soft-Drink Convention in San Antonio in early February 1977, a powerfully proreturnable advocate was given a platform, perhaps for the first time ever at a gathering of major bottlers. It belonged to a Royal Crown bottler from Corpus Christi as well as president of the national nonprofit group, Crusade for a Cleaner Environment. His multiplant operation had been surpassing his goal of 10 percent return on investment throughout the years he was arguing the flaws of the convenience packaging, and his fellow Texas bottlers did not confuse his environmental concerns with his or their business priorities as they listened to him speak.

"Is the so-called convenience package really the most convenient package in which to deliver our product to our customers while we're telling those same customers not to throw the non-returnable bottle and can into the trash but to . . . somehow recycle it?

Can anyone think of any merchandise you buy where you pay 40 percent of your purchase price for the package? Try to think of this 40 percent as though you paid $6 for a necktie and $4 for the tie box. Or $100 for a new suit and $40 for the suitbox. Sounds ridiculous, doesn't it? But that's what we as an industry have done to our customers. Stop and think about the fact that we are paying as bottlers 201 percent more for a case of 24 ten-ounce NR [non-returnable] bottles than we pay for the ingredients that we put in that case. Then ask yourself, who's being ridiculous?

He had few expectations about converting many of his audience to returnables, but he was also well aware that many of them were once just as hostile to
the one-way beverage containers. A 1962 article in *Bottling Industry* (now
known as *Beverage Industry*) spoke with alarm about the "developing cancer" of
one-ways and their introduction into a major southern California supermarket
chain. "The largest part by far . . . of the bottler's total investment . . . is tied up
with the returnable package." Outlining a whole program to save the deposit
business, the article highlighted the importance—indeed "the moral obligation"—of giving consumers the choice between the cheaper returnables and the
higher-priced convenience packaging.

Of course, the convenience package soon was king, but not necessarily because of any clear choice the consumers made. After the can had been around
several years, the supermarket chains found that there was a definite, though not
necessarily large, segment of the market that wanted a no-deposit, no-return container equipped with its own closure (no accessory for opening). That segment
didn't care about the closure rings tearing off or the telltale, metallic aftertaste
resulting from improper coatings inside the can, or any of the other problems
cans caused at that time. Seeing their opening, the chains quickly put their entire stock of private label brands into cans, and with the cost of the package
brought down by volume, just as quickly grabbed nearly a fifth of the market.
Coke and Pepsi got into the act, but the bottlers couldn't achieve the store
brands' efficiencies until the birth of the coop canning plants. The parent companies didn't really push the bottlers toward nonreturnables until they developed a formula for a reduced-weight glass package. Free of the returnable's extra
bulk, which it needed to withstand the physical punishment of multiple fillings,
the nonreturnable bottle was also an alternative to the can's bad aftertaste. Big
Coke and Big Pepsi now had the tools to take back what the private label brands
had taken away, and they tirelessly promoted the package across huge segments
of the market still very much at home with the returnables. It had nothing to do
with the consumer, said one executive from Owens-Illinois, a major packaging
manufacturer. "It's all in the internal workings of the intermediate market. The
consumer didn't want a can. They liked the convenience, but they didn't want a
can."

The conquest of convenience packaging thus had less to do with any clear
consumer preference than it did with the internal competition between the retailers and the soda makers. After the introduction of the can, bottlers were
more and more in the business of distributing prepackaged products shipped
from centralized plants farther and farther from their operations. An inexorable
shift in orientation from servicing to pricing had begun.

Despite this massive commitment to a primarily one-way system, convenience
packaging is, says our Texas bottler, more expensive than a returnable system,
just as it was when it was first introduced. His feelings were reiterated even more
strongly by a major Pepsi bottler from the mid-Atlantic region who commissioned some highly detailed studies by Charles River Associates and Franklin

Associates, two leading East Coast economic consultants. Based on the studies and other evidence, the bottler asserts that the returnable package far exceeds the economic efficiency of the nonreturnable. In fact, the studies conclude that even a wholly inefficient bottler dealing in returnables is more economically viable than the most efficient users of the one-way package, a finding allegedly confirmed by Sanford C. Bernstein and Company, a leading Wall Street investment firm. The bottler also asserts that, outside the East Coast, the returnable package accounts for more than half of all food store sales of Coke and Pepsi and nearly three-fourths of the promotional dollars spent by food stores to advertise soft-drink packaging.

J. Paul Austin himself admits that the returnable system would work flawlessly if everyone would return the containers, but this unfortunately requires a massive turnabout in habits that Coke and Pepsi encouraged. The predicament has led to hotly contested legislation for mandatory deposits from Maine to California. A whole array of powerful interests are lined up on the convenience side, including the wholesalers and big beer distributors, the major packaging firms and their trade associations, such as the Can Manufacturing Institute (CMI), the Glass Packaging Institute, and the Packaging Institute, USA. In 1977, these groups marshaled well over $4 million in "war chest" lobbying funds to fight deposit bills and referenda nationwide. Another vocal element in these debates was organized labor, which held that the tremendous loss in skilled jobs, such as glassblowers, would hardly be offset by the projected net gain in unskilled jobs.

These coalitions moved ahead vigorously to ward off passage of bills similar to those passed in Maine, Vermont, Iowa, Oregon, and Connecticut. Contentions that such bills were ineffective in controlling litter were difficult to defend, since Maine reported a container return rate of 90 percent while Vermont, Michigan, and Oregon came in at about 70 percent. In Michigan, there was a 41 percent decline in roadside litter during the first year of the legislation, and an 82 percent drop in litter from discarded beverage containers. Meanwhile, in many states, lobbyists were heavily behind privately financed anti-litter campaigns as a substitute for the proposed bottle bill legislation, yet Washington, among other states, was contemplating passage of a deposit law despite its model litter law and a $27 million, thousand-job recycling industry. After rejecting a bottle bill for several years running, the Massachusetts legislature narrowly passed one only to have it vetoed by Governor Ed King, despite two separate studies by cabinet secretaries which indicated that passage of a bottle bill would eliminate 75 percent of the state's can and bottle litter while reducing beverage costs and creating new jobs.

Nevertheless, Massachusetts was one of the states where political patronage and industry efforts paid off handsomely. In vetoing the bill, King downplayed the importance of his cabinet reports in favor of industry worries that the bill might raise prices, solve only a portion of the litter problem, and displace highly paid skilled workers. King's own aides agreed with the supporters of the bill that the action catered to the business-labor coalition which had put him in office.

Said one aide of the governor's veto, "I think his mind was made up the day he was elected."

A similar situation apparently existed in New York where Governor Carey was chided by bottle bill supporters for his solicitude for the beverage industry, whose lobbyist contradicted reports from bottlers in Oregon and Vermont when he wrote on the Op Ed page of *The New York Times* that the programs in these states were "dismal failures." Partly because of the war chests, New York and Massachuetts are among the few northern states well organized on the political front.

A third is Ohio, whose war chest of $1,650,000 contributed to a 72 to 28 percent plurality in favor of the industry position, the widest margin for a citizen initiative in the state's history. In addition to support from big labor, the highly organized campaign owed much of its success to the efforts of Hamerof and Milenthal, an advertising agency retained by the industry, whose first move was to undertake a complete study of the flaws in the Michigan campaign. Systematic polling programs located the strongholds of consumer support for the bottling bill, and those groups were effectively targeted by the ad campaign.

Action on a federal bottle bill has been contemplated with great hesitation in recent years. A 1975 Commerce Department study found that national legislation should not be enacted. "Benefits of the law could be much smaller while adverse impacts could be much more severe."

However, at a 90 percent bottle return rate—the best so far achieved in any state—the national energy saving eventually would amount to the equivalent of twenty-four million barrels of oil annually. Opponents argue that the law could curtail the search for less energy-intensive methods of package manufacture. The study did project a gain of between 95,000 and 115,000 unskilled jobs against a loss of 82,000 skilled jobs. The study's prediction of higher beverage prices received particular attention from a 1979 cabinet-level committee. The Environmental Protection Agency projected a lower shelf price for returnables while the industry-oriented Can Manufacturing Institute presented trends in the other direction in some states where the deposit law had already been enacted. In the end, the committee told President Carter it did not think a nationwide ban on throwaways was a good idea "because of uncertain impacts on prices and labor."

Even in the face of the huge investment necessary to convert back to returnables—one source puts the industry total at over $700 million—the small bottlers seem to share a widespread faith in the economic viability of the returnable. "Wherever container deposits have become law," reported *Leisure Beverage Insider* in late 1977, "bottlers in the areas eventually admit that profits have never been so good." One poll showed that 54 percent of the bottlers favored using returnables. A major father-son bottling chain with two Pepsi franchises has put together an expansive slide show promoting the returnable package while General Cinema, the largest independent Pepsi franchisee, commented in a recent study that 35 to 40 percent of its business was in returnables, a proportion it would like to maintain. More recent reports of big losses in the wake of bottle-bill legislation have, in many cases, been attributed to the old bugaboo of the bottler set—bad management. That is, before the deposit law was enacted, the franchises were poorly run by managers who refused to believe the law would ever pass, and criticized it endlessly when it did. "But," concluded the *Insider*, "the high level corporate studies never touch on this particular subject—even though it is common gossip in beverage and packaging circles in Oregon, Iowa, and Michigan, in particular.* Michigan consumers were reportedly far less perturbed by the legislation than the industry, many of whose hardships were avoided in Iowa. There, the franchise companies were better prepared, forming cooperative collection ventures with retailers and beer distributors that allowed them all to stay out of the garbage business and concentrate on selling their products.

As a result, sales in Iowa held steady in the wake of the bill's enactment while price increases there were far less than the 19 percent hike reported in Michigan. That state's higher prices reportedly had more to do with price wars and discounts among franchises owned by the parent companies or major conglomerates. As of early 1979, the experience of other states with deposit legislation, including Maine and Vermont, was more in line with that of Iowa than Michigan. According to the Can Manufacturing Institute, the average national price for a six-pack of cans was identical between states with and without a deposit law while the average price for bottles was about 10 percent higher in the deposit law states.

Coke and Pepsi have tempered their opposition to deposit legislation by backing statewide clean-up programs and research into recycling at the municipal level. PepsiCo has long been a supporter of the Washington-based National Center for Resource Recovery (NCRR), a non-profit corporation devoted to coordinating the efforts of industry, labor, and government in dealing with the mounting problem of solid waste. Kendall served as chairman of the board from NCRR's inception until early 1976, and has since remained a director along with John Ogden, president of Coke-USA. The worthy goal of cost-effective operations of municipal resource recovery plants is still five to ten years off, according to a senior project director of NCRR. In the meantime, any workable effort to recover packaging materials will have to involve the consumer in some fashion. Though they focus on only part of the overall problem, bottle bills do provide consumers with a decisive economic incentive to return empties and thereby stimulate a local recycling industry. But since the early seventies, the returnable question has been colored by an even greater uncertainty which, depending on its outcome, could alter forever the fundamental way business is conducted in the soft-drink industry. It has caused some strains in the bottler-parent relationship, prompted others that were already there to surface, and highlighted some of the seamier practices going on in all sectors of the industry.

On July 15, 1971, the Federal Trade Commission issued a complaint against

* *Leisure Beverage Insider*, August 13, 1979, p. 3

the Coca-Cola Company, PepsiCo, and five other major soft-drink makers alleging that the industry's time-honored use of exclusive territorial franchises restrained competition in violation of the Federal Trade Commission Act. It wasn't enough, the commission asserted, that Coke bottlers competed with Pepsi bottlers within a given territory. An exclusive territory still allowed bottlers to peg their prices at artificially high levels, which cost the consumers an estimated $1.5 billion annually. Not surprisingly, the industry bared its teeth at charges against a system that had been in use since the nineteenth century, and Coke and Pepsi led the effort in marshalling a response. Momentum in the turbulent case has shifted to and fro several times over the years, and the legislative and court battles stemming from it will carry on well into the eighties. Congress was hearing from Coke and its bottlers within a few weeks after the suit was filed. In fact, according to former Senator Fred Harris (D-Okla.), even before the FTC complaints were formally issued the company launched an intense lobbying campaign aimed at the Congress. With some nine hundred local bottlers at the time, Coke had more than enough voices to cover every congressional district. Through the Coca-Cola Bottlers Assn., the company raised a $280,000 "Franchise Defense Fund" from its bottlers to pay lawyers and lobbyists like Earl Kintner, who represented the National Soft-Drink Assn in this case. Kintner had been head of the FTC under Eisenhower, a fact which prompted congressional criticism among those suspect of the all-too frequent sweetheart arrangements in which top-ranking figures of the regulatory agencies slide back and forth from government to industry.

Coke's insistence that it was "not engaged in any sort of lobbying," while perhaps technically true, could not erase the impression of an overwhelming presence. The Coca-Cola Bottlers Assn. circulated a set of sample form letters for the bottlers to use in contacting their congressmen. One read:

> My Company is the Coca-Cola Bottling Company of _____. It is now owned by me and my father and prior to that was owned by his father. We are the main busines in the town of _____. We have a total of _____ employees, including _____ driver-salesmen. . . .

By early 1972, the FTC had received inquiries from over half the offices on Capitol Hill, some having contacted the commission more than half a dozen times with complaints from hometown bottlers. According to one FTC staffer, congressmen were calling from their districts during Christmas recess before having to face the local constituents. Another top figure at the FTC added, "We've had more letters than I've ever seen" while an aide in the Senate agreed. "This is the finest job of lobbying I've ever seen."

The upshot of the effort was a move toward legislative intervention which would, in effect, have granted the soft-drink industry a special antitrust exemption regardless of any conclusions the FTC might reach. The bill moved through committees in the Senate in the spring of 1973, gathering strength from

45 sponsors in that chamber as well as 175 in the House. Even staunch supporters of the pro-competition stances, such as Philip Hart (D-Mich.), chairman of the Senate's Anti-trust and Monopoly Subcommittee, gave up, since defying the bill meant bucking the overwhelming lobbying effort.

Other officials outside the legislative firing line were not swayed by the industry's claims. The Justice Department's Anti-Trust Division opposed the measure, saying its proponents must "show special and clearly convincing circumstances" which would entitle them to antitrust immunity. The assistant attorney general agreed as did the American Bar Association Antitrust Section. In a letter to Philip Hart, the section stressed that promoting competition is national policy and that those seeking exemptions bear a heavy burden to demonstrate the need for them. In the eyes of the ABA, the record did not justify the granting of congressional immunity.

Nevertheless, in June 1973, the Senate Judiciary Committee approved the bill and sent it to the floor with the lone negative vote cast by Edward Kennedy. The bill never became law, and through 1975 and 1976, action shifted to the House Judiciary Committee, which recommended passage of a similar bill with an amendment that delayed effective date of the measure until the FTC completed its investigation. This was a setback for the industry, since it defeated one of the central purposes of going to the Congress in the first place. The bill provided that the exclusive territories "shall not be deemed unlawful, per se," but that each case should be examined individually on whether it constituted restraint of trade. The bill died in committee, and two years later, in April 1978, the FTC submitted its final decision, upholding the original charges.

"We will fight this unjust and illogical decision with all the resources at our command," bellowed Pepsi's president John Sculley. "I have instructed our attorneys to work around the clock to prepare an immediate appeal." With characteristic reserve, Austin intoned Coke's intention of going to the Supreme Court, where recent developments have suggested that the case will probably be decided.

The complexity of the issues at stake was surpassed only by the enormity of the bottlers' financial and emotional investment. The fact that they were not formally named as respondents in the case hardly mattered. Many of them testified right alongside Big Coke and Big Pepsi, and their stake in the outcome was self-evident. Many of the small and medium-sized bottlers reacted to the decision in anger, fear, resentment, and disappointment. After all, this was the soft-drink business—full of a whole array of brands, every one of them competitive down to the last case, with every tenth of a point in the market share earned—and here was the government telling them they weren't competitive enough, and unveiling some of the more common business and pricing arrangements to make its case. Principal among these was "piggybacking," or carrying brands of several manufacturers. The practice is so common that the FTC found that "all brands of carbonated beverages are produced by one, two, or three bottlers in an area." The competition is thus really "between a small number of firms—an oligopoly—rather than between a number of brands. Piggybacking permits a bottler to control the pricing and marketing strategies for each piggybacked brand. . . . If a Coca-Cola bottler who piggybacks Dr Pepper finds that his price on a Dr Pepper promotion is cutting too deeply into his Coca-Cola sale, he may find it in his interest to raise the price of Dr Pepper rather than lower the price of Coca-Cola."

Anticipating the entry of Dr Pepper into the New York market, the Coke bottler there elected to piggyback Dr Pepper because "We would rather compete with ourselves than have somebody else compete with us." With a Coke or a Pepsi as his primary brand, said the FTC, a bottler would not price his piggy-backed brand to cut into the sale of the primary brand. Piggybacking increases the concentration of brands controlled by the strongest bottler in a given territory. More than restricting intrabrand competition, the exclusivity of that territory shields him from interbrand competition outside that territory. For instance, Pepsi sells more cheaply in the Washington, D.C. suburb of Warrenton, Va. than it did in the city. Because of the territorial exclusivity, the Warrenton Pepsi bottler is prohibited from selling in the city so that the Washington Coca-Cola bottler is protected from competition as well. A Coke bottler from the company-owned operation in Baltimore added, that without the territorial walls, "I think . . . that pricing would be more active than it ever has been. I think that it would mean that . . . to be competitive, and to get the business . . . we would be forced to reduce our price to the principal customers." The FTC concluded that this downward pressure on Coke prices would enhance interbrand competition throughout the industry because, according to the testimony of many bottlers, these other products were all in some measure competing with Coke.

"Dr Pepper," the drink's ads once proclaimed, "so misunderstood," but never so much as the bottlers were in the FTC's report. Written by one of the most pro-consumer members of the commission, Elizabeth Dole, wife of Republican Senator Robert Dole, much of it seemed to contribute, at least inadvertently, to the stereotypical perception still lurking about of the complacent bottler whose inefficient management skills became inbred over generations of protection from a true, free market. One bottler who observed the FTC hearings closely held that the commission quoted panelists accurately, but "used portions completely out of context." He indicated that answers were not "taken in the spirit in which they were given—with total honesty." In their bitterness, it was small comfort to the majority of bottlers that the FTC was mandated to protect the consumer from what it deemed anticompetitive practices, whether among the large bottlers in the major cities or the moderate-sized ones in the outlying suburbs. (The tiny rural bottler had no qualms either way—he was protected by geography.) Still the reaction was to take it personally. As one observer noted, "FTC wants to break up conglomerations by getting rid of the small guy." The commission acknowledged that protecting small firms from competition with big firms was not one of its priorities, but it did try to point out some of the possible advantages of its decision for the small bottler. Territorial restrictions may well have kept the small bottler small; whatever discounts or promotions he might offer, his success was limited by geographical boundaries. The FTC reasoned that since there were some small bottlers in the past who had been able to compete with large multiplant operations in their exclusive territories, certainly the same would apply to others after territorial restraints had been removed. For many, this argument had the empty ring of rhetoric; others, however, had learned from their own experience that perhaps there was hope in the new arrangement.

They were known with some opprobrium as bootleggers, and the name was not undeserved. They apparently confirmed the FTC's charges by their uncanny ability to haul dozens of cases of soft drinks up to a thousand miles and still undersell the local bottler in his protected franchise territory. A head of a northern California chain of convenience stores recently admitted that he purchased virtually 100 percent of the Pepsi and a good deal of the Coke sold in his stores over a period of two years from bootlegged product from as far away as Colorado and Missouri. Often, he paid as much as $1.25 less per case than if he had bought it from the local bottler, a saving of anywhere from 15 to 25 percent. As the chain store owner explained in congressional testimony, this wide price differential was made possible partially because the cost of store delivering a case of soft drinks on the franchise-owned trucks ranged from 25 to 900 percent more than the cost of delivering that same case from a grocery wholesale warehouse. (One dollar and eighty-two cents vs. twenty cents in 1974.)*

In New York and Los Angeles, cases of canned Coke and Pepsi can be obtained from sources as much as three hundred miles away. New York City in particular has been a hotbed of dumped Coke products hauled in on trailers by local beer wholesalers and sold at bargain prices in "beverage-barn" outlets on Long Island. In a sense, this is prima facie evidence that open territories would allow consumers to purchase soft drinks at a price below what currently exists in many areas. The bottling community is not optimistic that this set of circumstances would remain for long, since the road that runs into these major franchises, with their superior resources, also runs out.

Still, at least one bottler on the West Coast caused Coke great concern in the early seventies by standing up for what he saw as his right to bootleg like the big boys. For years, shipment of beverages across franchise lines was a commonly accepted occurrence, especially in southern California where some of the big supermarket chains insisted that the product be delivered to their warehouses. Though often located in the territory franchised to Coca-Cola of Los Angeles (Coke-LA), the warehouse would ship the soft drinks off to outlying branch stores in territories outside that of Coke-LA. Testifying before one of the early Senate hearings on the franchise legislation, Arthur MacDonald, board chairman of Los Angeles Coca-Cola Bottling Co., said that the long-standing practice

* U.S. Congress, House Committee on Interstate and Foreign Commerce, *Exclusive Territorial Franchise Act*, Hearings, 93rd Congress, 2nd Session, 1974, p. 854–6

included a rebate on each case shipped to the bottler in whose territory it had been delivered. He neglected to say that the arrangement worked smoothly for years until 1967 when Coke-LA terminated the payments to at least one of the bottlers because "developments in antitrust laws" appeared to invalidate exclusive territories, and therefore, the rebate agreement resulting from them. The shipments continued uninterrupted into the territory of a bottler who was soon to act on his belief that they could flow just as well into the Los Angeles territory.

W. Pope Foster owned and operated a tiny, three-man Coke franchise in Taft, California, located between Bakersfield and Los Angeles. In the early seventies, Foster was barely able to make ends meet and was under increasing pressure from Big Coke to sell out, when he received an order for thousands of cases of Coke from a big L.A. chain for delivery to its new warehouse in Taft. The order would allow him to make a decent profit, and still undersell Coke-LA. Foster saw the order as the beginning of a permanent relationship which could finance the development of plant and permit him to stay in business for years to come. But when he placed his first order for enough syrup to make fifty thousand cases, he immediately heard from Atlanta that the order would not be filled, and he was being placed on a strict syrup ration. The stated reason was that he was buying product in excess of the needs of his market for resale outside his territory. Seeing that Big Coke did nothing to stop the big bottlers from doing precisely the same thing, he decided to see a lawyer. A lengthy lawsuit resulted which was eventually settled out of court based on an agreement requiring that no one would discuss the details of the settlement.*

For Foster, the suit was an ordeal. As he told the Senate subcommittee:

> I think I mentioned that my father is ninety-eight years old and has been schooled in the Coca-Cola business. Anything and everything that Coca-Cola has said, he has never questioned it. . . . As soon as my lawyers contacted the Coca-Cola Company, I began to receive phone calls and visits from officials of the Coke bottlers association, from other neighboring bottlers, and even from a distant cousin I haven't heard from in twenty-five years who is a large Coke bottler back in Alabama.
>
> All of them told me basically the same thing: "Don't rock the boat, you're going to ruin it for all of us," or "What are you doing? You're disgracing the family name." The pressure was heavy but I resisted. After all, none of them suggested they would help solve my problems—they only wanted to stop me from upsetting their own apple carts." (State Health Department officials who hadn't been to Taft in years suddenly started showing up at Foster's plant.) ". . . maybe it was just a coincidence that they suddenly began making trips to Taft to inspect my plant, turn around and leave town again. It seemed that if I didn't go out of business voluntar-

---

*Coke does not like to air *any* of its dirty laundry—ever. It is a top corporate priority reflected, say some keen industry observers, in the company's willingness to pay exorbitant severance fees to dissident bottlers or disgruntled employees in return for one simple concession: a permanent and loyal silence on all sensitive aspects of company policy during their tenure.

ily, every means possible was going to be used to force me to close down or sell
out. . . . For years, I was petrified that the big boys would take it over. And the big
boys are taking it over.*

Foster had stood up to Coke and won—in a way—and though other bottlers
over the years would taunt the big franchises with similar tactics, the majority of
them did not aspire to such brazen heroics. Besides, they saw their oppression
coming from other quarters—Big Government—and who was better able to understand the plight of the misunderstood bottler than the parent? Didn't Coke
and Pepsi react with righteous, instantaneous anger at the announcement of the
FTC decision, firing off press releases and filing an appeal within hours? Didn't
Pepsi's Sculley show an equal amount of compassion in sending off a videotape
to 350 bottlers that counseled and reassured them in their moment of crisis?
Accordingly, many bottlers found that they didn't need to feel as angry, fearful,
or contemptuous as some of their peers were feeling. Big Coke and Big Pepsi
were venting those emotions on their behalf.

"It's my feeling," said a Southern bottler, "and along with a lot of bottlers I
talked to in Atlanta, that the parent companies need those of us who are left if
they want to go on getting those good annual growth figures. In the old days,
family-owned plants were working hard and digging out more cases and selling
more concentrate than the conglomerates can. When you're big business and
you have to reach way out, maybe seventy-five miles out, you just skim the potential. But local bottlers dig out those extra cases and that's where the real
strength of this industry lies. . . . I believe the big guys know this and that's why
they'll fight for our system."

Indeed they did. Throughout the congressional hearings on antitrust exemption, Big Coke and Big Pepsi dubbed the legislation a "small bottler bill," and
tried to explain how the basic laws of economics would act in the open marketplace in the absence of the franchised territories: the small bottlers would be
undersold, driven out of business, or swallowed whole in a rash of predatory acquisitions. Once the competition was gone, the once deflated prices would rise
to unprecedented levels, with the end result that a law intended to heighten
competition and lower prices would have done neither while wiping out the lifetime investment of a whole breed of small entrepreneurs.

It was a compelling argument which Congress kept coming close to endorsing
in the legislation, but always held back. They would pass a bill, then attach an
amendment requiring a case-by-case analysis, halting its implementation pending further review. As much economic sense as the argument made, there was an
unsettling, haunting reality in the companies' portrayal of what was in store, a
sense of certainty strong enough to make it seem that what they predicted had
already come to pass.

Buried without much discussion in the record of the congressional hearings

---

* U.S. Congress, Senate Committee on the Judiciary, *Exclusive Territorial Allocation Legislation*, Hearings, 92nd Congress, 2nd Session, 1973, Pt. 1, p. 104–21

were figures presented by the FTC which charted a trend well known to every-one in the soft-drink industry. Signaled by the declining numbers of bottlers—from 5,200 in 1947 to 2,300 in 1970—the trend revealed that "the small bottlers were going out of business because of economic forces that would not be aided by the antitrust exemption." Congressman John Sieberling (D-Oh) noted that forces intrinsic to the industry, including territorial franchises, were result-ing in the elimination of the small bottler through acquisitions. But he accepted industry concern over the small bottler at face value. Accordingly, he proposed an amendment to the 1976 legislation before the House that the antitrust ex-emption be applied *only* to small businessmen by limiting the protection to bottlers with annual sales of less than $10 million. Anticipating the opposition, Sieberling declared, "The big bottlers would not like this . . . but if we're really talking about protecting small businesses, this would do it." Sieberling's amend-ment did not meet with much acceptance, but increasingly perceptions began to build that perhaps the small bottlers weren't the uppermost consideration they were so diligently made out to be. This was a powerful and painful insight. For example, one of the first bottlers with this view was not a Coke bottler at all, but a competitor with the company-owned franchise in Chicago. A.J. Canfield & Co., a local soft-drink concern, filed suit against Big Coke charging that, for a period of one year, Coca-Cola of Chicago sold Coke at a price lower than the cost of making the product, thus forcing Canfield either to sell its product below cost or to lose its share of the market. Alleging the practice of predatory pricing, which violates antitrust law, Canfield sought triple damages for its losses during that year, as well as an injunction against Coke to cease its drastic underselling. Denying any knowledge of the suit to the *Wall Street Journal*, J. William Pruett, Coke's vice-president for public relations, added ". . . [pricing below cost] wouldn't be a sensible way to operate." However, the use of the practice was confirmed in the FTC report by John Ogden, executive vice-president of Coca-Cola USA. Ogden indicated that the company had operated its Chicago subsidi-ary at a loss for several years ". . . believing that leadership in a market ultimately moves to a profitable position."* This admission did not secure Canfield's case, since the bottler needed to prove Big Coke's intent was to drive Canfield out of business, but it aroused a groundswell of uncertainty in the bottling community over the parent companies' real motives in fighting the Federal Trade Commis-sion.

Doubts persisted in the wake of price wars instigated by the companies in the territories they owned. Bottlers hesitant to look malevolently at the intention of the franchisers still saw themselves caught in the old vise between Coke and Pepsi's struggle for control of the take-home market which was waged by blitz-ing a territory and subsidizing the loss. A landmark Wisconsin law that controls "Soda Water Trade Practices" was brought about by the underselling of local

---

* Though some of the bottlers were repelled by this practice, the FTC found nothing wrong in it, since the evidence also suggested that independent bottlers are also capable of operating at a loss.

bottlers as well as the excessive "footballing" (or dumping of product) by some of the giant syrup makers from their Chicago plants into Wisconsin. One bottler said in 1978, "If this cola war is showing concern for the franchise system and protecting the small bottler, which the big bottlers say is the main point of the legislation, give me the FTC. At least they make no bones about wanting to wipe us out. They are not saying one thing and doing another as the parent companies are."

Such sentiments would probably never have crossed a bottler's lips any time before the seventies but the sudden and powerful concern over protecting the bottler from the unfair competitive advantage of the parents' subsidiaries was addressed directly by the FTC (primarily as a result of requests by intervenors, the equivalent of friends of the court). The commission ordered relief in two related areas pertaining to confidential information:

> . . . during routine quality control inspections of bottling plants, respondents [the parent companies] can obtain access to the type of information which may reflect the innovations and methods a bottler may employ to reduce his production-line or plant costs, or increase his competitive potential.
>
> In addition, a bottler must obtain the Coca-Cola's approval before using new, previously unauthorized types of packaging, and as the record amply demonstrates, packaging decisions in this industry can be a vital aspect of a bottler's marketing strategy. The Coca-Cola Company would have advance knowledge of, and the right to approve, new packaging innovations and, unlike its independent bottlers, could begin to react to a bottler's innovation before it was actually introduced into the market.

The FTC final order prohibited disclosure of such information to Coca-Cola employees involved in the production and sale of finished beverages.

The sudden, powerful, and unprecedented alarm the bottlers felt toward the parent companies necessitated more in their eyes than the measures offered by the FTC. Six months before the FTC order was even issued, there was an undercurrent of support for a bill sponsored by Senator Gaylord Nelson, Wisconsin's celebrated small-business advocate. It called simply for divestiture by all the soft-drink manufacturers of their company-owned bottling plants. One bottler who headed a sprawling, multistate operation that showcased several national brands explained the conviction behind such legislation. "Without accusing anybody of wrongdoing, abuses in a highly competitive commodity business is one way of controlling the marketplace."* He was not alone in seeing those abuses arising from an accelerated vertical integration of bottling facilities which, he observed, was a highly unusual trend in any industry with as many small units of business as were still left in soft drinks. "I guess we don't have to

---

* *Leisure Beverage Insider*, October 10, 1977

argue over whether or not we're losing producers. We used to be seven thousand strong and now we're under three thousand. . . . If you believe in free enterprise in any case, the investment of multiple units of small ownership is a hell of a lot better for our economy than the concentration typical of the pattern in our industry."

The bottlers were beginning to distrust the parent companies' idealization of them as the classic embodiments of entrepreneurial individualism, and ironically, were beginning to look on the parents with a skepticism toward concentrated wealth that was once a hallmark of the American national character. The bottlers suspected the companies of ulterior motives concerning the inexorable consolidation of territories into larger and larger markets. Pope Foster had been among the first bottlers in the early seventies to sound the alarm of a master plan at Coke, reportedly admitted to him by former Coke president J. Lucian Smith, whereby the entire country was to be served by a total of seventy-eight territories, each administered by a huge, centralized production center.* (Former Coke vice-president Richard Harvey once commented that, according to studies done by Coke, the company would divide the country into thirty-two parts if no franchises existed.) In early 1978, a few top soft-drink executives were reported as admitting that it might help not to have franchised bottlers in some markets.† One obviously embittered independent said later that year that consolidation charts are "common interior decoration" at all the major soft-drink companies. More and more Pepsi bottlers have joined the ranks of their Coke colleagues in the conviction that the companies would battle the FTC only until they could achieve consolidation of the marketplace. Far from being done in the name of the small bottler, the preservation of the territorial franchise system was a priority: it would allow Big Coke and Big Pepsi to control the continual attrition in the ranks of the independents providing them in the process with ever greater leverage.

This scenario of what the companies intended to do if the territories survive bears a haunting resemblance to the picture *they* painted for Congress of what would happen without the territories. The companies were thus practicing a devilishly clever piece of sorcery. By dressing up reality in hypothetical clothes, they attempted to assure themselves that "what's past is prologue; what to come, in . . . [their] discharge."

In refusing to accept this portrait painted by the disenchanted independents, many other bottlers behaved as loyal apprentices to their sorcerers' scheme, and appeared by their parents' side to testify in these matters. No doubt, the presence of these independent bottlers weighed heavily on the Congress, and contributed to whatever spell was cast by the sophistry of Big Coke.

Just where the chips lay became more apparent with the Interbrand Competition Act (S. 598), the industry's latest proposed antitrust exemption legislation which held that the whole question of intrabrand competition between bottlers

---

* *Exclusive Territorial Allocation Legislation*, op. cit., p. 106 and 111
† *Leisure Beverage Insider*, February 11, 1978

was irrelevant. Competition between brands was the crux of the issue. A Capitol Hill attorney, an aide to Senator Howard Metzenbaum (D-Oh) who opposed the measure, indicated that since only four parent companies controlled over 50 percent of the syrup volume, a level generally considered to be the threshold where oligopolistic pricing practices emerge, "you begin with the proposition that even under the standard view, you don't have interbrand competition here." A Justice Department brief adds that the legal standards of the current legislation before the House Committee are so weak that they immunize territorial exclusivity "even where a bottler enjoys a near monopoly of sales in the territory so long as some other product is 'generally available.' "

The status of S. 598 and companion bills in the House is critical to the industry which is making an all-out effort for passage in 1980. "You can only bring up an issue so many times before it gets doomed to death by the fact that it's been around so long," one Washington source commented to the *Insider*. The 1980 presidential campaign, the Salt Treaty, the Iranian crisis, and the collapse of detente are all potentially devastating to lingering legislation. The Washington observer continued, "The industry now is at its maximum strength in Congress, so if they don't get the legislation through the 96th Congress, they probably won't be able to do it again."

The parent companies are not alone in their lust to acquire bottling franchises. In fact, they are relative latecomers to a very active merger and acquisition market that first blossomed back in the early sixties as superhighways, faster trucks, and improved technology made the territories scaled to the horse-and-buggy days obsolete. Bottlers holding contiguous territories began to merge in the hope of improving efficiency and cutting costs. Experienced bottlers confident of their know-how and eager to add volume set out to create chain operations. Coke-LA's Arthur MacDonald, a veteran of thirty-two years in the soft-drink business, dreamed of merging all the Coke bottlers on his borders, which extended in a radius of some fifty miles from City Hall. None of them was interested, and so MacDonald acquired bottlers in Fresno and Santa Barbara, California, as well as Las Vegas and Honolulu. His revenues shot from $20 million in 1962 to $45 million six years later.

But this sort of bottler-to-bottler arrangement was overshadowed in the late sixties and early seventies by a dramatic rise in the number of medium-sized conglomerates that bought into the bottling business in a major way. Wometco Enterprises of Miami; RKO General, New York; General Cinema in Boston were three of the big ones, and there were others. Soft drinks showed heavy cash flow and real growth potential in the leisure field, both of which are key criteria in these companies' decision to invest. Wometco was heavily involved in leisure holdings, including broadcasting stations, motion picture theaters, vending machines, and tourist attractions. It owned Coke plants in the United States, Canada, the Bahamas, and acquired the franchise in the Dominican Republic in 1973. General Cinema owned the nation's largest theater chain, and through its acquisitions of Pepsi plants beginning in 1968, became the nation's largest independent Pepsi bottler. In addition to its entertainment and communications holdings, RKO owned nine plants that handled Pepsi, Seven-Up, Dr Pepper, and others.*

These companies were among the first to diversify, and while none of them ever regretted it for a moment, the sugar crunch of 1974 and spiraling packaging costs vastly curtailed new entries and discouraged many from additional expansion. Wometco, a prodigious acquirer of Coke franchises, was no exception. As Philip de Tournillon, a company executive, explained, "Higher prices put a company like Wometco, or any large corporation, in a better bargaining position. We can absorb these higher costs far better than a small, independent bottler can. . . . Because of expansion, adding new equipment, they can't raise the capital and remain competitive. Many would have gone out of business had it not been for the large corporations acquiring them." Managers from virtually every other conglomerate agreed that it was necessary and inevitable for the small bottler to consolidate, and the impressive prices many of the franchises were commanding more than justified one manager's estimate that the small bottler was frequently overpaid by the conglomerate acquiring him.

Indeed, this overpricing of franchises was another factor slowing the conglomerate's entry into bottling in the mid-seventies. Many that had taken the plunge and discovered that they had perhaps laid out too much began to cut corners in unwise ways, especially if they were new at the soft-drink game. Having never before been a bottler's apprentice, they turned to their professional managers and their balance sheets, forgetting that soft drinks are a service industry and the small bottler whom they have just acquired is a tried and true expert in the special techniques of merchandising his products. Then, too, says another soft-drink executive, "Many of these companies have discovered that the soft-drink industry is rather divorced, marketing-wise, from their own concerns. They didn't realize the huge capital dollar expenditures involved in this industry. I mean, it isn't like marketing soap, there's a tremendous amount of advertising and marketing involved."

The late seventies witnessed a renewed wave of acquisitions, led this time by some of the premier conglomerates in this country. One of the reported reasons was a Supreme Court decision in the GTE-Sylvania case which many mistook as a death blow to the FTC's claim against territorial franchises.† The specter of

---

* Other conglomerates, too, participated heavily in the acquisition trend, though not necessarily handling Coke or Pepsi. Westinghouse Electric Corp. of Pittsburgh handled Seven-Up while International Telephone and Telegraph has been a more recent entry into the field with C&C Cola. Food companies have been very much in evidence: Beatrice Foods, Chicago: Royal Crown, Seven-Up, Canada Dry, and Gold Medal; Fairmont Foods, Chattanooga: Double Cola; Beverage Management, Inc., Columbus, Ohio: Seven-Up, Royal Crown, Squirt, Hires, Canada Dry, Frostie, Crush, Vernors, Schweppes, Lipton Iced Tea, Hawaiian Punch; Clorox Company, Oakland, California: Nesbitt.

† The FTC report was issued subsequent to this decision, and specifically addressed its inapplicability to its finding in the soft-drink industry. "The Coca-Cola Company's territorial restriction is a demonstrably more severe restraint on intrabrand competition than the dealer location clause imposed by GTE. GTE designates the location of its retailer dealer outlet, but apparently does not limit the area from which a retailer may draw its customers. The territorial restrictions involved here not only limit the area from which bottlers may solicit customers, they eliminate the retailer's option to do business with the Coca-Cola supplier offering the most competitive deals."

that case had been another recent deterrent to investment, but with the sun shining once again, the leisure-time industry rediscovered anew its natural affinity for soft drinks. Five companies were after the Coke franchises in Salt Lake City and Provo, Utah, but a British company, John Swire & Sons, Ltd., outbid them all and acquired the operations for seventeen times earnings, or 70 percent higher than the usual multiple in these deals. Warner Communications bought up 14 percent of Coke-NY while Twentieth-Century Fox diversified into Coca-Cola Bottling Midwest with a portion of the windfall from its hit movie, *Star Wars*. With its coffers swelling from its blockbuster movie *Jaws*, MCA, the Los Angeles-based entertainment conglomerate, moved in October 1977 to acquire Coke-LA, the second largest Coke bottler in the country, for $140 million. The franchise's management rebelled and sued to block the acquisition. The matter was resolved when Coke-LA agreed to sell out for $200 million to Northwest Industries, a midwestern industrial concern with a consumer subsidiary that imported Cutty Sark scotch, Finlandia vodka, and French wines.

From Atlanta, Big Coke must have watched this transaction with some concern, for the extensive involvement of many of its largest bottlers with major conglomerates could only work at cross purposes with its own priorities. The Interbrand Competition Act is an attempt to protect that priority by removing antitrust challenges to territorial exclusivity arising from any acquisition made by either parent company—provided there is sufficient competition between brands. Coke's recent $64 million purchase of its Atlanta franchise meant that its company-owned subsidiaries now supply about 10 percent of its domestic volume. On the other hand, Pepsi's company-owned bottlers account for nearly 20 percent of its domestic volume, and, says the *Wall Street Journal*, there is every indication that Coke may want to boost its percentage to stay competitive.*

That Coke may well have harbored this intention is attested to by its November 9, 1979 purchase of 1.8 million shares of Coke-NY from Warner Communications. The $14.8 million purchase gave Big Coke a 9.5 percent interest, just below the 10 percent level that would have changed its legal responsibilities as a major shareholder. "That's all they wanted," said a spokesman for Warner, which retained 161,000 of its shares. As the *Wall Street Journal* pointed out, Coca-Cola has no minority position in any other company, and a purchase of Coke-NY stock " 'solely for investment purposes' would be out of character for the Atlanta-based beverage maker. Instead, it may have been a ploy to fend off other companies interested in acquiring Coke of New York, whose depressed share price might make it an attractive takeover target." With operations in the Northeast, New England, and the Midwest, Coke-NY is frequently seen as a strategic arm of Big Coke's often denied long-range domestic consolidation program, and Atlanta would not want to see it go the way of Coke-LA.† ". . . According to a former Coke of New York official familiar with the situation," concluded the *Wall Street Journal*, "Coke of New York's shares have been of

---

* November 9, 1972
† *Leisure Beverage Insider*, May 7, 1979, p. 4

interest to at least three major consumer product companies . . . Coca-Cola may be trying to protect its key bottler."

Whatever the potential antitrust implications of these moves, Big Coke would take comfort in the precedent set a few years before when PepsiCo moved to acquire the Rheingold Corporation, which included a group of Pepsi bottlers even larger than Coke-NY's chain. In May 1964, Pepsi-Cola United Bottlers acquired New York's Rheingold Breweries for $26 million and became known as PUB United Corporation. Rheingold was then the nation's eleventh largest brewery with distribution in ten northeastern states. PUB United changed its name to Rheingold Corporation in 1965 when it claimed to be the largest independent Pepsi-Cola bottler in the world, with plants in Los Angeles, Mexico, Puerto Rico and, later, Florida. In October 1972, PepsiCo stunned the industry when it moved to acquire 51 percent of Rheingold's shares in a tender offer. The *Wall Street Journal* reported that bottlers around the country were puzzled and uneasy that Big Pepsi would undertake a tender offer for one of its own franchise holders, especially since the FTC complaint against the exclusive territories had only recently been issued. "I'm still in shock," said the president of a major Pepsi franchise. "I never thought Pepsi-Cola would raid a bottler." Others echoed the response, but did so anonymously, said the *Journal,* for fear of company reprisals. Rheingold promply filed suit to halt the tender offer and for good measure filed a $2.7 million complaint over alleged price-setting agreements at the Puerto Rico plant. Rheingold management tried to reassure its stockholders, telling them that PepsiCo's move violated a 1968 agreement with the FTC not to acquire any manufacturer or wholesaler of carbonated soft drinks. The agreement allowed Big Pepsi to take over franchised bottlers, but Rheingold claimed that its ownership of Flavette, a Florida soft-drink distributor, constituted a violation of that agreement. Rheingold was relieved when the FTC challenged Big Pepsi's move, but the whole matter was settled a year later when Big Pepsi simply agreed to divest itself of Flavette as well as the company-owned St. Louis bottling operation and to obtain FTC approval before acquiring any concentrate manufacturer or seller for a ten-year period.

In gauging potential antitrust problems connected with their acquisitions, both parent companies seem to be banking on a wide latitude based on the Rheingold precedent as well as anything that might result from pending legislation or the Supreme Court decision on the territories. Many small bottlers indicate that Big Coke and Big Pepsi have a handful of approaches for dealing with the antitrust climate which is obviously very much in flux as the eighties begin. When market and competitive conditions permit, parent companies are buying out available operations to stymie the inroads of outsiders. If they sense raised eyebrows at the Justice Department, they will help the bigger bottling operations make the acquisitions. Realizing that the smallest franchises are takeover targets for big business, they may even add to the market pressures these bottlers are already under to force a merger with a neighboring bottler or chain.*

---

* *Leisure Beverage Insider,* May 23, 1977; June 26, 1978

Bottlers who have pieced all this together started to meet quietly in early 1978 for counseling and strategy sessions. Both independents and conglomerate-owned, small and not-so-small, they have begun gradually to come to grips with a difficult situation. For some, the outside acquisitions are not so problematic. "But," said a large independent, "when we're faced, as bottlers are, with the dual distribution and dual profit structure of a highly integrated enterprise like Coca-Cola or PepsiCo, we've got problems. . . . If a bottler gives any kind of hang about his equity position in the industry, he has to know that the territories are a minor issue by contrast to vertical integration.* The new trend in thinking was: how can I protect my franchise from the sharks in my own industry?

One obvious measure was to be wary of too many private meetings between majority stockholders, especially if a bottler is sandwiched between two big territories. Another answer for many was a surprisingly elementary, concrete, but far-reaching return to square one of the bottling trade: returnables. Increasingly, bottlers began to see them as a major first step toward regaining a real toehold against all the forces closing in on them. Because of the need to pick up the empties, returnables greatly limited the distance between the bottler and retail outlets that can be serviced by any one bottling operation. Therefore, all the footballing and product dumping from far-away territories as well as other unfair trade practices and the sheer clout of the parent or unfriendly conglomerates could all, in some measure, be contained by the reintroduction of returnables. The FTC certainly rethought the issue in its opinion, since it ruled that any bottler who elected to use returnables would be entitled to territorial exemption for that portion of his trade, primarily because of the unavoidable chaos in trying to sort out the economic inefficiency and the rightful owner of the bottles in an unrestricted territory. There is some evidence, however, that the FTC's exemption for returnable bottles would do nothing to alleviate this chaos, and that the so-called "split-delivery" system, which would award territorial exclusivity to a portion of a bottler's trade, is unfeasible. The greatest fear among some proponents of returnables is that if the territories are ruled illegal, the returnable bottle will perish because of economic forces. Mandatory deposit legislation without the territories, they say, will simply result in spiraling costs and declining service to the consumer.

For example, the supermarket chains would no longer have to buy the big-name brands on a take-it-or-leave-it basis. It would become a buyer's market, serviced by a variety of sellers who would put a greater emphasis on delivery through the chains' warehouses instead of directly into the store. With the proliferation of private labels, the chain warehouses would be the center of action, and they would have less incentive to accept returnables unless the one-way had been outlawed.

Returnables aside, the end of exclusive territories would force the bottlers to operate more and more on a purely price basis, especially as they confront a continuing proliferation of private labels which constantly undercut the name

---

* ibid., October 10, 1977

brands like Coke and Pepsi. The change is part of shifting demographics. Even if the "graying" of the soft-drink market of the late sixties proves true, and the young consumers of those years take their habits with them into middle age, the industry still faces a declining population growth and thus a shrinking domestic market. Pricing can be the name of the game in the midst of a squeeze where growth in earnings is no longer coming from an expanding market or increased per capita consumption. Against this background, the bottlers' final crisis of the seventies emerges.

In May 1978, Coke bottlers were up in arms over Big Coke's proposed amendment to the hallowed, fifty-eight-year-old franchise agreement that, in addition to granting the exclusive territory "in perpetuity," had also fixed the price of Coca-Cola syrup, except for periodic fluctuations on the price of sugar. The move was supposedly prompted by economic considerations, several of which were credible in the bottlers' eyes, yet even these were offset by their own grievances. Introduced by Big Coke brass during a national bottlers' meeting in Atlanta, the proposed change would allow Coke to adjust the syrup price at will. Big Coke said it needed pricing flexibility to enhance the advertising and promotion of the brand. Industry sources like *Beverage Industry* were quick to point out that the company's domestic advertising expenditures in 1977 exceeded those in 1976 by a mere .3 percent and were only a fraction of what was spent on international advertising. Coke barely outspent Pepsi in domestic advertising of its premier brand—$19.1 million vs. $18.1 million—yet its domestic profits were substantial and overall earnings at a record height. The bottlers were unanimously disturbed. Just how much money did Coke intend to allocate to domestic advertising to justify this radical proposal? Nothing in the proposed amendment spelled that out. Moreover, though Coke said it would not change the price of syrup more than once a year, the amendment allowed "unforeseeable circumstances," such as rapid inflation and "unusual economic conditions" as a pretext for more frequent changes. What was an "unusual economic condition"? The amendment was silent on that too.

Coke-NY was demure in its reservations. "We cannot imagine surrendering this vital contractual provision without receiving something substantial in return." Other bottlers were not given to such understatement once assured of total anonymity by *Beverage Industry* and other trade journals. "It's laughable," one bottler said. "How they even have the guts to proceed with this is beyond me." Others noted that Pepsi, Seven-Up, and certain other major franchises maintained flexibility, but their bottlers received a concentrate instead of finished syrup which allowed them to buy sugar (or corn sweeteners) from the nearest source. Coke bottlers, on the other hand, had to pay freight and product charges to Big Coke, which bought the sugar from refiners at discount prices. In many eyes, Big Coke was something of a middleman, with a bit of the monopolist thrown in. "Coke's not in such bad shape," one bottler told *Beverage Industry.* "Their syrup price is based on the published price, but they're the world's largest sugar customer and they've been getting discounts right along and hedging their cost with futures."

An analyst at Drexel-Burnham, the Wall Street investment concern, affirmed that normally there is a difference of about 2 cents per pound between what Coke charges the bottlers and what the bottlers pay. Historically, the price of concentrate was fixed at 88 cents per gallon, and bottlers were charged according to the average price of sugar at the ten largest Northeast refiners during the first ten days of each quarter. In addition, the bottlers paid for 6 pounds of sugar per syrup gallon (which makes 832 ounces of finished product), but were getting only 5.663 pounds. Meanwhile, if Coke could procure its sugar under futures contracts below the quarterly average, it would pocket the difference. If not, it would absorb the loss, but as an analyst at First Boston Corporation suggested, the fact that this practice has been in use for six decades speaks for itself.

Big Coke apparently maintained its handle at the manufacturing end over the years by refusing its bottlers the option of purchasing concentrate rather than the finished syrup. While Pepsi has serviced every one of its domestic bottlers with only three concentrate plants, Coke continued to operate sixteen syrup plants despite the possibility that it could serve all of its bottlers with one concentrate plant located in Chicago. The system, said one bottler, was "a ridiculous extra cost that they've built into the system. . . . I think they want to maintain the profit they make on sugar." Few could overlook the fact that Coke supplied many of its foreign markets with a concentrate. Domestically, said one bottler, "the Coca-Cola Company wants the privilege of flexible pricing, but retain the sale of sugar."

In the face of such overwhelming opposition, Big Coke saw that it was going to have to make some concessions to bring the big bottlers into line. The amendment contained a clause requiring that bottlers representing 50 percent of Coke's domestic volume were needed before the amendment could go into effect. A handful of the big bottling chains and a couple of major territories could put them over the top, and once the ball was rolling, the holdouts would begin to dwindle. The strategy had many ramifications, including the company's obsession with avoiding any whiff of disharmony in its ranks. As the outcry swelled, Big Coke resolved to settle the matter swiftly, amicably, and far from any courtroom.

Its concession to give the bottlers the right to buy concentrate (by mid-1980, at least five bottlers who signed the proposal were taking advantage of this concession) set the plan in motion.* In addition, *after* the first increase, which amounted to a jump of some 24 percent, price hikes would be tied to changes in the Consumer Price Index. Wometco, one of the larger holdouts put off by the

---

* A second concession was aimed at bottlers who chose to stay with syrup rather than switch to concentrate. Instead of paying for 6 pounds of sugar, they would pay for only the 5.663 pounds that were actually contained in the syrup, and the price would be based on indicators that were more favorable to the bottler than had historically been true. And the company agreed that if another sweetener were to be introduced into Coke, the bottler would realize the saving. In early 1980, this concession took on added importance when Big Coke announced its historic move to substitute up to 50 percent of the sugar in Coca-Cola with a less expensive corn sweetener. (See Chapter 18.) Atlanta hoped that the bottlers' prospective savings on the sweetener would offset enough of its own proposed increases to induce the holdouts to sign.

vagueness of the original proposal, signed with a swan song. "We felt we were married to them, we want to stay on very good terms. They're entitled to some increases. So we went along as good corporate citizens."

Robert Moore, president of Coca-Cola Bottling Midwest, wasn't moved, primarily because Coke's "compromise" still pegged the price of the concentrate to that of finished syrup. "I think the price of concentrate should reflect the actual market condition, and not just be tied to their open pricing clauses for the syrup." As for funds to enhance advertising, Moore's initial reaction was typical of that of some of the larger bottlers Big Coke needed. "If they can sell their hardship theory they can sell the Brooklyn Bridge ten times over. Honest to God, we just can't buy their hardship story. . . . They have a lot of problems, but it's not money."

Big Coke's concessions weren't entirely accepted as such, and its cries of loss didn't jibe with the figures in the profit column, which hit another record in 1978. Atlanta responded to the resistance by trying to show bottlers what to expect for their cooperation. Measured advertising expenditures for all brands during the first nine months of 1978 exceeded Pepsi's by 36.7 percent, $51 million to $37.3 million. This was a 46.5 percent increase over the same period in 1977. Across the Coca-Cola bottling community however, the attitude was still reserved: give them extra funds for a couple of years and see what they can do with it in the advertising. But modify the sacred franchise agreement itself? The proposal seemed far more drastic than the stated reason justified, and suggested to the more sober observers that Atlanta was using the marketing fund problem as a discreet means of avoiding public airing of the more serious problem of a long-range profits crunch. "What Coke sees," said one industry source, "is not a continuation of a rate of industry growth in the 6 to 7 percent range. But more likely a rate of growth from here on out of maybe 5 percent this year, if the industry is lucky, though more in the 3, even 2.5 percent range." With inflation on top of that, "Coca-Cola sees that they are going to have to go for profits instead of unit growth. But they can't see an increased profit per syrup gallon sold unless they have the pricing flexibility."*

Some of the bottlers who sympathized with the view from Atlanta signed the proposal, saying in the same breath, though, that the solution wasn't to give a blank check to Big Coke. Others already suffering from the problems Atlanta was only anticipating feared that pricing flexibility foreshadowed part of a lengthy profits-growth crunch, and, as such, was part of the much-rumored long-range trend toward vertical integration.

These ruminations were colored by the pivotal role of Coke-NY in the year-long spat over the contract amendment. Its chairman, Charles Millard, was rumored to be among the firmest and most vocal opponents of the amendment. Nearly a year had passed since the bottlers met in Atlanta where the amendment was first broached, and here was Coke-NY's president, Ed Reilly, attending an

---

* *Leisure Beverage Insider,* June 12, 1978

Easter week solidarity meeting for the nearly one hundred holdouts in Chicago. Word was passing through the industry that Big Coke executives were on a deadline "to get this thing straightened out by the end of April." So Coke-NY was offered a break of some 58 cents in the ceiling they would be charged for the syrup price excluding the sweetener, which was then reduced from the proposed $1.675 to $1.095. With that offer, Coke-NY signed on April 17, 1979 followed promptly by indications that another major bottler, Coke-United, in Birmingham, would also sign. Although Atlanta was hoping to use the bigs to sway the smalls, it was relying a great deal on artful negotiation, and had a huge advantage since the bottlers were almost totally unorganized as a group. Collective bargaining simply played no part in their strategy, so that each bottler had to go head-to-head against Big Coke in its contractural negotiations. "We do know they're scurrying around the country, really working like little beavers, trying to round up the troops," said one bottler of Atlanta's approach. "They're not sparing the horses. The very top brass are making these calls on a one-to-one basis. That gets pretty hard for some bottlers to resist. They don't want to be remembered as the last guy to sign the amendment." Big Coke brass could play on that frailty and offer all kinds of options and incentives surrounding the basic lure of more promotion in the market. Enhanced advertising was the prime rationale given by the company for flexible pricing, but the degree of enhancement could vary from bottler to bottler depending on certain concessions (with the upper limit keyed to increases in the Consumer Price Index). With those kinds of stakes, said a bottler, "it takes a lot of fortitude to hang in there against a three-billion-dollar corporation."

The signing of Coke-NY misled many in investment circles to believe that the big money and the smart money were one and the same. Atlanta denied that 50 percent of the bottlers were holdouts, a rumor one bottler described as "the second best-kept secret in Atlanta—after the Coca-Cola formula." A Wall Street eager to celebrate the healing of this divided house hurriedly embraced speculation that the holdouts, which still included hundreds of plants around the country, would be rushing forward to sign. After all, Coke-NY was a massive, highly influential chain, which only a year before had reportedly offered to buy up every Coke franchise in Colorado. But many of these old-boy bottlers and family franchises refused to sign the pricing proposal, viewing the new contract as one more stark indication of how their position has eroded at the hands of the parent company. Moreover, in its haste to fondle once again one of the bluest chips in its history, the financial community neglected to read the shock running through the major bottlers in the industry, since there apparently had been at least an informal agreement among the big, publicly held Coke bottlers to hold out.

Wall Street, in fact, represented a different and in many ways opposing pressure on the parent companies to that exerted by the bottlers and the public. The bottlers' effort was geared to increasing business by offering the lowest feasible prices. The parent companies, on the other hand, seek to make their respective stocks more attractive with reports of higher revenues, bigger dividends, greater earnings, or, when these are in short supply, with the kind of short-run news that portends favorable figures in the future. Such reports might include promises to increase network advertising time, surrogate numbers on spiraling syrup gallonage or rising market share. Yet such measures amount to mere hedging in comparison with the unique, decisive price increase undertaken by Big Coke. Wall Street applauded Atlanta's move since it would pick up the action on Coca-Cola stock, especially because of the guarantee that the increased revenues were to be invested in marketing and advertising. Sources close to the soft-drink industry told *Leisure Beverage Insider* that "this puts pressure on Pepsi to sweeten *their* Wall Street image in the same way."

Aside from the effect of this price increase on its stock, Pepsi's rumored decision to raise its concentrate price some 17 percent was predicated on some of the same pressures that had prompted Coke, especially in the area of marketing. During the summer of 1979, said one industry observer, "Seven-Up will get a big, big effort behind it, and even the top colas are concerned about this. So I think Pepsi-Cola has no choice but to hike its concentrate price to exert the kind of marketing muscle expected of them in general, and specifically in this coming very, very rough ballgame."

In announcing a less drastic hike of about 15 percent, Purchase perhaps deferred to the heated response from its bottlers. One complained, "That figure [17 percent] is high as hell and unjustified as hell. Some of us heard them say they need more money for additional marketing and advertising, mainly in network TV. They say they can make better buys for us in bulk. Sure. But what they really want is control AND a lot of our money to run back-to-back advertising with all their other divisions" (Pizza Hut, Frito-Lay, Wilson Sporting Goods).

Like parent, like bottler, Pepsi's franchises were uniformly rougher, more physical, more earthy. They lack the apparent deference to Purchase most likely because they lack the hallowed "familyhood" of Coke. Though they undoubtedly love the soft-drink business, it tends to be just another business for them, and a very rough one at that—stripped of the trappings of faith and religious idealism that allows a Coke bottler to be bitter while a Pepsi one will most likely just get angry. "We're not stupid," commented another Pepsi bottler. "We don't want our money tied up like this, under their control. I'd hate to walk away from the coop fund, but. . ." More than their counterparts at Coke, or Seven-Up and Dr Pepper, for that matter, Pepsi bottlers complained about their parent's increased control of coop marketing funds for use on network television. "Network just doesn't get the damned job done . . . locally. It doesn't put the stuff on the shelves and it doesn't put the pop in the consumers' mouths."

Yet the last and most strategic frontier of control and one of the underlying wounds in the contractual squabbles at both companies lies with the fountain syrup, the original form in which soft drinks were marketed. Asa Candler saw nothing particularly promising in bottling. He deeded the rights to the whole country for a dollar that he never collected, and held fast to the fountain as the true marketing channel for his product. The franchise system spread his product so far over the next eighty years that "post-mix" seemed to lose its importance. More recently, however, sheer dissonant politics and dismal economics have left the bottling world wholly disenchanted, and given rise consequently to an eerie streak of archaism where many a bottler has come to value the raw stuff, or the rights to sell it, more fiercely than the finished product in the proud packages to which he has devoted the better part of his life.

Coke, of course, has always had a huge edge over Pepsi in fountain sales, which is one reason why Pepsi has pushed relentlessly in the take-home market since the days of Walter Mack. From its very beginnings, Pepsi gave away the fountain rights just as Candler had given away the bottling rights, and Pepsi's momentous commitment in 1960 to go after Big Coke in the take-home market did little to arouse interest in the fountain sales among the bottlers. When Pepsi succeeded in pulling even with Coke—some sets of figures even indicate that Pepsi has had a slight edge since 1976—Sculley and Kendall turned to the awesome prospect of going up against the giant's strength. To do this, they wanted absolute, centralized control of post-mix rights, and Purchase has thus made it its business to encourage bottlers to return the fountain rights. Having made no investment of time or energy, many did so without a whimper, and were then mobilized to exert pressure on some of their more recalcitrant colleagues with promises of "greater exposure for the trademark," as one bottler put it. That exposure was to come in exactly the kind of market any merchandiser would dream of.

"Saying used to be," said one bottler, " 'find a good location for a popcorn machine and build a movie theater around it.' Now the saying is: 'find a good location for a drink dispenser and build a restaurant around it.' Cold drinks subsidized this huge expansion in the fast-food industry." Kendall and Sculley probably eyed the success Coca-Cola had had with McDonald's and Burger King with a mixture of envy and alarm, but they would have risked spreading their resources too thin had they dropped their onslaught on the take-home market to go after fountains too soon. But once the take-home market was under control, they wasted no time in going full tilt after two major fast-food chains, Taco Bell and the highly successful Pizza Hut, whose owner, Frank Carney, became the second largest PepsiCo stockholder behind Herman Lay in the wake of Big Pepsi's $300 million takeover. "Some of us were lucky enough, visionary enough, that we saw what was going to come," one bottler remarked to *Leisure Beverage Insider* in 1979. "We spent the money to develop fountain sales. And we don't like the idea of the parent company moving in and then having all of us subjected to the directives of the fast-food chains."

The "us" here are the holdouts who are servicing the major fast-food accounts landed by Big Pepsi. The catch is that they are finding that they must serve them in ways that could quite easily make themselves obsolete within a very short time. The fast-food chains want bulk delivery of syrup to their centralized commissaries which will then distribute the syrup to their outlets. Commissary delivery—and total control of fountain syrup—is only a step removed from the appalling prospect of Big Pepsi's ten-thousand-gallon trucks invading the territory, delivering the concentrate directly to the chains, and letting them make the syrup. Such a tack would amount to violation of contract, but there are bottlers who do not put this extreme past Big Pepsi.*

While Pepsi bottlers are busy trying to hang on to their fountain rights, Coke bottlers have been struggling to win them in the midst of the negotiations over the franchise amendment. Big Coke has pushed for the same flexible pricing that exists in the rest of the industry, but they are not ceding the same privilege of making fountain syrup from concentrate which Pepsi bottlers have. In fact, the new amendment explicitly leaves fountain rights totally in the hands of Big Coke. To sell post-mix, a bottler must separately negotiate the right to distribution, and then buy it from Big Coke at parent company price. A veteran of both the cola makers commented, "If the Coca-Cola bottlers let the company get their hands on their original franchise [agreement] and leave them out in the cold on this syrup thing, they are idiots. . . . We all know that the syrup division of Big Coke always has made more than the bottling end, and that's more true today. The two divisions always have been very competitive. The fountain division has always worked hard to take accounts away from the bottlers."

From the assault on the territories to the erosion of the franchise, the bottlers' struggle for survival has turned them inexorably toward the essential substance of their trade. Other old verities like the returnable were exalted, but somehow they only served as a reminder that the better part of the old wisdom didn't have much value in the new world of soft drinks. The chaos left many bitter, searching for recourse, and others confused, blindly reaching for a tether. "We were always an army marching to a single drummer," said one bottler. "But now there are some discordant notes, and part of the army is out of step, going in several directions." Challenged in this climate, Coke apparently undertook a gambit at a bottlers' convention a few years back.

A large gathering of bottlers found itself standing before a soft, dome-shaped, inflatable structure made of a soft, dark material. They slowly entered the dome through a roundish tunnel of the same soft, dark fabric. Inside, it was so low and narrow that they were forced to stoop within a murky space. Suddenly, amid their jokes and whispers, images flashed on the huge, previously unnoticed screens. Shafts of brilliant light pierced the shadows, cacophonous music drowned the shudders. The sights and sounds moved swiftly, and with no period for adjustment, they conveyed sensations aside from pleasure or entertainment. The anxious unease was more pronounced as some began to perspire in a telltale fear. It was a long ten minutes before the darkness returned. Then the lights came up gradually until a brilliant glow centered on a familiar figure standing before them uttering words of cheer and comfort between warnings of mutual threats that assail "all of us if we don't stick together."

---

* *Leisure Beverage Insider*, February 19, 1979, p. 2

In an item entitled "Big Beverages Bend Bottlers' Minds," *Leisure Beverage Insider* pointed out that the smiling, reassuring Big Daddy was the president of "the billion-dollar franchiser." Unconfirmed reports elsewhere in the industry indicate that Coke hatched this "event," which is likely since Pepsi didn't pass the billion-dollar mark until 1976. This happening was a scientifically controlled regression exercise to bind the bottlers closer to the parent company. Similar exercises have occurred in a variety of Big Business concerns where the franchise relationship has been important in facilitating a high degree of vertical control. A variation of a bonding/binding regression technique was employed with a goal similar to that established in intensive individual or group therapies as well as cult groups. Through the use of assaultive sights and sounds, the subjects are "regressed" to a primitive mother-dependent state in which bonding to a loving, reassuring, substitute "parent" is the most natural response. According to one psychologist quoted in the *Insider*, this technique, if improperly used, is an extreme and even dangerous method of psychic persuasion. "Anything that involves taking someone back, way back to the toddler in all of us exposes that individual to terrible risk," including, he adds, psychotic breakdowns.

Even as they integrate their respective operations, the parent companies have marshaled their forces into a Brave New World of Soft Drinks. Those bottlers who saw it coming seemed most repelled, and if they were lucky, found the protection of a friendly conglomerate before succumbing to the corrosive forces of the marketplace. Those who didn't continued as malleable, loyal apprentices of a dying tradition, testifying on the merits of "small-bottler legislation" and the proud traditions of the individual entrepreneur. They were among the few who still saw the world more or less as the old bottlers had seen it, but the record suggests that the Georgia-green glass through which they gazed was really the bottom of an empty bottle. In it, they could see themselves roundly framed in a prophetic image of their destiny in bottling history. It is a work in progress conceivably entitled, "Portrait of a Monopoly as Free-Enterprise System."

CHAPTER TWENTY

The Cola Chronicles

"War doesn't help anybody. It's not even competitive. I wouldn't mind if the consuming public got the benefit. It's the retailer who's making the money. Eventually, when the business goes sour, the non-union and union help will feel the brunt of it. This is an unholy fight."

—*Labor leader, commenting on the impact of the Coke-Pepsi struggle*

IN 1979, AFTER fifty years of churning and yearning in Coke's wake, of suffering through dank old factories that pumped More Bounce into lines of used beer bottles, of fusillades of grinning, giggling advertising, of manic personalities, inscrutable alliances, and a slew of mergers, PepsiCo finally topped the Coca-Cola Company in total corporate sales. That year, PepsiCo's various divisions totalled $5.1 billion in business, $140 million more than Coke. Although Coke's profits at $420 million were still over 50 percent greater than PepsiCo's, the milestone shed once and for all the latter's long-held curse of being one of America's greatest underdogs.

Coca-Cola is still more profitable because of its greater soft drink sales—more Coke alone is sold than all of PepsiCo's soft drinks combined. Yet, here on Coke's turf, Pepsi's dervish-like efforts continue to make inroads, and in some categories, like take-home sales, the Pepsi brand has actually surpassed Coke. Pepsi's market share increased .3 percent in 1979 to 17.9 percent while Coca-Cola's dropped .4 percent to 23.9 percent. PepsiCo's superior performance over the years is a combination of its own persistent aggressiveness and Coke's failures. Caught for two decades between their self-importance and their fears, nervous Coke executives have recently broken into a cold sweat like an icy bottle on a hot summer's day.

Ever since the mid-fifties, when its scrappy rival could no longer be ignored, Coke has often been on the defensive, trapped in the peculiar neurosis of its own hallowed pride. Once too arrogant even to acknowledge other colas, Coke has never become fully accustomed to the pressures of fierce competition. Many were the Cokemen still on duty who longed for the era when Coke reigned as the unchallenged symbol of America's good life. Those dreamy days were long gone, particularly when Nixon took office and ejected Coke from the White House. Atlanta couldn't accept that this "imitator" had risen from bankruptcy to solvency to challenger to threat, then to be the virtual scepter in the king's hand. Even with the arrival of Jimmy Carter, Coke's aggrandized self-perceptions were exaggerated, its mystique sorely damaged.

Coke feigned indifference publicly, but behind closed doors, Pepsi was the unspeakable nemesis that besieged the fair Coke realm. "1980 is the critical year," warned a top-level memo circulated to Coke executives. "Coca-Cola must stop Pepsi's momentum. That means Coke must grow at least as fast as Pepsi." Yet, until Coke can reconcile its inflated ego with the realities of the marketplace, it can at best struggle for parity. "Ten years ago," said John Sculley, president of PepsiCo's domestic operations, "Coke could have clobbered us. Now they're stuck with us for good."

Coke's paranoia became panic in 1975 when PepsiCo introduced a campaign appropriately entitled "The Pepsi Challenge." Purchase discovered that in blind taste tests, slightly more consumers chose Pepsi than Coke. According to the *Wall Street Journal*, the preference for Pepsi resulted from its greater sweetness, but one flavor expert suggested that taste trends over the last twenty years have moved toward the "pepper" type accent characteristic of Pepsi, as opposed to the citrus note in Coca-Cola. (The subtle differences in each drink occur in the flavor base which, according to a veteran chemist of Coca-Cola, comprises an infinitesimal amount of the total drink—perhaps one part in 2,500. The flavor base is where the real romance lies, the realm of "base" notes and "top" notes which are the true art of the flavorist. The exotic lure of Coca-Cola and the mysterious Merchandise 7X, says the chemist, lies not so much in the taste as in the aroma. Flavorists often speak of the "nose" on the cola, and at least one chemist referred to a scientific breakdown of the Coke formula as an analytical problem in perfumery.) Based on the tests, they assembled a campaign touting the preference for Pepsi, and ran it in areas where Pepsi's market share was low, beginning in Dallas (see Chapter 15). Because comparisons tend to help only runners-up, Pepsi's use of comparative advertising was tactically sound, but this campaign was the first in which a major company made superiority claims based on criteria as subjective as taste.

Despite the sting of Pepsi's first strike, virtually everyone was shocked at the quickness and ferocity of Coke's response. Nowhere throughout the cola cosmos was the Coke/Pepsi feud more head-on, more fervid, more destructive than in comparative advertising. Cocky from success—the "Challenge" as much as doubled Pepsi's sales in some markets—Pepsi began to breach conventional wisdom by using comparisons in markets like Michigan where it was ahead of Coke. In New York City, Coke ran ads that claimed New Yorkers prefer Coke over Pepsi 2 to 1. Both companies implemented price-cutting wars, the marketing equivalent of trench warfare, catching other brands and their bottlers in the cross-fire. Pepsi escalated with a full page ad in *The New York Times*. "Truth in advertising is very important to us," read the copy, "and the truth is: Nationwide, more Coca-Cola drinkers prefer Pepsi to Coke."

"We decided to teach Pepsi a lesson," swaggered a Cokeman, but behind the bravado, Atlanta searched desperately for answers. Over Coke's illustrious history, some ads have certainly been better than others, but if the Coca-Cola Company has ever run *bad* advertising, it was its childish overreaction to the

"Pepsi Challenge." When Atlanta found that Pepsi fared well even in its own secretly conducted taste tests, it devised ads boasting that Coke was lighter in calories. In an apples-to-oranges comparison, another asserted that "one third of all consumers prefer Fresca to Pepsi," which allowed for the fact that two-thirds liked Pepsi. "It wasn't that we were trying to get people to switch from Pepsi to Fresca, . . ." a Coke marketing man recalled, "we presented it as a way to weaken the 'Pepsi Challenge.'" "We just laughed at the Fresca ad," said a Pepsi official. "If anything, it encouraged us to press on." In a series of inane spots, Coke tried to ridicule comparative advertising with the notion that "one sip is not enough." One featured a misfit who prefers tennis balls to either Coke or Pepsi because he likes fuzz. Another featured this dialogue after a consumer is asked to sample two glasses of cola: Consumer: "Come from a big city, don't you boy?" Interviewer: "Yes, I do." Consumer: "Thought so. You got one of those skinny little big city mouths. Now look here. Let me tell you something. You can't tell nothing from no test like this. Give me that bottle of Coke. I'll show you how we drink them down here. We don't sit around in no fancy bar taking little bitty sips and wearing skinny britches and pointy lizard shoes. You got to watch what you do down here, boy." Voice-over: "There's more to Coke. Coke adds Life." In another approach, Coke simply bought chunks of simultaneous time on all three networks to obstruct Pepsi. This solution suggests Coke's paranoia, for it was called "Project Mordecai" after the Biblical figure who saved the Jews from a plot to destroy them. Even while Coke floundered over the airwaves, it was still clutching to its antiquated sense of invulnerability. An inhouse movie was specially prepared that showed seven top Coke executives, playing themselves, in a Western-style six-gun shoot-out with the nasty "Big Blue Gang," a group of Pepsi executives. Of course, in their fantasy, the Cokemen were faster on the draw.

The pressure from Purchase had driven Coke from being too aloof to mention Pepsi by name, even within the sanctity of its own headquarters, to referring directly to its competitor in its own advertising. Coke's defensiveness was a sign of the extent of its wounds which perhaps surprised even Pepsi. With the 1976 election around the corner, the political lines had been drawn and Coke was in effect the challenger for the first time. Running on sheer instinct, the confused lion was itching for a fight, and when taunted in Dallas, it blew its Southern cool as never before.

Much of the soft-drink industry was aghast at the Coke/Pepsi slugfest. Choruses of industry representatives warned that such comparative advertising undermines all of advertising's credibility, and bottlers argued that Coke and Pepsi are fighting for each other's customers rather than trying to expand the market. Critics claimed that comparative tests should be used only to compare measurable qualities, and the market leader should never provide free advertising for the competition in its own ads. Yet logic had long been washed away.*

---

* Many saw hope when the National Advertising Division (NAD) of the Council of Better Business Bureaus announced its interest in the soft-drink war, but only a slight modification of current ads resulted rather than an end to the fracas.

Finally, at a National Soft Drink Association meeting in 1976, Donald Keough, president of Coca-Cola's domestic operations, announced to the cheers of participants that Coke was abandoning comparative advertising. Though Atlanta was undoubtedly motivated in large part by industry pressures and the lack of a successful counterattack, Keough called upon the old values and myths to help justify the decision. "Traditionally, we have marketed our products as refreshing good-tasting moments of pleasure befitting the desired lifestyle of consumers of the times," he declared, but cautioned, "We must never forget that the real competition facing soft drinks is first and foremost other types of liquid refreshment." Cooler heads had prevailed at Coke, but only temporarily.

Though unable to find a cogent response to Pepsi's onslaught, Coke soon resumed its counterattack. Its reactions were not so clumsy as before, and Atlanta is apparently relieved the "Challenge" has never been run nationally. Though victorious, Pepsi too has grown more cautious, and has recommended to bottlers that the campaign be used only for its original intent—the regional bolstering of low market share.

Coke's head-on rebuttal of Pepsi's "Challenge" was a gross miscalculation. Atlanta should have fully appreciated that the tests were foreign ground for soft-drink advertising and thus Pepsi, not Coke, was potentially vulnerable. However, by using direct references within its own ads to discredit the comparisons, such as "one sip is not enough," it virtually conceded Pepsi's success. And how could Coke hope to weaken the tests by deploying its own comparisons as it did with the Fresca ad? In effect Coke was playing the game on Pepsi's half of the court. It struggled to keep Pepsi from scoring, forfeiting in the process any offensive opportunities.

Much of the industry's alarm over the comparison battle lay in the fear that it would erode the precious images of both colas, and indirectly all soft drinks. Brand image—the consumer's perceptions of a product—was long recognized as a vital factor in selling soft drinks. While a car can offer better mileage and a detergent more cleaning action, soda ads cannot boast utilitarian values, and consequently must play to consumer emotions. Because of the similarities among soft drinks, image forges an identity that distinguishes a brand from the rest of the pack. Coke has become more preoccupied with brand image because of the traditionally heavy emphasis of its slogans on the product. But determining the most effective image is a difficult, tortuous, multimilliondollar task.

Coke's Archie Lee was a pioneer at crafting images, but Atlanta floundered when it lost his intuitive skill. Coke moved its account to McCann-Erickson in 1955 and soon began to build its advertising upon data collected from vast, ongoing surveys of American consumers. During the sixties, the company sought consumer feedback from focus groups, a common approach in which consumers are gathered to discuss their views. This technique was considered too subjective, and in the early seventies, Atlanta experimented with other methods then in vogue, including teleresearch and day-after recall (DAR).

Teleresearch took place at shopping centers, and involved screening commercials in a trailer to consumers recruited on their way to shop. Following the test, which involved several products, consumers were handed a book of coupons for the products screened. Coupons were also handed out to shoppers who were not shown the ads. At the end of the day, the difference in the number of coupons turned in for the various products by each group purportedly indicated the effectiveness of each product's advertising. DAR was a simpler method, involving phone calls to consumers the day following the airing of an ad to determine their recollection of it. Neither of these techniques was a particularly comprehensive indicator of brand image and whatever value they might have had in measuring impact in the most vital area of all—actual sales—was compromised by the fact that the techniques were applicable only to a campaign already in progress.

By the mid-seventies, Atlanta was seeking a crystal ball with which to predict a campaign's ultimate effectiveness before it invested its fortunes. For all its soul-searching over advertising, Coke seldom lost sight of the industry's consensus that advertising was but one of the factors impacting on sales—powerful but not all-powerful. Because merchandising considerations such as packaging and pricing are also elemental parts of the market-share equation, advertising couldn't be gauged by sales alone. True to its traditions, Coke deemed brand image to be the best indicator of its advertising's powers of persuasion, and to measure it, Atlanta devised its own in-house version of an approach used by many consumer companies and their advertising agencies.

Introduced in 1976, Coke's Quantitative Communications Test (QCT) is a large-scale exercise involving 400 subjects carefully matched into two identical groups. The first is asked to rate various brands on a 1 to 7 scale while the second group is shown the test commercials and then asked the same rating questions as the first group. After adjustments, the differences in scores supposedly reflect each ad's impact on brand image. In the rating questions, brand image is broken down into two sets of indicators. The first rates the product in connection with some of the body's physical responses—taste, thirst, refreshment, and lightness—and the second recognizes advertising's fundamental role as a mediator of social values and behavior. Coke's Roy Stout explains, "Coke and Pepsi's advertising try to get you to want to copy someone else. You want a Coke because you see certain people having a Coke." Thus, the questions reflect the product in social terms like "romantic," "fun," or "friendly."

This genre of "pre-tests" has come under serious fire from the advertising community itself. Detractors point out that the difference in scores between the same commercial tested on two separate occasions can vary as much as that between *any* two commercials selected at random. One frequently mentioned reason for this breakdown is that the artificial "movie-house" conditions under which the ads are tested bear little resemblance to the casual living room atmosphere that prevails during actual viewing. Moreover, the notorious unreliability of "pre-tests" applies *most* acutely to products like soft drinks, whose campaigns revolve almost completely around intangible or highly subjective product characteristics.

Unfettered by these drawbacks, Atlanta claims to have fashioned an accurate combination of these techniques which supplements QCT's "pre-tests" with both DAR and tracking studies that poll consumer image of the brand once the campaign hits the airwaves. The frequency with which an ad is aired is also part of the equation. After using this blend for four years, Coke claims to possess "a perfect predicter of brand image." How does brand image precisely co-relate with sales? That, says Atlanta, is a secret. Determining what brand images will be used in a campaign seems to be a trial-and-error process of seeing what the tracking studies detect as the most positive elements of brand image conveyed from a current campaign.

Pepsi, meanwhile, had an in-house "pre-test" system back in the sixties called Channel One, but apparently has never used it as a basis for major creative decisions. Focus groups have always played a bigger part in Pepsi's approach because of its orientation toward the user and his "problems." Because there is less emphasis on product-oriented slogans, there is less emphasis on measuring brand image. Pepsi's advertising remains largely in the hands of Alan Pottasch, regarded as a "superb advertising man" by Coke's Stout. He sees Pottasch as a figure in the intuitive tradition of Archie Lee and long-time Coke advertising manager Deloney Sledge, who were able to "forecast the weather better than the weather bureau."

However, another reason for Pepsi's avoidance of heavily quantified studies lies in resistance from its advertising agency. Like many agencies, BBD&O balked at the idea of having its work evaluated on the basis of highly quantified and frequently unreliable tests and allegedly threatened to drop the account if Pepsi were ever to go that route. Bill Backer, who had his hands full from time to time with strong-willed ad managers at Coke, adds that "researching image advertising is at best the ability to give educated guesses. It is not a definitive form."

Nonetheless, Coke, like Pepsi, pumped up its ad budget and set out to assuage a troubled nation with soda pop. One evening in May 1976, "Coke adds Life," adorned in a Bicentennial execution, was introduced in a simultaneous half-hour media blitz on all three networks. To complement what was only the fifth primary theme in Coke's history, the company implemented a whole new face lift, its first major overhaul since Project Arden in 1969. The campaign was upbeat during a guardedly hopeful election year and sought to position Coke for "better times." Implemented worldwide by McCann-Erickson, "Coke adds Life" was the first slogan designed to translate literally into any of the over eighty languages in which the Coke logo appears.*

When Coke debuted its campaign, Pepsi was reportedly ready to introduce "Pepsi's got your Taste for Life," but the similarities forced it to be scrapped. Instead, Pepsi returned with "Have a Pepsi Day," which was intended to reflect

---

* Such convertibility was no mean consideration. For example, when translated into Chinese, "Come Alive with Pepsi" read "Pepsi brings your ancestors back from the grave."

EDDIE MACH TAYLOR

DURANGO 1

the consumer's desire to "return to normalcy" after the country's recent upheavals. Described by the company as "joyful" and "positive," it was an extension of the "Pepsi Generation" and "Feelin' Free" themes. The campaign still featured scenarios of idyllic human interaction, including a family reunion, going to summer camp, enjoying an amusement park, and later, frog-jumping contests, frisbee football, and a boy and his first pony.

The pony commercial captured the "Pepsi moment" better than any. The scene is a well-to-do Western ranch somewhere in Big Land, U.S.A. A young boy's father, tall and Marlboro-like, and his mother, attractive though with a certain urbanity, ease their son toward the barn. Under the approving gaze of the ranch hands, the door swings open to reveal his very own pony. The camera focuses in on his beaming face, and in an affirmation of his coming of age, he mounts the horse and rides with the wind. He has just had a "Pepsi day." Said a Pepsi-Cola executive, "Some commercials shoot from the hip—we shoot from the heart."

Of course, Dr. Roy Stout, research director for Coca-Cola, disagrees with this approach, arguing that when a commercial is too much of a tear jerker or soap opera, the product message can be obscured. He claims that Pepsi's pony ad fared poorly on the QCT because it sold ponies rather than Pepsi. Bill Backer was unimpressed with the entire "Have a Pepsi Day" campaign, though he believes it succeeded in part because of the absence of a strongly executed Coke campaign. Like many, he preferred Pepsi's earlier "Live/Give" campaign.

"Coke adds Life," was followed by "Give me a Smile with everything on it, and I'll pass it on," which was recognized as ineffective. With discontent already brewing through Cokedom over the new bottling contract and Coke's uninspired performance, Atlanta ordered McCann-Erickson to engineer a stronger campaign or risk forfeiting the account. In 1979, the agency hurriedly brought its top minds to New York from around the world for a brainstorming session, and what emerged, besides forgettable trinkets like "Grab the World with a Coke," and "The Family of Man is the Family of Coke," was "Have a Coke and a Smile." This campaign, asserted a Coke vice-president, "extends and enhances the 'Coke adds Life' slogan that has now become a part of the American lexicon."

In a rare display of humility, this effort deliberately understated the traditional Coca-Cola promise, apparently because Coke brass believed there was a growing consumer resistance to exaggerated product claims. Though the orientation was still on the product rather than the consumer, offering a smile with your Coke was tame after promising the "Real Thing" or more "Life." "Coke is not going to change your life or make your day," said McCann-Erickson's Scott Miller, who succeeded Bill Backer on the Coke account, "but is a nice little thing you can do for yourself."

To whip up bottler enthusiasm over its new offering, Atlanta held a national meeting in the summer of 1979 to "get the family together again." They met three thousand strong in San Francisco and, sparing no expense, Coke renovated an unused nineteenth-century waterfront structure for its convention, which it later donated to the city. The family received "Have a Coke and a Smile" warmly, though a thirty-second spot nicknamed simply "Kid" stole the show.

"Kid," which stars defensive tackle Mean Joe Greene of the Pittsburgh Steelers, was a radical, one-time departure for Coke in that it featured drama and dialogue, and said Miller, worked toward dissolving the boundary between TV programming and commercials. Mean Joe, a massive but wounded warrior, is limping from the football field down a stadium runway. With his shirt off, baring mighty sinews and shoulder pads that accentuate his already heroic six-foot-four torso, he is silhouetted against the hazy sunshine of the field, pain etched on his face. Cut to a little boy following in awe, clutching a 16-ounce bottle of Coke with both hands. Sensing mighty Joe's discomfort, he offers him his Coke. Joe politely but impatiently refuses. Though Joe and the kid are never in frame together, their relative sizes are skillfully conveyed by upward and downward camera angles. Again, the kid offers him the Coke. Joe pauses and finally gives in to the boy's selfless sincerity. He grabs the bottle and in massive gulps all but inhales half its contents. The boy sighs and then meanders back up the runway, disappointed that the brief exchange has ended. "Hey, kid," Joe cries out to him behind a steel smile, ". . . catch!" Joe takes his game jersey off his shoulder and throws it to the boy. The child is overwhelmed with gratitude and Greene breaks into an even wider grin as "Have a Coke and a Smile" is flashed on the screen. Coke in hand, Mean Joe ain't so mean anymore.

"Kid" was brilliant at a time when McCann-Erickson needed results. Many hailed it as the best television ad of the year, and it ranks among Coke's all-time best performances. It was a well-crafted mini-drama that captured a contrived but highly effective encounter between a child of innocence and a hero cast in Homeric proportions. The commercial was so popular that a lore developed about its production. Reportedly, the ad took twelve hours to film, Greene had to drink eighteen Cokes in the process, and the little boy, a professional actor, kept flubbing his lines because he was genuinely in awe of the football star.

Coke was ecstatic over its aesthetic windfall. Roy Stout claims "Kid" did well in the QCT and was so effective in real life that mothers protested that their little boys raced to the refrigerator for a Coke every time they saw the ad. What saved "Kid" from the over-dramatization that Stout thinks plagues Pepsi's ads was the seven second close-up of Greene actually consuming the product.

In San Francisco, Coke offered visions of things to come. Campaigns have already been conceived for the eighties leading up to 1986, Coke's 100th anniversary. Based on its current advertising expenditures, Coca-Cola should shine nova-bright by then. The Coca-Cola Company's total national advertising budget, as estimated by *Advertising Age*, rose to $138,800,000 in 1978, up 56 percent from the previous year, and its worldwide ad expenditures increased 46 percent to $270,258,000. With the additional revenue from its new bottling contracts, domestic advertising for the Coca-Cola brand alone is estimated to be some $55 million for 1979, double that of just several years ago, but perhaps only half that projected for the eighties.

PepsiCo too has prepared for the eighties. Barely a month into the new decade, Pepsi sponsored a $2 million song and dance extravaganza in Las Vegas to rally its bottlers. Held in the Ziegfeld room of the MGM Grand Hotel, it was the first meeting of the clan since "Have a Pepsi Day" was debuted in 1976. A spectacle worthy of Al Steele and certainly its Las Vegas setting, the evening featured twenty professional performers and a history of Pepsi advertising since the 1930s. At one point, Pepsi president John Sculley, ever exuberant, appeared on stage in a white spangled tuxedo, only to later return clad in a green one, touting himself as president of "the Mountain Dew company."

The real hit of the show was a sixteen-foot replica of Pepsi's newest computerized vending machines which rose dramatically from the floor of the stage to the delight of the swooning bottlers. Jesse Meyers, publisher of *Beverage Industry*, called the evening a "combination of *Kramer vs. Kramer, Chorus Line, Superman, Star Wars*, Monopoly, and a Harvard Business School final in business tactics."

The festivities were staged to introduce the bottlers to Pepsi's advertising vision of the future: "A season of sharing, an era of emotion, relationships, and above all, family," all afloat in Pepsi-Cola. A departure from the "Me" decade of the seventies, Pepsi's commitment to rekindling traditional values is exemplified by its first campaign of the decade—"Catch that Pepsi Spirit. Drink it in!"

If Pepsi's executives were more extroverted than their Atlanta counterparts, so was their advertising. While Coke continues to make its promises, Pepsi continues to resolve consumer problems. Addressing itself in this case to a sense of malaise, the campaign focuses so strongly on the user that "Pepsi" again has been reduced to a mere adjective in the slogan. The ads are characteristically exuberant, their pace frenetic, their jingle spirited, and some executions still sport what Coke's Scott Miller calls "Pepsi's Master Race," caught in effulgent recreation. The campaign was still another extension of the fabulously successful "Pepsi Generation" theme for which Pepsi has spent $345 million over the last eighteen years. It not only remains an essential theme of Pepsi's advertising worldwide, but PepsiCo has licensed a line of Pepsi generation sportswear and offered a Pepsi generation club card which offers discounts to sporting and entertainment events as well as the opportunity to buy special Pepsi generation products like scarves and tote bags.

The competition between Coke and Pepsi extended throughout their respective soft-drink lines. For the eighties, Fresca is scheduled to be revamped with a new taste and packaging graphics. Ads that portrayed Tab as "lighter than light" greatly influenced Pepsi's decision to reformulate Pepsi Light as a citrus-flavored diet drink without any sugar. Diet Pepsi's campaign has evolved from "The taste that's changing the taste of America" to "You're drinking Diet Pepsi and it shows." Oddball Mountain Dew has become, according to a Pepsi official, ". . . a mature member of the soft-drink family." "We took it out of the outhouse and into the outdoors," said John Sculley. With the "Hello Sunshine, Hello Mountain Dew" campaign, sales soared. In 1979, this theme continued with "Reach for the Sun—reach for Mountain Dew," and for 1980, "Taste the Sunshine—

Mountain Dew." Even among the allied brands, neither company would give any quarter in the struggle for supremacy. Several years earlier when Pepsi claimed Mountain Dew was the fastest growing soft drink, Coke countered by claiming the honor belonged to its Sprite.

To compete in Mountain Dew's fast growing citrus-flavored category (not to be confused with lemon-lime drinks such as Sprite and Seven-Up), Schweppes introduced Rondo in 1977 and Coke followed a year later with a shameless imitation of Mountain Dew called Mello Yello. Mello Yello's ad campaign is hardly mellow though, as it abandoned the well-heeled emphasis on lifestyle for a hard sell that exalted brute consumption. The drink was designed with less carbonation and more sugar so it could be swallowed faster than other soft drinks. Coke then targeted those it believed belt down beverages quickly—thirteen- to-nineteen-year-old males from blue collar families—with the promise that Mello Yello is the "world's fastest soft drink." A new series of ads feature athletes dueling each other in Mello Yello speed-drinking contests, and promotional events staged similar competition with the public at selected beach areas during the summer of 1980. By focusing on the literal rate of intake, or in this case, its "chug-a-lugability," Mello Yello is in effect the fast food of soft drinks. This approach is shared by Rondo, whose ads tout: "The soda you can slam down fast," and "Rondo. The Thirst Crusher." Their strategy exemplifies the contrived lengths to which the soda makers will go to put a new face on consumption.

In 1972, Coke had introduced Mr. Pibb, recognized in the industry as a brazen imitation of the rapidly growing Dr Pepper, which was already distributed by scores of Coca-Cola bottlers.* Coke's goal was, of course, to woo its bottlers away from Dr Pepper with its own cherry cola, but the bizarre "Dr"-"Mr." nomenclature is suggestive of the famous Robert Louis Stevenson story where the tormented Dr. Jekyll turns into the predatory Mr. Hyde. Was Coke dropping some grossly inadvertent hint in choosing the name for this brand? Dr Pepper and Mr. Pibb—one "so misunderstood," the other something of a malingerer perennially lurking near the bottom of Coke's market share ratings with some ads that stressed that it isn't a "root beer" or a "cola," without saying what it is.

These drinks were but a conspicuous instance of the syndrome of "me-too" products running through every level of the soft-drink industry. A source at one of Coke's outside consulting firms and a veteran of the food industry indicated that Coke excelled at this game of product duplication primarily because of its superior marketing machinery, which simply eroded the competitor's share.

Coke's inability to grow as fast as PepsiCo was also the result of conservative

---

* With 6.6 percent of the market in 1979, Dr Pepper was fourth behind Seven-Up. Its biggest problem was the public perception that it contained prune juice and was therefore a laxative. "Get it from the horse's mouth," said W. W. Clements, the company's president, "there is no prune juice in Dr Pepper." To counter this impression, the company successfully ran campaigns that touted Dr Pepper as first "America's Most Misunderstood Soft Drink," and then "The Most Original Soft Drink Ever." Later, it urged consumers to "Be a Pepper."

corporate policies. Atlanta's acquisition program was more restrained than Purchase's, even though the former was renowned for its vast liquid assets. Over the years, Coke sat on its wealth while PepsiCo greatly expanded into lines of profitable businesses, enabling it to grow at a quicker rate than the rest of the soft-drink industry. Thus, some observers were surprised when, in 1977, Coke decided to turn its energies to, for Coke, a dramatically new business—wines. That year, Coke outbid PepsiCo and several other companies for Taylor Wines of New York, a $96 million concern.

Known for its New York State wines and Great Western champagne, Taylor had been in business since 1880, six years longer than Coke, and by 1976, ranked sixth among domestic wineries with 3.5 percent of the market. In eyeing Coke's resources and marketing prowess, the editor of an industry newsletter declared, "I see the entry of Coca-Cola as the most important marketing development of the industry's history."

The Coca-Cola Company got its start on cocaine, made its mark with caffeine, and now was reaching for alcohol. A break with Coke's tradition as a wholesome and upstanding alternative to spirits,* the Taylor acquisition was all part of a "master plan." Said Al Killeen, head of the wine division, "We want to be the Great American Wine Company."

But there were obstacles to national popularity. New York wines, such as Taylor, were accepted generally in the East, while California wines were preferred out West, particularly in the Golden State which consumed 25 percent of the country's total. To solve the problem, Coke first bought two respected California winemakers, Sterling Vineyards and Monterey Vineyards, and then began to market these wines as well as Taylor's under the California Cellars label. The strategy was brilliant. "Getting Taylor and California on the same label was a merchandising master stroke," said one wine producer. "In the East and Midwest, it will be seen as the best of both worlds." Coke's roster now had a national appeal as well as regional favorites.

Having found the marketing hybrid, Coke now had to publicize it. Since California Cellars were newcomers, Coke turned to the same ferocious advertising strategy which Pepsi had used against it. It asked twenty-seven wine afficianados to compare its wines with those of its major California competitors—Almaden, Inglenook, Sebastian, and C. K. Mondavi. Sure enough, its wines were generally preferred, and in 1978, it implemented a $1.5 million introductory campaign based on the results.

With its competitive instincts finely honed after some abuses from Pepsi, Coke went in for the kill, jolting the entire wine industry in the process. Prior to Coke's arrival, competition within the industry had been crisp but gentlemanly and high-minded. With the introduction of Taylor California Cellars, some manufacturers resented what they perceived as a bastardization of the industry's

---

* The company forsook some of its religious heritage to the consternation of several Methodist and Southern Baptist shareholders who threatened to sell their holdings if the wine deal went through.

viticultural integrity. No one, however, was prepared for the steamrolling taste tests that followed. One rival insisted the ads were "wholly inappropriate to the wine business." Another warned that the campaign heralded an "era of laundry bleach and detergent advertising." A third complained that the campaign "shoots the camaraderie of the industry all to hell."

Despite the controversy, Coke's gambit worked. "The ads made Taylor California Cellars a known brand in the California wine market," noted one company executive. Sales went up and observers expect the long-term effects to be a greater demand for wine and increased advertising efforts by the rest of the industry. When asked about the fairness of the campaign, the Wine Spectrum marketing director responded: "We clearly demonstrate the superiority of our product; the response is fear of the unknown and untried. Losers always complain about fairness issues." In effect, what was anathema for Coke's soft-drink business was fine for peddling its wines.

Thus, with fangs bared, Coca-Cola leapt upon an entire industry and sent it into retreat in much the same fashion as it did with the orange juice business seventeen years before. "The wine business is evolving from an agricultural production orientation to a marketing orientation," said Killeen with a touch of understatement. "We at Coca-Cola are comfortable in this evolutionary process. We have been through it before."

Since the total business of the Coca-Cola Company alone was equal to that of the entire wine industry, the Wine Spectrum will not impact significantly on Coke's books for some time to come. Its acquisition was consistent with the company's strategy to diversify cautiously, primarily into beverages. With the acquisition of the Belmont Spring Water Co. in 1969, and now Taylor, Coca-Cola runs a gamut of consumer liquid intake—from water and fruit juices to soft drinks, coffee, tea, wines, and champagnes. The exceptions included milk, hard liquors, beer, and mineral water.

Aside from Aqua-Chem, its largest subsidiary, and Cleaver-Brooks, the nation's leading supplier of steam and hot water generators, Coca-Cola is not likely to stray far from its consumer orientation. In 1978, its food division, which featured Minute Maid, still the leading citrus brand in the U.S., boasted of some $600 million in sales, which it will increase by expanding into Europe and Latin America to take advantage of higher growth opportunities.

PepsiCo meanwhile blossomed more rapidly through acquisitions. In 1978, its non-beverage sales accounted for over 60 percent of its total sales compared to less than a quarter for Coke. Frito-Lay was the premier division with sales since the 1965 merger increasing over 600 percent to $1.2 billion in 1978. Showing no signs of slowing down, it has already grabbed 35 percent of the $5 billion snack food business.

From 38 plants, a computer-scheduled truck fleet ships the products to thousands of retailers nationwide which are then serviced by an army of 7,200 salespersons who average 700,000 calls a week. The U.S. Army should deploy its troops and munitions so efficiently. Like Coke, Pepsi is pushing its non-soft drink wares overseas, particularly in Latin America. Time will tell if its marketing and merchandising skills can make its non-nutritive snack foods as successful as its soft drinks within some of the lesser-developed countries.

The big news at PepsiCo in the late seventies was its assault on Coke's lead in the fountain business. PepsiCo sought a major fast food chain in which to sell its soft drinks, and in November 1977, acquired the Pizza Hut chain, the industry's growth leader, in a deal reportedly valued at $300 million. Founder Frank L. Carney parlayed his first Pizza Hut in 1958 into the nation's largest pizza chain and the fourth largest fast food chain, behind McDonald's, Burger King, and Kentucky Fried Chicken. Pizza Hut begins the eighties as a cheesey empire of nearly 4,000 restaurants, half of which are operated directly by the company.*

Not content with one chain, PepsiCo acquired Taco Bell, Inc. a year later with an exchange of $148 million in stock. The largest Mexican fast food chain, Taco Bell has over 900 restaurants spread across the country. With its roots in the Southern California of the mid-fifties, the chain's hallmarks were Spanish mission-style architecture, vaguely resembling the Alamo, and a limited Mexican menu that could be prepared with no more than nine basic ingredients.

PepsiCo will have to wait for its cornucopia of growth, however. Almost immediately, the fast food business began to slow down, and in hindsight, it appears that Carney found big brother just in time. Increasing food and gasoline costs began to make fast food less of a bargain for many Americans, and the operating profits of PepsiCo's Food Division, the corporate roof for both chains, fell in 1978 from $73.6 million to $64.1 million.

Although America will long be the most profitable market for Pizza Hut, the headlong growth rate can best be found overseas. Carney's chain already has nearly 200 foreign restaurants in Canada and far-off locales like Japan, Australia, and Kuwait. "They know which countries to go into, and where to franchise and where to open company-owned units," said Carney. Indeed, his will be the conquering pizza.

Yet what made Coke and Pepsi great within their mercantile universe are those bubbly solutions of sugar, flavorings, and profitability. For years, there appeared no end to the amount of soft drinks the powerhouses could pump into the American bloodstream. Volume ballooned to the point where all the major manufacturers were growing and the only important growth indicator became a product's share of the market. No beverages have grown faster and at such expense to other liquids than soft drinks. During the decade since 1968, per capita consumption of soda increased 50 percent to 37 gallons, while milk, a more popular drink ten years ago, actually decreased by a third to 24.8 gallons. Within the same span, coffee declined 30 percent from its 37 gallon per capita consumption. Beer has steadily improved to 23.2 gallons in 1978, as have juices, although they have leveled off at 6.4 gallons since 1975. More Coke alone is sold than teas

---

* By virtue of the merger, Carney became a PepsiCo director and its second largest individual stockholder behind Herman Lay.

and wines combined or fruit juices. Most victimized has been an age-old favorite—water. From 64 gallons per capita in 1968, nature's essence has been reduced to 44.7 gallons in 1978 and is decreasing. What is happening is a determined reprogramming of America's drinking habits. One Coke executive optimistically projects that by 1990 nearly a third of all liquid consumption in America will be soft drinks, with each citizen guzzling an average of three cans a day. The time will come when Americans prefer soda pop to water.

In recent years, such trends have encouraged many to enter the business. One is the irrepressible ex-Pepsi boss, Walter Mack, who is trying to stir up some mischief again by manufacturing his own brew, King Cola. Still with more bounce to the ounce, even at 83 years of age, the pundit of pop and his associates, all industry veterans on the twilight side of 50 years old, fully intend to take the country by storm with King Cola and sugar-free Slim King. The new cola's inventor and company vice-chairman is chemist Thomas Elmezzi, a former Pepsi man of 43 years and one of the chosen few of that era privy to the Pepsi formula. Mack is selling 29 franchises, or "kingdoms" throughout the country and reportedly has a buyer from far-away Jordan who wants the first "kingdom" for the Coke-dry Middle East. His advertising will tout the "old switchola to the new King Cola" which he hopes will draw consumers to their supermarkets demanding in chorus, "I want my King Cola. Where the hell is it?"

While Mack and his oldtimers have raised a few eyebrows, the purchase of the new Seven-Up Company in the summer of 1978 by Philip Morris, Inc. (P.M.) for $520 million set the industry abuzz. Here now was a third mighty marketer that had earned its spurs on several fiercely competitive fronts. In the early sixties, P.M. took Marlboro cigarettes, endowed it with a macho Marlboro-man image, and advertised it until it was the world's premier brand. In 1970, P.M. again took a ho-hum product, Miller Beer, shot it up with a new image, and promoted it to the number two spot behind Budweiser of Anheuser-Busch, Inc. As a conglomerate larger than either Coke or Pepsi, Philip Morris then dove into the carbonated sea of soda and recreational hype. "The soft-drink party's gonna get rough," a Coke executive prophesied. "Philip Morris is a master at marketing. When they buy something like Seven-Up, you can be sure it's because they see some opportunity for profit there. . . . It's going to be a battle of the giants." A Seven-Up bottler gloated, "Philip Morris doesn't like to be second or third in anything."

With Seven-Up stagnant within its traditional lemon-lime category, which itself comprised only 12 percent of the soft-drink market, P.M. took the bold tack of trying to take on the leading colas directly, and thereby challenge taste preferences which Coke and Pepsi had spent fortunes to develop. It doubled Seven-Up's ad budget to a hefty $40 million to back a campaign built around the slogan, "America is turning Seven-Up." Presented as the "crisp, clear," toast of a happy-go-lucky status quo, Seven-Up became the favorite of exuberant sports-minded youth, long the symbolic province of Pepsi and, to a lesser extent, Coke. "This is exactly what Seven-Up needs," proclaimed one bottler. "It never had the dollars to compete with the Coke and Pepsis of the world." The entire industry locked the watertight doors and braced itself.

However, for all of P.M.'s herculean efforts, Seven-Up's sales actually decreased as did its market share from 5.9 percent to 5.6 percent, placing it further behind the Cola twins and barely ahead of Dr Pepper. The company was wrong to re-position Seven-Up against the well-entrenched colas, which had escalated their own advertising budgets considerably, and its campaign was too lackluster and undistinctive. Seven-Up made wholesale use of sports celebrities, a time-honored technique whose effectiveness was nevertheless damaged by its selection of injured, maligned, little known, or inarticulate stars. Moreover, Seven-Up's agency, N.W. Ayer, shot the ads in film rather than videotape so that the image appearing on the TV screen lost the sense of immediacy native to television. Full of sharpness and brilliant colors, the movie-like quality showed these heroes in literally an unfamiliar light which only added to the air of contrivance arising from the obviously staged action scenes. On the other hand, by avoiding action shots in its use of sports stars, McCann Erickson was able to use the intimacy of film in the touching sequence with Mean Joe Greene.

In the absence of a winning Seven-Up strategy, Philip Morris has decided to confront Coke and Pepsi with its own cola and eventually a full line of soft drinks. To advertise upcoming products, the company has hired Bill Backer, who now works out of his own agency, Backer & Spielvogel. Industry rumors suggest Seven-Up might experiment with a clear cola or one free of caffeine. There has also been talk that the company is interested in acquiring the Royal Crown Cola Co., which has introduced a cola free of sugar and caffeine called RC 100 to perk sales that have been flat since the sixties. Such a gambit by P.M. would certainly heat up competition, although it is unlikely that many Coke or Pepsi bottlers who handle Seven-Up would abandon their prize brands for Seven-Up's new cola.

There is a deeper, more ominous explanation for Seven-Up's fizzle. To the distress of soft-drink executives, their tidal wave of prosperity appears to be headed for the rocks. Industry-wide gains in 1978 were only 4 percent against 10 percent in 1977, and 13 percent in 1976, and early reports indicate that growth for 1979 is down to 2 or 3 percent. The first warning came in 1974 when sugar prices increased sevenfold. The retail prices of soft drinks rose and consumers, already inflation-weary, began to balk. In New York City, for example, a six-pack of Coke cost more than a six-pack of beer. "I've always wondered at what level we would meet price resistance," moaned a Coke executive at the time, "and now I've found out."

For the first time in memory, sales of the Coke brand decreased in 1974 and its overall share dropped slightly to 26.2 percent. Gains by Tab and Mr. Pibb, however, allowed the company's total market share to increase .6 percent to 35.3 percent. Even Pepsi lost business, dropping its market share slightly to 17.4 percent. Again, only gains from the other beverages enabled PepsiCo's whole line to increase .2 percent to 20.8 percent. The following year, the industry managed to rebound though not without some soul-searching and an ulcer or two. However, the long-term problems lay not so much within the industry as with the demographics of the marketplace.

The backbone of the soft-drink market has long been the 13 to 24-year-olds, whose 1976 per capita consumption was better than twice the national average. The post-World War II baby boom which had swelled the size of this group some 30 percent during the sixties is, of course, past, and this group is expected to decline by 8 percent. Some fear that as this populous "Pepsi Generation" grays around the temples, it will lose its lust for soft drinks.

In response to this latter trend, both cola makers are subtly adjusting their advertising for this aging "youth market." One Pepsi executive redefined the "Pepsi Generation" as "anything from 13 to 75. . . . It's a state of mind rather than being a physical age." Though still placing more emphasis on youth than Coke, Pepsi's new campaign, "Catch that Pepsi Spirit" is showing older consumers, such as the antics of an elderly skywriting pilot. Coke too is meeting these trends with ads more likely to show middle-aged and even elderly consumers. "A 50-year-old woman who's out there playing tennis three times a week is totally different from a 50-year-old woman of the 1940s and 1950s." Although "Coke Adds Life" was originally, and perhaps, says Backer, incorrectly aimed at the youth market, it can be read with a definite gerontological meaning. "This particular theme is adaptable to any age segment of our society," claims Donald Keough, but Coke seems unconcerned that its broad approach could dampen its appeal to the next generation of youths.

There are also signs that the domestic market is becoming saturated. Logic dictates that a finite market, regardless of how dynamic, simply cannot sustain indefinite growth. There is only so much soda an individual or a nation can be expected to consume. Annual per-capita consumption in 1980, which has tripled since the late fifties, approaches four hundred 12-ounce containers, or better than a soft drink every day for every man, woman, and child. "Domestic soft-drink consumption," said a beverage industry stock analyst, "is a function of the numbers of consumers and the average propensity to consume. Soft drinks are now almost universally available—and when things are that good, improvement is most difficult to achieve." The situation is aggravated by the energy crisis. The economy has slowed down, disposable income is reduced, tourism has decreased, and all away-from-home activities have been affected, particularly dining out.

The pressure within the corporate bottle is building. The major manufacturers have been spending more money on advertising, a traditional industry response to difficulties, yet in a static market, growth will come at the expense of the competition, rendering each incremental sales increase terribly costly. The industry can also woo consumers with packaging innovations and price cutting, though such a "commodities" approach to marketing can hurt both profits and crucial brand loyalty as the consumer shops for the best price only. "It doesn't take creativity to give a price allowance," snorted one Coke bottler, whose idea of inspiration is three five-foot, four-inch robots patterned after the famous android R2D2 from the movie *Star Wars*. Operated by remote control, they whirr and click along the aisles of supermarkets persuading shoppers to buy more soft drinks. One sports the Coke logo and is called Adds 2 Life 2.

Both companies will pay even greater attention to their non-U.S. expansion which has long exceeded their growth at home and contributes heavily to their steadily improving balance sheets. For Coke, 46 percent of its total sales and 62 percent of its soft-drink sales came courtesy of foreign markets. Despite over half a century of Coke's consumer proselytizing, many of these markets are still unpenetrated or embryonic, with annual per capita consumption outside the U.S. estimated at only ten cans. "The growth potential out there is unlimited," declared Austin. One of his vice-presidents elaborates, "If one talks about zero population growth in the U.S., we're talking about an over-population problem in much of the rest of the world. In the underdeveloped countries, you've got 50 percent of your population under 25."

The extent and success of their foreign business has endowed both companies, particularly Coke, with nearly mythic stature. Their expansion abroad will further wed their interests with those of policymakers worldwide, and both will continue to serve as corporate ambassadors of U.S. foreign policy. Besides Coke's political and financial clout, its technologies in critical areas such as agriculture and water purification provide it with still greater leverage with which to prod nations to accept American soft drinks. In this setting, the wisdom, patience, and resources of both companies, not to mention their prospective customers, will be tried as never before.

Both companies have already fallen prey to the pressures. In 1977, in the wake of the Lockheed scandal where management bribed overseas officials to secure contracts, Coke confessed that it too had bribed foreign officials. A company investigation, conducted by the law firm of Arnold & Porter, revealed that since 1971, Coke had made $1.3 million in questionable payments within twenty countries. These disbursements were for "government approvals," "termination of employees," political contributions, approvals of price increases, "efforts to expedite governmental matters in foreign countries," and "favorable business treatment and good will." PepsiCo, after an independent investigation requested by management, disclosed it too has made some $1.7 million in questionable payments abroad. Both companies assure that these practices have been terminated.

Entering the eighties, the most far-reaching problem for both companies is leadership. With retirement not far away, both Austin and Kendall will be tough acts to follow. Kendall bulldozed Pepsi through the competition finally to pull abreast of Coke, increasing sales some 400 percent in the process and molding Pepsi into one of the world's foremost consumer multinational corporations. Unlike Austin, he didn't inherit greatness; he made it, and on sheer toughness and opportunism. He was so dominant that the company and its products took on his aura—robust, competitive, and athletic, with a touch of macho. Kendall will be the Pepsi leader to which all others will be compared.

What has set both Austin and Kendall apart is their ability to exploit the political arena. Kendall actively sought political involvement, convinced that it was his responsibility to do so. He fashioned himself as an international spokesman for free enterprise and the American business community. So instrumental was he in Nixon's career that he undeniably helped shape modern history. Pepsi may never again enjoy a political association as daring or finely wrought. For Kendall, there was no "patronage" or "special interests," only participatory business. Austin was the paladin of the American presidency. If he was more discreet than Kendall, it was because he did not need introductions to the influential and the mighty. He was a peer in a world of commoners. If he appeared less patronizing, it was because the nation's policymakers were long convinced that the world would be better off swamped with Coca-Cola. When Coke needed to respond to Pepsi's alliance with Nixon, an old Georgia boy steeped in Coke's great Southern Democratic traditions was elected at the earliest possible moment.

Kendall welded PepsiCo to Republicanism. Besides Kendall, Lay, and Stewart, its board of directors included William T. Coleman, attorney and prominent black Republican. In 1959, he served on President Eisenhower's Commission on Employment Policy, and five years later, was an assistant counsel to the Warren Commission in its investigation into the assassination of John F. Kennedy. He served in various capacities for state and federal governments and, in 1973, declined an offer by Attorney General Elliot Richardson to become the Watergate special prosecutor. In 1975, President Ford appointed him Secretary of Transportation. He is a director of American Can Co., the Rand Corporation (of which Coke's Austin was board chairman), Brookings Institute, Chase Manhattan Bank, Pan American World Airways with Kendall, and International Business Machines Corp. Also on PepsiCo's board was another I.B.M. director and its former board chairman, T. Vincent Learson. He temporarily resigned from Pepsi's board in 1975 to serve as President Ford's Ambassador at Large and Special Representative. Learson's directorships include Chemical Bank, Caterpillar Tractor Company, and Kennecott Copper Corp. Another director with ties to Republican presidential politics is Casper W. Weinberger, currently a vice-president of the Bechtel group. He served as chairman of the Federal Trade Commission, director of the U.S. Office of Management and Budget, and Secretary of Health, Education and Welfare, all under Nixon.

Travelling in the loftiest of Republican circles, PepsiCo has connections to the party's front-running 1980 presidential hopefuls. Kendall contributed to John Connally's campaign, though the Texan withdrew early in the race for lack of popular support. The company's influence within Texas financial circles has brought it in contact with George Bush (see Chapter 14), and a key advisor to Ronald Reagan is its director, Casper Weinberger, who fancies himself as "very conservative." Weinberger can also plug Pepsi into the arcane wonders of global leadership as a member of the Trilateral Commission, whose ranks have also included, besides Carter and Austin, Bush and Republican maverick John Anderson.

While Austin was clearly in charge at Coke, venerable old Robert Woodruff, as chairman of the finance committee, still controls the purse strings. The total value of his company's stock was pegged by *Forbes Magazine*, at $5,420,000,-000 in 1978, ranking it 17th of all American corporations, and he and his family owned a reported 17.36 percent of it.* While hardly one of America's most colorful individuals, he is certainly one of its wealthiest, a fact he has played down well. One of the $40 Coke shares that his father bought from the Candlers in 1919 is reportedly worth $11,000 today. In what has been called the single largest private gift ever in American philanthropy, Woodruff gave Emory University three million shares of Coke in 1979, then valued at $100 million. This gift complemented the two million shares he had already donated. Every time Coke's stock rises a point, Emory gains by $5 million. After his school's trustees accepted the gift, the Emory chairman turned to his colleagues and implored, "All right, let's get out there and drink that Coca-Cola."

In Candler, Woodruff, and Austin, Coke has enjoyed three generations of spirited, Southern, fiscally conservative helmsmen, but the eighties bear many signs that the long exhausting struggle with Pepsi has begun to take its toll. "The Pepsi Challenge," Pepsi's greater market share in take-home, and its recently achieved advantage in total dollar volume—each new wound left scars of dissension on this once big, happy family. Austin himself increasingly was criticized for not diversifying into other product lines, as Pepsi did. Another ominous break with tradition occurred in 1980 when Coke borrowed $100 million in debt markets, the first such liability taken on by Atlanta since the Depression. Austin was further accused of devoting too much attention to foreign markets at the expense of weakening sales at home. One corollary here, of course, was the vastly deteriorating bottler relations which the company experienced during the late seventies. "Austin's slant was the overseas market," remarked Coke director J.T. Lupton, himself a descendant of one of the founding partners of the franchise system. "He left bottler relations to a succession of other people."†

The bottlers, of course, had long held prime space in the vision of Robert Woodruff, which probably explains the special feeling Woodruff had for Coke president J. Lucian Smith. A lifetime Cokeman from Mississippi, Smith was implicitly trusted by the bottlers and was credited with convincing many of them to agree to the controversial proposal from Atlanta permitting periodic price increase for Coke's syrup. Despite the long tutelage and grooming of Austin for the post of chairman, Smith was said to have been Woodruff's favorite man at the company and heir apparent to Austin, whose retirement at age sixty-five was to have become mandatory in early 1980. However, Smith's sudden and un-

---

* *CDE Stock Ownership Directory: Agribusiness* (New York: Corporate Data Exchange, 1979). p. 85–86. PepsiCo's stock value was ranked 50th at $2.3 billion.
† *Atlanta Constitution*, August 10, 1980, p. 9C

expected "retirement" in August 1979 paved the way not only for Austin to re-main on as board chairman, but also to take over the presidency as well.

The signs of a squeeze in this move were unmistakable. Austin clearly wanted to tighten the reins within the company and didn't want to have to go through Luke Smith to do it. Austin was undoubtedly emboldened to move against Smith out of a hunch that he wouldn't have to answer to Woodruff, who was bedrid-den with a lengthy illness that left him near death during much of Austin's ma-neuvering. Perhaps stirred by word of the wrangling, the feisty Woodruff made an unexpectedly swift recovery before Smith suffered an equally sudden, fatal heart attack. In August 1980, Austin's "retirement" was announced, effective the following March, and there was little suggestion anywhere in the press that his departure was voluntary. Despite all the other possible reasons, suggested one Atlanta journalist, the firing of Smith was the real reason for Austin's exit.

The choice of his successor had been a pressing issue in Atlanta even before Smith's demise, and it clearly preoccupied Austin after it. In November 1979, Coca-Cola announced that Austin would be staying on for another year, pre-sumably because Smith's departure left a vacuum that needed to be filled. The company also named six top executives to the newly-created post of vice-chair-man, and it was widely assumed not only that Austin's successor would be among them but also that in all but naming the vice-chairman, Austin was lay-ing the groundwork for remaining a power at the company well after his official departure. The vice-chairman represented a cross-section of the two main power centers at the company—those, like Smith, who were devoted to the domestic market and a strong bottling sector, and those who were more a part of the in-ternational managerial faction. The latter was largely a creation of Austin, just as the former has been the legacy of Woodruff, and one observer noted that the two groups can be divided between those who feel at home at Ichuay, Wood-ruff's baronial Georgia plantation, and those who don't. Austin's appointees to the new posts reflected his diversity. Donald Keough, for instance, former head of Coca-Cola USA, was a Coke old-boy while Claus Halle, head of soft drink operations in Europe, Africa, and the Middle East, was not. Neither were other powerful appointees like Albert Killeen, viewed as the number two man in the company and, barring his age, Austin's clear favorite for the top job. Like Aus-tin, Killeen had put in a long stint heading up the South African operations and returned home with a style so intimidating that he soon became known as "the man nobody talks to."* With South African-born Ian Wilson, the trio formed a powerful nucleus within the international-managerial faction known as "the South African Mafia," whose power became a source of increasing uneasiness as the disaffection with Austin mounted.

Perhaps to forestall a potentially devastating struggle for the throne, Wood-ruff and Austin pushed through the selection of a dark horse, former vice-chair-man Roberto Goizueta, who had only taken over the presidency from Austin

* *Wall Street Journal*, March 5, 6, 1980, p. 1

in mid-1980. The Cuban-born Goizueta, a chemical engineer, was a surprise in every fashion—a foreign national now heading a company heretofore led by dyed-in-the-wool Georgians; a technical, rather than a marketing, man was now at the helm of the world's greatest marketing organization. Goizueta is expected to reverse Coke's weakening position in the domestic market, and is viewed primarily as a strategist who will coordinate the rest of the operating management. He is free from the special interest areas that characterized nearly all the other candidates, many of whom can be expected to vie heatedly for the position of president which Goizueta vacated. More than anything else, then, Goizueta was the safest choice, the figure who could move most quickly to patch a divided house.

For the better part of his career Austin effectively straddled the extremes of the Coke empire, from its Old Boy bottlers to the grad-school managers, from Atlantans to Trilateralists. He integrated the foreign and domestic business just as he reconciled the almost contradictory forces of tradition and modernity. Paul Austin exemplified the breeding, assertiveness, and hubris of Coca-Cola. The company may never have a leader as appropriately qualified. In every respect, he was a great chief executive and certainly did what he was paid to do.

But Kendall did what he had to do.

It is unlikely that any successor to either Austin or Kendall will forge such spectacular successes. There are too few territories left to conquer. However, one can easily envision some future Coke or Pepsi leader scoring a public relations coup with some presidential assistance because his company landed the first soft-drink concession on the moon. Coke has already received inquiries for possible lunar franchises (do soft drinks fizz in zero gravity?).

Walter Mack once said that the war between Coke and Pepsi is a classic American struggle, a living testament to the national credo of free enterprise and competition. The historical links which both drinks shared with religious movements and, later, social institutions, forever wed them to some of the key shapers of the American character, and helped make them a trusted part of people's lives. Advertising harnessed the power of these bonds, elevating the drinks—and consequently, the companies—into sovereign symbols of American enterprise. More than practically any other companies embraced in bitter rivalry, Coke and Pepsi enjoyed a mandate to indulge openly in political solicitations, if not connivances, to achieve their ends.

The spectacle of their competition obscures a subtle and essential collaboration. On a strategic level, Coke and Pepsi operate within overlapping political and corporate networks that seek to preserve the marketplace favorable to both companies. On a symbolic plane, both contribute to an advertising structure that reinforces the values favorable to soft drinks. Thus, amid the warfare of the marketplace, the companies stand toe-to-toe in the center of a whole system merging economic and political organization with certain very basic patterns of social behavior—primarily consumption. The purpose of the system is to reduce social tensions and political frictions which in any way hinder consumption.

Advertising is aimed directly at the resolution of social conflicts, but its relentless emphasis on consumption is increasingly pitted against the reality of a world order threatened by scarcity. This contradiction is part of an age that is coming to see the corporate priority of all-consuming growth as self-serving and ultimately inimical to the greater well-being of society. Here lie the roots of a political conflict that the business sector has yet to resolve.

The battle between Coke and Pepsi has long flourished as though it would last until thirst itself passed away, but the consensus which has mandated that battle is now itself in question. Of course, their obsessive competition for shelf space and mind space endures as they continue to rend the very fabric of whole societies, but not without the gnawing sensation that the cola wars rage on shifting sands. In a time when virgin markets are few and global inflation saps the strength of developed ones, the "classic American struggle" faces the closing of the wide open frontier. A saga of men and myths—a tale of two sodas—the great rivalry between Coke and Pepsi engulfs a whole world whose thirst for their heroics may be one which the soda-makers will soon unavoidably quench.

SANTA FE COMMUNITY
COLLEGE LIBRARY